Research Methods and Statistics for Business

Robert N. Lussier
Springfield College

WAVELAND

PRESS, INC.

Long Grove, Illinois

For information about this book, contact:
Waveland Press, Inc.
4180 IL Route 83, Suite 101
Long Grove, IL 60047-9580
(847) 634-0081
info@waveland.com
www.waveland.com

Contents

PART I
THE RESEARCH PROCESS   1

2   The Introduction: Research Question and Review of the Literature   33

3   The Research Proposal, Completed Research Study, and Ethics   65

PART II
RESEARCH DESIGNS: DATA-COLLECTION METHODS   93

4   Methods: Research Designs   95

7   Survey Questionnaires

Preface

Why I Wrote This Book

According to Matulich, Papp, and Haytko,[1] today's students are called "Digital Millennial" or "NetGen" students. These students don't like to learn by passively reading for hours and listening to long lectures; they want to be actively engaged and develop skills they can use on the job, but they need guidance and clear directions to succeed. Because students have changed, so should the way we teach research methods and statistics.

I found the major business research methods textbooks to be too long (approximately 700 pages with 20 or more chapters). As a result, students don't want to read them, and instructors often struggle to decide which chapters to cover and which to leave out. In *Research Methods and Statistics* (*RMS*), I've addressed all the topics of the leading textbooks, but more concisely in only 14 chapters, so instructors can cover the entire book in one semester. I've also found that other books do not do an adequate job of teaching students to integrate research methods and statistics and to actually conduct research. So I wrote this book to be a more succinct "how to" book based on my experience, both in meeting the needs of today's students and in publishing hundreds of empirical research articles in conference proceedings and peer-reviewed journals.

Having taught research methods for several years, I haven't found a good textbook that actually teaches students *how to conduct research* effectively. Competing textbooks tend to focus on having students read about research rather than actually providing step-by-step instructions for conducting research. The course often becomes a passive reading and discussion of research, rather than an active learning experience. (With *RMS*, students actually conduct research!) To me, the difference is like talking about riding a bike versus actually getting on the bike and riding it. I wrote this book so we can take the ride together.

Unlike competitors' books that focus on reading text and examples, this book engages students through completion of exercises and problems. Students can actually learn by doing, by being guided through the step-by-step process of preparing a research proposal and completed study. To engage students, I've included more exercises and problems of greater variety and higher quality than those of the competitors. *RMS* provides three options—preparing a research proposal, completing a research study, and doing statistical analysis papers—including instructions and examples so that student can actually learn how to conduct statistical research.

Who Can Use This Book

The book is intended for use in research methods and statistics courses at the graduate and undergraduate levels. Although the title and applications are business oriented, the book is well suited to other disciplines such as psychology (especially industrial and organizational psychology) and education. *RMS* is an effective tool for teaching statistics from a research perspective, and it can be used during a one- or two-semester length course. The book is also an excellent reference book for professionals and professors who conduct research.

Easy to Read and Understand with Applications to Engage Students

Most students find research methods and statistics courses to be difficult. Statistical research can be a complex undertaking, and students are often frustrated because they learn *about* research rather than *how* to conduct research. Although it covers high-level methods and advanced multivariate statistics, this text is written in easy-to-understand language. It features examples, application exercises, and decision problems to help students apply the concepts to given research designs and to their own proposed research.

An integral part of the "how to" research process is the digital appendices in the CD that accompanies the book. The appendix in Part IV, The Research Proposal, contains an example of a student research proposal with hypotheses, accompanied by assignments with step-by-step instructions to the students for completing their own research proposal in four parts. The sample proposal in Part IV is transformed to a completed study in the Part V appendix, The Completed Research Study. Written Assignments sections at the end of each chapter are designed to work with these appendices, guiding students through the process of transforming their own research proposals into completed studies. For students who are required to use the style recommended by the American Psychological Association (the style required by many journals in research writing), the CD also contains a condensed guide to APA style, featuring examples of the most common errors students make in their research papers.

The digital appendix in Part VI, Statistical Analysis, features statistical assignments to help students understand the completed research project. Essentially, instructors may choose to have their students use their own research proposals and collect data from a convenience sample (possibly from other class members). Students can run the statistics and write the results and conclusions—in an APA journal-article format with an abbreviated introduction section. Although the data may not be valid, nevertheless it shows students *how* to conduct research. It is also a good method of practice for conducting an actual research project, thesis, or dissertation. All three appendices provide good examples of APA style.

Strong Integration of Research Methods and Statistics

While research methods books tend to do a good job of presenting methodology, they are weak at integrating statistics. At the same time, statistics books—even those targeting business and economics—are math books without a research foundation. Students are somehow supposed to take the research methods and statistics courses and put them together by themselves, which most can't do. So students never really learn *how* to conduct research-based statistical analysis. Therefore, I wrote this book with an eye toward truly integrating research and statistics by beginning with research methodology and then guiding students through the process of conducting their own statistical research. *RMS* takes the student from the initial process of selecting the research topic through the finished research proposal. It also explains *how* the proposal becomes part of the completed research project and teaches *how* to write the results and conclusions of the final research project using APA style.

Selecting the Appropriate Statistic Using a Decision Tree

Most students complete research methods and statistics courses without a clear understanding of which statistical test to use, or when, or why. Commonly, students are simply told which test to use. Most students have difficulty during the course, and after it is over they retain very little of what they learned. *RMS* solves this problem by providing a Decision Tree (in chapter 10 and included on the accompanying CD) that features five research designs and more than 30 bivariate and multivariate statistical tests. The chapter explains how to use the Decision Tree and requires students to select the appropriate statistic. After the course, students don't have to rely on memory—they can use the Decision Tree whenever they need it.

Hypothesis Testing

Most students are weak at hypothesis testing. Other textbooks don't do an effective job of teaching students how to write and test hypotheses, including reading and interpreting statistical computer printouts of p-values. Chapter 11 teaches hypothesis testing, including 16 exercises to assess students' understanding of Type I and II errors, p-values, and accepting or rejecting hypotheses. In addition, chapters 11 through 14 cover statistics using a five-step hypothesis-testing approach. Sample hypothesis tests are featured, along with computer printouts of test results with instructions on how to interpret them. Decision problems follow, for which students write and test hypotheses (including computer-printout analysis), accept or reject the null hypothesis, and answer pertinent related questions. Chapters 9 and 11 through 14 also feature statistics problems that use the computer, utilizing the same five-step approach to hypothesis testing. Students use the same data set for each chapter to understand how the same data can be used for multiple statistical tests. (The answers to all decision problems and computer problems are included in the Instructor's Manual.)

Pedagogical Features

- *Chapter outline*. Each chapter begins with an outline of the important topics of the chapter.
- *Conceptual objectives*. Each chapter has a list of conceptual objectives that students should be able to complete after studying the chapter. These objectives also appear in the text, directly following the information students need to understand and attain the objective. The answers to the questions posed by the conceptual objectives are given in the summary and glossary at the end of the chapters.

- *Skill development objectives.* Each chapter has a list of skills for applying the concepts from the chapter, with the exercises and/or decision problems that develop the skills.

- *Key terms.* As the last conceptual objective, the most important concepts are listed in the order in which they appear in the chapters. Within the body of the chapters the key terms appear again *with their definitions highlighted in bold and italics.* In the summary and glossary, the key terms appear a final time, in alphabetical order with their definitions directly below, as an interactive review.

- *Exercises.* At critical points in the body of each chapter, students are directed to stop reading and go to the section at the end of the chapter to complete exercises for skill development. Some of the exercises ask students about their own proposed research, while others present a situation that requires student input and presents questions they must answer.

- *Reading statistical test results in computer printouts.* Statistics chapters 9 and 11 through 14 include statistical printouts run primarily with IBM's Statistical Package for the Social Sciences (SPSS), version 19, with an explanation of how to understand the important information they contain.

- *Sample hypothesis tests.* Statistics chapters 11 through 14 include sample hypothesis tests using the five-step approach to accepting or rejecting the null hypothesis, along with discussion of the results.

- *Decision problems.* These problems, which appear in the statistical chapters 11 through 14, require students to implement the five steps of hypotheses testing to accept or reject the null hypothesis and to discuss the results. There are usually two for each type of statistical test.

- *Chapter summary and glossary.* All chapters end with the information required to realize the conceptual objectives and define the key terms.

- *Statistics problems for the computer.* Statistics chapters 9 and 11 through 14 include statistical problems using the computer. In chapter 9, five variables are given with data from 10 participants. Students use this same data set in all four chapters to understand how to statistically test the data in multiple ways, using the five steps of hypothesis testing.

- *A CD to accompany the text.* Included are examples of a research proposal, a completed research study, and a statistical analysis paper, along with checklists (grading rubrics) for students to use in their own research-writing projects, and a concise APA style guide. Actual data set documents are also included, in both SPSS and Excel, for students' use.

Written Assignments

Every chapter has written assignments that may be handed in at the instructor's discretion. If the end-of-chapter exercises and decision problems are not required assignments, students can do them on their own to improve their understanding and ability to conduct research.

Students may write a research proposal, completed study, and/or statistical analysis papers during this course. The assignments are briefly introduced in the chapters, and the detailed instructions are provided in the three appendices on the accompanying CD. In essence, these three items are completed in steps as students progress through the chapters of the book. The assignments accumulate throughout the chapters to the point where the students develop a completed research proposal and/or completed statistical study of their own. If this is the only course assignment, students may find that doing their papers in steps on a chapter-by-chapter basis greatly improves the quality of their work.

The Organization of the Book

The text teaches how to conduct and write statistical research by following the process involved in completing a research study. Part I of this book features the research process—the *introduction,* including the literature review to the research study. Part II addresses research design and data collection—the *method* of the research study. Part III deals with data analysis—the *results* and *discussion* of the research study. Students can use the examples of research writing in the digital appendices in Parts IV, V, and VI on the accompanying CD as templates for their own research projects.

Part I—INTRODUCTION

The research question/purpose of the study, literature review, and hypotheses.

Part I presents an overview of how to conduct research. Chapter 1 presents the research process and covers goals and types of research. Chapter 2 focuses on selecting the research question in connection with the literature review. Chapter 3 explains the elements of a research proposal and how the proposal becomes part of the completed study.

Part II—METHOD

Research design methodology for collecting data.

Part II presents research methods. Chapter 4 features the various research designs. Chapter 5 explains sampling methodology. Chapter 6 discusses data-collection methods, and Chapter 7 teaches development of survey questionnaires for data collection. Chapter 8 addresses methods of ensuring that reliable and valid measures are used when collecting data.

Part III—RESULTS AND DISCUSSION

Data analysis and interpreting results and discussion of the finding.

Part III presents data analysis to interpret results and discuss conclusions regarding the research findings. Chapter 9 presents organizing data, frequencies, and basic descriptive statistics. Chapter 10 teaches how to select the appropriate inferential statistic by using a Decision Tree that includes more than 30 statistical tests. Chapter 11 identifies the steps to test hypotheses and discusses Type I and Type II errors, as well as how to make decisions to accept or reject hypotheses based on probability values. Chapter 12 focuses on experimental designs and how to run and interpret tests of differences (T-test, Z-test, Mann-Whitney U, chi-square, and one-way analysis of variance—ANOVA). Chapter 13 includes how to run and interpret correlations (Pearson, Spearman, and partial); regression (bivariate, multivariate, with dummy variables, logistic); and model building (stepwise and hierarchical regression); plus a discussion of meta-analysis and canonical analysis. Chapter 14 teaches how to run and interpret two-way ANOVA and multivariate analysis of variance (MANOVA—one-way and factorial); plus coverage of factor and cluster analysis, statistical tests that use control variables (ANCOVA/MANCOVA, cross-tabulation—chi-square, AID, CHAID), and other advanced statistics (LISREL, path analysis, conjoint analysis, MDS, and time-series analysis).

Part IV—THE RESEARCH PROPOSAL

This digital appendix, on the CD that accompanies this book, provides an example of a research proposal to use as a template for developing an original research proposal as part of the course. The proposal is actually completed in four parts as students progress through the chapters. Instructions for each of the four parts are included at the end of the chapters and in greater detail in this appendix.

Part V—THE COMPLETED RESEARCH STUDY

Since completing a research study may be a requirement in the course, this digital appendix (also on the accompanying CD) provides an example of a completed study to use as a template for conducting a research study with either real or fictitious data. The study is actually completed in four parts as students progress through the chapters. Brief instructions for each of the four parts appear at the end of the chapters and are provided in more detail on the CD. Students have the option of extending their studies by conducting additional statistical analyses to learn how to run, interpret, and discuss the five statistical research-design statistical results.

Part VI—STATISTICAL ANALYSIS

As its title implies, this appendix, found on the accompanying CD, focuses on statistics. However, it is similar to the appendix on the completed research study in that through these seven assignments students select a research question, develop hypotheses and a questionnaire, collect data, run statistics, present results, and discuss the findings. The major difference is that students go beyond a typical completed study that uses only the statistics that are truly relevant. Through the assignments, students run one of each of the major statistical research designs: tests of difference (T-test, chi-square, one-way ANOVA) tests of association (Pearson, Spearman), tests of prediction (regressions), and tests of interaction (two-way ANOVA, MANOVA) to complete a study, even though any particular test may not be relevant to the research. Instructions for each of the seven assignments are included at the end of the chapters and in this appendix.

Supplemental Materials

- *CD*. The CD that accompanies the book has three parts. (1) the digital appendices to support the completion of a research proposal, actual study, and/or statistical assignments; (2) a concise review of grammar and APA style; and (3) a data set in both SPSS 19 and Excel (related to obtaining small-business loans) that is used throughout chapters 9–14 to illustrate the various statistical tests. Students can use this data set to run their own statistics.

- *Instructor's Manual*. Answers to all exercises and decision problems are included in the Instructor's Manual.
- *Test Bank*. The test bank includes two types of questions based on the objectives. Conceptual objectives include a variety of objective and short-answer questions. The skill development objectives feature questions similar to the exercises and decision problems in the book.

Note

[1] Matulich, E., Papp, R., & Haytko, D. (2008). Continuous improvement through teaching innovations: A requirement for today's learners. *Marketing Education Review, 18*(1), 1–7.

PART I

The Research Process

1

Basic Elements of Research

CONCEPTUAL OBJECTIVES

The conceptual objectives below also appear at appropriate places within the chapter at points when you will have accessed the information necessary to attain them. They appear again at the end of the chapter in the Summary and Glossary section, along with explanations that will enable you to meet the objectives.

After studying this chapter you should be able to:

1. Define research and explain when to use it.
2. Describe the difference between secondary and primary research.
3. Explain the difference between a concept and an operational definition.
4. Define *variable* and discuss the relationship between dependent and independent variables.
5. State the major differences between nominal, ordinal, and interval/ratio levels of measurement.
6. Describe the relationship between propositions/hypotheses and theories.
7. Describe the difference in the role of a theory and the role of a model, and explain their relationship.
8. List and briefly describe the characteristics of good research.
9. List the steps in the research process with their section titles.
10. Define the following key terms (listed in order of their appearance in the chapter).

research problem	conclusive research	variable
research	descriptive research	dependent variable (DV/Y)
goals of research	inferential research	independent variable (IV/X)
secondary research	theory	measurement
primary research	concepts	hypothesis
basic research	operational definitions	model
applied research	empirical research	research process
exploratory research		

SKILL DEVELOPMENT OBJECTIVES

The exercises that apply to particular skill development objectives are indicated directly beneath each numbered objective below. Periodic instructions within the chapter tell you when to stop reading and direct you to the end of the chapter to complete one or more of the skill development exercises.

After studying this chapter, you should be able to:

1. Identify research as secondary or primary, basic or applied, quantitative or qualitative, exploratory or conclusive, and descriptive or inferential.
   Exercises 1-1 through 1-6
2. Identify variables as dependent and independent, and their level of measurement and number of scales.
   Exercises 1-7 through 1-14

3. Identify and understand important parts of research and its terminology, including concepts, variables, propositions or hypotheses, theories, and models.
   Exercises 1-15 through 1-17

4. Identify characteristics of good research.
   Exercises 1-18 through 1-20

1.1 Why Study Research and Statistics?

Decision making is one of the most important responsibilities anyone can have. The decisions you make directly affect your performance in your personal and professional lives. Personal and business failure is often the result of poor decisions. With the trend towards globalization, the business environment is more complex than in the past. The trend toward large, complex organizational operations has increased the risks associated with decisions managers make. Thus, the need to make correct decisions based on information and research continues to increase. You need to know how to conduct and evaluate statistical research and how to use it to make decisions. You will improve your decision-making skills through this course.

The primary way research leads to better decision making is that it reduces uncertainty by providing information that improves the decision-making process. The one thing all science has in common is following the scientific method or process, which you will learn in this course. You will learn how to make decisions based on research rather than on simple opinion. The strategic decision-making process includes three interrelated stages:

- **Identifying problems or opportunities.** Managers can use research in planning strategies by determining the nature of situations, identifying the existence of problems or opportunities present in the organization. Research is also needed when conducting the external environmental analysis. Thus, you can use what you learn on the job.

- **Selecting and implementing a course of action**. An important part of decision making is analyzing the alternatives and selecting the most feasible. Research can be used to determine which alternative will be the most successful. Research is also useful in determining tactics required for the implementation of that course of action.

- **Evaluating the course of action**. After the strategic plan has been implemented, it is important to use research to determine the success of the chosen course of action. For example, performance-monitoring research is commonly conducted by organizations to ensure early detection of sales/revenues declines and other anomalies.

There are at least six situations in which you can benefit professionally from having statistical research skills:

1. **Improving your decision-making skills**. In your personal and professional lives, you have to make decisions. As stated above, by using research as part of your problem-solving and decision-making process you can improve your decision-making skills, whether you conduct the research yourself or if others do it. In either case, you have to know if the research was conducted properly and you must understand the research results to use them.

2. **Being current in your field**. With the rapid changes in all professional fields, it is important to keep up with the latest trends. You should be reading professional

journals to keep up in your field. Many of the better professional journals report statistical research results. By understanding statistical research methods, you will be able to read and understand professional journals and use this information on the job to improve your performance.

3. **Becoming an expert in your chosen field**. Your instructor may require you to conduct a literature review on a topic of your choice. In doing so, you will become an expert in your selected field. Being an expert in a topic area can help you to maintain your position or attain a better job.

4. **Developing your information skills**. By conducting a literature review, you develop your ability to collect and analyze information.

5. **Increasing the value of your employment skills**. During this course and/or after completing it, you may be required to conduct a research project. If you are presently employed, you may use your present organization, or another one, to select a problem, collect data, analyze the data, and recommend a decision for the problem. Through conducting a statistical research project, you develop your research skills that make you more valuable to your present or future employer. You may become known as a research expert and may be asked to conduct research studies or to give input into other studies. Other research studies could include being part of a team that selects an outside consultant to conduct a research study for your organization. You can give input into the research proposal, review the results to be sure they are properly done, and use the results in decision making.

6. **Qualifying for a research career**. If you find that you really enjoy research, you could seek a career as a research specialist with a large organization or a consulting firm. Through your courses you become an expert in your chosen major, and through research and statistics courses and conducting research projects in your field you become a dual expert.

> **STOP READING and turn to the end of the chapter to complete exercise 1-1.**

1.2 What Is Research and When Should It Be Used?

Now that you know *why* this course is important and how it can help you in your career, let's discuss *what* research is and *when* research should be used. Throughout this book you will learn *how* to conduct research.

Research Defined

Research can be described as a systematic and organized effort to investigate a problem; it is a series of steps designed and followed with a purpose and the goal of answering questions. *A **research problem** occurs when there are questions that need to be answered through research.* Thus, the research problem gives a purpose to conducting a study. In many journal articles the authors clearly state the purpose of their research in the beginning of the article so that the reader clearly understands what the research is all about.

A problem can simply refer to questions that are actually related to an opportunity (for example, if a company wants to offer a new product). However, it is classified as a problem for research purposes because questions need to be answered to enable the company to make a decision about whether to offer the new product. For example, managers may want the answers to the following questions before making the decision: Who are our potential customers? Who are our competitors? What is our competitive advantage over those competitors? What price should we charge? How many units can we sell? How much profit will we make? By conducting research, the company can obtain answers to these questions that will aid in making the decision.

Research encompasses the processes of inquiry, investigation, examination, and experimentation through which we discover new facts that help us to deal with problems. Research uses a *scientific method*. By *scientific* we simply mean that all researchers regardless of their discipline follow the same research process. People in business, economics, health, biology, psychology, sociology, education, and other fields all follow the same steps in conducting research to answer questions related to a problem within their disciplines. Thus, the research process is universal. You will learn how to conduct research in all disciplines.

To summarize and define, **research** *is the systematic process through which new knowledge is discovered through answering questions.* This systematic process is simply called the research process, which includes defining a problem and gathering and analyzing data to answer questions. We discuss this process in more detail later in this chapter. The definition of research suggests that gathering data is neither intuitive nor haphazard. Research (research) literally means to "search again." Thus, managers should carefully review the data multiple times to make sure that they get answers to their questions as well as answers to additional questions, and they may discover new questions that they also want to research.

Any decision that is made based solely on intuition or based on data that is not systematically gathered (haphazardly collected) is not a decision based on research. However, this does not mean that decisions must be made without the use of intuition. Successful managers (ones who make correct decisions) commonly use a combination of both research and intuition in decision-making.

When to Use Research in Decision Making

As stated above, decisions can be made with or without using research. However, research improves decision making by reducing the uncertainty of decisions, or it reduces the risk of making wrong decisions. But most decisions do not require the use of research. The four determining considerations of whether to use research in decision making include: (1) the type of decision, (2) the time constraints, (3) availability of data, and (4) cost-benefit analysis.

The type of decision.

There are primarily two types of decisions: programmed/routine and nonprogrammed/nonroutine. Programmed decisions are routine (such as how much inventory to order), and thus there is usually no need to conduct research (after the economic order quantity has been decided through research). Nonprogrammed decisions that are important and costly are not routine decisions (such as where to locate a new branch of the organization), and therefore research would be appropriate.

Time constraints.

Following the research process takes time, and there are situations in which a decision must be made quickly; thus, research cannot be used in making the decision. However, with the latest technology, such as the use of fax machines, computers, and the Internet, time constraints have become less of a problem.

Availability of data.

There are situations in which managers have enough information at hand to make a sound decision without conducting research. However, with the use of computers and the Internet managers have more data available and easily accessible for use in research than in the past. Thus, more decisions are being made based on research, but purchasing data can be costly.

Cost-benefit analysis.

Conducting research takes time, and the time people spend conducting research has a cost. Often research has direct costs, such as printing and mailing questionnaires. On the other hand, conducting research tends to reduce the risk of making a wrong decision. Consequently, the manager should ask, "Does the benefit of gaining information to improve the quality of the decision outweigh the cost of conducting the research?" Once again, the type of decision is important in the cost-benefit analysis, as well as the time constraints and availability of data.

CONCEPTUAL OBJECTIVE 1
Define research and explain when to use it.

**STOP READING and turn to the end of the chapter
to complete exercises 1-2 and 1-3.**

1.3 Research Goals and Types

Now that you know what research is and when to use it, let's discuss its goals and types. *The **goals of research** are to explain, predict, and control phenomena.* A phenomenon is a fact, occurrence, or circumstance observed through research. Phenomena can include human and animal behavior and/or objects.

The types of research can be classified in a variety of ways. Five contrasting types of research include secondary or primary, basic or applied, quantitative or qualitative, exploratory or conclusive, and descriptive or inferential.

Secondary or Primary Research

*Secondary research involves data that have been collected by others. **Primary research** involves data that have been collected by the researcher conducting the study.* There is a large variety of secondary data; libraries and the Internet are full of secondary data. Organizations also have lots of secondary data available to employees. All the data in the organization's computer system, and written data, are secondary sources. Thus, if you get data from the accounting department, for example, it is secondary data. Primary research includes gathering data through observation and survey. Many professional journals commonly publish primary research articles, which are secondary data to the readers.

Primary research is also called original research when the study has never been conducted in exactly the same way before. However, original does not mean that the researcher is studying something completely new. In fact, original research is expected to be based on prior studies. What makes the study original is the fact that new data are collected and analyzed. The focus of this book is on primary research.

During a research methods class, the data is commonly secondary, collected through the literature review of your topic. A research proposal is normally conducted and the primary data are collected after the course through a research project or thesis. However, the use of secondary data, such as stock market prices, is much quicker and easier to obtain than primary data, and statistical testing can be conducted with both types of data. In Chapter 2 you will learn about secondary data collection, and throughout the book you will learn how to conduct primary research and how to run statistics on either type of data.

CONCEPTUAL OBJECTIVE 2
Describe the difference between secondary and primary research.

Basic or Applied Research

Basic research is conducted to better understand concepts and theories as it attempts to expand the limits of knowledge. Basic research is also called pure research and is commonly conducted by academic professors. *Applied research is conducted as an aid in solving a specific problem.* Applied research, also called action research, is commonly conducted by people within an organization or by consultants. Basic research generally cannot be immediately implemented, whereas applied research can. While most of the professional journal articles are basic research, trade journals often tend to be more applied. The same research process you will learn in this book is used for both basic and applied research, but there are some differences, which we will discuss.

Throughout or after this course you may be required to conduct research. Your professor may specify which type of research you are required to conduct, or you may be given the option to choose. Students who are not employed often select basic research, whereas students who are employed often talk to managers within the organization they work for and conduct applied research.

Quantitative or Qualitative Research

Quantitative research generally includes a large sample size and reports statistical results. *Qualitative research* generally includes a small sample size and does not report statistical results. A large sample usually refers to at least 30 subjects. However, in some fields lower numbers are acceptable. Qualitative research is commonly conducted with a sample of 5 or fewer, but again, there are studies with larger numbers. Also, a single study can report both quantitative and qualitative findings. For example, a questionnaire could be sent out with both closed- and open-ended questions. The closed-ended questions could be reported using statistics and the open-ended without statistics.

Historical and philosophic research are usually qualitative. Below we will briefly discuss other differences between qualitative and quantitative research. However, as the name of this book implies, its focus is on quantitative research. Although Table 1.1 illustrates some of the common major differences between the two types when used in survey research, not all differences may apply to all research classified as one type or the other. We discuss the differences and types of qualitative and quantitative research designs in Chapter 4.

It's important to know when to use which type of research. Let's say that the research question refers to long-distance running. If you want to know descriptive things, such as how many runners use specific running shoes and how many miles per week they run, quantitative research is appropriate. However, if you want to understand *why* people are long distance runners, qualitative research is appropriate. With quantitative research you would have a large number of runners fill out a closed-ended questionnaire, and you would follow the procedures listed in column 1 of Table 1.1. For qualitative research, you would select a few long-distance runners and interview them in depth more than once, asking some of the same questions and new ones based on prior interviews to gain more understanding. (See the second column of Table 1.1.) The interviews could last for over an hour, whereas the questionnaires could be completed in minutes.

Some students jump to the conclusion that conducting qualitative research is easier because they really don't have to learn how to use statistics. However, quantitative research is more commonly used by students who must conduct primary research. With qualitative research it is common, especially for novice researchers, to wonder, "Should I interview the same people again? Should I interview more people? Do my results really tell me anything? What are my conclusions and are they correct?" These issues are much less common with quantitative research.

Also, qualitative research surveys require good interviewing skills that are not commonly taught in research and statistics courses. Effective interviewing requires more than simply coming up with a list of questions to ask during the interview. The interviewer

Table 1.1   Quantitative vs. Qualitative Research

Quantitative Research	Qualitative Research
1. Seeks to explain phenomena.	1. Seeks to understand phenomena.
2. Tests research questions (hypotheses).	2. Uses critical thinking to understand, rather than test.
3. Uses closed-ended, brief questions.	3. Uses open-ended, in-depth questions.
4. Uses a large sample size.	4. Uses a small sample size.
5. Data are collected, then analyzed once (questionnaire completed once).	5. Data are collected and analyzed as an ongoing process (may include multiple interviews with the same person).
6. There is a clear end to the data-collection process.	6. There is no clear end to the data-collection process.
7. Uses statistics to analyze data.	7. Does not use statistics to analyze data.
8. Results are objectively determined.	8. Results are subjectively determined.
9. Conclusions are reported to be generalized to population.	9. Conclusions are reported to help understand phenomena.

must be effective at listening and asking new, unprepared questions that result as the interviewee responds to the initial questions. Analyzing the interviews also takes skills that are not commonly taught in research and statistics courses. However, the skills needed to conduct quantitative research are commonly taught in these courses. Plus, it is usually easier to get help when conducting quantitative research.

Exploratory or Conclusive Research

*Exploratory research is conducted to provide preliminary data. **Conclusive research** is considered to provide the necessary information to make decisions.* Exploratory research is commonly used to provide qualitative data, whereas the conclusive research provides quantitative data. Exploration is often used to provide greater understanding of a concept or to help define a problem. Three interrelated purposes for exploratory research include (1) diagnosing a situation, (2) screening alternatives, and (3) discovering new ideas. This book focuses on conclusive research. Therefore, there is no further discussion of exploratory research other than an explanation of its three purposes, below. However, an understanding of conclusive research can help you to effectively conduct exploratory research.

Diagnosing a situation.

The exploratory research results indicate whether or not a conclusive study is needed. For example, human resource managers often want to diagnose a situation to answer questions (e.g., what are the employee's views on issues such as motivation and job satisfaction). If they believe there are no problems, a conclusive, full study is not needed. Thus, human resource professionals could talk to some employees to get an idea of the situation. Or if there is a specific problem suspected, it can be verified through exploratory data collection.

Screening alternatives.

This type of exploratory research is common in marketing. For example, Del Monte was considering selling a yogurt that did not need refrigeration. Rather than just come out with the product or conduct a complete study, Del Monte talked to people to "test the concept" and found that people did not believe yogurt was a product that did not need refrigeration. Del Monte decided that to overcome the belief would be too difficult and that the product would not be successful. As a result, they made the decision not to introduce the yogurt as part of their product line. A different product was selected.

Discovering new ideas.

Exploratory research is often conducted by getting a small group of employees together to discuss suggestions for increasing production, reducing costs, or improving safety. It is also used with customers or prospective customers to get ideas on product changes and new products. The focus-group interview, commonly used to gather exploratory data, is an unstructured, free-flowing interview with a group of between six and ten people. For example, a hospital could get a group of patients together to talk about improving the quality of health care. There are not a lot of predetermined questions. The moderator introduces the topic and encourages the group members to discuss the subjects among themselves. The group is encouraged to discuss their true feelings, anxieties, and frustrations, and to express their convictions in their own words. Again, these methods are exploratory and do not replace conclusive studies.

Descriptive or Inferential Research

Descriptive and inferential research are commonly considered to be conclusive research. As the term implies, descriptive research describes characteristics of a population or phenomenon. This type of research is designed to answer questions that ask who, what, where, when, or how much. *Descriptive research explains characteristics of participant data.* The governments of most developed countries collect descriptive data, which is available in libraries and on the Internet. Inferential research answers "why" questions. "Why do businesses fail?" is an inferential research question. *Inferential research goes beyond the descriptive to draw conclusions about the relationship among variables.* It is common to focus on the relationship between variables (e.g., What is the relationship between start-up business capital and business failure? What factors will predict business success versus failure?).

Descriptive and inferential are also the two primary types of statistics. Most inferential research studies include both descriptive and inferential statistics. For example, the major question could be, "Why do people smoke?" However, the researcher would also report descriptive statistics, such as "How many men vs. women smoke? At what age do people start smoking? How many times per day do people smoke?" Inferential is the highest level of research, with the goal of explaining and/or predicting and controlling phenomena. We will talk more about descriptive and inferential research in Chapter 4. You will learn how to conduct both descriptive and inferential statistics research in chapters 9–14. If you conduct research during or after this course, it probably will be inferential research.

> ### STOP READING and turn to the end of the chapter
> ### to complete exercises 1-4 through 1-6.

1.4 Research Terminology

No matter what types of research you conduct, there are important components that should be included in your research. Research includes concepts, definitions, variables, propositions or hypotheses, and possibly theories and models. Although academic research does focus on theory, much of the practical managerial research does not include a theory. Since it is important to know what a theory is, in this section we discuss important component terminology of all research within the framework of theory.

Before explaining what a theory is, let's take a minute to say what it is not. Some people contrast "theory" with "practice" by saying that something may be all right in theory but won't work in practice; such thinking conveys that theory is impractical. However, there is no contrast between theory and practice, because good theory leads to good practice—or good theories lead to correct decision making.

Theory and philosophy are not interchangeable terms. Plato, Aristotle, Locke, Marx, and Pareto were all philosophers who did not develop any theories. Nor is a theory the opposite of fact, although a theory and fact are each necessary for the other to be of value. Developing and testing a theory may lead to its becoming known as a fact. We all operate on the basis of theories. Theories explain what has happened in the past and predict what will happen in the future. Theories are, in a sense, generalizations you make about phenomena and the relationship among them. You use these generalizations to make decisions every day.

In simple terms, a theory is an explanation of a phenomenon. To be more specific, *a theory is a set of propositions or hypotheses based on interrelated concepts advanced to explain the relationship among variables.* Most theories are only partial, incomplete explanations that are often expanded and revised through further research. Notice that the goal of a theory is very similar to the goal of research in that they both attempt to explain an occurrence or circumstance observed through the research phenomena. Before you can fully understand what a theory is, you must understand what concepts, definitions, variables, propositions, and hypotheses are. Thus, we now discuss each part of a theory separately then pull them back together again under the umbrella of theory building.

Concepts

Concepts are basic to all thought and communication. *Concepts are abstract representations or characteristics of phenomena.* If we are to communicate about phenomena, there must be a common language with which to do so; this is the purpose of concepts. Hot, young, middle-class, leadership, motivation, quality, health care, organizational behavior, and research are all concepts that allow us to talk about abstract ideas and to understand what we are talking about. Concepts are created by classifying and categorizing phenomena beyond a single observation. When you hear or read the word *tree,* for example, this concept enables you to picture a large number of unique characteristics of a tree such as color, height, limbs, and leaves. This helps you to comprehend the concept of tree. We can overlook the ways in which pine, palm, and apple trees all differ from one another and grasp their generic resemblance via the concept. Concepts provide us with a perspective or way of looking at phenomena and classifying our experiences that allows us to generalize from them.

Concepts that are in frequent and general use have been developed over time through shared usage; we acquire them through personal experience. There are many concepts used in all organizations. Different cultures share many of the same concepts but often in different languages. However, there are concepts that do not translate well to other languages and there are concepts unique to a particular culture. New concepts are also developed through research.

Concepts serve as components of theories, and as such they are used to explain and predict phenomena. Concepts are critical elements in any theory because they define its content and attributes. For example, *supply* and *demand* are the pillars of economic theory; *power* and *legitimacy* define the substance of theories of governance. Isolated concepts are not theories. When we intentionally put concepts together for a given research and/or theory-building purpose, we have a *construct.* When we explain and predict how concepts relate to other concepts as a combined construct, we begin to construct theories. Thus, concept formation is an important part of theory construction.

Definitions

Research questions are based on concepts, and the success of your research is based on how well you conceptualize and how well others understand your research concepts. Therefore, it is important to clearly define the concepts you use in your research. There are two basic types of concept definitions: conceptual and operational. The difference between the two lies in the level of abstraction. Most people would define simple concepts such as *table* in a similar way. However, in the case of more abstract concepts such as *leadership* and *business failure,* people tend to define them in very different ways. If we defined leadership as the ability to influence others and business failure as a firm that is losing money, we still have a conceptual definition, because these are abstract definitions. Note that conceptual definitions also tend to use other concepts in their definition. *Operational definitions are concepts stated in measurable terms that can be tested empirically.* The measures must be so specific that any competent person using them would classify the phenomena in the same way.

As an example, let's say our research question is, "How motivated are our employees?" A conceptual definition could be that motivation is the willingness to work hard to achieve organizational objectives. To make our definition operational, motivation is the scaled score from 1 (not motivated) to 7 (highly motivated). Box 1.1 illustrates how the question could be asked.

As you can see, the answers to the question based on the conceptual definition of motivation will be very diverse, and it will be difficult to measure the motivation level of employees, but the operational definition is measurable. However, keep in mind that a concept and the operational definition are not the same thing. Operational definitions are commonly quite narrow and also open to interpretation, unless you get more specific and add more questions to measure willingness to work. Also, realize that the research question on motivation is a descriptive study of your organization and thus is not a theory of motivation. We will explain measurement in more detail with variables.

Box 1.1   Conceptual and Operational Definitions

Conceptual Definition: Motivation is the willingness to work hard to achieve organizational objectives.
How motivated are you?

Operational Definition: Motivation is the willingness to work hard to achieve organizational objectives. *Identify your level of motivation on the scale below by circling the number that best describes your motivation level.*

1	2	3	4	5	6	7

Not motivated ← ─────────────────────────────→ **Highly motivated**

Conceptual or empirical research levels. Conceptual and operational definitions are often referred to as being at the conceptual (abstract) level or the empirical level. Research articles are usually classified as conceptual or empirical. Conceptual research is generally based on secondary research; thus, the authors do not collect primary data and they develop propositions and theories without actually empirically testing them. Recall that secondary data include primary data of other researchers, so in a sense primary data may be used. On the other hand, *empirical research is based on collecting and analyzing primary data to test a research question or theory.* Empirical refers to sense "experience" in observation or manipulation of phenomena; statistics are commonly, but not always, used to analyze data. Most students who take a research course that includes or is followed by a research project/thesis will conduct empirical research. This book will show you how to do so.

CONCEPTUAL OBJECTIVE 3
Explain the difference between a concept and an operational definition.

Variables

The concepts that we are measuring and testing are on the empirical rather than conceptual level and are thus called variables. *A **variable** is an empirical-level concept of study with at least two values/scales of measurement.* In our example above, the concept of motivation has been operationally defined and is thus a variable under study. A variable can have any number of scales from two to infinity. Males and females are not two variables; gender is one variable with two scales of measurement: one for males and one for females. Our definition of motivation has seven scales of measurement. The ages of the people in a class can have many scales of measurement from, say, 25 to 60. A concept with only one level of measurement is called a *constant.* In our motivation question *employees* is a constant because it has only one level of measurement. However, the concept *employees* can become a variable by splitting it into groups such as nonmanagers and managers. Thus, you could compare the motivation level of nonmanagers to that of managers, as well as comparing males to females and comparing age groups.

Dependent and independent variables.

Researchers are interested in studying the relationship between variables. Therefore, variables are classified as independent or dependent to help explain the relationship. *The **dependent variable (DV/Y)** is measured for changes to explain relationships.* It is also called the *criterion variable. The **independent variable (IV/X)** is the hypothesized explanation of the change in the value of the dependent variable.* It is also called the *predictor variable.* The dependent variable is expected to be caused or influenced by the independent variable, or it is measured to assess the effect of the X. Table 1.2 features some sets of words that can help you classify variables. However, the same variable can change from one category to another to test different hypotheses. There are also control, moderating or interacting, extraneous, and intervening variables; we discuss them in the statistics chapter. For now, let's keep it simple and focus on DV/Y and IV/X.

In mathematics the dependent variable appears on the left-hand side of an equation and the independent variable is on the right-hand side. For example, in $Y = f(X)$, Y represents the dependent variable and X the independent variable, with f representing "is a function of." Thus, changes in the value of X are associated with changes in the value of Y, or X yields Y.

Table 1.2   Variables

Dependent Variable (Y)	Independent Variable (X)
measured change	manipulated to change value of Y
effect	cause
criterion	predictor
response	stimulus
consequence	preceding event

Example of a test of difference.

What if you want to explain whether motivation is related to type of job, or whether motivation is measured for changes between types of jobs, or whether the type of job affects motivation? To test the relationship, you would survey employees in different types of jobs (X) and compare motivation scores (Y). If the scores vary significantly among job types, then you can conclude that there is a relationship between these two variables. It is important not to reverse the Y and X, because you are not measuring the type of job.

Example of a test of prediction.

If you want to determine whether motivation is related to income, motivation is the Y (predicted to/criterion variable) and income is the X (predicted from/predictor variable), or the value of motivation can be predicted by the value of income. To test the relationship, you would survey employees and ask for their income and motivation levels. If the level of motivation increases with income, there is a positive relationship. Thus, if you know employees' income, you can predict their motivation level.

CONCEPTUAL OBJECTIVE 4
Define variable and discuss the relationship between dependent and independent variables.

Variable measurement.

The assignment of number values to variables is called **measurement.** Variables have three basic levels of measurement: nominal, ordinal, and interval/ratio. Numbers are used in three ways: (1) to nominally name variable scales, (2) to ordinally rank variable scales, and (3) to represent actual quantity.

The first and lowest level of measurement is *nominal,* which is *a labeling activity,* or a means of categorizing things by arbitrarily assigning values. For example, males could be given the value 0 or 1 and females 1 or 2. Types of jobs can be given a number for each type (e.g., manager = 1, salesperson = 2, etc.).

The second level of measurement is *ordinal, a ranking activity,* which is often an arbitrary assignment of values. For example, in Box 1.1 we are measuring motivation on a 7-point scale. However, it could have 3, 5, or any other number of scales, and the scales could be reversed with 1 as high and 7 as low.

The third and highest level of measurement is interval/ratio. *Interval measures* are standardized numbers such as IQ, college entrance, or TOEFL test scores, or a grouping of number values such as ages 1–10, 11–20, 21–30 and so on. With *ratio measures,* there is a lower limit or absolute 0 value, such as a minimum annual income of $40,000. With interval/ratio-level measures there is no arbitrary assignment of values. You would not arbitrarily assign someone an age or income; you would use the actual number. You will learn more about variables and measurement in Chapter 10.

CONCEPTUAL OBJECTIVE 5
State the major differences between nominal, ordinal, and interval/ratio levels of measurement.

With both nominal and ordinal levels of measurement, values are generally arbitrarily assigned. Therefore, the number of scales to use is an issue to consider at these two lower levels. However, with interval/ratio levels of measurement the number of scales is determined by the actual value of the numbers received through the data collection. In other words, the number of scales is known with nominal and ordinal variables, but it is not known with interval/ratio data. Therefore, in exercises 1-7 through 1-14, identify the number of scales for nominal and ordinal, but for interval/ratio just select unknown.

> ## STOP READING and turn to the end of the chapter to complete exercises 1-7 through 1-14.

Propositions and Hypotheses

Propositions and hypotheses are both tentative answers to a research question. However, a proposition is a statement about concepts that may be judged as true or false if the phenomenon is observable. For this reason, propositions are commonly used in conceptual studies/articles. When a proposition is stated so that the variables can be empirically measured and tested, it is called a hypothesis. Thus, hypotheses are commonly used in empirical studies/articles. *A hypothesis is a tentative answer to a research question stating the relationship between variables.* Hypotheses are critical to research because they force the researcher to clearly state how the research question will be answered in empirical (measurable and testable) terms.

As an example, let's use our research question, "How motivated are our employees?" A proposition could be that our employees are motivated. A hypothesis might be that our employees could have a motivation score of 5.5 or greater. Note that the hypothesis is a *tentative* answer—or it is what you *expect* the results of testing to be. Also note that this hypothesis does not explain the relationship between variables because there is only one variable—*motivation; employees* is a constant and is therefore an example of the less commonly used *descriptive hypothesis*. The statement, "Employees who have A, B, C jobs are more highly motivated than employees who have X, Y, Z jobs" does state the relationship between variables—an example of the more commonly used *relationship hypothesis.* The type of job (6 scales of nominal-level measurement) and motivation (7 scales of ordinal-level measurement) are the variables, and the relationship expected is that certain stated jobs are more motivating than others. Hypotheses, like the goal of research, are designed to explain, predict, and/or control phenomena related to variables under study. You will learn more about writing and testing hypotheses in Chapter 11.

The difference between a proposition/hypothesis and a theory.

A hypothesis is less complex than a theory because a hypothesis is usually a single statement about the relationship between two variables. Hypotheses *predict* a specific phenomenon while a theory *explains* a phenomenon. Theories are developed at the conceptual and empirical level, whereas hypotheses are tested at the empirical level. Therefore, a research study can have multiple hypotheses and not test a theory. Theories, on the other hand, are based on multiple propositions or hypotheses and variables for which the relationships must be explained.

The difference between conceptual and empirical use of propositions and hypotheses.

Two highly respected Academy of Management professional journals make a clear distinction between conceptual research articles that use propositions and empirical research articles that use hypotheses. In contrast, the *Academy of Management Review* includes conceptual articles that state propositions. The *Academy of Management Journal* includes empirical articles that state hypotheses. Furthermore, the *Journal* articles statistically test hypotheses, usually with primary data, while the *Review* does not statistically test propositions with secondary data. Articles in both journals usually present theories. Thus, the articles in both publications are very strongly based on—or use many references from—prior research articles.

CONCEPTUAL OBJECTIVE 6
Describe the relationship between propositions/hypotheses and theories.

Theory Building

Using our motivation example, for it to become a theory you must add more variables and explain or predict the relationship among the variables. However, you cannot just put together a series of unrelated hypotheses and variables and call it a theory. For example, to develop a theory you could propose that motivation is related to type of job and income level. A very simple theory could be that as employees get certain jobs and increase their income, their motivation level increases. More specifically, you hypothesize that people in certain jobs are more highly motivated than employees in other jobs and that employees with higher income levels are more highly motivated. To test your hypotheses/theory you would follow the steps in the research process, surveying people both in different jobs and at different income levels and compare their motivation scores. If the employees whom you expected to have a higher level of motivation do in fact have significantly higher motivation scores and higher incomes, then your theory has been confirmed by evidence. However, if scores and income are not significantly different, your results do *not* confirm (or they *refute*) your theory. You should also conduct research by examining the data in other ways, using other variables that were not included in your original hypotheses. For example, you could compare motivation by gender or race to see if there are differences in motivation of these groups. These findings could further explain motivation.

Another example of a theory includes three variables: fear of AIDS, knowledge of AIDS, and sexual promiscuity. The theory is that fear of AIDS is affected by knowledge and promiscuity. The hypotheses are that knowledge would be negatively related to fear (because knowledge would foster behavior that would reduce the risk of AIDS). Promiscuity was hypothesized to be positively related to fear (for the obvious reason that promiscuity is known to increase the risk of AIDS). Notice that the hypotheses are followed by the reasons for the predictions of the theory. For complete details of this study see Herzog, T. (1996). *Research Methods in the Social Sciences*. New York, HarperCollins, pp. 1–3.

If the results of your study confirm your theory, this does not "prove" that it is correct. Results only provide one piece of evidence that the theory is not wrong. Theories are often tested multiple times by different researchers to provide further evidence to support and to develop them. There are also multiple theories for many concepts. For example, principles of management textbooks commonly feature eight motivation theories (by Maslow, Alderfer, Herzberg, McClelland, Adams, Vroom, Locke, and Skinner). Although some of these motivation theories do not have strong empirically tested results they are still studied in courses today.

Most students simply test hypotheses rather than theories. In the above examples, because the theories are simple it may be better not to call them theories, but rather a test of hypotheses. Our sample theories, like most theories, only partly explain motivation and behavior. In our motivation example, other variables also contribute to motivation such as personality and values, coworkers, managers, the organizational culture, and so on. These variables could be added to further develop this theory. The same holds true for the theory about AIDS.

Through an extensive literature review, the important variables and methods for measuring and testing them are usually identified, and they give the study a strong theoretical foundation. Thus, the literature review is crucial to both hypothesis testing and theory building. You will learn more about the literature review in the next chapter.

Deductive and inductive reasoning.

Deductive reasoning is the process of deriving a conclusion from a known premise, or going from general to specific statements. For example, if we know that all employees are human beings, then we can deduce that employee Joel is a human being. *Inductive reasoning* is the process of establishing a general proposition on the basis of observations of a phenomenon, or going from a specific observation to a generalized statement. For example, Joel and the other the five employees I've seen in this organization are human beings. Therefore, all its employees are human beings.

Deduction is often associated with a top-down approach in which the researcher begins with a theory, whereas induction is often associated with a bottom-up approach in which the researcher begins with some observation and goes on to develop a theory. Theories can be, and often are, developed using both inductive and deductive reasoning.

Most students are interested in finding the answer to some research question, so they commonly use a sample group and generalize the results of the answers to the larger population. Distinguishing which type of reasoning or combination of reasoning you use in your research is not that important. Remember that students are usually concerned about testing hypotheses rather than developing theories.

Models

Research models are usually not physical replications; rather, they use symbols, concepts, and variables to illustrate results. More specifically, a model is a simplified representation of reality that delineates those aspects of the real-world phenomena the researcher considers to be relevant to the study. Models enable the researcher to formulate empirically testable propositions regarding the nature of these relationships. Ideally, after testing we will better understand the real-world phenomena. While the role of a theory is to explain the relationship among variables, this is not the role of a model. *A **model** is used to represent the reality of the phenomenon.* Thus, theories can be developed with or without the use of models, and models can be used without developing theories.

CONCEPTUAL OBJECTIVE 7
Describe the difference in the role of a theory and the role of a model, and explain their relationship.

Box 1.2 features an example of a prediction model. The research question is, "Why do some business succeed and others fail?" To better understand why, the author of this book reviewed the literature to determine the variables considered to be contributing factors to success or failure (S/F) and thus developed this success-versus-failure prediction model.

Box 1.2   Prediction Model

S/F = f (capital, record keeping and financial control, industry experience, management experience, planning, professional advisors, education, staffing, product timing, economic timing, age of owner, partners, parents owned a business, minority, marketing skills)

S/F is actually two scales of one Y (dependent variable), which is performance. Note that there are 15 X (independent variables) used to predict success or failure. All 15 variables were operationally defined to test the model. The model was tested using logistic regression (discussed later in the book). The model was significant at predicting success or failure. However, only 4 of the 15 X (planning, professional advisors, education, and staffing) were significant predictor variables of Y. For complete details of this study see Lussier, R. N. (1995). "A nonfinancial success versus failure prediction model for young firms," *Journal of Small Business Management* 33(1), 8–20. The model was later tested in Croatia: Lussier, R. N. and Pfeifer, S. (2000). "A comparison of business success vs. failure variables between U.S. and Central Eastern Europe Croatian Entrepreneurs," *Entrepreneurship Theory and Practice* 24(4). Most students do not develop models.

**STOP READING and turn to the end of the chapter
to complete exercises 1-15 through 1-17.**

1.5 Characteristics of Good Research

Now that you have a better understanding of research, let's talk about how you know whether your research, or someone else's, is good research. What criteria should we use to evaluate research? Your first thought might be that if my hypothesis or theory is confirmed, it is good research. However, as you will learn throughout this book, poorly designed and conducted research can lead one to make poor decisions without realizing it. You can identify good research by confirming that it meets four criteria: testability, generalizability or generalization, value, and replicability.

Is It Testable?

In prior sections, you learned about the need to clearly determine the purpose of the study, which is to answer some research question(s) through operationally defining variables so that they can be measured and tested. You also learned about the need for clearly stating propositions and hypotheses so that the research question(s) is clear, enabling you to determine whether the research question(s) has been answered. Most of this chapter relates to this topic, and below is a form of review for some of the material.

Statistical testing leads to findings that are more objective and thus provides credibility. Both basic and applied research data, as well as several secondary and primary research data, can be statistically tested. For example, if you want to know which type of customers—manufacturing or service—pay their bills to your company more quickly, you could go to the accounting department, get a secondary data sample of bills from both groups, and run a statistical test of differences to determine which (if either) pays more quickly. Quantitative and conclusive research are generally statistically testable, but qualitative and exploratory research are not. Descriptive research generally does use statistics, but it does not test anything; rather, it describes characteristics, while inferential research is statistically testable. Furthermore, propositions are not statistically tested while hypotheses are generally statistically tested.

Another very important factor in the testability of research is the design and methodology for collecting data and analyzing the results. It is important that the data-collection instrument (often a questionnaire) and the data collected meet the test of reliability and validity. (You will learn more about these concepts in later chapters.) Thus, being testable is an important characteristic of good research. By the time you have finished reading this book, you should be able to design a research study that can be tested, and you should be able to evaluate the research of others.

Is It Generalizable?

Generalization refers to the scope of applicability of research findings to multiple settings (*external validity*). This means, for example, that if employees are found to be particularly susceptible to peer pressure in one setting, the results would probably be the same in a different but related setting. Generally, the wider the range of applicability to the results generated by research, the more useful the research is.

Generalization widens with sample size, number of places and areas of observation, and variety of settings, as well as other factors. For example, as the size of the surveyed population increases—from one state, one region, or from the entire country or multiple countries—the generalizability of the findings will widen. Also, generalization is widened as studies are conducted by different researchers in different settings with similar results, or it is incremental as it builds over time.

Primary research usually ensures greater generalization than secondary research. Quantitative research is usually more generalized than qualitative research. Conclusive research has more generalization than exploratory. Inferential research is more generalizable than descriptive research because the former goes beyond the descriptive. Basic research has more generalization than applied research. For example, an academic researcher may ask the research question, "Are American workers motivated?" In contrast, an organizational researcher may ask the research question, "How motivated are our employees?" To gain generalization, the academic researcher would survey a large sample of employees, from multiple organizations, over a wide area, from different industries. The organizational researcher may also use a large sample but from only one organization, which may be from one location only, from one industry. However, this does not mean that basic research is more valuable than applied; it only means that their objectives are different.

Generalization is a major goal of basic research, not of applied. One of the values of basic research, in some cases, is to be a substitute for applied research or make it unnecessary. A major goal of applied research is to solve a specific problem through decision making. Thus, to make a specific decision, data from one organization are more valuable than general data (*internal validity*). However, the general data should be used as a foundation for the organization-specific research. In some cases, organizations may find a study similar enough to their own that they can use the results, enabling them to save the time and effort that would be involved in conducting the primary research.

Is It Valuable?

Research value provides new and useful answers to research questions. Let's begin this discussion by stating that all the types of research presented have the potential to be valuable. Research is valuable when it helps to answer a research question that provides new and useful information, regardless of the outcome. For example, if you hypothesize that your employees are motivated, and your findings confirm that they are, this is valuable information. Also, if findings do *not* confirm (i.e., refute) your hypotheses, it means that your employees are not motivated. This information is valuable because you can take corrective action to increase their motivation. From another perspective, knowing what does not work helps us to know what does; it keeps us from making mistakes or repeating the same mistakes or drawing wrong decisions. The Del Monte example of not offering the nonrefrigerated yogurt illustrates this point. Also, reporting the results of a theory that was not confirmed enables others to use it, revise it, and retest it.

On the other hand, research is not valuable if it answers research questions that are already answered or provides information that will not be used, regardless of the outcome. For example, from the organizational perspective, researchers have confirmed that, generally, today's workers want to participate in decision making. Thus, an organization having a suggestion system that collects data but whose managers use autocratic decision making and have no interest in using any of the ideas (or only a few great ones) are gathering data that is not valuable, because they have no real intention of using the information. Even the greatest employee ideas are useless if no action is taken. Besides, employees will catch on to the game management is playing and will stop making suggestions. Also, unfortunately, many managers ask for research yet don't use it if the results are not what they want to hear. These managers deny the reality of the situation and make their own decisions regardless of what the research shows.

From the student perspective, conducting a basic research study that simply duplicates prior research that has been confirmed many times is not very valuable. If a research topic has been studied multiple times over multiple periods, and few or no new studies have been undertaken in the last couple of years, there may be very little new to learn about the concept. To be valuable, the study should add some new information to increase the generalizability of the prior research. To this end, you could use prior research but use a sample with a different age, location, industry, or some other variable to see if results are the same, thus adding some new knowledge. Conducting applied research that will be used to make a decision for an organization can be very valuable.

Is It Replicable?

Being replicable ties in with the other three criteria for good research. Research is replicable if the research questions, design, and methodology/procedures for conducting the study are so clear that any person with reasonable research skills could conduct the same study and get the same test results. However, to replicate an exact study for the sake of replication is a waste of time. As you will learn, it is unnecessary if correct research methods have been used. Rather, research that can be reliably replicated serves as the basis for further research in the same area. A study conducted in one area that is then replicated in another area (e.g., by using samples of industry, age groups, and so on) and produces the same results increases the generalizability of the findings. Thus, replication that provides new knowledge related to generalization is valuable research. In fact, there are very few, if any, completely new research designs that are not based on some form of replication from prior studies. To claim total originality would be to claim that one does not use standard research methods. Researchers make the claim that they have followed sound research methods that provide valuable (new and useful) information. And testing makes the value of the research more credible.

A few words of caution: Be careful that the conclusions you draw from the data are confined to those justified by the data of the research and limited to those for which the data provide an adequate basis. In other words, do not broaden the basis of induction by including your personal experiences—and worse, your opinions—in your results and conclusions that are not actually tested through the research. Also, be careful not to overgeneralize your research findings. Generalizations are the usual or common circumstances, which often have limitation exceptions; so when you know them, state them. For example, we stated earlier in this chapter that ordinal data generally have arbitrary assignment of values. The limiting exception is when things are ranked, such as placement in a race. In these situations, there is an actual first and second (and so on) place that is not arbitrary. In all research, and especially applied research, results have limited generalizability and weaknesses, which are commonly called *limitations*. It's good research practice to present the limitations, which include any exceptions and weaknesses of a study.

CONCEPTUAL OBJECTIVE 8
List and briefly explain the characteristics of good research.

**STOP READING and turn to the end of the chapter
to complete exercises 1-18 through 1-20.**

1.6 The Research Process and the Plan for This Book

As stated in the introduction to this chapter, this book will enable you to become more familiar with the scientific method. If you say you don't like science, what you fail to realize is that what makes someone a scientist is not *what* they study but *how* they study it. The one thing all scientists have in common is that they follow the same scientific method, often referred to as the research process to make decisions. *The **research process** includes (1) the research question and literature review, (2) research design methodology for collecting data, (3) data analysis and interpreting results, and (4) making conclusions.* These research process steps refer to conducting empirical research.

Although journals are different and may use slightly different terms, if you look at a professional journal that publishes empirical research you may find that the steps in the research process are itemized in the headings within the article. Empirical articles commonly have (1) an introduction/purpose of the study/hypotheses, which may appear before or within the literature review; (2) methodology; (3) results; and (4) conclusions. This book follows the steps in the research process commonly found in empirical research articles. The table below briefly lists each step of the research process and where in the book you will learn more about it as you develop your scientific skills.

The Research Process

(1) The research question/purpose of the study, literature review, and hypotheses.	(2) Research design methodology for collecting data.	(3) Data analysis and interpreting results.	(4) Discussing results and making conclusions.
• *Introduction*	• *Methods*	• *Results*	• *Discussion*
Chapters 1–3	Chapters 4–8	Chapters 9–14	Chapters 9–14

The examples in this book lay out some of the basic style elements of the American Psychological Association (APA) research format the research studies use. Chapter 3 shows you how to develop a research proposal and accompanying study in APA style (the preferred style for scholarly research).

Part I of this book features research designs and data-collection methods, Part II addresses the research process, and Part III deals with data analysis. *Parts IV, V, and VI appear in the CD that accompanies this book (inserted on the back cover).* They are appendices containing a sample research proposal, a sample completed study, and a sample statistical analysis, respectively. The key elements of the research process sometimes overlap among these parts, as follows:

Part I. The Research Process: Introduction
The Research Question/Purpose of the Study, Literature Review, and Hypotheses

Part I outlines the various types of research. In chapter 1 you will learn about the development of the problem and research question. In chapter 2 the research question is again discussed, this time in connection with the literature review. These two topics appear in this same chapter because you start with a general idea for a topic/question and then refine it through the literature review. The appendix in Part IV, *The Research Proposal*, features a sample research proposal and instructions for completing an introduction and a literature review section for the research proposal. Chapter 3 explains the elements of a research proposal and how the proposal becomes part of the completed study.

Part II. Method
Research Design Methodology for Collecting Data

In Part II, chapters 4–8, you will learn the details of methodology for data collection. Chapter 4 features the various research designs, Chapter 5 explains sampling methodology, Chapter 6 discusses data-collection methods, and Chapter 7 teaches development of survey questionnaires for data collection. Chapter 8 addresses methods of ensuring that reliable and valid measures are used when collecting data. (Instructions are included for completing the Method section for a research proposal in the appendix in Part IV.)

Part III. Results and Discussion
Data Analysis, Interpreting Results, and Discussion of the Findings

In Part III, chapters 9–14, you will learn the details of data analysis using statistics to interpret results. Chapter 9 presents organizing data, frequencies, and basic descriptive statistics. Chapter 10 teaches how to select the appropriate inferential statistic by using a Decision Tree that includes more than 30 statistical tests. Chapter 11 identifies the steps to test hypotheses, discusses Type I and Type II errors, and shows how to make decisions to accept or reject hypotheses based on probability values. Chapter 12 focuses on experimental designs and how to run and interpret tests of difference (T-test, Z-test, Mann-Whitney U, chi-square, and one-way analysis of variance—ANOVA). Chapter 13 explains how to run and interpret correlation (Pearson, Spearman, and partial), regression (bivariate, multivariate, with dummy variables, logistic), and model building (stepwise and hierarchal regression). In addition, Chapter 13 is an invaluable aid in understanding meta-analysis and canonical analysis. Chapter 14 teaches how to run and interpret two-way ANOVA and multivariate analysis of variance (MANOVA—one-way and factorial); also discussed are cluster analysis, statistical tests that use control variables (ANCOVA/MANCOVA, Cross-tabulation—chi-square, AID, CHAID), and other advanced statistics (LISREL, path analysis, conjoint analysis, MDS, and time-series analysis). A sample completed study and instructions for completing the results section for a completed research study appear in the appendix in Part V, *The Completed Study*.

The three digital appendices in Parts IV, V, and VI on the accompanying CD augment what you learn in the book.

Part IV. The Research Proposal (Appendix RP)

This appendix provides a sample research proposal to use as a template for developing an original research proposal as part of the course. The proposal is actually completed in four parts as you progress through chapters 1–10. Instructions for each of the four parts are included at the end of the chapters and in this appendix.

Part V. The Completed Study (Appendix CS)

Completing a research study may be required in the course you are taking. This appendix provides a sample completed study to use as a template for conducting a research study with either real or fictitious data. The study is actually completed in four parts as you progress through the textbook chapters 1–14. Instructions for each of the four parts are included at the end of the chapters and in this appendix. You can extend the completed study by conducting additional statistical analysis.

Part VI. Statistical Analysis (Appendix SA)

As the name implies, this appendix focuses on statistics. However, it is similar to the completed study appendix in that through these seven assignments, one (1) selects a research question, (2) develops hypotheses and (3) a questionnaire, (4) collects data, (5) runs statistics, (6) presents results, and (7) discusses the findings. The major difference is that one goes beyond a typical completed study that uses only the statistics that are truly relevant. Through the assignments, one of each of the major statistical research designs is run to complete a study: test of difference (T-test, chi-square), test of association (Pearson, Spearman), test of prediction (regressions), and test of interaction (two-way ANOVA, MANOVA), even though a test may not be relevant to the research. Instructions for each of the seven assignments are included at the end of the chapters and in this appendix.

CONCEPTUAL OBJECTIVE 9
List the steps in the research process with their section titles.

SKI WEST STUDY

As we bring this chapter to a close, you should be able to:
- *understand the importance of studying research and statistics,*
- *know what research is and when to use it,*
- *describe five goals and types of research,*
- *define research terms,*
- *identify the characteristics of good research, and*
- *understand the process of this book.*

The appendix in Part IV features an example of a research proposal that becomes a completed study in the Part V appendix. Every chapter in this book ends with an explanation of how the chapter material was used in the Ski West Study. We begin the Ski West sections with a brief chapter overview and then apply the text concepts to the study. However, this first chapter provides an introduction to the study.

The Ski West Study was conducted by Matthew McLeish, a Springfield College graduate student majoring in industrial/organizational psychology. Matt completed the research proposal in 2008 and conducted the study and turned his research proposal into a completed study in 2009. This is an actual study, conducted at a real company and using its employee data. However, the name of the seasonal business has been changed to Ski West to preserve confidentiality. You can review this sample research proposal and completed study in appendices Parts IV and V at any time—before, during, or after you read this section in each chapter.

As you read the description of how Matt applied the concepts from Chapter 1 to his study, keep in mind that you are reading the finalized version. It took him lots of drafting and editing, as well as input from professors, to come up with his proposal and completed study. So you are not yet expected to have a clear idea of what you want to do for a study. The idea is to read what Matt did to give you ideas on what you want to study. So if you haven't already started to think about your own study, get going now.

Matt was interested in studying research methods and statistics because he had career plans in human resource management, and he understood that research skills would help him advance in his chosen field. Early in the course, Matt identified a couple of possible research topic areas that he could develop into a research question. Do you have any ideas yet? Matt understood that he would have to conduct primary research that was quantitative, and being career oriented he wanted to pursue applied research. He did conduct a conclusive research study that provided descriptive data about his sample, but the focus of the study was on inferential research.

Matt did not conduct a study that was highly theoretical, but he did develop hypotheses based on interrelated concepts advanced to explain the relationship between two variables. The two concepts of his study were personality testing and performance evaluations. These two concepts were operationally defined as the Conscientious Scale to measure personality and end-of-season evaluation to measure job performance. Conscientious Scale was his dependent variable measured on a test based on 100 possible points, and end-of-season evaluation was the independent variable, measured on a range between 10 and 50, and both variables are interval/ratio-level data. Other descriptive normative Xs included gender, age, and department. Matt's main hypothesis was: Conscientious Scale scores can predict the end-of-season evaluation scores.

Matt did not attempt to develop a theory or a complex model, but Matt's study of Ski West meets the characteristics of good research because it is: (1) testable—Matt conducted a test to determine if personality testing can predict job performance; (2) generalizable—the sample employee results presumably can be applicable to the entire company employee population; (3) valuable—his discussion makes implications that the HR staff can implement to improve job performance at Ski West; and (4) replicable—others have conducted similar studies before him and others can do so after him.

In the Part IV and Part V appendices you can read Matt's research proposal and completed study. Matt includes: (1) an introduction, stating the purpose of his study, and a literature review with hypotheses; (2) a research methodology section, stating his research design for collecting data and explaining how he conducted his study; (3) results, stating his statistical findings; and (4) discussion, stating his findings in nonstatistical terms, comparison of his findings to the literature, limitations, recommendations for further research, and implications.

CHAPTER SUMMARY AND GLOSSARY

The chapter summary is organized in a way that provides you with the answers necessary to help you meet the conceptual objectives for this chapter.

1. **Define research and explain when to use it.**
   Research is the systematic process through which new knowledge is discovered by answering questions. Research should be used when the decision is nonroutine and costly, time is available to conduct the research, data are available, and the benefits of conducting the research outweighs its cost.

2. **Describe the difference between secondary and primary research.**
   The difference between secondary and primary research is who gathers the data. Secondary data analyzed by the researcher have been gathered by others while primary data is collected through observation and/or survey by the researcher.

3. **Explain the difference between a concept and an operational definition.**
   A concept is an abstract definition, while an operational definition is stated in measurable terms that are empirically testable.

4. **Define *variable* and discuss the relationship between dependent and independent variables.**
   A variable is an empirical-level concept of study with at least two scales of measurement. The relationship between dependent and independent variables is one in which the value of the Y is expected to be caused or influenced by the X.

5. **State the major differences between nominal, ordinal, and interval/ratio levels of measurement.**
   Nominal- and ordinal-level variables are usually arbitrarily assigned number values while interval/ratio variables use their actual number values.

6. **Describe the relationship between propositions/hypotheses and theories.**
   Propositions and hypotheses are parts of theories. More specifically, theories combine multiple propositions or hypotheses to explain the relationship among multiple variables.

7. **Describe the difference in the role of a theory and the role of a model, and explain their relationship.**
   The role of a theory is to explain the relationship among variables, while the role of a model is to represent the reality of the phenomenon. The relationship between a theory and a model only exist when a theory includes a model.

8. **List and briefly describe the characteristics of good research.**
   The four characteristics of good research include:
   - *Testability*—good research answers questions by defining variables so that they can be measured and tested.
   - *Generalizability*—findings from one setting can be assumed to be the same in different but related settings.
   - *Value*—research has value when it provides new and useful answers to research questions.
   - *Replicability*—the research can be repeated with the same results.

9. **List the steps in the research process with their section titles.**
   The research process includes: (1) *Introduction*—the research question/purpose of the study, literature review, and hypotheses; (2) *Method*—research design methodology for collecting data; and (3) *Results and Discussion*—data analysis, interpreting results, and discussion of the findings.

10. **Define the following alphabetical list of key terms.** Select one or more methods: (1) fill in the missing key terms from memory, (2) match the key terms with their definitions below, or (3) copy the key terms in order from the list at the beginning of the chapter.

KEY TERMS

applied research	goals of research	primary research
basic research	hypothesis	research
concepts	independent variable (IV/X)	research problem
conclusive research	inferential research	research process
dependent variable (DV/Y)	measurement	secondary research
descriptive research	model	theory
empirical research	operational definitions	variable
exploratory research		

_____ occurs when there are questions that need to be answered through research.

_____ is the systematic process through which new knowledge is discovered through answering questions.

_____ explain, predict, and control phenomena.

_____ involves data that have been collected by others.

_____ includes data that have been collected by the researcher conducting the study.

_____ is conducted to better understand concepts and theories as it attempts to expand the limits of knowledge.

_____ is conducted as an aid in solving a specific problem.

_____ is conducted to provide preliminary data.

_____ is conducted to provide the information necessary to make decisions.

_____ explains characteristics of participant data.

_____ goes beyond descriptive research to draw conclusions about the relationship among variables.

_____ is a set of propositions or hypotheses based on interrelated concepts advanced to explain the relationship among variables.

_____ are abstract representations or characteristics of phenomena.

_____ are concepts stated in measurable terms that can be tested empirically.

_____ is based on collecting and analyzing primary data to test a research question or theory.

_____ is an empirical-level concept of study with at least two values/scales of measurement.

_____ is measured for changes to explain relationships.

_____ is the hypothesized explanation of the change in the value of the dependent variable.

_____ is the assignment of number values to variables.

_____ is a tentative answer to a research question stating the relationship between variables.

_____ is used to represent the reality of the phenomenon.

_____ includes: (1) the research question and literature review, (2) research design methodology for collecting data, (3) data analysis and interpreting results, and (4) making conclusions.

WRITTEN ASSIGNMENTS

Your instructor may have you write (1) a research proposal, (2) a completed study, and/or (3) statistical analysis papers during this course. These three assignments are briefly introduced within the chapters, and detailed instructions are provided in the three corresponding digital appendices, including examples of each of the three items.

In essence, the research proposal, completed study, and statistical analysis papers are completed in steps as you progress through the chapters of the book. The assignments are cumulative throughout the chapters, each building on previous assignments until you have developed a completed research proposal and/or completed statistical study.

Your instructor may or may not require you to complete any of the assignments or require you to turn any of them in. However, you can complete them on your own if you wish to do so. If your instructor requires only a completed research proposal and/or completed study, creating the paper in steps through the written chapter assignments will greatly improve the quality of your work.

A COMPARISON OF THE THREE WRITTEN ASSIGNMENTS

Before you conduct any research, you begin by writing a proposal that contains an *Introduction* section and a *Method* section. In essence, all three appendices include a proposal featuring these two sections. The difference is that the research proposal (Part IV, Appendix RP) stops at the proposal stage. The completed study (Part V, Appendix CS) goes on to the next two stages of the research process to include the *Results* and *Discussion* sections. The statistical analysis (Part VI, Appendix SA) requires only a brief introduction that stays the same for all the assignments, but the hypothesis and the Method section of these papers change with each individual paper, based on the statistical analysis required.

Therefore, although your completed study will use only the portion(s) of the statistical test(s) that answer your research question, the statistical papers presented in Appendix SA require the use of all the major statistical analyses presented in chapters 9–14.

ASSIGNMENT 1 FOR RESEARCH PROPOSAL, COMPLETED STUDY, AND STATISTICAL ANALYSIS PAPER

Although this is not an actual part of Assignment 1, it is good preparation for it.

List three to ten ideas on research questions that you would like to study. Include the following criteria from sections 1.3 and 1.4 of this chapter.

- What are your research goals, and what types of research are you interested in conducting?

- List any concepts, definitions, variables, propositions, or hypotheses you want to test.

There are no detailed instructions in the appendices related to Chapter 1.

EXERCISES

COURSE BENEFITS

1-1   State how you believe you will benefit from this course.

USING RESEARCH AND THE RESEARCH QUESTION

1-2   Give an example of how an organization you work(ed) for could use research.

1-3   Write the tentative question(s) you will answer through research during and/or after this course. In the next chapter, and through most of this book, you will refine your research question(s).

IDENTIFYING TYPES OF RESEARCH

For exercises 1-4 through 1-6, choose the best type of research for each of the situations described below.

(A) secondary or primary
(B) basic or applied
(C) quantitative or qualitative
(D) exploratory or conclusive
(E) descriptive or inferential

1-4 Select a research study conducted by an organization you work(ed) for. Identify the type of research it was using choices A–E above.

1-5 Select an article from a professional journal related to the approximate area of research for your question(s) of interest (or your instructor may assign a specific article). Identity the type of research reported in the article using choices A–E above.

1-6 Your instructor may require you to conduct specific types of research. If you have the option to select your own types of research, identify them using choices A–E above.

CLASSIFYING VARIABLES

For exercises 1-7 through 1-11, identify the dependent variable (DV/Y) and independent (IV/X) variables, their measurement level (nominal, ordinal, or interval/ratio), and their number of scales.

1-7 You want to know which gender smokes more cigarettes each day, so you survey people who smoke and test differences between the groups.

1-8 You want to know if you can predict whether a household has a personal computer if you know the weekly households' take-home pay. So you survey people and ask the amount of their weekly pay and whether they have a personal computer.

1-9 You want to know which graduate class (first to fourth semester) is more satisfied with their degree program (**1** Satisfied—**5** Not satisfied), so you survey students to compare differences.

1-10 You believe that if you know students' IQ scores you can forecast their grade point average, so you survey students and ask them their IQ and GPA, then run regression to see if the model works.

1-11 You want to know if there is a correlation between how many glasses of Coca-Cola purchasers drink each week and how much they say they enjoy drinking it (**1** really enjoy it—**9** don't really enjoy it).

1-12 Based on exercise 1-4, identify the variables in the study conducted by an organization you work(ed) for.

1-13 Based on exercise 1-5, identify at least two variables in the journal article.

1-14 Based on exercise 1-6, identify at least two variables you are interested in studying.

RESEARCH TERMINOLOGY

For exercises 1-15 through 1-17, answer questions A–D below. Give brief explanations of your answers.

(A) What was the overall research question/problem and the concepts studied?
(B) Was a proposition or hypothesis used?
(C) Was a theory presented?
(D) Was a model used?

1-15 This is a follow-up to exercise l-4. Identify A–D for the organizational study where you work(ed).

1-16 This is a follow-up to exercise l-5. Identify A–D for the journal article you selected.

1-17 This is a follow-up to exercise l-6. Identify A–D for your proposed study.

GOOD RESEARCH

For exercises 1-18 through 1-20, answer questions A–D below. Give brief explanations of your answers.

(A) Is the research question/hypothesis testable?
(B) Are/were results and conclusions generalizable?
(C) What is or will be the value of the research?
(D) Is the study replicable?

1-18 This is a follow-up to exercise l-4. Identify A–D for the organizational study where you work(ed).

1-19 This is a follow-up to exercise l-5. Identify A–D for the journal article you selected.

1-20 This is a follow-up to exercise l-6. Identify A–D for your proposed study.

2

The Introduction
Research Question and Review of the Literature

CONCEPTUAL OBJECTIVES

The conceptual objectives below also appear at appropriate places within the chapter at points when you will have accessed the information necessary to attain them. They appear again at the end of the chapter in the Summary and Glossary section, along with explanations that will enable you to meet the objectives.

After studying this chapter you should be able to:

1. Explain why it is important to write the research question and its value clearly.
2. Describe the differences among a research question, variables, and hypotheses.
3. State the procedure for selecting and testing a research question.
4. Differentiate the four types of literature and three types of articles.
5. Explain how to follow a reference chain.
6. Discuss reasons for completing reference summary forms.
7. List the four parts of the Introduction/research question section.
8. Explain why it is important to synthesize and compare articles in the review of literature.
9. Define the following key terms (listed in order of their appearance in the chapter).

introduction section	journal	informative article
research question	magazine	refereed article
research value	empirical article	periodic index
review of the literature	conceptual article	reference chain

SKILL DEVELOPMENT OBJECTIVES

The exercises that apply to particular skill development objectives are indicated directly beneath each numbered objective below. Periodic instructions within the chapter tell you when to stop reading and direct you to the end of the chapter to complete one or more of the skill development exercises.

After studying this chapter you should be able to:

1. Select, test, and refine a research question.
   Exercises 2-1, 2-3, 2-5

2. Conduct a database periodical index review of literature and obtain journal article abstracts.
   Exercise 2-2

3. Complete reference summary forms.
   Exercise 2-4

4. Write the introduction/research question and review of literature section of a research proposal/paper.
   Exercise 2-6

The Research Process

(1) The research question/purpose of the study, literature review, and hypotheses.	(2) Research design methodology for collecting data and statistics.	(3) Data analysis and interpreting results.	(4) Discussing results and making conclusions.
• *Introduction*	• *Method*	• *Results*	• *Discussion*
Chapters 1–3	Chapters 4–8	Chapters 9–14	Chapters 9–14

In Chapter 1 we listed the steps in the research process, reviewed above. In this chapter, we focus on the Introduction section. *The **introduction section** of a research study includes the research question and its value, the literature review, and hypotheses.*

In this chapter you will learn more about how to select a research question and conduct the review of literature. This material is presented in a step-by-step approach to the topic for those students who like structure (i.e., being told how to do things). The steps are designed to allow you to be successful without learning the hard way through trial and error. However, there are many different ways to approach this topic. You should feel free to try other ways to approach developing a research question and conducting a review of literature than the way presented in this chapter. Table 2.1 contains the suggested stages of the first step in the research process.

Table 2.1 Stages in Developing the Research Question and Literature Review

(A) *Select a research question.* • What interests you? • Do you want to conduct basic or applied research? • Decide on a tentative broad topic and problem/question.	(B) *Collect preliminary data.* • Talk to people familiar with your topic/question, or to get ideas for a question. • Start the literature review by getting abstracts of articles, books, and other secondary data on your topic to narrow your problem/question.	(C) *Continue the literature review, and write it, and write the research question.* • Read the literature to develop a specific research question. • Based on the literature, write the purpose of your research and its value. • Write the review of literature.

This chapter is written based on the assumption that you will have to develop a research proposal and/or conduct research as part of this course or after completing it. Thus, the focus of the chapter is to help you select a topic and conduct a literature review. However, you will first learn the importance of the research question and be given examples of completed work. After you understand the end results, you will learn how to select a research question and conduct a literature review to achieve your own results, using the examples as a guide. After you finish reading the chapter, come back and reread Section 2.1.

2.1 The Research Question

Clearly Stating the Research Question and Its Value

Recall that the starting place of research is with a problem or opportunity. A research problem occurs when there are questions that need to be answered through research. In other words, it's the reason or purpose for conducting a study. Albert Einstein said that the formulation of a problem is often more essential than its solution. To solve problems, you need to ask the right questions. Knowing what is to be accomplished is the foundation for the research process; it is the objective or "end" result. The methods of data collection are the "means" of answering the question. A problem definition error or omission usually results in a costly mistake that cannot be corrected in later stages of the research process. If the problem is not defined correctly, the research data will not solve the problem or answer the correct question.

The research question is placed in the Introduction section of the research proposal and the completed research project because it gives direction to the rest of the proposal and study. It is important to let the reader know early in the paper exactly what the study is all about. The research question should be accompanied by a presentation of the background of the problem, which is based on the literature. The background gives an explanation of the question/problem and why the study is valuable. Recall from Chapter 1 that research value provides new and useful answers to research questions. If the question is trivial and the answer has no value, why conduct the study? Thus, early in the paper it is important to identify the value of the study—who can use the knowledge and how. For example, in Table 2.2, question 1, if the research findings support the conclusion that giving positive reinforcement increases productivity, then managers can give reinforcement to increase productivity. If it doesn't, there is no benefit in management changing their policies to include reinforcement.

In the literature review you want to identify contradictions in research finding, or better yet, gaps—unanswered questions—that indicate the value of your study. You can get the reader's attention with a good research question and a statement of how your study is different from prior work and/or how it contributes new knowledge (value).

CONCEPTUAL OBJECTIVE 1
Explain why it is important to write the research question and its value clearly.

The Differences among the Research Question, Variables, and Hypotheses

The **research question** is a clearly stated purpose of the study that identifies the variables to be investigated and is the basis for propositions/hypotheses. There is a difference between a research question and hypothesis. In the last chapter you learned that a hypothesis is a tentative answer to a research question. It is not the research question itself. The research question is often referred to as the problem or purpose of the study. A clearly defined research question conceptually identifies the variables that are to be studied; it may also state the relationship between the variables. The variables are usually defined operationally in the Method section of the research paper. For examples of clearly stated research questions that identify variables and hypotheses, see Table 2.2.

You should realize that Table 2.2 is a final "end" result; the rest of the chapter gives you the details or means of how to get there. Researchers usually start with a very general research question and over a period of time, with the help of others and the literature, refine the question and variables and go on to state hypotheses. There may also be more than one variable and hypothesis for a research question. Also, note that the research question and hypotheses do not state the methods of measurement and testing. How the hypotheses are measured and tested is addressed in the Method section, which will be covered later. However, note that in example 3 *adolescents* is one variable with two scales—girls and boys. Also, in example 4 the variables/model would be listed in the report (refer to Chapter 1 if you want to see the list) and that success and failure are two scales of one variable—performance. Remember, at this stage you are developing a research question with its variables; you will operationally define the variables and how to test them later.

Table 2.2   The Research Question, Variables,* and Hypotheses

Research Question (purpose of the study)	Hypothesis (tentative answer to the question)
1. The purpose of the study is to determine if *positive reinforcement* influences worker *productivity*.	1. Workers who receive *positive reinforcement* have higher levels of *productivity* than workers who do not.
2. The researcher will investigate the relationship between *drug abuse* and *child abuse*.	2. Parents who *abuse drugs* also *abuse* their *children*.
3 The researcher will examine how watching television commercials affects the *buying behavior* of *adolescents*.	3. *Adolescent* girls *buy* more products advertised on television than adolescent boys do.
4. The purpose of this study is to determine the *variables* that distinguish business *success and failure*.	4. The *model* will predict business *success or failure*.

*The variables are *italicized*.

[handwritten] The purpose of this study is to ...
[handwritten] - The researcher will investigate/examine ...

Conceptual Objective 2
Describe the differences among a research question, variables, and hypotheses.

2.2 Selecting a Research Question

Now that you have a clear understanding of what a research question is, it's time to think about selecting one. Do you already have a research question? If not, don't be too concerned. The starting point is usually to select or discover a topic or problem area and then to develop questions by narrowing it down. The objective of this section is to help you select a research question.

Research Question Considerations

For beginning researchers, selecting a research question is often the most difficult step in the research process. Many students spend days in anxiety, worrying about where they are going to find a problem for their research assignment. Usually, the difficulty doesn't lie with the lack of possible questions. There is almost an unlimited supply of problems that need to be researched. The problem for students is often the lack of familiarity with the literature. Thus, there is a need to combine the search for a research topic with the search through the literature. An alternative option to selecting a topic is to let someone else pick the problem for you. This option can have drawbacks, as discussed under basic or applied research below.

Pick a topic of interest to you in which you would like to become an expert.
The starting point is usually to identify a broad problem/topic area that is related to your area of expertise/major and is of particular interest to you. What was your favorite course? What did you like about it? Recall that through conducting research you will become an expert in your chosen field. In what field do you want to be an expert?

The next step is to narrow down the broad problem/topic area to a specific researchable question. Remember, you are moving from a general question to more specific questions about the topic area. For example, you may be interested in leadership—but this is a very broad topic. What is it about leadership that you want to know? On the other hand, don't narrow the problem/topic so much that the answer to the research question is of no value. A review of the literature and a discussion with instructors/managers with expertise in the area can help you to narrow your problem/topic into a research question. A good research question has an answer to the dreaded questions: So what? Who cares? Think about something you would like to know.

Basic or applied research?

Are you interested in conducting basic (academic) or applied (management) research? Some students, particularly those working full-time, approach a manager in their organization, telling them that they will be doing a research project and would like to research a problem that would help the organization. Oftentimes managers have some good ideas for solving specific problems that currently exist. However, the topic may be of little interest to the student. Students may also suggest conducting research to answer their own question for the organization, in order to get approval and support to conduct the study. For example, students/workers often have ideas concerning a better way to do something—such as a way to increase productivity or improve morale—that is untested.

Other students go to an instructor and ask for ideas on topics or for ideas on narrowing down the topic. Instructors usually know the latest trends in their field and can help narrow a topic. Many of them have more ideas for research projects than they have time to conduct. A few students ask to work with an instructor to coauthor the research for publication. In this last case, the student is usually just told what to do by the instructor, which often limits the ability of students to conduct research on their own.

At this point, if you don't have any ideas, try talking to people. Even if you already have ideas, others can help you clarify them and make the transition from an area of interest to a research question. For example, one researcher was interested in the area of small business/entrepreneurship and wondered why some businesses succeed and others failed.

Talking to Knowledgeable People

Whether you are conducting basic or applied research, you should talk to people knowledgeable in your topic area. These important people, who can be instrumental in helping you with your research, are discussed below

Instructors.

Your instructor for this course is a good source but may not be the most knowledgeable about your topic. Besides, if you are required to write a research proposal for the course, your instructor will be helping you by talking to you and grading your proposal. If you will be conducting research and you have a research advisor, this is the key person to talk to because if your advisor does not accept your topic, you don't have a study. Another good source is instructors you have had in other classes who may be knowledgeable in your topic area. When you talk to one person who has not given you the help you need, ask for referrals to other people who can talk with you about your research question until you have a clear purpose and value for your study.

When you conduct your review of literature, you will get the names of authors and where they are from. If you have questions about your topic, you could try contacting these authors. However, if they are well-known researchers they may not talk to you, be very slow to get back to you, or not give you very much of their time. On a more positive note, when you contact them in writing, authors will often simply send you a copy of their questionnaire and other data that can be of help to you.

Managers/professionals.

If you want to conduct basic research, you may find it helpful to talk to some managers/professionals who are knowledgeable in you topic area, but it is not necessary. However, if you want to conduct applied research for one or more organizations, you must talk to the appropriate manager(s) to get ideas and, more importantly, to get permission to conduct the study. Without prior consent from the appropriate level of management you may not be able to collect the necessary data, and/or you may get yourself into some type of trouble.

Recall that you have two basic options: Approach managers, asking them to give you a problem to research; or propose a research problem that you are interested in researching. Students who are currently employed have an advantage of knowing managers to talk to within the organization. If you are not currently working or prefer to conduct research for a different organization and you want to conduct applied research, try to use currently employed contacts to give you access to managers for the purpose of conducting research. Your contacts include any friends and relatives who work for an organization for which you want to do research, and those who don't work for the organization but do know managers in the organization. It is important to have your contact either make the appointment for you, talk to the manager about you before you call to set up an appointment, or at least allow you to use their name when attempting to set up the appointment.

Others.

Other people you can contact to help you with your research question include your fellow students, coworkers, customers, suppliers, family, friends, and neighbors who may be able to help you come up with a question or clarify your existing question.

Testing a Research Question

The following ideas, which include a review of the above discussion, may help you select a topic that leads to a research question.

1. **Interest.** Do you have a topic that interests you? You will be spending a great deal of time and energy on your research proposal and possibly a resulting research project. Thus, an interesting topic is important to your motivation to finish and to do a good job. What was your favorite course and topic within the course? What prompted you to get the degree you are working on? Is there a question for which you would like to obtain the answer through research?

2. **Expertise.** Is your topic in an area in which you want to be an expert? Try to select a topic in such an area. Being an expert in a growing field can aid in your career development.

3. **Research value.** Will answering the question provide research value? *Research value provides new and useful answers to research questions.* Does it answer the "So what" and "Who cares" questions? Who will benefit and how? Explaining how your study is different than prior research also indicates research value. Addressing research value of the study along with the research question early in the paper gets

the reader's attention. For more discussion on research value, refer to Chapter 1, "Characteristics of Good Research—Is It Valuable?"

4. **Sufficient literature.** Are there enough prior studies on which to base your research? While it is good to select a new topic, if the topic is so new that there are few articles on it you can have real difficulty. Selecting a relatively new topic which is still popular but also has a critical mass of literature will help you to extend current work. Empirical research articles usually state the need for further research. Such articles will provide ideas to build on past work with some differences to extend the current work. However, duplicating prior work is acceptable when there are conflicting research findings.

5. **Feasibility.** Can you answer the research question, and if you can, within a reasonable time? Not all questions can be researched, and not all can be answered. For example, can you get the data you need? Is the research project realistic given other demands on your time and energy? Can you get it done in time to graduate? How much will it cost to do the research? Instructors and/or managers can often help you determine if your study is feasible.

6. **Openness to change.** Are you open to change? Don't necessarily stick with the first idea that comes to you. Be open to making changes as you work on the research. Your original question may already have been clearly answered; however, there may be a related question that is worth researching. Talk about your topic with students and instructors/managers to help you clarify your thoughts.

At this point you want to have a general topic idea that interests you, is in a desirable area of expertise, is of some value, and is feasible. However, you will not know if there is sufficient literature and a need for change until you go on to the next step and review the literature. But first, be sure to complete exercise 2-1.

CONCEPTUAL OBJECTIVE 3
State the procedures for selecting and testing a research question.

STOP READING and turn to the end of the chapter to complete exercise 2-1.

2.3 Preliminary Literature Collection

The next step in narrowing down your research question to make it clear is to conduct a preliminary literature review. There is no set order in talking to people and conducting the literature review. If you have a very broad topic area, it may be helpful to start by talking to people. If you have a narrow question, the literature review may be a good starting place. If you have decided to conduct applied research, you may also want to collect other secondary data.

The Need for a Literature Review

Once you have determined an area of interest (or better yet a tentative research question) and, if appropriate, you have talked to people about your topic, you are ready to conduct the preliminary literature review by using one or more periodical indexes. However, before we get into the details, let's define the review of literature and discuss why it is important.

Writing a research proposal and conducting a research study invariably involves a significant amount of reading. To be informed and to be an expert in your field, you must read and understand the important articles about your topic. Once you have tentatively selected a research question, reading the literature will give you ideas, let you know what other researchers have done, and help you to develop your research question or change it, if necessary. Through this course you also will learn how to read empirical articles with statistical analysis to help you make better decisions. A major purpose of this chapter is to help you to develop your research reading skills.

There are several reasons for conducting a literature review. *The **review of the literature** synthesizes and compares prior work related to the research question.* The following reasons make it well worth the time and effort:

1. The literature review helps you to refine your research question.

2. You may find the answer to your research question and decide that a study is not necessary.

3. The literature review is used to determine what has already been done that relates to your problem and what still needs to be done. As mentioned earlier, empirical research articles commonly state the need for further research. Comparing the results of multiple articles enables you to compare and contrast findings that indicate contradiction and gaps (work that has not yet been done and still needs to be done) that enhance the research value of your proposed study.

4. You become an expert in the area of your topic. The more thoroughly you read about your problem, the more of an expert you become.

5. You benefit by prior researchers' experience and can avoid mistakes. You will get ideas for collecting and analyzing data. To be more specific, the literature review will help you to operationally define your variables and help you determine how to measure them, how to statistically test your hypotheses, and which specific procedures you will use in conducting your research.

6. Finally, becoming familiar with previous research will facilitate interpretation of the results of your own study. Your results should be discussed in terms of whether they agree with (support) prior findings or *not* support (refute) the findings. If your study supports prior research, you can suggest a next step (the need for further research) to answer new, related questions. If your study does not support prior research, you can try to explain the possible reasons for the discrepancy. When prior research findings are inconclusive or discrepancies exist, you support or refute specific researchers.

Types of Literature and Reviews

There are four primary types of literature, three types of articles, and two types of article reviews. Let's discuss each separately.

Types of literature (books, journals, magazines, and newspapers).

There are differences between books, journals and magazines, and newspapers. You are familiar with *books*; you are reading this one now. *A **journal** generally presents scholarly* *articles with little or no advertising and is not sold in stores.* Scholarly work typically refers to empirical and conceptual studies conducted by professors and other professionals who are not paid for their articles by the publisher. A professional association commonly sponsors journals, and copies of the journal are sent to its membership and other subscribers, including libraries. Examples include the *Journal of Small Business Management* and the *Harvard Business Review. A magazine generally presents journalist articles with advertising and is sold in stores.* Journalists write articles and are paid for their work. Journalists may refer to scholarly studies and/or interview the authors, but they do not usually conduct extensive primary research. Magazines generally are sold to make a profit and thus have advertising and are sold on news stands, as well as to subscribers and libraries. Examples include *Time, Newsweek, Business Week, Fortune,* and *U.S. News & World Report.* Journals commonly use volume and issue numbers, whereas magazines commonly only use dates of publication. You are most likely knowledgeable about newspapers, which typically present articles written by feature newspaper reporters.

Types of literature articles.

There are at least three major types of articles. *An **empirical article** tests research questions/hypotheses based on literature reviews using primary data, and they often report statistical findings.* Recall from Chapter 1 that empirical qualitative research (e.g., case studies) does collect primary in-depth data with a small sample but does not report statistical results. *A **conceptual article** is based on secondary data and offers synthesis of the literature and research question propositions with recommendations for empirical study.* Some researchers start with a conceptual paper and go on to empirical study. *An **informative article** reports data and news and/or provides advice for the reader with limited, if any, literature review.* Informative articles are also called "how to" articles when they offer advice, which may include some reference to prior empirical and/or conceptual articles. Informative articles do not include a review of the literature or feature only a very brief review.

Empirical and conceptual articles are usually written by professors and often by professionals/managers whose articles commonly appear in journals, whereas informative articles are usually written by journalists and reporters and commonly appear in magazines and newspapers. It is usually easy to identify empirical articles because they use primary data and statistics. Also, the headings *Review of Literature, Method, Results,* and *Conclusions* are commonly used. However, some authors blend the conceptual and informative components together. Some professional associations have journals exclusively for one type of article. For example, The *Academy of Management Journal* publishes only empirical articles and the *Academy of Management Review* publishes only conceptual articles. The *Academy of Management Perspectives* publishes only informative articles, but they are heavily based on the literature to support advice to executives. Scholarly professional associations' journal articles are commonly written and read by professors and some professionals and managers. Occupational/trade professional association journal articles are often written by professors and professionals in the occupation or trade and are read by the professionals. Magazine and newspaper articles are commonly written by journalists and are read by the general population, which includes some professors, professionals, and managers.

In summary and general comparison, empirical journal articles report a research study and conceptual articles provide strong literature reviews with propositions and recommendations for empirical studies. Books are not based on research studies, but they often report informative research results of others (i.e., results that provide information and advice). Magazine and newspaper articles are also informative based on secondary sources of data and interviews. Thus, empirical journal articles, followed by conceptual articles, are the best sources of references in the review of the literature. In general, it's a good idea to make limited use of books, magazines, and newspapers, such as to report some factual data and to provide more references supporting journal articles.

CONCEPTUAL OBJECTIVE 4
Differentiate the four types of literature and three types of articles.

Types of reviews.

There are two major types of reviews—the process by which manuscripts get selected to be articles in journals and magazines. *A refereed article has been reviewed by the editor and peers.* Another less technical term is a *peer-reviewed article*. A *non-refereed article* has been reviewed only by an editor. Scholarly journals commonly referee or review articles, whereas magazines do not. The common approach used by scholarly journals is to accept unsolicited manuscripts. The editor reads the manuscript and determines if it is of the quality necessary for publication as an article in the journal. If it is, copies of the manuscript are sent to any number of reviewers, often three. These reviewers are usually professors with a proven record of publication and/or professionals and managers who are respected in their field. The reviewers are asked to make recommendations on the acceptability of the article and to make any recommendations for improvements. Using the reviewer recommendations, the editor makes the decision to reject, to accept contingent upon successful recommended improvements, or to accept the manuscript as submitted to become an article in the journal.

A journal or magazine may use a variety of types of reviews. The most objective method is the *double-blind review,* in which the editor selects reviewers without knowing who they are and sends articles to referees who do not know who the author(s) are. Numbers rather than names are used. A slightly less objective method is the *blind review,* in which the editor selects reviewers by name but the referees do not know the author(s)' name(s). The least objective method is the *author-known review,* in which the editor and reviewers know the author(s)' names. Generally, refereed articles are more prestigious than non-refereed articles and blind reviews are more prestigious than author-known reviews. However, there are exceptions—for example, the *Harvard Business Review* is a non-refereed journal, yet it is very prestigious to be published in the *HBR*.

Searching the Literature

In this section we discuss using the library and the Internet, database periodical indexes, and other sources of data.

Using libraries and the Internet.

A college or university library is generally your best place to search for literature. If you are not familiar with using the library for research, a *reference librarian* can help you find what you are looking for and possibly even find things you didn't know existed. Reference librarians have been taught to find information, and it's their job to help you find the information you need. If your library doesn't have a source of information you are looking for, such as a full copy of a journal article, your librarian can help you get it. If you go to the library, you will find computers that access the Internet an enable you to search for literature. You can most likely also access the college sources, including the database that includes periodical indexes, online. If you don't know how to do so, again, ask the librarian. (You will most likely need your college ID number.)

You may have done literature searches online using Google and other search engines. The Internet is generally not a good source for a literature search. The reason is that researchers generally don't put their work on the Internet—because, frankly, anyone can put just about anything on the Internet. Researchers want their work published in quality periodicals/journals. Thus, use a university periodical index, not the Internet. One exception is Google Scholar, a free online resource that allows you to quickly search hundreds of thousands of academic citations to articles, books, and more. However, I recommend using a good college database periodical index because you can do better advanced searches, it is better organized for researchers, and it gets less irrelevant results.

If your college doesn't have a good research library or if there is no library nearby (as sometimes can be the case when taking online courses), you can go to almost any university library. The only downside is that most libraries will not let you take anything (such as books) out of the library without a library card/college ID. However, what you really want is access to a good data periodical index, and you can make copies of what you need in the library anyway. If you don't have access to a college database, use Google Scholar.

Using an academic database periodical index.

Before you begin your literature search, you should identify your research question and the variables within your research question. Based on your chosen variables, make a list of key words or phrases to search. You are now ready to do a periodical index computer search. A periodical is a published work that appears in a new edition on a regular schedule. *A **periodical index** contains bibliographic data and abstracts of journal articles.* It may also have copies of some of the full articles.

If you have never conducted a computer literature search using a university's periodical index database, it is advisable to go to the library for at least the first use. The main reason for this is that you may not know which periodical indexes are available and which one (or more) you should use. There may be written instructions that are not online; and more importantly, there should be reference librarians available to help you conduct your computer literature search.

For business topic searches, two very good database periodical indexes are EBSCO *Business Source Premier* and *ABI/Inform*. They include journal articles from all aspects of business plus research reports, industry reports, company profiles, and SWOT analyses. *LexisNexis Academic Universe* is another good database. It has an enormous aggregation of news, business, legal, medical, and reference information. Another good source is *Proquest*. Your instructor may tell you which database(s) your college has and which to use. For your topic, some other database may be useful. You reference librarian can tell you which databases are available.

Search AND Boolean.

Most of the periodical index databases you use will have a variety of ways to search, such as by keyword, author, title, publication, and so on. Start with a keyword search. If you are not to sure of the exact keywords to use, try what you think is a good keyword. When you get results, see what keywords are used within the results and search with them as well. The more accurate your keywords are, the more pertinent the articles will be to your research topic.

A Boolean search uses the words AND, OR, and NOT to do an advanced search. If you type in four keywords with AND after each, only articles that have all four keywords will appear, which limits the results. If you don't use AND, most search engines will use OR and give you all articles with any of the four keywords. This broadens the search. If you don't know how to use the search features, there should be instructions in the on-screen menu under "help." If you are getting too many or too few results, ask the librarian for help.

Other secondary sources.

By far the most important secondary source of the review of literature is journal articles, which you find through a periodical index. The use of books and other secondary sources is usually given a lower priority than articles because books tend to reference articles and thus are often more outdated than the articles they cite. There is no one best way to prioritize and categorize abstracts. However, you may use other secondary sources such as books to help you find other sources (e.g., *Business Information Sources* and *The Encyclopedia of Management*); books on the specific topic; reference books such as those published by the government, including *Statistical Abstracts*; and publications of private businesses such as *Dun & Bradstreet, Standard and Poors,* and *Moody's.* Abstracts are also available, such as *Dissertation Abstracts, Psychological Abstracts,* and *Personnel Management Abstracts. Dissertation Abstracts* is not really a good reference source for your literature review, but it is helpful in selecting a topic because it tells you what research doctoral students are doing, and it can give you ideas on a research question. A conversation with a reference librarian can make you aware of the many resources your university has available to you.

When conducting applied research for an organization it is often necessary to use other secondary sources when writing the Introduction and the literature review. For example, you may want to write a brief history of the organization, which you can get from written sources such as annual reports and other documents. You may also need to give a background description of the problem, which may require obtaining data from purchasing, inventory, production, sales, and other records. The data you go on to collect and analyze may come exclusively from a secondary source or may be part of the data collected, along with primary data.

Reading, Recording, and Refining Strategies

Once you have searched, you have to cope with the literature review. One question you may have is, "How many references do I need?" Maybe little or nothing has been written about your research topic, or you may be overwhelmed by the volume of articles you have found. You may wonder how to read and organize it all. You may also find that your topic has already been extensively and thoroughly researched, in which case you may need to change or refine your research question. Next we give you some strategies to get you through these issues.

Number of references.

Beginning researchers often find it difficult to determine the number of references their literature review should include. There is no magic number. However, many research methods instructors and research project advisors will advise you on how many articles and/or pages a literature review should include. Also, if you have an interest in getting your research published in a specific journal, check through several articles in several issues to get an idea of how many references are included. If the average is between 20 and 30, you want to be in that range. Also, remember that the more articles you read related to your topic, the more of an expert you will be. So don't focus on limiting the number of references.

Too many articles.

If the expectation is, say, 25 articles and you get too many, do an advanced search (use AND so that you only get results containing *all* your keywords) to narrow the results and get fewer and more relevant articles. If you still have too many, select the articles that most closely relate to your proposed research. (We discuss this again under the section on prioritizing abstracts.) With a widely researched topic, such as leadership, there may be hundreds of articles from which to choose. Narrow the selection by picking only the more current empirical articles that are the most closely related to your specific topic; you may find that you need to go above the 25-reference guideline.

Too few articles.

On the other hand, with a new topic area there may not be many articles. In this case, broaden your search by using more keywords (use OR to get results containing *any* of your keywords). If there still aren't enough related articles, you have two choices. First, try broadening your search to other related topic areas. For example, take the topic of mental imagery in golf. Let's say there are only three articles specifically about mental imagery in golf. You would include these articles and go on to include the use of mental imagery in other sports, and you may have to use less than the recommended 25 references unless you use loosely related ones. If you still don't have enough references, you may want to select a new topic. If you get too many or too few articles, once again ask your reference librarian for help in searching.

Reading and recording the abstract.

The great thing about a database periodical index is that it provides an *abstract*—a summary overview of an article. Read the title of the article, and if it seems as if it is related to your research question, read the abstract. If it is relevant, record it. There are two forms of *recording*—print it and/or download it to a portable USB storage drive that you can take with you. If you are working from your own computer, you can download directly to your hard drive. Recorded abstracts eliminate the need to copy the reference down or make notes about the abstract by hand because it is already printed/stored for you.

Refining and retesting your research question.

Carefully read the relevant abstracts and rethink your research question. Is your research question interesting, will it make you an expert, does it have research value, is there sufficient literature, is it feasible? Do you want to change it in some way (e.g., do you want to reword it)?

It's all been done before.

This conclusion is almost always a faulty one. If you find that there are studies that have already answered your research question, look a little closer. It rarely happens that someone else has done *exactly* the same study. Your study is different if you include a different sample (e.g., use a new industry, different type of employees [different job, race, age], use larger- or smaller-sized organizations, use profit rather than nonprofit organizations, and so on). The location of the sample can be different. Do you have exactly the same variables? You can always drop, add, or change a variable. If you make changes, do another search using the new variable(s) as keywords. Discard any abstracts that no longer apply to your changed research question and add new ones. Even if a study has already been done, it will state its limitations and the need for future research—so the other study(ies) will even tell you *how* to make your research a little different.

Prioritizing abstracts.

The following ideas may help you come up with your own way to prioritize your abstracts. Prioritize by how closely related the abstracts are to your proposed study. The more closely related an article is to what your interest is, the higher the priority; also be sure to give a higher priority to empirical (statistical) articles than to conceptual and lastly to informative articles.

Another way to categorize abstracts is by year. On the abstract is the year of the publication, which is important because more recent work usually includes experience from prior research. If you find that there are few or even no current studies but that there have been many a few years ago, you may have an outdated topic. More recent publications are usually given a higher priority. If you have, say, 50 abstracts, it is not necessary to rank them 1–50. You could use a priority system such as empirical, conceptual, and informative. You can also prioritize them as directly related, somewhat related, and indirectly related (based on similarity to what you want to do). For example, if you read an abstract and it is empirical and directly related to your study, you can simply write the words *empirical* and *direct* or simply *E&D* on it; the year is also on the abstract. If the abstract is conceptual and indirectly related, you could label is *C&I*, and so on. Within your categories, you may prioritize by year of articles.

Unfortunately, it is not always easy to tell from reading the abstract what type of article it is. If this is the case, you will have to wait until you actually get copies of the articles to prioritize and categorize them. Also, once you start to prioritize, you may find a very large number in one priority and very few in others. Even if you have equal numbers in the various priorities, it may be helpful to use an additional system to help you better organize and understand your literature review.

> **STOP READING and turn to the end of the chapter
> to complete exercises 2-2 and 2-3.**

2.4 Review of the Literature

After you have collected the preliminary data (which primarily includes the abstracts of articles) and prioritized it, the next step is to get full copies of the high-priority articles and read them, then develop your own summary for each reference. Notice that we said get copies of your *high-priority* articles, not *every* article. You most likely found more articles than you can read, so you need to get the most important ones and read them. Do keep your lower-priority abstracts because you can include them in your bibliography and/or research paper as a reference, even though you don't read the articles.

Getting Copies of High-Priority Articles and Other Sources

This may sound like an easy step, but often this isn't the case, because the university library you are using may not have the actual article(s) or book(s) you need. Following is some advice to aid you in this step.

- **Copy/download from the database periodical index.** Some periodical indexes include full text of some of the articles, making it easy to get a copy.

- **Download from journal websites.** Another quick option is to go to the journal's website and download a copy of the article. The advantage is that this is quick and easy, but the downside is that many will charge a fee to download the copy.

- **Copy from your library.** For many articles, you will have to get the actual journal and make the copy yourself. Again, it may cost you to make the copy, but it is usually less costly than downloading from the journal's website.

- **Copy from another library (interlibrary loan).** For journals and books that are not available from your university, a reference librarian can usually tell you (or refer you to a source that states) where the reference can be found. If the library containing the source is relatively close by, you may visit the library and get a copy yourself. However, if distance is far, you can usually ask your university library to get a copy of an article, or have a copy of a book sent to the university library. There is usually a cost and a waiting time before it arrives. Thus, you may want to consider going to the library that has the source yourself, or if you know someone in the area of the other library, ask that person to copy it and send it to you.

- **Start now.** It is important to get an early start on obtaining your sources so that you allow yourself enough time to complete and write up your research. Another important point is to be sure you get copies of the articles and books so that they are at hand when you organize and write your literature review. Reading the articles in the library and taking notes does not work well, because later on you will most likely want to check or recheck for specific information that you did not think of initially. The money you spend for copies will be more than offset by the cost of the time you would waste going to the library again to reread the articles and by the quality of your work. Also, when you first start this course you may be weak in research methods and statistics (which is to be expected), and when you read the empirical articles you will not fully understand them. As you progress in this course, you will learn the information necessary to be able to understand the articles related to your study.

Following the Reference Chain

*The **reference chain** refers to using the citations included in one source to obtain additional sources.* As you read a journal article you will learn about other studies related to the one you are reading and, more importantly, to your proposed research. Thus, carefully review the list of references at the end of a journal article, or within a book somewhere, and if you don't have an abstract of any articles listed there that sound like they would be helpful to your study, get copies. When you obtain copies of those articles you did not find in your preliminary search, again follow the reference chain until you have all the good-quality references available. If you fail to follow the reference chain, you could get caught. For example, your research instructor and/or research project advisor may be knowledgeable in your area of study and realize that you have not included important references. Your literature review could be rejected and you could be told to do it again. Plus, to be an expert in a field, you want to find all the directly related references you can. How can you claim to be an expert in a job interview, when the interviewer asks if you have read a specific article and you have to say no?

Original sources.

To ensure accuracy you should get the original source to read and cite in your study. For example, you will read articles that discuss prior studies. However, you should not reference the author who cites another source. Follow the reference chain to obtain the original source, and cite the original source to ensure proper research procedures and accuracy. You may be surprised to find out that many authors who read about their work as presented by others often find that what they read is incorrectly interpreted.

Experts.

There is a very good chance you will find that the same authors have written multiple articles about your topic, and that they are cited and referenced in other articles. You can go back to the database and do a search by author name to find all of the expert's work that is listed in the database. By doing so, you may find some new articles to include in your literature.

Journal focus.

There is also a very good chance you will find that many of the articles come from the same journal. You can go back to the database and do a search to find all of the articles of the specific journal only. You can also go to the journal's website. In this manner you may find more new articles to include.

CONCEPTUAL OBJECTIVE 5
Explain how to follow a reference chain.

Reading and Summarizing Your References

Box 2.1 is a reference summary form that you may copy and use. If you write in your answers, be neat so that you can read what you have written later. Better yet, simply type the headings and the information for each section. Note that the form is geared toward the more important empirical research studies. Thus, your conceptual and informative articles will not have answers for statistics used and results, the source may not have any methods, and there may be propositions rather than hypotheses. Try to keep your summary forms to one page in length. You can always list page numbers within the article where you can turn for more details rather than write them all in your summary.

If you *type* the summary, you can exclude the unneeded sections and add others. You can also restrict each section to the desired size. If you have downloaded a copy of the article, you may be able to cut and paste some of the information into the summary form to save time and avoid errors.

An important point is to read each source (articles, books, etc.) and to fill out a summary for each. Your summaries will help you to focus on the important points of each article

Box 2.1   Reference Summary Form

Number/priority/outline/type of article:

Reference:

Research question/purpose/hypothesis:

Variables and measurement:

Research design and methods:

Statistics used and results:

Conclusions:

Important features that relate to your study and how you plan to use them:

(Attach a copy of the index abstract and a copy of the article to this form.)

and to organize them for writing the introduction and literature review for your research proposal and study. As you read each article, you may highlight areas of interest, but don't overdo it or the highlighting becomes meaningless.

Also, as stated above, don't be surprised if you don't understand everything you read at the beginning of the course. When you read something that you don't understand, place a question mark (?) in the margin. As the course progresses, you should get the information you need to understand the material. If you prefer, you can look up the information before covering it in this course. Now let's discuss what information is needed for each heading on the reference summary form.

Number/priority/outline/type of article.

You may want to number all your references—say, 1–42—for quick use in your outline. As discussed earlier, on the index abstracts you were developing a system of prioritizing articles. With the synthesizing outline (covered in the next section), you will determine where your articles will be reported. Place the codes (e.g., *E&D* or *C&I*, high-priority versus low-priority), which may be further developed as the answers with each heading, on the summary form. For example, the article could be coded for the outline 1-A—*E&D*. All you do is give the more relevant articles related to your study a higher priority by giving a lower number to the article. The type of article, in priority order, is empirical, conceptual, or informative.

Reference.

Write/type the reference in the proper form to be used in your proposal and research project. If you type it in the correct format, you can copy and paste it in the paper.

Research question/purpose/hypothesis.

Near the beginning of the article, possibly within the article's literature review, the research question(s) or purpose of the study should be listed. For empirical and conceptual articles there should be at least one hypothesis or proposition. Write the propositions/hypotheses in your own words, or copy them. If there are many hypotheses and/or they are long, you may want to simply list them with their page numbers where you can find them. If the article does not include any propositions/hypotheses (informative magazine articles, for example), state the purpose of the article.

Variables and measurement.

List the variables. For empirical articles also write the operational definition, which should include measurable terms. If there are many and/or they are long, you may want to list them briefly with the page number to find them in the article. The variables should be listed within the research question and hypotheses. However, the measurement (ratio, interval, ordinal, nominal) is usually listed within the research methodology section.

Research design and methods.

The research design guides the investigator's process of collecting, analyzing, and interpreting data. The methods are the specific procedures the researcher follows to collect, analyze, and interpret the data. Research design and methods are very important topics and are covered in chapters 4 through 8. Although you may not fully understand the methods, if you read the Method section of your articles you should be able to summarize some of the methodology used, such as the sample selection and size, and whether the data was collected by secondary sources, observation, or survey (questionnaire).

Statistics used and results obtained.

Because statistics are not covered until chapters 9 through 14, you may not understand the statistics used or the results of statistical testing until later in the course. However, by reading your articles' results section you should see the name of the tests used, such as Chi-square, T-test, ANOVA, correlation, and regression. Look at the tables; the titles often state the statistical test used. The results generally will state whether the hypotheses where supported or unsupported. Probability values (p-values, such as $p = .035$ or $p < .05$) are given to indicate the probability that an error was made. You will learn about them later.

Conclusions.

The conclusions generally state the results without the statistical terms and summarize the article. Many articles will also state the implications of the findings (the value of the results, or how they can be used by specific groups). This section of the article also commonly compares the results of the current study to that of prior research to support or not support prior work.

Conclusions generally will also state the *limitations* of the study (weaknesses) and recommendations for further research. *The recommendations for further research are very important* for getting ideas on how to take current research one step further; they are also valuable because the information can be used as a reference to support the research value of your study.

Important features that relate to your study and how you plan to use them.

Remember that you are not trying to come up with totally new ideas for your research. You want to base your work on prior work. Accordingly, as you read the articles think about what you would like to use in your study. For example, you may have found good statements supporting the value for your research, variables used and their operational definition to measure them, instruments/questionnaires used to collect data, procedures followed for collecting data, or statistical tests used.

CONCEPTUAL OBJECTIVE 6
Discuss reasons for completing reference summary forms.

**STOP READING and turn to the end of the chapter
to complete exercises 2-4 and 2-5.**

2.5 Research Writing and Style

Before you begin, it's important to familiarize yourself with the writing style you will use for your study. After reading some journal articles, you should realize that research writing and style are different from most other types of writing. For example, I wrote this book using a different style than I do when I write research journal articles. When editors refer to *style*, they mean the rules or guidelines a publisher uses to ensure consistent presentation in their publications, including scholarly journals, conference proceedings, and books. The research proposal and completed study must be written in appropriate research writing style of the organization for which it is prepared. Organizations usually supply a copy of their style to authors. Your college or university many have a style publication of some kind. Thus, **style** *refers to the rules or guidelines of the organization for which the research study is prepared.*

For applied business research, there are different styles and most businesses don't have a style manual. However, one of the important things to remember is to be consistent with the style you do select to use. Even if your college doesn't use strict APA (American Psychological Association) style, you can benefit from knowing a consistent research writing style. For scholarly publication, APA style is commonly used by professional association journals and conferences. Many journals as well as colleges and universities follow APA style. Look at the citations within articles and the reference sections at the end of articles you have from your literature review; is the style the same? Your college or university many have specific guidelines, as do many journals and conferences. Make sure you learn and follow the requirements specified.

Whichever style you follow, you must present your information clearly and analyze the needs of your primary audience. Many helpful sources are available for improving your writing style and analysis, including the *Publication Manual of the American Psychological Association, The Chicago Manual of Style,* the *MLA Handbook for Writers of Research Papers,* Strunk and White's *The Elements of Style,* and numerous others. A condensed version of APA style guidelines is included in the CD that accompanies this book.

2.6 Writing the Introduction

With your summary forms completed and attached to the articles, review your notes—and then you are ready to begin to write the introduction to your proposal/paper, which includes your research question and review of literature.

Introduction/Research Question

When using proper APA style, place the title of your study at the top of the second page (the first page being your title page—see Chapter 4 for full details). The title of your work should be as descriptive of what you are investigating as possible yet should not be too wordy and long. Reading the titles of the articles from your literature search should give you some good ideas for titles. Remember that your title can be refined later. For now, get yourself started on writing. Write first to get your ideas in print, then edit for improvements.

APA style does not include a heading for introduction, purpose of the study, or any other heading. Just start writing directly following the title. Begin by getting the reader's attention, stating why the problem area you are investigating is important or why it has research value. To do this, you must use references from prior work. No matter how much of an expert you are in your topic area, do not state your own opinions on why the research question is important. However, if you happen to look for and find other sources stating your ideas, use the references. As a general guide, in the Introduction/research question and brief literature review section (as opposed to the full literature review that will appear in Appendix B of your proposal/study), make sure every paragraph has at least one reference citation. The Introduction/literature review is meant to cite others' work, not state your opinions. However, if you have prior publications you may reference your own prior work. The key advice here is to read others' studies and reference them as the sources that explain why your study has research value—how it will fill a gap in the literature.

Parts of the Introduction/Research Question and Their Value

The introduction should answer the "So what" question. You must quickly get the reader's attention by stating the value of your research. The introduction to the research study includes four parts—importance of the topic, the research question/purpose of the study, the need for the research, and its implications. The Introduction is usually no longer than four paragraphs.

The importance of the topic.

Begin with a background that explains the research value of your topic. Be sure to cite references. If there are contradictory research findings in your literature review, you may list them to support the value of your research, especially recommendations for further research.

The research question/purpose of the study.

Now you are ready to state the research question/purpose of your study. Clearly state your questions and/or purpose of your research. List the variables and the differences among them based on the literature review, citing references.

The need for the research.

Here you should tell the reader how your research fills a gap in the literature. For example, does it help to answer a question identified in the literature, resolve a conflict in previous research, or will it help an organization in need of solving a problem or seeking an opportunity? If your study is in some way different from prior research, make this clear and cite references to prior work. If your research takes prior work a step forward or in a new direction, as suggested in prior recommendations for further research, this provides research value to your study.

Implications.

It is important to specify all those who can benefit from your study and how they can use your research. Implications clearly give support to the value of your research. Again, use references.

CONCEPTUAL OBJECTIVE 7
List the four parts of the Introduction/research question section.

Introduction/Review of Literature

Written in correct APA style for master's thesis/research projects and doctoral dissertations, the full review of literature is placed in Appendix B. It is commonly between 20 and 50 pages long. However, as you can see from the articles you have copied, such a long literature review is not practical for a journal article. Thus, in the introduction section of the proposal/paper a shorter version of the literature review (i.e., the best of the sources you have gathered) is placed directly after the research question/statement of the problem. Unlike journal articles, again there is no heading. (The heading *Review of Literature* appears only in the full version, Appendix B at the end of the paper.) Depending on the style of the journal manuscript (APA is double spaced), the brief literature review is usually only four to six pages long. For an example, refer to the Introduction in the Sample Research Proposal (Part IV, Appendix RP in this book).

Generally, it is a good idea to write the introduction/research question and state its value, then write your Appendix B Review of the Literature (the *full* version). Then come back to refine your introduction and go on to take the best of Appendix B as the *brief* review of literature in the body of the proposal/paper. Remember that it is through the literature review that you become an expert in your chosen topic area. Below are some specific steps recommended for conducting and writing a review of the literature. However, feel free to do it your own way.

Synthesizing the Review of Literature

First, let's discuss how to synthesize an outline for your *full* review of literature in Appendix B, then focusing on the best references to use in your *brief* literature review in the introduction section.

Step 1. Make a synthesizing outline.

Synthesizing is the process of uniting the parts into a logical whole that illustrates expertise in the topic area. This is what you will use in composing your Appendix B Review of Literature (full version). Identify your major topic areas, which will be written as first-level headings (using APA style—centered, with initial caps on all prominent words [sometimes called *title case*]). Then go on to develop subsections, which will be written as second-level headings (left justified, title case). (Again, refer to the Sample Research Proposal in Part IV, Appendix RP. Note that the full review of literature has four sections. You can also go on to create third-level headings, not shown.) Thus, the example would have the outline shown in Box 2.2 [the numbers in brackets within the outline will be explained shortly].

Unfortunately, there is no simple correct way to develop an outline. However, when looking at the articles you have read, you may find that the authors use an outline form that you can use or at least get ideas from. However, you cannot simply copy someone else's literature review. Another important consideration is the number of research ques-

---

Box 2.2   Review of Literature Outline with [Reference numbers]

Appendix B: Review of Literature
i.* (Introduction) [1, 20, 3, 6]
1. Personality Testing in the Workplace
    [1, 20, 41, 10, 17, 14, 39, 8, 22, 15, 21, 22, 41]
2. Job Performance
    [1, 18, 32, 41, 23, 5, 16, 43, 3, 11, 24, 12, 13, 19, 25, 27, 35]
3. Personality Testing to Predict Job Performance
    [1, 20, 7, 9, 33, 5, 10, 2, 29, 31, 38, 36, 40, 42]
4. Summary
    [1, 20, 16, 27, 22, 43, 4, 33]

*i = introduction of entire literature review.

tions you plan to answer, or the number of hypotheses you will test. It is a good idea to have a section for each planned hypothesis. You may want to get others' feedback about your outline before you finalize it.

Step 2. Determine under which outline section each reference can be used and write the reference number on the summary form.

If you have not already done so, on your coding system (number/priority/outline/ type of article) at the top of each summary form, place the number of each article—say, 1– 42—and the priority on each form. The next step is to review each reference and figure out where in the outline you should include it. Place the number representing the section heading and letter indicating the second-level subsection headings. Writing in pencil is recommended in case you change your outline. The number 1-1, 1-20, 1-41 appears on the reference summary form. In the outline in Box 2.2, Section 1, Personality Testing in the Workplace—1, 20, 41, etc., the 1 represents the section so it is not relisted with the reference numbers—[1, 20, 41, etc.]. These bracketed numbers represent the references (articles, books, etc.) that will be included in each section of the review of literature. You may find that some of your high-priority articles will be used in multiple places within your literature review, while others may be used only once. You may also find that you have articles that do not belong in any group. If so, the articles may be discarded and placed in the bibliography, used in a different section (such as the introduction, methods, results, discussion); or if there are several related, a new section may be added to the outline.

Step 3. Write the reference number in the outline where it will be included.

The outline in Box 2.2 indicates that several articles will be used in multiple places within the literature review. You may also have missing numbers if you discard any article. You now have a cross-reference check to be sure you use each article in its appropriate section.

Step 4(a). Group the articles and write, following your outline.

Group all the articles that should be used to introduce your entire review of literature (articles 1, 20, 3, 6 from Box 2.2) and write the Introduction section including the sources and listing the sections to come. Next, go on to your first heading Introduction (i), articles 1, 20, and 3. Review these articles and determine how they will be included to introduce your first section of the review of literature. Then write the Introduction in a way that gives an overview of the section and lists any subsections that are to come. Priority of articles should also be considered (start with the best, as discussed below).

Now group all the articles for section 1, article numbers 1, 20, 41, etc. Go on to the next until all sections are completed. However, be sure that each section has at least three paragraphs. If a section does not have at least three paragraphs, you need to add more to it or place the information within another section (reorganize). Try to stay away from using direct quotations; instead paraphrase the authors' work in your own words. Paraphrasing shows a better understanding of the literature.

Step 4(b). Focus on the best.

Start each subsection with the high-priority articles most related to your study. A good strategy is to discuss your empirical articles, and simply list the conceptual and informative articles that state the same thing. Your most relevant empirical articles, if any, should be the basis from your logical lead into your hypothesis (the tentative answer to your research question) for the subsection of your Introduction where you state a hypothesis. Your best articles (empirical, then conceptual) will most likely be used multiple times with details given, whereas your least relevant (informative) may only be used once, with little or no details. An important point here is to use the literature to develop a logical theoretical foundation for your hypotheses. (You will learn more about hypotheses in Chapter 11.)

Step 4(c). Write to compare and contrast the literature.

Be sure to organize the subsections logically into a whole section. Write about the articles to indicate their similarities and differences. Effectively synthesizing, comparing, and contrasting articles with different research methods and/or conclusions illustrates expertise in your topic area. For example, let's use section 1, article numbers 1, 20, 41, etc. You have 13 articles to include in this section. Let's say five of the articles are empirical and conceptual articles. You could begin the section by writing about these articles, in any number of paragraphs, by stating how organizations are using personality testing, again just listing the informative articles as backup for the empirical discussion. You need to get to the most important discussion of the results/findings and conclusions. Let's say that three of the articles reported the same results and two were different. You do not want to list them all separately, and it is helpful to try to explain the possible reason for differences. You can report similarities and differences and possible reasons as follows, using the same references. See the example below, taken from a literature review on the impact of job performance on employee turnover:

> Researchers found that disruption of performance is a negative organizational consequence of employee turnover (Adams, 2008; Rogers, 2005; Wilson & Commings, 2005). In contrast, Peterson et al. (1999) found that disruption of performance is not a negative organizational consequence of employee turnover. However, Peterson et al. (1999), was an earlier study that surveyed human resources managers in banks. It is possible that disruption of performance is not a negative consequence in banking but that it is in other industries, particularly retailing, which was supported. (Adams, 2008; Rogers 2005)

You could get more complex and report p-values. You will learn how to do so later. Table 2.3 summarizes the steps in conducting the review of literature.

Table 2.3   Steps for Conducting the Review of Literature

| 1. Make a synthesizing outline for your Appendix B: Review of Literature (the full version). | 2. Determine under which outline section each reference can be used, and write it on your summary form. | 3. Write the reference number in the outline where it will be included. | 4. Group the articles and focus on the best, writing to synthesize, compare, and contrast the literature as you follow your outline, and use the best references to write your *brief* literature review in the Introduction section of your proposal/paper. |

Synthesizing the written review of literature.

Following is a guideline for writing the long, full literature review.

When you do begin to write, you should introduce the entire review of literature by briefly listing and discussing the major sections of the literature review (first-level headings) with a few key references. Next, go on to write each section. The articles under the first-level headings will be used for this purpose.

Each major section (first-level heading) of the literature review should have three parts: (1) an introduction of the topics and a listing of its subsections, (2) the body or details of the literature, and (3) a brief summary/conclusion that ties together the importance of the section to your study, leading you into the next section. Each section should have at least three paragraphs.

End a lengthy review of the literature that has multiple sections with a summary of all sections. Here you would briefly restate in different words what you have reported, citing your best references again to highlight the research value of your study.

CONCEPTUAL OBJECTIVE 8

Explain why it is important to synthesize and compare articles in the review of literature.

Common mistakes made by students.

Avoiding these mistakes can improve your work.

- *Lack of comparisons.* Students often don't do an effective job of comparing articles. Some students simply take one article and report the findings, then go on to the next, and so on until all articles have been reported. To avoid this mistake, refer to the "employee turnover" example above for a good example of article comparison and contrast.

- *Procrastination.* Avoid waiting until the night before the assignment is due. Set a deadline for completion a few days before the actual deadline so that you have adequate time to edit your work and at least one other person's work in your class.

- *Marathon.* Do not try to write the entire review of literature in one sitting. Many shorter sessions (stopping after each section is done) will result in better quality work.

- *Editing.* Due to procrastination (which usually includes marathons), students often have no time to edit, or at least to do so effectively. After a marathon of writing, students are usually too tired to thoroughly edit their work. As a result, they may not edit at all, or they do a poor job of editing. It is very important to edit your work to find general writing errors and style errors. For example, is the entire literature review written in the past tense as it should be? Having another person in the class edit your work, and you theirs, is an excellent way to improve your work.

Hypotheses

When you conduct empirical research studies, you should include hypotheses. Recall that a hypothesis is a tentative answer to a research question. The hypothesis states the relationship between the variables. So you start with your research question, conduct a literature review, and based on the review you state the anticipated answer to the research question. It is common to have one overarching research question/purpose of the study with multiple hypotheses. When you do your literature review of empirical articles, you will find examples of the studies' introduction/research question and literature review with hypotheses. You should include some of the same articles, variables, and hypotheses as the literature.

STOP READING and turn to the end of the chapter to complete exercise 2-6.

2.7 The Researcher–Manager Relationship

In this section you will learn about some of the potential problems for managers in conducting applied research. The information in this section may seem as though applied research is not recommended for students. This is not the case. Applied research is actually encouraged. If you do conduct applied research for an organization, you are providing a valuable service that may aid in decision making—it could be very costly if a consultant were hired to do the research. The intent is to make you aware of some potential problems you may face.

Managers routinely collect data for decision making. However, they seldom have had formal training in research methods or research expertise gained by actually conducting a research project/thesis. There are times when the manager does not have the time to conduct research as well. In these cases, the job can be delegated to a researcher—which could be you, if you are interested in conducting applied research for a specific organization as part of your research requirements.

Managers often have questions/problem areas related to customers, employees, and competitors that, when researched, can lead to better decision making. As with basic research, applied research must have value to the organization. Otherwise, how will the organization use the information in decision making? If you decide to conduct applied research, here are some guidelines for both managers and researchers.

Managers should state their problems in terms of the decision they must make rather than to specify the data they want collected. As stated earlier, the development of a clear research question is important. If you do not have any input into what data need to be collected to answer the research question, you may find out too late that the data you collect do not answer the "right" research questions, and you will most likely be blamed.

Another possible problem is the fact that the manager may not allow you access to data that is needed to answer questions. For example, you may not be given access to confidential information, including personnel files and trade secrets. Thus, as a researcher you should be involved in determining the statement of the research question and what data will be collected. Once the research question is clearly stated, you are responsible for developing a research design that will provide the answers to the research question and hypotheses. You can expect to get help from this book, the instructor of this course, your research project advisor, and the manager you are working with to conduct the research project.

If you presently work for an organization and approach managers to conduct a research project, you should be aware of potential political problems. For example, if you approach your boss to conduct research, the boss may view you as a threat. To allow one's organization/department to be subjected to a critical study can be threatening, even though there is great potential for improvements. Some resistant managers may think that researchers are trying to make themselves look good (which is fine in and of itself), while at the same time making the manager look bad, or that researchers are incapable of doing the research job. You could even be suspected of trying to take your boss's job! So be careful in how you approach and work with managers. You want to make yourself look good, and possibly advance in the organization, without making the manager(s) feel threatened.

You also must be careful that you are not being used by managers who simply want you to come up with set answers to prove that they are right. As you will learn in Chapter 3, you need to be ethical. A good example of managers only finding what they want as answers in research questions has taken place in the tobacco industry, in which research reports were changed and/or not used in ethical decision making.

SKI WEST STUDY

As we bring this chapter to a close, you should be able to:
- *clearly state a research question and its value,*
- *describe how to select and test a research question,*
- *conduct preliminary and actual literature reviews,*
- *write the introduction of a research proposal or paper, and*
- *understand the researcher–manager relationship.*

As you read about how Matt applied the concepts from Chapter 2 to his research, you may want to review his completed study in the Part V Appendix before, during, or after reading further.

Matthew McLeish's research question was: Can personality predict job performance? His two variables were personality and job performance, and he stated his research question as a testable hypothesis: Conscientious Scale scores can predict the end-of-season evaluation scores.

At the time he selected his research question, Matt wanted a career in human resources (HR) management. Two important areas of this field are selecting the best job applicants and evaluating employee performance, two areas in which he had an interest and wanted to become an expert. He knew he wanted to do a practical applied research study, so he talked to a couple of his professors and a few HR managers. After making his research question more focused, he found that it passed the test of being interesting, promoting expertise, and having research value. He found sufficient literature, the research was feasible with the cooperation of the HR manager at Ski West, and he was open to change.

Using his college ID, Matt used the Business Source Premier database from home. His keyword search included personality and job performance. He selected empirical journal articles, made or downloaded copies of the best ones, and made copies of some abstracts for limited use. He followed the reference chain and found other articles. For example, Matt was looking for recent articles, and a 2004 article was an extension of a prior article published in 1991, and a 2009 article by the same author also referenced this same article, so he got a copy of that article.

After his literature search, Matt typed reference summary forms for each article. He wrote an outline for his study and listed which articles would be used in which sections by numbering the sections and placing the numbers on the reference summary forms. With his literature organized and ready to go, Matt was ready to write his Introduction section. First he wrote and re-edited his extended literature review in Appendix B of his research proposal. Then he wrote and rewrote the Introduction, including a brief literature review, followed by a list of hypotheses in the proposal.

Since he was doing an applied study for a specific organization, Matt did have to get a sponsoring company. Matt had worked for Ski West, so he talked to the HR manager, who agreed to let Matt conduct the study using Ski West employee data. A formal letter of approval was obtained, and a copy is included as Appendix D of his research proposal.

CHAPTER SUMMARY

The chapter summary is organized in a way that provides you with the answers necessary to help you meet the conceptual objectives for this chapter.

1. **Explain why it is important to write the research question and its value clearly.**
   The research question is the purpose for conducting a study. The research question has value when answering it will provide new and useful answers to what is being researched. If the question is not clear, the results of the study may not answer the right question, and the answer may have no value. Errors of purpose and value usually cannot be corrected in later stages of the research process.

2. **Describe the differences among research questions, variables, and hypotheses.**
   A research question identifies the purpose of the study. Variables provide measurement criteria in the research question. A hypothesis is a tentative answer to the research question, identifying the anticipated relationship among the variables. A study usually has one research question with multiple variables and hypotheses.

3. **State the procedure for selecting and testing a research question.**
   The procedure is to begin with a topic of interest to you in which you want to be an expert. Talk to knowledgeable professors, managers, professionals, and others for ideas on a topic and to refine your research question. The six steps of testing a research question are: Is the topic *interesting*? Is it a topic you want to be an *expert* in? Does the question have *research value*? Is there *sufficient literature*? Is the research *feasible*? Are you open to *changing* the question as you progress through the research process?

4. **Differentiate (a) the four types of literature and (b) the three types of articles.**
   (a) The four types of literature are books, journals, magazines, and newspapers. A *journal* generally presents scholarly articles with little or no advertising and is not sold in stores. A *magazine* generally presents journalists' articles with advertising and is sold in stores. *Books, magazines,* and *newspapers* commonly provide secondary information and advice.
   (b) The three major types of articles are empirical, conceptual, and informative. *Empirical articles* test research questions/hypotheses based on literature reviews by using primary data, and they often report statistical findings. *Conceptual articles* are based on secondary data and offer synthesis of the literature and research question propositions with recommendations for empirical study. *Informative articles* report data, news and/or provide advice for the reader with limited, if any, literature review.

5. **Explain how to follow a reference chain.**
   To follow a reference chain, start with one article and look at the references. For those related to your topic that you do not already have, you obtain these additional sources. From each new source in the chain, you continue viewing references until you have all relevant sources related to your research question.

6. **Discuss reasons for completing reference summary forms.**
   Some of the reasons for completing summary forms are to aid in organizing and comparing references in preparation for, and to be used when, writing the research question and review of literature.

7. **List the four parts of the Introduction/research question section.**
The four parts of the Introduction/research question section include: the importance of the topic, the research question/purpose of the study, the need for the research, and its implications.

8. **Explain why it is important to synthesize and compare articles in the review of literature.**
Synthesizing and comparing articles in the review of literature is important because it illustrates expertise in a topic by logically organizing prior work while presenting similarities and differences of the research.

9. **Define the following alphabetical list of key terms.** Select one or more methods: (1) fill in the missing key terms from memory, (2) match the key terms with their definitions below, or (3) copy the key terms in order from the list at the beginning of the chapter.

conceptual article	journal	reference chain
empirical article	magazine	research question
informative article	periodic index	research value
introduction section	refereed article	review of the literature

_____ of a research study includes the research question and its value, the literature review, and hypotheses.

_____ is a clearly stated purpose of the study that identifies the variables to be investigated and is the basis for propositions/hypotheses.

_____ provides new and useful answers to research questions.

_____ synthesizes and compares prior work related to the research question.

_____ generally presents scholarly articles with little or no advertising and is not sold in stores.

_____ generally presents journalist articles with advertising and is sold in stores.

_____ tests research question hypotheses based on literature reviews using primary data and often reports statistical findings.

_____ are based on secondary data and offer synthesis of the literature and research question propositions with recommendations for empirical study.

_____ reports data, news and/or provides advice for the reader with limited, if any, literature review.

_____ has been reviewed by the editor and peers.

_____ contains bibliographic data and abstracts of journal articles.

_____ refers to using the citations included in one source to obtain additional sources.

WRITTEN ASSIGNMENTS

This assignment is the same for completing a research proposal, completing a study, or statistical analysis papers. Essentially, you should conduct your literature review and begin to organize your paper. For details of the assignment, turn to Part IV, Appendix RP—Sample Research Proposal, RP-1, Research Proposal Introduction.

ASSIGNMENT 1 (FOR RESEARCH PROPOSAL, COMPLETED STUDY, AND STATISTICAL ANALYSIS PAPER)

To *complete* the research proposal's Introduction section, you must read and understand this chapter and Chapter 1. For this Chapter 2 assignment, however, conduct a literature review and complete three reference summary forms. There is overlap between exercise 2-4 below and Part IV, Appendix RP, Assignment 1 (i.e., whether you are doing a completed study or are only writing a research proposal, you *must* do a literature review).

EXERCISES

YOUR RESEARCH QUESTION

2-1   List a tentative research question/purpose of the study and test it by applying the six criteria below.

1. Interest
2. Expertise
3. Research value
4. Sufficient literature
5. Feasibility
6. Openness to change

PRELIMINARY LITERATURE REVIEW AND REFINING THE RESEARCH QUESTION

2-2   Conduct a periodical index review of literature and obtain, read, and prioritize journal abstracts for your research question. Briefly report your literature review results.

2-3   Based on completion of exercise 2-2, narrow or refine and retest your research question from exercise 2-l.

LITERATURE REVIEW AND REFINING THE RESEARCH QUESTION

2-4   Read journal articles and complete at least three reference summary forms for empirical research articles.

2-5   Based on completion of exercise 2-4, further refine and test your research question.

WRITE THE INTRODUCTION

2-6   Write the Introduction (one or two paragraphs) of your research proposal/paper.

3

The Research Proposal, Completed Research Study, and Ethics

CHAPTER OUTLINE

CONCEPTUAL OBJECTIVES

The conceptual objectives below also appear at appropriate places within the chapter at points when you will have accessed the information necessary to attain them. They appear again at the end of the chapter in the Summary and Glossary section, along with explanations that will enable you to meet the objectives.

After studying this chapter you should be able to:

1. List the parts of a research proposal.
2. Identify the major components of the Introduction section of the research proposal.
3. Identify the common second-level headings in the Method section of the research proposal.
4. List the parts added to the proposal to complete the study.
5. State a few of the writing strategies that you plan to use when research writing.
6. State the rights of participants.
7. Define the following key terms (listed in order of their appearance in the chapter).

research proposal	substantive hypothesis	discussion
research project	delimitations	implications
research defense	limitations	code of ethics goals
thesis	abstract	anonymity
dissertation	results	confidentiality

SKILL DEVELOPMENT OBJECTIVES

The exercises that apply to particular skill development objectives are indicated directly beneath each numbered objective below. Periodic instructions within the chapter tell you when to stop reading and direct you to the end of the chapter to complete one or more of the skill development exercises.

After studying this chapter you should be able to:

1. Write your proposed research title and classification of the research.
   Exercise 3-1
2. Write the running head for your research title.
   Exercise 3-2
3. Write the substantive hypothesis for your proposed research.
   Exercise 3-3
4. Write about your proposed participants and measurement instrument for your research.
   Exercise 3-4
5. Write your proposed statement of the problem, define DV/Y and IV/X variables and their measurement levels, and identify delimitations and limitations of your proposed research.
   Exercises 3-5 through 3-8

The Research Process

(1) The research question/purpose of the study, literature review, and hypotheses.	(2) Research design methodology for collecting data and statistics.	(3) Data analysis and interpreting results.	(4) Discussing results and making conclusions.
• *Introduction*	• *Method*	• *Results*	• *Discussion*
Chapters 1–3	Chapters 4–8	Chapters 9–14	Chapters 9–14

Chapters 1–2 presented the research process shown above. In this chapter we continue to focus on the research process. Again, unless your instructor says otherwise, the research proposal and completed study should be written in appropriate research-writing style (i.e., APA, or the style of your college or your employer). This chapter presents and explains the parts of the research proposal and the completed research study. Research writing and ethical considerations in research are also discussed.

3.1 Overview

Let's begin by defining some terms. A research proposal tells the organization how the research study will be conducted. In academia, the faculty advisor(s) wants to make sure the proposal is well done before the student actually conducts the research. In applied business research, management also wants to know how the research will be conducted. Thus, section 3.2 explains how to prepare a research proposal that can be used for either academic or business research. *The **research proposal** is a plan for conducting research that focuses on the Introduction and Method sections of the research process.* Once you get the approval of the proposal, you go on to complete the research study. *The **research study** includes the completed work—introduction, method, results, and discussion.*

On the academic side, the **research project** *is commonly completed with one faculty advisor, usually without a defense* (see below). It may be called an independent study or some other title. During the **research defense** of the proposal and completed study, the researcher commonly presents the work publicly to an audience of students, faculty, and administrators who can ask questions, can make recommendations for improvements, and may require changes before final approval of the work. Copies of the research study are commonly made available for people to read before the defense.

*A **thesis** is conducted at the master's degree level, usually with a limited defense.* The thesis is commonly completed with three faculty advisors, and the defense may be limited in some way, such as to the faculty advisors. *A **dissertation** is conducted at the doctoral degree level, usually with a full defense.* When the terms *thesis* and *dissertation* are used, the degree level (master's and doctoral) is not included, as the words thesis and dissertation identify the degree. College and university departments and libraries commonly keep copies of theses and dissertations completed by their students. *Dissertation Abstracts* is a published list of the abstracts of dissertations completed, which are considered unpublished dissertations. You may want to check with your professor and/or library to view theses and dissertations.

Completed dissertations are usually submitted for publication to journals and conference proceedings, and theses are sometimes sent as well. Research submitted for publication is commonly called a manuscript by a journal and a paper by a conference that publishes proceedings. Many journals and proceedings use the APA format, which is designed so that the researcher can essentially take the front end (excluding the appendices) of the completed study and submit it for publication. Many journals offer author guidelines within the journal for submitting a research study. Calls for papers to be submitted to a conference also provide author guidelines. However, we are getting ahead of ourselves. The first step in research is the research proposal.

3.2 The Research Proposal

There are different formats you can use to develop a research proposal. Although the sample research proposal, completed study, and statistical analysis papers that appear in the appendices to this book follow APA format, your college may have additional requirements to or in place of APA that you should follow. (Refer to Part IV, Appendix RP—Sample Research Proposal as you read this section—a picture is worth a thousand words.) The introduction and methods in the Sample Research Proposal include Appendix A–Research Design and Appendix B–Review of Literature.

Students completing a research methods course are commonly required to develop a research proposal. After the research methods course, the proposal is commonly refined with one to three faculty advisors, may be defended, and must be approved before the actual study can begin.

If you are wondering why you cannot skip the research proposal and just begin the research, the answer is provided: There is actually very little additional work in completing the research proposal before conducting the actual study, because the proposal becomes part of the completed research study. It increases the quality of the research study. Reviewers of your proposal can correct any errors and make suggestions for improvement.

CONCEPTUAL OBJECTIVE 1
List the parts of a research proposal.

The parts of the research proposal appear in Box 3.1. Let's discuss each section separately.

Box 3.1 The Parts of a Research Proposal		
• title page	• method	• Appendix B, review of literature
• table of contents	• references	• other appendices
• introduction	• Appendix A, research design	• bibliography

The Title Page

The *college title page* may vary from college to college, but it commonly includes the title of the proposed study, classification of the research (i.e., research project, thesis, or dissertation), the name of student and the college, the faculty advisors, and the date. (See the Sample Research Proposal in Appendix RP for a college title page.)

The title should be short, containing no more than 12 words. If the title takes more than one line, wrap the text in a pyramid shape with the second (or more) lines being longer than the first line. The running head begins on the title page (page one of the research proposal) and appears on every page of the proposal. It is usually the same as the title of the study (or an abbreviated version, if the title is a longer one). The running head is all uppercase and set flush left. It should be a maximum of 50 characters, including letters, punctuation, and spaces between words. See the Sample Research Proposal in Appendix RP for an example. Here is what it contains:

PERSONALITY TESTING AND JOB PERFORMANCE

Author's name, institutional affiliations, and date.

Type your name on a single line, along with your college/university or employer name. For a business report (see below), use a separate line to list the business name and any department and/or person who the report was conducted for or who authorized the study.

Business reports.

Research studies conducted for an organization are commonly called business reports. Researchers usually have to get permission from some level of management to conduct an organizational study. Thus, a report often includes a *letter of authorization* that states the sponsor of the research and gives the researcher permission (authorization) to conduct the study. (See the Sample Research Proposal, which includes in its Appendix C a simple letter asking for authorization and the authorization form.)

When an outside organization/consultant conducts a study for a client, the authorization is commonly called a *letter of transmittal*. In addition to authorizing the research, the letter includes any specific instructions or limitations placed on the project, as well as the purpose and scope of the study. The names of authorizers are placed on the title page; actual copies of the letters may be placed in the appendices. The last part is often the date of completion or submission.

Other information.

Your college may want specific information. APA style guidelines include an author note and contact information (mailing and e-mail address, and telephone number). See the Sample Research Proposal title page. Note that the sample is an academic paper as part of college requirements, but it is also a business report.

**STOP READING and turn to the end of the chapter
to complete exercises 3-1 and 3-2.**

The Introduction Section

The actual proposal begins on page 2. This section discusses all of the elements that should appear in the Introduction section of your research proposal.

The title.

The title of the research proposal—*not* the Introduction, which has no heading—is repeated at the top of page 2. The title is a first-level heading. Thus, it is centered in title case—however, it is not in bold type

Introducing the problem (1–2 paragraphs).

Begin the Introduction section with a clear statement of the research question—the purpose of the study—and its value; refer to Chapter 2, sections 2.1, 2.2, and 2.5 (Write the Introduction). However, be sure to write the Method section of proposal in the future tense. As illustrated, it is helpful to include the following components in the part of the Introduction section containing the research question (complete with reference citations):

- *The importance of the topic:* Does it help solve a problem?
- *The research question* (purpose of the study).
- *The need for your research:* What is its value? How does it fill a gap in the literature? Is there inconsistency in results of past work? Does it extend prior research? How is your study different and more relevant than past research? Justify the need for your further research.
- *The implications:* Who can benefit by the research, and how?

The literature review (3–5 pages).

After your Introduction, write your brief literature review. Although presented first, the literature review is actually written after the full review of the literature (Appendix B of your proposal). This brief version is a summary of the best of the literature, using the most relevant sources. The literature has already been written and published, so remember to write in the past tense.

Substantive hypothesis.

Following, and based on, the literature review, write your substantive hypothesis (or hypotheses, if you have more than one). *The **substantive hypothesis** is the results the researcher expects to find after completing the research study.* It is common to list multiple hypotheses with the literature supporting them. Although presented just before the research methodology section, the Method section and Appendix A are written before finalizing the substantive hypothesis. (See the introduction in the Sample Research Proposal.)

The use of headings in the introduction and throughout the paper.

Note that we call the beginning of the proposal the Introduction section; however, in APA style *the word* introduction *is not included as a heading.* However, with business publications it is common to have section headings for an Introduction and Review of Literature. Hypotheses are often placed in the literature review and sometimes even have a separate heading. The use of headings in business reports makes it easier for the reader to follow your presentation.

CONCEPTUAL OBJECTIVE 2
Identify the major components of the introduction section of the research proposal.

STOP READING and turn to the end of the chapter to complete exercise 3-3.

The Method Section

The research methodology section (or *Method section*) describes in detail how your study will be conducted. Different research designs require different methods, but describing your methodology allows the reader to evaluate the appropriateness of your methods and the reliability and validity of your results, and it allows other researchers to replicate your study.

Introductory paragraph.

The section titled *Method* appears with a first-level heading. The Method section begins with an introductory paragraph identifying the research question/purpose of the study and *research design* (discussed in Chapter 4). It also introduces the second-level headings that commonly include (a) participants, (b) measurement, (c) procedures, and (d) statistical analysis. However, although these subsections are the most commonly used, there may be other subsections as well. Your review of the literature may reveal other headings in the Method section that you may want to include in your proposal. The Method section of the Sample Research Proposal includes the heading Participants (Employee Records).

Participants.

The focus here is on data collection. Participants (a second-level heading) must be clearly identified. Be sure to identify the type of sampling (covered in Chapter 5) and expected number of participants you will have in the study. State the common demographic characteristics of expected participants, such as age range, experience, type of organization, location, and so on. After you collect the data, you include descriptive statistics (discussed in Chapter 9) of participants. Conclusions and interpretations should not go beyond the sample of the study. In the completed study you include the actual description of the sample size and response rate. With internal business reports, response rates are not usually issues as employees are requested to respond, or company data is used, such as in the Sample Research Proposal (Part IV) and Sample Completed Study (Part V) in the appendices.

Measurement.

Empirical research-methods measurement includes conceptual and operational definitions of the variables studied. The measurement instrument identifies how you will measure the variables you are studying. In experimental medical studies of weight loss, for example, a scale can be used to determine change in weight. For a blood-pressure drug test, blood pressure can be taken before and after taking the drug. With survey research, questionnaires are used as the measurement instrument. Try to obtain a survey instrument that has already been used and validated whenever possible.

When reviewing the literature articles, be sure to check the measurement instruments used by prior researchers. You may be able to get a copy of the instrument from them or from some other source, often at a cost. Helpful publications, including the *Mental Measurement Yearbook* and *Test Critique,* are available at the reference section of college/university libraries and online databases.

When writing about the measurement instrument you use, be sure to briefly identify the reliability and validity of the instrument (discussed in Chapter 8). If your measurements are not consistent and accurate, the value of your study will be questionable. Measurement instruments, such as questionnaires, are commonly placed in Appendix C of the research proposal.

Procedures.

The procedures state step by step exactly how the research will be conducted, with the emphasis on data-collection methods. There are four types of data-collection methods (covered in chapters 6–7): secondary sources, observation, survey interview, and questionnaires. You need to identify which method you will use to collect data. A well-written procedures section is written in enough detail that someone else could easily complete your research without having to ask you any questions about the methodology to use. The best way to test details is to ask someone who is not familiar with your study to read the Method section and tell you if they could conduct the research without any further input from you. If they can, it's probably detailed enough. If not, it probably needs more work.

Although procedures are required, they do not always have to appear as a separate section but can instead be presented in other sections. For example, in the participant section you can document the details of sampling procedures, describing the setting and location in which the data were collected. In the measurement section you can detail the procedures for measuring variables.

Statistical analysis.

This is the heart of the quantitative research study. It can also appear under the sub-heading *Data Analysis*. A common mistake of the novice researcher is to quickly develop a questionnaire and get responses without ever thinking about statistics until it's time to put the data into the computer and run the statistical tests. At this point, they often find out that they did not ask the right (important) questions, they don't know what statistics to run, or they can only run low-level descriptive statistics.

In the statistical analysis section, you must clearly identify the dependent (DV/Y) and independent variables (IV/X), and their measurement levels, and which statistical test(s) will be used to determine the answers to the research hypotheses and other research questions. When doing survey research, you should know which questions would be used as DV/Y and IV/X, which statistical test applies to each question, and which questions test which hypotheses. Many novice researchers without proper research education find out too late that they never actually statistically tested their hypotheses. By the time you finish this book, you should not get caught in the novice trap.

CONCEPTUAL OBJECTIVE 3
Identify the common second-level headings in the Method section of the research proposal.

STOP READING and turn to the end of the chapter to complete exercise 3-4.

The References

In the research proposal, the References appear after the Method section. Again, references only include sources cited in the Introduction and Method sections. Be sure to follow the required style of your business or school when working on the References. The first-level heading "References," followed by the list of double-spaced reference entries, is placed on a new page.

Business research reports may use footnotes or endnotes instead of the author-date system used in APA style. Footnotes also can be used with APA style in addition to references, but they should be kept to a minimum if used at all.

Appendix A, Research Design

Appendix A is an extension of the Method section, and it is not always required. The introductory appendix begins on a new page with an *introductory paragraph* of the topic, which is *not* indented. Write citations out in full as if you are writing them for the first time, with appropriate use of "et al." in subsequent citations. Appendix A includes the following first-level headings: (a) Statement of the Problem, (b) Definition of Terms, (c) Delimitations, (d) Limitations, and (e) Hypothesis(es). Although *Appendix A* and *Research Design* are both part of the same title of this section of the paper, they go on two separate lines and are not a first-level heading. they are not bold, but *Appendix A* is italicized. (See the Sample Research Proposal for an example of Appendix A.) Let's discuss the content found under the most commonly used first-level headings.

Statement of the problem.

In a sentence or two, state what you are investigating. The statement should include the relationship between the variables that are being measured. It should be similar to the research question/purpose of the study from the introduction section, but it should not be in the same words.

Definition of terms.

The most important terms to be included are those that you are measuring and statistically testing. They are referred to as operational definitions. Recall from Chapter 1 that *operational definitions* are concepts stated in measurable terms that can be tested empirically. Motivation, for example, can have many different definitions. However, for research purposes you must state *how* motivation is measured and tested.

Delimitations.

*The selected constraints of the study are called **delimitations.*** For example, you can select the geographic boundaries of participants. Will participation be worldwide? In one country? In one section of a country? How many different industries will be included in the study? Will you restrict the participants to a certain gender, age, race, job, illness, and so on? How many participants will be included in the study? Are you delimiting the measure of the variables in some way? Are you using single or multiple measures of the variable?

Limitations.

*The influences on the study that the researcher will not control for and are beyond the control of the researcher are called **limitations.*** In contrast to delimitation, you are not selecting constraints. For example, you generally cannot control the honesty of participants. Perceptions may be important, yet you cannot control participants' perceptions. There may be some bias that you should address.

Hypotheses.

You will recall from Chapter 1 that a hypothesis is a tentative answer to a research question that usually states the relationship between variables. The hypotheses in this section may be similar to the substantive hypotheses in the Introduction section, but they should not be repeated word for word. It is common to state the alternative hypotheses (there is a relationship) in the introduction and the null hypotheses (no relationship) in Appendix A. (You will learn about hypothesis testing in Chapter 11.) For now, if you only have one hypothesis, you use the word hypothesis (singular) and do not use the number 1, because there is no second hypothesis. If you have two or more hypotheses, you use the word hypotheses (plural) and number them consecutively.

**STOP READING and turn to the end of the chapter
to complete exercises 3-5 through 3-8.**

Appendix B, Review of Literature

Recall that the review of literature is very important because through it you become an expert in your chosen topic. The review of literature can be written as a separate journal article that could be submitted to a review journal for publication; thus, no reference should be made to the research journal article section; write citations out in full as if you are writing them for the first time, with appropriate use of "et al." in subsequent citations. (Refer to Chapter 2 for details on writing the review of literature in the past tense, and see the Sample Research Proposal for an example of Appendix B.) Note that although "Appendix B" and "Review of Literature" are both part of the names of this section of the paper, they appear on two separate lines and are not a first-level heading. Although it is not bold, *Appendix B* is italicized. The first paragraph is *not* indented. This style also applies to all other appendices.

Since the literature review verifies that you are an expert in your chosen topic, you need to read the entire journal articles, not just the abstracts. Again, synthesize the (similar and different) research and do not present each paragraph with a different study review. The last portion of this section should be a short summary that critically summarizes the research and then makes a transition for the reader, focusing on what is now needed in this research area.

Your instructor and/or research advisor(s) will most likely specify the expected length of your review of literature. However, the amount of literature available has an effect on the length. The Sample Research Proposal has a literature review of more than 13 pages (when double spaced). This is on the short side, to give you some idea. It is not uncommon for a research proposal submitted for a research methods class to have a shorter review of literature than the final research proposal accepted by the faculty advisor(s) of a study.

A Word about Headings: There are no commonly accepted headings recommended for use in the literature review. Create your own headings based on the literature.

Other Appendices

Almost all research proposals include additional appendices. is common to include the measurement instrument, such as a copy of the questionnaire, in Appendix C and the cover letter in Appendix D. The informed consent form is another common appendix. All appendices start on a new page in the proposal. (See the Sample Research Proposal for an example of appendices C and D.)

Order of presentation.

Other appendices are lettered sequentially (C through as many as needed) and each given a title. For ease in finding the appendices, be sure to list them in the order in which you write about them in the proposal. In other words, you would not write about a cover letter first and identify it as Appendix F and then write about the questionnaire and identify it as Appendix E.

Informed consent.

The informed consent form is commonly used with experimental designs that may possibly cause some type of harm to the participants in the study. If a participant is under legal adult age (18 in the USA), a parent or guardian must sign the informed consent form for the child to participate. However, if data is taken from school records rather than from children, informed consent is needed from a school administrator for permission to gain access to and to use the data in the study. Adults completing surveys generally do not have to sign an informed consent form, as completing the questionnaire is a form of giving consent. The college or university, not APA (the American Psychological Association), determines when an informed consent form must be used and what the form contains.

The Bibliography

The last part of the research proposal is the Bibliography. Recall that it includes all sources from the references (including those written about in the appendices that do not appear in the references), and it may include others that are not written about in the proposal. Be sure to familiarize yourself with the style requirements of your intended audience when working on the Bibliography. (See the Sample Research Proposal for an example of a bibliography in APA style.) The Bibliography is usually longer than the Reference section because it includes sources that are not in the Introduction and literature review to the study or in Appendix B.

3.3 The Completed Research Study

The research proposal is part of the completed study, but the tense is changed. Since the research proposal becomes part of the completed research study, you need to change the tense from the proposed future to the past tense after you complete the study. In addition, you add the new parts of abstract, results, discussion, and tables and figures. In this section we discuss only the new parts. See Table 3.1 for the parts of the completed research study. Notice that the major parts are bold and italicized. (See Part V, Appendix CS—Sample Completed Study for an example, and refer to it as you read the following sections on each part of its content.)

The Abstract

The abstract appears after the title page as the first actual part of the paper, but it must be written last to effectively summarize the entire study.

*The **abstract** includes a brief comprehensive summary of the research question, description of participants and variables, findings, and discussion.* An abstract allows readers to survey the contents of an article quickly and, like a title, it enables them to retrieve it from abstracting and indexing databases. In the business report, the abstract is often called the executive summary. Style, including length, varies by publication, but the abstract is usually between 50 and 150 words or a maximum of one or two double-spaced pages.

Table 3.1 Parts of the Completed Research Study

Part of Study	Required for Thesis or Dissertation	Required for Proceeding or Journal	Required for Business Report	Notes
College title page	Yes	NO	NO	
Table of contents	Yes	NO	Yes	(used with a report >6 pages, after the title page)
Title page	Yes	Yes	Yes	
Abstract	Yes	Yes	Yes	(with a report called the executive summary, focus discussion)
Introduction section	Yes	Yes	Yes	
Method section	Yes	Yes	Yes	(with a report, tends to be brief and could be an appendix)
Results section	Yes	Yes	Yes	
Discussion section	Yes	Yes	Yes	(with reports, discussion may come before method and results)
References	Yes	Yes	Yes	
Tables and figures	Yes	Yes	Yes	(all these "yes" parts are considered as the article or report)
Appendix A, Research Design	Yes	No	No	
Appendix B, Review of Literature	Yes	No	No	(can be a separate article sent to a review journal)
Other appendices	Yes	No	Yes	(can be sent with articles and are common in reports)
Bibliography	Yes	No	No	

Placement.

Again, the abstract is commonly on page 2 of the completed APA paper. With APA style/business reports, the abstract/executive summary is the *only* content on page 2. However, other styles place the abstract after the title and before the introduction. Note that although "Abstract" is a first-level heading, the abstract is typically only one blocked paragraph (not indented). (See the Sample Completed Study for an example of an abstract.)

Contents.

Although you talk about all of the four parts listed below, they are not headings in an abstract. The abstract includes a concise sentence or two for each of the four major parts of the study:

- *Introduction.* Describe the research question/purpose of your study.
- *Method.* Describe the research design, participants, variables measured, and statistical tests.
- *Results.* Report the findings of hypotheses testing.
- *Discussion.* State your conclusions and implications. Who can benefit from the study and how?

Tense.

Write in present tense to describe results and conclusions drawn with continuing applicability. However, use past tense to describe variables and outcomes measured.

Again, don't forget that the completed study uses the same *Introduction and Method sections* from the research proposal, but you change the tense from future to past tense.

Keywords.

For publication purposes, APA style places a list of keywords following the abstract. The publisher uses the keywords for database searching so that people can find your published work. If you are not planning to publish your work or place it on the Internet, a list of keywords is not needed.

The Results Section

The **results** *report the statistical findings of the hypotheses testing.* Results summarize the data collected and analyzed. Obviously, results cannot be part of the proposal. The results section is written in statistical terms that the general public may not understand, and you don't add any explanation for the results.

Note that unlike the Method section, there are no common headings in the Results section, nor are there common topics to address as in the Introduction and Discussion sections.

Tables and figures.

Complex statistical findings are commonly presented in tables and figures. However, they are a supplement to, not a replacement for, discussing the results. You must state the major results in the text and refer the reader to the tables and figures for more details.

Descriptive statistics.

It is common to begin with descriptive statistics of the variables, often in a detailed table. (We discuss descriptive statistics in Chapter 9.) Although descriptive statistics are run as results, it is common to go back to the Method section and include them with the discussion of participants.

Inferential statistics (hypotheses testing).

The inferential statistical results (discussed in Part III, chapters 9–14) of all tests are presented with probability values (p-value) stating whether the hypotheses are accepted/supported or rejected/refuted. In other words, you answer the research questions accurately without any bias. Typically you have one paragraph per hypothesis.

Headings.

Again, there are no commonly used headings in the Results section. Although second- and third-level headings are not commonly used, you can create your own headings (e.g., Descriptive Statistics and Inferential Statistics).

Placement.

Note that the results appear in a separate section from tables and figures. Results are placed near the middle of the paper, and their tables and figures are placed at the end of the paper.

The Discussion Section

Based on your methods and results, you now interpret your findings (draw inferences from inferential statistics), and make conclusions based on the results, especially as they relate to your hypotheses. *The **discussion** commonly includes a nonstatistical conclusion of the findings, a comparison of findings to the literature, implications, limitations, and recommendations for further research.*

With business reports, the comparison of findings to the literature is included briefly or not at all. Recommendations for further research may be stated, especially with exploratory studies and in cases when the results are not as expected, such as in the Sample Completed Study. Making recommendations for more research is one technique that consultants use to get more work for their business.

Nonstatistical conclusions of results/findings.

Conclusions represent inferences drawn from the results. You restate the results so that people not familiar with statistics can understand them. Thus, do not use the terms *significant* or *p-values* again. Instead, write with simple words and in clear statements. Were your hypotheses supported? If the results were not as expected, you can offer possible explanations. You are making generalizations from the sample to the populations, but don't draw conclusions that go beyond the data.

Comparison of findings to the literature.

State whether the findings support or refute prior research. Be sure to cite the specific authors of studies that your research supports or refutes. Discuss how your study adds to, or helps fill the gap in, the current literature.

Limitations.

You must be careful not to overgeneralize your findings and to state limitations. All research studies have their limitations, and good researchers state them. For example, the participants were from New England and the results may be different in other parts of the country.

Recommendations for further research.

What do you recommend other researchers do differently? For example, they could duplicate the study in other parts of the country, use a larger sample, could include different industries, and so on.

Implications.

*The **implications** identify who can benefit from the study and how.* Interpret the results/ conclusions by discussing the meaning of the findings, indicating any interpretations or insights that seem pertinent to the particular field of study. Refer to the introduction as to why the results are important. What should/could the study population do differently as a result of your research findings? With business reports, it is common to include *recommendations* for decision making.

Headings.

Note that although you write about all five parts above, they are not commonly your subheadings. They normally appear in separate paragraphs in the sequence presented above, but the order can be changed to fit the results. APA style does suggest ending with implications. It can be argued that using these headings make it easier for the reader.

If the Results and Discussion sections are short, as compared to the Introduction and Method sections, you can *combine the headings for results and discussion* (or results and conclusions) under one first-level heading. If you elect to use second-level headings, you can combine them. The Sample Completed Study uses four second-level headings, combining the *implications* and the *need for further research* subsections. These subheadings are put together because the results of the study were not as expected, leading to the need for further research to answer the research question. Why are the results different from the literature and not as expected?

Tables, Figures, and the Table of Contents

Don't forget that references are placed *before* the tables and figures; this is to acknowledge the work of others and to provide a way to locate the sources.

Recall that the statistics results are commonly placed in tables. However, note that the tables and figures are *not* placed with the results—they are placed *after* the references. Tables come first, followed by figures, if any. They are also listed sequentially in separate pages in the table of contents, if you include one. APA format calls for only one table and figure per page, regardless of how short they are. The review of literature can also include a table to highlight comparisons.

CONCEPTUAL OBJECTIVE 4
List the parts added to the proposal to complete the study.

3.4 Research Writing and Editing

This section focuses on getting ready to write and, when you are done writing, how to edit your work (macro view). We begin with the planning and organizing that should take place *before* you begin to write your paper, followed by discussion of writing strategies and editing.

Planning and Organizing

Before you begin writing, you should develop a plan (i.e., set objectives and a schedule for writing the sections) and organize your thoughts (the best system being an outline).

Length.

An important objective to consider is how many pages you are expected to have in the final paper. APA style suggests that less is better, as do many managers requesting organizational research reports. If you are writing for a course or graduation requirement, your instructor and/or college may have standard ranges of expectations. For business reports, discuss any expectations with managers. For journals or proceedings, check their typical length to determine the proper range.

Headings outline.

The nice thing about research writing is the fact that no matter what your field of study or topic is, before you start to write the paper you prepare an outline using the same basic headings that appear in the paper. See Box 3.2 for a listing of possible headings (levels 1, 2, and 3) and an outline for the research proposal and completed study. Your literature review can also provide you with ideas for headings.

Outline and references.   Before you begin to write, prepare your outline of headings and your references/abstract/article. Instead of note cards, you can use the computer abstract printouts and/or the reference summary form (discussed in Chapter 2). Each arti-

---

Box 3.2   Possible Headings and Outline

I. Introduction
The introduction may or may not actually be a heading in the paper, and the A–D headings below are *not* headings, but this section (one or two paragraphs) does include:
   A. Importance of the study
   B. Research question/purpose/hypotheses
   C. Need for the research
   D. Implications

II. Review of Literature
   A. Success factors
   B. Failure factors

III. Method
   A. Participants
   B. Measurement
       1. Success
       2. Failure
   C. Procedures
   D. Statistical analysis
       1. Hypothesis 1
       2. Hypothesis 2

IV. Results
   A. Descriptive statistics
   B. Hypothesis 1
   C. Hypothesis 2

V. Discussion
The heading may not be used in the paper, but this section should include:
   A. Conclusions/findings
   B. Results and the literature
   C. Limitations
   D. Further research
   E. Implications

cle should be on a separate sheet. You can fasten the abstract to the article or reference summary sheet. The abstracts and reference summary forms are excellent for writing your references and bibliography.

Matching the references to the outline.   With your outline and references in hand, place the outline numbers/letters on the reference form, indicating in which section and subsection the references will be used. If you plan to use the same reference multiple times, put multiple outline numbers/letters on it—for example, when you use a reference in the review of literature (II. A and B in Box 3.2) and use it again when you compare your results to the literature (V. B.).

If you are required to complete a long literature review in Appendix B, you may want to have two separate outline and numbering systems. Refer to Chapter 2 for a review of how to make an outline for Appendix B.

Piles.   Place your articles in piles that represent sections of your paper. It's helpful to have each batch together and ready to use when you write each section. As you write each section you move the reference to a new pile, either the "done with" pile (a nice feeling!) or the pile representing the next section in which it will be used.

Number of reference citations.   This varies by section, as follows:

- **Introduction.** Note that the Introduction (especially the literature review) and Appendix B employ heavy use of reference citations.
- **Method.** The Method section has far fewer citations if you are duplicating the methods of prior researchers, but you don't actually need any citations in the Method section.
- **Results.** The Results section commonly does not have any reference citations.
- **Discussion.** The Discussion section—where you compare your results to the literature—clearly needs reference citation, but other sections may or may not use citations. However, you can use limitations, recommendations for further research, and implications that you get from other researchers (which, of course, you need to cite). Don't forget that including others' recommendations for further research is a great reference to support your Introduction section.

Writing Strategies

Here are some ideas to implement as you write the paper:

- **Quiet time.** Try to find a quiet place to schedule your writing time when there is a minimum of distractions and interruptions.
- **Same location/folder.** Try to keep all your work in the same place (for example, in one folder) so that all your materials are easily accessible when you need them.
- **Interesting topic.** A paper is interesting because of the work itself, not because of the writing style. You don't need to be a creative writer; just make sure the reader understands what you are writing. This is explained in the next bullet.
- **Audience focus.** Keep your audience in mind and write in a style that the reader can understand.
- **Focus on the research question (objective or purpose and hypotheses).** The Introduction section states the objective or purpose of the study, the Method section states how you will measure and test the hypotheses, the Results section states

whether or not the hypotheses were supported, and the Discussion section states your conclusions about your hypotheses. To ensure that you have a consistent focus that the reader will understand, you need to edit your work.

- **Don't procrastinate.** Don't put off writing the paper. Procrastinating will only cause you stress and decrease the quality of your work. Don't wait until the night before the paper is due. An all-nighter may have worked in the past, but it will not work for quality research writing. Schedule time to write each section over several days or weeks, and get the work done. Some people recommend doing some work on your research every day.

- **Backward scheduling.** When scheduling writing time, work backwards from the due date and allow time for the possibility of something going wrong or taking longer than you planned for. For example, if the paper is due in four weeks, during week one you write the intro; week two the method; week three, results; week four, conclusions and editing.

- **Time estimation doubling.** Schedule more time than you think it will take to write the entire paper and each section. Estimate how long you think it will take to write the section, and then double it.

- **Long time blocks.** Schedule large blocks of uninterrupted time to keep your project moving forward. Most researchers get much more writing done in a two-hour block than in four-half hour sessions. Writing research is complex, so whenever you stop working, you waste time when you begin again, reorienting yourself to where you left off. So follow the next tip.

- **Note what's next.** When you break for a long period of time, write a note to yourself that summarizes where you ended and what you need to do next.

- **Set an early deadline.** Set a deadline earlier than the section/paper is due, so you have time to edit. For example, if the paper is due on Friday, have it done on Wednesday so you have Thursday to edit your work.

- **Write, then edit.** Write your ideas first and edit second. Quality usually increases if you write an entire section and edit afterwards. Don't try to write a paragraph and edit as you go.

- **Edit.** If you procrastinate, schedule insufficient time to write the paper, and don't schedule an early deadline, the odds are that you will not have enough time to edit your work. Marathon sessions will result in your being too tired to edit effectively. Editing is very important to the quality of your work. Some editing tips appear in the next sections. Although we discuss macro editing before micro editing, you can edit in either sequence based on your preference.

CONCEPTUAL OBJECTIVE 5
State a few of the writing strategies that you plan to use when research writing.

Macro Editing

Before we begin discussing macro editing, let's start with a few basics about editing. There are five major ways that you can *edit* (improve your written work). You can (a) add to it, (b) cut it, (c) rearrange it, (d) divide it, or (e) combine it. Edit on the computer, but read the hard (printed) copy out loud. At its simplest form, *run a spelling and grammar check* on the computer before printing. Although performing a spelling and grammar check doesn't guarantee accuracy, it helps.

When macro editing, you are looking at your work without reading it word for word. Macro editing is usually done with a printed copy of your work rather than reading it on the computer screen.

Length.

Is the length of the paper within the accepted standard? If your paper is too short, add to it; and if it is too long, cut it back.

Headings.

Check all your headings. Are there at least two parallel subheadings per heading? Are the heading levels (first, second, and third) correctly formatted? Should you add, cut, or rearrange the order to help the reader understand your ideas?

Paragraph length, references, comparisons.

Look at each paragraph to check its length. If any are too long (longer than three quarters of a double-spaced page) or too short (fewer than three sentences), make a note in the margin to fix them. Does each paragraph in the introduction and literature review have a reference? Does the literature review compare findings? If paragraphs only have one reference, there is no comparison. Include at least one reference to support what you are writing and a few to compare.

References ("and" versus "&," et al.).

Check to make sure all sources are cited correctly and that they appear in the Reference section (check for correct use of et al.). Edit your references and citations using the style recommended by your college or employer. If submitting your research for publication, make sure that the references and citations are in the style preferred for that publication.

Micro Editing

Edit each section, paragraph, and sentence carefully, as outlined in the editing checklist below.

Read and edit as you write sections.

This is not a contradiction to our previous advice to "Write and then edit." As you progress through the sections of the paper, go back to make sure you are consistent. Because a research paper is made up of different sections that must be consistent, writing new sections may affect what you wrote in earlier sections. For example, you may get ideas for prior sections when writing a different section. You may be in the Results section and decide to rephrase your hypothesis, which then will require changes in the Introduction section. The Introduction is very important because you need to get the reader interested quickly. Although it is short, it's difficult to write effectively, so plan to edit it several times. Refer to your literature for ideas on what to say and how to write it.

TBS (Topic Sentence, Body, Summary) and sentence length.

Does each paragraph have a topic sentence telling the reader what the paragraph is about (your one main idea)? Does the paragraph contain sentences to provide the details of that one idea? If the paragraph is long, does it have a summary/conclusion sentence? If not, edit the paragraph. Do the sentences in the paragraph vary in length but average around 15 words? If not add, cut, divide, or combine as appropriate.

One idea.

Does each paragraph have only one idea? Do all the sentences in the paragraph support just one idea? Do all sentences contain just one idea? If not, cut them or move them to separate paragraphs or sentences.

Transition.

Do all the sentences in the paragraph flow logically with the use of transition? If not, rearrange them and use transitions.

Grammar, diction, and punctuation.

Check each sentence in the paragraph for grammar, diction, and punctuation following the guidelines recommended by your college or employer (or following the preferred style of the journal to which you will submit your research for publication).

Grading/Rubric, Editors, and Re-editing

After your micro editing is finished, the following steps will ensure a well-written paper.

Grading/rubric.

Will your paper be graded with some form of a grade sheet/rubric provided by the instructor? Most instructors/managers will give you some indication of how they will evaluate your work. If so, check everything that they say is important (or everything presented on the grading sheet/rubric) to make sure you meet the criteria before you finalize and submit your paper.

Editors.

You may hire paid professionals or unpaid professionals, or you may recruit family, friends, classmates, or anyone who can help edit your work. If your college has some type of writing center, you may use it. It does help to have someone, even people not strong in English, to review your work and possibly recommend improvements.

Trade edits.

Teaming up with a classmate and editing each other's papers before handing them in can improve the quality and grade of your work (as well as completed work you submit for publication). To trade edits, remember that you need to set a deadline before the due date.

Re-edit one.

After editing your work as discussed above, re-edit (again). Read the hard copy aloud, following the steps outlined above. Even though this is called "re-edit one," you should actually edit several times before giving your paper to another person for review.

Re-edit two.

Based on your editors' comments, re-edit yet again. Well written papers do not come easily; they require several edits. Be sure to allow adequate time for your re-editing.

3.5 Ethics in Research

In these first few chapters we've discussed the research process and the basics of research writing. Now that you have a basic understanding of research, keep in mind that you must also be an *ethical* researcher. Writing-style requirements vary, but ethical and legal principles (right and wrong) underlie all scholarly disciplines. Virtually every professional association, such as the American Management Association, develops a code of ethics (which includes the ethical and the legal into one name—ethics). More than likely, your college has some type of student handbook discussing ethical topics such as cheating. Codes of ethics in research and publishing have three common goals. A *code of ethics ensures the accuracy of research, protects the rights of research participants, and protects intellectual property rights*. In this section we discuss these three goals.

Accuracy of Research

The essence of the scientific method is conducting research that can be repeated and verified by others. Accuracy is about honesty. Therefore, business researchers are ethical—they don't fabricate, falsify, modify, or omit data or results. *Conflicts of interest* can also influence you to be dishonest, such as when you are paid (as an employee or consultant) to conduct a study in which the organization wants the results to report findings that are favorable (or not unfavorable) to its business. Here we discuss some unethical practices that you may be tempted or pressured to engage in—but make sure you resist the temptation!

Fabricating, falsifying, or modifying data or results.

When you collect survey data and don't get an acceptable number of respondents or get a low response rate, you could be tempted to just add more data by filling in the questionnaires yourself or just reporting a higher number of responses (say, 100 instead of 50, or a response rate of 38% instead of 5%). Such changes are clearly wrong.

When you run your statistics and they don't support your hypotheses, you could be tempted to change them so that they do support your hypotheses. For example, if your results are p = .037, you could be tempted to change to p = .37 instead. But making unethical changes can lead to serious consequences to other people and to you, as you'll see below.

You could conduct a study for an organization (as an employee or consultant), and someone could ask you to change your data or actual results. For example, what if your study found a product to be ineffective, but someone asks you to changes the report saying the product is effective (or changes it themselves). Would you change the results yourself, or if someone else changed it would you just say nothing and let it go out of fear of losing your job? Or would you blow the whistle? Getting caught in any dishonest behavior (and some people *do* get caught) could result in discipline, job termination (or dismissal from college), and even a jail sentence.

If you read the Sample Completed Study in Part V, Appendix CS, you know that there were several hypotheses tested, and the results were unexpected, indicating the reverse—the employees with the lower personality test scores actually came out with higher performance evaluations. Would you have reported the finding accurately, as Matt did?

Omitting findings.

If an organization is paying you to conduct research (or grading your ability to do so), it can be tempting to make the results look better than they really are. Let's say you are testing three hypotheses and the results of two are as you predicted, and the third is not as predicted. You could be tempted to just take the third hypothesis out of the study. As another example, if you were conducting research to determine the effectiveness of a product and it was in fact effective but did have a negative side effect of some type, you could be tempted to make the results look better than they really are. Also, as discussed above, you could be pressured to leave out the information, or someone else could take out the negative findings. Clearly this is not an ethical research practice.

Rights of Participants

Participants in your study have at least six rights (your obligation to participants):

Nonparticipation and the right to withdraw at any time during the study.
It is unethical to force participants to be involved in your study or to force them to continue participating if they are unwilling to do so.

Full disclosure (no deception).
Participants have the right to know the purpose of the study. It is unethical to lie to potential participants to get them to agree to participate.

Right of privacy.
Privacy is equally as important as nonparticipation and full disclosure. When conducting observation research, you must take care not to violate participants' privacy by recording their behavior without their knowledge.

Right to either anonymity or confidentiality.
Participant data is pooled together so that no one knows any individual's participant data. *With **anonymity**, the researcher does not know who the participants are. With **confidentiality**, the researcher knows who the participants are but maintains their privacy.* The researcher should not state the names of participants, whether they be individuals or organizations, without their approval.

For example, a survey is mailed out to 200 people. Fifty are returned. If the researcher does not know which 50 returned the survey, this is anonymity. If the researcher knows which 50 return the questionnaires and which 150 did not but keeps their identities private, this is confidentiality. The benefit of confidentiality is that a follow-up request to nonrespondents of the survey can increase the response rate without a repeated request to the respondents who have already responded.

Right to experimenter responsibility.
With experiments such as drug testing, the researcher must give full disclosure and take precautions not to harm participants.

Informed consent.
Participants in experimental research should sign an informed consent form. With survey research, completing the questionnaire is commonly considered an informed consent. However, some organizations require a specific form—for example, to survey or study children you may need to get an informed consent from the parents. Recall that with organizational business report research you need a letter of authorization, which is somewhat similar to an informed consent. Some of the important parts include:

- an explanation of the procedures of the study,
- a description of any risks or potential discomforts and/or benefits—such as side effects of drugs,
- an offer to answer any inquiries, and
- instructions that the participant is free to withdraw at any time during the study.

If you as the researcher do not require a waiver of experimenter responsibility, this means you are responsible if you hurt someone.

CONCEPTUAL OBJECTIVE 6
State the rights of participants.

Intellectual Property Rights

You must obey copyright law. Not doing so is not only unethical, it is also illegal—you can be disciplined, fired (and/or kicked out of college), sued and fined, and possibly even jailed for violating copyright law. Here are a few examples of violations of intellectual property.

Claiming authorship.

It is clearly unethical to buy or otherwise acquire a paper and put your name on it, claiming to be the author. Doing so is not only unethical, it also cheats you out of the opportunity to learn how to conduct research. I recommend having others edit your work, but if others have essentially written or rewritten the paper—even if it is based on your own ideas—you cannot claim that you are the author.

Unauthorized help.

If it is inferred (or you are told) that you can't have anyone help you with your research, you must comply with the rules or you are being unethical. For example, you may be expected (or be told) to develop your own questionnaire, enter your own data, run your own statistics, or write your entire paper alone; failing to follow these instructions is unethical.

Plagiarism.

Stealing others' ideas without giving them credit for their work is called *plagiarism*. This practice is, of course, unethical. Besides, citing references of others' work is an important part of the research process.

Permission to use unpublished work.

It is unethical to use measurement instruments (e.g., questionnaires), procedures, or data developed by others and considered to be "theirs" without obtaining their permission. For example, let's say your friend developed a questionnaire in another course and you want to use it in your research course. You must obtain the person's permission and give them credit by citing them as the source.

Copyright permission.

Virtually all books and periodicals have copyrights that state that you can't use anything in the publication without the publishers' written permission. Obtaining permission usually takes time, and you are often required to pay a fee for using the material. However, with journal articles the questionnaire usually is not published, and if you ask the author(s) for a copy, you may get a copy at no cost. But this is not common with other forms of publications. For example, you can't just look in a management textbook and find a questionnaire (often called a self-assessment) and use it for your research without permission of the publisher. In most cases, the author legally can't even give you permission because the author doesn't own the copyright—the publisher does.

SKI WEST STUDY

As we bring this chapter to a close, you should:
- *understand the parts of a research proposal and how they become part of the completed study, and*
- *know how to plan and organize a study in an ethical manner.*

As you can see by looking at Matt McLeish's research proposal and completed study in the appendices, he learned to write in proper research-writing style (APA), and he completed a research proposal followed by a completed study (see Part V of the appendices). The first two sections of his research proposal become the first two sections of his completed study. He added results (with two tables) and discussion sections to complete the study, based on his data collection and analysis.

CHAPTER SUMMARY AND GLOSSARY

The chapter summary is organized in a way that provides you with the answers necessary to help you meet the conceptual objectives for this chapter.

1. **List the parts of a research proposal.**
   The parts of the research proposal include: (a) the college title page; (b) the table of contents; (c) the Introduction; (d) the Method section; (e) the References; (f) Appendix A, Research Design; (g) Appendix B, Review of Literature; (h) other appendices; and (i) Bibliography.

2. **Identify the major components of the Introduction section of the research proposal.**
   The Introduction section of the research proposal begins with the (a) title and is followed by the (b) research question (importance of the topic, purpose of the study, need for the research, and implications). Then comes the (c) literature review, and finally the (d) substantive hypothesis.

3. **Identify the common second-level headings in the Method section of the research proposal.**
   The common second-level headings in the Method section include: (a) Participants, (b) Measurement, (c) Procedures, and (d) Statistical Analysis. However, other headings may be used, and procedures may be included under other headings.

4. **List the parts added to the proposal to complete the study.**
   The abstract, results, discussion, and tables and figures are added to the proposal to complete the study.

5. **State a few of the writing strategies that you plan to use when research writing.**
   Strategies include finding quiet time; using the same location/folder to store materials; selecting an interesting topic; determining audience focus; focusing on the

research question; avoiding procrastination; employing backward scheduling and time-estimation doubling; scheduling long time blocks; noting what's next; setting early deadlines; and writing, editing, and editing again.

6. **State the rights of participants.**

   Participants in your study have at least six rights: (a) nonparticipation and the right to withdraw at any time during the research, (b) full disclosure (no deception), (c) the right to privacy, (d) the right to either anonymity or confidentiality, (e) the right to experimenter responsibility, and (f) informed consent.

7. **Define the following alphabetical list of key terms.**

   Select one or more methods: (1) fill in the missing key terms from memory, (2) match the key terms with their definitions below, or (3) copy the key terms in order from the list at the beginning of the chapter.

abstract	dissertation	research proposal
anonymity	implications	research study
code of ethics goals	limitations	results
confidentiality	research defense	substantive hypothesis
delimitations	research project	thesis
discussion		

   _____ is a plan for conducting research that focuses on the Introduction and Method sections of the research process.

   _____ includes the completed work—introduction, methods, results, and discussion.

   _____ is commonly completed with one faculty advisor, usually without a defense.

   _____ of the proposal and completed study means that the researcher commonly presents the work publicly to an audience of students, faculty, and administrators who can ask questions, can make recommendations for improvements, and may require changes before final approval of the work.

   _____ is conducted at the master's degree level, usually with a limited defense.

   _____ is conducted at the doctoral degree level, usually with a full defense.

   _____ are the results the researcher expects to find after completing the research study.

   _____ are the selected constraints of the study.

   _____ are the influences on the study that the researcher will not control for and are beyond the control of the researcher.

   _____ includes a brief _comprehensive_ summary of the research questions, description of participants and variables, findings, and discussion.

   _____ report the statistical findings—hypotheses testing.

   _____ commonly includes a nonstatistical conclusion of the findings, a comparison of findings to the literature, implications, limitations, and recommendations for further research.

_____ identify who can benefit from the study and how.

_____ are to ensure the accuracy of research, to protect the rights of research participants, and to protect intellectual property rights.

_____ means that the researcher does not know who the participants are.

_____ means that the researcher knows who the participants are but maintains their privacy.

WRITTEN ASSIGNMENTS

ASSIGNMENT 1 FOR RESEARCH PROPOSAL, COMPLETED STUDY, AND STATISTICAL ANALYSIS PAPER

This assignment is the same, whether you are completing a research proposal, conducting a study, or writing a statistical analysis paper. It is a continuation of the written assignment from Chapter 2. Hopefully, you have completed your literature search, part 1 (three reference summary forms), and part 3 (bibliography and title page) of Assignment 1. If not, finish them now.

Now that you have learned about research writing, including parts of the research proposal and research writing/editing tips, you are ready to write the Introduction section of your research proposal. For details of part 2 of the assignment, turn to Part IV (Appendix RP), Sample Research Proposal, Assignment 1, Research Proposal Introduction.

ASSIGNMENT 2

This second assignment is related to chapters 1 through 3 and is recommended for students doing the research proposal only, but an alternative is to extend the literature review. If you are doing a completed study, you may not be required to complete the assignment, which is to write Appendix B, Review of Literature. It is the expanded version of the brief literature review, consisting of 10 or more pages. It is usually completed after you hand in Assignment 1 and get feedback on your work. For details of Assignment 2, turn to Part IV (Appendix RP) and refer to the Sample Research Proposal's Appendix B, Review of Literature.

EXERCISES

COLLEGE TITLE PAGE (USED FOR COLLEGE RESEARCH PURPOSES)

3-1 Write your proposed research college title page information (title, author and affiliation, and other items).

TITLE PAGE (USED FOR PUBLICATION OR BUSINESS PURPOSES)

3-2 Write the running head for your research title (50 characters max) using APA style (or whatever style is recommended by your instructor/employer).

SUBSTANTIVE HYPOTHESES

3-3   Write your substantive hypothesis(es) for your proposed research.

METHOD

3-4   Write your proposed Method section (participants, measurement, procedures, and statistical analysis). We haven't yet covered research designs/data collection (Part II, chapters 4–8) or statistics (chapters 9–14), but your review of other articles should give you a good idea as to what methods and statistical test you will use.

APPENDIX A

Turn to Part IV, Appendix RP (The Research Proposal). See the Sample Research Proposal, and refer to Matt McLeish's Appendix A, Research Design. Using this as your template, complete the following exercises.

3-5   Write your proposed statement of the problem.

3-6   Write your proposed Y and X variables, their measurement levels, and their operational definitions.

3-7   Identify delimitations of your proposed research.

3-8   Identify limitations of your proposed research.

PART II

Research Designs
Data-Collection Methods

Methods
Research Designs

CHAPTER OUTLINE

4.1 Defining Research Design
4.2 Classification of Research Designs
      Type of Study (Exploratory or Conclusive/Formal)
      Data Collection (Secondary, Observation, or Survey)
      Data Triangulation
      Time Dimension of Data Collection (Cross-Sectional or Longitudinal)
      Research Environment of Data Collection (Fieldwork or Deskwork/Lab)
      Manipulating Variables (Experimental or Ex Post Facto)
      Purpose of Study/Data Analysis (Descriptive or Inferential/Causal)
      Goal of Data Analysis (Explain, Predict, or Control)
      Data Analysis (Qualitative or Quantitative/Statistical)
      Data Collection (Qualitative versus Quantitative)
4.3 Quantitative Inferential Statistical Research Designs
      Tests of Difference
      Tests of Interaction
      Tests of Association
      Tests of Prediction
      Tests of Interrelationship
      Primary and Secondary Research Designs
      Causal Inferences
4.4 Qualitative Research Designs
      The Case Study
      Focus Groups

CONCEPTUAL OBJECTIVES

The conceptual objectives below also appear at appropriate places within the chapter at points when you will have accessed the information necessary to attain them. They appear again at the end of the chapter in the Summary and Glossary section, along with explanations that will enable you to meet the objectives.

After studying this chapter you should be able to:

1. Identify and explain the parts of a research design.

2. List and contrast the three methods of data collection.

3. Explain the differences between qualitative and quantitative research.

4. Describe the similarity and differences between tests of differences and tests of interaction.

5. Describe the similarity and differences among the tests of association, prediction, and interrelationship.

6. Discuss the major advantage and disadvantages of the case study method.

7. Define the following key terms (listed in order of their appearance in the chapter).

research design	survey data	qualitative research
methods of data collection	data triangulation	quantitative research
databases	cross-sectional data	case study
observational data	longitudinal data	focus group

SKILL DEVELOPMENT OBJECTIVES

The exercises that apply to particular skill development objectives are indicated directly beneath each numbered objective below. Periodic instructions within the chapter tell you when to stop reading and direct you to the end of the chapter to complete one or more of the skill development exercises.

After studying this chapter you should be able to:

1. Classify your research design.
   Exercises 4-1 through 4-8

2. Identify your statistical research design.
   Exercises 4-9 through 4-12

The Research Process

(1) The research question/purpose of the study, literature review, and hypotheses.	(2) Research design methodology for collecting data and statistics.	(3) Data analysis and interpreting results.	(4) Discussing results and making conclusions.
• *Introduction*	• *Method*	• *Results*	• *Discussion*
Chapters 1–3	Chapters 4–8	Chapters 9–14	Chapters 9–14

Chapters 1–3 addressed the Introduction section of the research process, as shown above. This chapter shifts our focus from the Introduction to the Method section. The chapter begins by defining research design, followed by a presentation of eight research methodology design classifications. The last two sections discuss quantitative inferential statistical research designs and qualitative designs.

4.1 Defining Research Design

*The **research design** specifies the participants, variable measures, data collection, and data-analysis methods to answer the research question.* The research question is the starting point of the research process. Thus, the research study must be carefully designed to answer the research question. The Method section of the research proposal and study identifies the four key areas of the research design:

1. **Participants (sample)**. As discussed in prior chapters, you must determine whom the participants in your study will be. Participants are also referred to as cases or subjects. An important part of selecting participants is sampling. (We devote the next chapter entirely to sampling.)

2. **Variables and measures**. As discussed in prior chapters, you must clearly specify the dependent variables (DV/Y—measures changes to explain relationships) and independent variables (IV/X—explains the change in the value of the dependent variable) and their measurement as nominal/categorical, ordinal/ranking, and interval/ratio standardized and real numbers. You will learn more about variables and measurement in Part III of this book, Data Analysis: Results and Discussion.

3. **Data collection**. *There are three **methods of data collection**: secondary, observation, and survey.* You will learn more about data collection in the next section of this chapter and in Part II, Data Collection: Methods.

4. **Data analysis**. Data are analyzed qualitatively or quantitatively with statistics. In Part III, Data Analysis, you will learn about 30 different statistical techniques that can be used to analyze your data. Our focus on data analysis is on understanding which statistical technique to use for the research design selected to answer the research question.

The rest of this chapter focuses on the research design for data collection and analysis. When determining the research design for your study, *be sure to review the methods used in the literature.* Select the journal articles that are most closely related to your research question. Review their methods carefully, as you may want to use the same or similar methods in your study. Referencing others also supports the use of your research methods.

CONCEPTUAL OBJECTIVE 1
Identify and explain the parts of a research design.

4.2 Classification of Research Designs

There is no single accepted classification system for research designs. In Table 4.1 eight dimensions of research are presented and subsequently discussed in this section. You should realize that the classifications are interrelated and focus on data collection and analysis. Again, when selecting your design dimensions, focus on methods that will answer your research question and consider the research design methods identified in your literature search.

Table 4.1   Eight Classifications of Research Designs

Type of study	exploratory or conclusive/formal
Data collection	secondary, observation, or survey
• Time dimension of data collection	cross-sectional or longitudinal
• Research environment of data collection	fieldwork or deskwork/lab
Manipulating variables	experimental or ex post facto
Data analysis	qualitative or quantitative/statistical
• Purpose of study/data analysis	descriptive or inferential/causal
• Goal of data analysis	to explain, predict, or control

Type of Study (Exploratory or Conclusive/Formal)

As discussed in Chapter 1, *exploratory* research is conducted to provide preliminary data. *Conclusive* research provides the necessary information to make decisions. Conclusive studies are also called *formal* research designs. Exploratory studies are often the first step in research since they save time and money, because through a literature review you may find the answer to the research question, thus making a formal study unnecessary. Exploratory studies often begin by using a small sample; if results are positive, then researchers use a larger sample for the conclusive study to make the decision. Exploratory studies are also used to investigate topics so new that they need foundation work, such as to determine what the important variables are and to develop operational definitions to measure the new variables.

Generally, academic research studies (research projects, theses, and dissertations) are conclusive studies rather than exploratory. Again, if there is very little literature, you may want to select another topic rather than conduct exploratory research. The type of study is considered to be conclusive unless otherwise stated. Thus, in the Method section and Appendix A of the research proposal and paper it is not necessary to state that the study is conclusive.

Data Collection (Secondary, Observational, or Survey)

You have three major options for collecting your data. Recall that in Chapter 1 we contrasted *secondary* research (data collected by others) with *primary* research (data collected by the researcher conducting the study). Journals, magazines, and newspapers are a few examples of secondary data that you get through the literature search. However, *databases are secondary sources containing valuable data that can be used as part of your primary research study. Observational data are collected by watching behavior and recording results. Survey data are collected from others through interviews and questionnaires.* Surveys use self-reported data. Which of the three data-collection methods is used will vary, depending on the research question and area of research. For example, in finance secondary database sources (e.g., the stock market) are often used, in management survey research is common, and in athletic recruiting observation is used. Observation can also include the use of films, photographs, and video. Secondary, observational, and survey interviews are discussed in detail in Chapter 6. Survey research using questionnaires is discussed in Chapter 7.

CONCEPTUAL OBJECTIVE 2
List and contrast the three methods of data collection.

When selecting a data-collection methodology, consider your preferences: Do you like to talk to people and probe for details? If so, you may prefer interviewing. Do you like to watch people? If so, you may prefer observation. Do you like deskwork? If so, you may prefer using databases and survey questionnaires. Regardless of your preference, remember that you need to use methods that will answer your research question. You may not have a choice, and if you are already skilled in one of these areas you may want to develop new skills. You state which data-collection method (measurement instrument) will be (or was) used in the methodology section and research design (Appendix A) of the research proposal and paper. You can also use more than one method of collecting data—triangulation.

Data Triangulation

*Verifying the data collected using multiple techniques is called **data triangulation.*** Two methods that are less commonly used than single data collection are repeat-method triangulation (collecting data the same way more than once) and between-method triangulation (using more than one source or data-collection method). They are more commonly used in qualitative studies with small samples than in statistical studies with large samples.

Within-method triangulation.
With this method you use the same method at least twice to verify the accuracy of the data. For example, you can ask the same question differently a couple of times during the survey to make sure the answers are consistent. You can also interview/observe the same person two or more times, over a period of time, to make sure the answers/behavior are consistent.

Between-method triangulation.
With this method of triangulation, you use different sources or methods to verify the accuracy of the data. For example, in a case study to determine a manager's leadership style, you can interview the manager and question him to determine his leadership style. Then, you could talk to the manager's boss and/or use a questionnaire with employees to see if their perceptions agree with those of the manager, or you could observe the manager to see if she uses the leadership style she claims to use. The larger the number of different methods used, the stronger the support (validity) that the data are accurate.

Time Dimension of Data Collection (Cross-Sectional or Longitudinal)

When you collect your data, you have two major time-dimension options. *Cross-sectional data are collected at one point in time. **Longitudinal data** are collected and compared over different time periods to measure changes.* Between one and three years, and sometimes even longer, is a common period for time comparison. If you have a longitudinal study, it is a good idea to state so in the Method section and Appendix A; it is often in the title of the study. Academic management researchers tend to use cross-sectional data because a limited amount of longitudinal data are available in this field, and collecting it over the years is time consuming. Academic economics and finance researchers use longitudinal data because they are readably available. However, the data are considered cross-sectional unless otherwise stated, so it is not necessary to state in the Method section and Appendix A of the research proposal and paper that your data are cross-sectional. Because most students want to graduate sooner rather than later, they more commonly use cross-sectional data when longitudinal data are not available, rather than wait to collect the data. However, keep in mind that after graduation data can be collected again and compared to the original findings as a longitudinal follow-up to the academic work.

Research Environment of Data Collection (Fieldwork or Deskwork/Lab)

When you collect your data, you have two major environment options. With *fieldwork,* researchers go out "in the field" to collect research data. With *deskwork/lab work,* researchers stay put and collect data while sitting at a desk, sometimes in a laboratory. Fieldwork empirical data can't be collected without some kind of expedition, such as going elsewhere to interview managers, standing in a mall administering questionnaires, or sitting in a meeting to observe what takes place. Deskwork may include collecting questionnaire data via phone/mail/e-mail, the analysis of data collected by others (database), laboratory work, and literature searches in the library/online. Medical facilities, rooms with exercise equipment, and classrooms can all be used as labs to conduct research. Although a research environment is commonly classified as either fieldwork or deskwork/lab, you can have an element of both. Using the phone or mail/e-mail virtually takes you into the field while still sitting at your desk. If you go "out" to collect data, chances are you will analyze and write the results at a desk of some sort. Do you prefer going out to collect data or staying at a desk?

Manipulating Variables (Experimental or Ex Post Facto)

When you design your study, you have the option of manipulating variables. With an *experimental* design you attempt to control and/or manipulate the variables in the study. With the *ex post facto* research design you have no control to manipulate the variables. For example, an experiment can have participants follow a diet (or take a drug) and be tested to determine if the diet/drug experiment is working. Experiments are conducted in education by having courses taught with different methods in different classes to determine which method is more effective. In Chapter 12 (Tests of Difference: Experimental Designs), you will learn how to conduct and test experimental research designs. If you are interested in conducting an experiment, you may want to read Chapter 12 now. Secondary data collection and most survey research are ex post facto, as you simply collect data without manipulating variables. Observation either can be experimental, as the two examples illustrate, or it can simply report results without any manipulation.

Purpose of Study/Data Analysis (Descriptive or Inferential/Causal)

As discussed in Chapter 1, *descriptive research* is designed to explain characteristics of the data. *Inferential research* goes beyond the descriptive to draw conclusions about the relationship between variables. Descriptive studies answer "who," "what," "when," "where," and "how much" questions; whereas inferential studies can answer the "why" questions. Descriptive research only provides characteristics, such as who our customers are, what they buy, where they live, and how much they buy. For example, do men or women buy more of our products? With inferential research, you can discuss the relationship between variables and compare differences to make conclusions to answer "why" question (*Why* do men buy more of our products than women?). Inferential is also called *causal* when one variable causes the other variable to change (e.g., taking a drug causes a decrease in blood pressure).

Qualitative research commonly focuses on descriptive explanations of participants to better understand them. Although conclusions about the participants can be made, the support is limited because of the small sample size and lack of inferential statistical testing. Conversely, quantitative research commonly focuses on inferential statistics as it can support conclusions with statistical testing.

Goal of Data Analysis (Explain, Predict, or Control)

Another important consideration when designing the research is the goal of your research. Recall in Chapter 1 that the *goals of research* are to explain, predict, and control phenomena. As you will learn, different research designs (particularly statistics) are needed to: (a) explain the relationship between variables, (b) predict the value of the DV/Y based on the value of the IV/X, and (c) control the value of the Y based on the X. Your goal should be identified in the Introduction (research question/purpose of the study).

Qualitative descriptive research is commonly limited to explaining phenomena. Quantitative inferential research can commonly explain, predict, and control phenomena. Essentially all inferential research can explain phenomena, and some goes beyond to predict or to control phenomena, based on the research design (statistics).

Data Analysis (Qualitative or Quantitative/Statistical)

You have two primary options for data analysis—qualitative or quantitative. Here we expand our discussion from Chapter 1. *Qualitative research tends to use small samples and fieldwork, collecting data with surveys/interviews and observations that are analyzed without statistics to subjectively describe and explain research findings.* *Quantitative research tends to use larger samples, deskwork, collecting data with surveys, questionnaires, and databases that are analyzed with objective, descriptive, and inferential statistics to explain, predict, and control the relationships between variables.* An important concept is sample size, which will be discussed in the next chapter, but for now use at least 25 subjects for a large sample size.

Now that you understand the dimensions of research design, let's discuss the relationship between data collection and analysis. Although you can use triangulation, the method of data collection is commonly independent (or you select one method). For example, to study customers at Sears, you could choose to use secondary data, observe people shopping, or survey customers. However, specific data-collection methods are more commonly used with specific data analysis, as discussed below.

Data Collection (Qualitative versus Quantitative)

- *Secondary data* can be used with either qualitative or quantitative/statistical analysis. Databases can have lots of valuable data to answer your research question. With qualitative analysis, secondary data are often records found in libraries or archives.
- *Observation* is often more difficult and time consuming; thus, the sample size tends to be limited and qualitative analysis is commonly used. Animals and people are often observed to explain their behavior.

- *Survey* data collection is very common. However, the type of survey used tends to vary with data analysis. Survey *interviews* are more difficult and time consuming than a questionnaire; thus, the sample size tends to be limited and qualitative analysis is commonly used (but quantitative can be used with larger sample sizes). On the other hand, *questionnaires* are quicker and easier for getting a large sample size and using statistical analysis.

Goals and purpose of research and data analysis.
Data analysis is also related to the purpose and goal of the research.

- With the *goal to explain* with a *descriptive purpose*, the data analysis is commonly qualitative. However, with a large sample size, quantitative descriptive statistics can be used. The descriptive purpose (to explain characteristics of participants) is rarely used in academic research. Academics are expected to go beyond the descriptive to conduct inferential research. Although with qualitative analysis the researcher may make some inferences, support is weak.

- With the *goal to explain, predict, or control* the relationship between variables with an *inferential purpose,* the data analysis is usually quantitative, and inferential statistical research designs (our next topic) are run.

Differences between qualitative and quantitative research.
See Table 4.2 for a list of differences between the two designs (columns two and three), based on some of the other dimensions with other characteristics added (column one). Note that the type of study and time dimension are not listed because either exploratory or

Table 4.2   Differences between Qualitative and Quantitative Research

	Qualitative Research	Quantitative Research
Sample size	small	large
data-collection methods	survey (interview) secondary (often records/library) observation	survey (questionnaire) secondary (database)
data collection vs. data analysis	collection and analysis of data are ongoing	data collection first, and then analysis second
research environment	fieldwork	deskwork
manipulate variables	not common	with causal experimental designs
data analysis	qualitative (nonstatistical)	statistical
purpose of data analysis (measurement)	descriptive (written analysis) (subjective)	descriptive (descriptive statistics) inferential (explain variable relationships—objective)
goal of data analysis	explain	explain predict control
research designs	case study focus group	tests of difference tests of interaction tests of association tests of prediction tests of interrelationship

conclusive research and cross-sectional or longitudinal research can be used with either qualitative or quantitative research. The table also illustrates the relationship between data collection and analysis. Notice that there are similarities between qualitative and quantitative designs, and there are exceptions to this general guide.

CONCEPTUAL OBJECTIVE 3
Explain the differences between qualitative and quantitative research.

Many students fear statistics and consider conducting a qualitative study. However, quantitative studies are generally less time consuming and easier to conduct for the novice researcher. This chapter includes separate sections that further explain quantitative inferential statistical research designs (4.3) and qualitative research design (4.4). (See Table 4.2 for an overview.) Because the focus of this book is quantitative research, statistics are discussed throughout chapters 9–14. Data analysis (including specific statistics, when used), is discussed in the Methods section and Appendix A of the research proposal and paper.

STOP READING and turn to the end of the chapter to complete exercises 4-1 through 4-8.

4.3 Quantitative Inferential Statistical Research Designs

Your own research question must include the variables and their measurement levels so that you can proceed to select an inferential statistical research design.

When data analysis is quantitative and descriptive, you only use descriptive statistics, which include presenting frequencies (number of men and women), mean (average age), percentage (market share), median (middle salary), and mode (most frequent education level) of participants in the study. Academic research studies usually must go beyond the descriptive to include an inferential design. *Inferential statistics* provide data analysis results that are used to derive conclusions about the relationship between variables. In the five sample research questions below, be sure to realize the importance of identifying the variables, their dependency (DV/Y or IV/X), and their measurement level (see Chapter 1).

Tests of Difference

Tests of difference research designs compare the value of one dependent variable (DV/Y) among groups of one nominal independent variable (IV/X).

Research question: Do successful or failed businesses start with more capital? (Based on the literature, the substantive hypothesis would be that the successful businesses start with greater capital.)

Y = amount of capital (interval/ratio level of measurement)

X = gender—two groups/scales = male and female (nominal level)

You would run what is called a statistical T-test (see Chapter 12) to compare the mean/ average capital of successful businesses to the mean of failed businesses to determine which group started with the greater capital, if either. (You will learn about the T-test, Mann-Whitney U test, chi-square, and one-way analysis of variance in Chapter 12, as well as experimental and ex post facto/quasi-experimental research designs to test differences.)

Tests of Interaction

While *tests of interaction* research designs compare differences, they also determine if there is a best combination of three or more variables to maximize value differences; the dependent variable(s) is interval/ratio-level measurement and the independent variable(s) is nominal-level measurement.

Research question: Do any of our salespeople sell more of our products in any of our territories? (Looking at the data, you can see that one person does have higher sales in one territory, but you want to statistically test your hypothesis that there is a best combination of salesperson and territory.)

Y = sales (interval/ratio level of measurement)

X = salesperson—Moe, Linda, Joe (three scales, nominal level)

X = territory—north, south, east, west (four scales, nominal level)

For the first example, you should run a statistical two-way analysis of variance (ANOVA). The two-way ANOVA would run a test of differences (T-test) to determine which salesperson sells the most products, and it would also run a T-test to determine in which territory more sales are made. Plus, it can tell you if any salesperson sells more products in any specific territory. You will learn about two-way ANOVA, which needs at least two X, and MANOVA, which has two or more Y, in Chapter 14.

CONCEPTUAL OBJECTIVE 4
Describe the similarity and difference between tests of difference and tests of interaction.

Tests of Association

Tests of association research designs determine whether there is a correlational relationship among two or more variables that can be measured at either the ordinal or interval/ratio level of measurement.

Research question: Are the people with the highest income the most satisfied with their jobs? (You hypothesize that there is a positive correlation—as people's income increases, so does their level of job satisfaction.)

Y = income (interval/ratio level of measurement)

X = job satisfaction (ordinal measure of 1, very satisfied, to 7, not satisfied.)

You should run a correlation to test your hypothesis. With correlation, you assign either variable as Y or X as, unlike with the other tests, the statistical results will be the same. Some researchers classify correlations as descriptive because you can't determine that the IV/X causes the value of the DV/Y. We agree that tests of association are not causal, but correlations do go beyond simple descriptive statistics. Tests of difference also can't claim causation, but the tests are inferential. For example, you can say that there is a relationship between age and income, but you can't say that age *causes* income level. (You will learn about the Spearman and Pearson correlations in Chapter 13.)

Tests of Prediction

Tests of prediction research designs determine association, but they also forecast the value of the single dependent variable (DV/Y) based on the value of one or more independent variables (IV/X).

Research question: Can years of management experience, years of industry experience, gender, and education predict a business as successful or failed? (You hypothesize that they can: You have developed a predictive model—remember the Chapter 1 example about predicting employees' motivation level if you know their income).

Y = performance—profits (interval/ratio level of measurement)

X = years of management experience (interval/ratio)

X = years of industry experience (interval/ratio)

X = education (two nominal scales [college grad or not college grad])

You should run regression to test your hypothesis. For just about any test of correlation, you can run a higher-level statistical prediction test of regression. However, there are times when it is not logical to attempt to predict one variable based on the other. (You will learn about regression based on association in Chapter 13.)

Tests of Interrelationship

Tests of interrelationship research designs determine association but are used to organize a large number of variables into a smaller number of categories.

Research question: Why do people eat at McDonald's? (You ask 100 people, and you get 40 different reasons.)

X = 40 reasons/variables

You should run factor analysis to answer this research question. For example, of the 40 reasons, 12 are highly correlated, meaning they measure the same thing. Thus, you can limit the number of reasons to 12 in your results and conclusions. Notice that as with tests of association, there is no need to specify DV/Y and IV/X. Tests of interrelationship are commonly used in measurement research to validate questionnaires. (You will learn about factor and cluster analysis tests of interrelationship in Chapter 14.)

CONCEPTUAL OBJECTIVE 5

Describe the similarity and differences among the tests of association, prediction, and interrelationship.

Primary and Secondary Statistical Research Designs

You have learned about five statistical research designs. However, you should be aware that many research studies have a *primary* and one or more *secondary* research designs. The highest-level design is considered the primary design. In our business success versus failure example, the research study purpose was to develop a success versus failure prediction model. The primary design is prediction. Secondary designs could include tests of difference to compare successful and failed businesses on any of the other variables. Tests of association could also be run to determine if there is a relationship between variables, and a test of interrelationship could be used to group several IV/X together. However, a test of interaction could not be run to determine the best combination of IV/X to maximize success, because success and failure is a nominal variable and the Y must be interval/ratio level. You will learn more about statistics in Part III, chapters 9–14. See Box 4.1 for a review of the five major inferential statistical research designs that can be either primary or secondary designs.

Box 4.1   Five Inferential Statistical Research Designs

Tests of difference compare the value of one DV/Y among groups of one IV/X.
Tests of interaction compare differences but also determine if there is a best combination of three or more variables to maximize value differences. The DV/Y is interval/ratio, and the IV X is nominal.
Tests of association determine whether there is a correlation among two or more ordinal, interval, or ratio-level variables.
Tests of prediction determine association but also forecast the value of the one DV/Y based on the value of one or more IV/X.
Tests of interrelationship determine association but are used to organize a large number of variables into a smaller number of categories.

Causal Inferences

It's important to realize that all five inferential statistical research designs meet the goal of explaining the relationship between variables. Tests of prediction have the goal of prediction. The goal of control for *causation*, however, is limited to tests of difference and interaction with variable manipulation—experimental designs.

A causal inference occurs when the researcher concludes that one variable (IV/X) produces the value of another variable (DV/Y), or that one variable (IV/X) forces the other (Y) to change. Note that tests of difference and association are not the same as causation. In our previous examples, gender (X) doesn't *cause* one to have more or less capital (Y). There are other factors that also influence capital. Also, income (Y) does not *cause* job satisfaction (X) or vice versa. People do not work only for money, and there are many other factors that affect job satisfaction. Likewise, tests of prediction do not claim causation, but it is inferred that the value of Y (profits) is due to the value of the Xs (years of management, years of experience, gender, and education). Also, causation is not claimed with test prediction because other variables also contribute to the value of the Y that is not in the regression model of Xs. As you will learn in Chapter 14, to support causation you need to be able to control variables (e.g., give a drug to claim it is the cause of lower blood pressure).

As we bring this section to a close, you should realize the importance of the research question that includes a list of the variables and their measurement level, because the variables are the determining factor in which inferential research design you select, and the review of literature should provide inferential statistical research designs that you can use or adapt.

STOP READING and turn to the end of the chapter
to complete exercises 4-9 through 4-12.

4.4 Qualitative Research Designs

Recall that qualitative data are commonly collected through secondary data, observation, and survey interviews and that triangulation is commonly used. Observation and interview skills are very important for the qualitative researcher, and this book is not designed to make you an expert at either. There are entire courses offered to teach qualitative research, observation, and interviewing skills. You will learn more about collecting secondary data, observation, and survey interviewing in Chapter 6. Chapter 7 focuses on survey research using questionnaires. In this last section, we discuss the qualitative research case study and focus-group methods.

The Case Study

A *case study* provides qualitative, descriptive, detailed information about a specific individual, organization, or situation. The Harvard Business School is well known for the use of case studies as a teaching method. Faculty write case studies that Harvard and others sell to colleges and universities for class use. Many textbooks use cases to provide details about individuals and an organization. Have you taken a class that used the case study?

Case study or quantitative research?

A case study provides qualitative information, and a quantitative study provides statistics. An overlap between the two types of studies can cause confusion. A case study is of one organization. However, if you conduct a statistical study in one organization, it is not a case study. Thus, if you survey a large number of employees to determine job satisfaction, motivation, and so on, it's quantitative. An easy way to know the difference is based on the sample size and use of statistics; when you use stats, it's quantitative.

Triangulation.

Case study research for an organization commonly includes triangulation, collecting data using two or all three methods. Researchers may read secondary data, such as letters, memos, and reports. They also may observe what is taking place in the organization. They commonly interview employees, and sometimes customers and others who are familiar with the organization.

Potential bias.

Unlike in quantitative data analysis, in case studies the data are both collected and analyzed as the research progresses. Thus, there is no clear starting and ending point to data collection and analysis, making it more subjective. Because qualitative research is more subjective than quantitative, the researcher needs to be careful not to be biased. In other words, if you have a substantive hypothesis, you do not look for data to support it and ignore data that does not support it, or give it less importance.

Advantage of case studies (understanding).

The major advantage of a case study, compared to large sample sizes, is the detailed information that helps to really understand (which more fully meets the research goal to explain) a person, organization, or situation. For example, if you really want to understand what a person with AIDS goes through, it is better to spend personal time observing a person over time as his or her medical condition changes and to interview the person in depth many times over a period of time. You can also survey doctors, read medical records, and talk to the person's family and friends. Similarly, if you want to really understand why one business is successful, a case study works well.

Disadvantages of the case study (generalizations and subjectivity).
The major disadvantage of a case study is the lack of generalization of the findings. For example, the AIDS case findings may only be characteristic of the one participant; other people with AIDS may not have the same experience. Also, one business's recipe for success may not work in other organizations. In fact, companies have had problems because they try to copy methods that do not work in their business environment. In many fields of study, journals have many more quantitative studies (i.e., large-sample-size studies using statistics) to support the generalization of the findings.

A second disadvantage of the case study is its subjectivity. Although research questions and hypotheses are often developed, the support or rejection of the hypotheses is more difficult or weak without the use of statistical testing. There is also the question of potential bias in support or rejection of hypotheses.

Combining cases.
A qualitative study can combine the results of multiple cases. In doing so, the results can have greater generalization. If your research question is why businesses succeed, clearly combining the results of three, five, or ten separate company cases provides more generalization to all businesses than only one. But again, it is still weaker than statistical analysis.

Applied versus basic research.
Case studies tend to be more commonly used with applied research for specific organizations. Organizations tend to be more concerned about what works for *them* specifically. How the organization can solve problems and take advantage of opportunities are common research questions. Consultants conduct applied case research and quantitative research for an organization. However, academics who publish most of the empirical research journal articles are more concerned about getting published, and they study basic research using generalizable topics/theories with quantitative analysis.

CONCEPTUAL OBJECTIVE 6
Discuss the major advantage and disadvantages of the case study method.

Focus Groups

The focus group is an often-used method of exploratory research. *A focus group is led by a trained moderator who guides the members in an exchange of ideas, feelings, and experiences on a specific topic.* The typical focus group has 6 to 10 participants that meet for 1½ to 2 hours. The moderator is a researcher who is trained to use group dynamics to guide the discussion. Common topics of focus groups include developing a new product, getting feedback on new or improved products, and discovering all types of new and improved methods of conducting business.

Triangulation.

The moderator may read secondary data, such as letters, memos, and reports, as well as observing members' behavior during the meeting as part of the group dynamics. The moderator leads the discussion, which is a form of interview, and may interview others who are familiar with the topic.

Potential bias.

The moderator collects and analyzes data as the meeting progresses. The data collection and analysis influences the moderator's leadership in guiding the exchange of ideas, feelings, and experiences. Because qualitative research is subjective, the moderator needs to be careful not to be biased. In other words, if you lead a focus group, don't just try to get the members to agree with your substantive hypothesis. You need to try to get the group's consensus on the topic.

Advantage of focus groups (understanding).

Businesses need to understand their customers, and focus-group research is used for this purpose. In fact, the most common research use of focus groups is consumer topics related to the development and sales of products.

Disadvantage of focus groups (generalizations and subjectivity).

The major disadvantage of a focus group is the lack of generalization of the findings. Just because one group of 6–10 people like a product doesn't mean that thousands of others will, too. If the members have a clear consensus on the topic, the decision is supported. However, if there is no consensus, there is more subjectivity and managers can be biased towards their own preferences.

Combining focus groups.

A qualitative study can combine the results of multiple focus group results. In doing so, the results can have greater generalization. If your research question is which of three products to sell, clearly combining the results of three, five, or ten separate focus groups provides more generalization to all consumers.

Two-stage design.

Because of the disadvantage of generalization, focus groups are often exploratory, with the plan of conducting formal conclusive research at a later time. For example, if a company has three products to offer and wants to select only one to sell, it can first run focus groups. If the results are favorable, the product can then be offered only in a specific area and, if successful, sold nationally.

Applied versus basic research.

Focus groups are more commonly used than other methods with applied research for specific organizations, since they tend to be more concerned about what works for them. Focus group moderators are often consultants, and several large companies do have trained moderators. However, academics are more concerned about getting published, and focus-group research is rarely published. Also, most academics are not trained to conduct focus groups. Focus-group training is beyond the scope of this book, so unless you have this training, don't attempt to conduct focus-group research.

SKI WEST STUDY

As we bring this chapter to a close, you should be able to:
- *understand the four parts of the research design,*
- *classify research designs based on eight dimensions, and*
- *describe five different quantitative/inferential/statistical and two qualitative research designs.*

Matt McLeish proposed (and actual participants included) 50 employees from Ski West. His primary DV/Y was end-of-season evaluation and his X was the Conscientious Scale; other descriptive Xs included gender, age, and department. Data for his five variables were collected from secondary sources—employee records. Primary data analysis was regression.

Although not all classifications of his research design are covered in this chapter (you will learn about them in later chapters), it is useful to know that Matt's research proposal and study has the following design: The type of study was conclusive. Data collection (from employee records) was secondary and cross-sectional. Matt did not manipulative variables in an experiment; it was ex post facto. Data analysis was quantitative, statistical. The purpose of his study was inferential, with the goal of prediction.

The primary quantitative inferential statistical research design was a test of prediction (Can personality predict job performance?). Matt's secondary research design was six tests of difference, with the Ys being Conscientiousness and Evaluation, and the Xs being gender, age, and department. Although research designs can be qualitative or include an element of qualitative research, Matt made no qualitative analysis.

CHAPTER SUMMARY AND GLOSSARY

The chapter summary is organized in a way that provides you with the answers necessary to help you meet the conceptual objectives for this chapter.

1. **Identify and explain the parts of a research design.**
   The four parts of the research design are (1) participants, (2) variables and measures, (3) data collection, and (4) data analysis methods to answer the research question. Participants are the cases or subjects of the study. The dependent variable measures changes to explain relationships, and the independent variable is used to explain the change in the value of the dependent variable; they are measured as nominal/categorical, ordinal/ranking, and interval/ratio standardized and real numbers. Data are collected through secondary sources, observation, and survey. Data are analyzed qualitatively or quantitatively with statistics.

2. **List and describe the methods of data collection.**
   The three methods of data collection are secondary data, observation, and survey. Secondary data are collected by others. Observed data are collected by watching behavior and recording results. Survey data are collected from others through interviews and questionnaires.

3. **Explain the differences between qualitative and quantitative research.**
   Qualitative research tends use small samples and fieldwork, collecting data with survey interview and observation that are analyzed without statistics to describe and explain research findings. Quantitative research tends to use large samples and

deskwork, collecting data with survey questionnaires and databases that are analyzed with descriptive and inferential statistics to explain, predict, and control the relationships between variables. With qualitative research, data collection and analysis are ongoing without variable manipulation; whereas with quantitative analysis data are collected and then analyzed, and variables are manipulated with causal experimental designs.

4. **Describe the similarity and differences between tests of difference and interaction.**
   The tests of difference and interaction both test differences in the value of a dependent variable (DV/Y) between groups of a nominal independent variable (IV/X). The test of interaction also determines if there is a best combination of two or more nominal Xs to maximize the value of the interval/ratio Y(s). Also, a test of difference only has one Y and one X. However, a test of interaction can have more than one Y and has more than one X.

5. **Describe the similarity and differences among the tests of association, prediction, and interrelationship.**
   Tests of association, prediction, and interrelationship are all based on correlation. Prediction goes beyond correlation to forecast the value of the dependent variable (DV/Y) based on the value(s) of one or more independent variables (IV/X). Interrelationship uses correlation to reduce a large number of variables into categories.

6. **Discuss the major advantage and disadvantages of the case study method.**
   The major advantage of the case study is that it provides detailed qualitative information about a specific individual, organization, or situation. The disadvantages are that the results do not have generalization; support or rejection of hypotheses is subjective, making results weak without statistics and subject to bias.

7. **Define the following alphabetical list of key terms.**
   Select one or more methods: (1) fill in the missing key terms from memory, (2) match the key terms with their definitions below, or (3) copy the key terms in order from the list at the beginning of the chapter.

case study	focus group	qualitative research
cross-sectional data	longitudinal data	quantitative research
data triangulation	methods of data collection	research design
databases	observational data	survey data

   _____ specifies the participants, variable measures, data collection, and data analysis methods to answer the research question.

   _____ are secondary, observation, and survey.

   _____ are collected by watching behavior and recording results.

   _____ are collected from others through interviews and questionnaires.

   _____ is verifying the data collected using multiple techniques.

   _____ are secondary sources containing valuable data that can be used as part of your primary research study.

   _____ are collected at one point in time.

   _____ are collected and compared over different time periods to measure changes.

_____ tends to use small samples and fieldwork, collecting data with survey interview and observation that are analyzed without statistics to subjectively describe and explain research findings.

_____ tends to use large samples and deskwork, collecting data with survey questionnaires and databases that are analyzed with objective descriptive and inferential statistics to explain, predict, and control the relationships between variables.

_____ provides detailed qualitative information about a specific individual, organization, or situation.

_____ is led by a trained moderator who guides the members in an exchange of ideas, feelings, and experiences on a specific topic.

WRITTEN ASSIGNMENTS

The procedure for this assignment is somewhat similar for completing both a research proposal (RP) and a completed study (CS). However, in the statistical analysis papers the method will change based on the statistical testing, so it may not be required at this time.

APPENDIX RP, ASSIGNMENT 3 (METHOD AND APPENDIX A, RESEARCH DESIGN)

This assignment is a continuation of RP Assignment 1, in which you completed the Introduction section with literature review for your research. At this point it should have been reviewed and you should have improved it, if necessary. You do not need to complete RP Assignment 2 (Appendix B, Review of Literature) in order to complete this assignment. RP Assignment 3 is to complete the Method section and Appendix A: Research Design of the research proposal. For details of this assignment, turn to Part IV.

APPENDIX CS, ASSIGNMENT 2 (METHOD)

This assignment is a continuation of CS Assignment 1, in which you completed the Introduction section with literature review for your research. At this point it should have been reviewed and you should have improved it, if necessary. CS Assignment 2 is to complete the Method section of the research proposal, which becomes the method of the completed study. At this point you need to include a description of your research design in the Method section. For details of this assignment, turn to Part V.

APPENDIX RP, ASSIGNMENT 3 (METHOD AND APPENDIX A) AND
APPENDIX CS, ASSIGNMENT 2 (METHOD)

The Method assignment will actually be completed through chapters 4–8. For this chapter, insert the Method section headings and write the introductory paragraph and some of the information that goes in each part (see instructions in the assignment above). Refer to Chapter 3, The Method Section, for a discussion of the introductory paragraph and common method parts, and see Box 3.2 for a list of possible headings. You can also look at prior studies for ideas about headings that you may want to include in your Method section. Under the statistical analysis part, you may have some difficulty determining which statistical test to use. You may be able to determine the statistics to run based on the statistics used in the studies from your literature review. Also, in Chapter 10 you will learn how to determine the appropriate inferential statistical test to use for a given research design. Again, there is overlap between the exercises below and this assignment, but doing the exercises provides a good outline for RP Assignment 3 and CS Assignment 2.

EXERCISES

CLASSIFYING YOUR RESEARCH DESIGN
Identify the following items regarding your research design:

4-1 Type of study

4-2 Data-collection method

4-3 Time dimension

4-4 Research environment

4-5 Manipulation of variables

4-6 Purpose

4-7 Goal

4-8 Qualitative or quantitative design

INFERENTIAL RESEARCH DESIGN(S)
Identify your research study's primary inferential statistical design and secondary design(s) if you plan to use others.

4-9 The primary research design is a test of . . .

4-10 The DV/Y and IV/X variables, with their measurement level, are . . .

4-11 The secondary research design(s) is(are) a test(s) of . . .

4-12 The DV/Y and IV/X variables, with their measurement levels, are . . .

5

Sampling

CHAPTER OUTLINE

CONCEPTUAL OBJECTIVES

The conceptual objectives below also appear at appropriate places within the chapter at points when you will have accessed the information necessary to attain them. They

appear again at the end of the chapter in the Summary and Glossary section, along with explanations that will enable you to meet the objectives.

After studying this chapter, you should be able to:

1. Explain the difference between the systematic sample error and the random sampling error.

2. Describe how data-collection methods affect the population and generalization.

3. Explain the relationship between sample validity and sample size.

4. Discuss two qualitative considerations when determining the sample-size standards.

5. State the minimum sample-size requirements for conducting quantitative analysis.

6. Discuss the similarity and differences among the random sample methods.

7. Describe the similarity and differences between random and nonrandom samples.

8. Explain the difference between a random sample and a random assignment.

9. Define the following key terms (listed in order of their appearance in the chapter).

population	sample frame	cluster sample
sample	sample unit	systematic sample
valid sample	random samples	convenience sample
systematic sample errors	nonrandom samples	purposive sample
sampling errors	simple random sample	random assignment
sampling process	stratified random sample	

SKILL DEVELOPMENT OBJECTIVES

The exercises that apply to particular skill development objectives are indicated directly beneath each numbered objective below. Periodic instructions within the chapter tell you when to stop reading and direct you to the end of the chapter to complete one or more of the skill development exercises.

After studying this chapter, you should be able to:

1. Classify empirical research sample methods from the literature.
   Exercises 5-1 through 5-5

2. Classify your research sample methods.
   Exercises 5-6 through 5-10

The Research Process

(1) The research question/purpose of the study, literature review, and hypotheses.	(2) Research design methodology for collecting data and statistics.	(3) Data analysis and interpreting results.	(4) Discussing results and making conclusions.
• *Introduction*	• *Method*	• *Results*	• *Discussion*
Chapters 1–3	Chapters 4–8	Chapters 9–14	Chapters 9–14

Chapters 1–3 presented the first part of the research process. We began our discussion of method, the second part of the research process, in Chapter 4. This chapter focuses on sampling in the Method section. You will learn how to define your research population, sample frame, and unit. You will then learn about four random sampling and five nonrandom sampling methods, as well as how to select your sample. You will also learn how to conduct a random assignment.

5.1 Populations, Samples, and Sampling

We begin this chapter by explaining the difference between the population and sample of the research study, followed by a discussion of sample validity. We end this section with an overview of the sampling process, which is discussed throughout the rest of the chapter.

Population

A **population** *is a total group about which the researcher describes and makes inferences.* A *group* can include anything under study, such as animals, people, organizations, or things (e.g., machines). Common characteristics limit a population. For example, a study of employment would only include people getting paid; thus, children, retirees, and other unemployed people would not be included in the population. All small businesses in the state of Maine, or in the United States, can be a population. All employees in one company, or one department, can be a population. Researchers describe characteristics of the population under study. *Inferential statistics* provide data-analysis results that are used to derive conclusions about the relationship between variables in a population. So you have to determine the population of your study and whether your research purpose is to describe and/or make inferences about the population. If your population was the employees in one company and you surveyed every employee, you would survey a population, essentially conducting a *census*.

Sample

A **sample** *is a selection of participants that is used to describe and make inferences about a population.* Samples are commonly used in quantitative research. Even if you include every element in the population, it still meets the definition of a sample because you choose to select them all. Through your literature review, you most likely saw the term *sample* used in the Method sections.

There are many advantages to studying a sample rather than a population. One major advantage is that it usually takes less time and costs less to use a sample. Plus, researchers have argued that a sample can be more accurate than a population, even for taking the U.S. Census. A good sample can be used to describe and make inferences about the population it represents. However, a good sample must be *valid*, which will be explained in the next part of this section.

When to use a census versus a sample? Using a census is appropriate when you have a small population and the participants are quite different. For example, if you have only a few employees it is just as cost effective and fast to include them all. However, with large sample sizes and similar participants, it is appropriate to use a sample. Thus, populations are more commonly used with qualitative research and samples are more commonly used with quantitative research.

Sample Validity

*A **valid sample** accurately and precisely represents the characteristics of the population it purports to represent.* In measurement terms, to be valid a sample must be accurate and precise. We will talk more about validity in Chapter 8, but let's discuss accuracy and precision so that you can understand when a sample is valid.

Accuracy/nonrandom error.

Accuracy refers to being exact or correct. As it relates to sampling, it is the degree to which bias is absent from the sample. An accurate/unbiased sample has underestimators and overestimators balanced among the members of the sample. ***Systematic sample errors** occur when the sample is biased, causing errors in variable measures.* These errors are also called *nonrandom systematic sample errors.* Systematic sample errors usually occur due to researcher error in selecting the sample. For example, homes on the corner of the block are often larger and more valuable than those within the block. If a sample has too many corner homes, it is not accurate (it's biased), as the mean value of homes in the population will be overestimated. In other words, the sample does not accurately represent the population and thus is not valid as it contains systematic sample error/variance. As discussed throughout the book, you can also have *systematic nonsample errors*, in which the sample is fine but other systematic errors affect the research test results.

Precision/random error.

How well the sample represents the population reflects precision. However, no sample will fully represent the population in all aspects due to random fluctuation inherent in the sampling process. If you had a population of 100 and selected a sample of 25 four different times, the results would be slightly different each time due to the random chance by which participants are selected. Thus, ***sampling errors** occur due to chance in drawing the sample participants.* Unlike with systematic sample errors, sampling errors are not due to researcher error. Sampling error is also called *random sampling error.*

CONCEPTUAL OBJECTIVE 1

Explain the difference between the systematic sample error and the random sampling error.

Quantitative versus qualitative sample validity.

Statistically, sampling error is what is left after all known sources of systematic variance have been accounted for. Precision is measured by the standard error of estimate, a type of standard deviation measurement. The smaller the standard error of estimate, the more precise the sample is. On the other side of data analysis, qualitative research does not statistically test sampling error, making it difficult to know how well the sample represents the population. Thus, unlike with quantitative research, qualitative results are difficult to generalize to the population.

The need for a valid sample.

If your sample is not valid, the results of your study are not valid—you collected and analyzed data that is biased and not precise. Many wrong conclusions/decisions have been made due to invalid samples that do not represent the population. To increase the validity of your sample, follow the steps of sampling below.

The Sampling Process

The **sampling process** consists of five steps: (1) define the population, (2) define the sample frame and unit, (3) determine the sample size, (4) select the type of sample, and (5) draw the sample. However, you should realize that although the sampling process steps are numbered 1–5, it is not a simple linear process wherein you complete each step without the possibility of returning to prior steps. Also, some researchers select the type of sample before the sample size or select them together; thus, steps 3 and 4 are listed together in the steps of the sampling process in Table 5.1.

Table 5.1   The Sampling Process

1. Define the population.	2. Define the sample frame and unit.	3. Determine the sample size. 4. Select the type of sample.	5. Draw the sample.

5.2 Defining the Population, Sample Frame, and Unit

In this section we cover the first two steps of the sampling process—the sample must define the population. For example, say the purpose of the study is to compare job satisfaction of deaf employees and hearing employees. There are employees who are deaf and hearing all over the world. How will you delimit the population? Will your target population be one country (national), one region/part/state/city of a country? Within the field of business, what industry(s), profession(s), job(s), and so on are included in the population studied? The success-versus-failure prediction study discussed in prior chapters used a New England regional sample (six states) from all industries. You need to consider your data-collection method, generalization of your subjects, your personal goal for conducting the research, and the expectations of the acceptance of the study.

Data-Collection Methods and the Population Area

If your data-collection method is survey questionnaires, personal interviews, or observation, it is very difficult to have a large population area. Traveling all over the country would be expensive and time consuming. Thus, with personal interviews and observation it is common to have a smaller population area than when using survey questionnaires. It is relatively easy and inexpensive to mail questionnaires all over one country, and with e-mail, all over the world.

The Population and Generalization

The larger the population is, the greater the generalization. If your population is an entire country, the results can be generalized to the country. If your population is only one city/organization, the results may not be generalizable beyond that city/organization. There is a certain amount of trade-off between generalization and population size; it is usually easier to get participants on a local level, but it is more difficult to generalize from a relatively smaller population size.

Acceptance of the Study

Another important consideration in defining the population is your personal goal for conducting the research and the expectations of the acceptance of the study. With academic research (research projects, theses, dissertations), you will generally have between one and three advisors who must accept your research proposal and completed study. Thus, you need to know their expectations. What is the common population at your college for your type of research design?

Once your study is academically accepted, if your goal is to have it published you need to determine the expectations of the publication source (journal/proceedings). Review publication sources to determine the common population.

You can also collect data for academic research on a limited basis and later add more data from a larger target population. For example, you could do a thesis with a target population of your local region of the country. Later, add one or more regions to increase the population. For example, with the job satisfaction comparison of deaf and hearing employees, the student wanted to complete her research project and have it published. The data-collection method was survey questionnaire. Thus, the target population was defined as a national (U.S.) sample.

Sample Frame and Unit

*The **sample frame** is the list of population participants from which you draw the sample.* The list you use may delimit the population. For example, if you use a telephone book to contact participants, you must take into consideration that some people have unlisted numbers, others will have received a phone after the date of publication, and still others will have moved and no longer can be reached at the number in the book. Membership lists/directories, such as those of professional and trade associations, are commonly used. Online directories are generally more up-to-date than printed publications. In addition to directory problems, a list of people who belong to a professional or trade association or union may not include all of the population. You can also define a sample frame and buy a mailing list through professional mailing-list sellers. For example, SurveyMonkey.com and Zoomerang.com allow you to buy a sample frame, actually develop your questionnaire, and then collect the data for you online. You can also do an Internet search, such as "buy mailing lists" or "sellers of mailing lists," for information on obtaining mailing lists.

*The **sample unit** defines the participant as an individual, group, or organization.* The term *participant* is used to refer to any variable being measured, such as people, animals, places, things, products, events, and so on. Individual, group, or organization primarily refers to people. In the job satisfaction example of deaf and hearing employees, the sample unit is individuals. It could also compare groups/units/departments/divisions data, as well as organizational data. In the success-and-failure study the questionnaire was sent to the owner/manager of the small businesses for completion. Thus, the sample unit is organizational: Even though only one person completed the survey, the focus was data about the organization.

STOP READING and turn to the end of the chapter
to complete exercises 5-1 and 5-2.

5.3 Determining the Sample Size

This section covers the third step in the sampling process—determining the sample size. A common sampling question is: How large should my sample size be? Unfortunately, there is no simple answer. Keep in mind that sample size is only one aspect of sampling. A large, biased sample of a million is less useful than a representative sample of 100. However, if the sample is too small, results will not support generalization to the population. A small sample size also increases the probability of making an error in hypothesis testing.

General Guidelines

Now let's answer that question about sample size. Here are six general principles that influence sample size.

General rule of sample size.

The general rule of sample size is: The greater the sample size, the greater the accuracy and the probability that you have not made an error, and the easier it is to find relationships among variables.

Desired sample accuracy.

To minimize the possibility of error and maximize your confidence that you are making the right decision, a larger sample size will provide evidence of sample-accuracy validity. Importance of the research decision influences the sample size. For example, if the FDA considers allowing a new drug on the market with potential side effects that could seriously hurt or kill people, a large sample is needed to convince the FDA to allow the sale. You will learn more about probability values (providing confidence that you have not made an error) in Chapter 11, Hypotheses Testing.

Desired sample precision (variance in the population).

The greater the variance in the population, the larger the sample must be to provide evidence of sample precision validity. For example, if your variable is *income* and the range/variability within the population is between $1 million and $30,000, you need a large sample size to get an average that really represents the population. In other words, you have a high probability of having sampling error(s). Unfortunately, you often don't know the variance until you collect the data and run statistics. If the variance is small, it provides evidence of sample validity.

CONCEPTUAL OBJECTIVE 3
Explain the general rule of sample size and the relationship between sample validity and sample size.

The 10% guideline.

Some researchers recommend that the sample size should be 10% of the population. The 10% guideline is more relevant to descriptive studies than inferential studies. However, others disagree, calling the proportion rule a myth and stating that the absolute size of a sample is much more important than its size compared with the population. For example, if your population is *employees* and there are only 100 of them, 10% is only 10 participants, which is a small sample. Thus, it should be larger than 10%. If the population is one million, 10% is 100,000, which is larger than needed for almost any study.

So unless you are told to use a proportion guideline, don't worry too much about it. However, if you calculate the percentage of the population that you actually do survey, and it is a high percentage (more than 10%), stating the proportion can provide supporting evidence of precision validity for your sample size.

Subgroups.
The more subgroups in the study, the larger the sample size needs to be. If your population is the entire United States, you need a large sample size from every state to make comparisons among states. We provide more details below under the heading Quantitative Considerations.

Time and cost.
Most studies have time and cost considerations when selecting a sample size. Generally, with larger sample sizes, it takes more time to collect and analyze data and it costs more.

Qualitative Considerations

Recall that with qualitative research when the sample size is small, it can be a case study. Your academic research advisor(s) may ask you to complete multiple case studies and compare them to increase your sample size. Although the following suggestions have a quantitative element, they are given from secondary sources. It serves to separate them from the quantitative considerations. Based on your goal, what are the academic and literature standards?

Academic standards.
What is the common sample size at your college for your type of research design? In your Method section, if you can reference other research studies from your college that use a similar sample size, the sample may be large enough for your advisors to accept. You can also ask your faculty advisor(s) if your proposed sample size is large enough. If it's not, your research proposal will not be accepted unless the sample size is increased to meet the academic standard.

Review the literature for sample-size standards.
If you can reference other published research studies in your Method section that use a similar sample size, the sample may be large enough for publication acceptance. Generally, the better the journal, the larger the sample size needed to get your study accepted for publication.

CONCEPTUAL OBJECTIVE 4
Discuss two qualitative considerations when determining sample-size standards.

Quantitative Considerations

Statistically, the larger the sample size is, the greater the chance of finding a relationship between variables. Recall that a large sample size must have a minimum of 25 participants and preferably 30. This general guide varies with the statistical research design and topic. Be aware that these are minimum sample sizes. Your academic or publication standards may be higher and would take precedence over these minimums. You should also realize that if the sample size is smaller than the minimum, for tests of difference and association you could run nonparametric statistics in place of them, but relationships are harder to find and the results are weaker. We'll talk more about this in the statistics chapters in Part III.

Tests of difference.

To run a parametric test of difference, you need at least 25 per group and preferably 30 or more. So if you were comparing satisfaction with undergraduate college education by class (first, second, third, and fourth-year students), you would need a minimum sample of 100.

Tests of interaction.

As you add independent variables (IV/X), be sure that you continue to have at least 25 per group. For example, if you add *gender* to the satisfaction example, you need to have at least a 25–75 ratio of men to women, and you should have at least 10 participants for each X. So if you have five X, you need a minimum sample size of 50 and preferably more.

Tests of association.

Because you do not subsample the sample by group (male/female), you can have a minimum sample of 25 and preferably 30 or more to run a two-variable correlation.

Tests of prediction.

To run a test of prediction you should have at least the minimum correlation sample size of 25 and preferably 30 or more. However, you also need at least 10 participants, and preferably more, for each IV/X. So if you were trying to predict sales based on four X, the minimum sample is 40 and preferably more. In our prior example of the test to predict success and failure, there were 15 X (thus, the minimum sample was 150) with a sample size of 216.

Tests of interrelationship.

The tests of interrelationship require the largest sample sizes because you are reducing a large number of variables into a limited number of categories. For example, in a study on why people eat at McDonald's, there were 40 reasons/variables. At least 10 participants per X were needed. Thus, the minimum sample size would be 400 and preferably more.

CONCEPTUAL OBJECTIVE 5
State the minimum sample-size requirements for conducting quantitative analysis.

Power analysis.

A statistical test, *power of analysis*, can be run to determine the sample size needed to find differences. You will learn more about power analysis in Chapter 11.

Response versus nonresponse rate.

Not everyone selected for a sample will participate in your study, particularly with survey questionnaires through the mail/e-mail. We talk more about how to increase the response rate in Chapter 7. For now, you need to realize that if you want a sample of 100, you cannot just mail 100 questionnaires. In business academic research it is not unusual to get a 10% response rate. You would have to send out 1,000 questionnaires to get 100 back without extensive follow-up.

 STOP READING and turn to the end of the chapter to complete exercise 5-3.

5.4 Selecting and Drawing a Random Sample

In this section we discuss the fourth and fifth steps of the research process. There are two major classifications of sample types: probability (or random) and nonprobability (or nonrandom) samples. In this section we present the random sample types and how to draw them. In the next section (5.5), nonrandom methods are presented. Let's begin by defining and listing both types of sample categories. *Random samples use controlled procedures, assuring that each population participant is given a known probability of selection. Nonrandom samples use subjective procedures without a known probability of selection.* Keeping it basic, with simple random samples all members of the population have an equal chance of being selected, but with nonrandom samples some members of the population have a greater chance of being selected and others, no chance.

Random samples have several advantages. Only random samples provide controlled data-collection procedures, a known probability of being selected in the sample, support for sample validity, and support of generalization of the sample results to the population it represents. We will talk about and revisit these four advantages throughout this section and the next. Table 5.2 lists the types of samples, followed by a discussion of each.

Table 5.2   Types of Samples

Random/Probability	Nonrandom/Nonprobability
• simple • stratified • cluster • systematic	• convenience • purposive • volunteer • quota • snowball

Simple Random Sample

A *simple random sample provides each member of the sample frame an equal probability of selection.* Thus, the selection of one participant has no effect on the selection of another participant—neither increasing nor decreasing the chance of another's selection. The lottery system and bingo (with balls with each number) are examples. Although you could use a ball system, most researchers do not. Statistical packages are able to generate random numbers for you.

Selecting a simple random sample.
Below is a description of how to do simple random sampling by hand.

1. Get the *sample frame* (population list) and table of *random numbers*. If the sample frame does not number each participant in the population from 1 to N, do so.

2. Select the *number of participants* from the population that will be included in the sample. For example, if the list contains 500 and you want 10%, it's 50. Remember to include more to provide for the nonresponse factor. A set of random numbers appears at the end of this chapter. With some software programs, all that's necessary is to put the population into the program and it will randomly select the sample for you.

3. Determine *how many digits* you need from the table of random numbers. You need to use the number that represents the participants in the population, not the number you plan to select for the sample. If the list has less than 100, you need two digits. If the list has 100–999 you need three digits; 1,000–9,999 needs four. Using the list of 500, you need three digits. If you only used two digits (for the 50 you want to select), you could only have participants 1–99 included in the sample (100–500 would be excluded).

4. Develop a *plan* for using the random digits. Do not start at the top upper left-hand corner. Go down the column or across the row. Select the starting point by closing your eyes and putting your finger on the page.

5. Compare the number under your finger to the list of population participants. If found, the participant is selected for the sample; circle the number of the participant on the list. If not, skip the number. Notice that the random digit table has five digits. You ignore the digits higher than what you need. For example, if you are using three digits and the random number is 85072, ignore the 85. The number you use is 072, or 72.

6. Continue down or across as planned until you have the number selected for the sample.

Below are examples of random numbers. Assume this is your staring point and you are going across the row.

32404   45853   72218   14871   94051   69381   84187   (and so on)

Again, assume the sample frame has 500 and we want to select 50 for the sample. With the first number, ignore the 32, leaving 404, which is selected. Circle the number next to this participant to be included in the sample. The second number, 853, is higher than 500, so skip it. Select 218, skip 871, select 51, 381, and 187. So from this list of seven random numbers, we select five participants. Continue until you have 50 selected.

Although textbooks don't usually discuss it, students often ask about placing all the names of population participants in a hat and picking the sample. This is not a scientific method, and it does not give every participant an equal chance of being selected, because the pieces of paper tend to stick together and don't get fully mixed.

Stratified Sample

A **stratified random sample** *is a random sample with the sample frame broken into subgroups to ensure equal representation.* For example, when testing for differences between groups, it is sometimes important to make sure that each sample group is the same as the percentage in the population. Gender, ethnicity, age, and performance are examples. Notice that each member of the population does not have an equal probability of selection. For example, if a class has 60 African Americans and 40 Whites and you want to sample 25 of each, each White has a known greater probability of being selected.

Using with tests of difference and interaction.

The stratified sample is more commonly used with tests of difference and interaction because the researcher wants to compare the dependent variable based on the independent variables (subgroups). Stratified random samples are not commonly used with tests of association, prediction, and interrelationship because these statistical methods do not include subgroups.

Selecting a stratified random sample.

1. Using the sample frame, determine the strata (% of group members). Let's say there are 25% women and 75% men in the sample frame (divide the number of men and women by the number of the population). Following our example, of the 50 participants you would select 13 women (50 × .25 = 12.5) and 37 men (50 × .75 = 37.5).

2. Once you determine the number of each subgroup, you randomly select men and women participants until you have 37 men and 13 women. Once one subgroup stratified sample is complete, just pick from the other subgroup until the total is reached.

Cluster Sample

A *cluster sample* is *a random sample including groups as the sample frame.* Cluster is another term for group. Often the population is too large, or you don't have a list of all members of the population (sample frame). For example, if you attend a large university with 20,000 students and you want to use it as your population, it is too large to sit down and randomly select your sample. Also, there are situations in which there is a very low probability that you can get a copy of the list of all members of a population.

So how can you get your sample? You can use a cluster sample by selecting a required course, such as English, that all students must take. With several mixed-student classes sampled, the cluster sample should represent the population. The group could also be an organization. For example, if you wanted to know the opinion of employees, rather than of certain individuals, you randomly select organizations. Then you survey all people or a random sample within the group/organizations. Again, notice that each member of the sample frame doesn't have an equal probability of being selected.

To select a cluster sample:

1. Obtain or create a sample frame of groups/organizations.
2. Use simple random sampling to select the group(s) to be included as the sample.
3. Survey all participants in the sample group.

Systematic Sample

Systematic sample is *a random sample involving selecting every nth participant from the sample frame.* "Nth" stands for the *skip interval*—a number between 0 and the size of the sample that you want to select. For example, you would select every fifth name of the list in the sample. Although systematic sampling is somewhat easier than simple random sampling, it does not give each participant an equal chance of being selected in the sample. Thus, some question if it is a true probability sampling method, rather than a non-probability/nonrandom sampling technique.

Selecting a systematic sample.

1. Get or create a sample frame. Try to get a random list of participants because an alphabetical list decreases the chance of each participant being selected in the sample.

2. Determine the skip interval (nth). Divide the size of the sample frame by the size of the desired sample. Using the population of 500 and sample of 50, for example, you would select every "10nth" name.

3. Select a random place near the top of the list to begin. For example, throw a die. If it came up 6, the sixth participant on the list is selected for the sample, then select every "10nth" person after—numbers 6, 16, 26, 36, and so on until you get 50 to include in the sample. If you get to the end of the list before reaching the sample size, go back to the top of the list.

CONCEPTUAL OBJECTIVE 6
Discuss the similarity and differences among the random sample methods.

5.5 Selecting and Drawing a Nonrandom Sample

This section discusses the fourth and fifth steps of the research process for nonrandom sample types. Because the sample is selected based on subjective judgment, there are *no objective procedures* to follow when selecting the sample, as there are with random samples. Because they are not probability based, nonrandom samples are less likely to be representative of the population. Since random sample methods provide greater assurance that the sample is a valid representation of the population, it is highly recommended that you use a random method.

In some situations when it is difficult to use random samples, nonrandom methods are used. For example, during this course it is very difficult to actually develop a good research proposal and actually conduct the study. Therefore, students can conduct the study with a sample of classmates, or others, so that they can get the experience of actually running statistical analysis and making inferences about the relationships among variables, even though the results do not represent the actual population of the students' research. In addition, by using this book students can run all five types of statistics for their data, some of which are not actually part of their research proposal. Let's discuss five nonrandom sample methods, as shown in Table 5.2.

Convenience Sample

A *convenience sample* is a nonrandom sample including any available participants. Convenience samples are easy and quick to obtain. Professors and students doing academic research are tempted to use students at their college because they are conveniently accessible. For example, it is very convenient for a professor to agree to let a student researcher come to class and have the students in the classroom fill out his or her questionnaire. However, this convenience sample probably does not represent all college students in the nation/region/state/city of the population. This convenience sample is most likely not even a good representation of all the students at the college.

Purposive Sample

A *purposive sample* *is a nonrandom sample selected by the researcher as judged to represent the population.* It is also called *judgment sampling* because researchers handpick supposedly typical or interesting participants. Rather than randomly selecting participants, the researcher uses judgment that may be biased, and this is not random selection. For example, rather than randomly choosing workgroups to study, the researcher would select some of the groups that are believed to be representative of the population of workgroups. The purposive sample can snowball into a new sample.

Volunteer Sample

With *volunteer samples*, you ask members of the population to volunteer to participate in your study. This is common in athletic and medical research. Let's give an example combining both. A drug company has developed an energy vitamin and wants to know if it works. The company contacts athletic departments at colleges and asks for volunteers to take the vitamin over a period of time to determine results. Volunteers may be compensated in some way, such as pay and free vitamins for a period of time. You may have seen or heard such ads asking for volunteers. Volunteers have been shown not to be representative of the population, and not all population members have an equal chance of being selected. Also, rewards for participation bias the sample. Thus, volunteers are not random samples.

Quota Sample

Quota samples are commonly used with survey interviews, such as the Gallup Poll. It is commonly difficult to get a sample frame, such as of the people who are shopping at a mall. For example, people are hired to go to a mall and interview a set number of people in a certain profile, such as 50 women with children under 10 years old. The interviewer watches people walk by and asks them if they will answer some questions. They continue to survey until they have 50 sets of responses. Many people will refuse to answer, creating nonresponse error, and the ones that volunteer to answer may not be representative of the population. The location in the mall where the interviewer is standing does not give all of the population an equal chance to fill out the survey. The quota can also be within the sample— say, you need 25 men and 35 women. Thus, quotas are not a random method of sampling.

Snowball Sample

A *snowball sample* includes initial respondents who provide later respondents. If the researcher goes to a known participant from the population for data, the researcher may ask the participant for others they know with the sample characteristic from the population under study. Thus, each participant may lead to more participants. It is somewhat like following the reference chain. For example, let's say you want to survey croquet players. If you know some croquet players, you could survey them, ask them for names of others they know who play, and then ask those players for the names of others. If you don't know any croquet players, you could do a mail survey to 200 asking if they play and, if so, for the names and addresses of others who play. So you could get 5 or 10 who play and 25 referrals.

STOP READING and turn to the end of the chapter
to complete exercises 5-4 through 5-10.

Sampling Students and Employees

It is possible, in a sense, to make a convenience sample into a random sample with students and employees, as discussed below.

Sampling students.

From the student perspective, the easiest way to sample is to hang around the cafeteria or classroom building, asking people to complete their survey. The random way to go is to get a list of *all* students in the population (such as a student directory) and use a simple random or stratified sample. The population can be delimited to a major(s) and/or year(s) in college, and so on. Although it takes more time and effort to use a random sample, the quality of the sample representing the population increases the value of the research. With a simple convenience sample (such as the cafeteria sample), results and conclusions do not have generalization to the college population because the sample is not representative. With a random sample, the conclusions have generalizations to the college population. However, they may not have generalization to other colleges.

Sampling employees.

The best way to go when sampling employees is to get high-level management support for the research project. With management support, use random sampling or the population census if it is not large (the population can be delimited in any way). With a random sample, the results and conclusions have generalization to the organizational population. However, they may not have generalization to other organizations.

Random and nonrandom sample similarities and differences.

See Table 5.3 for a review of sampling similarities and differences related to the use of random and nonrandom samples. As you can see, there are two common similarities and four important sample *differences* (italicized) between them that are answered with yes and no responses. Again, the random sample methods are superior to the nonrandom sample methods because of these differences.

Table 5.3   Similarities and Differences between Sampling Types

	Random Sample	Nonrandom Sample
Large sample selected	yes	yes
Statistical data analysis	yes	yes
Controlled procedures of data collection	yes	no
Known probability of being selected in sample	yes	no
Sample validity supported	yes	no
Generalization of sample conclusions to population supported	yes	no

---

5.6 Random Assignment

This is often not considered as a step in the research process because it is only used with experimental research designs. ***Random assignment*** *is used in experimental research designs to allocate sample participants to control and experimental groups.* With random assignment, participants have already been selected in the sample. The issue is which group they will be a member of—the control group (no treatment) or the experimental (treatment) group. There are two methods of random assignment: simple random and the number system. Note that they are both random assignments. True experimental research designs require that each participant have an equal chance to be in either group. You will learn more about experimental designs in Chapter 12.

Simple Random Assignment (Two Groups)

With two groups, simple random assignment may be the easiest way to go.

1. Assign each participant a number 1–N, such as 1–60.
2. Use the random numbers table to select half the total, such as 30. Note that you are using two digits.
3. The other half are assigned to the other group.
4. Flip a coin to assign each group as control or experimental.

The Number System (More than Two Groups)

With three or more groups, the number system may be easier.

1. Assign a number for each group, (e.g., 1, 2, 3 / 1, 3, 5 / 2, 4, 6 / 3, 5, 8).
2. Use the random numbers table to assign by group number, such as 1, 2, 3. Note that you are using one digit. Start at the top of the participant list. That person is assigned to a group based on the random number.
3. Once one group has its equal share of participants, such as 20, stop assigning to that group.
4. Once the second group has its equal share of participants, stop the assignment to that group; you now have only one group left.
5. All remaining participants are assigned to the last group.

SKI WEST STUDY

As we bring this chapter that focuses on the sampling process to a close, you should be able to:
- *define a population and its sample frame and unit,*
- *state criteria for selecting a sample size,*
- *understand how to select and draw random and nonrandom samples, and*
- *explain how to make a random assignment.*

Matt McLeish followed the sampling process by (1) defining the population of all employees of Ski West and then narrowing it down to seasonal employees. (2) He received permission to use employee records as the sample frame, and the sample unit was individual employees. (3) Matt did not expect great variance in the population and selected a sample of 50, which met the academic standards. Under quantitative considerations, for his primary purpose of prediction he had only one X. To run regression he needed a sample size between 10 and 20, so his sample size of 50 was large enough. For his secondary purpose of comparing differences, he had close to 25 per group for gender and age, which is a good enough sample size but a bit small to compare three departments, at around 15 per group. (4) Matt used a large stratified random sample of 25 males and 25 females for equal representation; validity is assumed. (5) He drew the employee data for his five variables from the sample frame.

CHAPTER SUMMARY AND GLOSSARY

The chapter summary is organized in a way that provides you with the answers necessary to help you meet the conceptual objectives for this chapter.

1. **Explain the difference between the systematic sample error and the random sampling error.**
   Systematic sample errors occur when the sample is biased, causing errors in variable measures due to researcher error. Random sampling errors occur due to changes in drawing the sample participants, which is not due to researcher error.

2. **Describe how data-collection methods affect the population and generalizability.**
   Surveys, personal interviews, and observation usually have small populations and sample sizes, which lack generalization of the sample to the population. Survey questionnaires allow you to more easily sample larger populations, which allows for greater generalization.

3. **Explain the general rule of sample size and the relationship between sample validity and sample size.**
   The general rule of sample size is that the greater the sample size, the greater the accuracy and the easier it is to find relationships among variables in the research. A valid sample accurately and precisely represents the characteristics of the population it purports to represent. Thus, the greater the accuracy and precision desired by the researcher, the larger the sample must be to provide evidence of sample validity.

4. **Discuss two qualitative considerations when determining the sample-size standards.**
   Academic standards must be met. The literature, too, is used as a standard for sample size. Thus, the higher the standards, the larger the sample size needed for the research design to be approved.

5. **State the minimum sample-size requirements for conducting quantitative analysis.**
The minimum sample size per association and per group to compare differences is 25, and it is preferable to use 30 or more. When conducting tests of interaction, prediction, and interrelationship, multiple variables are being measured; there must be a minimum of 10 and preferably more participants per independent variable.

6. **Discuss the similarity and differences among the random sample methods.**
All random sampling methods use controlled procedures to ensure that each population participant is given a known probability of selection. The simple random sample gives all population participants an equal probability of being included in the sample. The stratified sample breaks the population into subgroups to ensure equal representation. Cluster samples use a group rather than an individual as the sample frame. The systematic sample selects every nth participant and does not provide an equal probability of being selected.

7. **Describe the similarity and differences between random and nonrandom samples.**
Random and nonrandom samples are similar in that they both commonly use a large sample size and statistical analysis. Random samples have four major differences from nonrandom samples: They provide (1) controlled procedures, (2) a known probability of selection in the sample, (3) support for sample validity, and (4) support for generalization of sample conclusions to the population. Thus, random samples are superior to nonrandom samples.

8. **Explain the difference between a random sample and a random assignment.**
Participants in a random sample are selected from the population for the sample; thus, not all are included. The random assignment is used in experimental research designs to assign sample participants to control and experimental groups; thus, all are included in some group.

9. **Define the following alphabetical list of key terms.**
Select one or more methods: (1) fill in the missing key terms from memory, (2) match the key terms with their definitions below, or (3) copy the key terms in order from the list at the beginning of the chapter.

cluster sample	random samples	sampling process
convenience sample	sample	simple random sample
nonrandom samples	sample frame	stratified random sample
population	sample unit	systematic sample
purposive sample	sampling errors	valid sample
random assignment		

_____ is a total group about which the researcher describes and makes inferences.

_____ is a selection of participants that is used to describe and make inferences about a population.

_____ accurately and precisely represents the characteristics of the population it purports to represent.

_____ occur when the sample is biased, causing errors in variable measures.

_____ occur due to chance in drawing the sample participants.

_____ consists of the following steps: (1) define the population, (2) define the sample frame and unit, (3) determine the sample size, (4) select the type of sample, and (5) draw the sample.

_____ is the list of population participants that is used to draw the sample.

_____ defines the participant as an individual, group, or organization.

_____ use controlled procedures assuring that each population participant is given a known probability of selection.

_____ use subjective procedures without a known probability of selection.

_____ provides each member of the sample frame an equal probability of selection.

_____ is a random sample with the sample frame broken into subgroups to ensure equal representation.

_____ is a random sample including groups as the sample frame.

_____ is a random sample involving selecting every "nth" participant from the sample frame.

_____ is a nonrandom sample including any available participants.

_____ is a nonrandom sample selected by the researcher as judged to represent the population.

_____ is used in experimental research designs to allocate sample participants to control and experimental groups.

WRITTEN ASSIGNMENTS

The Method assignment will actually be completed through chapters 4–8. For this chapter, write in the sampling method you will use for your study. Note that there is, however, a possible difference in sampling for completion of a proposal as opposed to completion of a study.

APPENDIX RP, ASSIGNMENT 3 (METHOD AND APPENDIX A)

Write your sampling method following the five steps of the sampling process (see Table 5.1) in the participant section. Try to use a random sample.

APPENDIX CS, ASSIGNMENT 2 (METHOD)

Write your sampling method following the five steps of the sampling process (see Table 5.1 in this chapter). If you are doing a completed study, there is a good chance that you will not have time to use a random sample. If not, state the actual sample method you do use to collect your data. For example, you can use a convenience sample with any available participants, you could enter the data several times for the same participant to increase the sample size, or you may even make up the data, randomly assigning possible values. Note that this is obviously unethical; however, the objective of your completed study is to learn to go through all the steps of a research study in one semester. If you can get the measurement instrument and collect the data using a random sample before the due date of the assignment, by all means you should do so.

Table of Random Numbers

39634	62349	74088	65564	16379	19713	39153	69459	17986	24537
14595	35050	40469	27478	44526	67331	93365	54526	22356	93208
30734	71571	83722	79712	25775	65178	07763	82928	31131	30196
64628	89126	91254	24090	25752	03091	39411	73146	06089	15630
42831	95113	43511	42082	15140	34733	68076	18292	69486	80468
80583	70361	41047	26792	78466	03395	17635	09697	82447	31405
00209	90404	99457	72570	42194	49043	24330	14939	09865	45906
05409	20830	01911	60767	55248	79253	12317	84120	77772	50103
95836	22530	91785	80210	34361	52228	33869	94332	83868	61672
65358	70469	87149	89509	72176	18103	55169	79954	72002	20582
72249	04037	36192	40221	14918	53437	60571	40995	55006	10694
41692	40581	93050	48734	34652	41577	04631	49184	39295	81776
61885	50796	96822	82002	07973	52925	75467	86013	98072	91942
48917	48129	48624	48248	91465	54898	61220	18721	67387	66575
88378	84299	12193	03785	49314	39761	99132	28775	45276	91816
77800	25734	09801	92087	02955	12872	89848	48579	06028	13827
24028	03405	01178	06316	81916	40170	53665	87202	88638	47121
86558	84750	43994	01760	96205	27937	45416	71964	52261	30781
78545	49201	05329	14182	10971	90472	44682	39304	19819	55799
14969	64623	82780	35686	30941	14622	04126	25498	95452	63937
58697	31973	06303	94202	62287	56164	79157	98375	24558	99241
38449	46438	91579	01907	72146	05764	22400	94490	49833	09258
62134	87244	73348	80114	78490	64735	31010	66975	28652	36166
72749	13347	65030	26128	49067	27904	49953	74674	94617	13317
81638	36566	42709	33717	59943	12027	46547	61303	46699	76243
46574	79670	10342	89543	75030	23428	29541	32501	89422	87474
11873	57196	32209	67663	07990	12288	59245	83638	23642	61715
13862	72778	09949	23096	01791	19472	14634	31690	36602	62943
08312	27886	82321	28666	72998	22514	51054	22940	31842	54245
11071	44430	94664	91294	35163	05494	32882	23904	41340	61185
82509	11842	86963	50307	07510	32545	90717	46856	86079	13769
07426	67341	80314	58910	93948	85738	69444	09370	58194	28207
57696	25592	91221	95386	15857	84645	89659	80535	93233	82798
08074	89810	48521	90740	02687	83117	74920	25954	99629	78978
20128	53721	01518	40699	20849	04710	38989	91322	56057	58573
00190	27157	83208	79446	92987	61357	38752	55424	94518	45205
23798	55425	32454	34611	39605	39981	74691	40836	30812	38563
85306	57995	68222	39055	43890	36956	84861	63624	04961	55439
99719	36036	74274	53901	34643	06157	89500	57514	93977	42403
95970	81452	48873	00784	58347	40269	11880	43395	28249	38743
56651	91460	92462	98566	72062	18556	55052	47614	80044	60015
71499	80220	35750	67337	47556	55272	55249	79100	34014	17037
66660	78443	47545	70736	65419	77489	70831	73237	14970	23129
35483	84563	79956	88618	54619	24853	59783	47537	88822	47227
09262	25041	57862	19203	86103	02800	23198	70639	43757	52064

EXERCISES

CLASSIFYING EMPIRICAL RESEARCH SAMPLE METHODS

For exercises 5-1 through 5-5 (see the table below) you must select three empirical research articles from your literature review. Place the article information (author, article title, journal, volume number, page number) in the first row and fill in the methods, following the five sampling-process steps, in the spaces provided. For step 5 of the sampling process select the data (which was already done in the study). If the author describes the process of drawing the sample, include it; if not, just include the response rate (number used in the study divided by number of surveys sent).

Reference	Reference	Reference
5-1. Population	**5-1.** Population	**5-1.** Population
5-2. Sample Frame and Unit	**5-2.** Sample Frame and Unit	**5-2.** Sample Frame and Unit
5-3. Sample Size	**5-3.** Sample Size	**5-3.** Sample Size
5-4. Sample Type	**5-4.** Sample Type	**5-4.** Sample Type
5-5. Drawing and Response Rate	**5-5.** Drawing and Response Rate	**5-5.** Drawing and Response Rate

CLASSIFY YOUR RESEARCH SAMPLE PROCESS METHODS

5-6 Define the population you will study.

5-7 Define your sample frame and unit.

5-8 Determine your estimated sample size. How did you come up with the sample size?

5-9 Select the type of sample to be used to collect your data. Why was this type of sample selected?

5-10 Draw the sample. (This may be done at a later date.)

6

Secondary Sources, Observation, and Survey Interviews

CHAPTER OUTLINE

CONCEPTUAL OBJECTIVES

The conceptual objectives below also appear at appropriate places within the chapter at points when you will have accessed the information necessary to attain them. They

appear again at the end of the chapter in the Summary and Glossary section, along with explanations that will enable you to meet the objectives.

After studying this chapter, you should be able to:

1. List the data-collection methods and explain which one is the most unobtrusive measure.

2. Describe the generalization/internal and external validity trade-off with observation.

3. Discuss similarities and differences between the panel of experts and the pilot test.

4. State what information is entered into the computer columns and rows for quantitative analysis.

5. Discuss the three characteristics that differentiate the three types of personal interviews.

6. Describe data-collection and data-analysis differences between the structured and unstructured interview.

7. Discuss some of the advantages and disadvantages of telephone interviews versus personal interviews.

8. Define the following key terms (listed in order of their appearance in the chapter).

unobtrusive measures	mutually exclusive	probing
observation	exhaustive	unstructured interview
ethnography	panel of experts	structured interview
frequency of observation	pilot test	semistructured interview
duration of observation	personal interview	telephone interview

SKILL DEVELOPMENT OBJECTIVES

The exercises that apply to particular skill development objectives are indicated directly beneath each numbered objective below. Periodic instructions within the chapter tell you when to stop reading and direct you to the end of the chapter to complete one or more of the skill development exercises.

After studying this chapter, you should be able to:

1. Know when secondary sources are the most appropriate data-collection method for your research proposal.
   Exercise 6-1

2. Know when observation is the most appropriate data-collection method for your research proposal.
   Exercises 6-2 and 6-3

3. Know when survey personal interview is the most appropriate data-collection method for your research proposal.
   Exercise 6-4

4. Know when the telephone interview survey is the most appropriate data-collection method for your research proposal.
   Exercise 6-5

The Research Process

(1) The research question/purpose of the study, literature review, and hypotheses.	(2) Research design methodology for collecting data and statistics.	(3) Data analysis and interpreting results.	(4) Discussing results and making conclusions.
• *Introduction*	• *Method*	• *Results*	• *Discussion*
Chapters 1–3	Chapters 4–8	Chapters 9–14	Chapters 9–14

In Chapters 1–5 we presented the research process shown above. Recall that there are three major methods of data collection—secondary, observation, and survey. This chapter discusses the data-collection methods of secondary, observation, and personal survey and telephone interviews. In the next chapter, we discuss survey questionnaires.

6.1 Secondary Sources

You'll recall that secondary sources have already been discussed in Chapter 2, because the literature review is always based on secondary sources. Remember that any work by others is secondary for you. However, you should give a much higher priority to using others' primary research studies. Bibliographies, indexes, and abstracts are useful in the literature review. For more information on the most relevant secondary sources and how to use them related to your topic, talk to your college reference librarian.

Secondary sources are listed here to remind you that they are one of the three methods of data collection. More importantly, some people use secondary-source *databases* as the data-collection method for their study. For example, some researchers analyze data from public-records databases, such as the stock market or government documents. Others use private company-records databases, such as medical records and all types of organizational data, for analysis. The big advantage of databases is that their data are often quicker and easier to obtain than data collected through observation and survey. The literature review is very important in the decision of how to collect data to analyze. Read the method sections of prior studies to determine how prior researchers collected data. Support your use of secondary sources by referencing other researchers who used the same sources.

Unobtrusive measures collect data without the influence of the researcher. Secondary research has the least unobtrusive measurement problems, as the researcher is reading data. Observational data collection may be obtrusive. For example, if a researcher sits in a class to observe behavior, the students may not behave the same as when the researcher is not in the class, particularly if the observer is a school principal or other administrator. Observation outside the class, looking through a two-way mirror, is used to make the measure unobtrusive. Survey can also have obtrusive measures. One problem area is focusing on the data that support the hypotheses while ignoring data that don't.

CONCEPTUAL OBJECTIVE 1
List the data-collection methods and explain which one is the most unobtrusive measure.

STOP READING and turn to the end of the chapter to complete exercise 6-1.

6.2 Observation

If you want to explain or predict a phenomenon, you can observe it as your primary data-collection method. We have already discussed selecting data-collection design methods in Chapter 4. This section discusses the definition of observation and its advantages and disadvantages. The next section (6.3) explains how to conduct an observational research study.

Defining Observational Research

Secondary sources require the researcher to read data, while a survey of people requires interviews or questionnaires to collect data. *Observation is the process of watching and recording behavior, objects, and occurrences to answer the research question.* Survey research includes verbal communication to obtain data. However, observation includes nonverbal communication. For triangulation, observation can be combined with secondary and/or survey research to increase the validity and reliability of the data collected to test one hypothesis. One such combined method is ethnography.

Ethnography

Ethnography is a methodology used to provide descriptions of human societies, primarily through observation. Ethnography studies people in their natural environments—where they live, work, shop, and play. It can provide you with a real-world understanding of consumer preferences, motivations, and needs by examining the environments consumers inhabit and the sociocultural influences on their behaviors. Organizations, including MTV, use ethnography to gain a deep understanding of who their customers are, how they act, and what they want, including unmet needs. In the business world, trained consultants are commonly used to conduct ethnography (consumer behavior studies).

Ethnographic Insight (http://www.ethno-insight.com) has this to say about ethnography: "In a business or marketing research context, ethnography is used to uncover, interpret, and understand the consumer point-of-view and the hidden rules of environments." Whereas focus groups and surveys (discussed later in this chapter) rely on self-reporting and memory out of context, ethnography provides a holistic view of consumers in the context of their daily lives. Ethnography overcomes the artificial nature of surveys and their standard question-and-answer format, which depend on self-reporting and the researcher's frame of reference. Ultimately, ethnographic research reveals the unspoken cultural and social patterns that shape consumer behavior.

Ethnography is a set of complementary techniques developed within the discipline of anthropology. Trained researchers establish rapport with people in various social contexts. By interacting with them through participation, observation, and dialogue, researchers can uncover their attitudes, beliefs, perceptions, and values, as well as the unspoken cultural patterns that shape their behavior. Such insights translate into strategic business opportunities, including improved customer loyalty and increased competitive advantage.

There really is no substitute for the opportunity to experience what consumers themselves experience. For example, consumers do not interact with your products and services in isolation; they are affected by changing family patterns, unseen cultural factors, and other products and objects in the proximate environment. Ethnographic research is the best means for getting at these unspoken cultural and social patterns that shape consumer behavior. Ethnography can be used as a stand-alone technique or can be used in conjunction with other qualitative and quantitative marketing research techniques.

Advantages and Disadvantages of Observation

While observation can be a valuable tool for the researcher, it also has some potential problems. The advantages and disadvantages of observation are listed below.

Advantages.

- *Exploratory study.* With a new topic that has no literature, observation can be used as an exploratory study to identify variables. Based on exploratory results, a formal conclusive study can be conducted.

- *No self-reporting bias.* The major advantage is the avoidance of self-reporting response bias through unobtrusive data collection. On a survey, people often say they behave in a desirable way, but when they are observed the real undesirable behavior may be seen. For example, managers know they should be participative leaders, so on a survey some tend to say that they practice participative leadership. However, when observed, they are actually autocratic leaders.

- *No communication.* Observation can be used with people who cannot communicate, such as children and the disabled, and with nonhuman subjects such as animals, objects, and occurrences/events. For example, toy makers observe children playing with prototype toys.

- *Internal validity.* Observation has strong internal validity, as the results represent the (usually) small population. Observation is the method of time-and-motion studies to improve job productivity.

Disadvantages.

- *Possibly obtrusive.* Data collection may cause obtrusive behavior of participants. Thus, two-way mirrors and cameras are used to avoid this potential problem.

- *Lack of external validity.* Generally, observation uses a small qualitative sample lacking external validity with generalization to a larger population.

- *Time and travel.* Time and travel can be costly. It is usually faster and easier to survey than to observe.

- *No cognitive measures.* Cognitive phenomena (motivation, expectation, intention) cannot be observed.

- *Possible observer bias.* Accurate measurement may be difficult. There can be observer bias, including judgment errors (seeing and recording what one wants to see while ignoring and not recording other behaviors that don't support the researcher's hypotheses).

- *Possible interrater errors.* Multiple observers may record observations differently, causing data errors. This underscores the need for training and interrater reliability (Chapter 8).

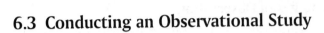

CONCEPTUAL OBJECTIVE 2
Describe the generalization/internal and external validity trade-off with observation.

 STOP READING and turn to the end of the chapter to complete exercise 6-2.

6.3 Conducting an Observational Study

The first step in conducting an observational study is to design the methods of data collection—answering the common who, what, when, where, and how questions; recording observation; and data analysis (in no particular order, as they are all interrelated). Let's use an observation example throughout this section to help you understand observational studies.

If you want to know who in a group talks most frequently and/or for the longest duration of time during a meeting, secondary sources of data are not available and survey data collection would not be reliable, because people tend to be poor judges of this topic. If you asked a group of five, you would probably get five very different answers about who talks the most often and for the longest time. Thus, observation is the best data-collection method to answer this research question.

What Will Be Observed?

As indicated in our definition of observation, the research question/purpose of the study determines the variables to be measured and affects the observational reporting system. Different variables can be observed differently. Operationally defined variables that clearly specify the behavior being observed are the key to successful observation. Observers must be able to clearly state that they have or have not observed the variable behavior. Thus, the behavior must be clearly observable and measurable.

In line with operational definitions of variables is *factual* or *inferential* observation. Most data collection by observation involves inference to determine whether the behavior actually took place. Asking a question or interrupting another group member is factual behavior. However, if the researcher has to determine whether the behavior was aggressive or assertive, the observation is more inferential and thus requires good operational definitions to distinguish between aggressive and assertive behavior.

In our example, the frequency and duration of talking is what will be observed. These variables are factual, as it is easy to observe when someone talks and for how long they talk in the group meeting.

Who Is Observed, Who Observes, and Who Gains Access?

The "who" question has three parts:

Who is observed?

Which participant(s) will be observed? What is the population, sample frame and unit, and sample size? Will the sample be a random or nonrandom sample? You may want to refer to Chapter 5 when answering these questions. In our example, five group members are being observed.

Who will observe?

Will there be one or more observers? With multiple observers, training is needed to ensure reliable measures (interrater reliability). The best way to train is with the use of video. All observers watch the video and record observations. If the results are basically all the same, they are reliable.

Who can gain access to observe?

In some situations, someone must get permission to observe. For example, in a company setting a manager must give approval to visit the workplace to observe, and in a school the principal or superintendent may require permission for classroom observation.

Sometimes the person observing could be an independent researcher or a group member (being careful not to be biased). This researcher may need approval from a manager and the group members.

When Will Observation Take Place?

Dates and times must be planned. You must consider the time of year, day of the week, and time of day that best represent the population behavior you want to observe.

How many times will the sample be observed? How many times observation will take place directly relates to the "when" question. In general, the more observations there are, the more reliable and valid the research study. However, time and travel constraints influence this decision. As discussed in other chapters, the standard of your college and publication sources can help you determine the number of observations. When the participants know they are being observed, it generally takes three to four observations before participants are comfortable with the observer and behavior is not affected.

In our example, you would observe multiple group meetings to be sure that the data collected do in fact represent the typical meeting conversation. It would be more practical to have multiple observations if the researcher is a part of the group.

Where Will Observation Take Place?

The research equipment often determines the place where observation will occur. In *field research*, you go to the natural environment of the participants, to their job or school, where they shop, and so on (ethnography). In *lab research* the participants come to you; you set up an unnatural environment to observe. A field setting generally has more external validity (generalization), whereas the lab setting has more internal validity.

In our example, the field setting would clearly be best for the research observation. Thus, the researcher goes to the group or the gathered data is sent to the responder.

How Does Observation Take Place?

There are three parts to the "how" question:

Direct or mechanical observation.

Will a person (direct) or a machine (indirect) observe? Audio or video recorders, traffic counters, UPC codes, or some type of Internet counter (e.g., number of visits to a website) are all different observation methods. Ethnographers commonly use both. They experience the situation and later review it for a better understanding.

Known or concealed observation.

Will participants know that a person or machine is observing them? Hidden recorders, cameras, and two-way mirrors can be used to conceal observation. When people know they are being observed, it can affect their behavior. However, there is an ethical question about the right to privacy and the absence of consent to full disclosure (discussed in Chapter 3) when participants don't know they are being observed. An ethnographer's presence can be known or concealed.

Participation in the group.

In some research the observer is a member of the group being observed. For example, you could observe the group dynamics of the department in which you work. Law enforcement agencies regularly send people undercover to observe criminal activity. Ethnographers do participate.

In our example, an audio/video recorder would be best for observation because it can be replayed a number of times to ensure accuracy of the observations. Participants can know of the observation, especially if it is intended to benefit the group in some way. However, you may want to hide the recorder so that group members will forget about it and conduct themselves as usual. Again, the researcher may or may not be a group member.

Recording Observations

There are four considerations involved in accurate recording of observations: (1) frequency versus duration of the observation, (2) continuous versus interval observation, (3) use of an observation recording form, and (4) review of the form by a panel of experts/pilot testing the form.

Frequency or duration?

Frequency of observation is a simple record of each time the participant conducts the behavior. Duration of observation is a record of how long the participant actually does the behavior. In our example, observing a small group meeting to study verbal communication, you could simply check off (on an observation recording form, discussed below) each time each person spoke, and/or you could time how long each person spoke. Thus, you could determine the frequency and duration of speaking for everyone in the group.

Continuous or interval?

With *continuous observation* you observe all behavior for the entire time period. With *interval observation* you only observe for a set period of time, such as 15 minutes out of every hour, which can change. For example, security guards make their rounds on an interval basis to observe whether there are any problems. Continuous observation would be most appropriate for our example group-meeting observation of talking.

Observation recording form.

With survey research you use a questionnaire, but with observation you use a recording form—a checklist of some type to collect the data. If you can use a recording form from a prior study, your work is done for you. If not, you must develop an observational recording form. Most published articles do not include copies of recording forms (or questionnaires), so you need to contact the author(s) to ask for a copy, along with permission to use it.

When developing the recording form, make sure that each observation category is mutually exclusive and exhaustive (that each observation fits into one of the categories).

Mutually exclusive means that all collected data fit only into one measurement category. Exhaustive means that all data collected fit into some measurement category. In Table 6.1, the left column is an example of a non-mutually exclusive and exhaustive measure (a measure can be in more than one category or in none), and the right column has a mutually exclusive and exhaustive measure (no overlap, and all measures can fit into one of the categories).

Table 6.1 Mutually Exclusive and Exhaustive Measures

No	Yes
_____ 1–3	_____ 0
_____ 3–6	_____ 1–3
_____ 6–10	_____ 4–6
	_____ 7–10
	_____ 11 or more

The sample form in Box. 6.1 could be used with our example group-meeting talking study. However, it would be better to leave more space between participants. Notice that the duration section could also be used to record frequency by counting the number of durations. Also be aware of the possibility of obtrusive measure. If you sit with the group to observe, you could influence the talking frequency and duration of members. Thus, a two-way mirror or audio/video recording could be used to provide an unobtrusive measure.

Have the recording form approved by a panel of experts, and pilot test the form.

Take your draft recording form to a panel of experts for improvement. *A panel of experts is a group of professors and professionals in the field of study who provide improvements to the measurement instrument.* The panel of experts commonly includes a mix of between two and five professors and professionals in the field of study. They read the form and suggest

---

Box 6.1   Observation Recording Form

Group Talking Observation Form

Group meeting date _____ Time _____

Group Members   Frequency (number of times talked during the meeting)*

Tom (1-1)   1 2 3 4 5 6 7 8 9 10 11 12 13 14 15 16 17 18 19 20

Judi (2-2)   1 2 3 4 5 6 7 8 9 10 11 12 13 14 15 16 17 18 19 20

Carl (3-1)   1 2 3 4 5 6 7 8 9 10 11 12 13 14 15 16 17 18 19 20

José (4-1)   1 2 3 4 5 6 7 8 9 10 11 12 13 14 15 16 17 18 19 20

Janet (5-2)   1 2 3 4 5 6 7 8 9 10 11 12 13 14 15 16 17 18 19 20

Group Members   Duration of times talked during the meeting**

Tom (1-1)   _____

Judi (2-2)   _____

Carl (3-1)   _____

José (4-1)   _____

Janet (5-2)   _____

*Check each time the person speaks.
**Record actual stopwatch time.

improvements. The professionals can include people from the population to be studied. An important issue we'll cover in more detail in Chapter 8 is *validity*: Are you actually measuring what you plan to measure through observation? Experts can help support validity.

However, before you actually perform the planned observation with the form you developed, you should usually conduct a pilot study to make sure the form works. *The **pilot test** simulates the actual data collection to make improvements to the measurement instrument*. It is also called the *pretest*. You can observe the actual sample to pilot test the form or, if this isn't feasible, you can observe people similar to the ones in the population. After the pilot test, you can use the results to improve the form again before collecting the actual data for the study. The pilot test also supports the validity of your recording form. If you can obtain a previously used observation recording form, it may have been developed with input from a panel of experts and pilot tested. Thus, the validity has been addressed and you don't need to use the panel or pilot test. But because data collection and analysis are ongoing, you can improve the form as you go.

In our example a panel of experts could have reviewed the form. Assuming there would be multiple observations, the pilot test could be the first meeting observation. After the meeting, the researcher listens to the audio/video record and records the observations on the form. The form can be improved, if needed.

CONCEPTUAL OBJECTIVE 3
Discuss similarities and differences between the panel of experts and the pilot test.

Qualitative or Quantitative Analysis?

As stated, observation is commonly considered a qualitative analysis, but it can be quantitative or both. For example, in Table 6.2 you can see that quantitative data is being gathered, with a small sample of five participants. You can provide descriptive statistics, but you can also go on to inferential statistics.

To enter nominal and ordinal data into the computer you must develop a coding system, as you cannot type in participants' names and gender as data to run statistics. Table 6.2

Table 6.2   Computer Data Entry

Variable Names in Columns, Data Entry in Rows*

Column ⇨ Row ⇩	Participant	Gender	Frequency Talking	Duration Talking Minutes
1	1 (represents Tom)	1 (male)	8	16
2	2 (represents Judi)	2 (female)	3	20
3	3 (represents Carl)	1	7	12
4	4 (represents José)	1	3	5
5	5 (represents Janet)	2	6	9
6				

*Information in parentheses is not actually shown on screen.

has a coding system. After each name is a number to represent the person (between one and five members). The second number (1 or 2) represents gender—male = 1 and female = 2.

Computer data entry.

Assume you collected the observed data on the form for the first meeting. For computer data entry, you would assign the variable names—frequency, duration, participant, and gender—to column headings in any order. The rows include data input cases. Notice that the data in Table 6.2 are from only one meeting. For multiple meetings, just label the frequency and duration by meeting date or number in the variable column, having two new variable columns for each meeting. If you don't want to compare meetings, you could just add the new meeting numbers with the existing ones to compare totals only.

Computer data analysis.

You could run two one-way ANOVAs (covered in Chapter 11) to compare how many times each member talks and/or for how long to determine the significance of the differences. In Table 6.2 we can see that Tom talks the most frequently and Judi for the longest duration. But is the difference significant? How sure are we that the difference is not due to chance? The variables to run the two one-way ANOVAs are as follows:

Y = Frequency   Y = Duration
X = Participant   X = Participant

You could also compare differences by running two T-tests (explained in Chapter 11) between male and female participants to determine which gender (if either) talks more frequently or for a longer duration. The variables to run the T-tests are as follows:

Y = Frequency   Y = Duration
X = Gender   X = Gender

You will learn more about computer data entry and data analysis in the next chapter, and in the statistics chapters 9–14.

CONCEPTUAL OBJECTIVE 4
State what information is entered into the computer columns and rows for quantitative analysis.

STOP READING and turn to the end of the chapter to complete exercise 6-3.

6.4 Survey Methods

Survey is the third type of data-collection method. There are five types of surveys: personal interviews, telephone interviews, Internet-based interviews, texting/instant message (IM) interviews, and questionnaires (self-administered surveys). Although questionnaires can be used for personal interviews and telephone interviews, we do classify them differently because they are self-administered, utilizing only one-way communication. The personal, telephone, and IM/texting interviews collect data providing two-way communication. The remainder of this chapter covers personal and telephone interviews, and the next chapter discusses questionnaires that can be used with any of the survey methods. We do not discuss IM/texting interviews separately because they have limited use, primarily with young people, and the same basic principles of personal and telephone interviews also apply to them. Although it is done with a phone, it is debatable if we can consider IM/texting to be telephone interviewing because interviewers and participants do not actually "talk," which is the primary function of a telephone interview. (Is texting/IM really talking?) However, texting/instant messaging with short questionnaires for marketing research targeting young people is on the increase.

A challenge to researchers planning to use survey methodology is to select a survey method for their research study. To help you decide, see Table 6.3 for a list of the advantages and disadvantages of each method. High, medium, and low is a rank comparison between the three methods. Time and travel are included as costs. The criteria will be explained with each type of survey. There is no single survey method that is best. They are all appropriate depending on the research question to be answered. You should also consider prior studies' data-collection methods from the literature review.

Table 6.3   Comparison of Survey Data-Collection Methods

Criteria	Personal Interview	Telephone Interview	Questionnaire Mail/E-mail/Fax
Cost	high	medium	low[1]
Response rate	high	medium	low
Sample size	low	medium	high
External validity	low	medium	high
Geographic area	low	medium	high
Probing	high	medium	low
Speed of data collection	medium	high	low[2]
Interview control	high	medium	low
Information depth	high	medium	low
Complexity of questions	high	medium	low
Interviewer bias possible	high	medium	low

[1] Cost is much lower with e-mail.
[2] The speed of data collection is much faster with e-mail than with regular "snail mail."

6.5 Personal Interview Surveys

A *personal interview* is a face-to-face survey through which the researcher asks the participant questions to answer the research question. Our definition emphasizes the importance of ensuring that the questions asked get the answers to the research question/hypotheses.

Types of Personal Interviews, Questions, and Forms

The three types of personal interviews are unstructured, structured, and semistructured. The three interview types of questions are the open-ended question (including hypothetical questions (such as "What would you do or say if . . . ?"), the closed-ended question (having a fixed answer such as yes or no), and the probing question. *Probing is the use of unplanned questions to stimulate discussion and obtain more information after an initial question has been asked and answered.* Note that while open- and closed-ended questions are planned, probing is not. However, probing questions are commonly open-ended questions. The types of questions and interview form you use will vary with the type of interview. Thus, we discuss them together below. In the next chapter you will learn how to develop questionnaires with a heavy focus on closed-ended questions.

Let's use an example of a personal interview that could be conducted in three different ways. Your research question is to explain manager–employee conflicts.

Unstructured interviews.

This type of interview requires a high level of interviewing skills. *The **unstructured** interview has broad, open-ended questions, relies heavily on probing, and uses notes as the question form.* Based on the research question, the researcher develops a few open-ended questions and plans to probe to get the details necessary to fully understand the answer. Asking good probing questions to get details is a skill that can be developed through training and experience. Counseling courses tend to focus on teaching unstructured interview skills.

Continuing our example, to conduct an unstructured interview the researcher would not list any possible conflict areas. The interviewee would simply be asked to identify any conflict areas with his or her boss. Probing questions would be used to get details in order to better understand the nature of the conflicts.

Structured interviews.

The structured interview requires the lowest level of interviewing skills. *The **structured interview** has primarily closed-ended questions, does not use probing questions, and has a set questionnaire that the interviewer fills out.* The difference between the self-administered questionnaire survey and the structured interview is essentially who fills out the questionnaire; in the latter the interviewee can ask the interviewer for clarification of the questions. Structured interviews are commonly used with census taking, door-to-door interviewing, and high-traffic areas—malls, conferences, and student unions. You will learn how to develop a questionnaire in the next chapter.

Continuing our example, the researcher would have a questionnaire (taken from the literature) that lists possible conflicts between managers and employees. The interviewer would simply ask each question and record the answer without any probing.

Semistructured interviews.

*The **semistructured interview** has a mix of closed- and open-ended questions, uses some probing, and has a set questionnaire with allotted space for probing answers.* It shares many of the characteristics of the other two types of interview. Human resources interviewing courses tend to focus on teaching semistructured interview skills.

Continuing our example, the researcher would review the literature and develop a list of questions based on the most common types of manager–employee conflicts. The researcher could ask the interviewee if he or she was experiencing a specific type of conflict. If yes, probing questions would be asked to get the details of what the conflict is and how and why it exists. The researcher would also ask for other conflicts not listed on the form.

In the next chapter you will learn how to develop survey questions to answer your research question. Although the questions are presented in survey questionnaires, it is also necessary to develop questions for structured interviews; questions can also be used for semistructured interviews, but they are less useful.

Panel of experts and pilot testing.

Regardless of the type of interview, you should have a panel of experts check your measurement instrument's questions to make sure your data will answer the research question, and then the questions should be pilot tested to improve the survey and provide support for reliability and validity of the questions and form.

CONCEPTUAL OBJECTIVE 5

Discuss the three characteristics that differentiate the three types of personal interviews.

Advantages and Disadvantages of Personal Interviewing

Before we list the advantages and disadvantages, you should realize that it is easy to conduct a bad interview and difficult to complete a good unstructured or semistructured interview—one that results in getting the interviewee to open up and provide the in-depth detail you need to understand the research question. Strong interviewers are good at probing. If you have strong interviewing skills it is an advantage for you, but if you don't have skills, it is a disadvantage to conduct personal interviews.

Advantages.

- *Understanding.* The goals of research are to explain, predict, and control phenomena. Personal interviews take explanation a step further to provide a more complete, in-depth understanding that generally can't be obtained through secondary sources, observation, and survey questionnaires. The researcher can also use data triangulation by observing the nonverbal behavior of participants.

- *Cognitive phenomena.* The interviewer can probe to better understand a person's feelings, attitudes, motivation, expectations, intentions, opinions, and so on. Personal interviewing is the best method for obtaining cognitive data, which cannot be observed.

- *Flexibility and demonstration.* The researcher can create a high or low level of structure for the interview and can ask unplanned questions as needed (probing). Products and other items can be demonstrated and questions asked about them.

- *Control.* The lack of a rigid structure allows the researcher to have great control over adapting questions as needed to target the most comprehensive data obtainable within the context of each interview. Personal interviews provide the greatest control of any data-collection method. There is no control over secondary data and little, if any, with observation and questionnaires. Of all the survey methods, it has the lowest number of unanswered questions.

- *High response rate.* Personal interviewing tends to have the highest response rate of survey methods. It's difficult to say no to a personal interview, which is a lot easier to do with other data-collection methods.

- *Internal validity.* Personal interviewing provides strong internal validity, as the results represent the generally small population.

Disadvantages.

- *Time, travel, cost*. Like observation, interviewing usually takes time and travel, which can be costly. In addition, many participants are paid for interviews.

- *Lack of anonymity*. The participant must be known to the interviewer, which can cause obtrusive measures. Without the anonymity of a questionnaire, some people are less apt to tell the truth or may not answer a confidential question when they are the known responders.

- *Lack of external validity*. Generally, personal interviews use a small sample size lacking in external validity (generalization to a larger population).

- *Possible interviewer bias*. Interviewers can cause obtrusive measures based on age, race, gender, appearance, and other factors. Interviewers may also be biased in how they ask questions (leading questions to get the answers they want) and record data (only recording what supports their hypotheses). Some unethical interviewers have simply filled in the answers to the questions to quickly meet the quota sample.

- *Possible interrater errors*. Multiple interviewers may record answers differently, which underscores the need for training and interrater reliability (discussed in Chapter 8).

6.6 Conducting a Personal Interview Study

Developing the interview questions that will answer the research question is critically important to successful personal interviewing. The details and mix of closed- and open-ended questions and probing vary with the type of interview. We discuss developing closed-ended questionnaires in more detail in the next chapter.

What Will Be Asked?

As with observation, the first step is to design the methods of data collection, answering the common questions of what, who, when, where, and how; recording answers; and data analysis (in no particular order as they are all interrelated). There is a lot of overlap between observations (which we have already discussed) and personal interviews related to the list of questions; thus, this section will be comparatively brief. The important factors to consider when planning a personal interview study are discussed below.

Who is interviewed?

Which participant(s) will be questioned? What is the population, sample frame and unit, and sample size? Will the sample be a random or nonrandom sample? Interviews can take place individually or in a group. Recall that a focus group has a moderator who is essentially an interviewer. Interviewing a group takes more skill than interviewing an individual, as the interviewer must know how to get everyone's answers and not let a few dominate the discussion. (You may want to refer to Chapter 5 when answering these questions.) However, participants for in-depth, unstructured interviews are usually chosen because of their experiences and attitudes that reflect the full scope of the issue, not because they represent the population.

Who will interview?

Will there be one or more interviewers? With multiple interviewers, training is needed to ensure reliable measures (interrater reliability). Generally, the larger the sample to be interviewed, the more structured the interview is. The less structured the interview is, the more training is needed.

Who grants/gains access to interview?

In some situations someone has to give permission to interview. For example, in a mall a manager may need to give approval for interviews of mall shoppers. The interviewer or some other party must determine who that person is and must obtain whatever permission is required.

When will the interview take place?

For personal interviews that are semi- or unstructured, it is best to set up an appointment. When setting up an appointment for an interview, follow the guidelines for conducting the interview (steps a–e below in the section on Conducting an Interview, the *Opening* section).

Where will the interview take place?

The interviewer typically goes to the participant(s) to conduct the interview. With structured interviews, the survey often takes place at a high-traffic area, such as a mall.

How many interviews take place?

The structured interview typically takes place only once with each participant. However, the unstructured interview may take place multiple times with multiple interviews to gain a more detailed understanding of the research question. For example, if you simply want descriptive data to find out why people run for exercise and/or athletic competition, you could develop a structured questionnaire, go to a race, and ask many runners the closed-ended questions after the race. However, if you really want to fully understand why people run, you could conduct several unstructured interviews with a few of the same runners.

Recording Responses

For the structured interview, the interviewer simply asks the questions and writes in the responses to the closed-ended questions on the survey form. For the semistructured and structured interviews the interviewer has two major choices.

Note taking or recording? Note taking gives you an instant record of key points, and you don't need to acquire any recording instrument. However, note taking can be distracting to the interviewer and/or inhibit the interviewee, and the interviewer may miss important points. Audio recording of the interview allows you to focus solely on interviewing, and you will not forget important points as you can listen to them multiple times. (Video recording adds the extra dimension of observing participants' nonverbal behavior.) However, recording may not be permitted, it may inhibit the interviewee, you must obtain the recording instrument, and you have to take notes as you listen to the recording. Some interviewers use both notes and recordings.

With the structured interview you must be sure that the questions are mutually exclusive and exhaustive. However, with the unstructured interview, due to the nature of the open-ended questions, there may be an overlap in answers to some questions.

A panel of experts should approve the questions and form, and the questionnaire form should be pilot tested.

Qualitative or Quantitative Analysis?

Quantitative analysis commonly uses closed-ended questions with a large sample size. However, open-ended questions, regardless of sample size, are difficult to computerize for running statistics and are thus used with qualitative analysis. The structured interview tends to use closed-ended questions with large sample sizes, which lends itself to quantitative analysis. In contrast, the unstructured interview uses open-ended questions, usually with a small sample size, which lends itself to qualitative analysis. For quantitative analysis, entering data into the computer and using a coding system are always the same, regardless of the method of data collection.

CONCEPTUAL OBJECTIVE 6
Describe data-collection and data-analysis differences between the structured and unstructured interview.

Conducting the Interview

There are three basic parts to conducting the interview:

- *Opening.* When opening the interview, you should develop a relaxed relationship of confidence and understanding (rapport) with the participant.

  (a) Tell the participant who you are and what organization or individual you represent.

  (b) Explain what you are doing in a way that will stimulate the participant's interest in conducting the interview. He or she must believe it will be a pleasant and worthwhile experience. Don't give too much detail; answer any questions and provide more detail as needed.

  (c) Tell the participant how he or she was chosen.

  (d) Tell the participant approximately how long the interview will take.

  (e) Overcome any reservations to be interviewed.

  (f) If you plan to record the interview, state why and ask for permission.

- *Interviewing.* During the interview, read the questions slowly and record responses in order on the form. Repeat and clarify questions as needed. Probe to gain additional data in an informal, relaxed manner. The interview should not seem like a cross-examination or quiz.

- *Closing.* In closing the interview, thank the participant for completing the survey. If there will be another interview, this may be a good time to make the appointment.

STOP READING and turn to the end of the chapter to complete exercise 6-4.

6.7 Telephone Interview Surveys

The telephone interview is the second survey data-collection method we discuss. *A telephone interview is a survey conducted via telephone through which the researcher asks the participant questions designed to answer the research question.* Telephone surveys essentially replace the personal structured interview to obtain the advantages listed below. Telephone surveys can be used with unstructured, structured, and semistructured interviewing methods. However, the telephone is more commonly used for structured and semistructured than for unstructured interviews.

The structured telephone interview is based on a questionnaire, which you will learn how to develop in the next chapter. Nielsen Media Research and Arbitron make thousands of telephone-interview calls each week to determine television viewing and radio listening habits. Political campaigns use telephone surveys to determine voter preferences, such as who they will vote for. People who don't complete the mail surveys can be called and asked to do so over the phone.

Regardless of the type of interview, you should have a *panel of experts* check your measurement instrument questions to make sure your data will answer the research question, and you should *pilot test* the questions to improve the survey and provide support for reliability and validity of the questions and form.

Advantages and Disadvantages of Telephone Interviewing

There are many reasons why an interviewer might prefer to use telephone interviewing over some other form of survey. A few of the advantages appear below, followed by some of the disadvantages inherent in interviewing by telephone.

Advantages.

- *Moderate to low cost, no travel.* Although more expensive than a mail survey, telephone interviewing is estimated to be about 40% less costly than personal interviews. These days, wide-area telecommunications services (WATS lines) and other telecommunications packages can be used to cut the costs of long distance calls, or flat rate charges can be applied, regardless of the number of calls.

- *Speed.* Telephone interviews are generally faster than personal interviews and mail surveys. If a computer (discussed shortly) is used, it can feature preset variables in the columns of the entry form; throughout the interview process, the interviewer can record data directly into the rows for quantitative data analysis.

- *Moderate response rate.* Although less frequently than in personal interviews, people are more willing to answers questions over the telephone then they are to complete a mail survey.

- *Clarification and probing.* If participants don't understand the questions, the interviewer can explain them and can ask additional unplanned questions.

- *Possible quality control.* If multiple telephone interviewers are employed, they can be trained and supervised from one location.

- *Possible external validity.* The use of the telephone can increase the sample size and geographic area, giving the results generalization to a larger population than personal interviews can. This is a trade-off with internal validity.

Disadvantages.

- *Noncontact callback.* It is common to call and get no answer, to be told the person is not available, or to get voice mail or an answering machine. Completing one survey often takes several calls. Some people with caller ID will not answer if they suspect telemarketing. In 2003, the Federal Trade Commission added to the noncontact problem with the "Do Not Call" registry. Businesses can't call these people, but this doesn't apply to academic researchers.

- *Cell phones and cable.* These days, many people don't have landlines—just cell phones. Cell phones cause problems when you want to survey a certain area. Landlines have area codes and three-digit prefixes that ensure you are reaching people in the area of your population. Cell phones and cable lines don't often have the same codes, so the people with these phone services may not be included in the sample— which can result in bias.

- *Time.* It takes a lot longer to call people and read them the questions than to send them the questions by mail/e-mail.

- *Less complex questions.* Generally, over the phone you need to keep the questions shorter and simpler than you would with personal interviews and mail surveys. Closed-ended questions generally work well, but giving too many answer options can be difficult to remember and may frustrate the interviewee. Thus, it is generally a good idea to try to use a scale (e.g., **1** satisfied to **9** dissatisfied) to be represented by the digits on the phone rather than giving the interviewee descriptive-choice (e.g., always satisfied, usually satisfied, sometimes satisfied, and so on through dissatisfied) answers. Trying to keep the responses identical is also advisable to make things easier and faster.

- *Length of survey.* Over the telephone, it is better to limit the length of the interview to 10 minutes or less. However, if you have an appointment for a phone interview, it can be longer.

- *Broken-off interviews and telemarketing.* More participants will hang up and terminate a telephone interview than will stop a personal interview. This is more often a problem with longer surveys. Telemarketing has resulted in people having a tendency to hang up quickly. The no-call list for solicitors can also limit the amount of interviews completed (in some cases participants think the caller is trying to sell something).

- *Possible interviewer bias and interrater errors.* Interviewers may want specific results and may try to get the interviewee to select the answers they want. Also, multiple interviewers can record the same answers differently, causing interrater errors.

- *Possible bias in sample frame.* Phone numbers can be inaccurate or nonfunctioning, and telephone books are consistently outdated. It has been estimated that 20% of the population moves each year, and 22% of the telephone numbers are unlisted. However, this may be overcome with the use of computerized random dialing, but the noncontact problem (as well as the cell and cable issues described above) can cause bias.

Now that you have read the advantages and disadvantages of the personal and telephone interviews separately, return to Table 6.3 for a side-by-side comparison of these two survey methods.

CONCEPTUAL OBJECTIVE 7
Discuss some of the advantages and disadvantages of telephone interviews versus personal interviews.

Computers and Telephone Interviews

There are three major uses of computers in telephone interviewing: random-digit dialing, computer-assisted telephone interviewing, and computer-administered telephone surveys.

Random-digit dialing (RDD).

Computer programs are available that can randomly dial telephone numbers, eliminating possible sample-frame bias. They also have the advantages of saving the interviewer dialing time. RDD is also part of CATI and CATS.

Computer-assisted telephone interviewing (CATI).

With this method, the computer essentially dials a number and the interviewer simply reads the introductory information and conducts prescreening from the computer screen. Then the actual questions are read from the computer screen and the answers typed directly into the database. The computer is programmed to eliminate non-possible answers. For example, if the scale of 1–9 is used and the interviewer presses 10, an error prompt will occur, requiring new data input. However, simple typographical errors can still occur.

Computer-administered telephone survey (CATS).

CATS takes CATI one-step further by replacing people with computers that actually conduct the interview and input the answers. However, CATS has a higher hang-up rate than when a real person conducts the interview, simply because it is easier for people to hang up on a computer than on an actual person. Also, only closed-ended questions can be used with CATS.

Conducting a Telephone Interview Study

Because the telephone interview is essentially a replacement for the personal interview, all of the "who, what, when, where, and how" questions are not addressed under separate headings here. Just follow the personal interview questions as you read this abbreviated version.

What will be asked is critical. Because the telephone interview is similar to the mail survey, see the next chapter for how to construct a questionnaire. The "who" can now be a computer, if you buy or rent the equipment or hire a professional firm to do the interviewing for you. However, students typically make all the calls themselves. When/where to call depends on whether you are calling a business (days) or residence (evenings). How many interviews? Usually just one. Responses can be written on the questionnaire, or you can type responses directly into the computer. It's easy if you wear a headset to keep your hands free, and it saves time. Telephone interviews typically collect and analyze quantitative data from large samples. See the information on Conducting the Interview under the Personal Interviews section for the steps to open, conduct, and close the interview.

STOP READING and turn to the end of the chapter to complete exercise 6-4.

SKI WEST STUDY

As we bring this chapter to a close, you should be able to:
- *decide which data-collection method you will use (secondary, observation, personal interview, telephone interview survey, or survey questionnaire), and*
- *collect data through secondary sources, observation, personal and telephone interviews.*

Of the three methods of data collection, Matt McLeish used secondary sources, employee records. Secondary databases have an advantage over observation and survey. Matt was able to collect his data quickly without having to be concerned with response rate. However, it does take some time to get permission to use secondary sources. In large companies it can take months to get approval to use employee records. In order to have Matt's completed study published in this book, it took a few months before corporate management gave approval.

Chapter Summary and Glossary

The chapter summary is organized in a way that provides you with the answers necessary to help you meet the conceptual objectives for this chapter.

1. **List the data-collection methods and explain which one is the most unobtrusive measure.**
   The data-collection methods are: secondary, observation, and survey (personal interview, telephone interview, and questionnaire). Secondary sources are the most unobtrusive measure because the researcher reads data, which does not influence participant response.

2. **Describe the generalization/internal and external validity trade-off with observation.**
   Observation tends to have strong internal validity and weak external validity. Observation from a small sample has internal validity, as results have strong generalization to a small population rather than generalization to a larger population for external validity. The researcher has a strong understanding of the observed participants but is trading off generalization, as the results may not be a valid for larger populations.

3. **Discuss similarities and differences between the panel of experts and the pilot test.**
   The goal of the panel of experts and the pilot test is the same: to improve the measurement instrument, providing support for its reliability and validity. The panel of experts consists of experienced professors and professionals in the field of study. When you pilot test, you observe people who are similar to (or the same ones who will be) participants in the actual study.

4. **State what information is entered into the computer columns and rows for quantitative analysis.**
   Variable names are entered into the column headings and the collected data is entered into the rows.

5. **Discuss the three characteristics that differentiate the three types of personal interviews.**
   The three differentiating characteristics are the use of open- and closed-ended questions, probing, and the interview form. The unstructured interview uses open-

ended questions, probing, and no actual form. The structured interview uses closed-ended questions, no probing, and a formal questionnaire form. The semis-tructured interview is a mix of the two.

6. **Describe data-collection and data-analysis differences between the structured and unstructured interview.**
   The structured interview tends to use closed-ended questions with a large sample size for data collection, which means that quantitative analysis is appropriate. Unstructured interviews tend to use open-ended questions with a small sample size, which means that qualitative analysis is appropriate.

7. **Discuss some of the advantages and disadvantages of telephone interviews versus personal interviews.**
   The telephone interview has some advantages over the personal interview: no travel, and speed in immediate responses. Telephone interviews can use larger sample sizes than personal interviews, allowing external validity. However, telephone surveys have a lower response rate, require callbacks, and have a greater chance of broken-off interviews than personal interviews do. In addition, telephone interviews generally must be briefer and less complex than personal interviews.

8. **Define the following alphabetical list of key terms.**
   Select one or more methods: (1) fill in the missing key terms from memory, (2) match the key terms with their definitions below, or (3) copy the key terms in order from the list at the beginning of the chapter.

duration of observation	observation	semistructured interview
ethnography	panel of experts	structured interview
exhaustive	personal interview	telephone interview
frequency of observation	pilot test	unobtrusive measures
mutually exclusive	probing	unstructured interview

_____ collect data without the influence of the researcher.

_____ is the process of watching and recording behavior, objects, and occurrences to answer the research question.

_____ is a methodology used to provide descriptions of human societies, primarily through observation.

_____ is a simple record of each time the participant conducts the behavior.

_____ is a record of how long the participant actually does the behavior.

_____ means that all data collected fit into only one measurement category.

_____ means that all data collected fit into some measurement category.

_____ is a group of professors and professionals in the field of study who provide improvements to the measurement instrument.

_____ simulates the actual data collection to make improvements to the measurement instrument.

_____ is a face-to-face survey through which the researcher asks the participant questions to answer the research question.

_____ is the use of unplanned questions to stimulate discussion and obtain more information after an initial question has been asked and answered.

_____ has broad open-ended questions, relies heavily on probing, and uses notes as the question form.

_____ has primarily closed-ended questions, does not use probing questions, and has a set questionnaire that the interviewer fills out.

_____ has a mix of closed- and open-ended questions, uses some probing, and has a set questionnaire with space for probing answers.

_____ is a survey conducted via telephone through which the researcher asks the participant questions designed to answer the research question.

WRITTEN ASSIGNMENTS

The Method assignment will actually be completed in chapters 4 through 8.

APPENDIX RP, ASSIGNMENT 3 (METHOD AND APPENDIX A) AND
APPENDIX CS, ASSIGNMENT 2 (METHOD)

For this chapter, if you haven't already done so, you can write in the data-collection method you will use for your study.

EXERCISES

SECONDARY SOURCES

6-1   Will you use secondary database sources as your primary data-collection method for your research proposal? Explain why or why not.

OBSERVATIONAL USE

6-2   Will you use observation as your primary data-collection method for your research? Explain why or why not. Be sure to discuss the advantages and disadvantages of observation as they relate to your study.

OBSERVATIONAL METHODS

6-3   If you will use observation as your primary data-collection method for your research proposal, answer the "who, what, when, where, and how" questions, explain how you will record your observations, and state whether you will use qualitative or quantitative analysis. If you will not use observation, state how it *could* be used for your study.

PERSONAL OR TELEPHONE INTERVIEW

6-4   If you will use the personal or telephone interview as your primary data-collection method for your research proposal, answer the "who, what, when, where, and how" questions, explain how you will record your observations, and state whether you will use qualitative or quantitative analysis. If you will not use the personal or telephone interview, state how they *could* be used for your study.

Survey Questionnaires

CHAPTER OUTLINE

CONCEPTUAL OBJECTIVES

The conceptual objectives below also appear at appropriate places within the chapter at points when you will have accessed the information necessary to attain them. They

appear again at the end of the chapter in the Summary and Glossary section, along with explanations that will enable you to meet the objectives.

After studying this chapter, you should be able to:

1. Identify the major advantages and disadvantages of the survey questionnaire, as compared to other survey methods.

2. Identify the first step in the survey research process, and discuss why it is the starting point.

3. Discuss the need for determining the use of each question and the statistical method to be used with it.

4. Explain the need to address nonresponse bias and how it is done.

5. Describe the characteristics of a good questionnaire.

6. Discuss general guidelines to the measurement level, scaling, coding, and numbering of questions.

7. Discuss the use of monetary and nonmonetary inducements.

8. Identify and describe four methods of increasing response rate.

9. Define the following key terms (listed in order of their appearance in the chapter).

questionnaire	contingency questions	checklist questions
cover letter	dichotomous questions	fill-in questions
response rate	rating-scale questions	matrix questions
nonresponse bias	ranking questions	funnel sequence

SKILL DEVELOPMENT OBJECTIVES

The exercises that apply to particular skill development objectives are indicated directly beneath each numbered objective below. Periodic instructions within the chapter tell you when to stop reading and direct you to the end of the chapter to complete one or more of the skill development exercises.

After studying this chapter, you should be able to:

1. Determine which survey method, if any, is most appropriate for your research design.
   Exercise 7-1

2. Follow the ten steps of survey research.
   Exercises 7-2 and 7-3

3. Write survey research questions.
   Exercise 7-4

4. Use methods to increase your response rate.
   Exercises 7-5 through 7-7

The Research Process

(1) The research question/purpose of the study, literature review, and hypotheses. • *Introduction*	(2) Research design methodology for collecting data and statistics. • *Method*	(3) Data analysis and interpreting results. • *Results*	(4) Discussing results and making conclusions. • *Discussion*
Chapters 1–3	Chapters 4–8	Chapters 9–14	Chapters 9–14

In prior chapters we presented the research process shown above. This chapter continues with survey research methods, focusing on the mail/e-mail self-administered questionnaire. We begin with a discussion of the advantages and disadvantages of questionnaires followed by the steps of conducting survey research. Based on these steps, we then provide details about how to construct a questionnaire and end with tips on how to increase response rate.

7.1 Questionnaire Survey Data Collection

The previous chapter presented the advantages and disadvantages of personal interview surveys and telephone interviews. We now present the third survey data-collection method, the questionnaire survey. *A questionnaire* is a type of *measurement instrument* with consistent questions and answers. *A **questionnaire** survey is a self-administered series of questions commonly delivered by mail/e-mail, the response to which enables the researcher to answer the research question.* Fax, hand delivery, or any other method of delivery is also acceptable. Recall that questionnaires are also used for personal interviews and telephone interviews, but we do classify them differently (based on interviews being two-way communication with probing and questionnaires being one-way communication with no discussion of questions and answers). However, the development process is the same for any type of questionnaire. Even if you don't plan to conduct survey research, being able to develop a good questionnaire is a valuable research skill. Have you ever filled out a service evaluation card at a hotel, restaurant, or car repair shop? Have you filled out a warranty card for a product you purchased? If the answer to any of these questions is yes, you have completed a research survey questionnaire.

Advantages of Mailed Questionnaire Surveys

- *Lower cost.* Mailed questionnaire surveys tend to be the least expensive survey method, although postage for large samples can be expensive. E-mail questionnaires cost even less. Time is a cost, and it doesn't take much time and effort to collect the data.

- *Large geographical dispersion.* The cost is the same to mail a letter anywhere in the United States and to e-mail anywhere in the world.

- *External validity (generalization).* Questionnaire surveys usually have a large sample size, so results can be generalized to a large population.

- *Reflection and convenience.* Participants have time to think about their answers and/or consult other sources, and they can complete the survey at their convenience (as long as they meet the deadline for returning the completed survey).

- *High unobtrusive measures and anonymity.* Although there can be bias in developing the questions, there is no interviewer bias with mailed surveys, and the participant can be unknown (anonymous) to the researcher.

Disadvantages of Mailed Questionnaire Surveys

- *Low response rate.* Many people simply throw the questionnaire away.
- *Slower data collection.* You must wait to get the data rather than gathering immediate responses, as with personal and telephone interviews.
- *No two-way communication.* Participants can't ask questions if they don't understand something. Also, no additional information can be asked through unplanned questions (i.e., no probing).
- *Lack of completion control.* The questionnaire may be completed by a different person than the one to whom the questionnaire was mailed. For example, in some cases an assistant who doesn't have full information may fill out the questionnaire for a busy manager.

We have now discussed the advantages and disadvantages of the three survey data-collection methods—personal interview, telephone interview, and questionnaire. For a comparison of the three methods, review Table 6.3 in Chapter 6.

CONCEPTUAL OBJECTIVE 1
Identify the major advantages and disadvantages of the survey questionnaire,
as compared to other survey methods.

 STOP READING and turn to the end of the chapter to complete exercise 7-1.

7.2 Ten Survey Research Steps

Notice that the title of this section features *survey research*, which includes personal and telephone interviews as well as questionnaires. These same steps can be followed for any survey method. Although it is geared toward self-administered questionnaire research, the questionnaire can also be completed by phone. The term for following a standard set of step-by-step procedures is the *total design method* (TDM). The TDM builds important considerations within the research process. A major problem is that students tend to think that questionnaire survey research is an easy process.

Don't be tempted to make the common mistake of jumping right into developing the questions. People who do usually find out that they have collected a lot of data that doesn't answer the research question, and they don't know what statistics to run for the data they do have. By following the ten steps in the survey research process you will avoid this common mistake, and you will provide support for the reliability and validity of your research-study data collection and develop good research skills along the way. However, you should realize that this is not a simple linear process in which you move sequentially from steps 1 through 10 without returning to prior steps to make changes that improve the study.

Step 1. Choosing a Research Question and Hypotheses

It bears repeating that a common error of novice researchers is the tendency to start by developing the questionnaire. Don't give in to that temptation! The starting place is to choose a clearly defined research question (purpose of the study) and hypotheses (tentative answers to the research questions—more to come on all this in Chapter 10). The well-written questionnaire is designed to get the answers to the hypotheses through specific questions. Your hypotheses need to be founded from a strong literature review, as it provides existing hypotheses that you can copy and/or use as the basis for your own questions, using references. See Box 7.1 for an example of a research question and hypotheses.

Box 7.1   Research Question and Hypotheses

The purpose of the researcher is to measure job satisfaction and compare differences between subgroups of employees.
  Hypothesis 1. Employees have a high level of job satisfaction.
  Hypothesis 2. Managers have a higher level of job satisfaction than nonmanagers do.
  Hypothesis 3. Men have a higher level of job satisfaction than women do.

CONCEPTUAL OBJECTIVE 2
Identify the first step in the survey research process, and discuss why it is the starting point.

Step 2. Choosing a Sampling and Survey Method

Who will participate in your study by completing the questionnaire? What are the population, sample frame and unit, and sample size? Refer to Chapter 5 and the material below when answering these questions and determining your completed survey and response-rate goals.

Which survey method will you use: personal interview, telephone interview, or questionnaire? It's important to know that you can combine survey methods. You can mail a survey, for example, and follow up with telephone interviews.

When determining the size of the mailing and the goals for completed surveys, you must remember to consider the response rate. When a survey is conducted within an organization, the response rate will most likely be very high—follow-up will not be a major task. However, if you are mailing/e-mailing to a wide general geographic area, your response rate after the first mailing may only be 10%, and follow-up will be a major task.

You should have a goal for a completed number of surveys based on the standards of your college/employer and prior studies—let's say 100 from a wide geographic area with a 33% response rate. You can take one of two approaches.

1. *A large mailing.* With an expected high response rate without follow-up, a large mailing works well. However, it does not work well with a low initial response rate. For example, with an expected 10% first return you would have to mail 1,000 questionnaires to get 100 completed. The problem is that the low response rate threatens the reliability and validity of the sample. Do the 10% who responded actually represent the population? Research-

ers have shown that there is often a difference between respondents and nonrespondents. More highly educated and professional people tend to have a higher response rate. If you have 100 surveys but you don't have the 33% response rate, to get the rate up to 33% you need 333 completed surveys (or 200 more), which will take a lot of follow-up time and effort.

2. *A moderate mailing*. With an expected low initial response rate, a moderate mailing with follow-up works well. Continuing our example, if you mail 333 randomly selected surveys, you will get around 33 responses the first time. However, your follow-up number is 77, which will take less time and effort as well as save mailing and possibly telephone follow-up costs. Let's say the number of responses is more important than the response rate. We will round off the number of surveys to mail at 400. If we get 100 completed we meet the total goal, but not the response rate, which would be 25%.

See Box 7.2 for an example of a research question, design, and sampling process (the steps listed in Chapter 5, Table 5.1).

Box 7.2   The Research Design and Sampling Process Methods

The purpose of the study is to measure job satisfaction and compare differences between subgroups of employees. The data-collection research design is a survey questionnaire with telephone follow-up. Data analysis is quantitative, using an inferential test-of-difference statistical design.

1. The population is the state of Massachusetts' (U.S.) employees.

2. The sample frame comes from a mailing-list company that provides a random list of 400 employees from Massachusetts, and the sample unit is individual employees from multiple organizations.

3. The sample size goal is 100 completed surveys with a 33% response rate.

4. The simple random sample method will be used.

5. The random sample of 400 will be drawn from the mailing-list company.

Step 3. Constructing the Questionnaire

Existing questionnaires.

Based on your review of the literature, is there an existing questionnaire that can be used to answer your research questions? If similar studies have been conducted, you can contact the researchers to ask for a copy of their questionnaire. Other sources offer a collection of questionnaires that have been developed and statistically tested for reliability and validity. One well-known source is the *Mental Measurements Yearbook* (MMY). You can check with your librarian to find out if your college has any books or online sources that you can search to find existing questionnaires. If you get an existing questionnaire, you could use it as is or make some changes and this step is done.

Making your own questionnaire.

If you don't obtain an existing questionnaire, you need to construct one that will get the answers to your hypotheses. We will discuss how to construct the questionnaire in the next section so we don't lose the flow of the steps. However, see Box 7.3 for examples of research questions to answer the hypotheses in Box 7.1. (The *italicized information* in Box 7.3 would not actually appear in the questionnaire; it is included there to enhance your understanding.)

Time frame and length.

First and foremost, the questionnaire must answer the research question/hypotheses. However, you also need to consider the time and length of the questionnaire. *Time* refers to how long it takes to complete the questionnaire, and *length* refers to how many questions to include. More complex questions tend to take longer to complete. Generally, the longer the questionnaire and the more complex it is, the less likely people will be to fill it out. As a general guide, try to keep the time to complete the questionnaire at 15 minutes or less; 10–15 minutes is a good range to encourage responses. Questionnaires that take more than 20 minutes often tend to result in nonparticipation. See step 6 for the way to determine the approximate amount of time it takes to complete your questionnaire.

Coding and planned computer data entry.

In the sample questionnaire in Box 7.3, note that the answers to all the closed-ended nominal and ordinal measurement questions have numbers as the coding so that the response data can be entered into rows on the computer; your goal is to have 100 questionnaires (100 rows). Each question is a variable that is typed in the columns (14 total). Part of the coding system is to number all questionnaires mailed so you can identify the nonrespondents for follow-up. When you use word processing it's easy to change the margins, font, type size, spacing, and so on to ensure that the questionnaire looks appealing and easy to complete.

Step 4. Determining the Use of and Statistics for Each Question

Recall novice researchers' tendency to rush off and get the questionnaires completed, and to worry about the statistics to run later after they get the data. This process does not work, as people who do so commonly find out that they cannot statistically test variables to answer their hypotheses with the data collected. They have to change their hypotheses or collect new data, both being poor choices. (This problem is virtually nonexistent when you follow step 4.) You will learn how to determine which statistical test to use and when in Chapter 10. The important thing for now is to realize how important it is to develop the statistical methods before collecting the data.

After writing the questions that will answer your hypotheses, the next step is to determine the use of each question. It is important to remember that a questionnaire that doesn't take too long to complete results in greater participation. So if any of your questions will not provide you with a response that will help you answer your research question/test your hypothesis, remove them from the questionnaire. The use of the question is also tied to statistics. On the questionnaire draft, write down the statistics for which each question will be used. In the example, it would be something like D–demographic, hypothesis–H1, H2, H3. If you have any questions for which you will not run statistics, ask yourself: Do you need the questions? Should they be cut?

See Box 7.4 (on p. 170) to continue our example. Note that descriptive statistics are run first, which is commonly done before hypothesis testing.

You may want to change hypotheses. As stated earlier, you may return to prior steps in the survey research process. When developing the questions (in step 3), you may find that you want to change hypotheses to better match the questions. Also, when you determine the statistics to use, you can change the wording of the questions and/or hypotheses, cut questions, or add new ones. For example, in Box 7.4 you could add hypotheses for any of the

Box 7.3   Questionnaire

Questions 1–8 answer Hypothesis 1: Employees have a high level of job satisfaction.
Researchers have identified six determinants of job satisfaction, on which the first six questions below are based. Please identify your level of satisfaction with each by circling the number that best describes your level of agreement with each statement on the continuum below. Then please rate your overall job satisfaction in question 7 and respond to the remaining questions 8–15.

Strongly disagree						Strongly agree
1	2	3	4	5	6	7

1. I have a positive attitude toward my job.

1	2	3	4	5	6	7

2. I enjoy the work I do.

1	2	3	4	5	6	7

3. I am fairly paid for my job.

1	2	3	4	5	6	7

4. I have a good boss.

1	2	3	4	5	6	7

5. I have good coworkers.

1	2	3	4	5	6	7

6. I have an opportunity for growth and upward mobility.

1	2	3	4	5	6	7

7. Overall, I am satisfied with my job.

1	2	3	4	5	6	7

8. Of the six determinants below, circle the number of the item that best reflects what is most important to your overall job satisfaction.
    1 my attitude, **2** the work itself, **3** my pay, **4** my boss, **5** my coworkers, **6** growth opportunity

Question 9 is needed to answers Hypothesis 2: Managers have a higher level of job satisfaction than nonmanagers do.
9. My position is a   **1** manager   **2** nonmanager

Question 10 is needed to answer Hypothesis 3: Men have a higher level of job satisfaction than women do.
10. I am a   **1** man   **2** woman

Questions 11–14 provide additional demographic information for describing the sample, and they can also be used to test differences between the subgroups, as with questions 9 and 10.

11. My job title is: _____
     It is best described as   **1** blue-collar work   **2** white-collar work

12. The one industry that best describes where I work is:
     1 Agriculture, forestry, landscaping, fishing, and so on
     2 Construction, building, painting, carpentry, heating, electrical, and so on
     3 Finance, insurance, real estate, and so on
     4 Manufacturing, printer, publisher, and so on
     5 Retail store, eating and drinking, apparel, florist, and so on
     6 Wholesale durable and nondurable, manufacturer's rep, and so on
     7 Services, repair (appliance, auto), business (advertising, computer), professional (accountant, consultant), personal (beauty, cleaning), health (nurse, doctor), education (teacher, counselor) and so on

Question 12 alternatives were not designed by the researcher; these are Dunn & Bradstreet classifications (validity).

13. The city in Massachusetts that is (or is closest to) the area in which I work is:
     1 Boston
     2 Worcester
     3 Springfield
     4 Pittsfield

14. My age is _____.

15. What could your organization do to increase your job satisfaction?
     Leave plenty of room for the respondent to write in the answer.

Thank you for completing this survey. Please return it in the self-addressed stamped envelope (SASE).

(If you don't provide an SASE to the respondent, provide the address to which the questionnaire should be returned. Note that when using SurveyMonkey the mailing address is not needed.)

Box 7.4   Statistical Methods

Descriptive Statistics. Demographic questions 9–14 in the questionnaire would be run to report data about the sample. For example, you would run the frequencies, percentages, mean, median, mode, and would report the percentage of managers to nonmanagers, men to women, blue- to white-collar, industry and area representation, and the mean age of the sample. Some of these questions are also used as the independent variables (Xs) to test hypotheses.

Hypothesis 1: Employees have a high level of job satisfaction.

(Questions 1–7) *Job satisfaction.* You would report the descriptive statistics for each variable/ question. If you use a questionnaire used in an earlier study, you could compare your sample results to the prior study's results to test for differences with a one-sample T-test.

(Question 8) *Most important determinant of job satisfaction.* You would report the descriptive frequency/percentage of each to rank them in order of importance to the sample. You could also run a chi-square test to see if there is a significant difference in the seven selections.

Hypothesis 2: Managers have a higher level of job satisfaction than nonmanagers.

(Questions 1–7) *Y = job satisfaction* (ordinal data measurement level, seven scales)

(Question 9) *X = job classification* (two scales—manager or nonmanager, nominal data)

You would run seven Mann-Whitney U tests to compare differences in level of job satisfaction for managers and nonmanagers to determine which group, if either, has a significantly higher level of job satisfaction.

Hypothesis 3: Men have a higher level of job satisfaction than women do.

(Questions 1–7) *Y = job satisfaction* (ordinal data measurement level, seven scales)

(Question 10) *X = gender* (two scales—men or women, nominal data)

You would run seven Mann-Whitney U tests to compare differences in level of job satisfaction for men and women to determine which group, if either, has a significantly higher level of job satisfaction.

You can plan to run other nonhypothesized tests.

(Questions 11–13) Type of work, industry, and area could also be used as Xs to test differences in Y—job satisfaction (Questions 1–7) that have not been hypothesized but could be added to the results and discussion sections of the completed study. You could also determine if there is a correlation between age (Question 14) and the level of job satisfaction (Questions 1–7).

(Question 15) In the results and/or discussion you can give ideas on how to increase job satisfaction.

non-original hypotheses using questions 11–14. For example, you may find a correlation identifying that older workers have a significantly higher level of job satisfaction than younger workers do. This result would be worth stating in your Results section.

Conceptual Objective 3

Discuss the need for determining the use of each question and the statistical method to be used with it.

Step 5. Developing a Cover Letter

The personal interview is introduced with an opening statement and the request for the interview, which is often personalized to the individual. The telephone interview commonly has an opening script that is read to the participant. With self-administered questionnaires, because there is no two-way communication a cover letter is needed. *The cover letter introduces the questionnaire with an inducement to complete it.* Remember to keep the cover letter short. The longer the letter, the greater are the chances that it will be thrown out with the junk mail. Use official letterhead and titles, and date the letter. Recall that the cover letter can be typed in as an *e-mail,* but plan to keep it the same for all in the mailing, unless you are making some personal adjustments as an inducement. Below is a checklist of important items that should be included in the cover letter.

- *Introduce yourself and your sponsor, if any.* Keep it brief.
- *State your research purpose.* Briefly state the research question and the expected benefits of the study. Who benefits from the study and how?
- *Inducement.* Why should the person respond? You need to answer the unasked question, "What's in it for me—why should I use my time to fill out your questionnaire?" We will discuss various inducements later in this chapter (in section 7.4 on increasing response rate). If you are offering results of the study as an inducement, be sure to have a system for doing so. Note that such a system is included in the cover letter in Box 7.5.
- *Confidentiality.* Let the participants know that only total results will be reported. Tell them that you have numbered the surveys so that you will know whose surveys have been returned to eliminate the need for follow-up.
- *Question contact.* Let participants know how to contact you if they have any questions.
- *Time frames.* Time has two meanings here: (1) Tell participants approximately how long it will take to complete the survey. You can find out how long it takes with a pilot test. (2) Tell the participants the date by which you need the survey returned (usually two weeks). Due dates may not increase response rate, but they tend to speed up returns.
- *Appreciation.* Thank participants for completing the survey and for helping you and whoever else will benefit.

Box 7.5 (on the following page) contains a sample cover letter. (The *italicized information* in the box would not actually appear in your cover letter; it is included there to enhance your understanding.)

STOP READING and turn to the end of the chapter to complete exercise 7-2.

Step 6. Using a Panel of Experts and Pilot Testing

As discussed in the last chapter, before you collect data you should have a panel of experts review your cover letter and questionnaire with an eye toward improving it. Afterwards, pilot test the questionnaire to determine further improvements. With the pilot group, ask if there are any questions that could be confusing or unclear and, if so, get input on how to improve the wording. A more formal approach to using a panel of experts is called *content validity ratio.* It is explained in the next chapter in the discussion of content validity. (Hold on, you are not ready to collect your data yet!)

Box 7.5   Cover Letter

College Letterhead
(return address)

Date of mailing

Are you satisfied with your job?

(introduction) My name is John Smith, a graduate student conducting a research project as part of my degree requirements. *(research purpose)* My study will determine the level of job satisfaction of employees at your company. I plan to publish the results in a journal article that will provide managers with information regarding how to increase the job satisfaction of their employees. *(inducement)*

I will be happy to send you a copy of the results of the study. Just provide your name and the address where you would like the results sent at the bottom of this letter and return it with your completed survey in the self-addressed stamped envelope enclosed.

(confidentiality) I assure you of complete confidentiality; only total results will be recorded. You have been randomly selected to represent many employees, so *I need your completed survey.* Your copy of the survey is identified by the number I have assigned to it, and your name will not be placed on the questionnaire unless you put it there. If you are not currently employed full time, please write: "not employed full time" on the first page of the questionnaire and return it in the enclosed SASE. *(question contact)* If you have any questions, please don't hesitate to call me at 999-999-9999 or write to me at the address above.

(appreciation and time frame) Thank you for helping me earn my degree! I appreciate your contribution, which will lead to a better understanding of the elements that contribute to employee job satisfaction. I need the survey back within two weeks *(date two weeks after date of mailing)*, if possible. Please complete the survey now; it will only take five minutes of your time.

Gratefully,
(signature)   *(signature)*
John Smith   Sue Doe, Ph.D.
Graduate Student   Professor and Research Advisor

Yes, I would like a copy of the results sent to:
(space for participants' name and address if they would like results sent to them)

Pilot test to determine the time to complete the questionnaire. Because it is helpful to tell participants how long it will take to complete the questionnaire, it's important to know how long it will actually take. So pilot test how long it takes each early participant, get the average time, and report it on the cover letter that goes out with the complete mailing. (Note that you must return to step 5—Developing a Cover Letter.)

Step 7. Addressing Reliability and Validity

An important part of your research methodology is how you will collect your data—secondary sources, observation, or survey. An observation form and questionnaire are measurement instruments that need to be reliable (i.e., measure consistently) and valid (i.e., measure what they claim to measure). Basing your research questions/hypotheses and variables on the literature, using a panel of experts, and pilot testing your questionnaire are methods of addressing reliability and validity. However, statistical testing provides strong support for the reliability and validity of the measurement instrument. We discuss reliability, validity, and statistical testing in the next chapter and in statistical chapters 9–14. Before you move on to step 8 and administer your survey, read Chapter 8 and possibly statistically test your questionnaire. Below we briefly discuss the possible use of statistical testing.

Possible statistical testing.

Notice that step 7 doesn't say you *must* statistically test your questionnaire. If you use a questionnaire that has already been tested, you don't need to do it again. Also, single-measure questions often don't need to be and sometimes can't be statistically tested, but multiple measures can and should be tested.

Single and multiple measures.

With multiple measures of a variable, statistical testing is needed to support the validity of combining the questions to answer a research question. In the questionnaire in Box 7.3 there are six questions to measure job satisfaction. However, we did not attempt to combine the six measures into one measure of job satisfaction. We asked participants to rate their satisfaction in question 7 (Overall, I am satisfied with my job: **1** strongly disagree, **7** strongly agree). With these single measures, you can't test statistically. However, if we were to combine the six prior job satisfaction questions into one measure, we would need to run statistics to support the validity of this multiple measure. We discuss statistical testing in the next chapter, so read it before collecting your data.

Step 8. Administering the Survey

OK! You should now have a good questionnaire that you developed by following the first seven steps of survey research to provide support for reliability and validity. You may have found that developing the questionnaire wasn't as easy as you thought it would be. It's likely that collecting the data will be difficult as well. Recall that a survey questionnaire can be completed through personal and telephone interviews; but this is often time consuming, and time is a cost. Self-administered questionnaires are commonly mailed, e-mailed, or e-mailed with a link to an outside source for online data collection. Let's talk about each method.

Mail.

This is by far the most costly method. Your college or university may be able to help you with the actual mailing to your sample-frame mailing list. Be sure to have a good printed copy of the cover letter and questionnaire. Make extra copies for the follow-up mailing. Don't forget to number each survey for follow-up purposes.

E-mail (as an attachment).

You can e-mail your cover letter to the participants in the sample with the questionnaire attached, to be returned via e-mail.

E-mail (with online data collection).

You can e-mail your cover letter to the sample with a link for the participant to click to complete the questionnaire. Recall that SurveyMonkey.com, Zoomerang.com, and other outside sources can be used to provide e-mail sample frame lists and to collect the data for you. This most modern approach is by far the fastest way to collect and record the data. With the old mail and e-mail approaches it's necessary to input the data by hand—but not with online data collection, as it's done for you. SurveyMonkey.com has gained acceptance in some research circles. In fact, as I was writing this chapter I received an e-mail from a doctoral student doing a dissertation at Kent State University who asked me as an expert in management theory to complete a survey using SurveyMonkey.com, which I did. If your field of research and your college accept this methodology, consider taking advantage of it. The websites provide you with instructions for using their services.

Step 9. Following Up (Monitoring the Response Rate)

Monitoring the rate of response is your next step. Since mail and e-mail both tend to have a low response rate, neither is preferred for addressing the problem of low response.

Low response rate is a major disadvantage of the self-administered survey question-naire. *The **response rate** is the percentage of returned questionnaires; it is the number of completed questionnaires divided by the number delivered.* For example, say you mailed 200 surveys. Ten came back uncompleted (nondeliverable, not part of the population, and so on). You received 72 completed questionnaires. The response rate is 38% (72/190).

In the last section of this chapter you will learn several methods to increase the response rate. Here we present only the best method—follow-up. After the two-week time period of waiting for responses, calculate the response rate. Unless you get an extremely high response rate, you need to follow up to increase it. Even if you exceed the goal (100 surveys) with a greater response rate (33%), do at least one follow-up mailing. In many studies, you will have to follow up more than once to meet your goals for completed surveys and response rate. Keep at it until you meet your goals (assuming they are realistic).

As the questionnaires come in, using the numbers, check off who responded so you don't follow up needlessly. Your first (optional) follow-up can be a postcard reminder (in one week). The next follow-up is to resend the questionnaire and SASE with an appropri-ately revised second cover letter to nonrespondents (in two weeks). The revision to the cover letter can be a simple addition to the top of the letter, as the example in Box 7.6 shows. This is just a bare-bones example. You can refine your letter to reflect your own needs and to best appeal to your participants.

Box 7.6   Second Cover Letter

College Letterhead
(return address)

Second mailing date

This is a follow-up to my original letter, a copy of which is attached. As of *(enter the two-week due date)*, I have not received your completed survey. If it is in the mail, thank you for responding. If you haven't yet responded, please do so, as **I really need your help!** It will take only five minutes or so to complete and return the survey so that I can complete the study and graduate on time.

(Attach the original cover letter to your follow-up letter.)

After four weeks, recalculate the response rate. If you haven't reached your goals, you need another follow-up. You can send a third revised cover letter, making a stronger plea for a return, or change your follow-up strategy to making telephone interviews. My preference is a second mailing rather than telephoning nonrespondents.

Telephone interviews require persistence. If you conduct telephone interviews as a follow-up, don't be surprised if it takes several calls to complete one survey. It's usually difficult to get people to return your call, so if someone other than the participant answers, ask for a good time to call back, and leave a message that you called and will be calling again. With voice mail or answering machines, leave a message stating who you are, why you are calling, and that you will call again.

If participants answer but tell you they are too busy, make a plea for help, stating that it will take very little time (approximately five minutes, if your questionnaire is efficiently constructed). If they still say they don't have the time, ask for an appointment so that you can call them at a time when they are able to answer the survey questions. Be sure to call back at the appointed time. Keep trying until you get the person to either answer the questions or outright refuse to do so, at least until you meet your goal response rate. Telephone interviews can also be a way of addressing nonresponse bias, our next topic.

Step 10. Addressing Nonresponse Bias

Nonresponse bias occurs when the participants of the survey do not represent the population. How do you know that the participants in your study *do* in fact represent the population? A random sample helps, but it does not answer the question. In other words, it is possible that the nonrespondents could have a higher or lower level of job satisfaction than the respondents? Their demographics could also be different (e.g., overrepresentation of more highly educated and professional participants). The lower the response rate, the greater is the possibility that the respondents do not represent the population. And if they don't, your study will report incorrect findings, which could mislead people into making incorrect decisions.

Whether you need to address nonresponse bias is based on two major considerations. One is the response rate. The lower it is, the more need there is to verify that nonresponse bias is not a problem. The second consideration is the academic standards of your college and the existence of prior studies. If other researchers with similar or smaller sample sizes and response rates do not address nonresponse bias, you may not need to. However, if you have a low response rate you should consider statistical testing to address nonresponse bias. It's not difficult.

Two ways to address nonresponse bias.

The first way to address nonresponse bias is with follow-up. If you keep at it, the rate of return will increase, which decreases the danger of nonresponse bias. The second way is to statistically test, as we discuss in the rest of this section.

Collecting data from 10% nonrespondents.

People who don't respond to at least two mailings are considered nonrespondents. Set a goal of 10% of the sample. In our example, 10% of 100 is 10. Select a random sample from the nonrespondents. Call them up and try to get them to respond to a telephone survey or visit for a personal interview. Remember that interviewing has a higher response rate than mail survey. If you do not reach your response rate goal, you can use telephone surveys to do so. The telephone surveys can also be used to test nonresponse bias. Once participants answer the questions, they are no longer nonrespondents. Thus, it is correct to categorize them as initial respondents, follow-up respondents, mail and telephone respondents, and so on.

Interview coding.

If you are addressing nonresponse bias, you need to make some indication on the survey that the data was collected by phone or personal interview, such as writing *telephone* at the top of the survey. Each instance of interview-survey data is entered in rows, as is the case with mail surveys. However, to identify the method of data collection you can set up a new variable column (called something like *data method*) and enter a 1 for mail/initial respondent and 2 for telephone/nonrespondent. This variable will allow you to compare differences between the respondent and nonrespondent data.

Statistically testing for nonresponse bias.

There are two methods to test for nonresponse bias statistically. The first method is a *test of difference*. You simply compare the answers of the original respondents to every closed-ended question with the answers of participants who initially were nonrespondents. If there are no significant differences on any questions ($p > .05$), you can make the statement that statistically testing (giving the name of the test—e.g., T-test, chi-square, etc.) found no significant differences; thus, nonresponse bias should not be a problem. However, you cannot say that there is no nonresponse bias. It would require you to get responses from the entire population to ensure that this is true.

If there are significant differences in responses to questions, you can drop questions, assuming there are not too many with major differences. If there are many questions with significant differences, you need to resample. One way is to keep following up with the nonrespondents until they become a large enough percentage of the sample that their answers are no longer significantly different, which will increase your sample size.

A second statistical method is *logistic regression*, which will predict if each sample participant is a respondent or nonrespondent. If the model (all the closed-ended questions) cannot accurately predict to which group each data set belongs, you can claim that nonresponse bias should not be a problem. Both statistics tests are actually easy to run. You will learn how in the statistical chapters 9–14. Box 7.7 continues our example, using the questionnaire in Box 7.3.

Box 7.7   Statistically Testing for Nonresponse Bias

Test of Difference
   Y = Questions 1–14 (different levels of measures and scales)
   X = new variable (nominal data, two scales, original respondent or follow-up respondent).
   You would actually run different tests of difference for some of the different questions based on their measurement levels.

Logistic Regression
   Y = new variable (nominal data, two scales, original respondent or follow-up respondent).
   X = Questions 1–14

CONCEPTUAL OBJECTIVE 4
Explain the need to address nonresponse bias and how it is done.

As a review, and to help you complete exercise 7-3, see Table 7.1. The right-hand column lists where in the research proposal (and completed study) the information in the left-hand column should appear.

Table 7.1   Survey Research Steps (for the Research Proposal Section)

1. Research question/hypotheses	(Introduction and Appendix A)
2. Sampling and survey method	(Method—participants)
3. Constructing the questionnaire	(Method—measurement instrument, an appendix)
4. Determining use of and statistics for each question	(Method—statistical analysis)
5. Developing a cover letter	(included as an appendix)
6. Using a panel of experts	(Method—measurement instrument)
7. Pilot testing	(Method—measurement instrument)
8. Administering the survey	(Method—procedures)
9. Following up (monitoring response rate)	(Method—procedures for follow-up methods in proposal. Actual response rate reported in Participants section of the completed study.)
10. Addressing nonresponse bias	(Method—procedures for how nonresponse bias will be handled, if it will be. Actual results of statistical testing, if used, will appear in a new subsection of the Method section of the completed study)

STOP READING and turn to the end of the chapter to complete exercise 7-3.

7.3 Constructing a Questionnaire

The questionnaire is the heart of survey research. In this section we discuss asking good questions, measurement, scales, and coding questions, as well as question content, types, format, and sequence, followed by avoiding bias. As we cover these topics, we'll use the job satisfaction questionnaire in Box 7.3 as the example.

Characteristics of a Good Questionnaire

Good questionnaires have three important characteristics: They ask the right questions (answer the research question), they are phrased the right way, and they allow appropriate responses. Let's discuss each separately.

Ask the right questions (answer the research question).

It sounds blindingly obvious, and we have repeated it, but it's where most questionnaires fail. What evidence do you have that your survey instrument includes the right questions—that it answers the research question? You will have evidence if: (1) the questionnaire is based on a clear research question/purpose and hypotheses, (2) you have good measures for *all* relevant variables providing descriptive statistics, and (3) you know how you will statistically use the question responses to test each hypothesis so that you provide support for or refute it. All three parts should be based on an extensive literature review. So review prior studies to help you determine your research question, all of the relevant variables related to your topic, and the statistics used to test the hypotheses. You will learn how to select and run statistics in chapters 9–14. The questionnaire in Box 7.3 states that the six determinants of job satisfaction came from the literature, which provides evidence that they are the right questions and that they answer the research question.

Questions must be phrased correctly.

What evidence do you have that your questions are phrased the right way? Following the guidelines here in this section will help you, especially in avoiding bias. However, remember that it is very important to base your terminology on the literature. It's also important that you use a panel of experts and pilot test the questions, making sure they are phrased so that participants can understand what is being asked and can respond appropriately. Since the questionnaire in Box 7.3 states that the six job satisfaction variables came from the literature, it provides evidence that they are phrased the right way, the questionnaire was panel tested with academics and professionals, and it was pilot tested to provide evidence of proper phrasing of questions.

The questions must allow appropriate responses.

Questionnaires usually provide a set list of responses, so remember that the responses must be based on the literature. Responses need to be mutually exclusive (only one answer), exhaustive (all possible answers are offered), and unbiased. (We discuss avoiding bias at the end of this section.) The questionnaire in Box 7.3 presents examples of responses that will help you develop a good questionnaire. They meet the criteria discussed in the rest of this section.

CONCEPTUAL OBJECTIVE 5
Describe the characteristics of a good questionnaire.

Measurement Levels, Scales, and Coding Questions

In this section we talk about scales and coding within the measurement levels.

Nominal level.

Nominal is the lowest level of measurement, which is a labeling activity or a means of categorizing things by arbitrarily assigning values. Many demographic data questions are measured nominally. For example, in Box 7.3, question 9 measures position with two scales—**1**, manager and **0**, nonmanager. The numbers 1 and 0 are arbitrarily assigned values. We could have reversed the numbers or selected 1 and 2 or any numbers. The values 1 and 0 are our coding method for entering the data into the computer rows. Questions 10 (gender) and 11 (job title) also have two scales coded 1 and 0. Question 12 is also nominal, but it has seven arbitrary industries (we could have more or less); question 13 has four scales.

Ordinal level.

The second level of measurement is ordinal, which is a ranking activity and is often an arbitrary assignment of values. In Box 7.3, questions 1–7 are at least ordinal-level data, and many consider it interval-level data. Notice that we have seven scales or points of measurement. However, it is an arbitrary number. We could have had five, four, three, or nine. We also could have reversed the scale so that 1 represented "strongly agree." The numbers 1–7 are also a coding system, as these are the numbers that will be entered into rows on the computer.

For our example hypothesis that managers have a higher level of job satisfaction than nonmanagers, we used a seven-point scale. Having only three ordinal scales makes the levels of measure very similar to nominal. Five scales are OK, and seven is generally a good number of scales. We will revisit this decision under the section on question format.

Interval/ratio level.

Interval is the third and ratio the highest level of measurement. When writing questions keep the difference in mind, but for statistical purposes they are essentially the same. Intervals are standard scores (e.g, IQ, college entrance SAT, and TOEFL test scores). Interval-level measurement also occurs when you set up ranges, such as 1–10, 11–20, and so on. Being the highest measurement level, ratio-level measurement has a true 0 value. Question 14 (age) is the only ratio-level question in Box 7.3.

Interval and ratio levels of measurement do not use any arbitrary scales or codes. Thus, for age (question 14), you don't assign scales and codes to represent a person's age; you use the actual age number.

Using the highest level of measurement for each question.

As you write questions to answer your hypotheses, be sure to keep the level of measurement in mind. Generally, you should use the highest possible level of measurement for each question. You can always decrease a measurement level, but you cannot increase a level of measurement after you collect the data. For example, question 14 could have been (a) nominal—young or old; (b) ordinal—youth, young adult, adult, middle age, senior citizen; (c) interval—20–29, 30–39, etc.; or (d) ratio—What is your age? Ratio-level measurement provides more data because you enter the actual age, and you have the option of lowering the level after you collect the data. However, for sensitive questions such as those relating to income and age, some researchers suggest using intervals to lessen the possibility of participants giving incorrect data.

Nominal coding values and question numbering.

In the questionnaire in Box 7.3, all the nominal questions have been given coded value numbers. You could have written the questions without the numbers and added the code values later. However, if coding the values is done at the questionnaire stage, it does not have to be done later; thus, there is less chance of data-entry error. It is also easier to enter data into the computer when each question has its own number, which represents one variable. Thus, each column represents one question. So, for example, don't have question 1, 2, 3a, 3b, 3c, 4 and so on.

Computer data entry.

In Box 7.3, questions 1–7 would all have separate columns for data entry and the numbers 1–7 would be entered in each row for each participant. Question 8 would have numbers 1–6, questions 9–10–11 numbers 1–2, question 12 numbers 1–7, question 13 numbers 1–4, and question 14's numbers would depend on the actual age of participants. Question

15 is an open-ended question and would not have data to enter into the computer. So we would have 14 variables/columns and 100 rows of data if we reach our sample goals.

CONCEPTUAL OBJECTIVE 6
Discuss general guidelines to the measurement level, scaling, coding, and numbering of questions.

Question Wording and Content

The question is the foundation of all questionnaires, so the wording and content are critically important. The content comes from the research question/hypotheses. The variables identified through the literature are formed into questions to answer the hypotheses. There are two types of related content questions—research and demographic, and factual and subjective—but before we discuss them let's begin with the wording of questions.

Wording.

Although you may be doing academic research, in which a high level of vocabulary is desirable, when you are collecting data you must be as clear as possible. Each question must be worded so that the participant understands its meaning, and the question must have the same meaning for each participant. In general, keep the structure of questions short, and the vocabulary simple and focused on the data you want to collect. Here is an example of a question using two different types of wording:

---

1. How long have you lived in Massachusetts?
2. How many years have you lived in Massachusetts?

You should realize that the second question is worded better. For the first question, although the short line helps to limit the answer, participants could respond with "since I was five" or "since I started college."

You must also use the appropriate wording for the population you are targeting. If you are studying computer programs, for example, feel free to use the technical jargon that programmers will understand. However, if you are studying people who use computers at home for information and entertainment it's best not to use technical jargon, or at least to define the variable terms clearly.

Provide operational definitions for any variables that may be interpreted in different ways by different participants (e.g., the word *liberal*). Notice that in our questionnaire the six determinants were presented before the overall job satisfaction question. This was done intentionally to set a foundation, as was also indicated in the introduction, to answer the overall question. If a foundation was not set, an operational definition based on the six determinants would be needed for question 7, overall.

Research and demographic questions.

The questions in the questionnaire are based on the variables that will answer the research question/hypotheses. Continuing our example, questions 1–8 are all measures of job satisfaction. However, questions 9–14 are all demographic questions that describe the sample that represents the population. Some of the demographic-data questions are also used to test hypotheses with research questions. For example, questions 1–7 measure job satisfaction as the dependent variable, and in questions 9 and 10, position and gender are used as the independent variables to test differences between the two groups in hypotheses 2 from Box 7.1 (managers have greater satisfaction than nonmanagers) and 3 (men have greater job satisfaction than women). Many, but not all, research questions are ordinal and interval/ratio measurements, whereas many demographic questions are nominal.

Factual and subjective questions.

Research-based questions can be both factual and subjective. Factual questions have a specific, correct answer that generally can be proven. Most demographic questions are factual. In contrast, subjective questions are based more on opinions, views, preferences, and so on. In Box 7.3, questions 1–8 are all subjective.

Types of Questions

The three types of questions are closed-ended, open-ended, and contingency questions.

Closed- and open-ended questions and quantitative/qualitative analysis.

We have already discussed closed- and open-ended questions. Questions 1–14 are closed-ended and will be used with quantitative data to run statistics that will test hypotheses. Questions 11 (first part) and 15 are open-ended and will be used for qualitative analysis.

Partially open-ended questions. These are similar to closed-ended questions, but one alternative answer is "other," followed by a blank space so that respondents can add their own answer if none of the other alternatives is appropriate. For example:

What business magazine do you prefer?
1 *Business Week*   **2** *Fortune*   **3** Other (specify) _____

Contingency questions. A **contingency question** *is a special-case, closed-ended question that applies only to a subgroup of participants.* The common format applies to instances where one subgroup answers one or more questions directly related to (and following) the contingency question, while the other subgroup of participants is directed to skip these questions. See the example of contingency questions below, relating to our prior job satisfaction example.

Questions 10 and 11 could be used to further describe the managers in the sample. Question 10 could be used to determine if there is a correlation between years of management experience and job satisfaction. Question 11 could be used to compare scales of job satisfaction by level of manager to see if any level experiences greater job satisfaction. However, with the sample goal of 100, subgrouped into managers and nonmanagers and then by level, the subsamples may be too small to test statistically. In addition, these research questions were not related to the hypotheses.

Contingency Questions
9. My position is a: **0** nonmanager   **1** manager If you are a manager, please answer the next two questions (10 and 11). If you are a nonmanager, please skip to question 12.
10. How many years have you been a manager? _____
11. What level manager are you?   **1** first-level, supervisor   **2** middle manager   **3** top level, executive
12. I am a   **0** woman   **1** man

Question Format

You can choose to write dichotomous, multiple-choice, rating-scale, ranking, checklist, constant-sum, and fill-in question formats. You can also use a matrix to format questions. The format of your question is based on the type of data you are collecting.

Dichotomous questions.

*There are only two possible answers to a **dichotomous question**,* and they are often opposites. True-or-false questions are dichotomous—for example, Are you employed full-time? (**1** yes **2** no). In our questionnaire example, questions 9 and 10 are dichotomous questions.

Multiple-choice questions (forced choice or not?)

Multiple-choice questions have three or more options from which to select. It's sometimes appropriate to offer *other, none of the above, does not apply* (and so on) as options so that you are not forcing a choice when the participant doesn't like the specific options offered. In Box 7.3, questions 11, 12, and 13 are multiple-choice questions. However, they don't include these "other" options because we wanted a forced choice—we felt that one of the offered options would be close enough for accurate participant response.

Rating-scale questions.

Rating-scale questions are subjective questions, with dichotomous descriptors at the two ends of a continuum. There are three types of rating scales: Likert scales, semantic differential, and numerical scales. They don't actually ask a question; they ask for a level of attitude or agreement regarding a dichotomous descriptive statement. Dichotomous descriptions include agree–disagree, good–bad, efficient–inefficient, and so on. The difference between these three types of rating scales is the number of descriptors (words to express the attitude) and the use of numbers on the scale.

A *Likert scale* tends to provide dichotomous agree-or-disagree statements, with each point having a descriptor and number rating. They are named after the researcher Rensis Likert (pronounced Lǐck'-ert), who is credited with making them a common question format. A *semantic differential scale* tends to have two dichotomous (often called bipolar) descriptors at either end of a rating scale *without numbers*. A *numerical scale* tends to have two dichotomous descriptors *with* numbers. See Figure 7.1 below for an example of each type of rating scale. We'll talk more about rating scales in Chapter 9.

Figure 7.1   Types of Rating Scales

Likert Scale

strongly disagree	disagree	uncertain	agree	strongly agree
1	2	3	4	5

Semantic Differential Scale

Fast ___ : ___ : ___ : ___ : ___ : ___ : ___ Slow

Numerical Scale

very dissatisfied						satisfied
1	2	3	4	5	6	7

Number of descriptors and level of measurement.   You have a choice whether or not to use a descriptor with each rating scale point—Likert or numerical. Some researchers consider numerical ranking to be a higher level of measurement (interval) than Likert scales (ordinal). This is because some consider numerical ranking to be more of a continuum, as a descriptor for each number breaks it down into more of an ordinal category rating. However, others believe that Likert scales are interval-level data and that numerical scales can be ordinal. There is also a third contingent, probably the largest, who simply say that they don't believe the number of descriptors matters—that both are interval or ordinal measures. Your decision regarding Likert or numerical should be based on the literature and your school's academic standards.

The disadvantage of Likert scales is that when you use seven or more points on the scale, it gets more difficult to describe them all, and often the middle descriptors don't really help anyway. With semantic differential scales you don't already have the numbers to enter into the computer, so why not include them, making it numerical? Numerical scales tend to have both point and numbering advantages. Questions 1–7 in Box 7.3 only feature *strongly agree* and *strongly disagree* at the two ends of the continuum with seven points—so it is a numerical scale, considered to be an interval-level measure.

Odd or even number of scales?   An odd number of scales provides a neutral or in-between option. However, if you want to force participants to lean towards one side or the other, use an even number of scales such as 8, as shown in the semantic differential scale in Figure 7.1.

Selecting the number of scales.   Although you don't have to use the same number, notice how many scale points were used in prior studies. As noted in our discussion on measurement, seven scales is a good number to use as a general guide. Here are more specific considerations to use when selecting the number of scales.

- As the number of scale points increases, the reliability of the measure increases. Seven is a good general guide.
- More scale points provide a better chance to find variances and statistical differences, so seven is a good general guide.
- As complexity increases, so should the number of scales. Low-involvement products that require little effort or thought to purchase (e.g., deodorant, a fast-food product, or a snack food) don't need so many scales. The three-point rating scale regarding color below is an example.

How do you like the color of our new deodorant compared to your current deodorant color?
1 worse   **2** the same as   **3** better than

So the general guide of seven can sometimes be ignored for a lower number. However, most academic research is complex, and it bears repeating that seven is a good general guide. It's always wise to consider what number has been used in prior studies and to take under advisement the academic standard at your college.

Rate the scales high that represent a higher level.   When you run statistics, it's easier to remember that the higher the mean = average, the higher is the result (rather than having to reverse the scale). In our example, for questions 1–7, strongly agree was purposely rated 7, which represents a high level of job satisfaction. Thus, if the means of the top three determinants were 5.3, 6.2, and 4.8 you would know that the 6.2, rather than the reverse 4.8, is the highest satisfaction rating. However, there is an exception to this rule, known as *responder bias*, which we discuss later in this section.

Stampel scales.   This type of scale uses a plus-to-minus scale—for example, +3, +2, +1 supervisor support –1, –2, –3. To make it more complex, respondents are commonly asked to give descriptors and rate them on the scale provided. However, this is a complex type of question to use with statistics, so it is not recommended for the novice. Instead, just use a numerical ranking scale that is something like "7, very supportive to 1, not at all supportive."

Ranking questions.
Ranking questions are used to show importance or priorities of options. In our example in Box 7.3, question 8 asks participants to select one determinant of job satisfaction as the most important—to rank it highest. However, many questionnaires ask to rank all options, not just to select one.

The data generated by ranking questions are more complex to enter into the computer, as you need a separate column for each variable that is ranked. Asking for the most important one will also give you the top ranking. You can also rank the answers without having to ask participants to do so. For our example, when you run the descriptive statistics, you can get the mean (average) of the six job satisfaction questions. The higher the mean, the higher the ranking of importance. However, if the research question/hypothesis is a ranking from best to worst, then use a ranking question. When you do use ranking questions, be sure to state which number is ranked first (best/most important = 1?) and which is ranked last (worst/least important = 6?). See the example below.

Checklist questions.
Checklist questions allow more than one response to a question. In our questionnaire, there is no checklist question. However, question 8 could be converted into one as shown below.

Ranking and Checklist Questions

8. *(ranking question)* Rank the six determinants of job satisfaction in order of importance to you. Place the numbers 1 (most important) to 6 (least important) on the lines before each item.

8. *(checklist question)* Of the six determinants of job satisfaction, which are important to you? Check all that are important.

_____ Having a positive attitude toward my job.

_____ Enjoying the work I do.

_____ Being fairly paid for my job.

_____ Having a good boss.

_____ Having good coworkers.

_____ Having growth and upward mobility.

Note that for ranking you would need a separate variable column for each of the six determinants; the same as for the checklist form. For ranking, the numbers 1–6 would be entered into the computer rows. For coding the checklist, 1 could be used to represent a check and 0 for no check. Statistically, ranking and checklist questions are more complicated than some other forms of questions. Thus, none were included in our questionnaire example. In essence, you can get the same results by asking for the top ranking only (as was done for question 8 in Table 7.3), because you can get the frequencies of each of the six options and rank them based on how many respondents selected each.

Constant-sum scales.

In this type of scale, participants allocate values (points/percentage/dollars) that must have a set total. See the two examples below. Notice that the constant-sum scale is somewhat similar to the ranking and checklist scales. Thus, it too is also more complex—you should use a separate column for each sum.

Constant-Sum Scales	
Please allocate 100 points for the importance of each of the following characteristics:	Please indicate how much of your $1,000 raise you want divided between:
_____ Food quality	_____ Salary
_____ Atmosphere	_____ Medical insurance
_____ Service	_____ Retirement plan
_____ Price	$1,000 Total
100 Total	

Fill-in questions.

Fill-in questions provide no option, requiring short factual completion. Do not confuse the open-ended question with the fill-in. In our questionnaire example (Box 7.3), questions 11 (job title) and 14 (age) are fill-ins; question 15 is open-ended. Fill-ins work well with ratio-level data, such as number of years of experience. When you use intervals rather than fill-ins with ratio-level data you lose information. For example, with incomes grouped in $20,000 intervals (<$9,999, $10,000–19,999, $20,000–39,999, $40,000–59,9999, $60,000–$79,000, 80,000+) what is the actual income? You don't know, so you end up putting the median/middle range of the interval into the computer, which could be incorrect by close to $10,000 in some intervals.

Matrix questions.

A **matrix question is** *structured to organize multiple rating questions with the same scales.* The matrix makes it easier and faster to answer the question rather than using a separate scale for each related question. In Box 7.3 questions 1–7 are a matrix.

Give every question its own number.   Some researchers use only one number for a group of matrix questions. In our questionnaire example the first seven questions are numbered 1–7. However, only question number 1 could have been used. Each question is numbered because each answer (1–7) to each question must be entered into a variable column's row. Questions 1–14 require 14 variable columns so the question and variable column numbers match, making things easier. It's more complex to have question 1 in 7 variable columns, then question 2 in variable column 8, and so on.

STOP READING and turn to the end of the chapter to complete exercise 7-4.

Avoiding Biased Questions

Biased questions lead to errors in the data collected. Here are some "do's and don'ts" to follow when constructing a questionnaire to avoid bias.

Loaded questions.

Don't use *loaded questions* that include nonneutral or emotionally laden terms. For example, consider these two wordings:

Should radical extremists be allowed to burn the American flag?   **1** yes   **2** no
Should people be allowed to burn the American flag?   **1** yes   **2** no

You should realize that the first version is a loaded question. Respondents are more apt to say no to the first version than to the second version. If you do need to use terms like "radical extremists," give a good operational definition to be sure everyone understands the term in the same way.

Leading questions.

Don't use *leading questions*—indicating to the participant that the researcher expects a certain answer. For example, look at the two pairs of question below:

You do have a high level of job satisfaction, don't you?   **0** yes   **1** no
Do you have a high level of job satisfaction?   **0** yes   **1** no
Shouldn't we increase spending?   **0** yes   **1** no
Do we need to increase spending?   **0** yes   **1** no

You should realize that the first options in each pair are leading questions.

Double-barreled questions.

Don't use *double-barreled questions* that contain more than one idea and have more than one answer (one for each idea). For example:

Do you have a good boss and coworkers?   **0** yes   **1** no
Do you have a good boss?   **0** yes   **1** no
Do you have good coworkers?   **0** yes   **1** no

In the first example, the question features two separate ideas that could have very different answers. Therefore, you need to have two separate questions, as shown in the second and third examples.

Mutually exclusive and exhaustive questions.

Make sure that each question is mutually exclusive and exhaustive. As defined and discussed in the last chapter, each question should have only one answer, and all possible answers should be offered. Refer to Chapter 6, Table 6.1, for an example. In the following example, the first question is not mutually exclusive and exhaustive, and the second question uses a fill-in format that is.

1. How much is your annual salary?

    _____ $30,000–50,000

    _____ $50,000–100,000

    _____ $100,000 or more

2. How much is your annual salary? _____

You should realize that in the first question a person making $50,000 and another making $100,000 have the same choice—the question is not mutually exclusive. Also, there are no options for people making less than $30,000—the question is not exhaustive. The second question can include any amount. Also, the second question provides a higher level of data—ratio versus interval. All of the questions in Box 7.3 are mutually exclusive and exhaustive.

Response set direction (same or mixed) and response bias.

This is not a simple "do or don't," because it depends on the number and complexity of the questions. As suggested, keep the rating-scale direction numbers the same—higher for the higher-level responses—and make the questions easy to answer and shorter with matrix questions.

However, there is an exception when you have a long list of long questions—say 10 or more questions with sentences exceeding 15 words per sentence. Participants may not actually read the questions, thinking that they know how to respond. In such situations, researchers recommend reversing the direction of the rating occasionally (mixing) to keep the reader's attention, or to detect when the participant is not actually reading and answering the questions accurately—response bias.

In Box 7.3, questions 1–7 have a one-directional response set, which is fine because there aren't many questions and they are short. But for illustrative purposes, below we reverse the wording of every other question (from a positive to a negative statement) to ensure that response bias is not a problem.

	strongly disagree 1 2 3 4 5 6 7 strongly agree
1. I have a positive attitude toward my job.	1 2 3 4 5 6 7
2. I do not enjoy the work I do.	1 2 3 4 5 6 7
3. I am fairly paid for my job.	1 2 3 4 5 6 7
4. I don't have a good boss.	1 2 3 4 5 6 7
5. I have good coworkers.	1 2 3 4 5 6 7
6. I don't have upward mobility.	1 2 3 4 5 6 7

A good example of the response bias problem is with standardized student assessments of professors. Students usually either like or dislike their professor, and some of them know that the response set is always in one direction. Consequently, these students don't bother to read the questions—they just give the same, or a similar, response to all questions without actually reading them. With a mixed-response set direction as in the examples above, students who actually want to give a high or low rating to the professor would have to read each question carefully to be sure to maintain the high or low rating. If students don't read the questions, many more professors would end up being rated in the middle as average because the high and low ratings would offset each other. The researchers who make up the questionnaires know, or should know, about this response bias. So why don't the researchers who design standardized student assessments of professors use a mixed response set? Why do administrators and faculty use these standardized one-directional response questionnaires that violate good research methodology with response bias? These are interesting research questions, and ethics could be an issue.

Sequence of Questions

After you write all the questions, making sure that they answer the research question/hypotheses and that there aren't any questions you will not use, you need to consider the placement order of the questions on the survey questionnaire. Here are few guidelines to consider.

Research questions followed by demographic questions.
Obviously, you want the participants to answer all of the questions. If you start out by asking for demographics (background information—age, gender, residence), you are off to a bad start that may end the response process. To entice the participant to complete the survey, start with the interesting research questions followed by the boring ones (to the participants, demographic questions would be the least interesting). How to move from research to demographic questions is illustrated in our example questionnaire in Box 7.3.

Less sensitive to more sensitive.
Respondents are more likely to answer sensitive questions (e.g., questions about income, drug use, sexual experience) after they have committed to answering questions of a less sensitive nature. At one bank a researcher stated that it is very difficult to get people to state their income, and it is not uncommon for them to lie about it (bias.) If you begin by asking for income, you are indeed off to a bad start.

Simple to complex.
We recommend starting with simple-to-answer questions and then asking the complex questions to encourage participants to complete their responses.

Funnel or inverted funnel sequence of questions.
The *funnel sequence* begins with broad questions followed by narrower questions. The *inverted funnel* begins with narrow questions followed by broader questions. Box 7.3 uses an inverted funnel, as questions 1–6 are narrower (more specific and less complex) than questions 7 and 8.

7.4 Increasing Response Rate

Recall that the major weakness of questionnaires is the low response rate that may lead to nonresponse bias. This section presents four things that you can do to increase the response rate, in rank order based on research, including (1) following up, (2) offering inducements, (3) gaining sponsorship, and (4) developing effective cover letters. We also discuss other ways to help increase response rates. But before we get started, let's address this question:

How Large Is an Acceptable Response Rate?

The obvious answer is, the larger the better. However, there is no set percentage. Some fields of research have higher levels than others. Compare your response rate to that of your college and look in the literature for similar studies. You must state your response rate in the completed study. If you are concerned that your response rate is not high enough, you may be able to reference other studies with similar response rates. You can also address nonresponse bias, as discussed.

Follow-Up

Researchers have shown that the leading method for increasing response rate is follow-up. The more contacts you attempt, the greater the response rate. The fewer the questionnaires returned after the original mailing, the greater the need for follow-up. We have already discussed follow-up as the ninth step in survey research, so here we summarize:

- Mail the original cover letter and questionnaire (week 1).
- Send a postcard reminder to return the survey (week 2). This method is not always effective, since it doesn't do any good when the questionnaire has been thrown out.
- Send a revised cover letter and questionnaire (week 4, or week 3 if a postcard hasn't been sent). Some researchers repeat this step twice (instead of the postcard or with the postcard).
- Follow up with certified mail or a telephone call (week 5). Not all researchers follow this step.

Inducement

Inducements are reasons for participants to complete the survey. The inducement, like the research question, needs to overcome the "so what" question. People are busy—why should they take the time to complete your questionnaire? Inducements can be classified as monetary and nonmonetary, and both types can be used together. You can use your creativity to get participants to complete your survey, and you need to be ethical.

Monetary inducements.

Monetary rewards can help increase response rates, and they don't have to be large. Tokens of appreciation do help. For example, researchers have mailed $5–$10 checks, books, or other small items upon return of completed questionnaires.

Rather than give every participant a monetary reward, some researchers have a raffle. For example, $50 (or some item) can be awarded to a person whose name is drawn from among the participants. Companies gaining information to help sell their products more commonly use monetary rewards than academic researchers do.

Nonmonetary inducements.

Although monetary inducements do work, the population and the type of questionnaire have to be considered. Monetary rewards are less important to high-income professionals, and pushing the inducement could possibly lower the response rate. Most academic researchers probably do not use monetary rewards.

An *altruistic appeal* (asking for help for yourself and/or the people who can benefit from the study) combined with an interesting study can often produce better returns than monetary rewards. Many people have a hard time saying no when asked for a favor. Students can write something like, "Please help me by completing this survey so that I can finish my degree and get on with my life." The cover letter in Box 7.5 includes an altruistic appeal.

Interesting research and questions.   Clearly stating the importance of the research (who can benefit from the study and how) can create an interest in completing the questionnaire. You can also ask questions to pique interest. (Notice that the cover letter, Box 7.5 began with a question—Are you satisfied with your job?)

Offering a copy of the results.   A next step related to interest is to offer to send a copy of the completed results to the participant. A student surveying small business owners wrote, "A better understanding of why small businesses succeed and fail can lead to greater success and less failure in the future." He also offered to send the results. Again, see the cover letter in Box 7.5 for an example.

CONCEPTUAL OBJECTIVE 7
Discuss the use of monetary and nonmonetary inducements.

Creativity.
You can also be imaginative with your inducement to help increase response rates. One student sent a cover letter stating that she would like to visit the participant to talk in person, but time and travel constraints would not allow it. She enclosed a tea bag and asked the participant to have a cup of tea and relax while completing the survey. Another student with computer skills was surveying small businesses, most of which do not have websites. He held a raffle with the prize being the development of a Web page for the winning participant. Do you have some special skill or talent that you could use as an inducement?

Ethical issues.
Don't forget about ethics in research. If you tell participants in the sample that you will send them some form of inducement, make sure that you actually send it. Follow through with any raffles. You also must be accurate in reporting your response rate.

STOP READING and turn to the end of the chapter to complete exercise 7-5.

Sponsorship

Sending a questionnaire that is authorized/legitimized by official respected sponsors can increase the response rate.

College or university and advisor.
It is common for students to send out cover letters on college stationery with the name and signature of their research advisor, as illustrated in the cover letter in Box 7.5. If you use e-mail, send the survey though the college e-mail system (preferably from your advisor's e-mail address) but have the results sent to you. With SurveyMonkey, having the data sent to you is easy to do, without the participant even knowing who gets the results.

Professional/trade organizations.
You may be able to get some professional organization to sponsor your research and allow you to use its membership list as the sample frame. If you can convince the organiza-

tion that your research can benefit the organization and/or its members in some way, they may sponsor you. In return for its sponsorship, the organization gets your completed results. Sponsorship level is negotiable and may range from simply letting you use the organization's mailing list and name to providing stationery. It could go as far as having the organization conduct the mailing and pay the cost.

For example, a deaf student was interested in conducting research to compare employees who were deaf with those who were hearing. She persuaded the National Association of the Deaf (NAD), of which she was a member, to be a cosponsor of her college research project. NAD selected a random sample of its members and mailed the cover letter and questionnaire for her. Her advisor got another organization to pay NAD for its expenses. With her advisor and co-sponsor as co-authors, two referreed journal articles were published from the study.

Is it possible to obtain a membership list? Although a professional organization might not sponsor you in any way, you may still be able to acquire a copy of its membership list to use as your sample frame. Without sponsorship you may not increase the response rate, but if you get a good sample frame of people with an interest in your topic it can increase response rate, as stated with inducements. But once again, remember to be ethical.

Management.

If you are conducting research for an organization, you usually need their permission to do so. Using a manager's name and stating that he or she is asking the employees to complete the survey generally results in an extremely high response rate.

STOP READING and turn to the end of the chapter to complete exercise 7-6.

Cover Letter

The cover letter is an integral part of the mail survey package, because it states the inducement to respond. Its primary purpose is to persuade sample members to become participants in the study. We already discussed developing the cover letter content in the fifth step in survey research.

CONCEPTUAL OBJECTIVE 8
Identify and describe four methods of increasing response rate.

Other Methods of Increasing Response Rate

There is strong research consensus that follow-up, inducements, sponsorship, and cover letters do in fact increase response rate. Here we list several methods that do not have consensus. In fact, while some studies have found that these methods do increase response rates, researchers and others find the increase is not significant enough to justify the extra cost involved. So you can decide whether to follow the advice below—and do take the cost into consideration, because it may outweigh the benefits of an undisclosed number of returned surveys that would not have been returned without such methods.

Valuing questionnaire time and length.

Common sense suggests that longer, more complex questionnaires have a higher chance of being thrown out, so try to make the questionnaire interesting and as short as possible. Around 10–15 minutes is a good time length, but remember that *getting accurate answers to the research questions* is the most important goal.

Valuing confidentiality over anonymity.

Research does not support using anonymity (not knowing who responds) over confidentiality (knowing who responds, but not telling anyone). Follow-up is more effective with confidentiality. Thus, use confidentiality unless your survey is of a very personal, private, sensitive nature.

Enclosing a return self-addressed stamped envelope.

Enclosing an SASE makes returning the survey easier, and research has shown that it increases the response rate, but is it cost effective? You can use special prepaid "business reply" envelopes so that you are only charged for surveys that are returned. If you use e-mail this is not an issue, and it is cost effective and very easy to follow up quickly.

Consider the type of postage.

In general, research does not strongly support any evidence of a significant advantage in using first-class mail over third-class, stamped versus metered mail, or a particular type or number of stamps. Thus, you probably need not be concerned about these things. Research does support using expedited delivery to increase response rate. However, the use of special FedEx/UPS/postal overnight delivery service is expensive, and the cost may not be greater than the benefits, especially for students with limited funds. With e-mail this is not an issue.

Personalization.

Research results are mixed as far as any significant advantage in including participants' names and addresses and a personal signature on the cover letter. If you have a title, use it. With mail merge, the personalization of names and addresses is very simple, and signing may not take you long. Your advisor may not want to sign but may give you permission to sign for him or her, but again, it may not be worth the time and effort. With e-mail this is not an issue, but be sure to use your college e-mail address.

Size, reproduction, and color.

Research results do not show any significant advantage in using a particular size of questionnaire, how it is copied (assuming it's not messy and is readable), or if it is on colored paper or uses color on the page(s). My personal preference is to have the package printed as a brochure on 11 × 17-inch paper, folded in half to make each page the U.S. standard 8 ½ × 11-inch size. The first page is the cover letter, and the next three pages contain the questions. It looks professional and you don't need stapled pages. However, shorter or longer questionnaires require different styles. Using online options such as SurveyMonkey helps take care of such details for you.

STOP READING and turn to the end of the chapter to complete exercise 7-7.

Some of the material in this chapter relates to the statistics covered in chapters 9–14, so you may not feel you have a complete understanding of all the material in this chapter. However, you should have a fairly good understanding of it. After you learn about statistics, you can review the concepts in this chapter, and you'll find that it will be clear and straightforward.

SKI WEST STUDY

As we bring this chapter to a close, you should be able to:
- *state advantages and disadvantages of mail/e-mail survey research,*
- *follow the 10 steps of survey research,*
- *construct a questionnaire, and*
- *know the methods to use that will increase response rates.*

Matt McLeish did not use survey research, so this chapter does not apply to his study. The advantage of Matt using secondary-source data collection rather than using a survey is that he did not have to develop a questionnaire or obtain one from another source, he didn't spend any time in interviewing or follow-up, and the response rate was not an issue.

CHAPTER SUMMARY AND GLOSSARY

The chapter summary is organized in a way that provides you with the answers necessary to help you meet the conceptual objectives for this chapter.

1. **Identify the major advantages and disadvantages of the survey questionnaire, as compared to other survey methods.**
   The major advantages of survey questionnaires are the low cost, large geographic sample size, external validity, and reflection and convenience. Disadvantages include the low response rate, slower data collection, and no two-way communication.

2. **State the first step in the survey research process and discuss why it is the starting point.**
   The first step in the research process is to develop the research question/hypotheses. A researcher cannot scientifically meet the purpose of the study unless there is a research question to answer. The other nine steps of the research process depend on the research question; they cannot be completed effectively without hypotheses.

3. **Discuss the need for determining the use of each question and the statistical method to be used with it.**
   The objective of the questionnaire is to answer the research question/test the hypotheses. If a question is not useful for this purpose, it should not be included in the questionnaire. The researcher must determine which questions will be used to statistically test the research question and which statistical test will be used *before* collecting the data to ensure that the research question will be answered (in other words, whether the purpose of the study will be met).

4. **Explain the need to address nonresponse bias and how it is done.**

   Nonresponse bias occurs when the participants of the survey do not represent the population. The smaller the response rate is, the greater the chance of nonresponse bias. With nonresponse bias the results are incorrect, which can lead to incorrect decisions. The two ways to address nonresponse bias are (1) to follow up to increase the response rate and (2) to statistically test it. To statistically test nonresponse bias, you interview nonrespondents (who subsequently become respondents) and compare their answers to the original respondents' data for differences (or prediction). If there are no significant differences or the answers to the questions cannot predict which participants are original or late respondents, you can claim that nonresponse bias should not be a problem.

5. **Describe the characteristics of a good questionnaire.**

   A good questionnaire has three important characteristics: (1) It answers the research question because it is based on a clear research question/purpose and hypotheses, thus creating good measures for *all* relevant variables providing descriptive statistics, and the question responses can be statistically tested to provide support for or refute the hypotheses. (2) Its questions are phrased the right way based on the literature, are reviewed by a panel of experts, are pilot tested, and are possibly statistically tested for multiple measures. (3) Its questions allow appropriate responses based on the literature, and they are mutually exclusive, exhaustive, and unbiased.

6. **Discuss general guidelines to measurement level, scaling, coding, and numbering of questions.**

   As a general guide, use the highest level of measurement possible for each question—ratio/interval, ordinal, or nominal. Use rating scales of seven. Code the questionnaire as part of its format for data entry. Give each question its own number.

7. **Discuss the use of monetary and nonmonetary inducements.**

   Both monetary and nonmonetary inducements increase response rate. Monetary inducements offer some form of tangible value for completing the questionnaire. Nonmonetary inducements focus on altruism and interest in the survey, and the researcher may provide the results of the study to participants as a nonmonetary inducement.

8. **Identify and describe four methods of increasing response rate.**

   Researchers can use follow-up, inducements, sponsors, and effective cover letters to increase response rate. *Follow-up* requires multiple requests to get more questionnaires completed. Monetary and/or nonmonetary *inducements* are offered to encourage survey completion. Researchers can gain *sponsors* from their college or university, professional/trade association, or management. They can develop an effective *cover letter* that includes an introduction, a statement of the research purpose, inducement, an assurance of confidentiality, contact information to answer questions, a statement of the approximate time it takes to complete the questionnaire, the due date for returning it, and an expression of appreciation for completing the questionnaire.

9. **Define the following alphabetical list of key terms.**

Select one or more methods: (1) fill in the missing key terms from memory, (2) match the key terms with their definitions below, or (3) copy the key terms in order from the list at the beginning of the chapter.

checklist questions	fill-in questions	questionnaire
contingency questions	funnel sequence	ranking questions
cover letter	matrix questions	rating-scale questions
dichotomous questions	nonresponse bias	response rate

_____ is a self-administered series of questions through which the researcher answers the research question, commonly sent to participants by mail/e-mail.

_____ introduces the questionnaire with an inducement to complete it.

_____ is the percentage of returned questionnaires; it is the number of completed questionnaires divided by the number delivered.

_____ occurs when the participants of the survey do not represent the population.

_____ is a special-case, closed-ended question that applies only to a subgroup of participants.

_____ have only two possible answers.

_____ are commonly subjective, with dichotomous descriptors at the two ends of a continuum.

_____ are used to show importance or priorities of options.

_____ allow more than one response to a question.

_____ provide no options, requiring factual completion.

_____ structure organizes multiple rating questions with the same scales.

_____ begins with broad questions followed by narrower questions.

WRITTEN ASSIGNMENTS

This survey questionnaire assignment may or may not be required for the type of study or assignment you are doing.

APPENDIX RP, ASSIGNMENT 3 (METHOD AND APPENDIX A: RESEARCH DESIGN)

If your research design's data-collection method is survey, develop a survey instrument or obtain an existing one from another source (e.g., measurement instrument books or the authors of a prior study). The survey instrument should appear in the appendix of the research proposal.

APPENDIX CS, ASSIGNMENT 2 (METHOD)

To complete a study during the course, you may not have time to obtain a questionnaire from other sources. Therefore, you may need to develop one now. To keep it simple, follow the instructions for Assignment 2 below.

APPENDIX SA, ASSIGNMENT 2 (QUESTIONNAIRE AND DATA COLLECTION)

For the statistical analysis papers you must develop a simple questionnaire, regardless of what type of data collection you plan to use. For instructions on developing a questionnaire, go to Part IV, Appendix SA (Statistical Analysis), Assignment 2.

EXERCISES

SURVEY RESEARCH

7-1   Will you use the survey questionnaire as your primary data-collection method? If so, why did you select this method? Be sure to discuss advantages and disadvantages. If not, how *could* you use a questionnaire?

COVER LETTER

7-2   State the major points you can/will make in the cover letter for your survey questionnaire study.

Introduction—yourself, and sponsor if any	Contact for further questions
Your research purpose	Expression of appreciation,
Your inducement	approximate time for completion,
Assurance of confidentiality	and due date

SURVEY RESEARCH IDEAS

7-3   What specific ideas from the survey research steps can/will you use when conducting a questionnaire study?

WRITTEN QUESTIONS

7-4   Compose at least one of each type of question that could be used with your study. Try to develop more research questions than demographic questions. Identify the measurement level, scales, and coding for each of your questions.

Dichotomous	Rating scale	Checklist
Multiple-choice	Ranking	Fill-in

INDUCEMENTS

7-5   What inducement(s) will/could you use to increase your survey questionnaire response rate?

SPONSORS

7-6   Are there any sponsors you will/could use to increase your survey questionnaire response rate?

OTHER INDUCEMENTS

7-7   Which other methods will/could you use, and not use, to increase your survey questionnaire response rate?

Measurement
Reliability and Validity

CHAPTER OUTLINE

CONCEPTUAL OBJECTIVES

The conceptual objectives below also appear at appropriate places within the chapter at points when you will have accessed the information necessary to attain them. They appear again at the end of the chapter in the Summary and Glossary section, along with explanations that will enable you to meet the objectives.

After studying this chapter, you should be able to:

1. Define and state the importance of reliability and validity measurement.

2. Describe the relationship between reliability and validity.

3. Compare the measures of criterion validity.

4. Compare the measures of construct validity.

5. List the steps to enhance validity.

6. Compare the measures of stability reliability.

7. Compare the measures of equivalence reliability.

8. Compare the measures of internal consistency reliability.

9. Explain the difference between intraclass reliability and the other tests of reliability.

10. Identify the minimal acceptable correlation coefficient levels for reliability and validity.

11. Define the following key terms (listed in order of their appearance in the chapter).

reliability	concurrent validity	stability reliability
validity	predictive validity	equivalence reliability
content validity	construct validity	internal consistency reliability
criterion validity	standard error	intraclass reliability

SKILL DEVELOPMENT OBJECTIVES

The exercises that apply to particular skill development objectives are indicated directly beneath each numbered objective below. Periodic instructions within the chapter tell you when to stop reading and direct you to the end of the chapter to complete one or more of the skill development exercises.

After studying this chapter, you should be able to:

1. Determine the reliability and validity of a measurement instrument.
   Exercise 8-1

2. Select the appropriate validity test.
   Exercises 8-2 through 8-8

3. Select the appropriate reliability test.
   Exercises 8-9 through 8-17

The Research Process

(1) The research question/purpose of the study, literature review, and hypotheses.	(2) Research design methodology for collecting data and statistics.	(3) Data analysis and interpreting results.	(4) Discussing results and making conclusions.
• *Introduction*	• *Method*	• *Results*	• *Discussion*
Chapters 1–3	Chapters 4–8	Chapters 9–14	Chapters 9–14

In prior chapters we presented the research process as shown above. This is our last chapter on the research design methodology for collecting data (method). The Method section, covered in chapters 4–8, shows you how to select a research design and sample. It also discusses how to select data-collection methods: secondary sources, observation, and survey (personal and telephone interviews and mail/e-mail questionnaires). In essence, this chapter is a continuation of Step 7 in the research process from our last chapter—Addressing Reliability and Validity. Now that you have a methodology for your data collection, you need to make sure that your measurement instrument is reliable and valid before going on to actually collect your data.

8.1 Measurement, Reliability, and Validity Overview

Let's start by reviewing measurement and levels of measurement, discussed in chapters 1 and 4. Then we present an overview of reliability and validity later in this section.

Measurement and Measurement Levels

In Chapter 1 you learned that measurement is the assignment of number values to dependent and independent variables. In statistical testing there are three levels of measurement: nominal, ordinal, and interval/ratio. Recall from the last chapter that identification of the level of measurement for rating scales as ordinal or interval is debatable. Here we make a distinction by the number of scales used: three or four for ordinal and five or more for interval, as discussed below.

Nominal.

This is the lowest level, in which numbers are assigned to at least two scales of the variable, commonly the independent variable. For example, gender is a variable with two nominal scales—men and women. You arbitrarily assign a number value of, say, 0 or 1 to men and 1 or 2 to women.

Ordinal.

The next level of measurement is ordinal, and rating scales with 3–4 scale points measure variables such as quality (**1** High, **2** Medium, **3** Low).

Interval.

There are at least three types of interval data that don't have an absolute zero (0) measure. The first type is rating scales, with five or more scale points to measure variables such as satisfaction. You arbitrarily determine the number of scales and assign number values to each scale, such as "satisfied—1 2 3 4 5 6 7—not satisfied."

The second type is ratio measures made into intervals. In other words, you arbitrarily determine the number of scale points and assign number values to each scale (e.g., age: 20–30, 31–40, 41–50). You don't arbitrarily assign ages, but you do arbitrarily assign the number of intervals (such as three) and arbitrarily assign a number to each interval (e.g., 1, 2, and 3; or use the middle age, such as 25, 35, 45). When making ratio-level data into interval-level data, you lower the level of measure.

The third type of interval-level measures include standardized tests (e.g, SAT, GRE, TOEFL, and IQ), where there is no arbitrary assignment of numbers.

Ratio.

Ratio-level measurements have an absolute 0 measure, and this type of measure is the highest level of measurement (e.g., fill-in questions on age and income).

Interval/ratio (statistics).

Some interval and all ratio variables have standardized or real numbers; thus, unlike nominal, ordinal, and rating-scale measures, no arbitrary assignment of numbers is done for variable scales. When statistics are run, interval and ratio measures use the same statistical test, but this isn't the case with nominal and ordinal measurement.

See Table 8.1 for a summary comparison of the levels of measurement. Note that the last column in this table has to do with metrics. In Chapter 12 you will learn that inferential statistical tests of significance are divided into two major categories: parametric and non-

Table 8.1   Levels of Measurement

Measure-ment Level	Mutually Exclusive and Exhaustive (categories)	Categories Can Be Ranked (order >)	Standard Unit Measure-ment (fixed intervals)	Meaningful Zero Point (0)	Numbers Are Arbitrarily Assigned (value)	Statistic to Test Hypothesis (metric)
nominal	yes				yes	non-parametric
ordinal	yes	yes			yes	non-parametric
interval	yes	yes	yes		no yes–rating	parametric
ratio	yes	yes	yes	yes	no	parametric

parametric tests. A *metric* is simply a unit of measurement. *Parametric tests* are powerful because they use interval/ratio level measures with random samples taken from a normally distributed population with equal variance. *Nonparametric tests* are less powerful because they use ordinal- and nominal-level measures and are used when parametric assumptions are not met. You already know that you want to use the highest level of measurement feasible for your study. Thus, we prefer to use parametric tests. You will learn more about statistically testing hypotheses in chapters 9–14.

Measurement instruments.

In the Method section of our research, we measure our dependent and independent variables. The common term for our choice of measurement is *measurement instrument*. For example, a survey/questionnaire, an IQ and TOEFL test, and a stopwatch/scale are measurement instruments. When we measure our variables, we must be sure that our measurement instruments are both reliable and valid.

The Importance of Reliable and Valid Measurement Instruments

No matter how much time and effort you spend developing the perfect research question and your hypotheses, if your measurement method/instrument is faulty, your methods, results, and discussion sections of your research process will all be faulty too. You will never really know if you answered your research questions correctly, and most likely you will be in error. Reliability has to do with how well you have carried out your research methods. As you learned in Chapter 1, good research is replicable, so if other researchers agree with your method and can carry out your study your research might be judged reliable.

Before you collect your data, an important part of methodology is to make sure that your measurement instrument is reliable and valid. Ask yourself the following questions: Are you sure that the measurement instrument is dependable (reliability)? Does the instrument measure what you claim to be measuring (validity)? If not, you will collect unreliable and invalid data that can lead to making wrong decisions. If the data analysis is unreliable and invalid, so are your discussion, conclusions, and recommendations. Thus, within the

Method section of your research project you must address reliability and validity—Step 7 of the research process described in Chapter 7.

Defining reliability and validity.

Reliability is the consistency and precision of a measurement instrument. When we say consistency, we refer to measures that are repeatable over time. For example, if I step on a scale and weigh 170 pounds, and I step back on the scale two more times and weigh 165 and 175, respectively, the scale lacks consistency—it is not reliable. (How much do I really weigh?) *Precision* refers to the accuracy of the measurement instrument. If I step on scale #1 and weigh 170, then step on scale #2 and weigh 175, at least one of these scales is not precise. Which one is more accurate? We discuss multiple test methods for reliability later in this chapter.

Validity is the extent to which a measurement instrument measures what it intends to measure. A scale does intend to measure weight. However, when using questionnaires to measure variables like attitudes, it's not so clear that you are truly measuring attitudes. In the next section, we discuss three forms of validity.

CONCEPTUAL OBJECTIVE 1
Define and state the importance of reliability and validity measurement.

The relationship between reliability and validity.

A measurement instrument can be reliable yet not valid, but it cannot be valid without being reliable. A measure can be reliable because it is consistent, but it can be consistently incorrect, making it invalid. Thus, reliability is a necessary but not sufficient condition of validity. Let's continue our scale example. Assume I step on scale #1 three times and weigh 170 pounds each time. Then I step on scale #2 three times and weigh 175 lbs each time. Both scales meet the consistency test of reliability. However, one or both of them are not precise—and therefore not valid. If I really weigh 175, then scale #1 is somewhat reliable (consistent but not precise) yet not valid, and scale #2 is reliable *and* valid. Although scale #2 is reliable, it would not be valid for measuring my body fat percentage. Thus, a reliable instrument is not valid when used incorrectly (as an ordinary scale is not intended to measure body fat).

CONCEPTUAL OBJECTIVE 2
Describe the relationship between reliability and validity.

Use previously validated measurement instruments.

As discussed in prior chapters, whenever possible you should use a measurement instrument that has previously been used and tested for reliability and validity. Doing so will save you a lot of time and effort. When one is not available, you must follow procedures to improve and possibly test your measurement instrument's reliability and validity by using the methods discussed in this chapter.

STOP READING and turn to the end of the chapter to complete exercise 8-1.

8.2 Validity

How do we know whether we are measuring what we intend to measure? When a teacher gives an exam, the purpose is usually to measure students' knowledge. However, do the students with the higher grades really have more knowledge? The problem is that the researcher never really knows for sure if differences in results obtained by the measurement instrument are truly valid, because the validity refers to the results of the test and not to the test itself. There is no such thing as complete validity or complete invalidity; it is on a continuum or progression of degree from low validity to high validity. The measurement instrument is also interpreted within the context in which it is used. For example, a valid geography test would not be valid if used in an algebra class. Validity is commonly classified into three types: content, criterion, and construct.

Content Validity

Content validity of a measurement instrument is the extent to which it provides adequate coverage of the variable. Content validity is also called face validity and requires both item validity and sampling validity. *Item validity* concerns how well the items represent measurement in the intended content area, and *sampling validity* concerns how well the instrument samples the total content area. Let's use a management questionnaire as an example. Content validity refers to the adequate coverage of the questions: Do all the questions actually measure the management variable? Are there enough questions to adequately measure the variable (i.e., are planning, organizing, leading, and controlling covered)?

Content validity (literature and panel-of-experts measurement).

This type of validity is a weak measure of validity because it doesn't actually assess the measurement itself; rather it is the extent to which a measurement instrument actually measures what it intends to measure. Although content validity is a subjective measure, following these steps can help support the validity of your measurement instrument:

1. Review and cite the literature as a foundation for your variable selection to study.

2. Write clear, measurable operational definitions of variables, based on the literature.

3. Write clear, measurable hypotheses, based on the literature.

4. Have a panel of experts review the measurement instrument as a source of validity.

We have already covered these steps in prior chapters—Chapter 7 for questionnaires. As a review, ask yourself the following questions: Does your measurement instrument (questionnaire) provide the data to answer the research questions/hypotheses? What statistical test will be run to test each hypothesis? There should be a statistical use for each question. The panel of experts reviews your measurement instrument to suggest any necessary changes, additions, or deletions. Your panel of experts provides validity to your measurement instrument (your questionnaire).

Content validity ratio.

The *content validity ratio* provides stronger support for the content validity of the panel of experts' judgment, making it structured and testable. It requires that each panel member is asked not only for improvements, but also to follow a structured format by rating each question of the survey instrument as essential, useful, or unnecessary. Essential questions are usually research questions. Useful questions are not essential; their answers commonly result in demographic data not used to test hypotheses. Unnecessary questions are not relevant to the study.

Although not a true statistical test, to measure the content validity ratio simply count how many panelists rate each question in each of the three categories. The more similar the rating ratios, the stronger the support for content validity is. Doing a good job of basing the questionnaire on the literature and knowing the statistical use for each question to answer the research question hypotheses should result in a high content validity ratio.

The size of your panel of experts affects the strength of content validity. The more experts you have, the stronger the support for content validity. There should be least three experts on a panel and preferably five or more. Remember that experts can be professors in the subject area and professionals working in the field of study.

Criterion Validity

The **criterion validity** *of a measurement instrument is its correlation score with other established measurement instrument scores.* For example, let's say you developed a new high-tech way to measure length. Current measures of length include rulers, tape measures, calipers, odometers, and so on. How do you know if your new measurement method is as good as, or better than, current (criteria) measures? If you measure distances with both your new measurement method and the old methods (criteria) and the length is the same or is more accurate (correlation), you have support for criterion validity of your new measurement method. An observation method that correctly categorizes families by current income level, for example, has concurrent validity.

Concurrent and predictive validity.

Criterion validity is classified as either concurrent validity or predictive validity, depending on the time sequence of measurement. *Concurrent validity measurement is taken at the same time as the criterion measure.* **Predictive validity** *forecasts a measurement in relation to the criterion measure.* With concurrent validity the new measurement instrument is compared to the standard measurement instrument at approximately the same time (concurrently). However, with predictive validity the measure of one variable is taken and may be correlated with the criterion measure at a later date to determine its prediction accuracy. Thus, with concurrent measures you get immediate statistical support for the validity of the new measurement instrument, but with predictive you generally have to wait to run the statistics to determine validity.

Concurrent criterion validity of new measurement instruments (correlation measurement).

Criteria exist for standardized tests—for example, tests to measure intelligence (IQ), scholastic aptitude (SAT), graduate record examination (GRE), graduate management admission test (GMAT), English foreign language (TOEFL), and so on. Let's say that you have developed a new shorter version of a standardized test (it would take only one quarter to one half the time to administer the test—1 or 2 hours instead of 4 hours). This new test would be a great time saver. The question is: How do you know whether the new, shorter test is as valid a measure as the existing test? To answer this question, follow the steps below.

1. Administer the new test to a sample of individuals.

2. Administer the criterion test (or acquire scores if already available) to the same group, at the same time, or shortly thereafter.

3. Correlate the two sets of scores (you want to know whether people get the same score on both tests).

4. Evaluate the results. If there is a correlation—if people get approximately the same scores on both tests—you conclude that your new test is valid and the new time-saving test can safely be used. In Chapter 13 you will learn how to run tests of correlation and regression to evaluate the results of concurrent and predictive validity.

Use a test of difference.   Although correlations are commonly run, you can also use a test of difference, using a matched pair T-test to determine if the two scores are the same (i.e., they support the new test) or statistically different (i.e., they do not support the new test). In Chapter 12 you will learn how to run tests of difference.

You can also compare a subjective measure to an objective measure.   For example, say you have a criterion observation form that sports scouts use to evaluate players. You can compare scouts' reports without using the criterion form to determine if there is a correlation in recommendations of the athletes scouted.

Sample size counts.   You should have at least 25 participants to run correlation. However, as with most statistical tests, you can run statistics with a smaller sample size using nonparametric statistics.

Predictive criterion validity (regression measurement).

If you were a college administrator, how would you know if criterion tests—standardized tests to predict college success at the undergraduate (SAT) and graduate level (GRE/GMAT)—can actually predict success at your college? To answer this question, follow the steps below.

1. Administer the predictive test to a sample of individuals (SAT and GRE are given by a testing company).

2. Wait until the predicted criterion behavior occurs (e.g., students complete their first year, students graduate).

3. Obtain measures of the criterion for the sample (cumulative grade point average—GPA).

4. Regress the two sets of scores (using correlation, SAT/GRE scores to predict GPA).

5. Evaluate the results. If there is a significant prediction/correlation between SAT/GRE and GPA scores, the test is a valid predictor of college success. In other words, the students with the highest SAT/GRE scores get the highest grades, and therefore the existing criterion tests are a valid part of admissions standards.

Notice that the major difference between concurrent and predictive validity is the time dimension of measuring the two scores. With concurrent validity you measure the new and old at approximately the same time, but with predictive validity you generally take the measure and wait until a later date to see if the forecasted performance is accurate. However, there is one way of getting around the waiting period, discussed below.

Prediction based on current performance (regression).

Although not as highly valid, you can save a lot of time by not waiting for the behavior to occur over a certain time period. For example, a researcher developed a business success-versus-failure prediction model. Rather than using a group of startup businesses and waiting for several years to determine if each succeeds or fails, the researcher used a sample of known successful and failed businesses and measured each business with a fifteen-variable model. The measures of the fifteen variables were used to predict whether each business was a success or failure. Because the model successfully predicted the known success and failure of these businesses, it is assumed that the model will also be valid for any new startup businesses.

Note that regression also helps to contribute to content validity, as it indicates which variables do in fact predict performance. You can add questionable variables to test their predictive powers. As a result, variables that are not significant predictors can be eliminated.

Your sample size should be at least 10 participants per independent variable (IV/X) and preferably 25. Thus, a prediction model with seven Xs requires a sample size of at least 70 and preferably 175.

The criterion test must be valid.

In the examples above there are clearly standard valid measures. However, when doing business research for an organization, the criterion may be set by the researchers, and thus the criterion test must be valid. For example, let's say that a company wants to develop its own pre-employment test to predict sales success. Thus, only candidates that do well on the test will be hired for the job. How do you know the test is valid before you run regression sometime in the future to determine if the test results do in fact correlate with sales success? To answer this question, a criterion test must have four qualities.

First, the criterion test should be relevant. Are the questions/variables true measures of sales success? You need to search the literature and organization to find out what it really takes to be a successful person for the company, and a panel of experts can help. Second, the test must be free of bias. Does everyone who takes the test have an equal chance of doing well? Again, a panel of experts can help. Third, the test also needs to be reliable. Will the candidates have the same score if they take the test multiple times? We discuss test-retest to address reliability later in this chapter. Finally, the information specified by the criterion must be available.

As discussed with prediction based on current performance, you can give the test to current salespeople and see if the salespeople with the higher test scores do in fact have higher sales. Hopefully, you have some poorly performing salespeople to make the distinction possible.

As discussed with predictive validity, you must use the test for hiring purposes. Later, maybe after one year on the job, run regression to determine if in fact there is a correlation between the test scores and actual sales. The test may need to be changed to improve its predictive power of accuracy. There are professional measurement-instrument people who develop and sell a variety of tests to predict job success, and other types of tests.

Validity records are mandatory.   If you do develop a pre-employment or promotion test of some type, you must have records of validity, as discussed above, because you can be brought to court and charged with discrimination claims that the test is not a valid predictor of job success. If you don't have any records (statistical tests, for example), you will lose the case and may be fined and forced to stop using the test. Professionally developed tests should include records of test reliability and validity.

CONCEPTUAL OBJECTIVE 3
Compare the measures of criterion validity.

Construct Validity

Construct validity assesses the theory and the measurement instrument. A *construct* is a nonobservable trait that cannot be measured directly (e.g., scholastic aptitude, intelligence, motivation, and leadership). A construct is based on a group of related hypotheses and variables that form a theory (i.e., it explains and/or predicts the relationship between the variables that form the theory). For example, intelligence is based on memory, comprehension, logical thinking, spatial skills, and reasoning. Thus, you first develop a theory of intelligence, then you develop and statistically test a measurement instrument to measure it (the IQ test). So construct validity is time consuming and often difficult to establish. It requires good operational definitions and hypotheses based on the literature.

Construct validity is established through statistical testing, and generally a number of independent studies are required to establish the credibility of a test of a construct. The theory of intelligence and the IQ test have credibility. Next we present three measures of construct validity; in later chapters you will learn how to run and analyze the statistic tests.

Convergent construct validity (correlation measurement).

Convergent validity is very similar to concurrent validity. However, a construct can't be directly measured—but a criterion, such as our example of length, can be. Constructs with multiple measures may have different tests to create a new criterion. For example, when developing the IQ test, there could have been one test to measure memory, another test for comprehension, and other variables. Thus, convergent validity may be based on multiple criterion tests—it can be multitrait, multimethod validity. As with criterion validity, the research expects high correlations; but with discriminant validity, low correlations are expected to support differences.

For your sample size, again the minimum for correlation is 25.

Discriminant construct validity (correlations or tests-of-difference measurement).

Discriminant tests are used with groups that are either determined by the researcher or are currently known to possess and not possess different levels of a construct. For example, one group is determined or known to be intelligent and the other is not. Both groups take the IQ test and their scores are either correlated or compared for differences using a T-test (discussed in Chapter 12). If the scores are not significantly correlated or significantly different, you can conclude that the IQ test discriminates levels of intelligence.

For your sample size, you should have at least 25 per group. Thus, in the IQ test you would need 50 participants.

Factor construct validity (factor analysis measurement).

A high-level statistical analysis to determine construct validity uses factor analysis, which groups a large number of interrelated factors. According to David Krathwohl (2009),[1] "Factor analysis is a statistical procedure that, by examining interrelationships among items, helps to identify the dimensions underlying a measure and hence what it is measuring" (p. 409). All factors that measure the variables of a construct should be grouped together, as in the following example.

Your goal is to measure attitude toward research as our construct, using three proposed variables or factors: verbal (V), mathematical (M), and oral presentations (OP). You develop an 11-item questionnaire to measure these three variables that make up our research construct. After administering the questionnaire, the first statistical step is to compute all the inter-item correlation coefficients for all 11 items on the questionnaire. The computer program computes factor loadings. The following factor loadings in Table 8.2 are fictitious ones that clearly represent how they are to be interpreted (real ones are more difficult to interpret for the beginner—note that you must add the proposed column, the *s, and the Xs, as well as label the factors (give the variables a name, because the computer can't name them).

If the questionnaire has construct validity there should only be three factors, and each proposed factor should *load* (in other words, it should be in the same factor group—determined by the highest correlation coefficient/number). As you can see in Table 8.2 below, this is not the case.

- "Star" the factor loadings above .40 (factor loadings are the highest correlation of the item in a row, with * indicating high factor scores in Table 8.2). Since there were four factors generated by the computer and only three variables/factors were originally proposed, the construct/questionnaire requires revision (assuming some logic can be placed on the items in the fourth factor).

- Item 3 (row X3) should be dropped since it double loads onto two factors and thus is not clearly representative of one or the other, and item 8 (row X8) should be dropped because it does not have a high correlation with any of the factors and is thus measuring some other factor not proposed as a variable of the construct.

Table 8.2   Factor Loading

Item	Proposed	Factor I	Factor II	Factor III	Factor IV
1	Verbal	.78*	.08	.111	.23
2	V	.12	−.11	.24	.43*
X3	V	.66*	.13	.63*	.01
4	Oral pres.	.22	.13	.55*	.22
5	Math	.13	.56*	.11	.08
6	V	.88*	.23	.18	.24
7	M	.34	.59*	.13	.11
X8	M	.11	−.13	−.34	.22
9	V	.13	.34	.25	.44*
10	OP	.34	.22	.49*	−.13
11	V	.69*	.34	.22	.08
		V	**M**	**OP**	**PT**

variables — what we say is measured — computer calculations

verbal — mathematical — oral presentations — attitude toward participant testing

- Factor I should be labeled *attitude toward verbal aspects of research* (V, as indicated at the bottom of the third column) since items 1, 6, and 11, which were all proposed to measure verbal attitudes, best represent it (i.e., they measure highest for this factor).

- Factor II should be labeled *attitude toward mathematical aspects of research* (M, as indicated at the bottom of the fourth column), and items/questions 5 and 7 are the items that measure highest for this factor.

- Factor III should be labeled *attitude toward oral presentations* (OP, as indicated at the bottom of the fifth column); items 4 and 10 are the items that represent this factor.

- An option to handle the fourth factor is to drop items/questions 2 and 9 to eliminate Factor 4. However, the question arises: Do you have a content valid questionnaire if you drop 4 of 11 questions/items? You may need more questions to replace the ones you drop—and you may actually have four variables in your construct.

- After looking more carefully at the wording of items/questions 2 and 9 (which were both proposed to be verbal but loaded high on Factor IV), you discover that they both have to do with testing the participants in studies. Conceivably there could be an attitude toward this phase of the research process. Thus, a revision in the number of factors may be needed, and Factor IV could be labeled *attitude toward participant testing* (PT, as indicated at the bottom of the sixth column), with items 2 and 9 representing this factor.

- Whenever you add new questions or change the wording of prior questions, you must retest the questionnaire by having participants complete it again and running factor analysis. This process continues until you have only the number of factors that match the number of proposed variables, and when all factors of the variable load together.

Note that factor analysis also contributes to content validity, as it helps you to determine which questions to change and delete.

To be a valid factor analysis, as with regression the sample size should be at least 10 (and preferably 25) participants per item. Thus, with 11 items/questions the minimum sample size needed is 110 and preferably 250. In a college with small enrollments in a research class, testing construct validity with factor analysis may not be feasible.

Standardized scores need statistical testing. You should realize that you cannot simply make up your own measurement instrument with multiple questions to measure a variable, take an average score, and call it a standardized score without running factor analysis to validate that all questions do in fact measure this variable. This is true even if you use a panel of experts. For example, let's say you want to measure employee motivation and write seven questions on a Likert scale of 1–7. You cannot get an average of the seven questions, such as 5.2, and call it the one/overall/standard level of motivation unless you run factor analysis and validate that all seven questions load on only one factor. Without factor validation you must analyze the results of each of the seven questions separately.

Recall that this is what we did in the last chapter with the job satisfaction example. We did not combine the six variables to get one overall job satisfaction score. We simply asked for the overall job satisfaction as a separate score. Clearly, running factor analysis to validate the combination of the six variables (multiple measures) into one score is a more valid measure than one simple question (single measure). However, to statistically test a questionnaire is time consuming and advanced beyond the skills of most novice researchers.

Remember to use a previously validated measurement instrument/questionnaire whenever possible so you don't have to waste time and effort validating your own. When using a previously validated instrument, report the validity statistical measures. Previously validated tests typically report the *Cronbach alpha correlation coefficients*: The higher the coefficients, the higher the level of validity of the measurement instrument. (We discuss correlations in more detail in Chapter 13.) Factor analysis results may also be given.

CONCEPTUAL OBJECTIVE 4
Compare the measures of construct validity.

Enhancing Validity

Although we discussed the three types of validity separately, they are actually interrelated. Experts suggest trying to address all three types of validity in your study. The common approach to enhance validity used by researchers is to:

1. First focus on the literature theory, which addresses content validity (using a panel of experts helps).

2. Then develop the measurement instrument (or use a previously validated one) to address content validity.

3. Finally, statistically test the measurement instrument with criterion and/or construct measures.

Before we discuss these steps in more detail, review Table 8.3 for a summary of the three types of validity.

Table 8.3   Types of Validity

Type of Validity	What is Measured	Measurement Methods*/ Statistical Test
Content	The extent to which it provides adequate coverage of the variable.	literature/panel of experts/ content validity ratio
Criterion	Its correlation score with other established measurement scores.	correlation/ tests of difference
• Concurrent	Current performance is taken at the same time as criterion measure.	regression
• Predictive	Forecast a future performance with criterion measure.	
Construct	Assesses the theory and the measurement instrument.	correlation
• Convergent	Similar to concurrent with nonobservable traits, multi-measures.	correlations/ tests of difference
• Discriminant	Tests known groups that do and don't possess trait for differences.	
• Factor	Tests the correlation of items with variable factors.	factor analysis

*Note that all measures should be based on the literature, which is the foundation for measurable operational definitions and hypotheses.

Using the correct measurement statistical test.

The research design commonly places more emphasis on one or more types of validity for measurement statistical testing. Thus, to enhance validity you must know when to use which validity measurement statistical test. Complete exercises 8-2 through 8-8 to develop your skill at understanding which type of validity measurement and statistical testing is most appropriate for a specific research design.

Steps to enhance validity.

By following these steps/methods you can enhance the validity of your measurement instrument:

1. Review and cite the literature as a foundation for your construct and variable selection to study.

2. Write clear, measurable operational definitions of variables, based on the literature.

3. Write clear, measurable hypotheses, based on the literature review and operational definitions.

4. Use a previously validated measurement instrument or have a panel of experts review your measurement instrument as a source of validity.

5. Pilot test the measurement instrument by using it. Having participants complete the instrument/questionnaire will help improve it and make sure it is used correctly (as discussed for questionnaires in Chapter 7).

6. Statistically test validity.

CONCEPTUAL OBJECTIVE 5
List the steps to enhance validity.

**STOP READING and turn to the end of the chapter
to complete exercises 8-2 through 8-8.**

8.3 Reliability

Recall that reliability refers to the consistency and precision of the measurement instrument. To be reliable, your measurement instrument must give approximately the same measure every time the same participant uses it, even under different conditions—if not, you have measurement error that lowers the reliability of your instrument. If your measurement instrument is not reliable, it can't be valid. Therefore, you have to address reliability—the eighth step in survey research. Reliability is concerned with minimizing measurement error, so researchers estimate reliability for stability, equivalence, internal consistency, and intraclass reliability. These are the topics of this reliability section. Although reliability tests are not as valuable as validity determination, reliability is much easier to assess.

Measurement Error and Decreasing Error

Reliability indicates the extent to which a measurement instrument contains variable errors. Any measure consists of a true component and an error component that indicates the measure's reliability. The obtained score is the score the participant gets on a test (an IQ test, for example).

Obtained score = True Score + Error Score

We never really know the true score, but we do know that there is an error score. Some of the possible reasons for error include:

Participant errors.

On the day of the test, if a participant was not feeling well, was anxious, had a memory block, was bored, was distracted, or was in a bad mood, any of these factors could result in an error score, lowering the reliability.

To decrease measurement error, be sure to properly prepare participants for the measure (i.e., providing good, clear instructions), and try to catch participants at the best time to reduce error and get a true score.

Situation errors.

Where the test is given can also result in error (e.g., if the room temperature is too hot or cold, if the test itself is hard to read, if the lighting is poor, and so on).

To decrease error, try to standardize the situation for all participants—each time it is measured.

Measurer errors.

The person giving the test could also cause an error score (e.g., if the tester gives poorly worded or incorrect instructions). An error could also occur during the scoring process. When dealing with subjective tests, different measurers could score the same answer to a question with a higher or lower score. An interviewer could record answers incorrectly. Two of the reliability correlation coefficients focus on testing the measurer.

To decrease error, be sure to train the measurers and conduct a test of stability for test administrators and an interrater test for equivalence.

Measurement instrument errors.

The measurement instrument (test or questionnaire) could have poorly worded questions that the participant does not understand. The measurement instrument is the major focus of several correlations to test reliability.

To decrease error, be sure to test stability with the test-retest, equivalence with parallel forms, and internal consistency with the split-half and alpha correlation formulas. These are discussed later in the chapter.

Relative reliability (correlation and test-of-difference measures).

If there is no error, the *relative reliability* is 1.00, indicating a perfect correlation score/coefficient between the two measures of the same instrument. The range of coefficients is +1.0 to –1.0. A coefficient of 0 would indicate no relationship between the two measures, or that the instrument is not reliable at all. (You will learn more about correlation coefficient measures in Chapter 13.) The greater the error, the lower the reliability < 1.00. For example, if we know that the score was 75 and we estimate the error score as 3, then reliability is .96.

Unfortunately, it's not that simple to measure reliability because we don't know the true score or error score—they are estimated. There are three correlation coefficients (stability, equivalence, and internal consistency) with which to measure relative reliability and tests of difference (intraclass). The relative correlation measures focus on the consistency of the measurer and the measurement instrument.

Absolute reliability (standard error measures).

The *absolute measure of reliability* focuses on the *precision* of the measurement instrument. It is the standard error (SE) of the measurement. SE estimates how often you can expect errors in a given test size. The obtained score is really an estimate of a true score. *The standard error (SE) estimates how much difference there probably is between participants' obtained scores and true scores.* The size of the difference (variance) is a function of the reliability of the test.

To determine the SE, you need to know the reliability coefficient and the standard deviation of the test scores. The SE is calculated for you, or it is given when you run several statistical tests. The lower the SE, the more precise is the measurement. However, SE is relative to the size of the test. For example, an SE = 5 would be large for a 20-item test because it means that an obtained score of 15's true score is between 10 and 20 (15 +/− 5). However, if the test has 200 items, SE = 5 is small, as the true score estimate is between 145 and 155. The range of estimated true scores (+/− SE) is also known as the *confidence interval,* which should contain the true score. The confidence interval can also be calculated for you when running statistical tests.

Stability Coefficients

Stability reliability measures the variability of scores using correlation coefficients of the measurement instrument itself (test-retest) and the measurer (test administrator) at two points in time. There are two types of stability coefficients: test-retest reliability and test administrator reliability. While the first (test-retest) focuses on the measurement instrument itself, the second (test administrator) focuses on the administrator of the test rather than the test itself. Stability is used primarily to test for participant and situational error measures from one time to another.

Test-retest reliability (correlation measure).

Test-retest reliability measures variance in scores using the same measurement instrument with the same participants at two points in time to determine stability of measures. The *variance* refers to the differences in scores at the two different points in time. For example, if you got an IQ score of 100 today and 99 tomorrow, the test is highly reliable. However, if you scored 100 and subsequently scored 130, it's not very reliable. To actually measure the stability coefficient, you correlate the test from time 1 and time 2 for the sample. You can also run a test of difference between the two test scores. The higher the correlation coefficient, the more support for the stability reliability of the measurement instrument. A coefficient of .80 or higher is considered acceptable, as you can expect errors. Remember that each test is subject to the four types of errors we already discussed. Here are two other possible errors.

Time and practice errors.   Two common errors can occur using the test–retest method—errors of time and practice. If the time between the two tests is short, participants may remember their answers from the last time and select the same answers, but if the time is too long, a change in other situational factors may be the cause of the new score. With some measures learning can take place though testing (a form of practice), so the participant might do better the second time.

Addressing errors.   How long a period should elapse between the two test measures will depend on the potential for time and practice error. With a test in which participants can learn or remember their answers, the elapsed time should be longer—often between two weeks and one month. However, if you wait too long the measure could change due to other factors, such as a change in attitude about job satisfaction. Something could have changed between measures—perhaps the participant got a raise or promotion—to increase the score on the second measure. With an IQ test, participants don't learn anything that will help them the next time they take the test. Because there are so many questions, participants will most likely not remember their answers and try to repeat them. Under such circumstances a short elapsed time like a day or a week is fine. Also, if you are conducting research you don't want to hold up your study any longer than necessary.

Test administrator reliability (correlation measure).

Test administrator reliability measures variance in scores using the same sole administrator/measurer with the same participants at two points in time. For example, a teacher gives an essay test or research paper to a class today. The same teacher corrects the test or research paper within two weeks of giving the test and re-corrects it a month later. Do the students get the same scores both times? You can run a correlation or test of difference to find out how reliable the teacher is at grading consistently. In another example, an interviewer reads 20 resumés (or watches a video of 10 job candidates being interviewed) and does an evaluation of each. The same interviewer reads the 20 resumés (or watches the same 10 candidates on video) again at a later date and re-evaluates them at that time to measure evaluator consistency. The time between test periods is subject to the same considerations as test-retest reliability.

Grading (job candidate evaluation) rubrics are being used today to help address this problem by making subjective judgments (e.g., essay test questions and candidate selection) more objective for both the students/job candidates and the teacher/hiring person. Students are given the grading rubric prior to taking the test or writing the research paper to help them do well, and the job candidates are given the job description and specification to help them prepare their resume and interview. The interviewer rating form is based on the job description and specifications, and the form is used to evaluate each candidate on these criteria.

CONCEPTUAL OBJECTIVE 6
Compare the measures of stability reliability.

Equivalence Coefficients

Equivalence reliability measures the variability in parallel forms of the measurement instrument and multiple measurers (interrater reliability) using correlation coefficients. The two types of equivalence coefficients are parallel forms and interrater reliability. The equivalent parallel forms focuses on the multiple measurement instruments measuring the same thing, whereas the interrater focuses on how reliable multiple measurers are. Equivalence is used primarily to test for participant and situational error measures at one point in time among tests and testers.

Parallel forms reliability (correlation measure).

Parallel forms include two or more versions of the same test given to the same group of participants at the same time. It is also called *equivalent-form reliability* and *alternative-form reliability*. The SAT and GRE college tests and TOEFL use multiple tests, as does the Registry of Motor Vehicles and other organizations. To test the reliability of the multiple tests, you give both versions of the test to the same people at approximately the same time to test the equivalency of the items from one test to another. You correlate the two test scores to determine if the coefficient is high enough to state that the multiple tests are equivalent. You can also run a test of difference to compare the two scores. "Approximately the same time" means that you can take a break between tests. For example, group 1 gets version A of the test and group 2 gets test B, followed by an hour break. Then group 1 takes test B and group 2 takes test A. (If there were only one version of these tests given many times, people could learn the questions and answers and might cheat.)

Errors and addressing errors.

One common problem is making both tests equal. To provide support of equivalency, each test should have the same number of items/questions/measures, at the same level of difficulty, and featuring the same examples, format, instructions, and time limits. This is difficult to do but can be statistically tested for reliability. Again, a correlation coefficient between the two tests of .80 or higher is an acceptable level of error.

As with test-retest, there is also the potential for practice to cause an increase in the second score. However, because the two tests are different, there is less chance for practice error in scores. To address this potential problem, some organizations like the SAT and GMAT actually encourage practice by offering "example tests" and test preparation courses given by other organizations. However, this doesn't work with all types of measurement instruments, so you need a delayed time between measures.

Interrater reliability (correlation measure).

Interrater reliability is used when multiple raters (rather than multiple versions of the same test) score the same participant at the same time. Some competitive sports, including gymnastics, figure skating, and diving, use a panel of judges to score participants to determine the winner. Using a panel rather than one judge makes the judging more reliable, and often the high and low scores are eliminated and the others averaged (or at least all the scores are averaged). You can statistically rate the judges by how much their scores vary from the average score for each participant. You can statistically run a correlation between the average score and the rater's score to test for this error. You can also evaluate each judge and compare them, using percentage of agreement with the average, using this simple equation.

$$\text{Interrater Reliability} = \frac{\text{Number of Agreements}}{\text{Number of Possible Agreements}} \times 100 \quad \frac{50}{75} = .666 \text{ or } 67\%$$

As you can see, one judge rated the athletes the same as the average rating only 67% of the time; thus the interrater reliability is not too high for this rater. You can calculate the reliability of each rater and rank them to determine which are more reliable than others. This same assessment can be used with job candidates. For example, six managers each evaluate 10 candidates with a rating form on a scale of 1–10. You get the average score and compare each manager's scores to the average to see who rated each candidate higher or lower. You could also have them rank the top five candidates and compare their selections for interrater reliability.

You can also test for bias. For example, some Olympic judges have been accused of rating the athletes from their country higher than those of other countries. If you are trying to claim bias, you must compare the number of agreements with the same country's athletes and the other countries' athletes. If the two sets of ratings are significantly different—say, a judge rates other countries' athletes the same as do the other judges 40% of the time but rates his/her own country's athletes higher 70% of the time, you have strong support for claiming bias. The same can be done with the candidate raters based on gender, race, or other factors. You may find that some managers rate people like themselves higher than those who are different from them.

In the business setting, some managers have been accused of bias against women and minorities when it comes to hiring, merit raises, and promotions. Corrective action can be taken against raters who significantly differ from the average of the ratings, or who are biased.

CONCEPTUAL OBJECTIVE 7
Compare the measures of equivalence reliability.

Internal Consistency Coefficients

Internal consistency reliability measures variability within the measurement instrument among items using the split-half and alpha methods. Internal consistency reliability is a concern when there are multiple questions/statements/trials/games measuring the same variable. For example, a personality test has six questions to measure the same dimension, or an athlete has many games during the season. How consistently do the test and the athlete perform? To find out, researchers can use one of the three methods discussed below. Although all three measures use correlations, you should realize that they are not simple correlations but rather are complex correlation formulas, which are taken care of by the computer statistics package.

Split-half reliability correlation measure (Spearman-Brown formula).

The *split-half reliability* measure gives one test to multiple participants at the same time. It tends to be used with measurement instruments that have several similar items (questions or statements) to which participants can respond. The similar items are commonly separated by odd and even numbers or two randomly selected groups of scores to determine equivalency within the one test (not between two measurement instruments, as is done in parallel form reliability). It also does not test stability reliability over time, as the test-retest does. If the correlation coefficient between the two halves (groups of scores) is high, the test has high internal consistency. Generally, the longer the test (or the more games played), the higher is the reliability. Thus, the Spearman-Brown correlation formula (see Chapter 13) is commonly used to adjust for the effect of test length and to estimate reliability of the entire test.

Alpha reliability correlation measure (Cronbach formula).

The *alpha reliability* test also gives one test to multiple participants at the same time. It tends to be used with multiple questions that measure the same variable, such as motivation and leadership. Alpha reliability is somewhat like factor analysis, but it is not as powerful a statistics test. With alpha, you take each item that measures the same factor/variable and run a correlation between each item to see if there is a high coefficient (in other words, whether they all measure the same thing). Items with a low correlation would be changed or dropped from the test to increase reliability. The common correlation formula is the Cronbach's alpha.

Dichotomous alpha reliability correlation measure (Kuder-Richardson formula).

The KR (Kuder-Richardson) formula is a quicker way to estimate the alpha coefficient with dichotomous (correct or incorrect) scoring, which is used with knowledge tests.

For our purposes, it's not important for you to know how to run these correlation tests now. However, if you read them in a report or journal article, you should understand what they mean. Chapter 13 will help you understand them better.

CONCEPTUAL OBJECTIVE 8
Compare the measures of internal consistency reliability.

Number of tests/testers and number of times a test is given.

Review Box 8.1 for a summary of reliability as it relates to the number of different tests and number of administration times a test is given. As you can see, internal consistency tests feature one test, given once. Stability tests include one test, given twice. Equivalence tests include two different measurement instruments (or testers/raters) that measure at one time. They are all compared for differences in measures. The higher the correlations, the stronger the support for reliability.

Box 8.1   Reliability by Number of Different Tests and Times

		Number of Different Tests or Tests/Measures	
		1	**2**
Number of Administration Times	**1**	*Internal Consistency* split-half alpha + dichotomous	*Equivalence* parallel forms interrater
	2	*Stability* test-retest test administrator	

Intraclass Reliability (Tests of Difference)

Intraclass reliability uses tests of difference in place of correlation coefficients as an analysis of variance. Although correlation coefficients are still used today, they are outdated; tests of difference are better for determining reliability for the following reasons:

- It is logical because reliability is really measuring differences. For example, it is more logical to test differences between test 1 and test 2 scores, rather than a correlation coefficient of stability that determines the relationship between the test and retest scores.

- With a test of difference you can compare the test scores of the same participant at time 1 and time 2 with a pair T-test (discussed in Chapter 12) or repeat measures. With correlation you can only compare all scores; one participant at a time is too small a sample size to run a correlation. Thus, the test of difference is a more robust test.

- With a test of difference you can analyze multiple possible sources of variability within the same statistical analysis (tests 1 and 2/measurers), but that's not possible with correlation.

- With a test of difference you can statistically analyze mean gains (e.g., on test 2 participants scored two points higher than on test 1), but you cannot do so with correlation.

Sample size is important. Recall that the sample size must be larger for tests of difference than for correlations. The minimum number for correlation is 25 total, and 25 per group for a test of difference, to run higher-level (parametric) statistics.

CONCEPTUAL OBJECTIVE 9
Explain the difference between intraclass reliability and the other tests of reliability.

Review Table 8.4 (on the following page) for a summary of the types of reliability covered in this section.

Using the correct measurement statistical test.

As with validity, the research design commonly places more emphasis on one or more types of reliability for measurement statistical testing. Thus, to enhance reliability you must know when to use which reliability measurement statistical test. Exercises 8-9 through 8-17 will help you develop your skill at understanding which type of reliability statistical testing is most appropriate for a specific research design.

**STOP READING and turn to the end of the chapter
to complete exercises 8-9 through 8-17.**

8.4 Assessing Reliability and Validity Coefficients

As we stated, reliability and validity are on a continuum between low and high. Table 8.5 illustrates their classification levels. A correlation coefficient of 1.00 would mean that

Table 8.4   Summary of Reliability

Type of Reliability	What Is Measured	Measurement Methods/ Statistical Test
Stability Test-retest Test Administrator	Measures the variability of scores of the measurement using correlations of repeated measurements of the instrument itself and measurer at two points in time. • measures variance in scores using the *same measurement instrument* with the same participants at two points in time. • measures variance in scores using the *same measurer* with the same participants at two points in time.	 Correlation Correlation
Equivalence Parallel forms Interrater	Measures the variability in parallel forms of the measurement instrument and multiple measurers using correlation. • measures variance with *multiple measurement instruments* measuring the same thing to determine their equivalence at one point in time. • measures variance when *multiple raters* score the same participants at the same time comparing the individual scores to the group scores	 Correlation Percentages/Correlation
Internal Consistency Split-half Alpha Dichotomous Alpha	Measures variability within the measurement instrument among items using the split-half and alpha methods. • measures the variance between the odd and even (random) item scores of a test at the same time to determine internal consistency. • measures the correlation of multiple items factor/variable with one measure at one time to determine if they are measuring the same thing. • estimates the alpha coefficient with dichotomous (right/wrong) scoring.	 Correlation formula (Spearman-Brown) Correlation formula (Cronbach) Correlation formula (Kuder-Richardson)
Intraclass	Uses tests of difference in place of correlation coefficients as an analysis of variance to determine reliability.	Tests of difference

Table 8.5   Standards of Reliability and Validity Coefficients

Reliability	Standard	Validity
.90 and higher	Excellent	.80 and higher
.80–.89	Good	.70–.79
.70–.79	Fair	.60–.69
.69 and lower	Poor	.59 and lower

every test/tester had the same score, or that there is no variance in scores. Some sources have lower standards of acceptable reliability and validity than shown in Table 8.5, and there are exceptions that make lower standards acceptable. Also, it is common to use the probability value that is given with the correlation coefficient. Based on multiple factors, you can have a high p-value (say, .82) with an unacceptable coefficient (say, .45). (You will learn more about p-values in chapters 11–14.)

CONCEPTUAL OBJECTIVE 10
Identify the minimal acceptable correlation coefficient levels for reliability and validity.

Considerations when Assessing Reliability and Validity

Although lower standards are acceptable, we can set a generally agreed-upon minimal acceptable level of .70 for reliability and .60 for validity, but here are some of the reasons that lower standards are acceptable.

Internal vs. external comparisons.

Reliability is an internal comparison (test/tester to test/tester). Validity is an external comparison (new test to criterion test). Therefore, it is more difficult to support validity than reliability. Thus, the acceptable standards are higher correlation coefficients for reliability.

Special groups.

When participants are younger, have disabilities, are beginners, or have other special attributes, it may be acceptable to use lower standards of reliability and validity.

Affective scales versus achievement and aptitude tests.

When measuring constructs, which cannot be measured directly, it may be acceptable to use lower standards of reliability and validity. However, when using achievement and aptitude tests it is usually acceptable to use higher standards of reliability and validity, as the decisions based on these tests are usually important (such as who gets a job and who gets accepted into a school).

Laboratory tests.

In laboratories when one can control conditions, it is usually acceptable to use higher standards of reliability and validity.

New research.

When researching a new area, it is usually acceptable to use lower standards of reliability and validity at first and to raise them for further studies.

Whole versus subscales.

When a test has subtests or sections measuring different things (recall that an IQ test has six subscales/tests), you can expect the whole or overall reliability and validity to be higher than the subscales because the reliability is partially a function of test length. Recall that the Spearman-Brown test (Chapter 13) adjusts for this. In other words, the whole is greater than the sum of its parts. However, all subscale coefficients related to the measurement of the study should be acceptable. When using a previously validated test, be sure to check the subscale coefficients.

SKI WEST STUDY

As we bring this chapter to a close, you should be able to:
- *define and compare reliability and validity;*
- *compare content, criterion, and construct validity;*
- *know how to enhance validity;*
- *explain measurement error and how to decrease errors;*
- *compare stability, equivalence, and internal reliability;*
- *understand how tests of difference rather than correlations can be used to test reliability;*
- *assess reliability and validity measures;*
- *identify which methods to use to address reliability and validity in your own study, and*
- *understand that if your measurement instrument is not reliable and valid, your results and conclusions will also be in error, which can lead to poor decisions.*

Matt McLeish's study addressed predictive criterion validity (regression measurement). The study included two measurement instruments. However, as he stated, neither the personality test nor the job-performance evaluation was checked for reliability and validity. Although Matt did not check reliability, what he actually investigated was the criterion validity of the personality measure. By testing with regression, he found out whether the test did in fact predict performance. As stated in the study, the personality measure was not validated at the .05 level.

Although the personality test was never actually tested, it did address content validity. As stated in the Ski West study, the HR department managers did develop the personality test based on the literature, and because they are HR specialists they can be considered a panel of experts. If any outside panel were used, it should have been stated.

CHAPTER SUMMARY AND GLOSSARY

The chapter summary is organized in a way that provides you with the answers necessary to help you meet the conceptual objectives for this chapter.

1. **Define and state the importance of reliability and validity measurement.**
   Reliability is the consistency and precision of a measurement instrument. Validity is the extent to which a measurement instrument measures what it intends to measure. If a measurement instrument is not reliable and valid, the methods, results, and discussion steps of the research process will be in error.

2. **Describe the relationship between reliability and validity.**
   A measurement instrument can be reliable but not valid, but it cannot be valid without being reliable. Thus, reliability is a necessary but not sufficient condition of validity.

3. **Compare the measures of criterion validity.**
   Criterion validity is measured in two ways: concurrent and predictive. They are similar in that they both compare a new measure to a criterion measure, but they differ on the time measure. Concurrent validity correlates a new measure with a criterion measure at the same time, whereas predictive validity forecasts a future measure in relation to the criterion. Thus, with concurrent measures you get immediate statistical support for the new measure validity, but with predictive measures you generally have to wait to run the statistics to determine validity.

4. **Compare the measures of construct validity.**

   Construct validity is measured in three ways: convergent, discriminant, and factor. They are similar in that they all assess the theory and the measurement instrument. However, convergent validity correlates multiple measures that cannot be directly observed, discriminant validity correlates or tests differences by groups that are known to possess and known not to possess different levels of a trait, while factor validity measures the interrelationship between multiple items/questions being measured and the factors/variables through factor analysis testing to be sure they are measuring the same thing.

5. **List the steps to enhance validity.**

   Step 1. Review and cite the literature as a foundation for your construct and variable selection to study.

   Step 2. Write clear, measurable operational definitions of variables, based on the literature. Write clear, measurable hypotheses, based on the literature review and operational definitions.

   Step 3. Use a previously validated measurement instrument or have a panel of experts review your measurement instrument as a source of validity.

   Step 4. Pilot test the measurement instrument by using it and having participants complete the instrument/questionnaire to help improve it or to make sure it is used correctly.

   Step 5. Statistically test validity.

6. **Compare the measures of stability reliability.**

   The two measures of stability are test-retest and the test of administrator reliability. They are similar in that they both measure how consistent one measurement is from time 1 to time 2. However, they are different because the test-retest measures the consistency of the test itself, whereas the test administrator measures consistency of the sole tester.

7. **Compare the measures of equivalence reliability.**

   The two measures of equivalence are parallel forms reliability and interrater reliability. They are similar in that they both measure the equivalence of multiple measures at one time. However, they are different because the parallel forms measures the equivalence of the multiple measurement instruments, whereas the interrater measures the equivalence of multiple testers.

8. **Compare the measures of internal consistency reliability.**

   The three measures of equivalence are the split-half, alpha, and dichotomous alpha reliability. They are similar in that they measure the correlation of multiple questions measuring the same variable at one time. However, they are different because the split-half correlates the odd and even numbered items, the alpha correlates all the items measuring the variable together, and the dichotomous alpha is used when the items are correct or incorrect.

9. **Compare the difference between intraclass reliability and the other tests of reliability.**

   They are similar in that they all test reliability. However, intraclass reliability uses tests of difference, whereas the other methods use correlation coefficients to measure the variance. The intraclass reliability is a stronger test.

10. **Identify the minimal acceptable correlation coefficient levels for reliability and validity.**
    The minimal acceptable coefficient level is .70 for reliability and .60 for validity. Reliability is an internal measure, whereas validity is an external measure; therefore, lower standards are set for validity.

11. **Define the following alphabetical list of key terms.**
    Select one or more methods: (1) fill in the missing key terms from memory, (2) match the key terms with their definitions below, or (3) copy the key terms in order from the list at the beginning of the chapter.

concurrent validity	equivalence reliability	reliability
construct validity	internal consistency reliability	stability reliability
content validity	intraclass reliability	standard error
criterion validity	predictive validity	validity

    _____ is the consistency and precision of a measurement instrument.

    _____ is the extent to which a measurement instrument measures what it intends to measure.

    _____ of a measurement instrument is the extent to which it provides adequate coverage of the variable.

    _____ of a measurement instrument is its correlation score with other established measurement instrument scores.

    _____ measurement is taken at the same time as the criterion measure.

    _____ forecasts a measurement in relation to the criterion measure.

    _____ assesses the theory and the measurement instrument.

    _____ estimates how much difference there probably is between participants' obtained scores and true scores.

    _____ measures the variability of scores using correlation coefficients of the measurement instrument itself (test-retest) and the measurer (test administrator) at two points in time.

    _____ measures the variability in parallel forms of the measurement instrument and multiple measurers (interrater reliability) using correlation coefficients.

    _____ measures variability within the measurement instrument among items using the split-half and alpha methods.

    _____ uses tests of difference in place of correlation coefficients as an analysis of variance.

WRITTEN ASSIGNMENTS

As previously stated, the Method assignment is actually completed through chapters 4–8. Method sections need to address reliability and validity regardless of the assignment, so it's essentially the same for all three assignments below.

APPENDIX RP, ASSIGNMENT 3 (METHOD AND APPENDIX A), APPENDIX CS, ASSIGNMENT 2 (METHOD), AND APPENDIX SA, ASSIGNMENT 2 (QUESTIONNAIRE)

In the research study's Method section, don't give a list of how you didn't meet all the various types of reliability and validity. Do focus on addressing how your measurements meet some reliability and validity requirements, using proper research terminology. See the appropriate instructions in the assignments in chapters 4–7 and in this chapter.

APPENDIX RP, ASSIGNMENT 4 (COMPLETED RESEARCH PROPOSAL)

The completed research proposal can be passed in after including the information from chapters 4–8. However, it can be passed in later after completing Chapter 10 to help understand which statistical test to state will be run in the Method section, statistical analysis subsection. Either way, the usual process is to turn in Appendix RP, Assignment 3 and get feedback for making improvements to the Method section. With the improvements made as you go from RP assignments 1 through 3 you have a completed research proposal. See Part IV, Appendix RP, Completed Research Proposal, Assignment 4, for instructions that include a few things that you haven't done in the prior three assignments.

EXERCISES

RELIABLE AND VALID MEASURE?

8-1   Hypothesis: Artificial football turf causes more player injuries than grass fields do. The measurement instrument is record of injuries in prior games. The researcher plans to count the number of injuries on artificial turf and on grass to compare differences. If there are significantly more injuries on artificial turf than on grass, the researcher will accept the hypothesis.
(a) Is the measurement instrument valid? Explain why or why not.
(b) Is it reliable?

WHICH TYPE OF VALIDITY IS NEEDED?

8-2   For new employees, you use a standard computer test to determine their computer skills. The test takes three hours and costs $100 per test. You want to develop your own test so you don't have to pay another company the $100 for using their test, and you also want to cut down on testing time. You have developed your new test, which should take about two hours. (a) How do you determine if your test is valid? Which (b) type of validity and (c) measurement/statistical test will you use to find out? (d) What is the minimum sample size you will need for your test?

8-3   You cannot find a previously validated questionnaire, so you develop your own. Which (a) type of validity and (b) measurement/statistical test will you use to ensure validity? (c) What is the minimum sample size you will need?

8-4   You want to make money in the stock market by developing a system that will allow you to pick stocks that will increase in value within one year. Based on the literature, you believe there are five important determinants of stock success within one year.

Which (a) type of validity and (b) measurement/statistical test should you use to determine the validity of your system? (c) What is the minimum sample size you will need for your test?

8-5 You want to determine why some employees are successful at your organization and others are not. Based on the literature and on talking to people in the organization, you have developed a list of reasons for the difference in performance. To determine if your variables are correct, you ask managers to give you the names of their most and least productive workers. Which (a) type of validity and (b) measurement/statistical test should you use to determine the validity of your variables? (c) What is the minimum sample size you will need for your test?

8-6 Your research focus is to develop an instrument that will measure employee job satisfaction. There are six variables in the literature. You have written 24 questions, four questions to measure each variable. Which (a) type of validity and (b) measurement/statistical test should you use to determine the validity of your questionnaire? (c) What is the minimum sample size you will need for your test?

8-7 Some theories say that effective leaders have intelligence, and other theories that they have emotional stability. There are standardized tests to measure these variables (IQ and EQ). You don't want to give leaders these two long and separate tests; rather, you would like to develop a leadership instrument that includes IQ and EQ. Which (a) type of validity and (b) measurement/statistical test should you use to determine the validity of your questionnaire? (c) What is the minimum sample size you will need for your test?

8-8 Which type of validity is most appropriate for your own research proposal design?

WHICH TYPE OF RELIABILITY IS NEEDED?

Note: Because tests of difference can be used rather than correlations, do not select differences/intraclass as your answer.

8-9 You have a long questionnaire measuring attitudes about leadership. Several of your questions focus on the same leadership traits. You want to be sure that the participants are answering the similar questions with the same attitudes. What reliability test is most appropriate for this research design?

8-10 You want to know if a manager gives consistent employee evaluations. Two weeks after the manager has completed employee evaluations for all 30 employees, you ask the manager to complete the same evaluation of the same employees once again. What reliability test is most appropriate for this research design?

8-11 You teach a course that has two sections. You teach research on Monday to one class and on Tuesday to another class. You fear that people who take the test on Monday will tell the students who take it on Tuesday what the questions are, thus giving them an unfair advantage to score higher. Which reliability technique can you adjust without actually testing in this situation?

8-12 You have developed a 60-question Language Arts test to assess grammar, diction, and punctuation skills (20 questions for each skill). Which test is most appropriate to assess the reliability of your test?

8-13 You have developed a test to measure people's opinions about politics. You are using Likert scales of 1–7 to measure opinions. A reviewer of your questionnaire thinks the questions are very general and recommends testing it to make sure people give the same answers if retested in a day or two. Which reliability test can you use to find out? What procedures will you follow?

8-14 A department of quality-control specialists all inspect the same computer product. You want to know if there is a variance in the results of their inspections. Which reliability test can you use to find out? What procedures will you follow?

8-15 You want to know if a 30-question ERG (existence, relatedness, growth) motivation test (with 10 questions at each level) really does measure these three levels of motivation. Which reliability test can you use to find out? What procedures will you follow?

8-16 You work for the registry of motor vehicles and you give the written test before the driving test. How many different versions of the written test should you have to ensure that people who have taken it can't tell others the answers? How can you test reliability of your written tests? What procedures will you follow?

8-17 Which type of reliability is more appropriate for your research proposal design?

Note

[1] Krathwohl, David R. (2009). *Methods of educational and social science research: The logic of methods* (3rd ed.). Long Grove, IL: Waveland Press.

PART III

Data Analysis
Results and Discussion

9

Data to Descriptive Statistics

CONCEPTUAL OBJECTIVES

The conceptual objectives below also appear at appropriate places within the chapter at points when you will have accessed the information necessary to attain them. They

appear again at the end of the chapter in the Summary and Glossary section, along with explanations that will enable you to meet the objectives.

After studying this chapter, you should be able to:

1. Explain item nonresponse and six options for dealing with it.
2. Describe the three activities of organizing data in preparation for statistical analysis.
3. Discuss the (a) role, (b) use, and (c) classification of statistics in research.
4. Compare the measures of central tendency.
5. Compare the measures of dispersion.
6. Discuss the difference between distribution shapes.
7. State the most appropriate descriptive statistics for each level of data measurement.
8. Define the following key terms (listed in order of their appearance in the chapter).

frequency distribution	measures of central tendency	range
measures of position	measures of dispersion	variance
statistics	measures of shape	standard deviation
role of statistics	mean	normal distribution
descriptive statistics	median	skewed distribution
inferential statistics	mode	kurtosis

SKILL DEVELOPMENT OBJECTIVES

The exercises that apply to particular skill development objectives are indicated directly beneath each numbered objective below. Periodic instructions within the chapter tell you when to stop reading and direct you to the end of the chapter to complete one or more of the skill development exercises.

1. Determine the type of variable and its level of measurement.
   Exercises 9-1 through 9-5 and problem 9-1

2. Calculate measures of central tendency.
   Exercises 9-6 and 9-7 and problem 9-1

3. Calculate measures of dispersion.
   Exercises 9-8 through 9-10 and problem 9-1

The Research Process

(1) The research question/purpose of the study, literature review, and hypotheses.	(2) Research design methodology for collecting data and statistics.	(3) Data analysis and interpreting results.	(4) Discussing results and making conclusions.
• *Introduction*	• *Method*	• *Results*	• *Discussion*
Chapters 1–3	Chapters 4–8	Chapters 9–14	Chapters 9–14

In prior chapters we presented the research process shown above. You began with your research question (1), and then you developed a research design and data-collection method (2). Now that you have collected your data, we are at the data-analysis and results interpretation stage (3) of the research process.

9.1 Organizing Data

Before you begin this first statistics chapter, be aware that most of the statistical computer printouts you will see in chapters 9–14 are from IBM's SPSS 19 (Statistical Package for Social Sciences) software. However, any other higher-level statistical software will give you the same information. (We will provide directions on how to run the various statistics in SPSS 19, so if you are not using SPSS, just ignore this information.) Note that SPSS uses the term *scale* to mean that a variable's measure level is *interval/ratio, or scale = interval/ratio.* Other programs may call interval/ratio data *continuous.* The SPSS software offers a "Help" section. Among other things, it includes a tutorial which is defined as:

> Illustrated, step-by-step instructions on how to use many of the basic features in SPSS. You don't have to view the whole tutorial from start to finish. You can choose the topics you want to view, skip around and view topics in any order, and use the index or table of contents to find specific topics.

Now let's begin by saying that although it's nice to have your data collected, before you can run statistics you must prepare your data and transform it into information—by editing, coding, and entering it into the computer statistical software program so that you can store it and run the statistics to answer your research question. Let's discuss each of these three activities separately in this section.

Editing Data

Editing is the process of getting data ready for coding and data entry by ensuring the completeness, consistency, and reliability of data. Editing is about finding and fixing errors and developing and selecting editing methods. By reviewing your data, you may find questions that are not answered correctly, are improbable, or have seemingly contradictory answers that need to be corrected (edited). For example, a participant may have reported weekly income instead of monthly, so you need to edit the answer by converting weekly to monthly pay; or participants may place a circle on a questionnaire form that overlaps two answers, so you need to make a judgment about which is their actual answer.

A key to successful editing is to develop a good questionnaire. Following the ten steps of survey research (Chapter 7) makes editing easier. A second key to success is to avoid bias—to be objective and ethical. The best approach is to have a plan with clearly defined rules on how to proceed with editing methods. If you are not the person who will edit the data, you need to be sure to train the editor to handle the process. Here are a few considerations that should be planned.

Disqualified participants.

You can receive completed questionnaires from people who are not in the sample frame and unit. For example, a responder could be too young, or if you are surveying family business owners you may get questionnaires returned from non-family businesses. You should discard their questionnaires from the data; you may adjust the response rate accordingly (Chapter 9).

Item nonresponse.

Recall that we discussed nonrespondents who don't return your questionnaire. You may also find that some participants don't answer all the questions. With a nonresponse item you have several choices:

- *Discard the questionnaire.* If the participant skipped several or most questions, you can drop the questionnaire from the sample. They are still respondents for the sake of response rate calculations, but the sample size (N) decreases.

- *Just leave the value blank.* However, realize that the N will vary with different questions, but this is not problematic.

- *Plug in a value.* You put in a value for the participant. With interval/ratio-level data, it is common to calculate the mean/average number and put in this value for all missing items. However, with a large sample, you should do this *after* coding and data entry to statistically calculate the mean. With ordinal/interval data, it is common to use the mid-point, such as 4 on a 7-point scale. With nominal data, such as yes or no, you can alternate answers based on expected proportion of responses. For example, you can use the statistical frequencies (e.g., if only 1 out of 5 participants are expected to say "yes, I will buy the product," alternate four "no" and one "yes" plugs).

- *Discard the question.* If you get too many nonresponse items, it is best to drop the question because you will more than likely have bias and the sample is not representative of the population, which can lead to poor decisions. For example, let's say you get only a 10% response rate and only half of the respondents answer the question. You really only have a 5% response rate. If the question is so sensitive (e.g., what's your income, do you use drugs, or do you have a venereal disease/AIDS) that participants don't want to answer the question, there is also a good chance that others lied about their answers. For example, people have been known to overstate their income and lie about drug and health issues. If you really need the answers to the question to answer your research question, the best option is to keep following up until you have an acceptable response rate, or use alternative sources.

- *Follow up.* If possible, you can contact the participants and ask them to give you the missing answer(s). This is obviously time consuming, but as stated in Chapter 7, follow-up is the best method for increasing responses, and this goes for item nonresponse too.

- *Utilize alternative data sources.* You can sometimes get the missing data through other sources. For example, if you know the person's zip code, you may be able to find secondary sources that tell you the average income and home value for the area, which you can plug in as the value.

CONCEPTUAL OBJECTIVE 1
Explain item nonresponse and six options for dealing with it.

"Don't know" answers.

If your questionnaire includes questions with a "don't know" or "does not apply" type of response, you need an editing plan. If the research question is to find out how many participants do and don't know something to test for differences between groups, then you want to keep the response as a separate option. See the examples below.

1. *Who developed the Situational Leadership model?*
   If you are not trying to find differences between groups, in a sense you have a non-response item. You can leave the value blank so that no data are entered for the question. Again, your sample size (N) will vary by question. Some researchers do use plug-in values, but this is a questionable method. A key question when deciding whether to leave an item blank or plug in answers is legitimate versus reluctant response: If the person really doesn't know and you are not comparing differences, you shouldn't plug in a value. However, if the person is reluctant, a plug-in is more acceptable. The hard part is knowing why participants picked the "don't know" response. The question itself helps you decide. See question #2 below.

2. *Do you like your job?*
   In the first question above, "I don't know" seems a legitimate answer, but the response to question #2 seems to be a case of reluctance to answer. Return to the material on questionnaire design in Chapter 7 for ideas on how to make better measurement questions. Also, when possible, don't develop questions with the "don't know" option.

Coding Data

Coding is the process of assigning numbers or other symbols to variables and question answers, so they can be grouped into a limited number of categories.

Coding variable categories.
Recall that with nominal, ordinal, and rating-scale interval data, you need to assign numbers. For example, with the variable *gender* you can't run statistics with the words male and female. You have to assign the male and female categories a number, such as 0 and 1 or 1 and 2. Recall that with standardized interval scales (e.g., IQ) and ratio variable data (e.g., age) you don't need to assign numbers, so coding categories is not necessary.

Coding variable questions.
The variable itself can be coded with symbols. For example, the variable *gender* can be coded as male and female or male could be coded as M and female as F. When you have a question to measure a variable, with most statistical software you have limited space to name the variable and categories, so you use some form of words, letters, and numbers to represent the variable and question. For example, if the question was "What are the major reasons that your business has been successful?" you could code the question as *success*, *suc*, or *suc1* (the 1 representing the question # or anything else you want it to represent). The idea is to code the variables and questions so that they are easy to identify. It is generally not a good idea to simply use the question number as the code because it's hard to remember what the question and variable are, simply based on the number.

Code while developing the questionnaire.
We have actually already addressed coding back in Chapter 7, in the discussion on developing the questionnaire. Return to the questionnaire in Box 8.3 and review how each question already has been coded. It is a good idea to give each question a different number. Also, don't forget that questions and their codes have to be exhaustive and mutually exclusive. When using most online questionnaires, you have to code while developing the ques-

tionnaire because the data is automatically entered for you. As you should realize, coding is necessary, and makes it easier, to complete the data entry.

Entering Data

Data entry is the process of getting the data into a medium for viewing and manipulating. After you have edited and coded the data, they have to be stored for use with a statistical software package so that you can further edit, code, and run your statistical analysis. You can enter data into an Excel spreadsheet and bring them into other software packages, such as SPSS.

Automatic data entry.

As just stated above, *online questionnaires* are great because the data are automatically entered for you. You can also use *optical recognition and scanning, voice recognition,* and *bar code* systems that also automatically enter the data for you.

Keyboarding.

Someone has to type in the data, a process called keyboarding. We provide exercises with data for you to use by keyboarding. Even with automatic data entry, someone most likely has to code the variable questions and categories for nominal and rating-scale questions. Variable names and categories are very important to have in the statistical software so that the codes appear on the statistical computer printouts. Hence, you can easily read and understand the results and make conclusions.

Virtually everyone is familiar with a computer keyboard, so you know how easy it is to use. If you have used spreadsheet software such as Excel, you already know how to enter data into columns (variables) and rows (participant answers). The more difficult part is entering the coding into the statistical software program. Because the coding methods vary, we will not attempt to teach you how to do so. If you don't know how to use a statistical software package, your instructor will address this issue, either by teaching you or having someone demonstrate in class or at a computer lab. Most colleges' computer labs have statistical software and lab workers to help you. Below is an example of a spreadsheet in Table 9.1. This is not an actual statistical software printout; we keep it simple by only showing six variables (amount, loan, income, age, education, and race) in the columns and six participant-response values in the rows. (There were actually 24 variables and questions and 94 participants in the sample: N = 94). The purpose of the study is to determine if race affects the likelihood of receiving a small business loan.

As shown in the data view in Table 9.1 (Part A), all you do is use the keyboard to type in the code names of the variables in the columns and the values in the rows. In the variable (coding) view (Part B), you type in the name of the variable. The label is the basic question. The value is where coding by assigning numbers comes in. Notice that you don't do any coding for standardized interval- and ratio-level variables because they have numbers. The column names in the coding view were taken from SPSS, however, not all columns are shown, just the most important. How you enter your codes will vary with the statistical software package you use.

Which data entry system should I use?

Major factors include availability of resources and your instructor's and college's requirement standards. Online questionnaire services like SurveyMonkey are becoming

Table 9.1   Loan Data by Race

A. Data View

	Amount	Loan	Income ($)	Age	Education	Race
1	35,000	0	60,000	31	5	0
2	4,000	1	40,000	45	3	1
3	7,500	1	35,000	51	2	0
4	10,000	0	52,000	25	6	1
5	60,000	1	102,000	47	1	1
6	25,000	1	73,000	36	4	0

B. Variable (Coding) View

	Name	Label	Value	Measure
1	Amount	Amount of loan applied for	None	Scale (ratio)
2	Loan	Loan received	0 = no, 1 = yes	Nominal
3	Income	Family income	None	Scale
4	Age	Age of loan applicant	None	Scale
5	Education	Level of education	1 = elementary, 2 = not done HS, 3 = HS, 4 = not done college, 5 = college, 6 = grad school	Ordinal
6	Race	Race of loan applicant	1 = African-American, 0 = white	Nominal

more commonly used. Another factor to consider is the number of questions and the sample size. The more questions, and the larger the sample size, the more time you save with automated data entry.

CONCEPTUAL OBJECTIVE 2
Describe the three activities of organizing data in preparation for statistical analysis.

Data entry with SPSS 19.

As mentioned earlier, at the time of this writing the latest version of IBM's Statistical Package for the Social Sciences is SPSS 19. Chapters 9–14 give you instructions for running the statistical tests we discuss in detail using SPSS 19; let's start now. Here's all you have to do to get started:

1. Open the SPSS program.

2. Click on the *Type in data* command on the right and then click *OK* at the bottom. Note that there are two views in SPSS as shown in Table 9.1: the data view and the variable view. Go between the two views by clicking the view you want at the bottom left of the screen.

3. Click *Variable view.* I like to start by going into variable view and setting up the variables, making it easier to be sure I'm entering the data in the correct variable column.

4. Type in the name of your variable and press *Enter.*

   (a) The entire row becomes visible.

   (b) Go to the *Label* column and type in the name of the variable(s) so that it (they) will labeled when you run statistics.

   (c) Go to the *Values* column and be sure to enter values in all nominal and rating-scale variables. Click in the right of the value column for a drop-down box that prompts for the entries. Values are your arbitrary numbers and labels are your variable names. But with interval/ratio (scale) you don't need arbitrary values because the entries are real numbers, so skip the values for scale variables.

   (d) Go to the *Measurement* column, click the box, and select either scale (interval/ratio), ordinal, or nominal.

5. Once you have entered all your variables, go to the bottom left corner of the screen, click *Data view,* and enter your value numbers in the columns for each variable.

6. Once all your data are entered (or before), save your data file.

7. *Back up your data.* After entering your data, be sure to save a copy on a portable storage device such as a Store'N'Go or DataTravler. You want a backup for two major reasons: People do lose data in hard drives, and if you use a college computer, be aware that many systems delete files on a regular basis.

Next time you want to run statistics from your stored data file:

• Click on the SPSS program,

• Click *Open an existing data source,* and

• Find your data file and open it. You are now ready to run your statistics.

9.2 Frequency Distributions

Descriptive data analysis is the process of transforming the raw data into a reduced collection of observations in a format that makes the data easy to understand and interpret. *Tabulation* is the process of arranging descriptive statistical data in a table or chart form. *A **frequency distribution** tabulates how many participants scored each value,* so the frequency refers to how many participants picked the same answer to the same question.

Tabulating the number of responses or observation in a frequency distribution on a question-by-question or item-by-item basis is commonly the first step in data analysis, but it is also done at the same time as running descriptive statistics. When tabulating data, you use the codes you developed and entered into your database. See Table 9.2 for an example that uses the data from our bank loan example.

Frequency (*f*) Distribution Form

The frequency distribution can be in two forms. The computer will make the frequency distribution for you. The distribution can be arranged in order from low value to high value (e.g., ranking test grades or incomes). This is commonly done with interval/ratio-level data. A second method is to arrange the values by the order of the question scales.

Running frequency distributions with SPSS 19.

You obviously have to run the SPSS program and open your file to run any statistics. I prefer to run statistics from the data view window. With ratio/interval-scale data, frequencies alone are not very relevant, but for ordinal and nominal values they are. Every time you run statistics, you begin by clicking *Analyze*. For frequency distributions, follow the steps below.

1. Click *Analyze* on the toolbar (the sixth item from the left, with *File* being the first). This results in a drop-down menu to select the statistic you want to run.

Table 9.2 Frequency Distribution

Years business owned before loan application.

		Frequency	Percent	Valid Percent	Cumulative Percent
Valid	1	6	6.4	6.4	6.4
	2	4	4.3	4.3	10.6
	3	7	7.4	7.4	18.1
	4	7	7.4	7.4	25.5
	5	9	9.6	9.6	35.1
	6	4	4.3	4.3	39.4
	7	9	9.6	9.6	48.9
	8	8	8.5	8.5	57.4
	9	10	10.6	10.6	68.1
	10	6	6.4	6.4	74.5
	11	5	5.3	5.3	79.8
	12	3	3.2	3.2	83.0
	13	3	3.2	3.2	86.2
	14	1	1.1	1.1	87.2
	15	8	8.5	8.5	95.7
	16	1	1.1	1.1	96.8
	17	1	1.1	1.1	97.9
	20	2	2.1	2.1	100.0
	Total	94	100.0	100.0	

(continued)

Table 9.2 *(continued)*

N	Valid	94
	Missing	0
Mean		.46
Std. Error of Mean		.052
Median		.00
Mode		0
Std. Deviation		.501
Variance		.251
Skewness		.174
Std. Error of Skewness		.249
Kurtosis		−2.013
Std. Error of Kurtosis		.493
Range		1
Minimum		0
Maximum		1
Sum		43

		Frequency	Percent	Valid Percent	Cumulative Percent
Valid	African-American	51	54.3	54.3	54.3
	white	43	45.7	45.7	100.0
	Total	94	100.0	100.0	

2. Select *Descriptive Statistics* and on the pop-up menu to the right click *Frequencies*.
3. Move your variables from the left into the variable(s) box on the right by selecting as many variables as you want and clicking the arrow between the boxes to move the variable. (You can also click and drag variables between the boxes.)
4. If all you want is frequencies, click *OK* and the frequencies will appear in the output window view.
5. If you also want descriptive statistics, click *Statistics* and check as many as you want; then click *Continue* and *OK*.
6. You can print the data by clicking the printer icon, and/or you can also save your data. It's easy to copy and paste data to a Word file by highlighting the data and pressing *Control c* to copy and *Control v* to paste.

Measures of Position

Measures of position indicate a value based on its relation to the other values in the distribution; measures include percentages, decals, and quartiles.

Percentage.

The *percentage* breaks the sample into parts based on 100. To calculate a percentage, you simply divide the value by the sample/total. For example, if a sample class of 30 has 20 men and 10 women, the percentage of men is 67% (20/30) and the percentage of women is 33% (10/30). With a frequency distribution (Table 9.2), the computer calculates the percentage of participants selecting each value.

Quartiles and decals.

These are both based on percentiles, the value of a variable below which a certain percent of observations fall. *Quartiles* break data into fourths (25, 50, 75), and *decals* break data into groups of 10%. Computers can calculate them for you. Quartiles and decals are meaningful when making comparisons. For example, test reports often state where the participant scored in relation to the others who have taken the test. Quartiles and decals are commonly used with standard tests rather than with empirical research studies. See Table 9.3 for an example of (A) quartiles and (B) decals for the income of applicants for a small business loan. The lowest income level was $15,500 and the highest was $133,000.

Table 9.3   Quartiles and Decals Frequency Distribution: Loan Applicant Income

Statistics

Income—Quartiles

N	Valid		94
	Missing		0
Percentiles	25		26900.00
	50		34500.00
	75		47500.00

Statistics

Income—Decals

N	Valid		94
	Missing		0
Percentiles	10		21000.00
	20		25000.00
	30		29000.00
	40		31000.00
	50		34500.00
	60		37000.00
	70		44500.00
	80		51000.00
	90		72000.00

Measures of position with SPSS 19.

Notice that when you run frequencies you get percentages. To run measure of position, you need to follow the same steps as getting to frequencies. Note that you can't run both quartiles and decals at the same time. So if you want both, follow the first set of directions below and then the other. To run quartiles:

1. Click *Analyze* on the toolbar.
2. Scroll down to *Descriptive Statistics* and then click *Frequencies.*
3. Move your variables from the left into the variable(s) box on the right
4. Click *Statistics* at the top right.
5. Click *Quartiles"* at the top left under *Percentile Values.* (Note that if you click both quartiles and cut points, you will get only cut points. You can also include other descriptive statistics with a check mark)
6. Click *Continue* at the bottom.
7. Click *OK* to generate the results in the data window.

To run deciles or any other percentage groupings, follow steps 1–4 again. Then:

- Click *Cut points for* and simply use the default of 10. However, you can change to any cut points, such as thirds.
- Click *Continue* and then *OK*, as with quartiles.

Other descriptive statistics.

When you are in the frequencies mode, if you click *Statistics*, as we just did for measures of position, you can also run descriptive statistics of central tendency, dispersion, and/or distribution by clicking any or all of them. Our next section presents an overview of statistics and discusses descriptive statistics in detail.

9.3 An Overview of Statistics

At this point your data should be stored and you can run frequencies (as discussed) and statistical analysis. Knowledge of statistics is essential for those who want to keep current in their field by reading journal articles that report empirical statistical findings. Statistics is even more important to those who must carry out, supervise, and evaluate research studies. If you were weak in statistics coming into this course, you probably had trouble reading and understanding the primary research articles with statistics for your literature review. Chapters 9 to 14 will discuss more than 30 popular statistical tests. For now, let's begin this section with a discussion of statistics and its role in the research process, followed by measuring variables and using statistics.

The Role of Statistics in the Research Process

Statistics are numerical facts collected for study. Statistics are used for data analysis to draw conclusions for the purpose of answering research questions/testing hypotheses. A *parameter* refers to the population, and a *statistic* refers to a sample. Inductive statistics works with a sample and generalizes the results to the population. Deductive statistics works with the population to generalize to a sample. For our purposes you will be learning inductive statistics. Insurance companies use deductive statistics to set premium prices for various segments of the population, for example.

*The **role of statistics** in research is to increase the probability of making valid and reliable decisions by explaining, understanding, predicting, and controlling phenomena that deal with relationships between variables.* The relationship is usually between dependent and independent variables.

Two Classifications of Statistics

The two major classifications of statistics are descriptive and inferential. Note that they coincide with descriptive and inferential research designs (see chapters 1 and 4).

1. *Descriptive statistics explain characteristics of the data or describe a large amount of data in an abbreviated fashion; they measure central tendency, variance, and the shape of the distribution.* Tables and charts are commonly used to present descriptive statistic data. (Pie charts, bar charts, and histograms containing descriptive statistics are presented later in this chapter.)

2. *Inferential statistics provide data-analysis results that are used to derive conclusions about the relationship between variables to answer the research questions/test hypotheses.* It is common to draw conclusions about the population based on the data collected from a sample.

In this chapter you will learn about descriptive statistics. In Chapter 10 you will learn when to use which statistic test, and in chapters 11–13 you will learn about inferential statistics.

CONCEPTUAL OBJECTIVE 3
Discuss the (a) role, (b) use, and (c) classification of statistics in research.

Variables and Statistics

Statistics are used to measure variables and to test the relationship between variables. Let's review what we know about variables. Recall that a *variable* is an empirical concept of study with at least two scales of measurement (Chapter 1). For example, gender is a variable with two scales/groups: male and female. If you had a study with only females, you would only have one measurement scale, or a *constant*. However, females could be a variable if you further classified them—for example, older and younger females (two scales); African American, Hispanic, and White females (three scales). An operational definition of a variable states how the variable will be statistically measured and tested.

Next, let's review the definitions of *dependent and independent variables and measurement levels.* We defined *dependent* variables (Y or DV) as measured for changes to explain relationships. In other words, the Y is observed and measured in response to another variable. *Independent* variables (X or IV) are the hypothesized explanation of the change in the value of the Y (or the X is selected and manipulated by the researcher to observe its effect on the Y). (See Table 1.2 in Chapter 1 for a review of Y and X). The variable's measurement level must also be determined in order to select the appropriate statistical test.

In some studies, the same variable is used to answer multiple research questions/test hypotheses. The same variable can also be used as both the DV/Y and IV/X for different hypotheses. See Table 8.1 for a review of levels of measurement (nominal, ordinal, interval/ratio) and Box 9.1 below for examples. Complete exercises 9-1 through 9-5 to develop your skill at understanding variables and measurement levels.

> ### Box 9.1 Variables and (Measurement Level)
>
> ***Example 1:*** You hypothesize that males have higher incomes than females. What you are observing/measuring/explaining is income and you are using gender as the explainer of the difference in incomes.
>
> Y = Income (K [3 or more] interval/ratio scales)
> X = gender (2 nominal scales—male and female)
>
> ***Example 2:*** You hypothesize that if you know students' level of satisfaction with the class, measured by rating scales **1** (satisfied) to **7** (dissatisfied), you can predict their class test scores (0–100). Test scores are to be predicted by the level of satisfaction/explainer or the reason for the grades.
>
> Y = Class test scores (K interval/ratio scales)
> X = Satisfaction (7 ordinal scales—1–7)

STOP READING and turn to the end of the chapter to complete exercises 9-1 through 9-5.

Descriptive Statistics

As listed in our definition of descriptive statistics, the three measures of descriptive statistics are:

1. ***Measures of central tendency*** *indicate where values center in a distribution; measures include the mean, median, and mode.*

2. ***Measures of dispersion*** *indicate the degree to which values are spread out in a distribution; measures include the range, variance, and standard deviation.*

3. ***Measures of shape*** *indicate the distribution curves shape; measures include skewness and kurtosis.*

Each measure is based on the frequency distribution. The three measures focus on the "middleness" (*central tendency*) of the distribution, how far apart the scores are (*variance*) in the distribution, and how the frequencies determine the *skewness* (left/negative or right/positive) and *kurtosis* (flatness or peakedness) of a distribution (*shape*). However, many research studies do not report the entire frequency distributions (especially with ratio-level data), only the descriptive statistics. In the next three sections we discuss each measure separately.

Note that it is not necessary to know how to calculate the descriptive statistics by hand. The computer will do the math for you. However, for those who have a better understanding by doing the hand calculations, we will show you how to run the descriptive statistics with a simple calculator. The most important thing is that you understand the terms and numbers and how to interpret and use them in research. Although using the computer to run the statistics is relatively easier than understanding the results, we can't show you exactly how to do so because there are several different software programs available. Your instructor and/or computer lab person can help you learn how to use the statistical software at your school.

We will continue our example from Table 9.3 by showing the descriptive statistics that were calculated by the computer with the frequency distribution in Table 9.4. Please note that this is an SPSS 19 printout. Results generated from other software programs may vary. However, they should contain the basic statistical terms presented here. Throughout the rest of this chapter you will learn how to calculate these descriptive statistics and to read, understand, and interpret them from computer printouts.

Descriptive statistics with SPSS 19.

Remember that when you run frequencies you can also run descriptive statistics by using the optional *Statistics* feature, which will also provide the median and mode (something that the *descriptives* mode will not provide). However, if you don't want frequencies and the median and mode, follow these steps:

1. Click *Analyze* on the toolbar.
2. Scroll down to *Descriptive Statistics* and on the right menu click *Descriptives* as the second selection.
3. Move your variables from the left into the variable(s) box on the right.
4. Click *Options* at the top right.
5. Check *Mean* and *Sum* and all the options under *Dispersion* and *Distributions*.
6. Click *Continue* and *OK*.

Table 9.4   Descriptive Statistics

Descriptive Statistics

	N	Range	Minimum	Maximum	Sum	Mean
	Statistic	Statistic	Statistic	Statistic	Statistic	Statistic
Income	94	108600	14400	123000	3734600	39729.79
Valid N (listwise)	94					

	Mean	Std. Deviation	Variance	Skewness		Kurtosis	
	Std. Error	Statistic	Statistic	Statistic	Std. Error	Statistic	Std. Error
Income	1932.196	18733.340	3.509E8	1.593	.249	3.480	.493
Valid N (listwise)							

9.4 Measures of Central Tendency

You'll recall that a measure of central tendency is a representative number that characterizes the "middleness" of the entire data frequency distribution. The three measures include the *mean, median,* and the *mode*.

Mean (M / $\overline{X}$)

*The **mean** is the arithmetic average; it is the appropriate measure of central tendency for interval/ratio-level data.* The mean is the most frequently used measure of central tendency. It is also used with ordinal ranking data, but it's not appropriate with nominal data. You have been calculating means for years, calling them averages. You calculate the mean as shown in the sample mean formula in Box 9.2. In Table 9.4, Descriptive Statistics, the sum is 3734600, and there are 94 questionnaires/cases; therefore, the mean income is $39,729.79, as is calculated and printed out for you. See Box 9.2 for the formula to calculate the mean.

Box 9.2 Calculating the Mean

$\mu, M \text{ or } \overline{X} = \dfrac{\Sigma X}{N}$

$M/\overline{X}$ = mean of the sample (pronounced "X bar")/μ = mean of a population ($\Sigma X/N$)

Σ = directs you to sum a set of values/scores (pronounced "sigma") = "the sum of" (σ)

Note: Σ can be used to represent the population variance.

X = individual scores

N = sample size, the total number of participants/cases/observations/responses

The mean of 5, 8, 10, 11, 12 = 9.20

Add up (Σ) the individual scores (X) and divide by the sample size (N).
(ΣX 46/N 5 = 9.20).

Weighted mean.

The weighted mean is calculated with different means taken from different samples, and the sizes may be different. For example, the mean standardized test scores in three schools are (1–220, 2–178, 3–192) and the sample size is (1–425, 2–470, 3–410). The weighted or grand mean is calculated as follows:

$$\overline{X} / M = \frac{220(425) + 178(470) + 192(410)}{220 + 178 + 192} = \frac{225,880}{590} = 433.69$$

A caution about using the mean with outliers.

Outliers are extremely high or low values that affect the mean. Look at these two examples to see how the SAT mean can be affected.

1. Mean = 450, 462, 473, 463/ 4 = 462

2. Mean = 361, 398, 420, 700/ 4 = 470 (new mean eliminating the outlier = 393)

In the first example all four students are about equal in scores. However, in the second example three students have low scores and the last has a perfect score. The one bright student pulls up the mean for the group, giving it a misleading average score. It is often better to eliminate outliers from the sample (as shown above), or use the median as the measure of central tendency. If your statistical software has it, you can use the *Winsorized mean* that adjusts for outliers by treating them differently than other scores.

Median (Mdn)

*The **median** is the midpoint that divides the distribution values into two equal parts; it is the appropriate measure of central tendency for ordinal-level data and with outliers.* When the distribution has an even number of values, the median is the average of the two middle values. For example, if the values range from 1 to 6, the median will be 3.5 (3 + 4 = 7/2 = 3.5). As another example, 9 10 12 13 15 18 (12 + 13 = 25/2) = 12.5.

Mode

*The **mode** is the value that appears most frequently in a distribution; it is the appropriate measure of central tendency for nominal-level data.* If there is one response in which most cases are concentrated, it is unimodal. However, it is possible to have no mode, two modes—bimodal, and many modes—multimodal.

Reporting measures of central tendency.

When reporting descriptive statistics, you may present all three measures of central tendency. However, if only one measure is presented, it should be the appropriate one for the level of data. Also, when using inferential statistics to test for differences, you must select the one test that compares the appropriate measure of central tendency.

Measures of central tendency with SPSS 19.

Note that if your menu choices are *Analyze, Descriptive Statistics*, and *Descriptives*, you will get only means, no median and modes. To get median and modes, choose *Frequencies* as your third option. Also, many of the inferential statistics have the option of including descriptive statistics means and standard deviations without median and modes, so it is a good idea to get descriptives through the *Frequencies* option.

CONCEPTUAL OBJECTIVE 4
Compare the measures of central tendency.

**STOP READING and turn to the end of the chapter
to complete exercises 9-6 and 9-7.**

9.5 Measures of Dispersion

Measures of central tendency describe data in terms of average value. They do not measure the extent of dispersion about this central value, nor the degree to which scores are spread out in a distribution. Measures of dispersion are also called *measures of variance*. *The **measure of dispersion** is the degree of spread or dispersion that characterizes a group of values and is the degree to which a set of values differs from some measure of central tendency.* It describes how a distribution of values cluster or scatter. The mean values of two distributions may be identical, but the degree of dispersion of their values might be different. One distribution's scores might cluster around the central value while another's are scattered. To illustrate:

Cluster (small variance) Distribution—24, 24, 25, 25, 25, 26, 26 = 175/7 = 25
Scatter (large variance) Distribution—16, 19, 22, 25, 28, 30, 35 = 175/7 = 25

The mean of both distributions is 25, but the variance is considerably different. Sample 1 is more homogeneous than sample 2. Therefore, you need an index to describe distributions in terms of variation of values. The indices are based on the level of data. The most common measures of dispersion are the range, variance, and standard deviation.

Range

The range measures variance in the span of the scores; subtract the lowest from the highest. The range of the cluster distribution above is 2 (26–24) and 19 (35–16) for the scatter; there is clearly a large range even though the means are the same. The range is sensitive to outliers, as they can increase the range dramatically. As shown in Table 9.4, Descriptive Statistics, the range is 108,600. The range is commonly used with ordinal-level measures, as variance and standard deviation are based on the mean and interval/ratio-level measures. The range is of limited value with nominal-level data as it is always based on the number of groups.

Variance

The variance is a measure of average score deviation from the mean squared. A *deviation* compares each score (X) to the mean (μ/M) to measure how much each varies. If every participant answered with the same value, the variance would be 0 (or no variance). A conceptual way to think of the variance is that it is the "total" distance of scores for the mean. In Table 9.4, Descriptive Statistics, the variance of 3.509 is given.

To calculate the variance in a distribution by hand, you subtract the mean from each of the scores/values and square it (multiply the number by itself). Then, you add up the sum of the squares and divide it by the number in the sample minus 1. You "minus one" from the sample to help eliminate bias, but you do not "minus one" when calculating a population variance. Let's use an example to illustrate in Box 9.3.

Standard Deviation (SD, μ = population SD, s = sample SD)

The standard deviation is the average distance of all the scores in the distribution from the mean; it is the square root of the variance. The variance does have one major drawback: It reflects a unit of measurement that has been squared. For instance, the mean sales figures will be in dollars, but the variance will be in squared dollars. To eliminate the discrepancy in measurements, you simply use the square root of the variance—the standard deviation. In Table 9.5, the standard deviation (SD) is 18,733.34. When the variance and standard deviation are small, their values are close together.

The variance and standard deviation are important because they are used in many statistical formulas. Like the mean, its counterpart measure of central tendency, the standard deviation is the most stable measure of dispersion because it takes into account each and every value. The standard deviation is the most commonly used measure of dispersion. Standard deviation is most appropriately used with interval/ratio-level data, and it is frequently used with ordinal data. However, it is inappropriate for use with nominal-level data, as the mean should not be used; thus, it makes no sense to calculate the standard deviation.

A caution about outliers.

Like the mean, the standard deviation is affected by large variations of a few scores, so you may want to eliminate outliers from the sample calculations.

Box 9.3   Sample Variance and Standard Deviation Formulas

$$s^2 = \frac{\Sigma(X-\bar{X})^2}{N-1} \qquad s=\sqrt{s^2}$$

The variance of 3, 4, 6, 8, 9 is 6.5 (26/4), as calculated below.

Standard deviation (s) is simply the square root of variance $\sqrt{6.5}=2.5$

X	$\bar{X}$	$X-\bar{X}$	$(X-\bar{X})^2$
3	6	−3	9
4	6	−2	4
6	6	0	0
8	6	2	4
9	6	3	9
n = 5			26

s^2 = symbol for sample variance/ σ^2 = population variance.

s = symbol for sample standard deviation/ σ = population standard deviation.

X = each value in the distribution.

X/M = mean.

Σ = directs you to sum a set of values/scores and square it.

N = sample size, the total number of participants/values/ N = population size (but don't "minus one").

Logic: The sum of deviations will always be zero. To fix it, square the difference, then average. Thus, variance is in a squared unit of measure, and standard deviation un-squares it.

Measures of dispersion with SPSS 19. You can run measures of dispersion in either *Descriptive Statistics/Frequency* or *Descriptive* options. Also, most of the inferential statistics have the option of including descriptive statistics, with the mean and standard deviation.

CONCEPTUAL OBJECTIVE 5
Compare the measures of dispersion.

**STOP READING and turn to the end of the chapter
to complete exercises 9-8 through 9-10.**

9.6 Measures of Shape

Shape, our last measurement of distribution, measures departures from normality. The number of frequencies within a distribution determines its shape. There are two primary measures of shape—*skewness* and *kurtosis*. The normal distribution (bell-shaped curve) is not skewed, and there can be left- and right-skewed distributions. Kurtosis refers to where the frequencies are distributed in making the curve shape—normal (mesokurtic), tall and thin (leptokurtic), and flat and broad (platykurtic) shapes. The best way to describe a distribution is to present it visually. See Figure 9.1 for measures of departure from normal shape—skewed and kurtosis distribution shapes. The scores of the variable are represented along the baseline, and the area under the curve represents the frequencies.

Normal Distribution

A basic understanding of the normal curve is important, because parametric inferential statistics are based on the assumption that the sample selected has a normal shape.

Large sample sizes ($\geq$ 30) tend to approximate a normal distribution.

We say "approximate" because you rarely, if ever, get a truly perfect normal distribution; there is usually some skew and kurtosis to the shape. Thus, the term *normal curve* is a theoretical construct not actually observed in the real world. It is used for statistical purposes. *A **normal distribution** is a theoretical frequency distribution with a bell-shaped symmetrical curve.* The *normal curve* shows the shape of a normal distribution. This discussion is based on the *central-limit theorem*, which states that as sample sizes increase, the distribution of the sample means, randomly selected, approaches a normal distribution. The larger

Figure 9.1 Distribution Shapes

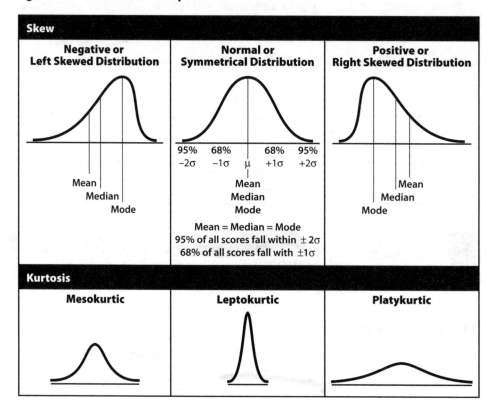

the sample size, generally, the taller the curve of the sample distribution. So with large sample sizes, you assume a normal distribution. The assumption of normal distribution is also needed to run parametric inferential statistics, so be sure to have large samples. (Review our discussion on sample size in Chapter 5.)

Following are the characteristics of normal distribution:

- It has a bell-shaped symmetrical curve, which means that the left and right halves of the curve are mirror images.

- The mode, median, and mean have the same value and are located at the center of the distribution, and it has only one mode.

- The tails of the curve have fewer scores, and the tails get closer and closer to the X axis but never touch it.

- The percentage of scores falling between the mean and any point on the X axis is the same for all normal curves. Based on the mean (M) and standard deviation (SD), you can determine what percentage of the values falls where. In the normal distribution, 68% of the values will fall within plus or minus one s of the mean. Also, approximately 95% will fall within two s (1.96 s is exactly 95%), and approximately 99% will fall within three standard deviation (2.58 s is exactly 99%). IQ tests have a mean = 100 and an s = ± 15 points. Approximately 68% of the population has an IQ score between 85 and 115, 95% between 70 and 130, and 99% between 55 and 145. The farther the IQ score is from the mean, the fewer the people with these outlier IQ scores.

Standard scores (Z-scores).

To make meaningful comparison between different distributions, they must have the same mean and standard deviation; however, this seldom happens in research data. *Standard scores (Z-scores)* allow you to compare scores from different distributions by expressing the distance between a specific score and the mean in terms of standard deviation units. For example, let's say you want to compare your grades in math and English on the first test. The means and standard deviations will not be the same, so you have to standardize the scores.

With the standard normal distribution, the mean of a Z-score is 0 and its standard deviation is 1. To calculate the standard Z-score you take the score minus the mean and divide by the standard deviation (score – M/SD). When known, you can use the population standard deviation. A Z of 1.3 informs you that the distance between a specific observation and the mean is one and one-third standard deviations. An advantage to the standard normal curve is that it provides information about the proportion of scores that are higher or lower than any other score in the distribution. The Z-score comparison determines if a score is higher or lower than the mean. A positive (+Z) indicates that a value is higher than the mean, and a negative (–Z) indicates that it is below the mean.

Skewed Distributions

A skewed distribution has more of the frequency scores near one end of a distribution than the other. In Table 9.5 the skew is 1.593, so it is positive—in other words, skewed to the right. You can get a rough visual of the distribution shape by looking at the frequency distribution. In the next section, you can visually see the shape of the distributions in the histograms in tables 9.6 and 9.7 (pp. 254–255 and 257–258, respectively). Take a quick look ahead now.

When the shape of the distribution is not symmetrical, it is positively or negatively skewed. The values of its mean, median, and mode are different, not the same as with normal curves. In a skewed distribution, there are more frequencies at one end than at the other (very high or very low) giving it more of a "tail" towards one end of the distribution than the other.

Negative/left- and positive/right-skewed distributions.
As shown in Figure 9.1, when the extreme scores are at the lower end of the distribution, it gives the shape a *negative or left-tailed skew*. When the extreme scores are at the higher end of the distribution, it gives the shape a *positive or right-tailed skew*.

The mean is "pulled" in the direction of the tail with the extreme figures (outliers) in the distribution. Since the mean is affected by extremes and the median and mode are not, the mean is always closer to the extreme tail, with the mode closer to the center of the distribution and the median between them.

Skew and measures of central tendency.
If you know the mean and the median, you can determine the shape without a frequency distribution. When the median is greater than the mean, the distribution is negatively skewed; when they are equal, the distribution is normal; and when the mean is greater than the median, the distribution is positively skewed. The greater the difference between the mean and the median, the more skewed the distribution is.

If you find it hard to remember, all you have to do is read the computer printout. In the next section, we will illustrate skewed distributions in tables and discuss the shapes.

Kurtosis Normal Distributions

Kurtosis measures the mesokurtic (normal), leptokurtic (peaked) or platykurtic (flat) shape of a normal distribution of frequencies. When we visualize a normal distribution, we tend to see a normal curve. However, recall that a normal curve is only theoretical for statistical purposes, so you can have different shapes of a normal curve. To visualize the differences, see the shape curves (in the bottom part of Figure 9.1, Kurtosis). Let's discuss the three separately.

Mesokurtic. The term *meso* means middle. Mesokurtic curves have a peak of medium height and distributions that are moderate in breadth.

Leptokurtic. The term *lepto* means thin. Leptokurtic curves are tall and thin with a high peak. They are leptokurtic because most of the scores are in the middle of the distribution, with few scores towards the tails.

Platykurtic. The term *platy* means flat or broad. Naturally, it follows that platykurtic curves are flat and broad. They are platykurtic because the scores are spread broadly among the distribution, rather than grouped in the middle.

Curve shape.
The *mesokurtic* distribution approaches the shape of a normal curve, being neither too peaked nor too flat. The *leptokurtic* curve is taller and thinner than a normal distribution; the *platykurtic* curve is shorter and broader than a normal distribution.

Kurtosis (positive and negative) values.
The kurtosis value of a mesokurtic distribution is close to zero (0), so generally the lower the value the better. The kurtosis value of a *leptokurtic* distribution will have a *positive* value, whereas the kurtosis value of a *platykurtic* distribution will have a *negative* value.

Measures of shape with SPSS 19.

You can run measures of shape in either the *Descriptive Statistics/Frequency* or *Descriptive* options, but most of the inferential statistics don't have the option of including shape.

You have probably figured out that you can check all the measures of central tendency, variance, and shape at the same time rather than running each one separately.

CONCEPTUAL OBJECTIVE 6
Discuss the difference between the distribution shapes.

9.7 Measurement Level and Descriptive Statistics

We've discussed that different descriptive measures are more appropriate for different levels of measurement. To further illustrate the three measures of descriptive statistics and measurement levels, we provide SPSS computer-generated printouts of the three statistical levels of measures. For consistency, in the examples in this chapter and in chapters 10–14 we have used an actual research study conducted by the author and his colleagues, "Bank financing discrimination against African-American owned small business," *Journal of Business & Entrepreneurship*, 10(1), 1998, pp. 82–93. (The complete statistical data are included in the CD that accompanies this book.) The researchers conducted the study to determine whether there is discrimination in bank lending to African American versus White small-business owners in Cook County (the Chicago area). The data presented here have been taken from the survey question results.

Charts and Graphs

In business and other fields, it is common to report descriptive statistics with graphs. Three commonly used graphs are the pie chart, bar chart, and histogram. Examples of charts and graphs are provided with each level of measure. (To save space, the graphics in tables 9.5 through 9.7 have been reproduced here in a smaller size than the originals generated in SPSS 19.)

Charts and graphs (frequencies) with SPSS 19.

As you can see, the charts are based on descriptive statistics, but you have to run them from the *Frequencies* option, not *Descriptives*. When you run frequencies, here's how you can elect to add charts to the data output.

1. Click *Analyze* on the toolbar to get the drop-down menu to select the statistic you want to run.

2. Scroll down to *Descriptive Statistics* and on the menu at the right click *Frequencies*.

3. Select as many variables as you want and move your variables from the left into the variable(s) box on the right.

4. Click *Statistics* and check as many descriptives as you want; then click *Continue*.

5. Click *Charts* and select either the bar, pie, or histogram option. With bar and pie you have the option of either frequencies or percentages, and with histograms you can include the normal curve (or not). End by clicking *Continue*.

6. Click *OK* to generate your results in the output view.

7. Print the data by clicking the printer icon, and save it if you wish by copying and pasting it into a Word file (highlight it, press *Control c* to copy and *Control v* to paste).

Nominal-Level Data

See Table 9.5 for a nominal-level computer printout of descriptive statistics and frequencies, followed by a computer-generated pie chart and bar chart.

Frequencies and measures of position (percentage).
As shown, the frequency of African Americans is 51 and that of Whites is 43 (N = 94). It is also helpful to know the *percentage* of each group. Of the sample, 54.3% were African American and 45.7% were White. The target sample size was 50 of each race. The valid percent is given in case there are problems with the data. The cumulative percent is also given. SPSS automatically generates percentages. We can see that the sample is pretty equal between the two groups. However, there are options to get more detailed percentages. Percentages, with the mode below, are the most appropriate measures of nominal-level data.

Measures of central tendency (mode).
- *Mean (meaningless).* With nominal data, the mean is *meaningless* and should be ignored. The mean of .457 is meaningless because the values 0 and 1, which are used to calculate the mean, are arbitrarily assigned. Also, if values were 1 and 2, the mean would be different.
- *Median (not informative).* The median is .000, which is also not very informative with nominal data.
- *Mode.* The mode is the most important measure of central tendency with nominal data. The mode tells us that the most frequent value is 0. Or, more importantly, that the sample has more African Americans than Whites. If we were to go on to inferential statistics, we could do a Chi-square to determine if there are significantly more African Americans than Whites. (The Chi-square, covered in Chapter 12, is based on comparing frequencies/modes.)

Measures of dispersion (not informative).
- *Range (not informative).* The maximum of 1.000 minus the minimum .000 is the range of 1.000. As with the median, the range is not informative with nominal data. Simply knowing the number of groups is more meaningful than the range.
- *Variance and standard deviation (meaningless).* The computer will give you the variance and standard deviation. However, the variance and standard deviation is based on the mean, which is meaningless, and thus is not an appropriate measure of nominal data. Therefore, these two measures are not included in Table 9.5.

Measures of shape (meaningless).
The shape of the curve to determine skewness and kurtosis are meaningless for nominal level data because they are based on the mean and standard deviation. So if the mean and standard deviation are meaningless, so are the measures of shape.

Charts and graphs.   Pie and bar charts are appropriate representations of nominal-level data and are shown as part of Table 9.5. However, histograms are not very meaningful without several scales and thus are not shown for the two scales.

Table 9.5   Nominal-Level Data Computer Printout

A. Descriptive Statistics: Race of the individual.

N	Valid	94
	Missing	0
Mean		.46
Std. Error of Mean		.052
Median		.00
Mode		0
Std. Deviation		.501
Variance		.251
Skewness		.174
Std. Error of Skewness		.249
Kurtosis		-2.013
Std. Error of Kurtosis		.493
Range		1
Minimum		0
Maximum		1
Sum		43

B. Frequency: Race of the individual.

		Frequency	Percent	Valid Percent	Cumulative Percent
Valid	African-American	51	54.3	54.3	54.3
	white	43	45.7	45.7	100.0
	Total	94	100.0	100.0	

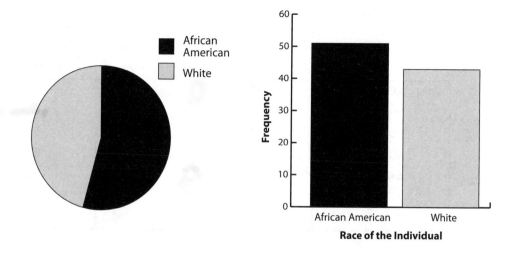

Ordinal-Level Data

See Table 9.6 for an example of an SPSS computer printout of ordinal data based on the level of education of the sample participants.

Measures of position (percentage).

Of the sample, the percentage of respondents for each value (1–6) are presented. Combined percentages give us 47.9% with less than a high school education and 42.6% with college educations (including grad school). Percentages are a good measure with ordinal data.

Table 9.6   Ordinal-Level Data Computer Printout

A. Statistics: Level of education.

N	Valid	94
	Missing	0
Mean		3.57
Std. Error of Mean		.214
Median		3.00
Mode		6
Std. Deviation		2.076
Variance		4.312
Skewness		.109
Std. Error of Skewness		.249
Kurtosis		−1.767
Std. Error of Kurtosis		.493
Range		5
Minimum		1
Maximum		6

B. Frequency: Level of education.

		Frequency	Percent	Valid Percent	Cumulative Percent
Valid	elementary	18	19.1	19.1	19.1
	not done HS	27	28.7	28.7	47.9
	HS	6	6.4	6.4	54.3
	not done college	3	3.2	3.2	57.4
	college	6	6.4	6.4	63.8
	grad school	34	36.2	36.2	100.0
	Total	94	100.0	100.0	

Table 9.6   *(continued)*

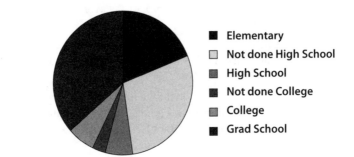

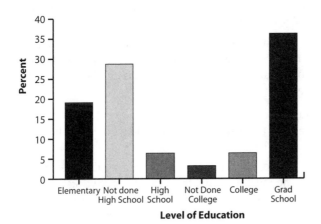

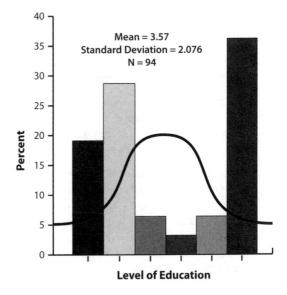

Measures of central tendency.

- *Mean.* The mean is 3.574, or the average education level is between high school and some college.
- *Median.* The median is the most commonly used measure of central tendency with ordinal data. The median is 3.000. Note that the median is based on the frequencies, not the scales 1–6 (3.5).
- *Mode.* The value with the highest frequency is 6 (or 34 participants have a graduate school education). The distribution is bimodal (there are high frequencies at both ends of the distribution). Note that this is a wide variance, and it is not a normal distribution (bell-shaped curve).

Measures of dispersion (range).

- *Range.* The maximum of 6.000 minus the minimum 1.000 is the range of 5.000. Range is the more common measure of ordinal data.
- *Variance and standard deviation.* The variance is 4.312 and the computer takes its square root as the standard deviation of 2.076. Because we don't have a mean based on actual number of years of education, standard deviation is not the best measure of variance, but it can be used.

Measures of shape (charts and graphs).

With several scales of measurement, the shape of the distribution can be easily seen in the bar chart and even more easily in the histogram.

- *Normal or skewed distribution?* By looking at the charts, we can see that the distribution doesn't look normal. To be more accurate, from the descriptive statistics, the skew value is .109, so we know that the distribution is positively skewed, with the tail stretching toward the right, to larger values (mode grad school).
- *Kurtosis.* As we can see from the charts, there are only a few scores in the middle of the distribution. A large proportion of the sample scores fall toward the two tails. To be more accurate, from the descriptive statistics table, the kurtosis value is –1.767, so we know that the distribution has a *platykurtic* kurtosis (it is flatter and broader than a normal distribution).

Interval/Ratio-Level Data

See Table 9.7 for an example of a computer printout. With interval/ratio data you have real numbers. Therefore, it is not necessary to label the values because it is easy to remember what the vales represent; they are years in Table 9.7. (The pie chart is not a recommended way to display the results in cases like this one, as you can see from the 20 different "slices.")

Frequencies and measures of position (not commonly used).

For a list of frequencies, return to Table 9.2. Of the sample, the percentage of respondents for each value (1–20) are presented. Although you do have percentages, the mean and standard deviation are better measures with interval/ratio data. Thus, frequency distributions are not commonly shown with interval/ratio data.

Split file. Above, we have presented the total sample descriptive statistics. However, by using the *Split files* command (in the data menu of SPSS) you could also run the descriptive statistics for the African Americans and Whites separately. With this research design to test differences between races, the split file should be run so you can get the descriptive for each group separately to compare similarities and differences.

Table 9.7   Interval/Ratio-Level Data Computer Printout

Statistics

Years business owned before loan application.

N	Valid	94
	Missing	0
Mean		7.94
Std. Error of Mean		.465
Median		8.00
Mode		9
Std. Deviation		4.512
Variance		20.361
Skewness		.508
Std. Error of Skewness		.249
Kurtosis		−.239
Std. Error of Kurtosis		.493
Range		19
Minimum		1
Maximum		20

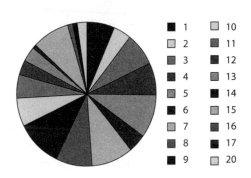

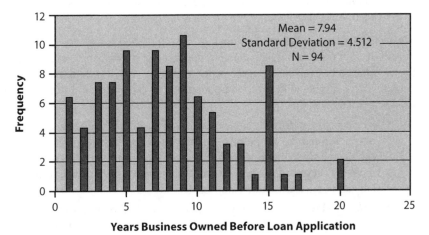

Mean = 7.94
Standard Deviation = 4.512
N = 94

(continued)

Table 9.7   *(continued)*

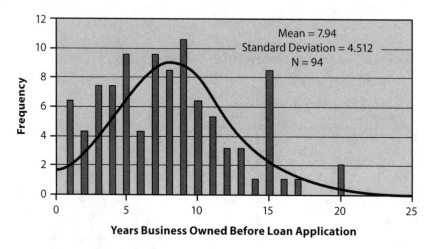

Years Business Owned Before Loan Application

Measures of central tendency.

- *Mean.* The mean is the most commonly used measure of central tendency with interval/ratio data. With the T-test (discussed in Chapter 12), the means are compared to determine if differences are significant between groups of nominal data—race.

- *Median (with outliers).* The median, or mid-point of the data, is 8.000.

- *Mode (limited information).* The value with the highest frequency is 9, or 10 participants have 9 years of prior business ownership.

Measures of dispersion (standard deviation).

- *Range.* The maximum of 20.000 minus the minimum 1.000 is the range of 19.000.

- *Variance and standard deviation.* The standard deviation is most commonly used with interval/ratio data. The variance is 20.361 and its square root is the standard deviation of 4.512. The standard deviation is fairly large.

Measures of shape (charts and graphs).

With several scales of measurement, the shape of the distribution can easily be seen in the bar chart and even more easily in the histogram of ratio data. Note that a pie chart becomes too complex with more than about seven categories and thus is not commonly used with interval/ratio data.

- *Normal or skewed distribution?* By looking at the histogram that accompanies Table 9.7 we can see that the shape of the distribution appears to be somewhat normal, but with the tail stretching toward the right, to larger values (more years, 15 and 20), it is positively skewed. We also know it has a positive distribution from the descriptive statistics because the skew value is .508.

- *Kurtosis.* As we can see, many of the scores are in the middle of the distribution and it looks tall. However, looks can be deceiving. Based on the descriptive statistic kurtosis value of −.239, we must conclude that the shape of the curve is actually platykurtic (flatter and broader than a normal distribution). Table 9.8 is a good review of the chapter, as it summarizes descriptive statistics.

CONCEPTUAL OBJECTIVE 7

State the most appropriate descriptive statistics for each level of data measurement.

Table 9.8   Descriptive Statistics

Measures of Descriptive Statistics	Measures with Descriptive Statistic Categories	Primary Level of Measurement
Position indicates a value based on its relation to the other values in the distribution)	• Percentage (percentage of *participants* with same score)	Nominal (all)
	• *Quartiles* (breaks data into fourths—25, 50, 75, etc.)	All (standardized)
	• *Decals* (breaks data into groups of 10%)	All (standardized)
Central Tendency where values center in a distribution	• *Mean* (arithmetic average)	Interval/ratio (ordinal)
	• *Median* (midpoint of distribution)	Ordinal (outliers)
	• *Mode* (the most frequent value)	Nominal
Dispersion the degree to which values are spread out in a distribution	• *Range* (span of the values; subtract the lowest from the highest)	Ordinal
	• *Variance* (a measure of average score deviation from the mean squared)	Interval/ratio (ordinal)
	• *Standard deviation* (*s*) (square root of the variance)	Interval/ratio (ordinal)
Shape the number of frequencies within a distribution that results in its shape	1. *Skew* (negative or left and positive or right)	All
	2. *Kurtosis* (mesokurtic—normal curve, leptokurtic—tall and thin, and platykurtic—flat and broad shaped)	All

---

SKI WEST STUDY

As we bring this chapter to a close, you should be able to:
- *organize data (edit, code and enter);*
- *understand the role of statistics in research;*
- *be able to make frequency distributions;*
- *calculate and understand descriptive statistics to measure central tendency (mean, median, mode); variance (range variance, standard deviation); and distribution shape (skew and kurtosis); and*
- *know which descriptive measurements are the most appropriate to use based on the level of your data. (See Table 9.12 for an overview of descriptive statistics.)*

Matt McLeish ran descriptive statistics. Some of the descriptives are stated in his completed study (Appendix CS) in Table 2, Tests of Difference: Conscientious Scales and End-of-Season Scores by Gender, Age, and Department, which also includes measures of central tendency (means) and measures of dispersion (standard deviations).

CHAPTER SUMMARY AND GLOSSARY

The chapter summary is organized in a way that provides you with the answers necessary to help you meet the conceptual objectives for this chapter.

1. **Explain item nonresponse and six options for dealing with it.**
   Nonresponse items are questions that have not been completed by participants. There are six options for dealing with nonresponse: (1) Discard the entire questionnaire when several important questions are not answered. (2) Just leave the value blank and use different sample sizes with different questions. (3) Plug in values. With interval- and ratio-level data, plug in the mean. With ordinal and scale intervals, plug in the midpoint. With nominal data, plug in values, alternating answers based on expected proportion of responses. (4) Drop the question. When too many respondents don't answer the question it can cause bias. (5) Follow up by contacting the participants and asking for the missing information. (6) Use alternative sources of data when you can't get participants to respond.

2. **Describe the three activities of data organizing in preparation for statistical analysis.**
   The three activities of data organizing are editing, coding, and entering. *Editing* is the process of getting data ready for coding and data entry by ensuring the completeness, consistency, and reliability of data. *Coding* is the process of assigning numbers or other symbols to variables and question answers, so they can be grouped into a limited number of categories. *Data entry* is the process of getting the data into a medium for viewing and manipulating, including statistical analysis.

3. **Discuss the (a) role, (b) use, and (c) classification of statistics in research.**
   (a) The role of statistics in research is to increase the probability of making valid and reliable decisions by explaining, understanding, predicting, and controlling phenomena that deal with relationships between variables. (b) Statistics are the tools that are used for interpreting the results of data analysis and drawing conclusions to answer research questions/test hypotheses. (c) The classification of statistics is descriptive or inferential. Descriptive statistics explains characteristics of the data or describes a large amount of data in an abbreviated fashion. Tables and charts are commonly used to present data. Inferential statistics are used to draw conclusions and make statements about the population, to answer the research questions/test hypotheses.

4. **Compare the measures of central tendency.**
   The mean, median, and mode are similar in that they all measure where the values center in a distribution. However, the mean is the arithmetic average and is primarily used with interval/ratio and ordinal data as the measure of central tendency. The median is the midpoint of the distribution and is primarily used with ordinal data and when the mean has outliers. The mode is the most frequent value and is primarily used with nominal data.

5. **Compare the measures of dispersion.**
   The range, variance, and standard deviation are similar in that they all measure the degree to which the values spread out in a distribution. However, the range is simply the difference between the largest and smallest value and is primarily used with ordinal and sometimes interval/ratio-level data. A deviation compares each

value to the mean to measure how much each varies. The variance is the average of the squared deviations, and it is not commonly used. The standard deviation is the variance squared, and it is primarily used with interval/ratio-level data.

6. **Discuss the difference between the distribution shapes.**
   There are two primary measures of departure from normal shape—skewness and kurtosis. A *normal* distribution is a theoretical frequency distribution with a bell-shaped symmetrical curve. A *skewed* distribution has more of the frequency scores near one end of a distribution than at the other end. When the extreme scores are at the lower end of the distribution, this gives the shape a negative or left-tailed skew; when the extreme scores are at the higher end of the distribution, this gives the shape a positive or right-tailed skew.

   Kurtosis measures the mesokurtic (normal), leptokurtic (peaked) or platykurtic (flat) shape of a distribution of frequencies. The mesokurtic distribution approaches the shape of a normal curve, being neither too peaked nor too flat. The leptokurtic curve is taller and thinner than a normal distribution, and it has a positive value. The platykurtic curve is shorter and broader than a normal distribution, and it has a negative value.

7. **State the most appropriate descriptive statistics for each level of data measurement.**
   With nominal-level data, frequencies with measure of position, percentages, and the mode are the most appropriate measures; the mean and median, variance and standard deviation, and shapes are meaningless. With ordinal data, the most appropriate measure of central tendency is the median and the variance measure is the range; the mean and shape are sometimes used. With interval/ratio data, the most appropriate measure of central tendency is the mean and for the measure of variance the standard deviation is the most appropriate measure. The shape of the distribution is measured for skewness and kurtosis.

8. **Define the following key terms.**
   Select one or more methods: (1) fill in the missing key terms from memory, (2) match the key terms with their definitions below, or (3) copy the key terms in order from the list at the beginning of the chapter.

descriptive statistics	measures of dispersion	range
frequency distribution	measures of position	role of statistics
inferential statistics	measures of shape	skewed distribution
kurtosis	median	standard deviation
mean	mode	statistics
measures of central tendency	normal distribution	variance

   _____ tabulates how many participants scored each value.

   _____ indicate a value based on its relation to the other values in the distribution; measures include percentages, decals, and quartiles.

   _____ in research is to increase the probability of making valid and reliable decisions by explaining, understanding, predicting, and controlling phenomena that deal with relationships between variables.

   _____ are numerical facts collected for study.

_____ explains characteristics of the data or describes a large amount of data in an abbreviated fashion by measuring central tendency, variance, and the shape of the distribution.

_____ provide data-analysis results that are used to derive conclusions about the relationship between variables to answer the research questions/test hypotheses.

_____ indicate where values center in a distribution; measures include the mean, median, and mode.

_____ indicate the degree to which values are spread out in a distribution; measures include the range, variance, and standard deviation.

_____ indicate the distribution curve's shape; measures include skewness and kurtosis.

_____ is the arithmetic average; it is the appropriate measure of central tendency for interval/ratio-level data.

_____ is the midpoint that divides the distribution values into two equal parts; it is the appropriate measure of central tendency for ordinal-level data and with outliers.

_____ is the value that appears most frequently in a distribution; it is the appropriate measure of central tendency for nominal-level data.

_____ measures variance in the span of the scores; subtract the lowest from the highest.

_____ is a measure of average score deviation from the mean squared.

_____ is the average distance of all the scores in the distribution from the mean; it is the square root of the variance.

_____ is a theoretical frequency distribution with a bell-shaped symmetrical curve.

_____ has more of the frequency scores near one end of a distribution than the other.

_____ measures the mesokurtic (normal), leptokurtic (peaked) or platykurtic (flat) shape of a normal distribution of frequencies.

WRITTEN ASSIGNMENTS

The research proposal does not include any statistical analysis; therefore, there are no instructions for this until Chapter 10. Instructions do continue for both assignments below.

APPENDIX CS, ASSIGNMENT 3 (RESULTS)

You will create the results section of the completed paper in chapters 9–14. For this chapter, run the descriptive statistics for all of your variables described in your research methodology section, as discussed and presented in this chapter. Return to your Method section and add your descriptive statistics to the Results section in your study. You may also make a table to present the descriptives. For more details of this assignment, turn to the results section in Part V, Appendix CS, Completed Study.

APPENDIX SA, ASSIGNMENT 3 (INTRODUCTION, METHOD AND DESCRIPTIVE STATISTICS)
See the instructions for developing the introduction and method sections of this assignment. Run the descriptive statistics for all of your variables in your questionnaire, as discussed and presented in this chapter. For examples of a statistical analysis paper, turn to Part VI, Appendix SA, Statistical Analysis.

EXERCISES

VARIABLE AND MEASUREMENT LEVEL

9-1   A cost accountant is concerned about keeping the cost of rejected products down in the production department. The cost accountant wants to know if there are more rejected products later in the workday. In other words, is there a correlation between the number of hours worked and the number of rejected products? The cost accountant goes to the records and determines how many products are rejected during various hours of the work shift for 40 different days. Identify the dependent (Y) and independent variables (X) and their measurement levels, as in Table 9.1.

9-2   A government statistician keeps track of the Consumer Outlook Index. So for this year the same random sample of 1,000 people will be called each quarter and asked: "Do you believe the economy will get better in the next quarter? The economy will remain the same? Or that the economy will get worse in the next quarter?" The 1,000 scores (1–3) are entered into the computer after each quarter. The second-quarter data has been entered into the computer. The statistician wants to know if the index has changed between the first and second quarters. Identify the Y and X and their measurement levels.

9-3   The manager of a major league baseball team wants to estimate his team's winning percentage for the season. The manager believes that the players' batting averages (BA) and runs batted in (RBI) can be used. So, he runs the statistics to find out. Identify the Y and Xs and their measurement levels.

9-4   The sales manager is interested in determining the profile of buyers of the company's products. The manager wants to compare the ages and incomes of buyers and nonbuyers to determine if there is a best combination of age and income to target for sales calls. Identify the Y and X and their measurement levels.

9-5   The production manager is concerned about the quality of the product made. The manager listed 25 different questions, using the highest level of measurement for all questions, to ask the company's best 50 customers about the quality of the product. However, the manager wants to know if these different questions about quality can be grouped together in some categorical method so results are easier to understand. Identify the Y and Xs and their measurement levels.

CALCULATING MEASURES OF CENTRAL TENDENCY

For the two exercises below, calculate the sample size (N), mean, median, and mode.

9-6   Cases 18 17 15 14 13

N =   mean =   median =   mode =

9-7   Value (X)   Frequency (f) = Xf

7	1
6	3
5	2
4	5
3	4
2	1
1	1

N =   sum =

mean =   median =   mode =

CALCULATING MEASURES OF DISPERSION

9-8   What is the range of 5, 5, 2, 5, 3?

9-9   Using the data in 9-8, what is the variance and standard deviation?

$$X \qquad \bar{X} \qquad X - \bar{X} \qquad \left(X - \bar{X}\right)^2$$

9-10   Using the data in 9-8 and 9-9, what is the range in which 68% of total values will fall?

USING THE COMPUTER: DESCRIPTIVE STATISTIC PROBLEM 9-1

You must use a statistical software program to run statistics to solve this problem. Be sure to make a hard copy of your statistics (your instructor may want you to hand it in with this assignment) and save your work on a portable storage device. (Computer problems also appear in the other statistical chapters 11–14.)

1. Set up variable columns for the following five variables for a research study about political parties.

2. Then place the values in each column from below. You had 10 people fill out a simple survey for this data. You should have 5 variable columns and 10 rows of data. Numbers 1–10 identify participant rows.

    Gender: (1) male, (2) female, (3) m, (4) f, (5) m, (6) m, (7) f, (8) f, (9) f, (10) f
    (Code gender as 1 = male, 2 = female)

    Income: (1) medium, (2) low, (3) high, (4) l, (5) m, (6) m, (7) m, (8) h, (9) m, (10) m
    (Code income as 1 = low, 2 = medium, 3 = high)

    Satisfaction: (1) 5, (2) 5, (3) 3, (4) 3, (5) 4, (6) 4, (7) 4, (8) 6, (9) 7, (10) 2
    (Code as dissatisfied 1 2 3 4 5 6 7 satisfied)

    Political Party: (1) republican, (2) democrat, (3) independent, (4) r, (5) r, (6) r, (7) i, (8) d, (9) d, (10) d
    (Label 1 = repub. = 2 democrat, = 3 indep.)

    Age: (1) 25, (2) 33, (3) 36, (4) 41, (5) 47, (6) 57, (7) 29, (8) 38, (9) 44, (10) 52
    (No need to label age scores.)

3. Run the frequencies and descriptive statistics listed in this chapter, present them in tables like the ones below, and complete items 4–7 below, using the statistics.

4. At the same time, make at least one type of graph (pie, bar, histogram) of the data for each variable.

5. Complete the following information using the data in item 2 above.

Variable	Measurement level	# of scales/ groups	Appropriate measure of central tendency	Appropriate measure of variance/position
Gender				
Income				
Satisfaction				
P Party				
Age				

6. Complete the following information from your descriptive statistics printouts.

Variable	Mean	Median	Mode	Range	Variance	s	Skew	Kurtosis
Gender								
Income								
Satisfact.								
P Party								
Age								

7. Identify the distribution shape for each of the following variables: left/negative, normal/symmetrical, or right/positive skewed, and whether kurtosis is mesokurtic, leptokurtic, or platykurtic.

   Gender

   Income

   Satisfaction

   Political Party

   Age

10

Selecting the Appropriate Inferential Statistic
A Decision Tree

CONCEPTUAL OBJECTIVES

The conceptual objectives below also appear at appropriate places within the chapter at points when you will have accessed the information necessary to attain them. They appear again at the end of the chapter in the Summary and Glossary section, along with explanations that will enable you to meet the objectives.

After studying this chapter, you should be able to:

1. Discuss (a) tests of difference, (b) the number of variables and measurement levels of the dependent and independent variables, and (c) matched pairs.

2. Define tests of interaction and state the number of variables and measurement levels of the dependent and independent variables with two-way and multivariate ANOVA.

3. Discuss (a) what tests of association measure, (b) the appropriate measurement levels of the variables used with correlation, and (c) when to use a test of difference rather than correlation.

4. Describe tests of prediction and the number of dependent and independent variables and their measurement levels.

5. Discuss tests of interrelationship and the number and level of measurement of the variables.

6. Define the following key terms (listed in order of their appearance in the chapter).

inferential statistical tests	tests of association
tests of difference	tests of prediction
matched pairs	tests of interrelationship
tests of interaction	

SKILL DEVELOPMENT OBJECTIVES

After studying this chapter, you should be able to select the appropriate statistical technique for a research design. Note that all of the exercises (10-1 through 10-31) are to be completed *after* you read and understand the entire chapter.

The Research Process

(1) The research question/purpose of the study, literature review, and hypotheses.	(2) Research design methodology for collecting data and statistics.	(3) Data analysis and interpreting results.	(4) Discussing results and making conclusions.
• *Introduction*	• *Method*	• *Results*	• *Discussion*
Chapters 1–3	Chapters 4–8	Chapters 9–14	Chapters 9–14

In prior chapters we presented the research process shown above. We are now in the data-analysis portion of the book, but you must state in your Method section which statistical test you will use to test your hypotheses. In this chapter you will learn *how* to select the appropriate statistical test so you can include this information in your Method section. In chapters 11–14, you will learn how to interpret statistical hypothesis tests. The Decision Tree in this chapter will enable you to select, from 30 statistical tests, the appropriate test for a given research design.

10.1 Using the Decision Tree: What Are You Testing?

The title of this chapter is "Selecting the Appropriate *Inferential Statistic*: A Decision Tree"—so let's begin by recalling that in chapters 4 and 9 we discussed *inferential statistics*, which provide data-analysis results that are used to derive conclusions about the relationship between variables. We are going beyond simple descriptive statistics, in most cases, to draw conclusions about a population based on data collected from a sample.

Rather than memorize over 30 statistical techniques, the author and his colleague, Dr. Mary Ann Coughlin, have developed the Decision Tree (shown in Figure 10.1) to help you to easily select the appropriate inferential statistic. To determine the appropriate statistical technique, use the Decision Tree by answering a series of three to six questions. The first question you will always ask is, *What are you testing?* (See the black box in the upper left-hand corner of the figure.) Simply answer the question by making your choice from the first column (directly below the black box), and then follow the sequence of the Decision Tree from left to right until you come to the last column, which indicates the type of statistical test to use.

Recall from Chapter 4 that there are five statistical research designs for tests of: (1) *difference*, (2) *interaction*, (3) *association*, (4) *prediction*, and (5) *interrelationship*—the five major classifications of **inferential statistical tests.**

The next five sections in this chapter cover each of the classifications of statistical tests, and chapters 12–14 detail how to conduct most of the various statistical tests for each of the five types of test. Each type of statistical test is presented, followed by an example of how to use the Decision Tree to select the appropriate test. In various boxes throughout the chapter are examples that tell you to use the Decision Tree to select the appropriate test. When you come to these examples, turn to the Decision Tree in Figure 10.1 and follow along to answer the questions—in other words, look back and forth between the examples and the Decision Tree. (You may want to print a copy of the Decision Tree from the CD that accompanies this book, so you do not have to turn the book pages to see it when reading examples and doing the exercises at the end of the chapter.)

10.2 Tests of Difference

Tests of difference compare values of any level of dependent variable between the nominal independent variable groups. Note on the Decision Tree that you run different statistical tests based on the number and level of the dependent variable(s) (DV/Y). The Y is always what you are measuring or comparing between the groups. The groups compared with any number of scales/groups are always the Xs (the nominal independent variable or IV/X). When the Y measurement level is ordinal or interval/ratio, you have one Y and one X, with any number of groups. When the Y is nominal, you can have any number of nominal Xs, providing you have a large enough sample for the number of Xs, as will be explained in Chapter 12 with the chi-square test of difference.

Groups within a Nominal Independent Variable

With a nominal IV/X, you take a sample and compare differences between scales. In other words, you break a nominal X into groups or subsamples by its scales to compare differences between the groups. For example, you can test for differences in a Y (income) between an X group(s)/scale(s) (gender), as in Box 10.1 (on p. 272).

Remember that males and females are not two variables; they are two groups of one variable—gender. Thus, the major role of nominal-level variables is to provide descriptive statistics, to compare differences between higher-level variables, and to compare differences between all nominal variables. The nominal X groups can be unmatched or matched.

Figure 10.1   Decision Tree

What Are You Testing?	Number and Level of Measurement of DV (Y)	Number of Nominal IV (X)	Number of Groups of X	Groups of X	Statistic
Difference (chapter 12)	1 Nominal	1 or more	2	Unmatched	Chi-Square
				Matched	McNemar
			3+	Unmatched	Chi-Square
				Matched	Cochran Q
	1 Ordinal	1	2	Unmatched	Mann-Whitney U
				Matched	Wilcoxon Matched Pairs
			3+	Unmatched	Kruskal-Wallis ANOVA
				Matched	Friedman ANOVA
	1 Interval / Ratio	1	2	Unmatched	t or z-test
				Matched	Paired t or z-test
			3+	Unmatched	One-way ANOVA*
				Matched	One-way Repeated Measures of ANOVA
Interaction (chapter 13)	1 Interval / Ratio	2 or 3+	2 or 3+	Unmatched	Two-way (Factorial) ANOVA*
				Matched	Repeated M. Factorial ANOVA
				Mixed	Mixed Factorial ANOVA
	2 or 3+ Interval / Ratio	1	2 or 3+	Unmatched	One-way Multivariate ANOVA+
				Matched	Repeated Measures MANOVA
		1 or more	2 or 3+	Unmatched	Factorial MANOVA+
				Matched	Repeated M. Factorial MANOVA
				Mixed	Mixed Factorial ANOVA

* adding control covariate variable(s) results in using ANCOVA for any of the ANOVAs
+ adding control covariate variable(s) results in using MANCOVA for any of the MANOVAs

What Are You Testing?

Association (chapter 12)

Lowest Level of All Variables	Number of Variables	Statistic
Ordinal	2	Spearman ρ (Rho) or Kendall τ (Tau)
Ordinal	3+	Kendall Partial Correlation / Kendall τ (Tau)-W
Interval / Ratio	2	Pearson R
Interval / Ratio	3+	Partial Correlation

Prediction (chapter 12)

Number of DV (Y)	Level of Measurement of CV (Y)	Number of IV (X)	Levels of Measurement of IV (X)	Statistic
1	Interval / Ratio	1	Interval / Ratio	Bivariate Regression
		2 or 3+	Interval / Ratio	Multiple Regression—Stepwise / Hierarchical
			Mixed / Nominal	Regression with Dummy Variables
	Nominal / Ordinal	2 or 3+	Interval / Ratio	Logistic Regression / Discriminanat Analysis
			Mixed / Nominal	
2 or 3+	Interval / Ratio	2 or 3+	Interval / Ratio	Structural Equation Modeling / Canonical / Path Analysis
			Mixed / Nominal	With Dummy Variables

Interrelationship (chapter 13)

One Variable—Purpose	Level of Measurement	Statistic
Reduce a number of variables into a limited number of factors	All	Factor Analysis / LISREL
Reduce a number of participants by classifying into groups	All	Cluster Analysis /
	Interval / Ratio	Multidimensional Scaling
	Nominal / Ordinal	Latent Structure Analysis

Box 10.1   Tests of Difference

Y values compared between X for differences in Y values

   Y = Income (interval/ratio level)
   X = Gender (nominal level, two scales/groups)

The mean income of men and women are compared to determine if men or women have significantly higher incomes.

Matched and Unmatched Pairs/Groups

A *matched pairs* group occurs when the dependent variable measure is repeated two or more times to compare differences of the same participant. The most common matched pairs design compares the same participant's Y scores on two occasions—thus called *repeated measures and pre-post test design*. For example, if a researcher developed a program to improve employee job satisfaction and surveyed the same employees one year later to determine whether the level of satisfaction had increased, she would be using a matched pairs pre-post test design. As Box 10.2 shows, this researcher has an option to use the matched or unmatched design. The matched option is shown first because it is the more appropriate design for her situation.

Unmatched measures.

Even when you have the option to use matched pairs (as in the example above), with repeated measures it is more time consuming (and therefore more expensive) to keep track of each person's responses. Also, it is sometimes difficult to reach the same people twice. The sample will most likely drop some participants from period 1 to period 2 as people move, and so on. In addition, in a company with a very high employee turnover that uses a yearly survey, such as in a fast-food restaurant, many of the employees measured the first time are gone for the repeated measure that occurs over several years. In addition, if the survey questions change (new ones added, old ones dropped over time), the validity of using the same participant repeatedly decreases. Plus, if the same employees are used for

---

Box 10.2   Matched and Unmatched Groups

Matched vs. Unmatched Design—employee satisfaction with and without a program

   Y = Satisfaction (interval, 7 levels)

(A) Matched

   X = Pre-post test (nominal—survey the same employee before and after program)

   or

(B) Unmatched

   X = Year 1 and 2 (nominal—survey different employees, no program implemented between surveys)

The mean level of satisfaction in period 1 is compared to period 2 to determine if the level of satisfaction has changed and hopefully has increased over time.

---

several years, does the sample still represent the population? Newer employees may not share the same views. Human resources departments regularly use yearly employee surveys. However, if an organization does not take any action to change the survey results and the survey is used over several years, unmatched groups are more commonly used. Thus, in Box 10.2 the unmatched group (the second X) would be appropriate.

Notice that the matched pairs example in Box 10.2 uses the term *pre-post test* and the unmatched pairs example uses *year 1* and *year 2*. Pre-post test should be used only with matched repeated measures, because there is a difference in how you enter data into the computer and how the computer runs the data for pre-post test versus for years 1 and 2.

Most groups are *unmatched* because they cannot be matched. For example, in Box 10.1 a comparison is being made between men's and women's income. Also, you generally cannot match political party, race, religion, and others groups to compare matched pairs differences.

Matched natural groups.

A less common *matched* method includes using a natural pair group, such as husband's and wife's Y satisfaction with marriage or a product scored on a scale of **4** satisfied, **3** somewhat satisfied, **2** somewhat dissatisfied, **1** dissatisfied. The natural group does not have the problem of getting the same participants' values twice, because you only take the measurement once and compare it between the natural pairs and totals or unmatched totals.

Independent (unmatched) and dependent (matched) groups.

The grouping variable is also called *independent groups* rather than unmatched, and *dependent groups* rather than matched pairs. The reason we use unmatched and matched is to avoid confusing these terms with dependent and independent variables. Remember, as shown on the Decision Tree, the groups are always the scales of a nominal independent variable. So don't be confused when a statistical package uses the terms *dependent groups* for matched and *independent groups* for unmatched. If you forget, the test names you see will either have or not have the words *paired* or *repeated measures* to remind you if you are correct.

A comparison of statistical calculations of matched and unmatched pairs.

The unmatched statistical test compares only the total mean (frequency or median/rank mean), and you often have an unequal number in the groups. The matched statistical test is a stronger test because it compares each participant's DV/Y value 1 and Y value 2, and the totals of both groups are compared for significant differences. Thus, the matched pairs test is better for comparison purposes. However, as discussed, it is not always possible or feasible to use matched pairs, and not all statistical software offers this matched pairs test.

Matched pairs can be used only with tests of difference and tests of interaction.

Even if you use matched pairs to collect data and run tests of association, prediction, or interrelationship (discussed later in the chapter), groups are not used with these tests. Therefore, you need to know *what you are you testing*. If it isn't differences or interaction, don't use matched pairs to collect your data.

Control-variable grouping.

A final method, which is less commonly used, is to create a control-variable matched pairs group based on specific qualities. For example, successful and failed businesses that are similar in age, location, size, and type could be considered a matched pair based on four control variables. Thus, a failed three-year-old restaurant in Chicago with 20 employees is compared to a successful five-year-old restaurant in Chicago with 15 employees to control for the possible impact of these variables on differences. Through the control variable group, you ensure that you are not comparing the failed restaurant to a 20-year-old manufacturing firm in Dallas with 2,000 employees—or an unmatched paired group.

With the control-variable matched pair it is much more difficult and time consuming to get participants with multiple control-variable characteristics. The greater the number of control variables, the more difficult and time consuming it is to get the matched pairs. Some researchers also argue that control-variable matching should take place, but that a nonmatched testing procedure should be used. Therefore, there is disagreement in classifying control-variable groups as matched or unmatched. Also, only the tests of difference and interaction allow for using matched or unmatched groups.

Various tests of difference.

With any test of difference, you answer the same six questions. What changes is the measurement levels (nominal, ordinal, interval/ratio) of the one DV/Y, and the number (two or more) and types (unmatched or matched) of groups of the one IV/X. In Chapter 12 you will learn how to conduct the T-test, one-way ANOVA, Mann-Whitney U test, and chi-square tests of difference, as well as how to analyze the test data to make decisions. See Box 10.3 for an example of a test of difference. Be sure to use the Decision Tree as you read it.

Box 10.3   Using the Decision Tree to Select the Appropriate Test of Difference

Winnie wants to know if high- or low-income customers buy more ice cream products. In other words, which group's sales are larger?

Instructions

Using the Decision Tree (Figure 10.1), follow the arrows as the answers to the italicized questions are given.

Solution (Decision)

Question 1: What are you testing? We are testing differences, so follow the arrow down to Difference.

Question 2: What are the number and levels of measurement of DV(Y)? We have 1 Y = sales, which is measured in actual sales volume, and its measurement level is interval/ratio, so follow the arrow to the right to Interval/Ratio.

Question 3: What is the number of nominal IV/X? We have one X, so continue to follow in a straight line to the right.

Question 4: What is the number of X groups? We have two groups (high and low), so follow the top choice (2).

Question 5: What type of X groups? We have unmatched groups because we are not comparing the same participant matched value twice. So follow the top choice (unmatched).

Question 6: What type of statistic? T- or Z-test (the top choice).

CONCEPTUAL OBJECTIVE 1

Discuss (a) tests of difference, (b) the number of variables and measurement levels of the dependent and independent variables, and (c) matched pairs.

10.3 Tests of Interaction

Tests of interaction determine the best combination of three or more variables to maximize value differences; the dependent variable(s) is interval/ratio and the independent variable(s) is nominal level. Note on the Decision Tree that you run different statistical tests based on the number of DV/Y and IV/X.

The test of interaction also performs a test of difference (called a main effect), plus it takes things a step further by determining whether there is an interaction (called a differential effect). A test of interaction determines whether there are differences for multiple variables or a best combination of variables to maximize values.

When to Use a Test of Interaction

There are four criteria for using a test of interaction rather than a test of difference:

1. You must have at least three variables.

2. The DV/Y(s) must be interval/ratio level, which can include rating scales (at least five scales).

3. The IV/X(s) must be nominal level. If Xs are ordinal or interval/ratio you must assign nominal values to them to form groups, as Winnie did in Box 10.3 with income, making it categorical with high or low scales. Again, if you have all nominal Xs, regardless of the number you must use a chi-square test of difference.

4. You should be interested in determining whether there is an *interaction*. If you are not interested in a best combination of variable values, you can often simply run two or more tests of difference rather than a two-way *analysis of variance (ANOVA)* or *multivariate analysis of variance (MANOVA)*.

Whether you run a two-way or multivariate ANOVA depends on the number of Ys and Xs. When you have one Y and two or more Xs you are calculating a two-way ANOVA; and when you have two or more Ys and one or more Xs you have a MANOVA design. MANOVA is the only test in this book that has two or more Ys; all others use one Y or none (a test of interrelationship, discussed later in the chapter). The measurement level of Y and X is the same for both two-way ANOVA and MANOVA tests, as shown below:

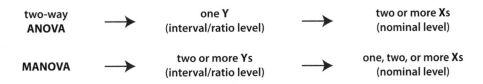

There are *no* variable measurement level differences between two-way ANOVA and MANOVA.

As with a test of difference, with tests of interaction you must determine if you have matched or unmatched IV/X groups. However, with a test of interaction you also can have a *mixed group* design with an X that is matched and an X that is not matched. The three types of group designs with two-way ANOVA and MANOVA are explained below.

Two-Way Analysis of Variance (ANOVA)

The *two*-way ANOVA is so named because you have at least two IV/Xs; it is also called factorial and randomized two-way ANOVA. However, you still only have only one DV/Y, as in a test of difference. In other words, you take a test of difference and add a second X so you can look for a combination of Xs to maximize the value of Y (interaction). Following are examples of unmatched, mixed, and matched two-way ANOVA designs.

Unmatched groups two-way ANOVA.

Let's use satisfaction with student activities as the Y, college class years 1–4 as X, and a second X—major, with seven groupings of majors. You can run a test of difference with ordinal data, but you should not do so with two-way ANOVA. Therefore, we use rating scales of "not satisfied 1 2 3 4 5 6 7 8 9 satisfied," referred to as *interval data*. Notice that we make the design more complex (or a higher-level statistical test) by making the Y the interval-measurement level needed for tests of interaction—making it a true rating scale with nine scales rather than an ordinal measurement level.

The interaction is the best combination of X to maximize the value of the Y. In other words, is there one year of college and one major that are more satisfying than the others? (If we didn't care about an interaction, we could run two lower-level tests of difference between satisfaction and year and satisfaction and major.) Box 10.4 summarizes this design.

Box 10.4   Unmatched Two-Way ANOVA Groups Design

Y = Satisfaction with student activities this year (interval level, nine scales)
X = College year (nominal—first-, second-, third-, and fourth-year students)—*unmatched*
X = Major (nominal level, seven different groupings)—*unmatched*

The mean of satisfaction is compared among the year and major to determine whether there is a significant difference/effect, and whether there is a best combination of year and major that maximizes satisfaction.

Mixed groups two-way ANOVA.

The matched pairs comparison is appropriate and is commonly used with an experimental design, which includes a control group, an experimental group, and a treatment. For example, Carlos, a golf pro who gives lessons, wants to know if his lessons improve trainees' golf scores, so he develops the one-tailed hypothesis and action in Table 10.1. In the table, Ho is the null hypothesis stating that there is no difference. Ha is the alternative hypothesis stating that there is a difference. Only one is selected, based on statistical analysis.

Carlos can design the study using unmatched pairs and compare the combined mean score of all students before and after lessons, or he can choose a stronger design, comparing the score of each trainee, pre (before) and post (after) lessons with a matched pairs design.

Table 10.1   Mixed Groups Two-Way ANOVA Hypothesis and Action

Hypothesis*	Action
Ho: My golf lessons do not improve trainees' scores (mean scores are equal before and after lessons).	Do not advertise an improvement in golf scores of my trainees.
Ha: People who take my lessons improve their scores (mean scores are lower after lessons).	Advertise a specific improvement in scores of my trainees if it is by five or more strokes, and state only that they improve scores if it is between one and four strokes.

*Ho = null hypothesis, Ha = alternative hypothesis

To test his hypothesis, Carlos designs the *classic experimental pre-post test control and experimental groups design*. Carlos gets 50 people to agree to participate in the study, randomly assigning 25 people to an *experimental group* that gets the lessons (called a *treatment*) and the other 25 people to a *control group* that does not get golf lessons (*no treatment*). (You will learn more about true experimental and quasi-experimental designs in Chapter 14.)

Near the middle of the golf season, on test day one (*pre-test*) all 50 participants play golf and their scores are recorded. For the next five weeks, the control group plays golf as usual and the experimental group gets the lessons. After five weeks, on test day two (*post-test*) all 50 participants play golf again and their scores are recorded again.

Carlos hypothesizes that there will be no significant difference in the pre-post test scores of the control group (no lessons), and there will be a significant difference/effect in the pre-post test scores of the experimental group that got the lessons (treatment). The best combination (interaction) is post-test experimental group to maximize the difference in golf scores. If the interaction does occur, Carlos can claim that his lessons do improve or "cause" the improvement in golf scores. Box 10.5 presents the mixed groups design variables.

Box 10.5   Mixed Two-Way ANOVA Groups Design

Y = golf scores (interval/ratio level)

Unmatched groups
X = Control group [doesn't get lessons] and experimental group [gets lessons]; two scales

Matched groups
X = Pre-post golf scores compare "same" participants' scores of test days 1 and 2

The hypothesized interaction is post-test experimental group to maximize the difference in golf scores (i.e., the people who get the lessons improve).

Matched groups two-way ANOVA.

Unlike the mixed groups, matched groups do not include a control and test group. The commonly used matched groups design has all participants take both the actual treatment and a placebo (fake) treatment. For example, say you developed a natural vitamin pill you call Energizer to increase energy levels. You get 60 participants to volunteer to try the product for 8 weeks (56 days). Participants are told that you have two Energizer pills (not a placebo) to compare to see if one is superior. (This information is given so that the study is not biased by people guessing if they are taking the real pill or the placebo pill and scoring accordingly.) Before the study begins, you ask everyone what their usual energy level is on a rating scale of "low 1 2 3 4 5 6 7 8 9 high."

You randomly assign 30 participants to group one, and they get the real Energizer pill for the first four weeks (28 days). The other 30 are in group two, and they get the placebo non-vitamin sugar pill. The pills look alike and come in a special container with clear days and weeks marked. Each week is scheduled so that taking the pill begins on a Monday and ends on a Sunday. For each week, on Sunday each participant rates his or her energy level for the week on a special mail-in form, using the same scale used before the study began. The data is mailed in weekly. After four weeks, all participants are asked their energy level again for another pre-change treatment. This time, group one now gets the placebo and group two gets the real Energizer pill. The same packaging and data-collection methods are used.

Both pre-treatment scores are entered into the computer for each four-week period, to calculate the post-treatment energy levels for each participant. So each participant has an energy level before (pre) both treatments, a mean energy level for the month using the Energizer, and a mean energy level for the month using the placebo pill. The pre-post test for each participant will be run using the matched two-way ANOVA.

The hypothesized interaction is that the participants who are taking the real Energizer pill will have a higher mean energy level than before they started the study and than when they were taking the placebo. If participants have higher energy levels when taking the Energizer, you can claim that it increases energy. If participants have the same level of energy before and during the study using both pills—or worse, if energy levels when taking Energizer are lower than when taking the placebo or than pre-test energy levels—you cannot claim that it works. The design is shown in Box 10.6.

Multiple Analysis of Variance (MANOVA)

MANOVA gets its name because you have multiple (two or more) DV/Ys and possibly IV/Xs. In other words, you can take a test of difference and add one or more Ys and even Xs. However, there must be a correlation between the Ys; you run a correlation between Ys to determine if there is a relationship. If they are not correlated, run separate tests of difference or two-way ANOVA. Below are examples of unmatched, mixed, and matched two-way ANOVA designs.

Box 10.6 Matched Groups Two-Way ANOVA (Repeated Measures)

Y = Energy level (interval/ratio 1–9)
X = Pre-energy level before taking the placebo pill (nominal)
X = Post-energy level after taking the placebo pill (nominal)
X = Pre-energy level before taking the Energizer pill (nominal)
X = Post-energy level after taking the Energizer pill (nominal)

The hypothesized interaction is that participants have higher levels of energy when taking the Energizer pill.

Unmatched groups MANOVA.

Using the MANOVA design in Box 10.7 to determine if students are satisfied with the student activities by class, you could make the design a more complex, higher-level statistical test by adding another Y variable that you believe is related to satisfaction (e.g., satisfaction with the student union building facilities, measured on a Likert scale of 1–9).

Box 10.7   Unmatched Groups MANOVA Design

Y = Satisfaction with student activities (interval/ratio level 1–9)
Y = Satisfaction with student union facilities (interval/ratio level 1–9)
X = Class year (nominal, years 1–4 students)—*unmatched*

The mean of both satisfactions is compared among the four classes to determine if there is a significant difference/effect in satisfaction.

Matched groups MANOVA.

Using husbands' and wives' levels of satisfaction with their marital relationship, we can add a related Y, satisfaction with having children. See Box 10.8 for an example of this design.

Box 10.8   Matched Groups MANOVA Design

Y = Satisfaction with spousal relationship (interval/ratio level 1–9)
Y = Satisfaction with having children (interval/ratio level 1–9)
X = Husband and wife (nominal)—*matched*

The mean of satisfaction is compared between the matched husband and wife to determine if there is a significant difference/effect in satisfaction.

Mixed factorial MANOVA groups.

A senator has not been getting good ratings for trustworthiness and performance in voter opinion polls. The senator has decided to try to increase public opinion by working to pass a bill that would please many voters. The senator randomly selects 200 voters, who are called and asked on a scale of 1–9 how they would rate the senator on performance and trustworthiness. After getting the bill passed and publicized, the same 200 voters are called and asked to rate the senator again. The senator is also interested in knowing if there is a difference in rating scores by gender; see Box 10.9 for an example of this design. (Note that this is a factorial design because it has more than one X.)

In Chapter 14 you will learn more about two-way ANOVA and MANOVA and how to analyze the test data to make decisions. See Box 10.10 for an example of a test of interaction. Be sure to use the Decision Tree as you read it.

Box 10.9   Mixed Factorial MANOVA Groups Design

Y = Senator's performance score (interval/ratio level 1–9)
Y = Trustworthiness score (interval/ratio level 1–9)
X = Pre-post legislation performance rating by the *same people* (nominal)—*matched*
X = Pre-post legislation trust rating by the *same people* (nominal)—*matched*
X = Gender (nominal)—*unmatched*

Box 10.10   Using the Decision Tree to Select the Appropriate Test of Interaction

Judy has invented a new product. To keep sales prices down, Judy wants the product to come in only one color (either white, gray, or green). She is also considering two different advertising campaigns. Judy wants to know if there is a best combination of color and ad campaign, or at least which color and ad will result in the highest level of sales.

Instructions

Using the Decision Tree, follow the left-to-right progression as the answers to the questions are given.

Solution (Decision)

Question 1: What are you testing? We are testing interaction. Choose that selection from the column below the black box in the upper left-hand corner.

Question 2: What are the number and level of measurement of Y? There is one Y, *sales*, and it's interval/ratio level. Follow the arrow to the top choice on the right.

Question 3: What is the number of X? There are two: *color* and *ad*. Continue in a straight line to the right.

Question 4: What is the number of X groups? Two Xs—One *color* (three paint color groups—sales of white, gray, green products) and one *ad* (2 campaign groups). Continue to the right.

Question 5: What type of X Groups? Unmatched. The colors and ads are independent of each other. You are looking for a best combination of the two Xs, such as green/ad one, to maximize sales. Continue moving right, to the Statistic column.

Question 6: What type of statistic? Two-way (factorial) ANOVA.

10.4 Tests of Association

Tests of association measure the correlation between two or more ordinal and/or interval/ratio-level variables. Note on the Decision Tree that you run different statistical tests based on the level of variables. Commonly used terms to identify association include relationship, correlation, and covariance. The test of association uses correlation to measure the covariance between variables.

When to Use a Test of Association

The key to selecting association versus differences is the measurement level of the variables. Both tests of differences and tests of interaction are based on comparing the DV/Y scores between the nominal IV/X groups. With the test of association (prediction and interrelationship, discussed later in the chapter) you do not have a nominal X for the purpose of splitting the total sample into groups to make comparisons. In fact, when you don't have a nominal X you cannot compare differences, but you can run a correlation.

Covariance, the relationship between variables, is generally hypothesized to have a positive or negative linear slope. The covariance is positive (an upward sloping curve) when both variables increase together or move in the same direction. The covariance is negative (a downward sloping curve) when one variable increases as the other decreases or moves in the opposite direction. If there is no slope, or a relatively straight line, there is no linear relationship between the variables.

Correlational Designs

This section discusses how to plot correlations both by hand and by using the computer, what you need to know about association, why the Decision Tree does not include a test of association for nominal-level variables, and why the Y and X are interchangeable with correlation.

Hand plotting correlations.

Let's illustrate with hypotheses. *H1: There is a positive association (or linear covariance) between income and age.* To test H1 you ask 20 people who appear to be 40 to 60 years old to tell you their age and income (both variables are interval/ratio). The 20 responses are plotted in Figure 10.2A (you place an X at the income by age for each participant).

H2: There is a negative association (or linear covariance) between energy level and age. To test H2 you ask the same 10 people their energy level on an interval scale of "low 1 2 3 4 5 6 7 8 9 high." The 10 responses are plotted in Figure 10.2B.

After plotting your results, the next step is to draw a line that best fits the data (i.e., comes closest to connecting the plotted Xs). If you have a perfect linear relationship, which rarely if ever happens, all the plotted Xs will be in a straight positive (left to right) or negative (right to left) linear line. The positive association moves from the bottom to the top of the figure and the negative association moves from the top to the bottom. After drawing your line, you determine whether there is a linear relationship. As we can see in Figure 10.2A & B on p. 282, H1 has a positive correlation and H2 has a negative correlation or covariance. In other words, we made a good guess without statistically testing the hypotheses.

Using the computer.

As you will learn in Chapter 13, the computer will plot the data for you, draw the line, tell you the covariance strength and direction of the relationship, and give you the *p-value* (or probability of making a *Type I error*—claiming there is a relationship when there really is none). See Chapter 11 for a detailed discussion of p-values and Type I and Type II errors.

What you need to know about association.

For now, to select the appropriate test of association you must understand three things:

1. *You must clearly understand what a test of association is and when to use correlation.* The information above and the next two points will also help you to understand the proper use of the test of association.

2. *Use multiple scales.* When you statistically test a hypothesis with an association using ordinal or rating scales, be sure to use multiple scales (at least five and preferably seven). If you only use a few scales you have a much greater chance of making a *Type II error* (saying there is no relationship, when there really is).

3. *Do not run a test of association with a nominal variable; run a test of difference.* Even though you can statistically do a test of association with a nominal variable, you don't know the direction of the relationship because the data is not linear, so it makes no logical sense. You cannot claim that nominal variables such as gender or political party are continuous scales of data.

See Table 10.2 for an illustration of an illogical nominal-variable correlation testing *H3: There is a relationship between gender and income* and *H4: There is a relationship between income and political party.*

Figure 10.2   Test of Association

A. *H1: There is a positive association between income and age (correlation results).*

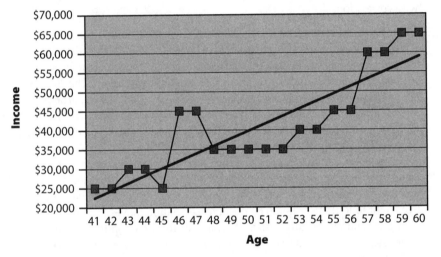

B. *H2: There is a negative relationship between energy level and age (correlation results).*

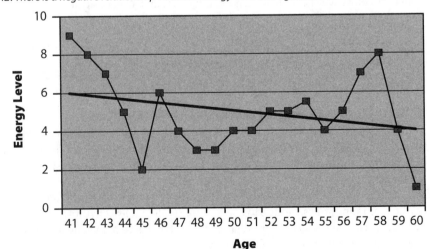

Table 10.2   Illogical Nominal-Variable Correlation

H3 and H4 Correlation results plotted with the frequency of the response			
Income ($)			
65,000		1	
60,000	2		1
55,000		1	2	2
50,000	1	2	3	1
45,000		1		2
40,000	2	1	2	1
35,000	1	1		
30,000	1		1	1
25,000	3	4	1	2
	Males	**Females**	**Republicans**	**Democrats**

The Decision Tree does not include a test of association for nominal-level variables.

Because it is more logical (and is a stronger test) to conduct a test of difference than a test of association with a nominal variable—even though tests called the Phi, Cramer V, Lambda, and Mantel-Haenszel do exist to test association with nominal data. These tests do not appear on the Decision Tree so that you realize you are not using the most appropriate test with nominal-level data. Thus, if you go to the Decision Tree and you answer question two, "What is the lowest level of all variables?" as nominal, you will not find an arrow to nominal. You should realize you are making a mistake and go to the test of difference, where you will find the use of the nominal IV/X using groups for comparisons.

Partial and multiple correlations.

The Decision Tree does illustrate that you can run correlations with three or more variables. However, bivariate (two-variable) correlation is much more commonly used than correlation with multiple variables. Using multiple variables in correlations is common with the test of prediction. Therefore, in order to avoid confusion we only use bivariate correlations for the tests-of-association methodologies. In Chapter 13 you will learn about Pearson and Spearman correlations and how to analyze the test data to make decisions.

CONCEPTUAL OBJECTIVE 3

Discuss (a) what tests of association measure, (b) the appropriate measurement levels of the variables used with correlation, and (c) when to use a test of difference rather than correlation.

The dependent and independent variables are interchangeable with association.

Unlike with the tests of difference and interaction (and also tests of prediction, discussed later in the chapter), it is not necessary to determine which variable is the Y and which is the X because you will get the same results either way. For example, in Figure 10.2 income is plotted on the Y axis and is, therefore, the DV/Y; age is plotted on the X axis and is the IV/X. However, you could plot age as the Y and income as the X. If you want one of the variables to be placed on the Y axis, make it the Y. If you don't care which is on the Y and which is on the X axis, don't worry about it—just enter the computer commands to make it run. See Box 10.11 for an example of a test of association. Be sure to use the Decision Tree as you read it.

> ## Box 10.11 Using the Decision Tree to Select the Appropriate Test of Association
>
> Dewayne wants to know if the people at City Hospital with the highest level of income are the most satisfied (**1** satisfied, **2** somewhat satisfied, **3** somewhat dissatisfied, **4** dissatisfied) with their jobs. In other words, is there a relationship between level of satisfaction and income?
>
> **Instructions**
> Using the Decision Tree, follow the path to the right as the answers to the questions are given.
>
> **Solution (Decision)**
> *Question 1: What are you testing?* We are testing association, so follow that progression (on page two of the tree, top part).
> *Question 2: What is the lowest level of all variables?* Age is interval/ratio measure. Satisfaction is ordinal level, so follow the right-hand path to ordinal. In other words, all variables have to be interval/ratio to follow that progression. Age is a continuous variable and has no minimal size unit. Satisfaction is a discreet variable and has a minimal-size unit (1–4). When you have mixed variables, as Dewayne does, you use the lower-level test, as stated, because you can always break a higher-level variable down into a lower-level variable but not the other way around.
> *Question 3: What is the number of variables?* We have two variables, so follow the arrow in the top row to two.
> *Question 4: What type of statistic?* Spearman Rho (ρ) or Kendall tau (τ).

10.5 Tests of Prediction

Tests of prediction forecast the value of any level of dependent variable based on the value of any level of independent variable(s). However, all variables can't be nominal level. When all variables (two or more) are nominal-level with unmatched groups, chi-square is the appropriate statistical test. Note on the Decision Tree that you run different statistical tests based on the level of the one DV/Y and the level and number of IV/Xs. Xs are the explainer or reason for the Y value. As with a test of interaction, rating scales with five or more scales can be considered interval data with tests of prediction.

When to Use a Test of Prediction

The relationship between association and prediction is somewhat similar to the test of difference versus the test of interaction. Prediction is based on correlation, but it takes things a step further. It is a more advanced statistics test. With the test of association your primary hypothesis is that there is a relationship between variables. You must measure the direction (positive or negative), the strength of the relationship, and the p-value of making a Type I error. You are not trying to predict the value of one variable based on the value of the other(s); however, with prediction you are. For example, you could hypothesize that if you know how many hours students have studied for a test, their IQ scores, and their GPA, you can predict their test scores (or that test scores can be explained by studying, natural intelligence, and prior success at test taking).

Correlation or regression?
Many tests of association can be tests of prediction (a higher-level statistic) by using one or more variables to predict the DV/Y. However, if one variable really does not predict

the other but they move in the same or opposite direction, or if you have no idea which variable should be Y and which X, maybe you really just need a test of association. Also, correlation is more commonly used with only two variables and regressions with one Y and multiple Xs, as illustrated in Box 10.11, because there are usually multiple variables needed to predict or explain the value of Y.

Regression.

Regression is the primary statistic of prediction, and there are multiple variations of regression (see the Decision Tree). Which regression technique to use is based on the number and levels of measurements of the variables. You can only have one Y, but you can have one, two, or more IV/Xs, and the measure of all variables can be of any level. Regression is one of the most, if not *the* most, commonly used statistical tests because almost all organizations forecast variables such as sales, interest rates, inflation, prices of materials, labor cost, and so on. For example, a real estate agent wants to be more accurate at predicting the selling price of a house. The following IV/Xs in Box 10.12 are selected as the predictors or explainers of the price of a house (Y).

Box 10.12   Regression Variables to Predict the Price of a House

Y = Price of house (interval/ratio in $)
X = Size of house (interval/ratio in square feet)
X = Size of lot (interval/ratio in square feet)
X = Condition of the house and lot (interval/ratio rating 1–9)
X = Number of bedrooms (interval/ratio actual number)
X = Location (nominal—city or area of the city)

Dependent and independent variables with prediction.

In contrast to tests of association (and the same as with tests of difference and interaction), the Y and X must be clearly identified. In regression, select one Y to be predicted or explained and one or more X to be the predictors or explainers. With the test of prediction, you are saying, "If I know the values of the X(s) I can always predict the value of the Y." Even if you change the values in the X(s), you can predict the value of Y. The DV/Y is always plotted on the y axis and the IV/X(s) on the x axis. See Box 10.13 for an example of a test of prediction. Be sure to use the Decision Tree as you read it.

CONCEPTUAL OBJECTIVE 4
Describe tests of prediction and the number of dependent and independent variables and their measurement levels.

Box 10.13   Using the Decision Tree to Select the Appropriate Test of Prediction

Chris is a cost accountant at Samuel Enterprises. Products are custom manufactured, it's a job shop, and Chris bids on contracts to get orders. Bids have not been very accurate, so Chris wants to develop another method for determining the bid price of a job to ensure a set profit margin. Chris hypothesizes that if the job size is known (the customer requests a set number of the custom product), one can predict the number of labor hours to complete the job (labor cost per hour is known). *H1: the number of the product can be used to predict labor hours.* Chris will use data from past jobs to test the hypothesis.

Instructions

Using the Decision Tree in Figure 10.1, follow the path of arrows to the right as the answers to the questions are given.

Solution (Decision)

Question 1: What are you testing? Prediction. Follow the Decision Tree arrow to page 2 (second test down).

Question 2: What is the number of Y? One Y, labor hours.

Question 3: What is the measurement level of Y? You don't arbitrarily assign a number, so it is interval/ratio. Follow the top choice to the right.

Question 4: What is the number of X? One X, number of customer products ordered.

Question 5: What is the measurement level of X? Interval/ratio. Follow the top choice to the right (interval/ratio).

Question 6: What type of statistic? Bivariate regression.

10.6 Tests of Interrelationship

Tests of interrelationship reduce a large number of associated variables or participants, of any measurement level, into a limited number of dimensions or groups. Note on page 2 of the Decision Tree that you run factor or cluster analysis based on what you are grouping.

When to Use a Test of Interrelationship

With a test of interrelationship, you have independent variables (Xs) only. With the other four tests (test of difference, interaction, association, and prediction) you have both dependent and independent variables. A test of interrelationship is similar to the test of association and prediction because it is based on correlation. However, it is also different because with the test of interrelationship you're looking for the relationship between many IV/Xs, or you have no DV/Y. Box 10.14 summarizes the dependent and independent variable differences between the five types of statistical tests.

Box 10.14   Variable Differences among the Five Types of Statistical Test

Y and X need to be identified (differences, interaction, prediction).
Y and X are interchangeable (association).
Xs have only independent variables (interrelationship).

Recall from Chapter 8 one of the limiting criteria for using tests of interrelationship: *factor analysis*, the need for large sample sizes to validly run the statistics. You need a minimum of 10 cases/observations/participants per IV/X and preferably 25. The measurement level of the Xs can be any level. In this chapter we will identify only if the test is factor or cluster analysis, not the level of measures of the Xs.

CONCEPTUAL OBJECTIVE 5
Discuss tests of interrelationship and the number and level of measurement of the variables.

The Difference between Factor and Cluster Analysis

The two major tests of interrelationship are factor and cluster analysis. Factor analysis begins with a well-defined group composed of two or more distinct sets of characteristics (test questions) in search of a set of variables to separate them (what the question measures). Cluster analysis starts with an undifferentiated group of participants (e.g., people, animals, events, objects) and attempts to reorganize them into homogeneous subgroups (buyers of a product, medical patients, inventory, products, employees). Cluster analysis is especially similar to factor analysis when the factor is applied to people instead of to variables. Thus, *factor analysis* groups variables (concepts), and *cluster analysis* groups participants (measures of participants: financial status, political affiliation, market segment characteristics, symptom classes, product competition definitions, productivity attributes).

Factor analysis.

Review Chapter 8 for a discussion of how factor analysis is used as a test of validity of a questionnaire. Another type of example appears below:

You work in the admissions office of your college and you want to know why students attend your college. You hypothesized that if you can identify a list of reasons, you can improve recruiting by emphasizing these reasons in your promotions of the college. Accordingly, you randomly surveyed 500 first-year students at your college, giving them the following introduction and asking them this open-ended question: "The admissions office would like to know why students attend our college. Please list the reason(s) why you selected our college. You may give multiple responses."

From the responses you have identified 25 commonly stated reasons why students attend your college. Each reason is a separate variable. The question you may ask yourself is, "How can we group the 25 variables that are related together to make understanding the reasons easier?" In other words, maybe you can come up with three to five groups under which there are multiple responses that are related—that measure the same thing.

Cluster analysis.

Cluster analysis is commonly used as a marketing tool to segment markets. Marketing segmentation is the process of grouping (clustering) potential customers together based on similar characteristics that lead them to buy a specific product. If you can clearly identify the characteristics of people who buy your product, you can target (cluster) them as good sales prospects and focus sales promotions on them for specific products; you don't waste time and money going after poor customer prospects (clusters).

For example, you work for Ford Motor Company and you want to segment the car-buying population into various distinct market segments or types of customers. Using cluster analysis, you define the variables on which to measure distinct types of customers. You select age, income, and family size as the variables to measure types of customers to be clustered together. The cluster of customers buying the Mustang and the cluster of customers buying the Windstar minivan are different.

In Chapter 14 you will learn more about factor and cluster analysis. See Box 10.15 for an example of a test of interrelationship. Be sure to use the Decision Tree as you read it.

Box 10. 15   Using the Decision Tree to Select the Appropriate Test of Interrelationship

Ted has data on his company's best 500 customers. Ted wants to develop a limited number of classifications for these customers to segment them so that different product features and advertisements can be developed for each group.

Instructions

Using the Decision Tree in Figure 10.1, follow the arrows to the right as the answers to the questions are given.

Solution (Decision)

Question 1: What are you testing? We are testing interrelationship, so follow the first column below the black box down to interrelationship.

Question 2: What is our purpose? We are grouping a large number of customers (participants) into a limited number of clusters, so follow the arrow that pertains to participants.

Question 3: What is the measurement level? Any level.

Question 4. What is the statistic? Cluster analysis.

10.7   What to Do if You Aren't Sure What You Are Testing (Another Starting Point before the Decision Tree)

After reading about the five types of tests with their accompanying examples, you should be able to answer the first question, "What am I testing?" However, answering this question requires an understanding of and ability to define the types of variables and their measurement levels, as well as the five types of tests, without looking up the definitions. So take the time to memorize these important concepts before trying to do the exercises. A good method for learning these key terms is to write the definition on one side of a 3 × 5 card and the key term on the other side and test yourself until you can define them all without looking at the answers.

If you have memorized the key terms but still cannot figure out what you are testing, you can try a different starting point that will help when you get to the other questions. List (a) the DV/Y and IV/X variable(s), (b) the Y and X measurement levels, and (c) the number of Y and X and scales.

SKI WEST STUDY

As we bring this chapter to a close, you should be able to use the Decision Tree to select the appropriate statistic of the research design.

Using the Decision Tree to test H1 (Personality testing can predict job performance), Matt's research design was a test of prediction. He had one interval/ratio Y and one interval/ratio X. Therefore, the appropriate statistic was bivariate regression, which Matt did run.

Using the Decision Tree to test H2a,b and H3a,b, Matt tested differences. He had one interval/ratio Y (personality) and another interval/ratio Y (performance) with the same nominal Xs, gender and age. Both gender and age have two unmatched groups. Therefore, the appropriate statistic was the T-test for all four H tests, which Matt did run.

Using the Decision Tree to test H2c and H3c, Matt tested differences. He had one interval/ratio Y (personality) and another interval/ratio Y (performance) with the same nominal X (department). Department has three unmatched groups. Therefore, the appropriate statistic was one-way ANOVA, which Matt did run.

CHAPTER SUMMARY AND GLOSSARY

The chapter summary is organized in a way that provides you with the answers necessary to help you meet the conceptual objectives for this chapter.

1. **Discuss (a) tests of difference, (b) the number of variables and measurement levels of the dependent and independent variables, and (c) matched pairs.**
   (a) Tests of difference compare values of the dependent variable (DV/Y) between the nominal independent variable groups (IV/X). (b) There is one dependent and one independent variable. The Y level of measurement can be nominal, ordinal, or interval/ratio. (c) A matched pairs group occurs when the dependent variable measure is repeated two or more times to compare differences of the same participant.

2. **Define tests of interaction and state the number of variables and measurement levels of the dependent and independent variables with two-way and multivariate ANOVA.**
   Tests of interaction are used to determine the best combination of three or more variables to maximize differences. Two-way ANOVA has one interval/ratio dependent variable and two or more nominal independent variables. MANOVA has two or more interval/ratio dependent variables and any number of nominal independent variables.

3. **Discuss (a) what tests of association measure, (b) the appropriate measurement levels of the variables used with correlation, and (c) when to use a test of difference rather than correlation.**
   (a) Tests of association measure the correlation between (among) two (or more) variables. (b) All variables should be ordinal or interval/ratio-level measurement. (c) A test of difference is used when one of the variables is a nominal-level measurement.

4. **Describe tests of prediction and the number of dependent and independent variables and their measurement levels.**

   Tests of prediction are used to forecast the value of the dependent variable based on the value of the independent variable(s). There is only one dependent variable, which can be of any measurement level. There can be any number of independent variables, which also can be of any measurement level. However, all variables can't be nominal level.

5. **Discuss tests of interrelationship and the number and measurement level of the variables.**

   Tests of interrelationship are used to reduce a large number of associated variables or participants into a limited number of dimensions or groups. There is no dependent variable and there can be any number of independent variables. The measurement can be at any level.

6. **Define the following alphabetical list of key terms.**

   Select one or more methods: (1) fill in the missing key terms from memory, (2) match the key terms with their definitions below, or (3) copy the key terms in order from the list at the beginning of the chapter.

   inferential statistical tests   tests of difference
   matched pairs   tests of interaction
   tests of association   tests of interrelationship
   tests of prediction

   _____ are tests of (1) difference, (2) interaction, (3) association, (4) prediction, and (5) interrelationship.

   _____ compare values of any level of dependent variable between the nominal independent variable groups.

   _____ occurs when the dependent variable measure is repeated two or more times to compare differences of the same participant.

   _____ determine the best combination of three or more variables to maximize value differences; the dependent variable(s) is interval/ratio and the independent variable(s) is nominal level.

   _____ measure the correlation between two or more ordinal and/or interval/ratio-level variables.

   _____ forecast the value of any dependent-level variable based on the value of any independent-level variable(s).

   _____ reduce a large number of associated variables or participants, of any measurement level, into a limited number of dimensions or groups.

WRITTEN ASSIGNMENTS

All three written assignments require selecting the appropriate statistic to test the hypotheses that you develop.

APPENDIX RP, ASSIGNMENTS 3 AND 4, AND APPENDIX CS, ASSIGNMENT 2

If you haven't included the statistic in the statistical analysis material that you will use in your Method section, or if it is incorrect, go back and state the appropriate statistical tests.

APPENDIX SA, ASSIGNMENTS 4 THROUGH 6

Each of these statistical analysis assignments requires the use of a different statistic. Therefore, you will need to change the statistic for each assignment. You will be instructed to do so in each instance, so you can return to the Decision Tree for assistance in the future.

EXERCISES

SELECTING THE APPROPRIATE STATISTICAL TECHNIQUE

For each of the research designs, select the appropriate statistical test using the Decision Tree in Figure 10.1. (It is easier to have a copy of the tree right in front of you than it is to go back and forth between the pages.) Be sure to clearly list each step resulting in the statistic, as illustrated in boxes 10.3, 10.10, 10.11, 10.12, and 10.14. You may find it helpful to identify the DV/Y and IV/Xs, their measurement level, and groups (if any) before answering the Decision Tree questions.

10-1 Use the information in Box 10.2, part A, to select the appropriate statistic.

10-2 Use the information in Box 10.2, part B, to select the appropriate statistic.

10-3 Use the information in Box 10.11 to select the appropriate statistic.

10-4 You want to know which political party (republicans, democrats, or independents) are more satisfied with your proposed tax bill (scales: good bill, fair bill, poor bill). Select the appropriate statistic.

10-5 Use the information in Chapter 9, Table 9.1 (part A) to select the appropriate statistic.

10-6 Use the information in Chapter 9, Table 9.1 (part B) to select the appropriate statistic.

10-7 Use the information in Chapter 9, Exercise 9-1, to select the appropriate statistic.

10-8 Use the information in Chapter 9, Exercise 9-2, to select the appropriate statistic.

10-9 Use the information in Chapter 9, Exercise 9-3, to select the appropriate statistic.

10-10 Use the information in Chapter 9, Exercise 9-4, to select the appropriate statistic.

10-11 Use the information in Chapter 9, Exercise 9-5, to select the appropriate statistic.

10-12 You work for an insurance company and want to know if there is a relationship between age and the number of accidents a person has had over the past two years. You go to your files and randomly select 50 files to analyze. If a relationship does exist, you will adjust insurance rates accordingly to be fair, based on driving record. Select the appropriate statistic.

10-13 You want to know if you can forecast your annual sales (in dollars) based on the amount of money you spend on advertising (in dollars). You get data based on the last five years' sales and advertising expenditures. If advertising is effective, you will use the data to forecast next year's sales; if not, you won't use it. Select the appropriate statistic.

10-14   Your company sells sporting goods. People in the marketing department think that people of color perceive your products to be of higher quality than the products of your competitors. Therefore, the marketing people want to develop a special advertising campaign geared to people of color. You disagree, then conduct a study to find out if the marketing people are right by asking 500 people (half white and half of color) to rate your products (as high or low quality). You plan to tabulate the number in a two-by-two frequency distribution table for analysis of proportions. Select the appropriate statistic.

10-15   You have developed a new drug that should lower blood pressure. To test the drug, you select 100 people with high blood pressure. You start by giving each person a blood pressure test (pre-test blood-pressure number). You randomly select 50 of them to take the real drug and the other 50 to take a sugar pill placebo for 30 days (experimental and control group); then you give them another blood pressure test (post-test blood-pressure number). You will compare the participants' pre-test blood-pressure numbers to their post-test blood-pressure numbers to see whether the drug reduced blood pressure. You hope that the best combination of X is post-test and experimental group. Select the appropriate statistic.

10-16   You are a police chief in a metropolitan area. You want to know why people commit crimes. You go to the jail and ask 50 prisoners at random why they committed a crime. They provide their responses (20 different reasons). You decide to run a statistical test to see if these reasons are correlated in some way so that you can limit their number into fewer categories of reasons. Select the appropriate statistic.

10-17   You want to know if people are good prospects to call on to make sales, so you won't waste your time calling on non-buyers. You want to be able to forecast accurately whether a potential customer will be a buyer or non-buyer. You run your data with five variables (age, income, occupation, residence, gender) that should help you identify the buyers and non-buyers among 100 customers. Select the appropriate statistic.

10-18   You are a restaurant owner and want to know if the people with the highest level of satisfaction with your restaurant (1 very satisfied—5 very dissatisfied) are the customers who come to dine most often (number of times per month). In other words, is there a relationship between satisfaction and dining? Select the appropriate statistic.

10-19   You want to know which group of employees (managers or staff) takes the most vacation days (number). Accordingly, you pull all the records for the 30 managers and 200 staff to test your hypothesis: Managers take more vacation days off than staff. Select the appropriate statistic.

10-20   You have a listing of 100 different pedigrees of dogs. You would like to somehow condense this number so that the amount of categories can be lower, making it easier to work with the data. Select the appropriate statistic.

10-21   You want to know if the level of satisfaction with your product varies between men and women and across different ethnic groups. Satisfaction is measured using a reliable and valid instrument/questionnaire that provides one standardized score (up to 100 points) for 20 questions. Individuals are sent the satisfaction questionnaire with their one-year warranty information. You plan to run a test to compare differences between both male and female responses and the ethnic groups to determine if there is a best combination between gender and ethnicity. Select the appropriate statistic.

10-22   A political debate will be held about whether or not abortion should continue to be legal. You have been selected for a debate team. You want to know people's opinions on several issues, including which gender has the strongest level of agreement (**1** agree—**4** disagree) with abortion upon demand. Accordingly, you conduct a survey to compare answers. Select the appropriate statistic.

10-23   You are the human resources manager responsible for hiring new sales reps, and you want to know if you can predict a candidate's sales performance based on years of sales experience, IQ score, age, and prior knowledge of the product (yes or no). You want to run a test to see if your predictors are accurate at selecting the best sales candidates based on past records. Select the appropriate statistic.

10-24   You want to know if the three ERG (existence, relatedness, growth) needs developed by Clayton Alderfer are better met by employees with or without disabilities. The measurement instrument has been validated. The questionnaire has five questions for each need, and you get one standardized measurement for each of the three needs. You plan to compare the level of needs being met for all three needs by each type of group. You are not sure if there will be any best combination. If the needs of the disabled are not being met at the same level as those of the non-disabled, you will push for public policy changes to further help the disabled in the workforce. Select the appropriate statistic.

10-25   You want to know who has the highest level of education (noncollege graduate, undergraduate, or graduate degree—coded 1, 2, 3, respectively) by business owner (failed or successful). You want to compare frequencies to determine which group has the greatest proportion of higher-level education. Select the appropriate statistic.

10-26   You work in the production department and you make one product. That product is expensive, and each is individually tested for quality control before being sent to the customers. Quality is measured on a standardized measure of 1–10. To pass quality inspection, the product must get at least a 7. Lately, more products have been returned as not lasting for the lifetime warranty of the product. You think that the problem may be the quality control test: The test may be giving a higher rating than it should, causing faulty products to pass inspection. Therefore, you have decided to test a sample of 25 products three times, rather than the just once as usual, and compare quality ratings of each product to determine if the quality changes from test 1 to test 2 to test 3. If quality rating of the same product changes significantly, you will determine that the standardized quality control measure is in error and take corrective action to ensure consistency in quality ratings. Select the appropriate statistic.

10-27   You are a marketing manager and want to better understand your customer profile. Accordingly, you compare the gender and race of your customers as compared to your top competitor's customers to determine if you have more of any one sex and race. Select the appropriate statistic.

10-28   You are an accountant and want to know if there is a negative correlation between the percentage of accounts receivable that get paid/collected and the age of the accounts receivable. You hypothesize that the longer an accounts receivable is outstanding, the lower the percentage of payment. Select the appropriate statistic.

10-29   You work as a general manager for a theater that puts on plays. You want to know if the ratings of enjoyment of a play are the same right after a play and one week later, and if there is a difference in ratings between season ticket holders and those who aren't season ticket holders. Right after the play, as people are leaving, you randomly ask 25 people if they enjoyed the play (yes or no) and whether they are season ticket holders; you also get their telephone numbers so you can call the same people to ask the enjoyment question again in one week. Select the appropriate statistic.

10-30   You work for a candy company and you have designed five different Easter bunnies. You want to market only two of the five designs. You get a group of 50 families with a husband, wife, and child to look at the five bunnies and to rate them by preference: **1** like the most to **5** like the least. The two bunnies with the highest ratings will be sold. Select the appropriate statistic.

SELECTING THE APPROPRIATE TECHNIQUE FOR YOUR RESEARCH DESIGN PROBLEM

10-31   Write the hypotheses that you plan to test in your research project, then list the Y and X(s) and their measurement level and scales. Next, use the Decision Tree to select the appropriate statistical technique to test your hypothesis. Use the following list to assist you.
Hypotheses:
DV/Y and measurement level:
IV/X and measurement level and scales:
What are you testing?
What is the appropriate statistical test?

11

Hypothesis Testing

CHAPTER OUTLINE

CONCEPTUAL OBJECTIVES

The conceptual objectives below also appear at appropriate places within the chapter at points when you will have accessed the information necessary to attain them. They appear again at the end of the chapter in the Summary and Glossary section, along with explanations that will enable you to meet the objectives.

After studying this chapter, you should be able to:

1. List the steps in hypothesis testing.

2. Discuss the two parts of a hypothesis, which one is statistically tested, and why.

3. State when one-tailed and two-tailed hypothesis tests are used.

4. Compare (a) Type I and Type II errors, (b) the three situations of setting the critical value, and (c) which critical values academic and business researchers generally use.

5. Describe statistical power and its purpose.

6. State what a probability value tells the researcher.

7. Describe the hypothesis test decision rule.

8. Define the following key terms (listed in order of their appearance in the chapter).

steps in hypothesis testing	two-tailed test	critical value
null hypothesis	Type I error	statistical power
alternative hypothesis	Type II error	p-value
one-tailed test	level of significance	confidence interval

SKILL DEVELOPMENT OBJECTIVES

The exercises that apply to particular skill development objectives are indicated directly beneath each numbered objective below. Periodic instructions within the chapter tell you when to stop reading and direct you to the end of the chapter to complete one or more of the skill development exercises.

After studying this chapter, you should be able to:

1. Write hypotheses.
   Exercises 11-1 through 11-4 and Problem 11-1

2. Select critical values.
   Exercises11-5 through 11-8

3. Interpret p-values.
   Exercises 11-9 through 11-12 and Problem 11-1

4. Make hypothesis decisions.
   Exercises 11-13 through 11-16 and Problem 11-1

The Research Process

(1) The research question/purpose of the study, literature review, and hypotheses.	(2) Research design methodology for collecting data and statistics.	(3) Data analysis and interpreting results.	(4) Discussing results and making conclusions.
• *Introduction*	• *Method*	• *Results*	• *Discussion*
Chapters 1–3	Chapters 4–8	Chapters 9–14	Chapters 9–14

Prior chapters have presented the research process shown above. We now focus on data analysis and interpreting results, stage three of the research process. We run statistics to answer research questions stated as hypotheses that we developed in the first stage of the research process, based on the research design methodology and the data collected to run the statistics.

11.1 Hypotheses

After completing the descriptive statistics, you progress to inferential statistics to make generalizations, draw conclusions, and make recommendations for the purpose of making decisions. It is common to compare measures of central tendency (mean, median, mode) between groups and to measure relationships between variables through hypothesis testing. To answer questions and make decisions we use *hypothesis testing,* the process of making decisions/conclusions based on statistics. Take the following example.

Sam is the human resources director at Bailey Manufacturing. Sam wanted to know if employees are satisfied with their jobs and if he should do anything to improve job satisfaction. In order to answer his questions and make decisions, Sam followed the steps in hypothesis testing that are discussed throughout this chapter. We cover each step in separate sections of this chapter so that you will understand how to test hypotheses, using Sam's research as the example.

*The **steps in hypothesis testing** are to:*

1. state the hypothesis,

2. set the critical value,

3. select the methodology of data collection and statistical test,

4. run the statistics to obtain the p-value, and

5. make the decision/draw the conclusion.

CONCEPTUAL OBJECTIVE 1
List the steps in hypothesis testing.

In step 1 of hypothesis testing you state the hypothesis by identifying a problem or opportunity, your purpose for conducting the study, questions to be answered, and the action to be taken when the decision is made. The questions are commonly stated as hypotheses, and the answers to the questions are used to make decisions. In our example, Sam wants to know if employees are satisfied with their jobs (question). If employees are satisfied with their jobs, he will keep things the same (one possible action). If employees are not satisfied with their jobs, Sam will do something to improve job satisfaction (another possible action). His decision is to determine which alternative is the best action to take.

Recall from Chapter 1 that a *hypothesis* is a tentative answer to a research question stating the relationship between variables. The term *relationship* is broadly used and can mean that there is a difference in means between groups or a correlation between variables, that one or more variables can predict another variable, that there is a best combination of variables, and so on. In other words, in developing the hypothesis you transform your questions into statistically testable terms to help you make decisions.

The Null and Alternative Hypotheses

A hypothesis has two parts called the null hypothesis and the alternative hypothesis. *The **null hypothesis** (Ho) states that there is no relationship between variables.* In other words, there is no variance, no correlation, no difference between groups, no effect, no change, no improvement. The status quo is given the benefit of the doubt. We assume the Ho is true until evidence suggests otherwise.

The **alternative hypothesis** (Ha or H1) *states that there is a relationship between variables.* It is the logical opposite of the null hypothesis. We need evidence to support our Ha claim. When conducting organizational research, we should also state the action to be taken with the two parts of the hypothesis so that the decision-making part is predetermined.

As discussed in Chapter 3, the *substantive hypothesis* is a statement about the expected results. It is usually the alternative hypothesis. The substantive hypothesis is stated in the introduction of the paper before the Method section. However, the null hypothesis is usually stated in the Appendix A section of your proposal/paper, which is not included as part of a journal article.

The Ho and Ha must be mutually exclusive and exhaustive. In other words, both cannot be true, but one must be true. Plus, the action for the Ho and Ha must be different. Sam's primary research question is, "Are employees satisfied with their jobs?" Sam believes that employees are not satisfied with their jobs (Ha), so he writes the hypothesis below. Notice that the Ho and Ha are not stated in statistically testable terms and that Sam has a different action written for both parts of his hypothesis.

Hypothesis	Action
Ho: Employees are satisfied with their jobs.	Keep things as they are now / take no action.
Ha: Employees are not satisfied with their jobs.	Develop a program to increase job satisfaction.

Researchers' versus managers' stated hypothesis and action. As presented above, managers should write the Ho and Ha and the action for each because they are making decisions for organizations. However, academic researchers realize that each hypothesis has an Ho and Ha, which are the opposite. Therefore, they do not write both the Ho and Ha. Depending on the style of the publication they send their articles to, they write either the Ho or the Ha. Researchers select the hypothesis that has literature support.

It's important to realize that academic researchers do not actually make decisions like managers do. Rather, they make conclusions to state that there either is or is not a relationship between the variables they are studying. Therefore, it is not necessary for them to state the action next to the hypothesis like managers should do. However, researchers do make conclusions about the implications of the study, or they make recommendations to people who make decisions. So when you read a journal article, you know why there is only one hypothesis—either an Ho or an Ha—and no action statements.

Statistically Testing the Null Hypothesis

Only the null hypothesis is actually statistically tested. Based on the test, technically, you either "do not reject" (fail to reject) the Ho or "reject" the Ho. A hypothesis cannot be proved; therefore, it cannot really be "accepted." Hypothesis testing gives only a chance to (1) reject or (2) fail to reject the null hypothesis. For example, suppose you hypothesize that statistics textbooks contain an index. If you check the back of one statistics book and find an index, you haven't proved your hypothesis; you only have one piece of evidence supporting your hypothesis. But if the book does not have an index, your hypothesis is disproved. One text-book is enough to disprove your hypothesis, but 1,000 textbooks are not enough to prove it. There may be textbooks without an index that are not in your sample. You remain uncertain.

Because you cannot prove your hypothesis, NEVER USE THE TERM *PROVE* with statistics. You either support or fail to support (or refute) the hypothesis through statistical testing. Statistical results do vary and you rarely, if ever, really know which is correct. For example, in an early study researchers concluded that margarine is better for you than butter. In a later study, researchers concluded that margarine and butter are equally healthy. In a more recent study, researchers concluded that butter is better for you than margarine. How could all three researchers have correctly "proven" results?

Though technically incorrect, for many students it is easier to say and understand "accept" Ho or Ha rather than "do not reject" Ho (which results in accepting Ho for the decision) and "reject" Ho (which results in accepting Ha for the decision). For the sake of understanding, both forms are presented throughout this book.

CONCEPTUAL OBJECTIVE 2
Discuss the two parts of a hypothesis, which one is statistically tested, and why.

One-Tailed and Two-Tailed Hypothesis Tests

The one- or two-tailed tests are commonly used when conducting tests of difference to compare two means. A normal curve has two tails (as discussed in Chapter 9). In a *two-tailed test* the region of rejection of the Ho is located at both left and right tails, whereas in a *one-tailed test*, the region of rejection of the Ho is located in the one tail predicted.

The one-tailed test.

The **one-tailed test** *is used when one mean is expected to be greater than the other and when the direction of a correlation is predicted.* Sam wants to know if employees are satisfied with their jobs. So, with several other questions, he asked employees this rating-scale question:

Identify your overall level of satisfaction with your job:

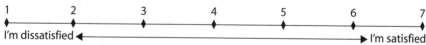

If the mean (M) is equal to or less than ($\leq$) 2, Sam will conclude that employees are dis-satisfied with their jobs—he will reject Ho (accept Ha). If the mean is greater than (>) 2, he will conclude that employees are satisfied with their jobs—he will not reject Ho (accept Ho). Now we can add statistically testable terms to the hypothesis, as shown in Table 11.1 to illustrate the one-tailed test.

The two-tailed test.

The **two-tailed test** is used when means are expected to be different, but when we're not sure which will be greater, and when the direction of a correlation is not predicted. Sam is also interested in knowing if the men and women of Bailey Manufacturing have an equal level of satisfaction with their jobs. If Sam is not sure which sex has the greater level of sat-isfaction, he could write the following two-tailed test in Table 11.2.

With a two-tailed test, you are comparing two statistically run obtained means. Therefore, no difference in M is represented by 0 (zero), which appears in the center of the normal distribution, and the standard deviations are shown to the left and right to illustrate the differences. We will not use mean numbers now because they are based on p-values,

Table 11.1   One-Tailed Hypothesis Test

Hypothesis	Action
Ho: Employees are satisfied with their jobs (M is > 2).	Keep things as they are now/take no action.
Ha: Employees are not satisfied with their jobs (M is ≤ 2).	Develop a program to increase job satisfaction.

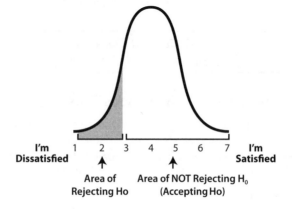

Table 11.2   Two-Tailed Hypothesis Test

Hypothesis	Action
Ho: The level of job satisfaction by gender is equal (M are =).	Keep things as they are now, take no action.
Ha: The level of job satisfaction by gender is not equal (M are ≠).	Develop a program to increase job satisfaction of the gender with the lower mean.

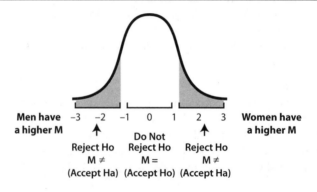

which are discussed later in this chapter. For now, you need to understand that the greater the difference in means, the further out in a tail the difference is. The direction of the difference, toward the tail, is based on which gender has the greater and lower mean.

The one-tailed test is statistically more powerful.

Logically, you are being more precise when using a one-tailed test and are more likely to reject Ho (saying there is no relationship between variables) than you are when using a two-tailed test. In other words, it is more difficult to reject Ho with a one-tailed test. We will explain the reason more fully when discussing statistical power. Since Sam selected 2 as the value to accept or reject Ho, he is using a one-tailed test, and he will also select this critical value for differences within the sample means. This is explained in the next section. Before you read further, write hypotheses in exercises 11-1 through 11-4.

Conceptual Objective 3
State when one-tailed and two-tailed hypothesis tests are used.

STOP READING and turn to the end of the chapter to complete exercises 11-1 through 11-4.

11.2 Type I and Type II Errors and the Critical Value

When you make decisions—reject or fail to reject the Ho (select Ho or Ha)—there is always the probability of making an error. The two types of errors you can make are called Type I and Type II errors. You must evaluate the cost of making each type of error and set the critical value to avoid the most costly error (or both types of errors).

Type I Errors

A *Type I error* occurs when the null hypothesis is rejected in error; the conclusion is made that *there is a relationship when there really is none.* You are rejecting a true Ho. The probability of committing a Type I error is referred to as *alpha* and is symbolized by its sign α; $1-\alpha$ is the probability of making a Type I error. In other words, you are rejecting Ho (accepting Ha) when Ho is correct (you should accept Ho). When you make a Type I error, you are assuming that there is a difference/relationship when there really is none.

Continuing our example, if Sam calculated the statistics and the mean job satisfaction was 1.7 (he may have caught many employees having a really bad day, or there was some other sampling reason for an error [see Chapter 5] when on a better day the mean would have been around 2.5), he would reject Ho (accept Ha) and assume employees are *not* satisfied. As a result, he would develop an *unnecessary* program to increase job satisfaction.

Type II Errors

A *Type II error* occurs when the null hypothesis is NOT rejected in error; the conclusion is made that there is NO relationship when there really is. You are retaining a false Ho—you fail to reject the null hypothesis when it is false. The probability of committing a Type II error is referred to as *beta* and is symbolized by its sign β; $1 - \beta$ is the probability of making a Type II error and it is commonly called the *power of a test*. In other words, if you commit a beta error you are not rejecting Ho (accepting Ho) when Ha is correct (you should accept Ha). When you make a Type II error, you are assuming that there is NO relationship when there really is one.

In Sam's case, what if employees were afraid to tell the truth and placed their level of job satisfaction higher than they actually had so the mean was 4.5, or there was some other reason for an error to occur? Sam would assume that employees are satisfied with their jobs, and he would *not* develop a program when he should.

When hypothesis testing, we can make either a right or wrong decision based on statistical inferences. For a presentation of the four possible outcomes of hypothesis testing— two ways to be right and two ways to be wrong—see Table 11.3.

Table 11.3   Type I and Type II Errors

Decision (Action) Based on Sample	The Truth about the Ho	
Take no action.	**Ho is true** (should accept) Employees really are satisfied with their jobs.	**Ho is false** (should accept Ha) Employees really are *not* satisfied with their jobs.
Do not reject the Ho.	**No Error** Sam does *not* develop a program.	**Type II Error** β (You assume there is *no* relationship when there really is.) Sam does *not* develop a program when he should.
Reject the Ho (accept Ha) Develop a program to increase employee satisfaction.	**Type I Error** α (You assume there is a relationship when there really is none.) Sam develops an *unnecessary* program.	**No Error: Correct Decision** Sam develops a necessary program.

Evaluating Type I and Type II Errors Based on the Level of Significance

When hypothesis testing, you cannot be sure that you will not make an error. However, you can assign a probability of making an error based on what is called the level of significance.

Level of significance.

*The **level of significance** is the probability that a Type I error will be made.* If you want to be 95% confident that you are not making a Type I error, you select the .05 level of significance $(1 - .05 = .95$ or $100\% - 5\% = 95\%)$, which means you may falsely reject 5% of the true hypotheses you test. If you select .10, 10 times out of 100 you may make a Type I error. *The **critical value** is the researcher's predetermined level of significance needed to reject the null hypothesis.* Thus, the critical value lies exactly on the boundary of the region of rejection. The more certain you need to be that you are not making a Type I error, the lower the level of significance needs to be, and vice versa. The lower the significance level is, the lower the alpha value (.01, .05, .10). The .05 level of significance is the most commonly used critical value for research. Researchers focus more on Type I than on Type II errors, partly because the latter are hard to detect.

The trade-off between Type I and Type II errors.

There is a trade-off—an inverse relationship—between Type I and Type II errors. Thus, a decrease in the probability of making a Type I error leads to an increase in the probability of making a Type II error.

By increasing sample size, however, you can simultaneously decrease the probability of making both types of errors. Large sample sizes are generally more valid than small samples. (Sam has a large sample of 200.) However, larger sample sizes are more expensive, and the trade-off between error types still exists. Errors in business usually have some cost. Therefore, you calculate the cost of both errors. However, in many decisions actual costs are difficult and even impossible to calculate. Therefore, subjective cost-benefit analysis is often needed.

Costs of Type I errors.

The Type I error is more easily controlled than a Type II error. If Sam makes a Type I error, he develops a program to increase job satisfaction which is not needed. Sam could estimate the cost. He may never discover the error, or he may discover it only after a period of time in which he resurveys employees to determine if the program worked. If the program was not necessary, job satisfaction may not increase. Sam may conclude that the program did not work and try another program rather than realize that employees are actually satisfied with their jobs.

Costs of Type II errors.

The Type II error is difficult to control. If Sam makes a Type II error, he does not develop a program to increase job satisfaction when one is needed. If employees are not satisfied with their jobs but Sam does nothing to address the problem, morale and productivity may suffer. The costs of low morale and lost productivity due to lack of job satisfaction are very difficult to estimate.

Setting the Critical Value

The second step in hypothesis testing is to set the critical value. Theoretically, the critical value should be set before the data are collected, or at least before the hypothesis is statistically tested. Once the critical value is set, you generally should not change it after the statistical test results are known. In practice, however, some business decisions are made without setting a critical value, and when the results do not support the wanted hypothesis critical values are changed. When this happens, you should determine if the behavior is ethical (see Chapter 3).

The three situations of Type I and Type II errors.

Because there is an inverse relationship between making a Type I and a Type II error, there are three possible situations (the third being the possibility of making both types). Based on evaluating both types of errors, determine which situation you are in and set the critical value accordingly.

*Situation 1 (**low critical value**) ≤ .01: A Type I error is costly and a Type II error is not costly.* Do not worry about making a Type II error in this type of situation. Set a low critical value of .01, or lower, so you are 99% certain that you will make the correct decision (the probability that you make a Type I error is 1 in 100). If you are making parachutes, for example, you need to be certain that they work properly. One death could put you out of business, so you need a very low critical value. Let's give a more detailed example.

Example: Goodstone Tire Company has been caught and fined for false advertising several times. A project team has developed a tire that it claims will last 75,000 miles. It presents a report to management, which wants evidence to support the claim. Goodstone's hypothesis and action would be as shown below.

Hypothesis	Action
Ho: The tire will *not* last 75,000 miles (M < 75,000).	Do *not* produce and advertise the new tire; don't make the claim.
Ha: The tire will last 75,000 miles or longer (M ≥ 75,000).	Do produce and advertise the new tire as lasting 75,000 miles. If at least 70,000 consider producing with the lower claim.

To develop and advertise a new tire that did not last 75,000 miles (a Type I error) would be very costly; the government checks ad claims regularly. Tires that were sold and did not last 75,000 miles as claimed under warranty would likely result in a fine and a recall to take back the tires, refunding money or giving away new replacements. The cost of not marketing the new tire would be the cost of the time and effort of the project team that developed it. The cost to not market the tire is much less than the cost to market it in error. Therefore, a Type I error is costly and a Type II error is not costly. Goodstone should set a low critical value of .01 so it is 99% certain that it does make the correct decision. Because of the high cost of error, a large sample size is also recommended to decrease the chances of error. Goodstone used a sample of 100 tires.

*Situation 2 (**high critical value**) ≥ .10: A Type II error is costly and a Type I error is not costly.* Do not worry about making a Type I error. Set a high critical value of at least .10 so that you are somewhat (depending on the critical value selected) certain that you have made the correct decision.

Example: Koors Beer used descriptive statistics to claim that 58% of Spud drinkers prefer the taste of Koors Extra Gold. Koors does not advertise the use of inferential statistics to test its hypothesis. Koors' hypothesis and action are shown below.

Hypothesis	Action
Ho: Spud drinkers do *not* prefer the taste of Koors (Koors % = ≤ Spud).	Do *not* advertise that Spud drinkers prefer the taste of Koors.
Ha: Spud drinkers prefer the taste of Koors (Koors % > Spud).	Do advertise that Spud drinkers prefer the taste of Koors.

The difference of 58% versus 42% could be due to chance, sample error, or other errors rather than to actual taste preference. Without the actual data we cannot determine the real significance level, but a guess of at least .85 could be close. In other words, Koors is only about 15% certain that Spud drinkers do in fact prefer the taste of Koors. In other words, there is an 85% probability that Koors made a Type I error in rejecting Ho (accepting Ha).

Koors may have run a T-test to compare preferences. However, because most people, including managers, do not understand p-values (which we will discuss shortly), businesses do not report them to the general public.

If Koors did do a hypothesis test, the rationale for allowing such a high alpha critical value is the fact that they were in Situation 2 (high critical value): A Type II error is costly and a Type I error is not costly. Do not worry about making a Type I error. Set a high critical value, as Koors did. The reason Koors conducted the study was so that it could advertise and get some Spud drinkers to switch to Koors. The advertising is not considered a cost of an error; the cost is the expense of conducting the study and not being able to advertise the claim.

Because most people do not understand inferential statistics, they may switch brands based on a test with very, very weak statistical results. The familiar Pepsi challenge (comparing the taste of Coke to that of Pepsi) and other product comparisons would also have very high critical values, or no critical value. In general, businesses are not concerned about making a Type I error and often make decisions based on descriptive statistics (e.g., 58%). So reading this book should take you out of the realm of the general public (who don't understand statistics and will often switch brands based on weak findings).

*Situation 3 (**medium** critical value) .05: Both Type I and II errors are costly.* Set a medium critical value of .05 so that you are at least 95% certain that you have made the correct decision, and use a large sample for important, potentially costly decisions. While large samples decrease the chances of making both types of errors, increasing the sample size is especially helpful in decreasing the likelihood of a Type II error.

Example: Returning to Sam's situation, referring to his earlier hypothesis and action will tell you that it could be considered costly to make both Type I or Type II errors. Therefore, Sam set a critical value of .05 and used a very large sample of 200. However, he selected a mean of 2, which is low on a scale of 1–7 without knowing the actual .05 mean. This was done to illustrate how to test hypothesis using only descriptive statistics. A low mean of 2 does help ensure that employees really are dissatisfied with their jobs.

Box 11.1 summarizes the three situations of Type I and II errors, and it illustrates how the acceptance region is larger in both tails as the critical value gets lower. In other words, it is more difficult to reject Ho at the .01 level than at the .05 level, and the higher you go over the .10 level of significance, the easier it gets to reject Ho.

Researchers' versus managers' selection of the critical value (researchers' .05).

Academic researchers are generally concerned about making both types of errors. Therefore, the most commonly used level of significance by researchers, as reported in journal articles, is .05. However, researchers commonly include the actual p-values so that readers, who include managers, can make their own decision to reject or not reject Ho (accept Ho or Ha). Many researchers also report results as being significant at the .10 level. Academic researchers do not usually determine their error situation; they just use the standard .05.

When business researchers and managers set the critical value, they should select their error situation and use the recommended critical value. However, unlike researchers they may use critical values much higher than .10. In fact, they commonly use descriptive statistics only, as was discussed with the Koors example above.

Box 11.1   Three Situations of Type I and Type II Errors

Situation 1 (low critical value) ≤ .01: A Type I error is costly and a Type II error is not.
Situation 2 (high critical value) ≥ .10: A Type II error is costly and a Type I error is not.
Situation 3 (medium critical value) .05: Both Type I and II errors are costly.

A. One-tailed Test Comparing Acceptance and Rejection Regions for the Three Situations

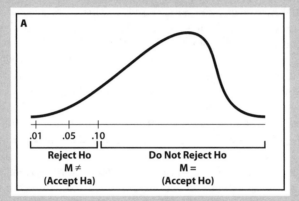

B. Two-tailed Test Comparing Acceptance and Rejection Regions for the Three Situations

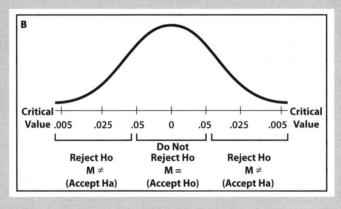

CONCEPTUAL OBJECTIVE 4

*Compare (a) Type I and Type II errors, (b) the three situations for setting the critical value,
and (c) which critical values academic and business researchers generally use.*

Descriptive statistical testing of hypotheses versus inferential statistical testing.
    You can test a hypothesis using only descriptive statistics, as in the Koors example, by
comparing the obtained mean (or percentage) to the predetermined mean. However, you
can state the confidence that a Type I error is not being made by obtaining p-values (discussed later in this chapter).

In testing Sam's hypothesis, "Employees are satisfied with their jobs," Sam selected the critical value of a mean of 2. The critical value could have been 3 or another number. Means will almost always be different. The real question is, are the differences significant? The way to determine if differences and relationships are significant is by obtaining p-values through inferential statistical testing. Recall that inferential statistics are based on the measures of descriptive statistical central tendencies (mean, median, mode); they take them one step beyond the descriptive, making them more powerful statistics for decision making. Sam can use inferential statistics to determine the exact mean, rather than guess at 2 by using p-values.

If Sam has a yearly survey to determine if the job satisfaction level is changing, he can use inferential statistics to compare results over time. Sam could also use inferential statistics to test other hypotheses—for example, is there a relationship between job satisfaction and other variables such as salary, type of job, length of service, employee age (and so on)?

To determine whether there is a difference between the job satisfaction level for men and for women, Sam uses the inferential statistical T-test. Therefore, he will obtain a p-value and will be able to state the probability that a Type I error occurred. Sam wants to be 95% certain that he is not making a Type I error, so he selected the .05 critical value.

STOP READING and turn to the end of the chapter to complete exercises 11-5 through 11-8.

Power Analysis

Statistical power is the probability of correctly rejecting a null hypothesis (or to reject a false hypothesis correctly). You reject an Ho correctly when it is in fact false. In other words, you are finding a relationship that does exist. This is commonly what researchers want to do. They commonly hypothesize that a relationship exists, and they test to find out if they are correct. Power analysis focuses on avoiding the Type II error; $1 - \beta$ (saying there is no relationship when there really is). Again, the one-tailed test is more powerful than the two-tailed test.

The purposes of power analysis.

We use power analysis to determine the sample size necessary to detect a difference that will reject Ho. Both before and after a study is conducted, a power analysis test is run. We run power analysis to determine the sample size necessary to reject the Ho before the study is conducted. We also run it to evaluate a completed study and determine the power of that test. In other words, if a study did not correctly reject the Ho, there really may be a difference—but it was not detected, perhaps because a sample size is too small. Therefore, how large a sample size is needed to detect a difference?

The larger the sample size, the greater the chances of rejecting Ho.

Remember that if you increase the sample size, you decrease the chances of making both Type I and Type II errors. If you are like most researchers, you want to find a relationship—thus, be sure to use a large sample size.

Power analysis is not commonly calculated and reported with research studies for at least two reasons. First, many statistical packages do not include a program that will run the power analysis. Second, many times data are not available to estimate effect size. Sigma (σ) is unknown, as is the mean for the Ho and Ha. Thus, it cannot be run. Do not be concerned about calculating power of analysis. If you use a large sample size, you are covered. For now, you should simply understand what statistical power is, its purposes, and the importance of a large sample size.

CONCEPTUAL OBJECTIVE 5
Describe statistical power and its purpose.

11.3 Data Collection and Statistical Tests

The third step of hypothesis testing is to select the methodology of data collection and statistical test. Recall from Chapter 6 that there are three major classifications of data collection:

1. *Secondary sources,* such as company records, periodicals, library reference sources, the Internet, and so on;

2. *Observation,* such as counting the number of rejected items on a production line, watching people buying a product, scouting competitors' prices in their stores, and so on; and

3. *Survey sources,* such as using a questionnaire to get answers to your questions by mail, by telephone, or personal interview.

It may be helpful to review chapters 4–7 for details of data collection. The method of data collection for exercises 11.1 to 11.8 is included in the next section with the statistical results.

As discussed in the chapters that discuss data collection, it is important to determine in advance which statistical technique you will need to test your hypotheses. If you don't, you may find out that you failed to get the data needed to answer the research question through hypothesis testing. Also, conducting the wrong statistical test can lead you to believe you are 95% confident that you have not made a Type I error, when in fact you have.

In Chapter 10 you learned how to use the Decision Tree to easily select the appropriate statistical test without having to memorize over 30 different tests and knowing when they should be used. The approximately 30 statistical tests discussed in chapters 12–14 are grouped together based on the five major types of statistical testing methodology from Chapter 4. These are also in the Decision Tree in Chapter 10. The Decision Tree is an excellent tool that you can use in this course and in your career.

11.4 The Significance of Probability Values

The fourth step in hypothesis testing is to run the statistics to obtain the probability or p-value. To calculate the obtained descriptive statistics and p-values, you perform the statistical test selected in step 3 of hypothesis testing. When you use a computer-based statistical software package to test a hypothesis, the obtained values are printed out for you.

A *probability* is the expected relative frequency of a particular outcome, such as rejecting hypotheses correctly or in error. *The **p-value** is the calculated probability that a Type I error has occurred.* In other words, what are the odds that we are saying there is a difference between group means when there really isn't any difference? When printed out, the p-value is commonly labeled *probability value* (appearing, for example, as p = .028), or *significance level*, or just *sign*.

The p-value can be considered the equivalent of the bottom-line profit in accounting; in essence it is generally considered the most important number in inferential statistics. The larger the obtained p-value, the less difference there is between means (or the weaker the relationship between variables); inversely, *the lower the p-value, the greater the difference or the stronger the relationship.* When conducting research you usually expect what the Ha predicts. Therefore, you generally expect to obtain a small p-value—the smaller the better. Researchers most commonly use $p \leq .05$.

Of the more than 30 statistical tests in the Decision Tree, all have a p-value which is interpreted in the same way. Therefore, if you clearly understand the simple concept of p-values in this chapter, inferential statistics will not be difficult for you. Even if you don't clearly understand p-values now, you should understand the concept after completing the multiple inferential statistic tests.

Sam calculated all descriptive and inferential statistic tests (N = 200, men n = 100, and women n = 100). The sample's obtained mean level of job satisfaction was 4.35. However, the mean for men was 5.6 and the mean for women was 4.1. You do not get a p-value when you run descriptive statistics, so there is no p-value for the overall mean of 4.35. However, when running the T-test of difference between men and women, Sam got a value of p = .0321. This obtained p-value tells us that only 3% of the time a difference of at least this size would occur when the men's and women's mean scores are actually equal in the population. In other words, Sam can be 97% confident that he did not make a Type I error (stating that there is a difference when there really isn't a difference). The data-collection methods and p-values for exercises 11-1 through 11-8 are presented in exercises 11-9 through 11-11.

**STOP READING and turn to the end of the chapter
to complete exercises 11-9 through 11-12.**

CONCEPTUAL OBJECTIVE 6
State what a probability value tells the researcher.

11.5 Confidence Interval

Although we focus on the p-value for making decisions, you should realize that you can also use confidence intervals (CI) to support your decision and even as a criterion for making decisions. A CI is commonly used to estimate the population mean based on the sample mean. A *confidence interval contains a range of sample means with a probability that it contains the population mean.* Like the p-value, the common significance level for the CI is

.05. For example, let's assume a large bank wants to know the average amount of money in its savings accounts. It decides to take a random sample of 50 accounts. The mean of the savings-account sample is $1,176. At the .05 level of significance, the CI is $1,081.65 to $1,270.35. Thus, the bank is 95% certain that its average savings account is between these means (CI). In the next chapter we discuss CI in more detail, including computer printouts.

11.6 Decision Making

The last step in hypothesis testing is to make the decision, which goes in the Conclusion section of a paper/report. The decision you make is based on answering your question and rejecting or not rejecting the null hypothesis (accepting Ho or Ha). In this section we discuss ways to make decisions using descriptive and inferential statistics, and the importance of technical accuracy in the decision-making process.

Types of Statistical Decision Making

Below we discuss descriptive and inferential statistics as ways of decision making, continuing with the example of Sam's research on employees' job satisfaction levels.

Descriptive statistic decision making.

To make your decision using only descriptive statistics, you compare your selected critical value to the obtained value. Sam selected a critical value of a mean of 2 and the obtained mean was 4.35. Hence, (the obtained mean) 4.35 > 2 (critical value), therefore, Sam does not reject Ho (accepts Ho) and assumes that employees are satisfied with their jobs. Because employees are overall satisfied with their jobs, Sam as the human resources director should make the decision *not* to take action, *not* develop a program, to improve overall job satisfaction.

The inferential statistic hypothesis decision-making process.

To make the decision using inferential statistics, you compare the critical value you selected with the p-value you obtained—statistically calculated. Remember, the smaller your p-value, the greater the difference in your hypothesis test means. The decision rule based on a critical value of .05 is as follows:

- When the critical value you set ≤ p-value from the computer printout, you should accept Ho (reject Ha) because there is NO relationship (.05 < .29 or 95% > 71%— there is only a 71% probability you are not making a Type I error).
- When the critical value you set > p-value from the computer printout, you should accept Ha (reject Ho) because there is a relationship (.05 > .03 or 95% < 97%—there is a 97% probability you are not making a Type I error).

The Importance of Technical Accuracy

We never really accept Ho because we can never be completely sure (100%) that there is no relationship. Technically, for academic research decision-making purposes you generally state only Ha and whether it is supported or not supported. However, most students find it much easier to understand the simple statement that we accept Ha or Ho. Also, in managerial decision making it is common to write both the Ho and Ha because there is a difference in the action taken based on the results of statistical testing. Therefore, since we focus on managerial decision making, we will write both Ha and Ho with their actions and keep it simple by accepting Ho, even though it is technically not correct to do so.

Making the decision.

Sam also tested the difference in level of satisfaction of men and women. The critical value is .05, which is greater than the obtained p-value of .03. Therefore, Sam should accept Ha (reject Ho). In other words, he wants to be 95% certain that the level of satisfaction is truly different and not due to chance. Sam is 97% certain that he is not making a Type I error, so he concludes that there is a significant difference in the level of job satisfaction for men and for women. Based on the statistics, Sam should make the decision to determine *why* women are less satisfied than men and take action to improve job satisfaction for women.

> ## STOP READING and turn to the end of the chapter
> ## to complete exercises 11-13 through 11-17.

CONCEPTUAL OBJECTIVE 7
Describe the hypothesis test decision rule.

Let's put the five steps of hypothesis testing together to illustrate the process. Read the example in Box 11.2, then do problem 11-13 to put all five steps together to test a hypothesis.

Box 11.2   Hypothesis Test to Measure Business Success vs. Failure

In this example, a researcher wanted to determine what factors contribute to success versus failure of small businesses. The one variable under hypothesis testing (there were others not presented here) is management experience prior to starting a business. It is generally believed that an entrepreneur with prior management experience has a greater chance to succeed than a manager with no prior experience. The sample included 216 small business owners (108 successful and 108 failed matched pairs). Owners were surveyed by mail and telephone in the six New England states of the USA. This research design is a test of difference.

Instructions
- Clearly list the five steps of hypothesis testing and answer these questions within the appropriate step.
- For *step 1*, be sure to clearly write the null and appropriate one or two-tailed alternative hypothesis with actions.
- For *step 2*, which of the three situations of Type I and II errors is present? What should the critical value be?
- For *step 3*, list the dependent and independent variables with their measurement level and appropriate statistical test.
- For *step 4*, the computer printout is given below; however, list the step, then write the percentage of confidence that the mean difference is significant.

(continued)

- For *step 5*, answer the following questions as part of making the decision: (a) What are the two means, and which is higher? (b) Is the difference between means significant at the .05 level? (c) Should the null hypothesis be rejected? (d) What action should be taken?

T-Test Simulated Computer Results

Two-sample T-test for C1 vs. C2

N	Mean	StDev	SE Mean
C1 108	9.2291	7.744	1.062
C2 108	7.6916	8.224	1.031

T-Test mu C1 = mu C2 (vs not =): T= 1.51 P = 0.133 DF= 214

Solution (Decision)

Step 1. State the hypothesis and action.

Hypothesis[1]	Action[2]
Ho: Failed and successful business owners have an equal number of years of *management experience* prior to starting their firm (M =) (two-tailed).	Conclude that there is *no difference* in the number of years of management experience.
Ha: Successful business owners have more years of management experience prior to starting their firm (M ?). (one-tailed).	Conclude that there is a difference in the number of years of management experience

Step 2. Set the critical value.

Critical value is .05. Because it is a researcher, this is Situation 3 (both Type I and Type II errors are costly).

Step 3. Select the methodology of data collection, measurement level of the variables, and type of statistical test.

Survey was the method used for data collection. The dependent variable (management experience) was a ratio-level measure, and the independent variable (performance) had two nominal groups being compared (success and failure). Therefore, the matched pairs T-test is the appropriate statistical test.

Step 4. Run the statistics to obtain the p-value.

As shown in the simulated computer printout, the researcher is approximately 87% (1 – .133 p) confident that a difference exists between successful and failed business managers' experience levels.

Step 5. Make the decision.

a. The failure mean is 9.2991, and it is higher than the success mean of 7.6916.

b. No. The obtained value is .133 > .05, the critical value. The researcher wanted to be 95% certain of not making a Type I error, but there is only an 87% probability that the difference is not due to chance.

c. No—do not reject (accept) Ho.

d. The failed business owners' responded mean (number of years) was greater than that of successful owners, but the means are not significantly different. Therefore, the researcher's action was to conclude that both failed and successful small-business owners started with equal levels of management experience. The researcher concluded that this variable is not a distinguishing factor.

[1] Recall that academic researchers do not state both the null and alternative hypotheses. Both are shown for illustrative purposes only.

[2] Recall that academic researchers do not state the action with the hypotheses. Action is shown for illustrative purposes only.

11.7   Significance and Importance of Statistical Results in Decision Making

Results that are significant are not necessarily important, and important results aren't necessarily significant. Sam's hypothesis test of overall job satisfaction was not considered to be significant. However, the results were important for decision-making purposes. Because employees are satisfied with their jobs, overall action focusing on both men and women was not necessary to improve job satisfaction—a decision which saves time and money.

However, the test of difference between men's and women's level of satisfaction was significant and explains the overall satisfaction rating. The men are more satisfied with their jobs than women are (5.6 vs. 4.1). The overall mean of 4.35 is misleading and reflects this difference. When examining the results, Sam should realize that there is a problem with job satisfaction for women but not for men, and he should take action to correct the problem for women only.

Significance depends on three factors: (1) variability in the actual groups within the sample (e.g., men and women); (2) the sample sizes; and (3) how well the sample represents the population. First, the greater the variance between groups, the greater is the chance that the difference will be significant. Second, in very large samples even small differences can be significant, whereas in small samples even larger differences may not be significant. Sam used a good-sized sample of 100 women and 100 men to test his hypothesis. If he had compared a random sample of just 10 men and 10 women, the results could have been very different due to sampling errors (discussed in Chapter 5). Large sample sizes tend to be normally distributed and more reliable than smaller ones. Third, samples that do not represent the population can lead you to believe that you are making the right decision, based on a high level of significance in the sample, when in reality you are making the wrong decision. In other words, when there is no difference in the population it is supposed to represent, there can be a significant difference in the sample because of sampling error—so if you infer that the results of the sample apply to the population, you are in error. In other words, statistics are only as good as the sample, methods, and measurement you use. (It may be helpful to review chapters 4–8, which cover this material in detail.)

Ethics

When researchers and managers do not get the results they want, they can be tempted to make unethical changes to alter the results to say what they want them to say (discussed in Chapter 3). Sometimes managers may be tempted to prevent the results from being known. The tobacco industry, for example, has been accused of knowing the harmful effects of tobacco and taking no action to fix the problem. If you worked for a tobacco company, would you have blown the whistle and made results available to the public—knowing that doing so could hurt sales and that you could lose your job as a consequence?

Significance versus Importance

Returning to the point of a statistic being significant but not important, here is an example from the success versus failure study. The failed business owners actually had a significantly higher number of years of education than the successful owners (M 15.32 SD 2.98 vs. M 14.53 SD 2.59, p = .042). The difference between the means is only .79. Can we really conclude that getting less than one more year of college education will have a negative effect on business success? Certainly not! Yes, this difference is significant, but it is not important.

Why is a small difference significant? Let's review our significance, examining the three factors above. First, notice the large standard deviations of close to 3 years and 2½ years. Also, the sample size was 216, with 108 in each group (recall that with a large sample size it is easy to find differences). We don't really know how well the sample represents the population. However, even though the sample size is 216, the population of all the small businesses in New England is very large, so the sample may not really be a true representation of the population. Thus, the real reason for the difference in level of education may be due to one or more of these factors. The moral of the story is that you can't just go by the numbers—you have to think logically.

SKI WEST STUDY

As we bring this chapter to a close, you should be able to:
- *understand and write one- and two-tailed hypotheses,*
- *know the difference between Type I and II errors,*
- *interpret probability values so you can test hypotheses and make decisions, and*
- *explain why something can be significant but not important.*

Matt McLeish followed the five steps of hypotheses testing:

1. **State the hypotheses.** Matt developed one primary hypothesis to test whether personality test scores can predict job performance at Ski West. He also developed six secondary hypotheses (H2 a, b, c and H3 a, b, c) to test for differences between personality and performance by gender, age, and department.

2. **Set the critical value.** Matt set it at .05 so that he could be 95% confident that he was not making a Type I error (saying that personality can predict performance when in fact it doesn't). He also used the critical value of .05 for each test of difference so that he could be 95% confident that he was not making a Type I error (saying there is a difference when there really is none).

3. **Select the methodology of data collection and statistical test.** Matt's method was to use Ski West measurement instruments and collect data through secondary sources from employee records. His statistical analysis included: bivariate regression to test H1, T-test to test H2a,b and H3a,b and one-way ANOVA to test H2c and H3c.

4. **Run the statistics to obtain the p-values.** Matt did so.

5. **Make the decision/draw the conclusion.** Matt rejected H1 ($p = .309$) and concluded that personality testing cannot predict job performance at Ski West. Any resulting decision would be made by management, which could include revising the personality test or stopping its use altogether because it is not a valid predictor of job performance.

Only one of the six H was accepted, H3a. Males did score higher on job performance than females ($p = .031$). However, the conclusion was that the difference is significant but meaningless (M 27.96 v. M 30.48, difference 2.52 or 5% out of 50 possible points). The decision was not to give preference to males in the hiring process.

CHAPTER SUMMARY AND GLOSSARY

The chapter summary is organized in a way that provides you with the answers necessary to help you meet the conceptual objectives for this chapter.

1. **List the steps in hypotheses testing.**
   The steps in hypothesis testing are: (1) state the hypothesis, (2) set the critical value, (3) select the methodology of data collection and statistical test, (4) run the statistics to obtain the p-value, and (5) make the decision.

2. **Discuss the two parts of a hypothesis, which one is statistically tested, and why.**
   The two parts of a hypothesis are the null (there is no relationship between variables) and the alternative (there is a relationship). The null hypothesis is tested because a hypothesis cannot be proved; it is tested to determine the probability that a correct decision is being made to accept or fail to accept the Ho.

3. **State when one-tailed and two-tailed hypothesis tests are used.**
   A one-tailed hypothesis is used when researchers believe they know which mean will be greater, or the direction of the correlation. The two-tailed hypothesis is used when researchers believe there is a difference, but they are not sure which mean is greater, or the direction of the correlation.

4. **Compare (a) Type I and Type II errors, (b) the three situations of setting the critical value, and (c) which critical values academic and business researchers generally use.**
   (a) A Type I error occurs when the null hypothesis is rejected in error—you say there is a relationship between variables when there really is none. A Type II error occurs when the null hypothesis is *not* rejected in error—you say there is no relationship when there really is a relationship. (b) The Three Situations of Type I and II errors are: Situation 1 (low critical value) ≤ .01: A Type I error is costly and a Type II error is not; Situation 2 (high critical value) ≥ .10: A Type II error is costly and a Type I error is not; and Situation 3 (medium critical value) .05: Both Type I and II errors are costly. (c) Academic researchers generally use a critical value of .05 and business researchers generally set a high critical value or just use descriptive statistics.

5. **Describe statistical power and its purpose.**
   Statistical power is the ability to correctly reject a null hypothesis. The purpose of power analysis is to determine the sample size necessary to detect a difference that will reject the null hypothesis. The larger the sample size, the greater the chances of rejecting the null hypothesis.

6. **State what a probability value tells the researcher.**
   The probability value (or p-value) is the calculated probability that a Type I error has been made. The lower the p-value, the smaller the probability that a Type I error has been made. The p-value tells the reader the probability that a null hypothesis has been rejected in error—in other words, it's the percentage of chance that the researcher concludes there is a relationship between variable values when there really is none.

7. **Describe the hypothesis test decision rule.**
   The hypothesis decision is made as follows. The critical value is selected by the decision maker based on the three situations. The p-value is calculated by the com-

puter for the decision maker. The two values are compared to determine whether to accept or fail to accept the hypothesis. When the critical value ≤ p-value, do not reject Ho (null hypothesis). When the critical value > p-value, accept Ha (alternative hypothesis) or reject Ho.

8. **Define the following alphabetical list of key terms.**
   Select one or more methods: (1) fill in the missing key terms from memory, (2) match the key terms with their definitions below, or (3) copy the key terms in order from the list at the beginning of the chapter.

alternative hypothesis	null hypothesis	steps in hypothesis testing
confidence interval	one-tailed test	two-tailed test
critical value	p-value	Type I error
level of significance	statistical power	Type II error

_____ are: (1) state the hypothesis, (2) set the critical value, (3) select the methodology of data collection and statistical test, (4) run the statistics to obtain the p-value, and (5) make the decision/draw the conclusion.

_____ states that there is no relationship between variables.

_____ states that there is a relationship between variables.

_____ is used when one mean is expected to be greater than the other and when the direction of a correlation is predicted.

_____ is used when means are expected to be different but when the researcher is unsure which will be greater, and when the direction of the correlation is not predicted.

_____ occurs when the null hypothesis is rejected in error (the conclusion is made that there is a relationship when there really is none).

_____ occurs when the null hypothesis is *not* rejected in error (the conclusion is made that there is *no* relationship when there really is).

_____ is the probability that a Type I error will be made.

_____ is the researcher's predetermined level of significance needed to reject the null hypothesis.

_____ is the probability of correctly rejecting a null hypothesis or of rejecting a false hypothesis correctly.

_____ is the calculated probability that a Type I error has been made.

_____ contains a range of sample means with a probability that it contains the population mean.

WRITTEN ASSIGNMENTS

All three written assignments require hypotheses to be stated. However, the research proposal does not actually collect the data and run the statistics to test the hypotheses. The completed study and statistical assignments do test hypotheses.

APPENDIX RP, ASSIGNMENTS 1 AND 3 (APPENDIX A) AND
APPENDIX CS, ASSIGNMENT 1 (INTRODUCTION)

If you haven't included one or more clear and accurate hypotheses at the end of your literature review, or if it is not correct, go back and include the appropriate hypothesis(es). Also, be sure to follow the five steps of hypotheses testing in your study.

APPENDIX SA, ASSIGNMENTS 4 THROUGH 6

Each of these statistical analysis assignments requires the use of a different hypothesis and statistic. Therefore, you will need to change the hypothesis and statistic for each. You will be instructed to do so in each assignment, so you can return to this chapter and the Decision Tree in the Chapter 10 to help you with future assignments.

EXERCISES

WRITING HYPOTHESES

11-1 An editor of an investment magazine wants to know if the stock market will go up, go down, or remain about the same during next year. Write the null and alternative hypotheses to be tested, with the action for each. (a) Write it the first time as a two-tailed hypothesis, assuming the editor thinks the stock market will change but is unsure in which direction it will go. (b) Write it again as a one-tailed hypothesis, assuming the editor thinks the market will go up.

11-2 A social scientist wants to know whether the incomes of two countries are different. Write the null and alternative hypothesis to be tested with the action for each. (a) Write it the first time as a two-tailed hypothesis, assuming the scientist thinks that one of the two countries has a higher income but is unsure which is higher. (b) Write it again as a one-tailed hypothesis, assuming the scientist thinks that country 1 has a higher income level than country 2.

11-3 The McKing fast-food franchiser is considering building a restaurant at a specified location. To be acceptable, a site must have a mean of 100 or more pedestrians passing the site per hour. (a) Write the null and alternative hypotheses to be tested with the action for each. (b) Is this a one- or two-tailed hypothesis?

11-4 The Wayne Restaurant has never advertised before. Mr. Wayne wants to know if there is a relationship between advertising and sales, so he decided to try advertising. For each of three months he progressively increased advertising levels. If sales have continued to increase during the three-month period, he will again increase advertising in month four. Write the null and alternative hypotheses to be tested with the action for each.

SETTING CRITICAL VALUE

11-5 Evaluate the cost of making a Type I and Type II error for the financial editor in Exercise 11-1. (a) Be sure to clearly state what errors would be made for both Type I and Type II. (b) Determine which of the three situations applies to the financial editor and recommend the appropriate critical value. (c) Would you recommend a large sample size? Why or why not?

11-6 Evaluate the cost of making a Type I and II error for the social scientist in Exercise 11-2. (a) Be sure to clearly state what errors would be made for both Type I and Type II. (b) Determine which of the three situations applies to the scientist and recommend the appropriate critical value. (c) Would you recommend a large sample size?

11-7 Evaluate the cost of making a Type I and II error for McKing in Exercise 11-3. (a) Be sure to clearly state what errors would be made for both Type I and Type II. (b) Determine which of the three situations McKing is in and recommend the appropriate critical value. Also, (c) would you recommend a large sample size? Why or why not?

11-8 Evaluate the cost of making a Type I and II error for Mr. Wayne in Exercise 11-4. (a) Be sure to clearly state what errors would be made for both Type I and Type II. (b) Determine which of the three situations applies to Wayne and recommend the appropriate critical value. (c) Would you recommend a large sample size? Why or why not?

EXPLAINING PROBABILITY VALUES

11-9 The financial editor in Exercise 11-1 used a survey to collect the data. The editor called 15 stock market experts and asked for their forecast. The editor elected to use the chi-square test of difference and ran the statistics. Assume the editor set the critical value at .10, which may or not be what you recommended in Exercise 11-5. Eight experts said the stock market would go up, five said it would go down, and two said it would remain the same. The obtained p-value was .6723. (a) Explain what the p-value means, or what it tells you as it relates to this situation. (b) Is it ethical to consult experts and then make a forecast based on theirs without telling the readers that your forecast is based on those of other experts? Unlike most managers, the financial editor will know if a Type I or Type II error or no error was made (i.e., find that a correct decision was forecast after the time period is over).

11-10 The social scientist in Exercise 11-2 collected secondary data, means, and standard deviations of the two countries in a database and converted them into dollars. A T-test to compare mean income data in dollars was run. Assume the researcher set the critical value at .05, which may or not be what you recommended in Exercise 11-6. The mean in country 1 was $22,635 and the mean for country 2 was $38,291. The obtained p-value was .0401. Explain what the p-value means, or what it tells you as it relates to this situation.

11-11 McKing in Exercise 11-3 collected data by observation—the number of pedestrians was counted, on 20 different occasions, on different days and times of day. Assume the researcher set the critical value at .01, which may or not be what you recommended in Exercise 11-7. Descriptive statistics were run; then a T-test was run, comparing the standard acceptable mean of 100 and standard deviation of 10 pedestrians passing the site per hour, to the obtained mean of 105 and standard deviation of 20. The obtained p-value was .0199. Explain what the p-value means, or what it tells you as it relates to this situation.

11-12 Mr. Wayne in Exercise 11-4 ran ads in the local newspaper for three months. In each month, ad spending was increased. Data were collected by secondary records: The actual money spent on advertising and sales figures for each month were used from the accounting files. Advertising expenses were $1,000, $2,000, and $3,000; sales were $10,000, $12,000, and $12,500, respectively. Sales prior to advertising averaged $8,500. Assume Mr. Wayne set the critical value at .05, which may or not be what you recommended in Exercise 11-8. Running a Spearman correlation (see Chapter 13) between the three advertising and sales figures, there was a positive relationship between variables, and the obtained p-value was .0253. Explain what the p-value means, or what it tells you as it relates to this situation.

HYPOTHESIS DECISION PROBLEMS

Decision problems 11-13 through 11-16 below use the information in exercises 11-1 through 11-12. Since steps 1 to 4 of hypothesis testing have already been completed in the exercises, only the decisions will be made now.

11-13 The editor in exercises 11-1, 11-5, and 11-9 set the critical value of .10 and planned to make a strong statement that the stock market would go up. As reported in 11-9, the p-value was .6723. (a) Should the editor reject or not reject the null hypothesis (accept Ho or Ha)? (b) What action should the editor decide to take? (c) Would your answer change at the .05 or .01 levels?

11-14 The social scientist in exercises 11-2, 11-6, and 11-10 is a researcher, not a manager, so the most commonly used critical value of .05 was used. As reported in exercise 11-10, the p-value was .0401. (a) Should the scientist reject or not reject the null hypothesis (accept Ho or Ha)? (b) What action should the scientist decide to take? (c) Would your answer change at the .10 or .01 levels?

11-15 For the McKing site in exercises 11-3, 11-7, and 11-11, to be acceptable there must be more than 100 pedestrians passing the site per hour. The critical value was set at .01. As reported in exercise 11-11, the mean was 109 and the p-value was .0199. (a) Should McKing reject or not reject the null hypothesis (accept Ho or Ha)? (b) What action should McKing decide to take? (c) Would your answer change at the .05 or .10 levels?

11-16 Mr. Wayne in exercises 11-4, 11-8, and 11-12 set a critical value of .05, and he plans to continue to advertise more each month until there is no longer a linear relationship between sales and advertising. As reported in exercise 11-12, with the advertising and sales figures the p-value was .0253. (a) Should Mr. Wayne reject or not reject the null hypothesis (accept Ho or Ha)? (b) What action should he decide to take? (c) Would your answer change at the .10 or .01 levels?

YOUR HYPOTHESES AND METHODS

11-17 For this exercise, use your own research proposal. Follow the steps of hypothesis testing.
Step 1. Write hypotheses that you plan to test. (Specify whether they are null or alternative and one- or two-tailed tests.)
Step 2. What critical value will you set? (Specify what situation applies to your study.)
Steps 3–5. Briefly state your data-collection method and the appropriate statistical test. Review Chapter 10 if you need help. (As you know, you cannot complete steps 4 and 5 of hypothesis testing in a proposal.)

Hypothesis Testing Problem

11.18 Merkk Drug Company developed a new AIDS drug. It is going to test the new drug against the competitors' combined-drugs program. Merkk believes its drug is superior. Merkk got 100 newly diagnosed AIDS patients to volunteer for the study; they get free treatment for participating. Of the sample, 50 are randomly assigned to take the Merkk drug and the other 50 take the competitor's drugs. Three months later, Merkk measures results based on a scale of **1** ineffective to **10** effective. Merkk set the critical value at .25. Merkk plans to bring the results to the FDA to seek its approval of the AIDS drug, if it is significantly superior to the competitor's drugs.

Unlike exercises 11-13 to 11-16, this problem is not based on prior exercises. Therefore, follow the five steps of hypothesis testing to test this hypothesis. *Clearly list each of the five steps* as is done in Box 11.2 and answer the same questions for all the steps. In step 1, write the one-tailed hypothesis to be tested. In step 4, the mean for the competitor was 6.3 and the mean for the Merkk drug was 6.8. The obtained p-value was .2473. The information for other steps is provided within the problem information above.

12

Tests of Difference
Experimental Designs

CONCEPTUAL OBJECTIVES

The conceptual objectives below also appear at appropriate places within the chapter at points when you will have accessed the information necessary to attain them. They appear again at the end of the chapter in the Summary and Glossary section, along with explanations that will enable you to meet the objectives.

After studying this chapter, you should be able to:

1. Explain the difference between experimental and quasi-experimental designs and state which one has the greater cause-and-effect relationship and why.

2. Discuss (a) internal and external validity, (b) the trade-off between the two, and (c) their impact on decision making.

3. Describe the difference between parametric and nonparametric tests of significance.

4. Explain the difference between: (a) the T-test and the paired T-test, (b) the one-sample T-test and the T-test, and (c) the Z-test and T-test.

5. Discuss differences between the T-test and Mann-Whitney U test.

6. Compare the T-test, the Mann-Whitney U test, and the chi-square test.

7. Compare the T-test and one-way ANOVA.

8. Define the following key terms (listed in order of their appearance in the chapter).

experimental designs	internal validity	one-sample T-test
quasi-experimental designs	external validity	Mann-Whitney U test
control groups	parametric tests	chi-square (X^2)
experimental groups	nonparametric tests	one-way ANOVA
factorial designs	T-test	

SKILL DEVELOPMENT OBJECTIVES

The exercises that apply to particular skill development objectives are indicated directly beneath each numbered objective below. Periodic instructions within the chapter tell you when to stop reading and direct you to the end of the chapter to complete one or more of the skill development exercises. *The decision problems that test hypotheses in chapters 12–14 are more complex than the exercises in prior chapters.*

After studying this chapter, you should be able to:

1. Test a hypothesis using the T-test.
   Decision problems 12-1 and 12-2, and 12-9 through 12-11

2. Test a hypothesis using the Mann-Whitney U test.
   Decision problems 12-3 and 12-4

3. Test a hypothesis using the chi-square test.
   Decision problems 12-5 and 12-6

4. Test a hypothesis using one-way ANOVA test.
   Decision problems 12-7 and 12-8

The Research Process

(1) The research question/purpose of the study, literature review, and hypotheses. • *Introduction*	(2) Research design methodology for collecting data and statistics. • *Method*	(3) Data analysis and interpreting results. • *Results*	(4) Discussing results and making conclusions. • *Discussion*
Chapters 1–3	Chapters 4–8	Chapters 9–14	Chapters 9–14

At this point in the research process, we run the statistical tests selected in the Method section with a focus on reading computer printouts to test hypotheses and using the results for decision-making purposes.

12.1 Experimental Designs: Tests of Difference and Interaction

This section classifies experimental designs, covers the criteria required for a research design to be considered an experiment, presents experimental designs, discusses cause and effect, and explains internal and external validity.

Experimental Design Classification

Experimental designs compare the measure of central tendency (covered in Chapter 9), frequency, mean (M), median (Mdn), or mode of the dependent variable (DV/Y) with the independent variable (IV/X). You are claiming that the difference in the values of the Y is the effect of the value of the X. The X must have a least two groups to compare differences (e.g., gender, same participants' values compared twice). Before we actually get into the statistics, we need to understand the two types of designs used with tests of difference, so in a sense we are returning to chapters 4 and 10 (research designs) to further refine our test-of-difference designs.

Experimental versus quasi-experimental designs.

When testing differences and interaction, the data-collection methodology (step 3 of hypothesis testing) is called either experimental or quasi-experimental design. *In experimental design the independent variable(s) is manipulated by a treatment with a matched experimental group to cause the difference in the value of the dependent variable(s). In quasi-experimental design the independent variable(s) may not be manipulated by a treatment, and the independent variable helps understand and explain the difference in the value of the dependent variable(s) groups.*

These definitions will become clearer as you read this section, as they are in essence a summary. For now, it's easier to understand that sometimes we can have an experiment (e.g., giving a group a drug and comparing differences before and after the treatment), but at other times we cannot have an experiment because we can't assign groups (e.g., gender: We are either male or female). There are also times we can't control the treatment (e.g., the *environment* in which women developed from childhood to adulthood). For these reasons we have what are called *quasi-experimental designs*. Even if your major research design is experimental association or prediction, you can also include quasi-experimental differences between participants based on descriptive statistics, such as gender.

Although we use the term quasi-experimental design, the term *quasi-experimental* is not commonly used in research studies. The term *experimental design* is only used with a true experiment, and if research is quasi-experimental in design, it is not stated as such. Simply calling the research design a test of difference is sufficient to let the reader know it is quasi-experimental.

In Chapter 11 you learned about the matched repeated measures, pre-post test design, and the classical experimental pre-post test control and experimental group designs. You also learned about unmatched period 1 and period 2 and unmatched groups, such as males and females. These are considered quasi-experimental designs. Many tests of difference are quasi-experimental designs, whereas many tests of interaction are experimental designs.

Criteria for Experiments

With experiments the difference in the Y is assumed to be caused by the manipulation (or treatment) of the X, called the *cause-and-effect relationship*. You can only claim cause-and-effect relationships with experimental designs, not with quasi-experimental. We discuss this in more detail under the heading Cause and Effect. Here are the three criteria necessary to be considered an experimental design. If you can't meet all three criteria, you don't have an experimental design for your study; it is quasi-experimental.

1. Requiring an experimental group.

To consider your research design as an experiment, you must have an experimental group, but you don't have to use a control group. *The **control group** does not get the treatment in experimental designs to compare differences with the experimental group. The **experimental group** does get the treatment in experimental designs to compare differences with the control group and/or to compare differences of participants in the experimental group.*

Random group assignment (randomization). When you do use both control and experimental groups, you need a random group assignment (Chapter 5) so that all participants have an equal chance to be in either the control group or experimental group. Randomization is necessary as a control to help ensure that the groups are relatively equal to begin with. If groups are not equal, the results of the experiment may not in fact be due to the treatment. Remember that control groups are not necessary, but when the groups are randomly assigned, the term *randomized design* is commonly used. The control group serves as the baseline. If the experimental group's dependent variable is greater than the control group's, you assume the difference is due to the treatment—our next topic.

2. Manipulating a time-ordered independent variable treatment.

To consider your research design as experimental, you must manipulate an independent variable treatment (e.g., giving a drug, a test, or a program), and the treatment must occur first (or at the same time) to ensure that the changed value of the dependent variable (DV/Y) was due to the treatment of the independent variable (IV/X)—the cause-and-effect relationship. The time-ordered treatment also can't be time sensitive. In other words, if you give a treatment and the time between measures is long, the treatment may no longer be the actual reason for the change in the Y.

3. Comparing matched groups' dependent variable values.

In order to be sure that the treatment is the cause of the change in the Y, you need to compare a matching set or group of participant values for differences. The strongest test is to compare the same participant before and after the treatment, often called *repeat measures*, as used with pretest-posttest designs. But you can also compare a control group to its matched experimental group score, as in posttest-only designs.

No extraneous variables and nonspurious relationships. There is one more consideration that we don't include as a criterion for experiments because for simple designs that meet the three criteria it is not usually an issue, and extraneous variables can be controlled. However, if you have extraneous variables without controls in your study, what you really have is a quasi-experimental design. Meeting the other three criteria is a form of *control* over extraneous variables, something we discuss later in this section.

Part of being an experiment includes the assumption of no extraneous variables resulting in a nonspurious relationship—you have to control for them. A *nonspurious relationship* (also called *confounding*) means that the change in Y was actually caused by the treatment of the independent variable (IV/X) rather than some other X or flaw in the experiment. A *spurious* relationship means that the change in Y was actually caused by an extraneous variable, not the X. For example, at large fires there are more fire trucks. However, the appearance of more fire trucks is clearly an extraneous variable that could result in a spurious relationship, because *the number of fire trucks does not cause the size of the fire*. Selecting variables from the literature and employing proper controls (the other two criteria) help to prevent spurious/confounding relationships caused by extraneous variables. You can also add a third control variable to test the relationship. We discuss extraneous variables again under the quasi-experimental time-series design, in the Cause and Effect heading within this section.

We've established that if any of the criteria defining an experiment are not met, the design is quasi-experimental. But don't assume you shouldn't use a quasi-experimental design. Although experimental designs have strict requirements, giving them a stronger design than quasi-experimental designs, it isn't always possible or feasible to use an experimental design.

Ethics is not listed as a criterion because it is assumed that the research will be conducted in an unbiased, ethical manner. If you are not accurate in conducting and reporting results, if you violate the rights of participants or if you abuse intellectual property rights, your experiment or quasi-experiment is not valid. Participant rights are especially relevant to experiments (i.e., the right to nonparticipation and withdrawal at any time, the right to full disclosure—no deception, and the rights to privacy, anonymity or confidentiality, experimenter responsibility, and informed consent). Review the section on ethics in Chapter 3 for details on the right to accuracy, participant rights, and intellectual property rights.

Experimental Designs

The experimental designs we discuss below are pretest-posttest and posttest only, with and without a control group.

Pretest-posttest control and experimental group.

The classical pre-post test design includes using both a control group and an experimental group, with each participant being in both groups and with pretest-posttest in each group. The pre-post test design is a stronger design than just posttest, but it is not always possible or necessary to use a control group or a pre-post test. Refer to Chapter 10 to review the material on golf pro Carlos's test of golf scores as an example of pre-post test experimental design.

Pretest-posttest without a control group.

Once gain, you don't always have to have a control group. Continuing with the Chapter 10 example, Carlos wants to know if his golf lessons improve the scores of his trainees. Carlos has an experimental group and a control group with a score before and after treatment to compare differences. However, Carlos does not need the control group to claim that his golf lessons improve scores. All he really needs to do is compare two sets of scores of the same group of people before and after they took his lessons to see if they improved. Why go through the time and expense of having a control group?

Criteria for experiment? As with the pretest-posttest control and experimental groups, Carlos meets the three criteria for an experimental design because he (a) has an experimental group, (b) does manipulate a treatment of golf lessons (IV/X), and (c) does compare golf scores (DV/Y) of the same participants. Therefore, Carlos has a true experimental design with no control group. The reading program in the example below also could be conducted without a control group.

Posttest-only control and experimental groups.

As the heading implies, in this situation you have both groups but only give the test once. For example, the Woody Reading Program teaches people how to read faster with a higher level of comprehension. Woody hypothesizes that people who take the reading program have higher reading scores. Reading score is an interval/ratio variable measured by a combined speed and comprehension formula to determine words read per minute. Woody has developed one valid and reliable test instrument to measure reading scores.

Woody would like to test reading scores before and after the reading program. However, he only has one measurement reading test. Woody cannot have people take the same test before and after taking the program because they will remember the story and have higher scores based solely on prior reading. Therefore, Woody has decided to use a sample of 50 people: Half are randomly assigned to the control group that will do nothing different for five weeks, and half to the experimental group that will take the reading program for five weeks. At the end of five weeks, all 50 participants take the reading test (*posttest-only design*). The mean reading scores of the control and experimental groups will be compared. If the reading scores of the experimental group are significantly higher than those of the control group, Woody will reject Ho (accept Ha) and claim that his program increases reading speed and comprehension.

Criteria for experiment? Woody has a true experiment because his design (a) has an experimental group that (b) does get the reading program treatment (X) and (c) is considered to be a matched pair, because it has both a control group and an experimental group that both take the same test to compare results (Y). Therefore, Woody has a posttest-only control and experimental groups design.

Quasi-Experimental Designs

This type of design is appropriate when you can't assign participants to groups and/or manipulate a treatment. For example, you can't assign participants to gender or race to compare differences, so you have to use a quasi-experimental design to compare male and female values. Again, you simply call the design a test of difference. Next we discuss four quasi-experimental designs—nonrandom assignment to groups, one-shot, static group, and time-series—and explain why they are *not* experiments.

Nonrandom assignment to groups.

Recall that when you have a control group and an experimental group, you must randomly assign participants to either group. Unfortunately, there are situations in which you can't make random assignments (e.g., gender), and if you are conducting business research and want to compare products/departments/companies, they are already categorically assigned. Also, if you are conducting educational research and you want to compare two teaching methods used in two different sections of the same course, you can't randomly assign students to the two sections—the registrar's office does the assignment without randomization.

Criteria for experiment? Even though you don't have a true experiment because (a) you don't randomly assign participants to groups, you can still have (b) a time-ordered treatment (X), and (c) a matched group comparison (Y). This is a strong type of quasi-experimental design that is sometimes referred to as a *compromise design*.

One-shot (after-only) design, no experimental group.

The *one-shot* quasi-experimental design has only one measure at one point in time, usually subsequent to some phenomenon that allegedly produced change. For example, an employee training program could be conducted without determining employee knowledge before the program, so if you only measure their knowledge at the end of the program you can't determine a change in knowledge.

Criteria for experiment? The group in the training program above represents a one-shot design that does not meet the criteria for an experiment because (a) there is no experimental group, (b) there is a treatment training program, (c) and there are no matched pair comparisons. Therefore, it is classified as a one-shot quasi-experimental research design. The design could be changed to a stronger experimental design by using an experimental group and comparing pre-post test knowledge in order to measure the change in knowledge that can be assumed to be caused by the training program.

As stated, the training program above could be changed to be an experiment. However, there are situations in which it is very difficult to make changes—in which you can't have an experiment. For example, when a company offers a new product to consumers, it is difficult to have an experimental group, treatment, and match. Also, if an organization introduces a new policy it is difficult to have an experiment. But you can do a one-shot after-only quasi-experiment to determine if the new product or policy is performing to expectations.

Static group control and experimental group.

With the static group design you have a control and an experimental group, but you do not randomly assign participants to each group. For example, there is a major disaster (e.g., a fire, flood, or tornado) that is the treatment and a consequence (trauma, loss) that is the measured outcome. A pretest before the disaster is possible, but if you can't predict where or when the disaster will occur; therefore, you can't pretest close to the time of the disaster. You compare the consequence of the "static group" (the control group) that did not experience the disaster to the experimental group that suffered the consequences to compare differences.

Criteria for experiment? The static control group is not an experiment because, although there is an experimental group (a), the requirement of random assignment of participants to control and experimental groups is violated. However, it does meet the criterion of (b) having a treatment, and (c) there is a match of a control and an experimental group. Therefore, it is a static group quasi-experimental research design.

Time series.

A *time series* takes repeated measures over a long period of time to distinguish between temporary and permanent changes and trends in dependent variables. It is commonly used in economics and to forecast sales. For example, the Obama administration implemented an economic stimulus plan, which is a treatment. The federal government takes all kinds of economic measures that can determine its success.

Criteria for experiment? Because time series is so broad, let's use the Obama stimulus plan as the example of why time series is not considered an experiment. Technically, you could say the economy is an experimental group (a), it has a treatment (b), and you can compare before-and-after results (c). Recall that to be considered an experiment your design has to control the situation and must have nonspurious variables. The problem is in the complexity of the economy (i.e., so many variables that affect the economy can't be controlled). If the economy improves, it could be due to many variables other than the stimulus plan. Also, with long-term repeated measures the treatment effect can be short lived, with other spurious variables taking over to account for the change. (Running a time-series analysis is discussed in Chapter 14.)

Complex Designs

Complex designs can have a mixture of experimental and quasi-experimental design features. Three complex designs include the *completely randomized design, randomized block design,* and the *factorial design.*

Completely randomized and randomized block designs.

Completely randomized designs are those the researcher can manipulate by causing participants to receive different levels of a treatment to investigate the effects of a single X. *Randomized block designs* extend the completely randomized design by including a single extraneous (spurious/confounding) variable that might affect test results/participant responses to the treatment, and the effects of this variable are isolated by being blocked out.

Factorial designs.

Before we get into factorial designs, let's define factor. *Factor* is commonly used to denote an independent variable (IV/X). Thus, factor analysis in a test of interrelationship only has Xs, no Y. Both the completely randomized and block designs have a single factor, whereas factorial designs have two or more Xs.

Factorial designs include two or more independent variables and are identified by the number of independent variables and the number of groups/scales in each. Thus, the test of interaction—two-way (factorial) ANOVA (see Chapter 14) is a factorial design. A factorial design has an inordinate number of possible design combinations based on the number of Xs and the number of groups/scales of each X. For example, a 2×3 factorial design indicates that there are two Xs. The first has two groups/scales (such as male and female) and the second X has three groups/scales (such as Jewish, Catholic, Protestant). A $2 \times 2 \times 2$ factorial design indicates there are three Xs, all with two groups/scales. Identify a $4 \times 2 \times 3 \times 2$.

Main effect and interaction effect. In factorial designs the statistical analysis provides two results called the main effect and interaction effect. The main effect provides separate results for each of the Xs, as with running a one-way ANOVA (discussed later in the chapter). The interaction effect gives the combined effect of all the Xs. A major advantage of the factorial design is its ability to measure the interaction effect, which may be greater than the total of the main effects. (You will learn more about factorial designs and statistical testing in Chapter 14).

Before we move on to cause and effect, let's review the three categories of experimental designs in Box 12.1.

Box 12.1   Test-of-Difference Designs

Experimental design (has an experimental group, IV/X treatment, and matched comparison of DV/Y group values)
• Pretest-posttest control and experimental groups
• Pretest-posttest without control group
• Posttest-only control and experimental groups

Quasi-experimental design (a test of difference that does not meet the criteria of experiment)
• Nonrandom assignment of groups
• One-shot (after-only, no experimental group)
• Static group (has a control and experimental group, but not a direct comparison)
• Time-series (repeated measures over time, so may have extraneous-variable spurious relationships)

Complex design (can be a mix of experimental and quasi-experimental designs)
• Completely randomized (one IV/X)
• Randomized block (one IV/X)
• Factorial (two or more IV/X)

Cause and Effect

Let's discuss the differences between cause and effect versus understanding and explaining differences.

Experimental designs assume cause and effect.

Recall from Chapter 1 that the role of statistics is to understand, explain, predict, and control phenomena. Of the five types of statistical tests, the experimental design is the strongest test to support that the change in a Y is *caused* by manipulating the treatment through control and experimental groups in the X (cause and effect). The quasi-experimental design is weaker because you cannot claim causation.

Quasi-experimental designs help understand and explain differences, not causation.

Although the experimental design is a stronger design than the quasi-experimental design, you often cannot meet the three criteria and must use a quasi-experimental design. For example, researchers have documented that even after 30 years of equal pay for equal jobs in the United States, women still get paid less than men. However, you cannot claim that being a woman is the "cause" of a lower income because there has been no random assignment of group members to control and experimental groups, even though there has been a treatment—the Equal Pay Act. Surely, gender is an *explainer* (as the X is commonly called) of the reasons for the pay difference, but it is not the *cause*. There are other extraneous (spurious/confounding) variables that can also explain the difference in pay. Generally, men and women get paid about the same for the same non-managerial job. However, fewer women make it to high-paying top management jobs, and many women tend to take white-collar jobs in fields dominated by women that have traditionally paid less than blue-collar jobs more traditionally held by men. These are also "explainer" variables of why "all" women are paid less than all men. In other words, gender helps us to understand and *explain* pay differences, it is not the *cause*.

CONCEPTUAL OBJECTIVE 1
Explain the difference between experimental and quasi-experimental designs,
and state which one has the greater cause-and-effect relationship and why.

Internal and External Validity

Although we will be discussing the trade-off between internal and external validity with the test of difference, you should realize that it is heavily based on the sample and is, therefore, relevant to all five types of statistical research designs and statistical tests.

We stated in Chapter 8 that a test instrument is valid when it measures what we say it will measure. We now discuss two other types of validity in detail: internal and external validity. *Internal validity is the extent to which the differences in the values of the dependent variable can be attributed to the manipulation of the independent variable.* *External validity is the extent to which the results of a study can be generalized.* In other words, how well does the sample represent the population? (This topic is covered in chapters 1 and 5). However, a study can have neither internal nor external validity. For example, if the measurement instrument is not valid then the study is not valid, so you can't have internal or external validity. Things can happen that pose a threat to each type of validity.

Threats to internal validity.

Threats include nonequivalent control and experimental groups, history, maturation, testing, the measurement instrument, regression to the mean, and experimental mortality. We will not give details for each of these threats, however. For our purposes, it's enough to know that if you meet the criteria of an experimental design, you help to control external factors that could explain the difference in Y values rather than the manipulated X (treatment) causing the change; there is less threat to internal validity.

Threats to external validity.

The two major threats to external validity are the representativeness of the sample and the reactive arrangements in the research procedure. The first threat can be controlled for to some extent with sample size so that the sample truly represents the population (see the discussion on good random samples in Chapter 5). The reactive arrangements refer to the environment. Clearly, you can have more control in a laboratory setting than in a field-based research design (out in the business world).

Trade-offs between internal and external validity.

Internal and external validity have an inverse relationship (they move in opposite directions). Thus, managers and researchers can take measures to increase either type of validity, but not both simultaneously. The wider the geographic population, sample size, and diversity of the sample, the more generalizable the results of the test and the more external validity it has (and vice versa). Recall the example of Carlos, the golf instructor. If Carlos conducts the golf test, there is very high internal validity and very low external validity. If an academic researcher randomly tests five golf teachers in one state, the internal validity goes down as the external validity increases. If the researcher takes a national sample of 100 golf teachers, internal validity goes down again as external validity increases.

In experimental versus quasi-experimental designs, here's a general guide: Experimental designs provide greater internal validity (cause and effect), while quasi-experimental designs provide greater external validity (generalization).

Internal validity and business research.

When making decisions, managers are generally more concerned about internal validity. In other words, managers want to be able to say that the test results are valid for *their* organization, although results may not be generalizable to other organizations. Continuing our example, Carlos is much more concerned about the sale of his golf lessons than that of other golf pros. Carlos is not concerned that just "any" golf lessons improve scores—he wants to be able to claim that *his* golf lessons improve scores, so people will come to him for lessons. Similarly, managers generally tend to use more narrow or focused samples (just their own organization) than researchers do (many organizations).

External validity and the academic researcher.

When testing hypotheses and making decisions, academic researchers are generally more concerned about *external* validity. In other words, researchers are more concerned about being able to say that their test results are valid for *all* organizations in the population. Conversely, they are generally less concerned about being able to say that the results of their test are only valid for one organization and may not be generalizable to other companies (e.g., an academic researcher would be more concerned about explaining effective golf lessons that can be used by *all* golf teachers than about only Carlos's golf lesson sales). Therefore, more academic researchers focus on external validity. Also, externally valid results are more frequently published because they are generalizable to a wider audience readership. When you did your literature review, how many articles were just one-company studies?

CONCEPTUAL OBJECTIVE 2
Discuss (a) internal and external validity, (b) the trade-off between the two,
and (c) their impact on decision making.

12.2 Parametric versus Nonparametric Tests

The inferential statistical tests of significance are divided into two major categories: parametric and nonparametric tests. As we first mentioned in Chapter 8, a *metric* is simply a measurement. *Parametric tests are powerful because they use interval/ratio level measures using random samples taken from a normally distributed population with equal variance.* **Nonparametric tests** *are less powerful because they use ordinal- and nominal-level measures and are used when parametric assumptions are not met.* You already know that you want to use the highest level of measurement feasible for your study. Thus, parametric tests are always preferable.

Parametric assumptions.

As indicated in our definition of parametric tests, there are four major assumptions that should be met to use a parametric test. They are ranked here by level of importance.

1. The measurement level of the DV/Y is interval or ratio.
2. The sample participants are selected from a normally distributed population.
3. The population should have equal variance.
4. The sample participants are randomly selected from the population.

Use a large sample size. You can't always know whether the population is normally distributed and has equal variance. However, when you use a large sample size (a minimum of 25–30 per group) you can generally make these two assumptions.

Parametric tests place different emphasis on the importance of assumptions. Some tests hold up well even when the assumptions are not met. Thus, you may use a parametric test even if you have not met, or are not sure you met, all assumptions. People do use parametric tests when they don't have random samples.

Rating scales ≥ 5. However, don't use a parametric test without interval/ratio-level data. Again, if you use rating scales with at least a scale of 1–5, you have interval/ratio-level data and may use parametric tests.

CONCEPTUAL OBJECTIVE 3
Describe the difference between parametric and nonparametric tests of significance.

Parametric and nonparametric tests and the Decision Tree.

There are parametric and nonparametric tests of difference. For each parametric test of difference there is a similar nonparametric test. Take another look at the Decision Tree in Figure 10.1, Selecting Appropriate Statistical Techniques. Note that the T-test is a parametric test and that the Mann-Whitney U and chi-square test are its nonparametric substitutes. We talk more about this later on when we explain each of these tests.

There is a lower probability of finding significant differences with nonparametric tests.

Because nonparametric tests make fewer assumptions than parametric tests, they are weaker and require a higher probability that differences are not due to chance (that you are not making a Type I error, saying there are differences when there are none). Thus, if you run a parametric T-test (scale of 1–5) and a nonparametric Mann-Whitney U test, you almost always will get a different p-value (unless it's .0000, because you cannot go lower). The p-value of the T-test will be lower than the p-value of the Mann-Whitney U test. As a result, although it does not happen very often, you could have p-values of, say, .041 and .053. The decision would be to reject the Ho using the T-test (.041 < .05—concluding that there is a difference in means), but not to reject Ho using the Mann-Whitney (.053 > .05—concluding there are no differences). Remember too that the larger the sample size, the greater the probability of finding significant differences. Thus, another way to look at things is to say that a nonparametric test with a sample of 100 will provide the same statistical testing power as a parametric test with a sample of 95, or nonparametric tests have a 95% efficiency rate as compared to parametric tests. The important thing to remember is that a parametric test is more powerful, and you should use it whenever possible.

In the next four sections you will learn about the parametric T-test (IV/X 2 groups) and its nonparametric alternatives, the Mann-Whitney U and chi-square tests of difference. Then we discuss the parametric one-way ANOVA (IV/X 3+ groups) and its nonparametric alternatives.

12.3 T-Tests and Z-Tests

In this section we discuss the T-test, the paired T-test, the Z-test, and the one-sample T-test. But first, let's discuss the T-test assumptions and one-tailed and two-tailed T-test hypotheses.

T-Test Assumptions

T-tests are all parametric, and thus the data should meet the four assumptions. However, with a T-test the assumption of a normal distribution is not critical. Because we are comparing means (M [total sample] m [subsample]), variance and its standard deviation (SD/s = sample) is an important consideration. One simple way to check to make sure the variance is not too large is to compare the variance of the two groups.

Check for and remove outliers.

If the variance of one group is four times larger than the other, you are probably violating the assumption of equal variance. If the variance is too large, recall from Chapter 9 that outliers can make the mean misleading due to large variances, and if you eliminate outliers from the data it can affect the variance. If you have unequal variance, check for outliers and eliminate them and you may have equality to run the T-test.

Some statistical software packages have menus that require you to select *equal or unequal variance assumed*. Many statistical packages also pool variance of the two samples when you assume equal variance. So you can make the > 4 variance-between-groups comparison above to make the assumption. However, some statistical packages like SPSS 19 will run the T-test giving both equal and unequal results and run Levene's test of equality of variance with an F and p-value to let you know whether the variance is equal. So you can test the variances with an F-test for equal variances. Many times the difference between equal and unequal variance is small.

The formula for the t-ratio appears in Box 12.2. However, don't worry about calculating the T-test by hand as the computer statistical software will do it for you.

One- and two-tailed hypotheses testing.

With null two-tailed hypotheses, you predict that the means are equal (Ho M1 = M2)—there is no significant mean difference. Thus, two-tailed alternative hypotheses predict that

---

Box 12.2   T-Test Ratio Formula

$$t = \frac{m_1 - m_2}{\sqrt{\dfrac{s_1^2}{n} + \dfrac{s_2^2}{n}}}$$

For example, in a test of difference of mean level of satisfaction on a Likert scale of **not satisfied** 1 2 3 4 5 6 7 8 9 **satisfied**:

	Sample size (n)	Mean (m)	Sample standard deviation (s)
Men	61	7.31	2.38
Women	39	5.63	3.16

t = 2.857

the means are significantly different (Ha M1 ≠ M2). However, you are not predicting which group has the higher mean.

With one-tailed null hypotheses, you again predict no difference. However, alternative one-tailed hypotheses predict that one of the two means is greater than the other (Ha M1 > M2, or M1 < M2).

T-Tests

*The **T-test** compares mean differences of one interval/ratio dependent variable between one nominal independent variable with two groups.* Thus, the descriptive statistics (see Chapter 10) that the T-test uses is the measure-of-central-tendency mean with the standard deviation (s) as its variance measure. The T-test is also commonly called the "independent groups T-test" to distinguish it from its paired T-test, which uses matched groups. Recall that a mean difference is also called a *treatment effect*, or just *effect*.

When calculating means, you'll find that there is almost always a difference between group means. The real question is, "Is the difference significant or just due to chance (such as a random occurrence or sampling error variance)?" Thus, we test the mean differences through hypothesis testing.

Your substantive hypothesis is usually that the means are significantly different. Thus, you predict that you will reject the Ho (accept Ha) and claim that there is a difference between groups. If you do not find evidence to reject the Ho (accept Ha), one of two possibilities is true:

1. The means are equal or very similar. No error has been made as there are no differences.

2. The means are different, but you are not able to detect the difference because:
   (a) the sample size is too small,
   (b) there is large variability in the values of the DV/Y, or
   (c) both.

A Type II error is made because you claim there is no difference when there really is a difference. Using a large sample is often a possible way to help decrease Type II errors; testing for equal variance, discussed above, is another method.

Independent groups T-test.

The *independent groups T-test* compares the means of two unmatched groups/scales. Recall that independent and unmatched groups are the same. The independent groups T-test is used with a quasi-experimental design because you do not use paired groups and usually do not manipulate a time-ordered treatment. The best way to understand the T-test is through examples with computer printouts of results that explain how to interpret them for decision-making purposes (see Box 12.3). Box 12.4 contains a sample hypothesis for a T-test.

T-test with SPSS 19.

1. Click *Analyze* on the toolbar.

2. Scroll down to *Compare Means* and on the menu at the right click *Independent Samples T Test*.

3. Click and drag your dependent variable(s) from the left into the test variable(s) box on the right.

4. Move your independent variable to the grouping variable box directly below.

Box 12.3   Reading Independent Groups T-Test Results

You have two salaried sales employees and you want to know if either one has significantly higher sales. If one does have higher sales (.05 critical value), that employee will get a merit pay raise. So, you get a random sample from the last 12 months, 8 and 9 sales figures in units, and run a T-test with confidence intervals, which is presented below.

Data: Enter all sales numbers (17) in the same Y column. In the next column, enter 0 = Tom's sales (8) and 1 = John's sales (9).

Tom = C1:   90   72   61   66   81   69   59   70
John = C2:   62   85   78   66   80   91   69   77   84

Group Statistics

	gender	N	Mean	Std. Deviation	Std. Error Mean
sales	Tom	8	71.0000	10.25392	3.62531
	John	9	76.8889	9.54521	3.18174

Independent Samples Test

		Levene's Test for Equality of Variances	
		F	Sig.
sales	Equal variances assumed	.000	.995
	Equal variances not assumed		

Independent Samples Test

		t-test for Equality of Means			
		t	df	Sig. (2-tailed)	Mean Difference
sales	Equal variances assumed	-1.226	15	.239	-5.88889
	Equal variances not assumed	-1.221	14.440	.242	-5.88889

Independent Samples Test

		t-test for Equality of Means		
			95% Confidence Interval of the Difference	
		Std. Error Difference	Lower	Upper
sales	Equal variances assumed	4.80192	-16.12394	4.34616
	Equal variances not assumed	4.82352	-16.20479	4.42701

(continued)

Below, the important values from the SPSS 19 computer printout are explained. Note that the variable names are printed out based on the values entered as data into SPSS. The statistical results are presented in priority order. You must understand the first two (p-values and mean comparisons), and the others are helpful.

P-Value/Sig (2-Tailed Sig). The bottom line in all inferential statistical tests is always the p-value. The p-value (2-tailed sig) tells you that 24% (.239 and .242) of the time a difference of at least this size would occur when the two population means are equal. You wanted to be 95% certain (.05 critical value) that the difference is not due to chance. The p-value of .240 tells you that you are only 76% (1.00 − .24 or 100% − 24%) certain of not making a Type I error and saying that one employee has significantly higher-level sales than the other, when in fact this is not the case. There isn't enough evidence to support the difference. Thus, do not reject Ho (accept Ho .05 < .24); although John has higher-level sales, the difference is not significantly higher. Therefore, do not take any action (do not give a merit raise).

You must be careful about testing one- or two-tailed hypotheses, because the p-values are different based on the number of tails. Recall that you were not sure which employee had the higher level of sales. Therefore, you correctly used the two-tailed test.

Error in number of tails. If you used the test with the wrong number of tails, you can change the number of tails in SPSS and rerun the T-test or easily convert to the other test. For example, the two-tailed p-value is .24; to make it a one-tailed test you would double the p-value = .48 (to get the full p-value in one tail). Conversely, to go from a one-tailed to a two-tailed p-value (to get the p-value into two tails) you divide .48 by 2 = .24.

Means. The means tell you who sold more, and how many more, units per month. You can see that employee C2/John sold more units per month than C1/Tom (76.89 vs. 71). However, the difference is not significant, as interpreted through the p-value. If there is no significant difference, it is not too important which mean is higher. You often just ignore non-differences because you do not take any action (or do not give the raise, in this example). If there is a significant difference, then it is important to know which mean is higher, because this tells you which employee should get a raise.

Be careful to interpret the means correctly. The higher mean is not always the best performance—for example, with faster times being lower. Also, you do not always get the results you expect. In this instance, you could have expected Tom to have the higher level of sales. If you analyzed only the p-value without looking at the means, you could give the raise to the wrong person.

T-Statistic. The t-statistic is a measure of the test of difference. The larger the t-statistic is, the greater the difference between means. However, it is very difficult to interpret by itself, which is why the p-value is so important. A major value of the t-statistic is: If it is positive (no sign before the t-value) you know that C1 has a higher mean than C2; if it is negative (minus sign before the t-value) you know that C2 has a greater mean than C1. The t-value is −1.22; thus, John has the higher level of sales. However, the p-value is what's really important because it tells you whether or not the difference is significant.

Levene's Test for Equality of Variances. *Caution:* The sig .995 is not the T-test p-value—it is the Levene's F-test of equality. The F-value is the ratio of the variances within the two samples. The t-ratio compares the variance between sample means. If the p-value is not significant (> .05), there is equal variance within the sample and you use the equal t- and p-values. *Note:* The p-value of the Levene test is the opposite of the T-test p-value. The greater the Levene P, the less variance there is between groups. Therefore, if the Levene p is > .05 you use the equal numbers (p = .239); if it is < .05 you use the unequal numbers (p = 242). In this T-test, notice that there is little difference in the numbers of the p-value for the standard error and confidence intervals (see below).

Standard Deviation (SD) and Standard Error (SE) of the Mean. Recall that the SD is the square root of the variance. SE mean is another measure of variance; it is the sample variance. The

SE mean Tom (3.6) is calculated by dividing the standard deviation (10.3) by the square root of N (8 = 2.828). The same calculations are used for the John SE mean. In SPSS the *Levene's test* is based on variance, and thus by using the unequal numbers *you are adjusting for the large variance.* Based on the data, however, we use the equal variance in this example.

Large SD/SE and outliers. As we've discussed, if you have an SD of one group that is four times larger than that for the other group, it could be due to a few outliers that are distorting the mean Accordingly, check the data, eliminate them, and run the T-test again.

Confidence intervals (CI). CI tell you the range within which you are 95% confident the actual difference in the means (–5.89) lies. You don't really need to have both CI and p-values; they provide different probability information. P-values are a stronger test of hypothesis than CI. Therefore, you want to use p-values with two sample T-tests.

(N = Sample Size). The N tells you the number of participants' values in each group. Tom had 8 sales months and John had 9. It is a good idea to check it to make sure all the data have been entered into the computer. The sample size is used in determining the Confidence Intervals because it affects the SE mean, and it also affects the degrees of freedom (see below), which affects the p-value.

Degrees of Freedom (df). The df is the number of values in a sample that are free to vary. The df is based on the number of sales observations in each of the two groups. It is just the total Ns (17) minus 2 = 15. Don't worry about the calculations; the computer does it for you. However, you should realize that df are used together with the t-value to determine the p-value. Recall, with small sample sizes, that you increase the chances of making a Type II error by not finding a difference between means when there really is a difference. Thus, the larger the sample size, the greater the df, and the greater the chances of finding a difference when there is one.

Box 12.4   Example of a Hypothesis for a T-Test

Education Levels

Chris would like to claim that people who use the company product are smarter than people who use the competitor's product. However, this is a difficult measure. So, Chris decides to find out if the company customers are more highly educated than those of its leading competitor. If customers are more highly educated, this will be advertised as a means of taking customers away from the competitor. Chris decided to use survey research and randomly asked the company's customers and the competitor's customers their education level. Chris asked for the actual number of years of full-time education. Thus, a grade school graduate would have 8 years, a high school grad 12, two years of college (associate's degree) 14 years, bachelor's 16, masters 17–18, doctorate 19 plus. Chris selected a large sample size, with a goal of around 170 for both groups, because there is a greater chance of finding a difference with a large sample size (a better chance of avoiding any violations of T-test assumptions).

Instructions

Clearly list the five steps of hypothesis testing and answer these questions within the appropriate step.

For *step 1*, be sure to clearly write the null and appropriate one- or two-tailed alternative hypotheses with actions.

For *step 2*, which of the three situations of Type I and II errors applies to Chris? What would you set as the critical value? Is there a significant difference in means at your critical value level?

For *step 3*, list the dependent and independent variables with their measurement level and the appropriate statistical test.

(continued)

For *step 4*, see the data in the simulated computer printout below; however, list the step and write the percentage of confidence that the mean difference is significant.

For *step 5*, answer the following questions as part of making the decision: (a) What are the two means, and which is preferred? (b) Is the difference between means significant? Regardless of your answer to this question, use .40 as the critical value. Is the difference important? (c) Should Chris fail to reject Ho (accept Ho) or reject Ho (accept Ha)? (d) What action should Chris take? (e) If Chris advertises, would it be helpful to give the education level means to the general public? Is not giving the means legal and ethical? Would you give the means in Chris's position?

Solution (Decision)

Step 1. State the hypothesis and action.

Hypothesis	Action
Ho: The mean number of years of education of our customers is equal to the competitor's (M =).	Do not advertise that our customers are more highly educated than the competitor's.
Ha: The mean number of years of education of our customers is greater than the competitor's (one-tailed M ?).	Advertise that our customers are more highly educated than the competitor's.

Step 2. Set the critical value.

Chris is in situation 2—high critical value. A Type II error (saying there is no difference when there is one) is costly because Chris cannot advertise. A Type I error (saying there is a difference when there really isn't any) is not costly; if a legitimate test is conducted you have legal protection to avoid a possible lawsuit. Therefore, Chris should set a high critical value of .40 to be certain of not making an error. Recall that for legal purposes all you need is descriptive statistics (as with the Koors example of 58% in Chapter 11). There is a significant difference at the .40 level.

Step 3. Select the methodology of data collection and statistical test.

The Y is interval/ratio (years of education) and the X is nominal (customers or noncustomers). Thus, the T-test is the appropriate test.

Step 4. Run the statistics to obtain the p-value.

Because we already just showed an entire computer printout, to save space we give you only the numbers you need to make the decision.

T-test for Independent Samples of EDUC (education of the individual)

Variables	N	Mean	SD	SE of Mean
EDUC individual				
Customers	161	14.174	2.76	.217
Competitors	171	13.105	2.72	.208

Mean Difference = 1.069

Chris is over 99% confident that the difference between means is significant.

Step 5. Make the decision (a–e).

(a) The customer mean of 14.174 is larger than the competitor mean of 13.105, which is preferred.

(b) The difference between means is significant (p-value .00 < .40 critical value). The importance of the difference is questionable. It is important in the sense that the ad can be run. However, it is not so important that your customers are a little over one year more educated than the customers of your competitor's. Can we really conclude that a person with a little over two years of college is significantly more educated than a person with a little over one year of college? Statistically, Chris is over 99% certain that an error has not been made, or that there really is a difference. (*Note*: Recall that with large sample sizes it is easier to find mean differences that are significant than it is with small sample sizes.)

(c) Chris should reject Ho (accept Ha) because there is a significant difference (p-value .00 < .40 critical value). (*Note*: Recall that the smaller the p-value, the greater the probability that there really is a difference or that a Type II error—assuming there is no difference when there really is one—is not being made.)

(d) Chris should advertise that the company customers are more highly educated than the competitor's.

(e) Giving the education levels to the general public will not help to convince customers to change to Chris's company product. It is legal not to give the means. (*Note*: Keebler once stated on the front of the package that its Chips Deluxe were preferred to Chip's Ahoy Chocolate Chip Cookies. On the front of the package it said to see the back for details. However, the only information provided there was that the claim was based on a national sample—no numbers were given.) There is no simple answer to the ethical question. What do you think about this? Would you give the means to be ethical?

5. Click *Define Groups* and enter your codes (0-1, 1-2) that represent your groups, then click *Continue*.

6. You can also click *Options* and set the confidence intervals if you don't want the default 95%, which is the recommended level.

7. Click *OK* to generate the results in the data window.

Note that you can run multiple T-tests at the same time with several Y, but with only one X.

After printing the output results it's a good idea to save them. Close the output window to return to the data view window. (These directions apply for all statistical tests that you run in SPSS 19.) You can run many different statistic tests and leave the results in the output window, but it can get messy, mixing up different types of tests in the same printout. It is not so bad with a file saved in Word, because you can split the tests yourself onto different pages, making them easier to read.

STOP READING and turn to the end of the chapter to complete decision problems 12-1 and 12-2.

Paired T-Tests

The *paired T-test* compares mean differences of one interval/ratio dependent variable with the same measurement taken at two different times.

Differences between the independent groups T-test and the paired T-test.

The independent group T-test has one Y and one X (with two groups/scales). With a paired T-test you really don't have one Y and one X—you have two Ys. The comparison of pairs is between the means of the two Ys, versus the T-test comparison of the mean of the two groups of the X (i.e., men and women).

The independent groups T-test is commonly used with a quasi-experimental design and the paired T-test is more commonly used with an experimental design because of the need for repeated measures. However, the paired T-test can also be used with quasi-experimental designs when the groups are matched but one of the other four criteria of experimental designs is not met (e.g., no treatment is used).

Data entry.
The T-test and the paired T-test have different methods of data entry, and you must be sure to enter the data correctly for each. With the T-test you enter the values of the interval/ratio Y (e.g., age) and the nominal X (e.g., gender) in two separate columns. But with the paired T-test you enter the same Y value twice (e.g., pre-test and post-test score). Below is an example of an experimental design using the reading scores before a reading program treatment (pre-test) and the reading scores after completion of the reading program (post-test).

Pair Participant	Variable 1 Pre-test	Variable 2 Post-test
1	54	65
2	49	53
3	30	50
50	31	47

The paired T-test will compare the reading scores before and after the reading program to determine if the means are significantly different. Just by looking at the data above we can see that every reading program participant's score did improve, but we need to run the test to know if the difference is truly significant, or how confident (95%) are we that our reading program does in fact improve reading scores.

Paired T-test with SPSS 19.
1. Click *Analyze* on the toolbar.
2. Scroll down to *Compare Means* and on the menu at the right click *Paired Samples T-Test*.
3. Move your first variable into the variable 1 column and the other into variable 2 column.
4. You can also click *Options* and set the confidence intervals if you don't want the default (95%, which is the recommended level).
5. Click *OK* to generate the results in the data window.

Z-Tests

Recall at the end of Chapter 9 we talked about standard scores—Z- and T-tests. With a Z-score, the mean is 0 and the standard deviation (s) is 1. In order to run a Z-test rather than the T-test, you must know the s of the population. However, in most studies, the population standard deviation is not known. Thus, the T-test is much more commonly used in research, but not in production quality control. An example of a one-sample Z-test appears in the computer printout in Box 12.5.

The Z and t distributions are similar but different. The Z distribution is a perfect bell-shaped curve; however, the t distribution has a lower peak and fatter tails and a wider variance. Thus, you can run a T-test even if the population distribution is not a good normal curve, so long as it is not extremely skewed.

One-Sample Z- and T-Tests

*The **one-sample T-test** compares a sample mean to a population/standard mean.* The Z-test is calculated using the known population standard deviation (called *sigma*) while the T-test uses the sample standard deviation. Therefore, when comparing one-sample mean to a population mean, when you know the population standard deviation you should use the one-sample Z-test; if you don't know, use the more common one-sample T-test.

The difference between the one-sample test and the T-test.

An important difference between the T-test and the one-sample T-test is the fact that with the one-sample T-test you are comparing your study's total data mean to an external mean (and sigma with Z-test) given in the literature or in some way called the standard. With the T-test you are actually using your total data but splitting it by groups/scales of the IV/X. When running the one-sample T-test, unlike with the T-test you must type in the standard/population mean, and with the Z-test you type in the mean and sigma. The one-sample T-test is commonly used in manufacturing because you know what you want for the results (product specifications) and you test to ensure that the product meets the standards (quality control).

When to use the one-sample test.

Let's give an example of when a one-sample T-test would be used instead of a T-test. A manager wants to measure the job satisfaction of employees, so she develops a rating scale of **1** not satisfied—**9** satisfied. The manager has only one group/sample. Thus, she cannot run a T-test. However, the manager can set a standard mean of, let's say, 7 and compare it to the sample employee mean. Consider another possibility: If the manager read in a journal that the study mean was 6.5 and standard deviation 1.3, she could use the study data (population/standard) to compare to her employee data using the Z-test.

The one-sample Z-test is commonly used in production/operations management (POM) to determine if a sample mean meets the product standard mean. The population mean can be specified (or not) in the Z- and T-tests. When it is not specified, a mean equal to zero is used. The best way to understand the one-sample and T-tests is through examples with computer printouts of results that explain how to interpret them for decision making (see the simulation of an EXCEL printout in Box 12.5). Because the T-test and one-sample T-test are so similar to interpret, there are no sample or decision problems. However, there is a computer problem for you to run at the end of the chapter.

Box 12.5   Reading One-Sample T-Test Results

Comparing Mean Candy Bar Weight

You work for Hershey as a production manager making five-ounce candy bars. The standard/population mean is 5 oz. You know that the standard/population standard deviation (sigma) is .2 oz. In other words, if the candy weight is greater than +/− .2 oz, it does not meet the standard. For illustrative purposes, let's also assume that you do not know sigma. You have to be sure that you are not shipping candy bars that weigh significantly more or less than 5 oz. You have nine cases of candy bars and randomly grab one candy bar from different boxes to see if they have an acceptable mean, critical value .05. If they do, they will be shipped; if not, they will not be shipped. To make your decision, you run a Z-test (using sigma of .2) and T-test (no population

(continued)

standard deviation, the sample standard deviation is used) with confidence intervals for both. Note that we are specifying the population mean at 5, rather than not specifying and letting the computer use 0 for Z testing.

Data in Ounces

   4.9   5.1   4.6   5.0   5.1   4.7   4.4   4.7   4.5

Excel Z- and T-test Results

	A	B
1	Z-Test: (Sigma Known)	
2		
3	Test of MU = 5.0000 vs MU ≠ 5.0000	
4	Sigma	0.2
5	Sample Mean	4.7889
6	Standard Deviation	0.2472
7	Standard Error of Mean	0.0667
8	Observations	9
9	Z-Statistic	-3.17
10	p-value =	0.0016
11	90% Confidence Intervals	4.6792, 4.8986

	A	B
1	t-Test: (Sigma Unknown)	
2		
3	Test of MU = 5.0000 vs MU ≠ 5.0000	
4		
5	Sample Mean	4.7889
6	Standard Deviation	0.2472
7	Standard Error of Mean	0.0824
8	Observations	9
9	t-Statistic	-2.56
10	p-value =	0.033
11	90% Confidence Intervals	4.6356, 4.9422

Because much of the same information is in the T-test and the one-sample T-test, our focus is primarily on the differences between these two tests and between the z- and T-test.

   Z-test and T-test and p-Values. You will recall that the bottom line is always the p-value. The Z-test p-value tells you that less than .16% of the time a difference of at least this size would occur when the means are equal. The T-test p-value tells you that less than 3.3% of the time a difference of at least this size would occur when the means are equal. You wanted to be 95% certain (.05 critical value) that the difference is not due to sample variance or chance. The Z-test p-value of .0016 (T-test p-value of .033) tells you that you are over 99% (Z) and 96% (T) certain that the candy bars do not weigh 5 oz. There is strong evidence to support the difference. Thus, do reject Ho (accept Ha .05 > .0016 and .033). Therefore, the action is not to ship the candy bars as is.

   You may be wondering why the Z- and T-test p-values are not the same. The reason is that the Z-test is a stronger test because it uses sigma (.200), not the sample standard deviation (.2472) like the T-test. Thus, with a smaller variance it is easier to find differences with the Z-test than with the T-test. For example, if the critical value were set at .01, you would reject Ho (accept Ha) with the Z-test and not ship the candy. However, with the T-test you would not reject Ho (accept Ho) and would ship the candy—two opposite decisions based on the same data. Thus, when using the T-test, which is more common than the Z-test outside of production sampling, you may want to set a higher critical value than with the Z-test when the cost of making a Type II error (saying there is no difference when there really is) is costly and a Type I error (assuming there is a difference when there really is not) is not costly. This is situation 2 of the three situations of Type I and II errors.

   Confidence Intervals (CI). The Z-test CI tell you that on average 90% of the candy bars in the sample weigh between 4.6792 and 4.8986 oz.; and with the T-test 4.6356 and 4.9422. You should realize that the CI should also be slightly above and below the 5.000 oz value. This is an indicator that the sample mean is different than the standard/population mean. If you are doing routine testing, CI may be preferred to p-values. However, if you are testing nonroutine hypotheses, use p-values.

   Means. The mean tells you the estimated average weight of the candy bars ready to be shipped for sale. With routine testing, simply comparing the mean to the standard is often all that is done. If the mean is between standard CI—say 4.8 and 5.2 oz (based on sigma .2)—the product passes inspection; if not, it fails (the candy bars are not shipped). Thus, CI and p-values are not always used. However, notice that if CI and p-values are not used the mean may be rounded off to 4.8 oz and the candy bars would be shipped, a different decision than the one based on p-values and CI.

CONCEPTUAL OBJECTIVE 4
Explain the difference between: (a) the T-test and the paired T-test,
(b) the one-sample T-test and the T-test, and (c) the Z-test and T-test.

One-sample T-test with SPSS 19.

1. Click *Analyze* on the toolbar.

2. Scroll down to *Compare Means* and on the menu at the right click *One-Sample T Test*.

3. Click and drag your one variable into the test variable box.

4. Type your *Test Value* (the population/standard mean you want to compare to your sample mean) in the box.

5. You can also click *Options* and set confidence intervals if you don't want the default (95%, which is recommended).

6. Click *OK* to generate results in the data window.

Decision Tree.

You may have noticed that on the Decision Tree, the test of differences does not feature a one- and/or two-sample Z- and T-test. The reason is that when you compare two means—whether it be a population mean to a sample mean, or whether you compare two sample means—you still have two groups (population and sample, considered one sample; or sample and sample, considered two samples). Thus, when you use the Decision Tree you should be able to come to the Z- or T-test and understand whether you use the one- or two-sample test. Also, because the two-sample tests are much more commonly used when people are not sure which test to run, the one-sample test is not needed on the Decision Tree.

12.4 Mann-Whitney U Test

The Mann-Whitney U test is the nonparametric ordinal-level alternative to the T-test. *The Mann-Whitney U test compares ranked values of one ordinal dependent variable between one nominal independent variable with two unmatched groups.* In this section we discuss the U test and its alternative (Wilcoxon matched pairs, discussed later in the chapter).

Differences between the T-Test and Mann-Whitney U Test

- The T-test (t) is a more powerful parametric test, whereas the Mann-Whitney U (MWU) is a nonparametric test.

- The MWU DV/Y is ordinal level; the t Y is interval ratio.

- The MWU compares ranked values; the t compares means.

- The MWU does not need to meet the t assumptions of a random sample taken from a population with a somewhat normal distribution with an equal variance.

Nonparametric tests are often called distribution-free statistics. The parametric T-test is a more powerful statistic than the Mann-Whitney U; thus, if you ran a T-test and a MWU test with the same data, the MWU would tend to give a larger p-value, making it more difficult to claim differences by rejecting Ho. In other words, it is easier to make a Type II error (saying there is no difference when there really is) when using the MWU test than when using the T-test. Therefore, when selecting methodology measurement level, use interval/ratio levels of measures when feasible—wide rating scales of at least 5.

What to do if your statistical software does not include the Mann-Whitney U test.
    If the software package you are using does not have the MWU test, run the parametric alternative T-test. If the p-value results are not close to the critical value, don't worry about it; the T-test is fine. But if the p-value and critical value are close (such as p = .041 and cv = .05), you may want to find software that includes the MWU and run the test again or make the decision not to reject Ho and claim that there is a difference (effect) and make a Type I error (saying there is a difference when there is none).

Ranking (median).
    Recall that the ordinal-level data measure of central tendency is the median (Chapter 9). The Mann-Whitney U test utilizes a ranking procedure as an integral part of the calculations. Remember that the median uses a ranking process by placing the observations in order and selecting the one that falls in the middle. Thus, the measure of central tendency of ranked data is actually the median. However, depending on the software, the Mann-Whitney computer printout may use one of the terms *rank mean, median, or mean*. Whatever it is called, it is a ranking process and not an arithmetic mean.

Calculating the Mann-Whitney U.
    First, list the entire set of scores from lowest to highest (as when determining the median). Then assign each score its corresponding rank, with the lowest ranked 1, the next lowest ranked 2, and so on. Next, place the participants' ranks back into the original two groups. Now, if there is a significant difference/effect in rank means, one group will have significantly more ranks at the lower end of the distribution compared to the second group. The nice thing about tests of significance is that the p-values are all interpreted the same way: The lower the p-value, the greater the differences/effect in ranks/medians. Don't worry about doing the hand calculations, let the computer do it for you. Review the computer printout in Box 12.6 for the MWU test, continuing with our bank-loan example. Note that the education scale is 1–6 (1 = elementary, 6 = grad school; see Chapter 9, Table 9.6 for frequency distribution), and the X is race.

Box 12.6   Reading Mann-Whitney U Test Results

You want to know if either race has the higher level of education, so you run a Mann-Whitney U test and get the following SPSS results.

Hypothesis Test Summary

	Null Hypothesis	Test	Sig.	Decision
1	The distribution of Level of education is the same across categories of Race of the individual	Independent-Samples Mann-Whitney U Test	.000	Reject the null hypothesis

Asymptotic significances are displayed. The significance level is .05.

Sig (p-value). The bottom line is always the p-value. The p-value (.000) tells you that almost 100% of the time a difference of at least this size would occur when two population rank means are equal. You wanted to be 95% certain (.05 critical value) that the difference is not due to chance. The p-value of .000 tells you that you are over 99% (you can never be 100%) certain of not making a Type I error and saying that one race has a higher level of satisfaction than the other, when in fact this is not the case. There is strong evidence to support the difference.

Hypothesis Decision. Thus, as printed out for you, reject Ho (accept Ha .05 < .000), conclude that one race has a higher level of education.

Descriptive Statistics. Unfortunately, running a Mann Whitney doesn't give you the means of each race to compare. All you have to do to get the means is run a T-test. The actual means on a scale of 1–6 were African Americans 4.33 and Whites 2.67. Therefore, we conclude that in our sample African Americans have a higher level of education than Whites.

Mann-Whitney U test with SPSS 19.

For some reason, SPSS will not let you run a Mann-Whitney U test with ordinal data, so if you want to run the MWU, go to the Variable view, make sure your Y is labeled as scale, and then:

1. Click *Analyze* on the toolbar.
2. Scroll down to *Nonparametric Tests* and on the menu at the right click *Independent Samples*.
3. In the Fields view, enter your Y(s) (labeled as scale) as the *Test Field* and X as the *Group*.
4. At this point you have two options. First, go to step 5 and let the computer pick the test for you, using the default setting "Automatically Compare Distributions across Groups" in the Objective view. Alternatively, you can go to the Objective view, check *Customize Analysis*, and then go to the Setting view, check *Customize Tests*, and select *Mann-Whitney U test*.
5. Click *Run* to generate the results in the data window.

CONCEPTUAL OBJECTIVE 5
Discuss the differences between the T-test and the Mann-Whitney U test.

STOP READING and turn to the end of the chapter to complete decision problems 12-3 and 12-4.

Wilcoxon Matched Pairs Test

As the Mann-Whitney U test is the alternative nonparametric statistic to the parametric T-test, the Wilcoxon matched pairs test is the nonparametric alternative to the paired T-test. The *Wilcoxon matched pairs test* compares ranked mean differences of one ordinal dependent variable between one nominal independent variable with two matched groups/scales. The research design is a repeated-measures design in which one group of participants receives two treatments. The treatments can be two experimental conditions, an experimental and control condition, or a pretest and posttest.

As with a paired T-test, the DV/Y values of each participant are compared to each other, typically pre-post to test differences/effect. If you can understand a Mann-Whitney computer printout, you can read a Wilcoxon matched pairs computer printout. Thus, no computer printout, example, or decision problems are included.

Wilcoxon matched pairs test with SPSS 19.

For some reason, SPSS will not let you run a Wilcoxon with ordinal data, so if you want to run one, go to the Variable view, make sure your Y is labeled as scale, and then:

1. Click *Analyze* on the tool bar.

2. Scroll down to Nonparametric Tests and on the menu at the right click *Related Samples*.

3. In the Fields view, enter your two (labeled as scale) matched-pairs variables.

4. At this point you have two options. You can go to step 5 and let the computer pick the test for you, using the default setting "Automatically Compare Distributions across Groups" in the Objective view. Alternatively, you can go to the Objective view, check *Customize Analysis*, and then go to the Setting view, check *Customize Tests*, and select your own Wilcoxon matched-pairs signed-ranks test.

5. Click *Run* to generate the results in the data window.

12.5 Chi-Square Tests

To a large extent you can avoid using the Mann-Whitney and the Wilcoxon tests by using ranking scales of at least 5 points (7 is better), considering the level of measure to be an interval, and running a T-test. However, you can never assume that nominal-level data is interval/ratio, so when you have two nominal-level variables you need to use chi-square. Thus, the chi-square is the nonparametric nominal-level alternative to the parametric T-test and the ordinal-level alternative to the Mann-Whitney U test. *Chi-square* (X^2) *compares nominal frequency distribution differences of any number of unmatched groups.* X^2 tests for independence, homogeneity, and goodness of fit. Somewhat like the one- and two-sample T-tests, yet different, the chi-square has a one-variable test (called one-way X^2) and a two or more variable (called two-way X^2) test. There is also the McNemar, a form of X^2 for two matched/dependent groups, and the Cochran Q, a form of X^2 for three or more matched/dependent groups. We discuss all four types of X^2 in this section. But before we get into the different types, let's discuss how chi-square is different from other tests, and then we address the rule of 5.

Comparing the T-Test, Mann-Whitney U Test, and Chi-Square Test

- The T-test (t) is a more powerful parametric test, whereas the Mann-Whitney U (MWU) and X^2 are nonparametric tests.

- The t DV/Y is interval/ratio and X is nominal, the MWU DV/Y is ordinal and X is nominal, and the chi-square has all nominal variables.

- The t compares means, the MWU compares mean ranks/medians, and the chi-square compares frequencies. In other words, each test uses a different measure of central tendency (discussed in Chapter 9).

- The t and MWU have two variables, whereas the chi-square can have any number (1, 2, 3, or more—3+).
- The MWU and chi-square do not need to meet the t assumptions of a random sample taken from a population having a somewhat normal distribution with an equal variance.
- With the t and MWU, you must correctly identify the DV/Y and IV/X. However, with chi-square, as with correlation, it doesn't matter—the results are the same if you reverse the variables.

See Table 12.2 for an illustration of these differences. The chi-square can actually be run with ordinal data too. However, you really should use the stronger Mann-Whitney U test instead. This is somewhat like not running a correlation with nominal data.

Table 12.2   Differences among the T-Test, Mann-Whitney U Test, and the Chi-Square Test

	Metric	Level of DV/Y	Level of IV/X	Compares	# of variables
T-test	parametric	interval/ratio	nominal	means	2
Mann-Whitney U	nonparametric	ordinal	nominal	rank means–median	2
Chi-square	nonparametric	nominal	nominal	frequencies	1, 2, or 3+

CONCEPTUAL OBJECTIVE 6
Compare the T-test, Mann-Whitney U test, and the chi-square test.

Test of difference between T-test interval/ratio DV/Y versus nominal data.

It is very important to realize that the X^2 compares frequency distributions/counts, often called *proportions*, rather than means or rank means. The difference is illustrated in Box 12.7 on the following page. Also note how higher-level data can be converted into lower-level data, but not the other way around.

The statistic test used is the chi-square comparing *frequency distribution* of category of purchase size of men and women. The formula for chi-square appears in Box 12.8. (Do not worry about calculating the X^2 by hand, as the statistical software will do it for you.) See the two-way chi-square test in Box 12.9 for the actual computer printout of this study.

The chi-square is the weakest statistical test of differences because it is based on the lowest level of measurement—nominal data. Thus, it is easier to make a Type II error, saying there is no difference when there really is, than when using the T-test and Mann-Whitney U. Thus, the first design using interval/ratio data allows the use of a stronger statistical test. You should realize how you lose important information in this example. Wouldn't you like to know the actual size (mean) of the purchase of both men and women and to compare their means? Again, use the highest level of measure feasible.

The rule of 5.

Some statisticians say you should not use chi-square if more than 20% of the cells/ groups have expected frequencies of less than 5 and if *any* have less than one; others say none of the cells should have less than 5 frequencies. When you have < 5, some statistical programs will run the appropriate Fisher Exact or Yates' Corrections test with a 2 × 2. Some soft-

---

Box 12.7   Tests of Difference

Ha: Women make larger purchases than men.

Design 1. Highest level of measurement—interval/ratio.

Y = purchase (interval/ratio, actual amount bought)

X = men and women (women [code 1], men [code 2])

Data entry into computer (gender—1 = women, 2 = men):

Variable 1 Gender	Variable 2 Size of purchase
1	1.25
1	6.29
1	etc. (you can enter all "women" values)
2	5.45
2	2.25
2	etc. (you can enter all "men" values)

The statistic used is the T-test comparing *mean* purchase of men and women

Design 2. Lowest level of measurement—nominal conversion of interval/ratio data to nominal.

Y = purchase (nominal groups: small < \$10 [code 1], large ≥ \$10 [code 2])

Coding could be any range and number of size purchases/scales with codes, such as < \$0–4.99, (1) \$5.00–9.99 (2), 10 and over (3).

X = men and women (women [code 1], men [code 2])

Variable 1 Gender: 1 / 2	Variable 2 Purchase size: 1 = small (< \$10); 2 = Large (≥ \$10)
1	2
1	etc. (you can enter all "women" values)
2	2
2	1
2	etc. (you can enter all "men" values)

Box 12.8   Chi-Square Formula

$$X^2 = \frac{\sum(fo - fe)^2}{fe}$$

$\sum$ = sum of

fo = frequency observed in data

fe = frequency expected, usually even distribution between groups

Example: You asked 222 people if they liked a politician before and 6 months after s/he was elected.

	Before	After	Total
Yes	36 (69%)	80 (47%)	116
No	16 (31%)	90 (53%)	106
Total	52	170	222

$X^2 = 8.1$

ware will also remind you of the rule of 5 by stating how many cells have frequencies of less than 5 in them. To use the more powerful chi-square rather than Fisher, you can also often combine some cells to increase the frequencies. For example, with a small sample, instead of having four college classes (freshman, sophomore, junior, senior) use two cells (upper classes and lower classes). We'll talk more about the rule of 5 with computer printouts.

One-Way Chi-Square

The one-way chi-square compares differences of frequencies of one nominal variable group's scales—for example, are there significantly more men or women in your sample? Are there significantly more first-, second-, third-, or fourth-year students? Reading a one-way computer printout is so similar to reading a two-way printout that we only show the two-way.

One-way chi-square with SPSS 19.

1. Click *Analyze* on the toolbar.
2. Scroll down to *Nonparametric Tests* and on the menu at the right click *One Sample.*
3. In the Fields view, enter your variables.
4. At this point you have two options: You can go to step 5 and let the computer pick the test for you, using the default setting "Automatically Compare Distributions across Groups." Alternatively, you can go to the Objective view, check *Customize Analysis,* and then go to the Setting view, check *Customize Tests,* and select *Compare Observed Probabilities to Hypothesized (Chi-Square Test).*
5. Click *Run* to generate the results in the data window.

Decision Tree.

Note that on the Decision Tree in Chapter 10 under tests of difference there is no separation of one-way and two-way chi-square. The tree lists the two-way, like the two-sample T-test. However, you should realize, as stated on the Decision Tree, that you can run chi-square with one or more nominal variables. Thus, if you have one variable, you use one-way and if you have two or more, you run two-way. (Most actual computer printouts do not stipulate one-way or two-way chi-square.)

Two-Way Chi-Square

The two-way chi-square compares differences of frequencies of two or more nominal variable groups/scales—for example, do men or women prefer Ford or Chevy cars?

Two-way chi-square with SPSS 19.

Here are the steps to run a two-way chi square using SPSS.

1. Click *Analyze* on the toolbar.
2. Scroll down to *Descriptive Statistics* and on the menu at the right click *Crosstabs.* Note that you can't run a two-way chi-square from the "Nonparametric Tests Analysis" function, and you can't run a one-way chi-square in crosstabs.
3. Click and drag your nominal variables to the right in the *Row(s)* and *Column(s)* boxes.
4. Click *Statistics* on the right, check *Chi-square,* and then click *Continue.*

5. You can also click the *Cells* button on the right (directly under Statistics) and check off *Row, Column,* and/or *Total* in the *Percentage* box.

6. You also have the option of clicking *Display Clustered Bar Charts* (under your list of variables) to get a bar chart.

7. Click *OK* to generate the results in the data window.

Box 12.9 is an example of actual results generated using the options selected in the directions above. Box 12.10 shows how to read the printout in Box 12.9, and Box 12.11 shows an example of hypothesis testing using the same printout.

Box 12.9   Two-Way Chi-Square SPSS 19 Printout

Race of the individual. * Bank loan actually received. Crosstabulation

			Bank loan actually received.	
			no	yes
Race of the individual.	African-American	Count	35	16
		% within Race of the individual.	68.6%	31.4%
		% within Bank loan actually received.	63.6%	41.0%
		% of Total	37.2%	17.0%
	white	Count	20	23
		% within Race of the individual.	46.5%	53.5%
		% within Bank loan actually received.	36.4%	59.0%
		% of Total	21.3%	24.5%
Total		Count	55	39
		% within Race of the individual.	58.5%	41.5%
		% within Bank loan actually received.	100.0%	100.0%
		% of Total	58.5%	41.5%

Race of the individual. * Bank loan actually received. Crosstabulation

			Total
Race of the individual.	African-American	Count	51
		% within Race of the individual.	100.0%
		% within Bank loan actually received.	54.3%
		% of Total	54.3%
	white	Count	43
		% within Race of the individual.	100.0%
		% within Bank loan actually received.	45.7%
		% of Total	45.7%
Total		Count	94
		% within Race of the individual.	100.0%
		% within Bank loan actually received.	100.0%
		% of Total	100.0%

Chi-Square Tests

	Value	df	Asymp. Sig. (2-sided)	Exact Sig. (2-sided)	Exact Sig. (1-sided)
Pearson Chi-Square	4.701[a]	1	.030		
Continuity Correction[b]	3.834	1	.050		
Likelihood Ratio	4.725	1	.030		
Fisher's Exact Test				.037	.025
Linear-by-Linear Association	4.651	1	.031		
N of Valid Cases	94				

a. 0 cells (.0%) have expected count less than 5. The minimum expected count is 17.84.
b. Computed only for a 2x2 table

(continued)

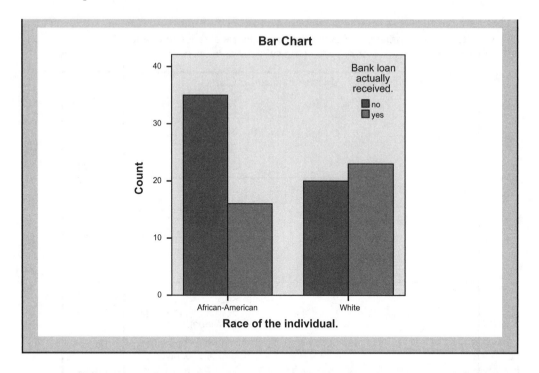

Bar Chart

Race of the individual.

Box 12.10 Reading Chi-Square Test Results

Following are explanations of the values from the two-way chi-square computer printout in Box 12.9. The variable names are printed out based on the values given when entering the data into SPSS.

Chi-Square-Statistic and p-Values (Pearson Significance). The X^2-statistic is a measure of the test of difference. The higher the value is, the greater the difference in frequencies. However, it is very difficult to interpret the value by itself. The X^2 value is 4.701. However, it is really the p-value that is important because it tells you whether or not the difference is significant.

Pearson: When you run the SPSS X^2 through Crosstabulation, the chi-square is the Pearson. (Yes, there is also a Pearson correlation: Don't get them confused.) The likelihood ratio is not really necessary and is beyond the scope of this text. Note that the difference in Pearson is significant at the .05 level.

The two-tailed p-value (.030) tells you that 3.0% of the time a difference of at least this size would occur when the two population frequencies are equal. You wanted to be 95% certain (.05 critical value) that the difference is not due to chance. The p-value of .030 tells you that you are 97% (1.00–.030%) certain of not making a Type I error and saying that one race gets more loans than the other, when in fact this is not true. There is evidence to support the difference. Thus, reject Ho (accept Ha .05 > .030). However, this assumes the hypothesis was a two-tailed Ho. Recall that for a two-tailed p-value to be converted to a one-tailed, you need to double the p-value, making a one-tail p = .06. For a one-tailed test Ho would be accepted.

Crosstabulation Frequencies. Frequencies, also called proportions, tell you how many African Americans (AA) and Whites received a loan. Thus, we can see that of the 51 African Americans, 35 (68.6%) did not get a loan and 16 (31.4%) did get a loan. Of the 43 Whites, 20 (46.5%) did not get a loan and 23 (53.5%) did get a loan. Again, it is important to look at the frequencies, not just the p-value to determine differences.

Minimum Expected Count. See Note a. below the Chi-Square Tests box. The sample size is 94 and there are four cells; thus, to have a perfect frequency distribution there would be a count of 23.5 (94/4) in each cell. The greater the difference in the four cells, the lower the p-value. As shown, the minimum expected count is 17.84, and only 16 African Americans got a loan, thus giving us a p-value that is significant.

Number of Cells with < 5. Again, in note a. below the Chi-Square Tests box, if you have any cells with a count of < 5, the computer will print it out for you. The note says "0 Cells have expected counts less than 5." If you have violated the rule of 5, use the Fisher's Exact Test values (.037 and .025). Another option for violating the rule of 5 is to merge groups together when you have more than a 2 × 2 crosstab. Using the example from Box 12.7, if you had three size purchases, you could combine two of them into one variable.

Box 12.11   Example of a Chi-Square Hypothesis Test

Bank Loan Received by Race

The results of the above X^2 computer printout in Box 12.9 are presented below through hypothesis testing.

Instructions

Clearly list the five steps of hypothesis testing and answer these questions within the appropriate step. For *step 1*, be sure to clearly write the null and one- or two-tailed alternative hypothesis. For *step 2*, select .05. For *step 3*, list the dependent and independent variables with their measurement levels and the appropriate statistical test. For *step 4*, see the computer printout in Box 12.8; however, write the percentage of confidence that the frequencies are significant. For *step 5*, answer the following questions: (a) Who received more loans? List the frequencies. (b) Is the difference between frequencies significant? (c) Should we fail to reject Ho (accept Ho) or reject Ho (accept Ha)? (d) What conclusion should be made?

Solution (Decision)

Step 1. State the hypothesis and action.

Ho: African Americans and Whites received loans equally in frequency.

Ha: One race received more loans. (two-tailed)

Ha: Whites received more loans than African Americans. (one-tailed)

Step 2. Set the critical value (.05).

Step 3. Select the methodology of data collection and statistical test.

The DV/Y is nominal (bank loan actually received) and the IV/X is nominal (African Americans and Whites). Thus, the chi-square is the appropriate test.

Step 4. Run the statistics to obtain the p-value.

See the computer printout. As discussed in Box 12.10, we are 97% confident that the difference between frequencies is significant, or that we are not making a Type I error (saying there is a difference when there really is none).

Step 5. Make the decision.

(a) Whites get more loans than African Americans (23/53.5% vs. 16/31.4%).

(b) The difference between frequencies is significant (.03 < .05 critical value) for a two-tailed test. We wanted to be 95% certain of not making a Type I error, and we are 97% certain. However,

(continued)

for a one-tailed test we need to double the p-value to .06 > .05. So for a one-tailed test we are only 94% certain—not 95% or higher.

(c) We should reject Ho (accept Ha) for a two-tailed test because there is a significant difference. However, we should accept Ha for a one-tailed test because the difference is not significant at the .05 level.

(d) We can conclude that Whites get more loans than African Americans, but based on this one test alone we can't say why. Maybe the Whites in this sample were more highly qualified to receive a loan, or maybe not. To find out, tests should be run to compare differences, such as income, years of experience, loan size requested, and so on.

 STOP READING and turn to the end of the chapter to complete decision problems 12-5 and 12-6.

McNemar

The *McNemar* X^2 compares nominal frequency distribution differences of two matched groups/scales. Thus, the McNemar is similar to the paired T-test and Wilcoxon matched pairs test. It is a stronger test than the chi-square as it uses a repeat measure to compare the same participant DV/Ys' values. If the McNemar is not available on your statistical software, you have two options: Find one that has the McNemar, or run the regular chi-square. If you run the chi-square and the significance result is not close to the critical value, you should be OK. However, if the p-value and critical value are close, find a McNemar. Reading the McNemar computer printout is essentially the same as reading a chi-square; an example is not provided.

McNemar matched pairs test with SPSS 19.

1. Click *Analyze* on the toolbar.
2. Scroll down to *Descriptive Statistics* and on the menu at the right click *Crosstabs*.
3. Click and drag your nominal variables to the right in the *Row(s)* and *Column(s)* boxes. Note that you are moving the same paired variable with two tests: test 1 and test 2.
4. Click *Statistics* on the right and check the *McNemar* box, then click *Continue*.
5. You can also click the *Cells* button on the right (under *Statistics*) and check *Row, Column*, and/or *Total* in the *Percentages* Box.
6. You can also click *Display Clustered Bar Charts* (under your variables) to get a bar chart.
7. Click *OK* to generate the results in the data window.

Cochran Q

The *Cochran Q* compares nominal frequency distribution differences of three or more matched groups/scales. For example, you can compare gender (two scales—men and women) and class (four scales—freshmen, sophomores, juniors, and seniors). Thus, the Cochran Q is similar to the Friedman ANOVA (ANOVA is our next test). It is a stronger test than the chi-square as it uses a repeated measure to compare the same participant's values. If the Cochran Q is not available on your statistical software, you have two options. Find a software package that has the Cochran Q or run the regular chi-square. If you run the chi-square and the p-value is not close to the critical value, you should be OK. However, if the p-value and critical value are close, find a Cochran Q. Since reading the Cochran Q computer printout is essentially the same as reading a chi-square printout, one is not provided.

Cochran Q matched pairs test with SPSS 19.

1. Click *Analyze* on the toolbar.
2. Scroll down to *Descriptive Statistics* and on the menu at the right click *Crosstabs*.
3. Click and drag your nominal variables to the right in the *Row(s)* and *Column(s)* boxes. Note that you are moving the same paired variable with two tests, test 1 and test 2, as the two variables.
4. Click *Statistics* on the right and check *Cochran's* and *Mentel Haenzel statistics* at the bottom, and then click *Continue*.
5. You can also click the *Cells* button on the right (under Statistics) and check *Row, Column*, and/or *Total* in the *Percentages* box.
6. You can also click *Display Clustered Bar Chart* (under your variables list) to get a bar chart.
7. Click *OK* to generate the results in the data window.

12.6   One-Way ANOVA Tests

The **one-way ANOVA** *compares mean differences of one interval/ratio dependent variable among one nominal independent variable with at least three groups.* The one-way ANOVA is also called independent groups one-way ANOVA. Recall that a one-way analysis of variance (ANOVA) has one IV/X, and a two-way ANOVA has two or more IV/Xs, also called factors. You are analyzing means for differences/effect.

Comparing the T-Test and One-Way ANOVA

- The T-test and one-way ANOVA are similar because they both compare means of one interval/ratio DV/Y between one nominal IV/X.
- The real difference between the T-test and one-way ANOVA is that a T-test compares means of two groups, and the one-way ANOVA compares three or more group/scale means. If you run a one-way ANOVA with only two groups, the results would be essentially the same as the T-test.
- The one-way statistic is an F ratio rather than a t-ratio.
- Both are parametric tests and thus should meet the assumptions of a random sample taken from a population having a somewhat normal distribution with an equal variance. With SPSS, both tests run the Levene test of equality of variance to test the third assumption. However, the T-test provides p-values for the assumption of equality and nonequality of variance. The one-way does not provide an alternative analysis if the variance is not equal. Thus, researchers hope that the Levene p-value

is greater than .05 so that the equality assumption is met. However, other statistical software uses the pooled variance from all groups.

- The one-way also provides "between-groups" and "within-groups" variance. The *between-groups* variance compares the variance among all groups of the X as a total. The *within-groups* variance compares the variance of all participants within each group. In other words, how far away from the mean are each participant's values/scores from their group's mean?

Like the T-test, one-way ANOVA can be used with unmatched or matched groups, and there are nonparametric alternatives using ordinal DV/Y—Kruskal-Wallis and Friedman one-way ANOVAs. However, we will only illustrate the unmatched test of difference, because if you can analyze the one-way ANOVA computer printout you can analyze the other ANOVA printouts. Also, if you use rating scales with at least five points you can consider the data as interval/ratio, so you can use the parametric tests.

CONCEPTUAL OBJECTIVE 7
Compare the T-test and one-way ANOVA.

The formula for one-way ANOVA appears in Box 12.12. However, do not be concerned with doing the calculations by hand as the computer will do it for you.

Box 12.12   One-Way ANOVA Formula

Source of Variation	Degrees of Freedom	Sums of Squares	Mean Squares	F-Statistic
Treatments	$k-1$	SST	$MST = \dfrac{SST}{(k-1)}$	$f = \dfrac{MST}{MSE}$
Error	$n-k$	SSE	$MSE = \dfrac{SSE}{n-k}$	
TOTAL	$n-1$	SS (Total)		

One-way ANOVA with Tukey SPSS 19.

Remember, if you only have two groups (gender) in the X, you are running the wrong test; run the T-test instead. To run an ANOVA with three or more groups, follow these steps.

1. Click *Analyze* on the toolbar.

2. Scroll down to *Compare Means* and on the menu at the right click *One-Way ANOVA*.

3. Click and drag your scale variable to the *Dependent* list at the right and your nominal independent variable into the *Factor* box.

4. Click *Post Hoc*, check *Tukey*, and then click *Continue* to compare the differences between the three means. Tukey tells you which of the three or more means are significantly different.

5. Click *Options* and check the *Descriptive* box, then click *Continue* to get the means and standard deviations of your Y.

6. Click *OK* to generate the results in the data window.

Box 12.13 contains an SPSS computer printout. In Box 12.14 we explain how to read the printout, and Box 12.15 contains an example of a hypothesis test for the printout.

Box 12.13   One-Way ANOVA with Tukey

Descriptives

Amount of loan applied for.

	N	Mean	Std. Deviation	Std. Error	95% Confidence Interval for Mean Lower Bound	Upper Bound	Minimum	Maximum
none	8	4937.50	1474.485	521.309	3704.80	6170.20	3000	7000
family and friends	28	34571.43	27218.497	5143.812	24017.20	45125.66	9000	100000
credit card	58	29025.86	30851.714	4051.029	20913.82	37137.91	4000	200000
Total	94	28627.66	29285.482	3020.567	22629.41	34625.91	3000	200000

ANOVA

Amount of loan applied for.

	Sum of Squares	df	Mean Square	F	Sig.
Between Groups	5.488E9	2	2.744E9	3.362	.039
Within Groups	7.427E10	91	8.162E8		
Total	7.976E10	93			

Post Hoc Tests

Multiple Comparisons

Amount of loan applied for
Tukey HSD

(I) Sources of borrowed capital.	(J) Sources of borrowed capital.	Mean Difference (I-J)	Std. Error	Sig.	95% Confidence Interval Lower Bound	Upper Bound
none	family and friends	-29633.929	11453.018	.030	-56922.60	-2345.25
	credit card	-24088.362	10774.712	.071	-49760.86	1584.14
family and friends	none	29633.929	11453.018	.030	2345.25	56922.60
	credit card	5545.567	6574.291	.677	-10118.75	21209.88
credit card	none	24088.362	10774.712	.071	-1584.14	49760.86
	family and friends	-5545.567	6574.291	.677	-21209.88	10118.75

* The mean difference is significant at the 0.05 level.

(continued)

Homogeneous Subsets

Amount of loan applied for.

Tukey HSD [a,b]

Sources of borrowed capital.	N	Subset for alpha = 0.05	
		1	2
none	8	4937.50	
credit card	58		29025.86
family and friends	28		34571.43
Sig.		1.000	.840

Means for groups in homogeneous subsets are displayed.

a. Uses Harmonic Mean Sample Size = 16.858.
b. The group sizes are unequal. The harmonic mean of the group sizes is used. Type I error levels are not guaranteed.

Box 12.14   Reading One-Way ANOVA Test Results

Amount of Loan Applied for by Source of Financing

ANOVA F-Statistic and p-Value. The F of 3.362 is the measure of variance, which is difficult to interpret alone. The important number is the p-value (sig) .039, which tells you that 3.9% of the time a difference of at least this size would occur when the four population means are equal. Or, you are 96% (1 – .039) confident that you are not making a Type I error and claiming there is a difference, when there really is none. Confidence intervals are also shown.

Means. As stated in the directions for running a one-way ANOVA, you need to go into the options and check *Descriptives* to get the three means. So people who use no source of financing asked for an average loan of $4,937.50, those borrowing from family and friends asked for $34,571.43, and those using credit card asked for $29,025.86.

Post-Hoc Test. Note that *Descriptives* provide the means, and the p-value tells us if there is a significant difference/effect between them. However, we have not tested to determine if each mean is significantly different than each other mean by pairs. To compare each mean pair, you can run the post-hoc tests such as Tukey, as shown in the multiple comparisons table. If the difference between the means is not significant, you don't need the post-hoc test. But we have at least one significant difference in this analysis, so we use the Multiple Comparisons Tukey analysis. In essence, what a Tukey does is run a T-test between each variable in pairs.

Multiple Comparisons—Tukey. As we can see, people who apply for a loan and do not borrow any money ask for a significantly smaller loan than those who borrow from friends and family (p = .030); however, there is no significant difference between not borrowing and using a credit card (p = .071). People who borrow from family and friends borrow more than those who don't borrow money (p = .030) but don't ask for significantly less than people who start their businesses with a credit card (p = .677). Further, those who use a credit card to borrow money don't ask for a significantly larger loan than those who don't borrow any money or those that borrow from friends and family (p = .071, p = .677).

Box 12.15   Example of a One-Way ANOVA Hypothesis Test

Amount of Loan by Source of Financing

Instructions

Clearly list the five steps of hypothesis testing and answer these questions within the appropriate steps. For *step 1*, be sure to clearly write the null and one- or two-tailed alternative hypothesis. For *step 2*, select .05. For *step 3*, list the dependent and independent variables with their measurement levels and the appropriate statistical test. For *step 4*, see the computer printout in Box 12.13; however, write the percentage of confidence that the means are significantly different. For *step 5*, answer the following questions using this information: (a) which group asks for the largest and smallest loan? (Give means.) (b) Should we fail to reject Ho (accept Ho) or reject Ho (accept Ha)? (c) If there is a significant difference, which group or groups is different?

Solution (Decision)

Step 1. State the hypothesis.

Ho: There is no difference in the amount of loan by the method of financing a business.

Ha: There is a difference in the amount of loan applied for by the method of financing a business. (two-tailed)

Ha: People not borrowing money to finance their business ask for the smallest loans. (one-tailed)

Step 2. Set the critical value.—.05

Step 3. Select the methodology of data collection and statistical test.

The DV/Y is interval/ratio and the IV/X is nominal (three groups/scales). Thus, one-way ANOVA is appropriate.

Step 4. Run the statistics to obtain the p-value.

The p-value is .039, so we are 96% confident that we are not making a Type I error (saying there is a difference in loan request by method of financing the business when there really is none).

Step 5. Make the decision.

(a) Amount of loan applied for: People who do not borrow any money to start their business ask for an average loan of $4,937.50, those financing with a credit card ask for $29,025.86, and those borrowing from friends and family ask for an average loan of $34,571.43.

(b) Reject Ho (accept Ha) because the calculated p-value .039 < the .05 critical value. You're about 96% sure the means are different, not 95%.

(c) People who apply for a loan and do not borrow any money ask for a significantly smaller loan than those who borrow from friends and family; however, there is no significant difference between not borrowing and using a credit card. People who borrow from family and friends borrow more than those who don't borrow money, but they don't ask for significantly less than people who start their businesses with a credit card. Further, those who use a credit card to borrow money don't ask for a significantly larger loan than those who don't borrow any money or those who borrow from friends and family.

**STOP READING and turn to the end of the chapter
to complete decision problems 12-7 and 12-8.**

One-Way Repeated Measures ANOVA

The *one-way repeated measures ANOVA* compares mean differences of one interval/ratio dependent variable with the same measurement taken three or more times. The purpose of a one-way ANOVA and a repeated measures ANOVA is the same: to compare means. But because the comparison is clearly different, the terms *within-subject* or *within-participant* are used as a descriptor of the repeated measures ANOVA.

Comparisons between the paired T-test and one-way repeated measures ANOVA.

Recall that the *paired T-test* compares mean differences of one interval/ratio dependent variable at two different times. Now we have the one-way, which repeats the same measure three or more times. If you think back to our reading score pre-test and post-test, you could add a third measure in the middle of the program—you just have three Y variable scores. You could also use the same reading test four times, for example pre-test, one-quarter-test, one-half-test, and post-test.

The paired T-test and one-way repeated measures ANOVA are commonly used with the *experimental* research design, and the independent T-test and one-way ANOVA are used with the *quasi-experimental* design. As with the paired T-test, you need to be sure you understand how to enter data into the computer to run the repeated measure.

Repeated measures ANOVA with SPSS 19.

Running a repeated measure in SPSS 19 is a more complicated process than with the other statistical tests you have run so far. To run it, follow these steps.

1. Click *Analyze* on the toolbar.

2. Scroll down to *General Linear Model* and to the right click *Repeated Measures*.

3. Type in the variable name you want to use in the *Within-Subject Factor Name* box. Note that you have to make up a new name, such as "compare test results."

4. Next, in the *Number of Levels* box type the number of repeated measures you have (three or more) and click *Add*.

5. Now, in the *Measurement Name* box, type in a different name for what you are measuring (again, you are making up a new name, such as "grades"), click *Add*, and then click *Define*.

6. Move the three or more repeated measures (such as three different test grades) in the correct sequence in the *Within-Subject Variables* box.

7. Click *OK* to generate the results in the data window.

Note that you don't have to put anything in the *Between* or *Covariate* boxes to simply compare the results of your repeated measure. For example, you could just check to see if you got a significantly higher test grade on three tests throughout the semester.

Kruskal-Wallis One-Way ANOVA

The *Kruskal-Wallis one-way ANOVA* compares rank mean differences of one ordinal dependent variable among at least three unmatched groups/scales of one nominal independent variable. Thus, it is the nonparametric alternative to the one-way ANOVA.

Kruskal-Wallis with SPSS 19.

To run this test, follow the steps below:

1. Click *Analyze* on the toolbar.

2. Scroll down to *Nonparametric Test, Independent Samples.*

3. In the Fields view click and drag your dependent variable into the *Test Field*. Again, note that you must label your ordinal Y as a scale level of measurement to get SPSS to accept it. Next, place your X in the *Groups* box.

4. In the Settings view click *Customized Tests* and *Kruskal-Wallis 1-way ANOVA k samples*. In the *Multiple Comparisons* drop-down menu click *None*. Note that you can also run a Kruskal-Wallis test with matched/related groups test by selecting *All Pairwise*.

5. Click *Run* to generate the results in the data window.

Friedman One-Way ANOVA

The *Friedman one-way ANOVA* compares mean rank differences of one ordinal dependent variable among one nominal independent variable with at least three matched groups/scales. Thus, it is the nonparametric alternative to the one-way repeated measures ANOVA.

Friedman one-way ANOVA with SPSS 19.

1. Click *Analyze* on the toolbar.

2. Scroll down to *Nonparametric Test, Related Samples.*

3. In the Fields view, click and drag your two repeated-measure variables into the *Test Field*.

4. In the Settings view click *Customized Tests* and *Friedman 2-way ANOVA by ranks (k samples)*. In the *Multiple Comparisons* box click *All Pairwise*.

5. Click *Run* to generate the results in the data window.

Note that one- or two-way refers to the number of independent variables. In all the tests in this chapter we have had only one X. Friedman is listed as two-way because you enter two variables in the same box.

SKI WEST STUDY

As we bring this chapter to a close, you should be able to:
- *explain the difference between experimental and quasi-experimental research designs and parametric and nonparametric statistical tests, and*
- *read computer printouts and test hypotheses using the*
  —*T-test (interval/ratio DV/Y with 2 IV/X groups),*
  —*Mann-Whitney U (ordinal DV/Y with 2 IV/X),*
  —*chi-square (any number of all nominal-level variables), and*
  —*one-way ANOVA (interval/ratio DV/Y with three or more IV/X groups).*

Recall from the last chapter that Matt McLeish had a secondary focus and six hypotheses: tests of difference. His research design was quasi-experimental because he did not manipulate the Xs. Although Matt has a comparison of a personality pre-test and a job performance evaluation post-test, he couldn't use a paired T-test because it is not a matched pair—the two tests are very different measures (50–100 and 10–50). For a repeat measure you need to take the same (or similar) measure two or more times.

Matt tested six hypotheses with tests of difference, using the T-test for personality and performance by gender and age (two groups), and one-way ANOVA for personality and performance by department (three groups). Only one of the six hypotheses was accepted, H3a. Males did score higher on job performance than females (p = .031). However, the conclusion was that the difference is significant but meaningless (M 27.96 vs. M 30.48, difference 2.52 or 5% out of 50 possible points). The decision was not to give preference to males in the hiring process.

CHAPTER SUMMARY AND GLOSSARY

The chapter summary is organized in a way that provides you with the answers necessary to help you meet the conceptual objectives for this chapter.

1. **Explain the difference between experimental and quasi-experimental designs, and state which one has the greater cause-and-effect relationship and why.**
There are three criteria necessary for research to be considered an experimental design: (a) it has an experimental group, (b) there is a manipulation of a time-ordered independent variable treatment, and (c) matched groups dependent variable values are compared. If any of the criteria is missing, the design is quasi-experimental.
The experimental design has a cause-and-effect relationship because it meets the criteria of an experiment. The quasi-experimental design helps to understand and explain the differences between groups, but one cannot say that the difference in the dependent variable is caused by the independent variable because it is not an experiment.

2. **Discuss (a) internal and external validity, (b) the trade-off between the two, and (c) their impact on decision making.**
(a) Internal validity is the extent to which there is a cause-and-effect relationship, whereas external validity is the extent to which the results of a study can be generalized. (b) Internal and external validity have an inverse relationship. Thus, the trade-off is that as one type of validity increases, the other decreases. As a general guide, experiments have more internal validity and quasi-experimental designs have greater generalization to the population. (c) Managers are generally more concerned about internal validity because they are making decisions about their organizations. Researchers are generally more concerned about external validity because they seek findings that are generalizable to many organizations.

3. **Describe the difference between parametric and nonparametric tests of significance.**
Parametric tests are more powerful than nonparametric tests because they use interval/ratio-level measures and assume a random sample is taken from a normally distributed population with equal variance. Nonparametric tests are less powerful because they use ordinal- and nominal-level measures and are used when parametric assumptions are not met.

4. **Explain the difference between: (a) the T-test and the paired T-test, (b) the one-sample T-test and the T-test, and (c) the Z-test and T-test.**
(a) The T-test is run with unmatched pairs, whereas the paired T-test uses matched pairs. (b) The one-sample T-test compares a sample mean to a population/standard

mean. The T-test compares two sample means. (c) The Z-test is run when the population mean and standard deviation (sigma) is known, whereas the T-test is run when the mean is known but sigma is not known.

5. **Discuss differences between the T-test and Mann-Whitney U test.**
   The T-test is a parametric test with an interval/ratio dependent variable; it compares mean differences and meets the assumptions of a random sample taken from a population with a somewhat normal distribution and equal variance. The Mann-Whitney U test is the nonparametric alternative of the T-test, comparing rank mean differences of one ordinal dependent variable between one nominal independent variable with two unmatched groups/scales.

6. **Compare the T-test, Mann-Whitney U test, and chi-square test.**
   They are all similar in that they are all tests of difference. However, the T-test is a parametric test and the Mann-Whitney U and chi-square (X^2) tests are nonparametric. They all have a different level of measurement of the dependent variable that is compared between groups of the independent variable: T-test is interval/ratio comparing means, Mann-Whitney is ordinal comparing rank means, and X^2 is nominal comparing frequencies. The T-test and Mann-Whitney are run with two variables, whereas the X^2 can be run with any number of variables.

7. **Compare the T-test and one-way ANOVA.**
   The T-test and one-way ANOVA are similar because they both compare means of one interval/ratio dependent variable between one nominal independent variable. Both are parametric tests and thus should meet the assumptions of a random sample taken from a population with a somewhat normal distribution with an equal variance. The real difference between the T-test and one-way ANOVA is that a T-test compares means of two groups and the one-way ANOVA compares three or more groups'/scales' means

8. **Define the following key terms.**
   Select one or more methods: (1) fill in the missing key terms from memory, (2) match the key terms with their definitions below, or (3) copy the key terms in order from the list at the beginning of the chapter.

chi-square (X^2)	factorial designs	one-way ANOVA
control groups	internal validity	parametric tests
experimental designs	Mann-Whitney U test	quasi-experimental designs
experimental groups	nonparametric tests	T-test
external validity	one-sample T-test	

   _____ are when the independent variable(s) is manipulated by a treatment with a matched experimental group to cause the difference in the value of the dependent variable(s).

   _____ are when the independent variable(s) may not be manipulated by a treatment, and the independent variable helps understand and explain the difference in the value of the dependent variable(s) groups.

   _____ does not get the treatment in experimental designs to compare differences with the experimental group.

_____ does get the treatment in experimental designs to compare differences with the control group and/or to compare differences of participants in the experimental group.

_____ include two or more independent variables and are identified by the number of independent variables and the number of groups in each.

_____ is the extent to which the differences in the values of the dependent variable can be attributed to the manipulation of the independent variable.

_____ is the extent to which the results of a study can be generalized.

_____ are powerful because they use interval/ratio level measures using random samples taken from a normally distributed population with equal variance.

_____ are less powerful because they use ordinal- and nominal-level measures when parametric assumptions are not met.

_____ compares mean differences of one interval/ratio dependent variable between one nominal independent variable with two groups.

_____ compares a sample mean to a population/standard mean.

_____ compares mean rank differences of one ordinal dependent variable between one nominal independent variable with two unmatched groups.

_____ compares nominal frequency distribution differences of any number of unmatched groups.

_____ compares mean differences of one interval/ratio dependent variable among one nominal independent variable with at least three groups.

WRITTEN ASSIGNMENTS

All three written assignments require selecting the appropriate statistic to test the hypotheses that you develop. However, only the completed study and statistical analysis require running the statistics.

APPENDIX CS, ASSIGNMENTS 3 (RESULTS) AND 4 (DISCUSSION)

Based on your methodology, you may need to complete chapters 9–14 before you can complete your study. If your methodology includes tests of difference, run them now and write your statistical findings in the Results section of your study.

APPENDIX SA, ASSIGNMENT 4 (CHI-SQUARE AND T-TESTS)

This assignment is a continuation of Assignment 3 in Appendix SA. You will be running a chi-square and T-test with your data.

DECISION PROBLEMS

T-TEST

12-1   Continuing the bank-financing discrimination example, we want to know if there is a difference in the number of years a person owned a business before applying for a loan and whether he or she actually received a loan. In other words, does having owned a business for a greater number of years before applying for a loan actually increase the chances of getting the loan?

Instructions
The five steps of hypothesis testing are listed below. For steps 1–4, follow the instructions in the example in Box 12.4. For *step 5*, answer the following questions: (a) What are the two means and which is preferred? (b) Is the difference between means significant? (c) Should you fail to reject Ho (accept Ho) or reject Ho (accept Ha)? (d) What conclusion should you make? (e) Would your answers change if the critical values were set at .10 and .01; if so, how?

Solution (Decision)
Step 1. State the hypothesis.
Step 2. Set the critical value. As a researcher, use .05.
Step 3. Select the methodology of data collection and statistical test.
Step 4. Run the statistics to obtain the p-value.
Step 5. Make the decision (a–e).
An SPSS 19 computer printout is done for you below:

Group Statistics

	Bank loan actually received.	N	Mean	Std. Deviation	Std. Error Mean
Years business owned before loan application.	no	55	7.62	4.794	.646
	yes	39	8.38	4.101	.657

Independent Samples Test

		Levene's Test for Equality of Variances		t-test for Equality of Means		
		F	Sig.	t	df	Sig. (2-tailed)
Years business owned before loan application.	Equal variances assumed	1.046	.309	-.810	92	.420
	Equal variances not assumed			-.832	88.705	.408

Independent Samples Test

		t-test for Equality of Means			
		Mean Difference	Std. Error Difference	95% Confidence Interval of the Difference	
				Lower	Upper
Years business owned before loan application.	Equal variances assumed	-.766	.946	-2.646	1.113
	Equal variances not assumed	-.766	.922	-2.598	1.065

12-2   Continuing the example, we want to know if there is a difference in the ages of African American and White business owners who applied for a loan.

Instructions

The five steps of hypothesis testing are listed below. Follow the instructions in Problem 12-1.

Solution (Decision)

Step 1. State the hypothesis.

Step 2. Set the critical value. As a researcher, use .05.

Step 3. Select the methodology of data collection and statistical test.

Step 4. Run the statistics to obtain the p-value.

Step 5. Make the decision (a–e).

An SPSS 19 computer printout is done for you below:

Group Statistics

	Race of the individual.	N	Mean	Std. Deviation	Std. Error Mean
Age of the individual.	African-American	51	38.14	7.950	1.113
	white	43	39.44	4.905	.748

Independent Samples Test

		Levene's Test for Equality of Variances	
		F	Sig.
Age of the individual.	Equal variances assumed	9.075	.003
	Equal variances not assumed		

Independent Samples Test

		t-test for Equality of Means			
		t	df	Sig. (2-tailed)	Mean Difference
Age of the individual.	Equal variances assumed	-.936	92	.352	-1.305
	Equal variances not assumed	-.973	84.773	.333	-1.305

Independent Samples Test

		t-test for Equality of Means		
			95% Confidence Interval of the Difference	
		Std. Error Difference	Lower	Upper
Age of the individual.	Equal variances assumed	1.394	-4.073	1.464
	Equal variances not assumed	1.341	-3.971	1.362

MANN-WHITNEY U TEST

12-3 Continuing the bank-financing discrimination example, we want to know if there is a difference in the education level (**1** elementary—**6** grad school) by gender.

Instructions
Clearly list the five steps of hypothesis testing and answer these questions within the appropriate step. For *step 1*, be sure to clearly write the null and one- or two-tailed alternative hypothesis. For *step 2*, select .05. For *step 3*, list the dependent and independent variables with their measurement level and the appropriate statistical test. For *step 4*, see the computer printout; however, write the percentage of confidence that the rank mean difference is significant. For *step 5*, answer the following questions as part of making the decision: (a) What are the two means? (b) Is the difference between rank means significant? (c) Should we fail to reject Ho (accept Ho) or reject Ho (accept Ha)? (d) What conclusion should be made? (e) Would the answers change if the critical value were set at .10 and .01; if so, how?

Solution (Decision)
Step 1. State the hypothesis.
Step 2. Set the critical value.
Step 3. Select the methodology of data collection and statistical test.
Step 4. Run the statistics to obtain the p-value.
Step 5. Make the decision (a–e).
An SPSS 19 computer printout is done for you below:

Hypothesis Test Summary

	Null Hypothesis	Test	Sig.	Decision
1	The distribution of Level of education is the same across categories of Gender of the individual	Independent-Samples Mann-Whitney U Test	.864	Reject the null hypothesis

Asymptotic significances are displayed. The significance level is .05.

12-4 Continuing the example, we want to know if there is a difference in the level of education based on getting a loan. In other words, do the people who get the loans have a higher level of education than those that do not?

Instructions
The five steps of hypothesis testing are listed below. Follow the instructions in Problem 12-3.

Solution (Decision)
Step 1. State the hypothesis.
Step 2. Set the critical value. As a researcher, use .05.
Step 3. Select the methodology of data collection and statistical test.
Step 4. Run the statistics to obtain the p-value.
Step 5. Make the decision (a–e).

Hypothesis Test Summary

	Null Hypothesis	Test	Sig.	Decision
1	The distribution of Level of education. is the same across categories of Bank loan actually received..	Independent-Samples Mann-Whitney U Test	.381	Retain the null hypothesis.

Asymptotic significances are displayed. The significance level is .05.

CHI-SQUARE

12-5   Continuing the bank-financing discrimination example, we want to know if there is a difference in the frequencies of getting a loan by gender. In other words, who gets more loans: women or men?

Instructions

The five steps of hypothesis testing are listed below. For steps 1–4, follow the instructions in Box 12.11. For *step 5*, answer the following questions: (a) Which gender received more loans? List the frequencies. (b) Is the difference between frequencies significant? (c) Should you fail to reject Ho (accept Ho) or reject Ho (accept Ha)? (d) What conclusion should you make? (e) Would your answers change if the critical values were set at .10 and .01; if so, how?

Solution (Decision)

Step 1. State the hypothesis.
Step 2. Set the critical value. As a researcher, use .05.
Step 3. Select the methodology of data collection and statistical test.
Step 4. Run the statistics to obtain the p-value.
Step 5. Make the decision (a–e).

Gender of the individual. * Bank loan actually received. Crosstabulation

			Bank loan actually received.		
			no	yes	Total
Gender of the individual.	female	Count	6	7	13
		% of Total	6.4%	7.4%	13.8%
	male	Count	49	32	81
		% of Total	52.1%	34.0%	86.2%
Total		Count	55	39	94
		% of Total	58.5%	41.5%	100.0%

Chi-Square Tests

	Value	df	Asymp. Sig. (2-sided)	Exact Sig. (2-sided)	Exact Sig. (1-sided)
Pearson Chi-Square	.949[a]	1	.330		
Continuity Correction[b]	.450	1	.502		
Likelihood Ratio	.935	1	.334		
Fisher's Exact Test				.374	.250
Linear-by-Linear Association	.939	1	.333		
N of Valid Cases	94				

a. 0 cells (.0%) have expected count less than 5. The minimum expected count is 5.39.
b. Computed only for a 2x2 table

12-6 Continuing the bank-loan discrimination example, we want to know if there is a difference in the frequency of gender by race. In other words, is the proportion of men to women who receive loans the same for African Americans and Whites?

Instructions

The five steps of hypothesis testing are listed below. Follow the instructions in Problem 12-5 above.

Solution (Decision)

Step 1. State the hypothesis.
Step 2. Set the critical value. As a researcher, use .05.
Step 3. Select the methodology of data collection and statistical test.
Step 4. Run the statistics to obtain the p-value.
Step 5. Make the decision (a–e).

Gender of the individual. * Race of the individual. Crosstabulation

			Race of the individual.		
			African-American	White	Total
Gender of the individual.	female	Count	6	7	13
		% of Total	6.4%	7.4%	13.8%
	male	Count	45	36	81
		% of Total	47.9%	38.3%	86.2%
Total		Count	51	43	94
		% of Total	54.3%	45.7%	100.0%

Chi-Square Tests

	Value	df	Asymp. Sig. (2-sided)	Exact Sig. (2-sided)	Exact Sig. (1-sided)
Pearson Chi-Square	.399[a]	1	.528		
Continuity Correction[b]	.110	1	.740		
Likelihood Ratio	.397	1	.528		
Fisher's Exact Test				.562	.368
Linear-by-Linear Association	.395	1	.530		
N of Valid Cases	94				

a. 0 cells (.0%) have expected count less than 5. The minimum expected count is 5.95.
b. Computed only for a 2x2 table

ONE-WAY ANOVA

12-7 Continuing the bank-financing discrimination example, you want to know if any one of the three types of business owners has a significantly higher income level.

Instructions

The five steps of hypothesis testing are listed below. For steps 1–4, follow the instructions in the one-way ANOVA example in Box 12.15. For *step 5*, answer the following questions: (a) Which group has the highest income? (b) Is the mean difference significant? (c) Should we fail to reject Ho (accept Ho) or reject Ho (accept Ha)? (d) What conclusion should be made?

Solution (Decision)

Step 1. State the hypothesis.
Step 2. Set the critical value. As a researcher, use .05.
Step 3. Select the methodology of data collection and statistical test.
Step 4. Run the statistics to obtain the p-value.
Step 5. Make the decision (a–e).

Descriptives

Income

	N	Mean	Std. Deviation	Std. Error	95% Confidence Interval for Mean	
					Lower Bound	Upper Bound
partnership	4	36000.00	10230.673	5115.336	19720.72	52279.28
corporation	6	39666.67	22250.094	9083.563	16316.63	63016.71
propritorship	84	39911.90	18944.894	2067.057	35800.61	44023.20
Total	94	39729.79	18733.340	1932.196	35892.83	43566.75

Descriptives

Income

	Minimum	Maximum
partnership	27000	50000
corporation	21000	75000
propritorship	14400	123000
Total	14400	123000

ANOVA

Income

	Sum of Squares	df	Mean Square	F	Sig.
Between Groups	58455167.173	2	29227583.587	.082	.922
Within Groups	3.258E10	91	3.580E8		
Total	3.264E10	93			

12-8 Continuing the bank-financing discrimination example, you want to know if any one of the three industry types of business in the study has a significantly higher income level.

Instructions

The five steps of hypothesis testing are listed below. Follow the instructions from Box 12.15.

Solution (Decision)

Step 1. State the hypothesis.

Step 2. Set the critical value. As a researcher, use 0.5.

Step 3. Select the methodology of data collection and statistical test.

Step 4. Run the statistics to obtain the p-value.

Step 5. Make the decision (a–e).

Descriptives

Income

	N	Mean	Std. Deviation	Std. Error	95% Confidence Interval for Mean	
					Lower Bound	Upper Bound
food service	14	34335.71	14109.986	3771.052	26188.85	42482.58
general service	54	41405.56	22110.378	3008.841	35370.58	47440.53
retail	26	39153.85	11952.213	2344.022	34326.24	43981.45
Total	94	39729.79	18733.340	1932.196	35892.83	43566.75

Descriptives

Income

	Minimum	Maximum
food service	17000	60000
general service	14400	123000
retail	22000	72000
Total	14400	123000

ANOVA

Income

	Sum of Squares	df	Mean Square	F	Sig.
Between Groups	5.676E8	2	2.838E8	.805	.450
Within Groups	3.207E10	91	3.524E8		
Total	3.264E10	93			

ADDITIONAL T-TEST DECISION PROBLEMS

Instructions

Unless your instructor tells you otherwise, for decision problems 12-9 through 12-11, clearly list the five steps of hypothesis testing and answer these questions within the appropriate step, following prior examples. For *step 1*, be sure to clearly write the null and one- and two-tailed alternative hypotheses. For *step 2*, the critical value is given with each problem. For *step 3*, list the dependent and independent variables with their measurement levels and the appropriate statistical test. For *step 4*, see the computer printout; however, list the step and write the percentage of confidence that the mean difference is significant. For *step 5*, answer the questions given in each problem.

12-9   You are the production manager, and you are going to buy a new machine. You have narrowed the alternatives to two models—A and B. Model A claims to be faster and is much more expensive than Model B. If Model A is significantly faster, you will buy it. If not, you will buy Model B. To test the two models, you have both models set up in your shop and take random samples. Each sample represents the number of units produced in a one-hour period. Test results are given below.

Follow the instructions in steps 1–4 above. For *step 5*, (a) What are the two means, and which model is faster? (b) Is the difference between means significant using .01 as the critical value? (c) Should you fail to reject Ho (accept Ho) or reject Ho (accept Ha)? (d) Which machine should you buy? (The simulated computer printout below contains the numbers you need.)

Simulated Computer-Generated T-Test Results
Two sample T for C1 vs C2

	N	Mean	StDev	SE Mean
MODEL A	12	326.0	44.0	14
MODEL B	12	285.0	40.0	13

T-Test M C1 = M C2 (vs >): T = 2.15 P = 0.00 DF = 22

12-10 Dr. Schneider conducted a study to determine whether vitamin and mineral supplements help fight infections. Participants included 96 men and women age 65 and older. Half took the vitamin and half took the placebo. The number of days of illness from infections for each participant, ranging from colds to pneumonia, were recorded. Results (below) were published in the British journal *Lancet* (November, 1992).

Follow the instructions in steps 1–4 above. For *step 5*, (a) What are the two means, and which is preferred? (b) Is the difference between means significant using .05 as the critical value? (c) Should you fail to reject Ho (accept Ho) or reject Ho (accept Ha)? (d) Can Dr. Schneider claim that vitamin and mineral supplements strengthen the body's immune system? (e) Would the answers to the questions change if the critical value were .01 and .10?

Simulated Excel-Generated T-test Computer Results

	A	B	C
1	t-Test: Two-Sample Assuming Unequal Variances		
2			
3		Vitamins	Placebo
4			
5	Mean	39.46	43.81
6	Standard Deviation	12.96	11.95
7	Standard Error of the Mean	1.32	1.22
8	Observations	96	96
9	Degrees of Freedom	190	
10	t-Statistic	-1.71	
11	p(T≤t)one-tailed	0.045	

12-11 You are a business professor who believes that females get higher grades than males. To find out, you took a random sample of students with at least two semesters of grades to record cumulative GPAs to compare for differences. Computer results appear below.

Follow the instructions in steps 1–4 above. For *step 5*, (a) What are the two means, and which gender has the preferred mean? (b) Is the difference between means significant using .10 as the critical value? (c) Should you fail to reject Ho (accept Ho) or reject Ho (accept Ha)? (d) Can you claim that females have higher grades? (The simulated computer printout below contains the numbers you need.)

Simulated Computer-Generated T-Test Results
Two sample T for C1 vs C2

	N	Mean	StDev	SE Mean
FEMALES	65	2.67	0.75	0.0930
MALES	50	2.59	0.66	0.0933

T-Test M C1 = M C2 (vs >): T= 1.217 P=0.3194 DF= 113

Using the Computer

Tests of Difference Using Data from Chapter 9

Instructions: For each of the following problems 12-12 to 12-20 use the data from Chapter 9 about political parties, with a sample size of 10. For each problem, write the steps of hypothesis testing, similar to the hypothesis example boxes and problems. With each problem, additional information about steps 1–4 will be given.

Step 1. (Introduction) For the hypothesis, based on the information write the "one hypothesis" (Ho or Ha, one- or two-tailed). Because this is basic research rather than applied (management decisions), action is not used.

Step 2. The critical value will be given.

Step 3. (Methods) Methods information will be stated. However, all statistical tests use unmatched (independent) groups/pairs. (a) Be sure to clearly list Y, X and their measurement levels and number of groups/scales of X. (b) State the appropriate test of difference you will run.

Step 4. Run the statistics. State whether there are any violations in your test of difference. For *step 5* of all problems, label and answer these questions:

(a) What are the means/rank means/frequencies compared for differences and which, if any, is preferred?

(b) (Results) Is the difference significant? How certain are you that there is a difference (that you are not making a Type I error)?

(c) (Decision) Should you fail to reject Ho (accept Ho) or reject Ho (accept Ha)?

(d) (Conclusion) Put a–c together to make a clear conclusion about your research.

12-12 For *step 1*, you want to determine whether there is a significant difference between gender and political party. You hypothesize that there is no difference.
Step 2. Set the common critical value for researchers (.05).
Do steps 3–5 as instructed, using the computer problems from Chapter 9.

12-13 For *step 1*, you want to determine whether there is a significant difference between gender ages. You hypothesize that one gender is older, but you're not sure which.
Step 2. Set the common critical value for researchers (.05).
Do steps 3–5 as instructed, using the computer problems from Chapter 9.

12-14 For *step 1*, you want to determine whether there is a significant difference between age of the members of the political parties. You hypothesize that Republicans are older.
Step 2. Set the common critical value for researchers (.05).
Do steps 3–5 as instructed, using the computer problems from Chapter 9.

12-15 For *step 1*, you want to determine whether there is a significant difference between males and females. You hypothesize that there is no difference.
Step 2. Set the common critical value for researchers (.05).
Do steps 3–5 as instructed, using the computer problems from Chapter 9.

12-16 For *step 1*, you want to determine whether there is a significant difference between the level of satisfaction with the current president/prime minister of your country between your sample and a recently conducted national poll. The mean of the national poll was 3. You hypothesize that there is no difference.

Step 2. Set the common critical value for researchers (.05).
Do steps 3–5 as instructed, using the computer problems from Chapter 9.

12-17 For *step 1*, you want to determine whether there is a significant difference between male and female incomes. You hypothesize that there is no difference.
Step 2. Set the common critical value for researchers (.05).
Do steps 3–5 as instructed, using the computer problems from Chapter 9.

12-18 For *step 1*, you want to determine whether there is a significant difference between satisfaction levels with the president, by political party. You hypothesize that Independents are more satisfied.
Step 2. Set the common critical value for researchers (.05).
Do steps 3–5 as instructed, using the computer problems from Chapter 9.

12-19 For *step 1*, you want to determine whether there is a significant difference between satisfaction levels with the president/prime minister by gender. You hypothesize that there are no differences.
Step 2. Set the common critical value for researchers (.05).
Do steps 3–5 as instructed, using the computer problems from Chapter 9.

12-20 For *step 1*, you want to determine whether there is a significant difference between income levels of political party members. You hypothesize that Republicans have higher-level incomes.
Step 2. Set the common critical value for researchers (.05).
Do steps 3–5 as instructed, using the computer problems from Chapter 9.

YOUR RESEARCH STUDY

12-21 Which test of difference can/will you use for your research study? Explain your choice of test.

Tests of Association and Prediction

CONCEPTUAL OBJECTIVES

The conceptual objectives below also appear at appropriate places within the chapter at points when you will have accessed the information necessary to attain them. They appear again at the end of the chapter in the Summary and Glossary section, along with explanations that will enable you to meet the objectives.

After studying this chapter, you should be able to:

1. Discuss (a) covariance, (b) the direction and strength of a correlation coefficient, and (c) one- and two-tailed hypothesis tests.

2. Describe the conclusions that can and cannot be made about correlation tests.

3. Compare the Pearson r and Spearman rank rho correlations.

4. Compare correlation and regression.

5. Write the bivariate regression model and state what the symbols represent.

6. Compare the coefficient of determination (R^2) and the error variable.

7. Compare bivariate regression, multivariate regression, and regression with dummy variables.

8. Discuss (a) model building, (b) multicollinearity, (c) stepwise regression, and (d) hierarchical regression.

9. Compare multivariate regression and logistic regression.

10. Define the following key terms (listed in order of their appearance in the chapter).

covariance	bivariate regression	stepwise regression
correlation coefficient	coefficient of	hierarchical regression
Pearson r correlation	determination (R^2)	logistic regression
Spearman rank	multivariate regression	discriminant analysis
rho correlation	regression with	
partial correlation	dummy variables	
regression	multicollinearity	

SKILL DEVELOPMENT OBJECTIVES

The exercises that apply to particular skill development objectives are indicated directly beneath each numbered objective below. Periodic instructions within the chapter tell you when to stop reading and direct you to the end of the chapter to complete one or more of the skill development exercises.

After studying this chapter, you should be able to:

1. Test a hypothesis using correlation.
   Decision problems 13-1 through 13-4, 13-8 and 13-9

2. Test a hypothesis using regression.
   Decision problems 13-5 through 13-7, 13-10 through 13-13

The Research Process

(1) The research question/purpose of the study, literature review, and hypotheses.	(2) Research design methodology for collecting data and statistics.	(3) Data analysis and interpreting results.	(4) Discussing results and making conclusions.
• Introduction	• Method	• Results	• Discussion
Chapters 1–3	Chapters 4–8	Chapters 9–14	Chapters 9–14

In prior chapters we presented the research process shown above. Now we are running the statistical tests selected in the Method section to test hypotheses/generate results to help us make sound decisions. In this chapter you will learn about the Pearson and

Spearman correlations used to test relationships between variables. You will also learn about regression, which uses correlation to predict the value of the dependent variable. Thus, regression is a more advanced statistical test than correlation. Refer to Chapter 11 for a discussion of correlation. Later in this chapter we discuss the difference between correlation and regression and when to use each.

13.1 Correlation

Recall that in Chapter 10 (section 10.4) you were introduced to tests of association. This kind of test (Pearson and Spearman) measures the direction and strength of the linear relationship between variables. In this section we discuss covariance and its coefficient followed by the Pearson and Spearman correlations. It's important to remember that with correlation, the dependent variable (DV/Y) and independent variable (IV/X) can be changed because you get the same results, but this isn't the case with regression. We end this section with a discussion of advanced partial correlation.

Covariance and Coefficient

Let's begin by stating the assumptions that must be met to run correlations.

- *Linear relationships*. This is explained with covariance, but if you don't have a linear relationship between variables you can't run correlations.
- *Homoscedasticity*. (*homo* meaning same, *scedastic* meaning scattered) The variables must have the same level of relationship throughout the range of the independent variable. In other words, the values must be spread throughout the distribution. If all the values are in the middle of the distribution, you don't have a real linear relationship.
- *At least ordinal data*. If you have nominal-level data, run a test of difference.
- *No outliers*. Recall that extreme scores distort the mean by making it larger or smaller than when it is removed. The same holds true with correlation. Outliers inflate the value of the coefficient. Thus, check your data visually by looking at the variable values of extreme values/scores or plot the data to see if a value is outside the normal range of data values. If you have outliers, remove them and rerun the correlation and you will have more reliable test results.

The relationship must be correctly specified. In addition to the assumptions above, it is important that the model (set of variables) does not exclude important causal variables or include extraneous variables, because they can change the beta weights and hence the interpretation of the importance of the independent variable(s). This is explained under the advanced correlations subsection.

Covariance and the direction of the association.

Covariance is a measure of the linear relationship between two random variables (in other words, the manner in which one variable changes in relation to another). The relationship between variables is generally hypothesized to have a *positive* or *negative* linear relationship (or slope). *Linear* refers to making a straight line with the values of the participants. The covariance is positive (an upward sloping curve/line) when both variables increase together, or move in the same direction. The covariance is negative (a downward sloping curve/line) when one variable increases as the other decreases, or moves in the opposite direction, or when it is an inverse relationship. If there is no slope, a relatively straight line, there is no linear relationship between the variables.

Return to Chapter 10 (Figure 10.2, Tests of Association) to review how to hand plot the relationship between income and age and energy level and age, and to see a positive and negative covariance. Recall that you can have the computer draw the scatterplots, similar to the hand-plotted correlations in Figure 10.2, so that you can visually look at the relationship between variables to see if it is linear. Remember that correlation only measures *linear relationships*. Since nominal-level variables are not linear, they should not be used in correlation; instead use a test of difference (chapters 10 and 12).

One- and two-tailed (directional) hypotheses.

If you believe there is a positive or negative relationship between the two variables, you use a one-tailed hypothesis test. When you believe there is a relationship but you are not sure in which direction, use a two-tailed test. As with a test of difference, it is easier to find a relationship with a two-tailed than with a one-tailed test because the p-value is smaller in the tails (it doubles in one tail).

Correlation coefficient.

*The **correlation coefficient** (r) is the measure (+1 to –1) of the strength and direction of the linear relationship between variables.* The correlation coefficient measures between +1 to –1. The direction of the relationship is indicated by the sign: a plus sign (+) or no sign = positive relationship, and a negative sign (–) = a negative relationship.

The number indicates the *strength* of the relationship. The closer to the absolute value of 1 the coefficient, the stronger the relationship between variables. The closer to 0 the coefficient, the weaker the relationship.

In some research designs the coding of the data may create a negative relationship. For example, 1 is the preferred score/status in high school class rank, while a high SAT score is preferred. Thus, we would expect that as class rank increases, SAT scores would decrease.

Strength of the relationship and p-value.

Many researchers, including myself, prefer two levels (a coefficient < .4 does not have a strong relationship, whereas a coefficient > .4 has a strong relationship). Thus, as with the t-ratio and chi-square, the strength of the relationship is difficult to assess by itself. Again, the bottom line in inferential statistical testing is the p-value.

The p-value tells you whether the relationship is significant for the given data. The p-value tests if the coefficient is significantly different from 0. Unlike with the test of difference, we conclude with statements about the association, relationship, or correlation between variables. We will be using p-values with Pearson and Spearman correlations. Remember that the larger the sample size, the greater the probability of finding a significant correlation with a lower correlation coefficient. It is not unusual to find significant correlations with low coefficients.

CONCEPTUAL OBJECTIVE 1
Discuss (a) covariance, (b) the direction and strength of a correlation coefficient, and (c) one- and two-tailed hypothesis tests.

Correlation conclusions (understanding and explaining—not true cause and effect).
With correlation you can conclude that there is an association/relationship between variables. Correlation helps us to understand and explain variables' covariance. However, unlike true experimental designs, you cannot conclude that the IV/X causes DV/Y unless you meet the requirements of a true experimental design. But note that correlation does not, and cannot, use a matched pairs design; thus, making this conclusion is questionable when based on correlation alone. Thus, we may conclude that Y (age) is positively or negatively associated/related/correlated with X (income). We can also discuss the strength of the relationship, if it is significant, and discuss the probability of making a Type I error (saying there is a correlation when there is none). But we cannot conclude that Y (age) causes X (income), or vice versa.

CONCEPTUAL OBJECTIVE 2
Describe the conclusions that can and cannot be made about correlation tests.

Pearson r Correlation

The **Pearson r correlation** *measures the strength and direction of the linear relationship between two interval/ratio variables.* Its proper name is the Pearson Product-Moment Correlation Coefficient.

Pearson uses interval/ratio data and a normal distribution, so it is a parametric test. With a large sample size (25–30 or more participants) we can assume a normal distribution. The Pearson formula appears below. However, the computer will do the calculations for you.

Pearson Product Moment Correlation Coefficient

$$r = \frac{N\Sigma XY - (\Sigma X)(\Sigma Y)}{\sqrt{\left[N\Sigma X^2 - (\Sigma X)^2\right]\left[N\Sigma Y^2 - (\Sigma Y)^2\right]}}$$

Box 13.1 contains a computer printout to help you understand how to read Pearson r correlation results. Box 13.2 contains a sample hypothesis test for Pearson r.

Box 13.1   Reading Pearson r Correlation Results

You believe that people marry others of similar education level. You decide to test your hypothesis by asking students the education levels (number of years) of their mothers and fathers. A simulation of the results in EXCEL are presented below.

	A	B
1	Pearson Correlation Coefficient	
2	coefficient	0.331
3	p one-tailed	0.000
4	Sample	112
5	2-tailed significance	

(continued)

Coefficient and p-value. The coefficient of .3106 tells us that the direction of the relationship is positive, or as the education levels of fathers increases so does the level of mothers, and the strength is .311. However, the coefficient is difficult to analyze by itself, therefore, it is the p-value that is the more important number. The p-value of 0.000 tells us that we are more than 99% confident that there is a linear relationship, or that .311 is significantly different from 0 (no relationship).

N. You asked 112 people their parents' education level. The size of the sample (N) is 112.

Box 13.2   Example of a Hypothesis for Pearson r

Education Levels

Instructions

Clearly list the five steps of hypothesis testing and answer these questions within the appropriate step. For *step 1*, be sure to clearly write the null and one- or two-tailed alternative hypothesis. For *step 2*, select .05. For *step 3*, list the Y and X variables with their measurement levels and the appropriate statistical test. For *step 4,* see the computer printout in Box 13.1; however, write the percentage of confidence that the relationship is significant, or that you are not making a Type I error (saying there is a relationship when there really is none). For *step 5*, answer the following questions as part of making the decision: (a) What is the coefficient r? Is the relationship positive or negative? Explain, using the variables. (b) Is the relationship significant? (c) Should we fail to reject Ho (accept Ho) or reject Ho (accept Ha)? (d) What conclusion should be made?

Solution (Decision)

Step 1. State the hypothesis and action.

Ho: There is no relationship between the education levels of married people.
Ha: There is a relationship between the education levels of married people. (two-tailed)
Ha: There is a positive relationship between the education levels of married people. (one-tailed)

Step 2. Set the critical value.

As a researcher, use .05.

Step 3. Select the methodology of data collection and statistical test.

The Y is interval/ratio (father's education level) and the X is interval/ratio (mother's education level). (*Note:* Recall that the Y and X are interchangeable.) Thus, the Pearson r is the appropriate test.

Step 4. Run the statistics to obtain the p-value.

See the computer printout in Box 13.1 above. We are more than 99% confident that there is a relationship between education levels (or that we are not making a Type I error, saying there is a relationship when there really is none).

Step 5. Make the decision (a–d).

(a) The "r" is .311. There is a positive relationship; as the education level of fathers increases, so does the education level of mothers.

(b) The relationship is significant (p-value .000 < .05 critical value). We wanted to be 95% certain of not making a Type I error, and we are 99% certain.

(c) We should reject Ho (accept Ha) because there is a significant relationship.

(d) We should conclude that there is a positive linear relationship between the education levels of married people.

Pearson r correlation with SPSS 19.

To run a Pearson correlation, follow these steps.

1. Click *Analyze* on the toolbar.

2. Scroll down to *Correlate* and click *Bivariate*.

3. Enter your two scale variables. The correlation coefficient default is *Pearson*, so it should be checked for you.

4. In the *Test of Significance* box select a one- or two-tailed test.

5. You may click *Options* in the *Statistics* box, check off *Means and standard deviations* and then click *Continue*.

6. Click *OK* to generate the results in the data window.

STOP READING and turn to the end of the chapter to complete decision problems 13-1 and 13-2.

Spearman Rank Rho Correlation

*The **Spearman rank rho correlation** measures the strength and direction of the ranked linear relationship between two variables that are at least ordinal.* Its proper name is the Spearman Rank Correlation Coefficient. Recall from the Decision Tree that the decision on which correlation test to use is based on the lowest level of measurement of all variables. Thus, our definition states *at least ordinal data* because one of the variables can be ordinal and the other interval/ratio.

If your statistical software package does not have the Spearman rho correlation, you have two options: Find one that has Spearman, or run the Pearson r correlation. If the p-value is not close to the critical value, you should be OK; if they are close you should use Spearman.

Unlike Pearson, which is parametric, both variables do not have to be interval/ratio and be from a normal distribution. Spearman is distribution free; it is the nonparametric equivalent to the Pearson. Rho is the alternative to r. In other words, they both tell you the same thing but use different assumptions, data levels, and calculations.

Spearman, being an ordinal measurement level, calculates the coefficient rho based on ranking data. Spearman generates a separate ranking for each participant on both variables. The relationship between the order of the rankings for both variables is what is used to calculate the coefficient. Again, don't worry about the calculations because the computer will do them for you.

The Spearman rho computer printout gives you exactly the same three values as the Pearson. The only difference is that the values are calculated differently. Therefore, we don't include an example of how to read a Spearman correlation printout.

There are other ordinal-level correlation coefficients. As shown on the Decision Tree, the *Kendall tau* correlation measures the direction and strength of the linear relationship between two variables that are classified as at least ordinal. As the two definitions indicate, Spearman and Kendall are very similar. Kendall is used when the data have categories that are not so focused on ranking. (There are other tests for nominal-level data that don't appear on the Decision Tree.)

Spearman correlation with SPSS 19.

To run a Spearman correlation, follow these steps.

1. Click *Analyze* on the toolbar.

2. Scroll down to *Correlate* and click *Bivariate*.

3. Enter your two ordinal variables (or one scale and one ordinal). Uncheck the correlation coefficient default (*Pearson*) and check *Spearman*.

4. In the *Test of Significance* box select a one- or two-tailed test.

5. You may click *Options* in the *Statistics* box, check off *Means and standard deviations*, and then click *Continue*.

6. Click *OK* to generate the results in the data window.

CONCEPTUAL OBJECTIVE 3
Compare the Pearson r and Spearman rank rho correlations.

**STOP READING and turn to the end of the chapter
to complete decision problems 13-3 and 13-4.**

Partial Correlations

The Decision Tree also includes running correlations with three or more variables. Let's discuss partial correlation briefly here, and we will discuss it in more detail in the regression section.

Partial correlation defined.

Partial correlation is run with three or more variables, removing the effect of the additional variable(s) from the coefficient of the remaining two variables. The third variable is usually a control (or extraneous) variable. Think of a control variable not as being a research variable that you want to study, but rather as a variable that you don't want to affect your results. A control variable is held constant so that the results of the two research variable correlations are unaffected. It can block the effect of one or multiple extraneous variables. For example, there is a correlation between educational level and income. However, age is an extraneous variable because there is a positive relationship between age and income. So you could run a correlation between education level and income and control for age, through partial correlation, to take out the effect of age. This way, you are sure the relationship is not being influenced by age. As another example, when correlating the variables of successful companies you might control for two extraneous variables: the size of the business (number of employees) and the number of years it has been in operation.

You can also use partial correlation to determine if the relationship between two variables is the result of some third extraneous variable that influences both of the measured variables (a spurious relationship, discussed in Chapter 12). For example, a study found that the number of appliances in the home had a strong correlation with the use of preventive medical care. Can you think of some other variable that would cause this spurious relationship? If you said income or having medical insurance, you are correct. The reason people have more appliances is because they have higher levels of income, and usually health insurance too. So if you ran a correlation with the three variables, income—not appliances—is the true correlation with preventive medical care. Partial correlation is commonly used with regression, so we discuss it again in connection with hierarchical regression.

Partial correlation with SPSS 19.

To run a partial correlation, follow these steps.

1. Click *Analyze* on the toolbar.
2. Scroll down to *Correlate* and click *Partial*.
3. Click and drag your two test variables into the *Variable* box.
4. Move one or more variables into the *Controlling for* box.
5. In the *Test of Significance* box select a one- or two-tailed test.
6. You may click *Options*, check off *Means and standard deviations*, and then click *Continue*.
7. Click *OK* to generate the results in the data window.

13.2 Linear Regression

A logical question to ask is whether one of the variables can predict or explain the other. Recall from Chapter 10 (section 10.5) that regression can replace correlation and that regression is based on correlation. You cannot have a regression without a correlation, and it is a higher-level statistic. Refer to Chapter 10 for an explanation of when to use correlation versus regression. Again, with correlation the dependent variable (Y) and independent variable (X) are interchangeable, but not with regression; the Y is the criterion variable and the Xs the predictors or explainers. In other words, if you know the value of the Xs, you can predict the value of the Y, or the change in X results in a predicted change in the value of Y.

With all types of regression you can conclude prediction, but unlike with true experimental designs, you cannot conclude that the X causes the Y value unless you meet the requirements of a true experimental design. However, note that regression does not, and cannot, use a matched pairs design, thus making this conclusion questionable based on regression alone. For example, in Figure 13.1 we may conclude that age predicts income, running regression to verify, but we cannot conclude that age *causes* income. However, causality is often assumed because the change in the value of the Y is the result of a change in Xs.

Regression predicts the value of one dependent variable on the basis of one (or more) independent variable(s). There are various types of regression based on the measurement level of the one dependent variable, the number of independent variables, and their measurement levels. The most common types of regression, bivariate and multivariate, are discussed in this section. In sections 13.4–13.6 we discuss some variations of multivariate regression.

CONCEPTUAL OBJECTIVE 4
Compare correlation and regression.

Bivariate Regression

Bivariate regression predicts the value of one interval/ratio dependent variable with one interval/ratio independent variable. (Bivariate regression is also commonly called simple regression.) Note that with bivariate regression you get the same r coefficient result as with correlations, but you also get the R-square and additional analysis.

The bivariate regression model.

See Box 13.3 for an analysis of the regression model, which is also called the *regression equation*; for the income and age example see Figure 13.1. Note that with the equation, a predicted score may be made for any value of X within the range of data.

Box 13.3   Bivariate Regression Model

$$Y = \beta_0 + \beta_1 X + \epsilon \quad \text{or} \quad Y = a + bX + \epsilon$$

Y = dependent variable that is to be explained or predicted.

β_0 = constant or intercept, the point at which the regression line "intercepts" the Y-axis. It is the average value of Y when X is 0, or the amount of Y that is constant or present when the influence of X is null—0. The Y-intercept is zero; if not, you can get some strange results, such as negative prices.

β_1 = the slope of the regression line. It is the average value of a one-unit change in Y for a corresponding one-unit change in X. Thus, the slope represents the direction and strength of the line. See *least squares* below for explanation of how the line is determined/drawn.

X = independent variable, which is the explainer or predictor of Y.

ϵ = (ϵ is the Greek letter epsilon) the error variable that represents the variability of Y that cannot be explained by the linear relationship between X and Y; it is a random variable(s) missing from the model. For example, in Figure 13.1 the value of ϵ will vary from person to person for age and income, even if X remains constant due to the type of job, time on the job, and other variables that are not in the model. ϵ is associated with homoscedasticity. As ϵ is an advanced concept, some do not include it in the model. We'll keep it simple. Note that in Figure 13.1 every plot not on the line is an error, + above the line and – below it.

When you run regression, you are testing if $\beta = 0$. The Ho states that $\beta = 0$, and the Ha states that $\beta \neq 0$. The greater the slope, the greater the coefficient (+1 to –1), or the stronger is the relationship between X and Y. If the slope is 0, you would see a horizontal/flat regression line.

Conceptual Objective 5
Write the bivariate regression model and state what the symbols represent.

The least squares method.

The heart of regression analysis centers on fitting a straight or linear line through the points on the scatterplot. In Figure 13.1 scatterplots are the diamonds (♦), and you can see the linear line. Every plot (♦) not on the line is in error, + above the line, and – below it. The computer determines the regression line using the least squares method, which minimizes

Figure 13.1   Regression Analysis

Ha: Age can predict income (results).

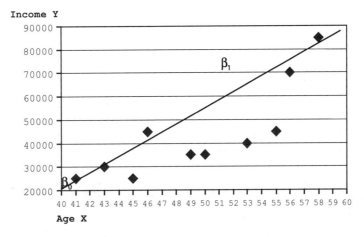

the distance between each plot (♦) and the regression line—in other words, it finds the least error. The deviation in fitting the line within the data is called the *error term*. The linear/straight line essentially is the regression model.

Note that in Figure 13.1 the β_0 constant (or intercept) is not at zero and that it has a positive slope. The slope is the direction and intensity of the line, and the intercept/constant can be thought of as the starting point of the line. The slope represents the amount that the Y increases or decreases in response to a one-unit change in the X.

Coefficient of determination (R^2) and error variable.

The R (multiple R, R-square, and adjusted R-square) is calculated when running regression; R is basically the Pearson r that measures the direction and strength of the relationship between the Y and X. More accurately, the R is a measure of the goodness of fit of the estimated regression equation. Recall that the higher the r (closer to 1), the stronger the relationship.

Of course we want to know how accurate our regression model is. The coefficient of determination indicates the explanatory power of the regression model. When we square the r value (R^2), we have the coefficient of determination, which ranges from 0 to 1. It is the amount of the shared *variance* between X and Y. The **coefficient of determination** (*R^2 or R-square*) *measures the amount of variance in the regression model's dependent variable that is explained by the variance in the independent variable(s).* The higher the R^2 the lower the error variable, and vice versa. Age is certainly not the only X that is a predictor of income, thus, there is an error variable ($\in$ missing variables) in the model. For our purposes, the *error variable* is the missing independent variable(s) needed to improve the regression model's explained variance in the dependent variable; it is the unexplained variance.

R^2 is often referred to as effect size in regression, because we want to know if X does affect Y and how strong the effect is. In simple terms, think of an R^2 of .80 meaning that 80% of the Y scores is explained by the X. Conversely, the remaining 20% is unexplained, or there is $\in$ (random variables missing from the model and random errors). However, again, r and

R^2 will not tell us if the model is a significant predictor. Thus, we need p-values. We discuss R^2 and p-values with computer printouts and examples throughout this chapter.

CONCEPTUAL OBJECTIVE 6
Compare the coefficient of determination (R^2) and the error variable.

Bivariate regression is severely limited in that one X can rarely fully explain the variance in the Y; thus it is prone to have an error variable(s). Thus, multivariate regression (using multiple Xs) usually decreases error variables, but it rarely if ever eliminates the error variable from the regression model. But let's not get ahead of ourselves—we'll talk about multivariate (multiple) regression after we review bivariate regression printouts, examples, and problems in boxes 13.4 through 13.6.

Box 13.4   Bivariate Regression

Related to the Pearson r correlation computer printout in Box 13.1 and the example in Box 13.2, you want to know if you can predict the education level of the child, based on the education level of the father. You decided to take a national survey (you received 1,066 responses) to determine if you can predict the education level. The more important values are explained from computer printout below.

Model Summary[b]

Model	R	R Square	Adjusted R Square	Std. Error of the Estimate
1	.482[a]	.232	.232	2.568

a. Predictors: (Constant), Years of education of father
b. Dependent Variable: Years of education of child

ANOVA[b]

Model				F	Sig.
1	Regression			322.37	.000[a]
	Residual				
	Total				

Coefficients[a]

Model		Unstandardized Coefficients		Standardized Coefficients		
		B	Std. Error	Beta	t	Sig.
1	(Constant)	9.451	.209		12.31	.000
	Years of education of father	.347	.019	.482	17.95	.000

a. Dependent Variable: Years of education of child

Box 13.5   Reading Bivariate Regression Results

F-Statistic and Sig F. The F-statistic of 322.37 is the measure of the variance of the model. The F tests if the slope $\beta = 0$. In other words, if the slope is 0, the predicted value for child's education is the same regardless of the father's education, or the model does not work. Higher F-statistics indicate that there is a relationship (slope) between the Y and X. However, it is difficult to interpret the F by itself.

Therefore, it is the Sig F of .000 that is the most important value because it tells you if the model works (or whether you can predict the education level of the child based on the education level of the father). You are over 99% certain that the model works (or that you are not making a Type I error by concluding that the model will predict, when in fact it will not). However, with a sample size of 1,066 the chances are good that the model would be significant.

Coefficients (Rs). The F statistic actually tests the Rs, which is the same as testing the model as a whole. You should use the adjusted R-square because it is the most accurate of the three Rs. In the sample, .232 (23%) of the variance in education level of the child is explained by the father's education level. Or, 77% of the variance is explained by variables not in the model, the error variable. Thus, the model can be improved by adding variables to the model—making it a multivariate (multiple) regression model.

T-Statistic and Sig T. The t-statistic of 17.95 is the measure of the relationship between X and Y. The T-test of the slope is B = 0. Higher T-statistics indicate that there is a relationship between the Y and X. However, it is difficult to interpret the T by itself. Therefore, it is the Sig t (two-tailed) of .000 that is the most important value because it tells you if the X predicts Y. With bivariate regression, the F and T significant values are the same because the entire model includes only one X variable. The T is important for multiple regression, not bivariate.

Slope (B) Unstandardized Coefficients. The B value .347 tells you the slope of the regression line. It is not 0. Thus, a change in the value of 1 unit of X results represents the amount of the change in the Y. The greater the value of B, the greater the affect a change in X has on a change in the value of Y.

Beta (β_0). Standardized Coefficients. The beta coefficients are adjusted B and are therefore the ones that are reported and used for decision making. The standardized version of the B coefficients are the beta weights, and the ratio of the beta coefficients is the ratio of the relative predictive power of the Xs. The Y changes B units because the X changes 1 unit.

Constant and False Sig. The constant/intercept (β_0) 9.451 tells us whether the regression line goes through the origin (the point at the intersection of the two axes; it is the point where both variables are 0). We would predict 0 years of education for a child whose parents had 0 years of education. However, the intercept is not at the origin; thus, you would predict 9.45 years, because that is the intercept/constant.

The constant has a significance value, but it is just placed there by default, so ignore the sig of the constant because it is not relevant.

Standard Error. Approximately 68% of all Y scores/values/plots should fall within +/– one standard error from the regression line. Thus, it can be used to set confidence intervals for Y.

Box 13.6   Example of a Bivariate Regression Hypothesis Test

Predicting Education Levels of Children
Below are the results of the computer printout in Box 13.3, presented through hypothesis testing.

Instructions

Clearly list the five steps of hypothesis testing and answer these questions within the appropriate step. For *step 1*, be sure to clearly write the null and alternative hypothesis. Note that we test the two-tailed Ha only. For *step 2*, select .05. For *step 3*, list the model and the appropriate statistical test. For *step 4* see the computer printout in Box 13.3; however, write the percentage of confidence that the model is significant (or that you are not making a Type I error, saying that the model predicts when it really does not). For *step 5*, answer the following questions as part of making the decision: (a) What is the important coefficient R, and what does it tell you? Explain, using the variables. (b) Is the model significant? (c) Should we fail to reject Ho (accept Ho) or reject Ho (accept Ha)? (d) What conclusion should be made? (e) Calculate the education level of children whose fathers are high school and college graduates—12 and 16 years of education.

Solution (Decision)

Step 1. State the hypothesis.

Ho: The education level of the child cannot be predicted by the education level of the father. ($\beta = 0$)

Ha: The model can predict education levels. ($\beta \neq 0$)

Step 2. Set the critical value. As researchers, use .05.

Step 3. Select the methodology of data collection and statistical test.

$Y = \beta_0 + \beta_1 X + \epsilon$

Child education level = 9.451633 + .347027 × (father's education level). Bivariate regression is the appropriate test.

Step 4. Run the statistics to obtain the p-value.

See the computer printout in Box 13.3. We are more than 99% confident that ($\beta \neq 0$) the model predicts, or that we are not making a Type I error (saying it predicts when it really does not).

Step 5. Make the decision (a–e.)

(a) The adjusted R^2 is .232. In other words, 23% of the variance in the education level of children is explained by the education level of the fathers. Thus, 77% is explained by other variables ϵ.

(b) The model is significant (p-value .0000 < .05 critical value). We wanted to be 95% certain of not making a Type I error, and we are more than 99% certain.

(c) We should reject Ho (accept Ha) because the model will predict education levels.

(d) We should conclude that there is a positive linear relationship between the education levels of fathers and their children; as the education level of the father increases, so does the child's. Also, the education level of the father will predict the education level of the child. However, there are other variables that also predict education that are not in the regression model.

(e) Using the equation in *step 3* above, as the father's education increases so does the child's:

High School Y = 9.45 + (.347 × 12) 4.164 = 13.614

College Y = 9.45 + (.347 × 16) 5.552 = 15.002

(*Note*: Regression does not use a matched pairs design, as in experimental designs; therefore, if you compared one actual father to his child, the education level of college graduates would probably be equal to or greater than college grad—16 years of education.)

Bivariate regression with SPSS 19.

The only difference in running a bivariate versus multivariate regression is the number of Xs, so the only step that changes is *step 4*.

1. Click *Analyze* on the toolbar.

2. Scroll down to *Regression* and click *Linear*.

3. Click and drag your one scale Y into the *Dependent* box.

4. Move one scale X into the *Independent(s)* box.

5. You may click *Statistics* and check off a variety of analysis options, and then click *Continue*.

6. You may also click *Options*. One nice feature is *Missing Variables*. You can check *Replace with mean* so that you don't have to exclude data (drop your sample size) due to missing values.

7. Clicking *Plot* will give you a visual of the data used in the regression analysis.

8. Click *OK* to generate the results in the data window.

**STOP READING and turn to the end of the chapter
to complete decision problem 13-5.**

Multivariate Regression

Multivariate regression (or multiple regression) predicts the value of one interval/ratio dependent variable with two or more interval/ratio independent variables. It is an extension of bivariate regression because it adds Xs to increase the predictability of the model. Thus, multivariate regression has essentially the same assumptions as correlation and bivariate regression. However, multivariate regression having interval/ratio Y and X variables can also add ordinal and nominal-level Xs. With multivariate regression, the simple model is expanded as discussed below in Box 13.7.

What sample size (n) is needed to effectively run multivariate regression? Although there is no agreement among statisticians, 10 cases/participants/observations per X (and preferably more, 20 per X) is a good sample size. Therefore, a regression model with four Xs should have a minimum sample size of 40, and 80 participants is preferred. But remember

---

Box 13.7   The Multivariate Regression Model

$$Y = \beta_0 + \beta_1 X + \beta_2 X \ldots + \in \quad \text{or} \quad Y = a + bX + cX \ldots + \in$$

The Y, β_0, β_1 X and $\in$ are the same for both bivariate and multivariate regression. See the bivariate regression model in Box 13.3 for an explanation of all but the ellipsis. What changes is the"β_2 X +...." The β_2 X represents the second variable in the model and the ellipsis represents any number of other variables in the model. Thus, a model with five Xs would have β_5 X or fX (the sum of 5 Xs).

The ellipsis means that any number of Xs can be included, but you need at least 2 Xs; otherwise you have a bivariate model.

that the larger the sample size, the greater the chance that the model can predict (or that you are not making a Type II error by saying the model cannot predict when it really can).

Because bivariate and multivariate regression are so similar, let's go right to the computer printout in Box 13.8, how to read it in Box 13.9, and an example of a hypothesis test using multivariate (multiple) regression in Box 13.10.

Box 13.8   Multivariate Regression

You are the sales manager of a large company. You have been hiring salespeople based on subjective data, with mixed results. You want to be more objective, and to consistently select the best candidates for the job. You believe that sales performance (measured on an index based primarily on sales) can be predicted based on intelligence quotient (IQ), years of sales experience (YSE), personality test score (PTS), and age. You ran a regression on the data of 22 of your salespeople, 10 of whom had performance indexes of less than 100. The computer printout is below. If the model is an accurate predictor of success, you will hire applicants with the highest performance index; but only candidates with a performance index equal to or greater than 100 will be hired. The more important values are explained in Box 13.9.

Model Summary[b]

Model	R	R Square	Adjusted R Square	Std. Error of the Estimate
1	.845[a]	.714	.677	3.878

a. Predictors: (Constant), Age, IQ, Personality test score, Years of sales experience.
b. Dependent Variable: Sales

ANOVA[b]

Model		Sum of Squares	df	Mean Square	F	Sig.
1	Regression	637.415	4	159.354	10.595	.000[a]
	Residual	255.769	17	15.040		

a. Predictors: (Constant), Age of the individual. , IQ, Personality test score, Years of sales.
b. Dependent Variable: Sales

Coefficients[a]

Model		Unstandardized Coefficients		Standardized Coefficients		
		B	Std. Error	Beta	t	Sig.
1	(Constant)	75.437	37.762		.035	.000
	IQ	.173	.069	.334	2.516	.022
	Years of sales experience.	.068	.133	.081	.513	.615
	Personality test score	.212	.069	.410	3.086	.007
	Age	-.353	.086	.636	-4.107	.001

a. Dependent Variable: Sales

Box 13.9   Reading Multivariate Regression Results

F-Statistic and Signif F. The F-statistic is the same for bivariate and multivariate regression. The F of 10.595 measures the variance of the model with four Xs. The F tests if the slope $\beta = 0$. In other words, if the slope is 0, the predicted performance value for the sales person is the same regardless of the values of the four Xs, or the model does not predict. Again, it is the Signif F of .000 that is the most important value because it tells you if the model predicts performance. You are over 99% certain that the model works (or that you are not making a Type I error by concluding that the model will predict, when in fact it will not).

T-Statistics and Sig T of Xs. Unlike with bivariate regression, the F and T are not the same because you have multiple Xs. Each T and its sig tell you if each X is a significant predictor of performance. Of the four Xs, *IQ, personality test score*, and *age* are significant predictors of performance ($p = .022, .007, .001$). However, *years of sales experience* is not a significant predictor of performance ($p = .615$). Any X that is not significant is usually dropped from the model.

Note that the best X predictor of Y is the one with the lowest sig T (p-value); Rs are not used to determine which one X is the best predictor, or to rank them. In other words, sig Ts give you individual X performance, whereas Rs give you combined X results.

Coefficients (Rs). All three Rs tell you the same basic thing: the amount of the variance in Y that is explained by all the Xs together. Generally, the more variables in the model, the greater the R value is. Thus, you should use the adjusted R-square because it is the most accurate of the three Rs, as it adjusts for the number of Xs. In the sample, .677 (68%) of the variance in performance level of the sales staff is explained by the Xs in the model, and 32% of the variance is explained by variables not in the model (the error variable).

Slope (B and beta). The B values .173 to –.353 tell you that the slope of the regression line for each X is not 0. Thus, a change in the value of the Xs results in a change in the Y. The greater the value of B, the greater the effect a change in X has on a change in the value of Y. Notice that age has a negative correlation with performance or that as age increases performance decreases. Again, use standardized beta values. While the multiple R is the measure of the correlation of the model (combined Xs) on the Y, the beta is the coefficient between each X and the Y.

Constant. The constant/intercept 75.437 tells you whether the regression line goes through the origin (the point at the intersection of the two axes; it is the point where both Y and Xs are 0. The constant value is used in predicting the performance, as you will see in Box 13.10 (e). Again, the sig of the constant should be ignored because it is not relevant.

Box 13.10   Example of a Multivariate Regression Hypothesis Test

Predicting Sales Performance

Instructions

Clearly list the five steps of hypothesis testing and answer these questions within the appropriate step. For *step 1*, be sure to clearly write the null and alternative hypotheses. Note that we test the two-tailed Ha only. For *step 2*, select .05. For *step 3*, list the model and the appropriate statistical test. For *step 4*, see the computer printout in Box 13.8 above; however, write the percentage of confidence that the model is significant. For *step 5*, answer the following questions as part of making the decision: (a) What is the important coefficient R^2 and what does it tell you? Explain, using the variables. (b) Is the model significant? (c) Which Xs are and are not significant, and which has the greatest explanatory power of Y? (d) Should we fail to reject Ho (accept Ho) or

(continued)

reject Ho (accept Ha)? (e) What conclusion should be made? (f) You have two candidates: Chris has a 100 IQ, 5 years experience, a personality test score of 110, and is 40 years old. Sandy has an IQ of 105, 10 years of experience, a personality test score of 100, and is 30 years old. Using your model, with all significant variables at the .05 level, should you hire either candidate as a salesperson? If yes, which one would you hire?

Solution (Decision)

Step 1. State the hypothesis.
   Ho: The four variable model can not predict sales performance. ($\beta = 0$)
   Ha: The model can predict sales performance. ($\beta \neq 0$)

Step 2. Set the critical value. As researchers, use .05.

Step 3. Select the methodology of data collection and statistical test.
   Y/Performance = $\beta_0 + \beta_1 IQ + \beta_2 YSE + \beta_3 PTS + \beta_4 Age$
   Multivariate regression is the appropriate test.

Step 4. Run the statistics to obtain the p-value.
   See the computer printout in Box 13.8. We are more than 99% confident that ($\beta \neq 0$) the model predicts (or that we are not making a Type I error, saying it works when it really does not).

Step 5. Make the decision (a–f).
   (a) The adjusted R-square is .677, or 68% of the variance in the performance is explained by the model. Thus, 32% is explained by other variables that are not in the model.
   (b) The model is significant (p-value .0000 < .05 critical value). We wanted to be 95% certain of not making a Type I error, and we are more than 99% certain.
   (c) Years of sales experience is not significant; all other variables are. Age is the greatest predictor, based on having the lowest sig t (.001 vs .007), but not by much.
   (d) We should reject Ho (accept Ha) because the model will predict performance.
   (e) We should conclude that there is a positive linear relationship between IQ and personality test score. However, age has a negative relationship, and years of sales experience is not related to performance. Also, the performance of salespeople can be predicted by the model: IQ, personality test score, and age. The model has explanatory power of performance.
   (f) Hand calculations for selecting Sandy:

Y = A + B₁ × IQ + B₃ × PTS + B₄ × Age*
```
Sandy   PI  104.211 = 75.436  +   28.775
                      75.436  +   (.173)  (105)  =  18.165  (B₁)
                              +   (.212)  (100)  =  21.2    (B₃)
                              −   (.353)  (30)   =  10.59   (B₄)
                                                   28.775

Chris   PI  101.936 = 75.436  +   26.5
                      75.436  +   (.173)  (100)  =  17.3    (B₁)
                              +   (.212)  (110)  =  23.32   (B₃)
                              −   (.353)  (40)   =  14.12   (B₄)
                                                   26.5
```

* Notice that B₂, years of experience, has been dropped from the model because it is not a significant predictor.

Note that the regressions appearing throughout the rest of this chapter are considered advanced statistics and may not be covered in this course. However, you should read the material to gain a better understanding of some of the other advanced options used with regression. Also, in the future you may find the information helpful. For example, if you read a journal article that uses regression using stepwise or hierarchical regression, regression with dummy variables, and/or logistic regression you will understand what is being done and how to analyze the results. Plus, someday you may go on to actually use these statistical techniques in your own research. Thus, you can refer to this book for help in analyzing the computer printouts.

STOP READING and turn to the end of the chapter to complete decision problem 13-6.

Multivariate regression with SPSS 19.

The only difference in running a bivariate versus multivariate regression is the number of Xs, so the only step that changes is #4.

1. Click *Analyze* on the toolbar.

2. Scroll down to *Regression* and click *Linear*.

3. Click and drag your one scale Y into the *Dependent* box.

4. Move two or more scale Xs into the *Independent(s)* box.

5. You may click *Statistics* and check off a variety of analysis options, and then click *Continue*.

6. You may also click the *Options* button. One nice feature is *Missing Variables*. You can check *Replace with mean* so that you don't have to exclude data (drop your sample size) due to missing values.

7. Click *Plot* to get a visual of the data used in the regression analysis.

8. Click *OK* to generate the results in the data window.

13.3 Regression with Dummy Variables

Bivariate and multivariate regression are both true linear models using all interval/ratio-level variables. However, we can improve many linear models by adding nonlinear nominal variables, called dummy or indicator variables. *Regression with dummy variables is used when the dependent variable is interval/ratio measurement level and the independent variables are mixed between interval/ratio and nominal.* Thus, this form of regression is an extension of linear multivariate regression to include nonlinear nominal variables. If all the Xs are nominal, then you don't use regression; you use two-way ANOVA as stated in Chapter 10. So far, all the variables used in our regression examples and problems have been interval/ratio. However, there are nominal variables that do help to predict the value of Y.

Recall that regression assumes a linear relationship. Also, recall that nominal variables are not linear, or we do not use them with correlation. However, with regression using dummy variables, nominal variables are treated as interval/ratio by creating an "interval" of one between 1 and 0.

Regression T-tests don't test dummy variable mean differences. Logically a true T-test compares means, and means have no real value with nominal variables, so it makes no sense to interpret the T-test of dummy variables like the interval/ratio variables. Thus, regression T-tests are not used directly for dummy variables, even though SPSS and other statistical packages print them. Also note that the T-test is a test only of the unique variance an independent variable accounts for, not of shared variance it may also explain, as shared variance while incorporated in R^2 is not reflected in the B coefficient. Therefore, the significance of dummy variables must be assessed as a set, using the R-square change method. The computer printout in Box 13.11 provides a simple way to interpret a dummy variable.

Developing Dummy Variables with Two Groups/Scales

Dummy variables, also called *indicator variables*, take on only two scales, and the values most commonly used are 1 and 0. One value represents the existence of a certain condition and the other value indicates that the condition does not hold. You generally code the variable scale that you expect to have the higher value as 1 and code the 0 to the expected lower value. In our bank loan problem, we assume Whites have a higher income (coding White = 1 and African American = 0) and run the regression; the results appear in the computer printout in Box 13.11, and the accompanying discussion appears in Box 13.12. Note that with a variable having only two groups, you use only one variable. However, with a variable having three or more groups/scales, you need to have two variables so that one category is left out. Let's read regression with and without dummy variables, and then take a look at how to code a variable with three groups.

Running regression with and without dummy variables.

The best way to interpret regression with dummy variables is to run a regression without the dummy variable and again with the dummy variable to see whether the model improves. Using our bank loan example, you want to predict income (Y) based on your independent variables, and you select four interval/ratio variables. Then you run a regular regression. Next you run the regression with the addition of the dummy variable *race* to see if it improves the model. We discuss the difference in the T-test and significance section in Reading Dummy Variable Regression, Box 13.11.

Box 13.11   Dummy Variable Regression

Model Summary

Model	R	R Square	Adjusted R Square	Std. Error of the Estimate
1	.616[a]	.380	.345	15166.897

a. Predictors: (Constant), Years of prior work experience., Percentage of capital borrowed to start the business., Percentage of capital used to start the business., Age of the individual. , Amount of loan applied for.

ANOVA[b]

Model		Sum of Squares	df	Mean Square	F	Sig.
1	Regression	1.239E10	5	2.479E9	10.776	.000[a]
	Residual	2.024E10	88	2.300E8		
	Total	3.264E10	93			

a. Predictors: (Constant), Years of prior work experience., Percentage of capital borrowed to start the business., Percentage of capital used to start the business., Age of the individual. , Amount of loan applied for.
b. Dependent Variable: Income

Coefficients[a]

Model		Unstandardized Coefficients		Standardized Coefficients	t	Sig.
		B	Std. Error	Beta		
1	(Constant)	16488.773	9502.119		1.735	.086
	Amount of loan applied for.	-.044	.069	-.069	-.639	.525
	Percentage of capital used to start the business.	.420	.085	.538	4.964	.000
	Percentage of capital borrowed to start the business.	140.098	61.993	.203	2.260	.026
	Age of the individual.	438.681	269.520	.158	1.628	.107
	Years of prior work experience.	-167.351	490.868	-.033	-.341	.734

a. Dependent Variable: Income

Model Summary

Model	R	R Square	Adjusted R Square	Std. Error of the Estimate
1	.618[a]	.382	.339	15225.946

a. Predictors: (Constant), Race of the individual., Amount of loan applied for., Years of prior work experience., Percentage of capital borrowed to start the business., Age of the individual. , Percentage of capital used to start the business.

ANOVA[b]

Model		Sum of Squares	df	Mean Square	F	Sig.
1	Regression	1.247E10	6	2.078E9	8.964	.000[a]
	Residual	2.017E10	87	2.318E8		
	Total	3.264E10	93			

a. Predictors: (Constant), Race of the individual., Amount of loan applied for., Years of prior work experience., Percentage of capital borrowed to start the business., Age of the individual. , Percentage of capital used to start the business.
b. Dependent Variable: Income

(continued)

Coefficients^a

Model		Unstandardized Coefficients B	Unstandardized Coefficients Std. Error	Standardized Coefficients Beta	t	Sig.
1	(Constant)	16140.992	9558.981		1.689	.095
	Amount of loan applied for.	-.036	.071	-.056	-.498	.620
	Percentage of capital used to start the business.	.411	.087	.527	4.751	.000
	Percentage of capital borrowed to start the business.	131.966	63.879	.191	2.066	.042
	Age of the individual.	429.515	271.056	.154	1.585	.117
	Years of prior work experience.	-178.576	493.180	-.035	-.362	.718
	Race of the individual.	1878.331	3326.872	.050	.565	.574

a. Dependent Variable: Income

Box 13.12   Reading Dummy Variable Regression Results

Predicting Income

T-test and significance. The dummy variable *race* added to the regular regression is not significant (p = .574), but it is only set by default; you can't interpret this t and significance like the interval/ratio-level variables. The significance of dummy variables must be assessed as a set, using the R-square change method. Let's keep it simple: When we ran regular regression without the dummy variable *race* the adjusted R-square was .345, but when we ran it with dummy variable *race* it was .339. Thus, the R-square went down (from .345 to .339), the model F-statistic went down (from 10.776 to 8.964), but the significance stayed the same. Of the t significance values, three of the four were lower without the dummy variable *race*—only years of work experience (p-value) went down from .734 to .718, but the variable is not significant anyway. Thus, the model is not improved by adding race as a variable, so use the model without it.

Dummy Variable. When the B value of the dummy variable is positive, the 1 code scale is greater than the 0 code scale. Thus, Whites do have higher income levels and African Americans have lower incomes. In the model equation you would use a positive B number (1878.336) for Whites and use the same B number with a negative value for African Americans. However, scales can be reversed, as we do with logistic regression. Again, the model is not improved by adding race.

Developing Dummy Variables with Three or More Groups/Scales

Because dummy variables can only have two scales (0 and 1), when you have a nominal variable with three or more groups/scales, you must develop K-1 dummy variables (or one group is dropped). Assume that in our bank loan problem we had a third race category of *other*. Thus, 3 – 1 = 2 dummy variables (D) that are needed. Coding would be as follows:

D_1 = 1 (if race is White)
　　　 0 (if race is not White)
D_2 = 1 (if race is African American)
　　　 0 (if race is not African American)

Of course, once the conversion is made, if we know a case's value on all the levels of a categorical variable except one; that last one is determined. In other words, the dummy variable group that is missing is the group that is attributed to making the change in the dependent variable. Thus, select the group in the dummy variable to be left out as the one that you want to test. We also have to leave one of the levels out of the regression model to avoid perfect multicollinearity (discussed in the section 13.4). The omitted category is the reference category because B coefficients must be interpreted with reference to it.

Regression with dummy variables with SPSS 19.

The only difference in dummy variable regression and multiple regression is the inclusion of at least one nominal X, so the only step that changes is #4.

1. Click *Analyze* on the toolbar.

2. Scroll down to *Regression* and click *Linear*.

3. Click and drag your one scale Y into the *Dependent* box.

4. Move one or more scale Xs and one or more nominal Xs into the *Independent(s)* box.

5. You may click *Statistics*, check off a variety of analysis options, and then click *Continue*.

6. Before you run the results you may also click *Options*. One nice feature is *Missing Variables*. You can check *Replace with mean* so that you don't have to exclude data (drop your sample size) due to missing values.

7. You can also click *Plot* to get a visual of the data used in the regression analysis.

8. Click *OK* to generate the results in the data window.

CONCEPTUAL OBJECTIVE 7
Compare bivariate regression, multivariate regression, and regression with dummy variables.

**STOP READING and turn to the end of the chapter
to complete decision problem 13-7.**

13.4 Stepwise Regression and Hierarchical Regression

Let's begin by discussing model building and multicollinearity, and then how stepwise and hierarchal regression are used to develop models.

Model Building

As the name implies, *model building* is the process of attempting to improve a regression model's (set of Xs to predict the Y) predictive powers, by improving either the adjusted R-square and/or p-value. Two common methods of improving models are adding and dropping independent variables, and running multiple models.

Adding variables and variable selection.

We have already stated how we can add Xs to models to improve them; recall that we added race as a dummy variable to predict income, but it didn't improve the model. However, we don't want to add correlated X. Thus, you should not just add every variable that you can think of into your regression model. The variables selected for inclusion in the model should be based on the literature. When ample studies provide literature, select Xs based on prior predictive powers. However, if researchers have mixed results (i.e., some say the X is a predictor and others say it is not), include the X in your model to support or refute each prior study. We can also improve models using the stepwise and hierarchical methods of regression, which we discuss after analyzing multicollinearity. One potential problem with adding variables to a regression model is multicollinearity.

Dropping variables.

Recall that when you run multiple regression, you usually drop any Xs that are not significant. By doing so, and running the regression with the new model, you are model building. For small samples, the F test of the overall regression model may be nonsignificant even though T-tests for some B coefficients are significant. Dropping variables with nonsignificant B may lead to a significant F in this situation.

Developing multiple models.

In model building it is helpful to develop more than one model. After running a regression, you can rerun the regression using only the significant variables, thus providing multiple models. A *full model* includes all the Xs, whereas a *reduced model* includes only the significant Xs of the full model variables. You can also develop different models by only including some mixture of the variables in different sets/models, giving you a full model and reduced models, or you can also create multiple models by changing X to Y variables. In addition, you can use a different Y with the same Xs, which is common with complex statistical hierarchical regression designs published in the *Academy of Management Journal*.

Residual analysis.

When building models, you want to be sure not to violate any of the correlation assumptions. One way to check for violations is through residual analysis. *Residuals* are the difference between the observed values and those predicted by the regression equation. Residuals thus represent error, as in most statistical procedures. Residual analysis is used for three main purposes: (1) to spot violations in heteroscedasticity (i.e., increasing error as the observed Y value increases), (2) to spot outliers, and (3) to identify other patterns of error (i.e., homoscedasticity error associated with certain ranges of Xs). The actual residual analysis is beyond the scope of this book. But keeping it simple, you can look at the data and scatterplots for a visual check to see if any of these problems is present in your regression data.

Multicollinearity

When running regression we want the Xs to be correlated with the Y. However, we do not want the Xs to be correlated among themselves. *Collinearity* exists when two independent variances are highly correlated. *Multicollinearity exists when three or more independent variables are strongly correlated.* Multicollinearity does not affect the F-test of the significance of the model. However, it does affect the T-test of each X.

When correlation is excessive, standard errors of the B and beta coefficients become large, making it difficult or impossible to assess the relative importance of the predictor variables. Multicollinearity is less important where the research purpose is sheer prediction, since the predicted values of the Y remain stable, but multicollinearity is a severe problem when the research purpose includes causal modeling.

Multicollinearity is a problem when R > .7.

Although researchers try to select Xs that are not correlated, multicollinearity exists in virtually all multivariate regression models. Therefore, the question is not whether multicollinearity exists, but rather whether it is problematic. According to the simple rule-of-thumb test, multicollinearity is a potential problem if the value of one X R coefficient is > .9 or R > .7 for several independent variables, which is a very strong correlation. Recall that we said that anything > .4 was a strong correlation, so there is a good chance that you will not have multicollinearity problems.

Analyzing Multicollinearity

Let's discuss the different tests of multicollinearity.

Bivariate correlation Rs > .7.

To determine multicollinearity, you can run bivariate correlations between all the Xs to determine the r values and significance levels. Are any > .7? Many journal articles that run regression report the correlations between all the Xs. However, you can test for multicollinearity when you run regression. Two measures are the tolerance and the variance-inflation factor (VIF).

Tolerance < .20 is problematic.

Tolerance is $1 - R^2$ for the regression of that X on all the other independents, ignoring the Y. There will be as many tolerance coefficients as there are independents. The higher the intercorrelation of the independents, the more the tolerance will approach zero. As a general guide, if tolerance is less than .20 a problem with multicollinearity is indicated.

Variance-inflation factor (VIF) ≥ 4 is problematic.

VIF is simply the reciprocal of tolerance. Therefore, when VIF is high there is high multicollinearity and instability of the B and beta coefficients. Standard error is doubled when VIF is 4.0 and tolerance is .25, corresponding to R = .87. Therefore VIF ≥ 4 is the common cut-off criterion for deciding when a given X displays "too much" multicollinearity: values above 4 suggest a multicollinearity problem. Some researchers use the more lenient cutoff of 5.0.

Handling multicollinearity.

One way to deal with multicollinearity is to increase the sample size because it decreases the standard error, which is the basis for B and beta coefficients. Some researchers will drop one of the highly correlated variables, as is done with stepwise regression. However, when the variables are based on the literature and theory development, simply dropping a variable without a theoretical foundation is not a good idea. It may be possible to combine the variables into one new variable based on a theoretical foundation.

Multiple regression and collinearity with SPSS 19.
You are running a multiple regression and testing to determine if collinearity is a problem, so the only step that changes is #5.

1. Click *Analyze* on the toolbar.
2. Scroll down to *Regression* and click *Linear*.
3. Click and drag your one scale Y into the *Dependent* box.
4. Move two or more scale Xs into the *Independent(s)* box.
5. Click *Statistics* and check off *Collinearity Diagnostics* to get tolerance and VIF; then click *Continue*.
6. You may also click *Options*. One nice feature is *Missing Variables*. You can check *Replace with mean* so that you don't have to exclude data (drop your sample size) due to missing values.
7. Click *Plots* to get a visual of the data used in the regression analysis.
8. Click *OK* to generate the results in the data window.

Part of a printout is reproduced below, showing only the collinearity statistics (which appears on the far right of the coefficient printout section). There is also a collinearity diagnostic section, but it is not needed. As we can see, the tolerance is greater than .20 and the VIF is less than 4. Therefore, the results of the collinearity statistics test indicate that multicollinearity is not problematic.

Collinearity Statistics	
Tolerance	VIF
1.000	1.000

Stepwise Regression

Stepwise multiple regression (also called statistical regression) can be used to build models. *Stepwise regression is a model-building method in which the computer adds or removes independent variables from the model to optimize R-square (R^2).*

Forward and backward.
Stepwise regression includes only those Xs in the model that improve the model's fit—significance level of R-square. Stepwise regression is an interactive procedure that adds and deletes one X at a time. The decision to add or delete a variable is made on the basis of whether that X improves the model R-square. With *forward* stepwise regression the strongest X correlation with the Y is selected in the model, then the second X, and so on until adding an X no longer improves the model or until all Xs are entered. Alternatively, the process can work *backward*, starting with all variables and eliminating Xs one at a time until the elimination of one makes a significant difference in R-square. Forward and backward will give you essentially the same results.

Proper use of stepwise regression.
Stepwise is used in the exploratory phase of research or for purposes of pure prediction, not for theory testing. Theory testing should be based on selecting variables, and their order, from the literature, not on a computer stepwise regression process. It is inappropriate to use stepwise because it capitalizes on random variation in the data and produces results

that tend to be difficult to replicate in any sample other than the study sample. Thus, stepwise limits the ability to make generalizations from the sample to the population. Stepwise methods can yield R^2 estimates that are substantially too high, significance tests that are too lenient (i.e., allow Type I error), and confidence intervals that are too narrow. Also, stepwise methods are even more affected by multicollinearity than regular methods are. However, stepwise can be used to eliminate correlated variables from a model.

Academic versus business research.

In one academic study, the original 15 X full model was not significant. However, after running stepwise a new reduced model was developed that included three of the original fifteen variables. Not good theory, but it did develop a significant model. In business research, managers are not concerned about testing theory; they generally want to predict how the Y will change based on Xs. Thus, stepwise is generally considered a valuable tool in business research but a poor tool for developing models to test academic theory.

Box 13.13 contains a computer printout using multivariate regression decision problem 13-6 (at the end of the chapter), running the same multivariate regression model to predict income (Y) based on five Xs using the stepwise regression method, rather than Enter method, in SPSS. Also notice that the computer printout in Box 13.14 includes testing for multicollinearity.

Box 13.13   Running Stepwise Regression

Model Summary

Model	R	R Square	Adjusted R Square	Std. Error of the Estimate
1	.573[a]	.329	.322	15430.777
2	.598[b]	.358	.344	15177.253

a. Predictors: (Constant), Percentage of capital used to start the business.
b. Predictors: (Constant), Percentage of capital used to start the business. Percentage of capital borrowed to start the business.

ANOVA[c]

Model		Sum of Squares	df	Mean Square	F	Sig.
1	Regression	1.073E10	1	1.073E10	45.069	.000[a]
	Residual	2.191E10	92	2.381E8		
	Total	3.264E10	93			
2	Regression	1.168E10	2	5.838E9	25.343	.000[b]
	Residual	2.096E10	91	2.303E8		
	Total	3.264E10	93			

a. Predictors: (Constant), Percentage of capital used to start the business.
b. Predictors: (Constant), Percentage of capital used to start the business., Percentage of capital borrowed to start the business.
c. Dependent Variable: Income

(continued)

Coefficients[a]

Model		Unstandardized Coefficients	
		B	Std. Error
1	(Constant)	33043.834	1877.482
	Percentage of capital used to start the business.	.448	.067
2	(Constant)	31054.312	2091.806
	Percentage of capital used to start the business.	.418	.067
	Percentage of capital borrowed to start the business.	120.114	59.326

Coefficients[a]

Model		Standardized Coefficients			Collinearity Statistics	
		Beta	t	Sig.	Tolerance	VIF
1	(Constant)		17.600	.000		
	Percentage of capital used to start the business.	.573	6.713	.000	1.000	1.000
2	(Constant)		14.846	.000		
	Percentage of capital used to start the business.	.536	6.228	.000	.953	1.049
	Percentage of capital borrowed to start the business.	.174	2.025	.046	.953	1.049

a. Dependent Variable: Income

Box 13.14   Reading Stepwise Regression Results

Stepwise method and excluded variables. Notice that the prior regressions used the Enter method, with all variables entered together to test the model. However, with the Stepwise method (forward), the variables were entered one at a time until no more variables improved the model. The strongest X (*capital*) correlated with Y (*income*) was entered first and *borrowed* second. Thus, age and years experience did not improve the model, so they were not included (were dropped from the model).

Significance. Note that there are two significant models, so choose which one you want to use. In the ANOVA, both models have the same sig at .000. So we are more than 99% confident that both models can predict income.

When we look at the Model Summary Rs, Model 2 is higher for all three, again with adjusted R being the more important because it adjusts for the number of variables in the model. Therefore, select Model 2 (*capital* and *borrowed* together) as the best model to predict income.

Looking at the Coefficient X sigs, note that *capital* is lower than *borrowed* (.000 and .046). This should be the case because the stepwise method selected *capital* as the best predictor of income and *borrowed* second. Also, notice in the Excluded Variables that age and years experience are not significant. Recall that when we ran these Xs to predict income with regular regression and with the dummy variable *race*, *capital* and *borrowed* were the only two significant variables.

Collinearity. Collinearity is a measure of multicollinearity, as was discussed. Notice the high tolerance (much > .2) and low VIF (much < 4) values of collinearities; thus, although these variables were dropped from the model, multicollinearity is not a problem. Also, if two variables are highly correlated, only one will be included in the model; that is why no collinearity values are given with the coefficients left in the model.

Examples and decision problems are not included—if you can read a multivariate regression printout using the Enter method, you can read one using the stepwise method.

Stepwise regression and collinearity using SPSS 19.

You are running a multiple regression with the stepwise function, and you are also testing to determine if collinearity is a problem, so add a new step 6.

1. Click *Analyze* on the toolbar.

2. Scroll down to *Regression* and click *Linear.*

3. Click and drag your one scale Y into the *Dependent* box.

4. Move two or more scale Xs into the *Independent(s)* box.

5. Click *Statistics* and check off *Collinearity diagnostics* to get tolerance and VIF; click *Continue.*

6. In the *Method* box (under the Xs), click the drop-down menu and select *Stepwise.* You could also select backward or forward rather than stepwise.

7. You may also click *Options.* One nice feature is *Missing Variables.* You can check *Replace with mean* so that you don't have to exclude data (drop your sample size) due to missing values.

8. You can also click *Plot* to get a visual of your data used in the regression analysis.

9. Click *OK* to generate the results in the data window.

Hierarchical Regression

Hierarchical multiple regression (not to be confused with hierarchical linear models) is similar to stepwise regression, but you (rather than the computer) determine the order of entry of the variables. Using hierarchical regression, you can see how most variance in the Y can be explained by one or a set of new X, over and above that explained by an earlier set. Hierarchical regression is a higher-level statistic than stepwise because the researcher uses theory, not the computer, to determine the variables in the model, and it uses control variables.

Hierarchical regression is a model-building method in which the researcher enters variables one at a time or in sets to compare changes in model R-squares and to control for the effects of extraneous variables. Hierarchical regression is not commonly used to simply enter your Xs one at a time to compare differences. Let's discuss the use of control variables, R-square changes to compare models, and the use of partial correlation to control for the effects of extraneous variables.

Control variables.

All Xs are commonly entered altogether, and control variable(s) are entered in another step to control for their effect on the Y. *Control variables* are extraneous variables that could affect the results of a study. You don't want them in your model (you don't want them to affect the results of your model), so you want to take out their effects. For example, in a study developing a model to predict success and failure, control variables included age of the business, the location of the business, the size (number of employees), and the type of business (i.e., retail vs. manufacturing). Common control variables for individuals include age, gender, and education.

In the first step (block 1) of hierarchical regression, it is common to enter the control variables and then to enter the Xs as the second step (block 2) so that you can test whether the control variables do in fact affect the results by comparing the R-squares. In essence you get two models, one for each step (or block of variables entered). Model 1 includes only the control variables, and Model 2 includes the control and X variables. SPSS and other software will give you the R-square for both steps, give the change in them, and compare the difference in the R-squares.

R-square change (ΔR^2).

The change in the Y is measured by the change in R-square, so you use *Significant F Change* to determine if the change is significant from one model to the next model. ΔR^2, also called R^2 *increments*, refers to the amount R^2 increases or decreases when a block variable(s) is added to or deleted from the equation. The R^2 *difference test* refers to running regression in a series of blocks, subtracting each R^2 and testing the significance of the difference by generating an R^2 value each time. Subtracting each R^2 from the prior one also gives the R^2 increment. R^2 increments are tested for significant changes, and they are an important part of hierarchical regression.

R-square change with stepwise regression. The R-square also changes with stepwise regression, so you can also compare R-square with stepwise regression. However, in stepwise you know the change improves the model, so it is doesn't add much to your analysis. Using SPSS in stepwise, at the *Statistics* stage, just click *R-square change*.

Regression correlations.

In addition to getting an R-square, with multiple regression there are three correlations you can run that are used in relation to controls. Recall, back in our discussion of correlation, that *partial correlation* is run with three or more variables, removing the effect of the additional variable(s) from the correlation of the remaining two variables, and that partial correlation is also used with regression. However, recall that with correlation it did not matter which variable was the Y and the X, but it does matter with regression. In SPSS you need to make only one check to get all three correlations: zero-order, partial, and semi-partial or part.

Zero-order correlation is used in regression as a bivariate coefficient between the Y and one of the Xs. You get a bivariate coefficient for each of the Xs and the Y. Having the bivariate correlation coefficient gives you an idea of how strong the relationship is between each

X with the Y. The coefficients provide a base for comparing the results of the partial and part correlations.

Partial correlation in regression is the coefficient of one X with the Y variable, with the effects of other Xs removed from both the Y and X variables. In other words, it measures the relationship between an X and the Y, holding constant (or *partialing out* the effect of) all other Xs on both the Y and X. The partial correlation in regression gives you the percentage of the variance in the Y that is explained by a single X without the effects of the other Xs. The effects of the other variables are removed from both the Y and X variable. You get a coefficient for each and every X in the model, controlling for all the other Xs.

Semi-partial (part) correlation is the coefficient of one X with the Y, with the effects of other Xs removed from that one X variable only. When squared it indicates the proportion of variance in Y shared by that specific X after variance shared with the other predictors has been removed from that one X only. Like partial correlation, it is measuring the relationship between one X and the Y, but notice that part correlation does not control for the Y, as partial does.

The computer printout in Box 13.15 is an example of a hierarchical regression. Again, we use *income* as the Y, but this time we use *age* as a control variable (we could use multiple control variables and the *percentage of capital used to start the business*, the *percentage of capital borrowed to start the business*, and *years of prior work experience* as the three Xs. Box 13.16 explains how to read the results.

Box 13.15   Hierarchical Regression

Model Summary

Model	R	R Square	Adjusted R Square	Std. Error of the Estimate
1	.267[a]	.071	.061	18153.076
2	.614[b]	.377	.349	15116.351

Model Summary

Model	R Square Change	F Change	df1	df2	Sig. F Change
1	.071	7.041	1	92	.009
2	.306	14.559	3	89	.000

a. Predictors: (Constant), Age of the individual.
b. Predictors: (Constant), Age of the individual. , Percentage of capital borrowed to start the business., Percentage of capital used to start the business., Years of prior work experience.

(continued)

ANOVA[c]

Model		Sum of Squares	df	Mean Square	F	Sig.
1	Regression	2.320E9	1	2.320E9	7.041	.009[a]
	Residual	3.032E10	92	3.295E8		
	Total	3.264E10	93			
2	Regression	1.230E10	4	3.075E9	13.458	.000[b]
	Residual	2.034E10	89	2.285E8		
	Total	3.264E10	93			

a. Predictors: (Constant), Age of the individual.
b. Predictors: (Constant), Age of the individual. , Percentage of capital borrowed to start the business., Percentage of capital used to start the business., Years of prior work experience.
c. Dependent Variable: Income

Coefficients[a]

Model		Unstandardized Coefficients B	Unstandardized Coefficients Std. Error	Standardized Coefficients Beta	t	Sig.	Correlations Zero-order	Correlations Partial	Correlations Part	Collinearity Statistics Tolerance	Collinearity Statistics VIF
1	(Constant)	10976.577	10996.938		.998	.321					
	Age of the individual.	742.324	279.764	.267	2.653	.009	.267	.267	.267	1.000	1.000
2	(Constant)	16071.352	9448.015		1.701	.092					
	Age of the individual.	428.786	268.177	.154	1.599	.113	.267	.167	.134	.755	1.325
	Percentage of capital used to start the business.	.391	.071	.501	5.526	.000	.573	.505	.462	.853	1.172
	Percentage of capital borrowed to start the business.	129.064	59.338	.187	2.175	.032	.290	.225	.182	.945	1.058
	Years of prior work experience.	-146.939	488.194	-.029	-.301	.764	.189	-.032	-.025	.753	1.328

a. Dependent Variable: Income

Box 13.16   Reading Hierarchical Regression Results

Method. Age (control) was entered in block 1, creating Model 1. The four Xs were entered in block two, creating Model 2, but note that the control variable stays in the new Model 2.

Significance of the models. The first thing we want to know is: Do the two models predict income? As we can see, the ANOVA sig are both < .05 (.009 and .000), so we can conclude that we are 99% confident that the models can predict income, and Model 2 is the better model.

Rs and ΔR^2 and significance. We focus on the adjusted R-square; notice the great improvement from Model 1 to Model 2 (.061 to .349). The question is: Is Model 2 better than Model 1, or is the change significant? Note that it is the F test of change that measures R-square change significance. Ignore the significance of Model 1 because it only compares the control variable to the intercept model. As we can see, the sig F change for Model 2 is significant (or we are 99% confident that Model 2 is better than Model 1, which is what we assumed).

Significance of the Xs. Note that in Model 1 *age* is significant, but it is not in Model 2 (.009 to .113). *Age* is the control variable. Our conclusion is that age does not affect the results of our three

Xs, because its affect is not significant in Model 2. Whether or not the control variable is significant, it is not included in the model (unless you change it to an X, which should be based on support from the literature theory). Notice that *years of experience* has a negative coefficient; this indicates that having more years of experience does not help to predict income. But we are only talking about less than one year (−.029), and it is not significant, so we can't conclude that having more years of experience has a negative effect on income.

Two of the three Xs are significant (*percentage of capital used* and *percentage borrowed*) and one is not (*years of experience*). So our new model is: Income can be predicted based on percentage of capital used to start the business and percentage of capital borrowed to start the business.

Correlations. The *zero-order* is the bivariate correlation between Y and each of the Xs. As we can see, *percentage used* and *percentage borrowed* are the highest coefficients (.573 and .290) and they are sig, but *years of experience* has a low coefficient (.189) that is not significant. *Partial* correlation is the coefficient between the Y and each X, partialing out the effect of the other Xs on both the one X and the Y. In essence, it makes the values of the other variables equal so they don't affect the results. Notice that the coefficients go down from the zero-order. This is due to the shared variance with the other Xs that is taken out of the results. Part correlation is the coefficient of each one independent variable with the dependent variable, with the effects of other independent variables removed from that one independent variable only; it does not remove the effects from the Y. Thus, once again it is expected that the coefficients will go down.

Because hierarchical regression is an advanced statistic, we do not include any examples or decision problems.

CONCEPTUAL OBJECTIVE 8

Discuss (a) model building, (b) multicollinearity, (c) stepwise regression, and (d) hierarchical regression.

Control and effect.

When you run hierarchical regression, you get the results for the control variable(s) and for the Xs. The *effect* (or *main effect*) is the term used to describe the results of one X. So there is one effect for each X. The X results (B and beta coefficients) have been shown in all the regression examples but have not been labeled *effect* because no controls or interactions were used in the regression models. Without control and interaction variables, the regressions are called main effect models.

Interaction.

In addition to getting a control and effect results, you can also get an interaction by combining Xs. Interaction *cross-product variables* are added to the model to incorporate the joint effect of two or more variables (income and education) on a Y (conservatism) over and above their separate effects. Cross-product X may be highly correlated with other Xs, so check for multicollinearity. Interaction is beyond the scope of this book. But in simple terms, you examine the interaction of two or more variables with their coefficients combined as a new cross-product standardized X with one set of coefficients. So you can get:

- *Model 1.* The effect of each control variable (block 1 control variables entered).
- *Model 2.* Controls and the effect of each X (block 2 Xs entered).

- *Model 3.* Controls, effects of Xs, and the interaction of cross-product standardized Xs (block 3 cross-products entered). When two Xs are combined, it's called a two-way interaction.

- *Model 4.* You can also have three-way interactions, and more, based on how many Xs you combine into one new cross-product variable (block 4).

Interaction effects are sometimes called *moderator effects* because the interacting third variable, which changes the relation between two original variables, is a moderator variable (i.e., moderates the original relationship). For instance, the relation between income and conservatism may be moderated based on the level of education.

Creating cross-product standardized variables. To create a new interaction variable X12 from variables X1 and X2, simply issue the command COMP X12 = X1*X2.

Hierarchical regression with change in R and partial correlation with SPSS 19.

Note that in SPSS you enter the control variables in the same box for independent variable(s); don't enter any variables in the *Selection, Case,* or *WLS* boxes.

1. Click *Analyze* on the toolbar.

2. Scroll down to *Regression* and click *Linear.*

3. Click and drag your one scale Y into the *Dependent* box.

4. Move the control variable(s) in the *Independent(s)* box in Block 1 of 2; then click the *Next* button; it will change to Block 2 of 2.

5. Move your X into the *Independent(s)* box.

6. Click *Statistics* and check *Model Fit, R squared change,* and *Part and partial correlations.* Note that you can also check *Collinearity diagnostics* (already discussed) and *Descriptives.*

7. You may change the *Method* and also click *Plots* and *Options* for further analysis.

8. Click *OK* to run the results in the data window.

13.5 Logistic Regression

So far we have discussed linear regression models and have extended linear models to include nonlinear nominal/dummy variables. We now discuss a nonlinear regression model, and an alternative to it, using a nominal Y. However, you should have at least one interval/ratio X; as stated in Chapter 10, when you have all nominal-level variables you should run chi-square. *Logistic regression is used when two or more interval/ratio or mixed independent variables are used to classify observations into categories of a nominal dependent variable with two groups/levels.* The two groups/scales of the dependent variable can be any category (e.g., male or female, success or failure, and received a loan or did not receive a loan). If the Y has three or more groups/scales, such as religion, you must make two scales (e.g., Jewish or non-Jewish) or you cannot use logistic regression. If you try to run logistic regression in SPSS with three groups/scales, the computer will state that you made an error and will not give you any results.

However, with three or more groups/scales of the Y you can use discriminant analysis (also called *discriminant function*), which is also an advanced statistic not covered in this book. You should, however, know its definition. *Discriminant analysis is used when two or more interval/ratio or mixed independent variables are used to classify observations into categories of a nominal dependent variable with two or more groups/levels.* However, nominal X should be dummy variables to create interval-level data for both logistic regression and discriminant analysis.

Reading Logistic Regression Results

See the computer printout in Box 13.17 for logistic regression, along with an explanation of the results in Box 13.18. Because logistic regression and discriminant analysis are very similar, we show only logistic regression.

Box 13.17   Logistic Regression

Continuing our bank loan example, now let's determine if we can predict who gets a loan (**Y** = yes or no) based on *race* (**0** = White, **1** = African American) and *gender* (female = **1**, male = **0**) dummy variables and *capital, borrow, educ* (education level), *workexp* (work experience), and *income* as Xs. Therefore, we ran logistic regression.

Omnibus Tests of Model Coefficients

		Chi-square	df	Sig.
Step 1	Step	11.782	7	.108
	Block	11.782	7	.108
	Model	11.782	7	.108

Model Summary

Step	-2 Log likelihood	Cox & Snell R Square	Nagelkerke R Square
1	115.793[a]	.118	.159

a. Estimation terminated at iteration number 4 because parameter estimates changed by less than .001.

Classification Table[a]

			Predicted		
			Bank loan actually received.		
Observed			no	yes	Percentage Correct
Step 1	Bank loan actually received.	no	45	10	81.8
		yes	23	16	41.0
	Overall Percentage				64.9

a. The cut value is .500

(continued)

Variables in the Equation

		B	S.E.	Wald	df	Sig.	Exp(B)
Step 1[a]	capital	.000	.000	.461	1	.497	1.000
	borrow	.004	.009	.241	1	.624	1.004
	educ	.082	.125	.438	1	.508	1.086
	workexp	.019	.066	.088	1	.767	1.020
	income	.000	.000	1.898	1	.168	1.000
	race	.832	.499	2.774	1	.096	2.298
	gender	-.475	.662	.516	1	.473	.622
	Constant	-1.436	1.614	.791	1	.374	.238

a. Variable(s) entered on step 1: capital, borrow, educ, workexp, income, race, gender.

With dummy variables the B plus (no + sign .832) indicates the group assigned 1 has the higher value, and a negative (–.475) indicates the 0 category (White) has the higher value. Thus, Whites and females have the higher values.

Box 13.18   Reading Logistic Regression Results

Below we discuss the more important parts of the computer printout results.

Chi-square and sig. The chi-square of 11.782 replaces the F-statistic in regression because the Y is nominal. It examines the goodness of fit with all variables. The model chi-square tests the null hypothesis that the coefficient for all the Xs in the model, except the constant, are 0. The significance is the p-value (.108) to test the model. Thus, we are only 88% confident that the model is a predictor of receiving a loan. In other words, the model will reliably predict a group of loan applicants as received or not received more accurately than random guessing 88% of the time, which is 38% higher than random guessing at 50%.

Classification table. How well the model classifies the observed data is another way to determine how well the model fits (or how well the model performs). Classification is conducted by comparing the model's predictions to the actual observed outcomes. The classification table shows whether the estimated probability is greater than or less than one-half. The overall accuracy percentage is 64.9%. Or, if random guessing produces a 50% correct classification, then the model is 15% more reliable at classifying *received* or *did not receive* a loan.

Coefficient R-square. As in regression, the R value (.118 and .159—let's use the more accurate Nagelkerke R) explains the correlation variance in the Y explained by the Xs. In other words, the model variables only explain 16% of the variance in getting or not getting a loan. Thus, 84% of the reason for getting or not getting a loan is explained by Xs not in the model (error variables).

–2 log likelihood. The model is tested to examine how "likely" the sample results are given the parameter estimates. The –2 log likelihood (LL) compares the model to a "perfect" model in which all cases would be correctly classified. The –2 LL statistic indicates whether the model differs significantly from the "perfect" model. How well the model fits the data is the goodness-of-fit statistic; it compares the observed probabilities to those predicted by the model. The larger the LL value, the better the model. However, the p-values are actually represented in the model Chi-square and significance level. Thus, again, it is the p-value that is important.

Conclusions. The results of the logistic regression to test the Ho (the model cannot be used to predict if a business owner will receive a loan) is accepted at the .05 and .10 level (p .108 > .05 and .10). The model has a lot of missing variables.

However, at higher significance levels the model is significant. Although higher significance levels are not acceptable to academic researchers, they might be to business research. Overall, as stated, the model is better than random guessing. However, business lenders legally can't use race and gender as criteria for granting loans, but they clearly do use income and other variables when making such decisions. One important missing variable is a business plan that illustrates the financials that will provide the revenue to pay off the loan.

Logistic regression with SPSS 19.

Following are the steps for running logistic regression (also called "binary," because you have a nominal Y with only two levels/groups).

1. Click *Analyze* on the toolbar.

2. Scroll down to *Regression* and click *Binary*.

3. Click and drag your one nominal Y into the *Dependent* box.

4. Move your Xs into the *Covariates* box. If any of the Xs are nominal, you can click *Categorical* and move the nominal X(s) into the *Categorical Covariates* box. This will provide a frequency distribution for your nominal Xs without affecting your regression test results.

5. You may click *Options*, but these selections are advanced statistical analysis operations beyond the scope of this book.

6. Click *OK* to generate the results in the data window.

Discriminant analysis with SPSS 19.

Here are the steps for running discriminant analysis commonly used with a nominal Y having three or more levels/groups, but it can also be used with two levels.

1. Click *Analyze* on the toolbar.

2. Scroll down to *Classify* and click *Discriminant*.

3. Move your one nominal Y into the *Grouping Variable* box.

4. Click the *Define Range* box and enter your codes for Y, such as 0-1, 1-3, in the *Minimum* and *Maximum* boxes and click *Continue*.

5. Move your X into the *Independents* box.

6. You may click *Statistics* to get descriptives, and in the *Discriminant Analysis* box you can just use the default setting without clicking *Classify*.

7. Click *OK* to generate the results in the data window.

CONCEPTUAL OBJECTIVE 9
Compare multivariate regression and logistic regression.

13.6 Meta-Analysis and Canonical Analysis

Meta-analysis and canonical analysis are advanced statistical techniques that use regression. Because they are advanced techniques beyond the scope of this book, we will simply define them and give examples of how they are used.

Meta-Analysis

Meta-analysis uses existing research studies that address a set of related research hypotheses for its data (rather than collecting new data), using regression for statistical analysis. For example, you can have a study of 25 samples versus the typical single-sample regression study, with a much larger total sample size. Meta-analysis is commonly used when there are many prior studies; new research is not needed. Meta-analysis synthesizes what has been learned through prior research, so to use it you need to have enough prior studies, and they must be testing the same hypotheses.

Major advantages of meta-analysis over one-study regression include the fact that it derives statistical testing of overall effect size in related studies, giving it higher statistical power to detect an effect than a single study would, and thus enable the researcher to make generalizations to a greater population of studies. You can also control for between-study variations and include moderators to explain variation.

The effect size provides information about how much change is evident across all studies and for subsets of studies. In regression, effect size is primarily measured by correlation (r). In other words, does a body of studies have the same results? The higher the correlations, the more similar are the results of the prior studies.

Let's say your research question was, "Why do some businesses succeed and others fail?" If you conduct a literature review and find 40 prior empirical studies, you can conclude that there is already a large body of research. So rather than collect your own data, you could conduct a meta-analysis—based on, say, 30 of the studies that meet your criteria—to answer your research hypotheses. A recent study used data from 8,757 teams in 39 studies to determine the effect of contextual factors in work team diversity, for example.

Canonical Analysis

Canonical analysis is a multivariate regression technique concerned with determining the relationships between groups of variables in a data set. It is used with two or more dependent and independent variables. It is flexible in that you can run canonical analysis with all interval/ratio-level variables or with dummy variables, and there is even a nonparametric test so that you can use any level of data.

Multiple dependent variables. Note that all the other regression techniques have only one Y, so the major difference is that canonical analysis has two or more Ys. In the next chapter we discuss multivariate analysis of variance (MANOVA), which also uses multiple Ys. The primary difference is that canonical analysis is used primarily with interval/ratio Ys and Xs, whereas MANOVA has interval/ratio Ys and nominal X(s). When you learn about MANOVA, you will have somewhat of a better understanding of canonical analysis.

For example, a researcher has collected data on two psychological variables (personality and motivation), three academic variables (SAT, GPA, and college entrance exam test scores), and gender for 500 college students. She is interested in how the set of psychological variables relates to the academic variables and gender. In particular, the researcher is interested in how many dimensions are necessary to understand the association between the two sets of variables.

SKI WEST STUDY

As we bring this chapter to a close, you should be able to:
- *read computer printouts to test hypotheses and make decisions/draw conclusions for*
  —*Pearson and Spearman correlations,*
  —*bivariate and multivariate regression,*
  —*regression with dummy variables, and*
  —*stepwise, hierarchical, and logistic regression; and*
- *define meta-analysis and canonical analysis.*

The major hypothesis of the Ski West study was that personality test scores can predict job performance. The statistical design to test this hypothesis was a test of prediction. Matt ran a bivariate regression. The regression results did not support the hypothesis (p = .309) and the r values were low (R-square .022). Thus, the conclusion is that personality tests are not a valid predictor of job performance at Ski West.

CHAPTER SUMMARY AND GLOSSARY

The chapter summary is organized in a way that provides you with the answers necessary to help you meet the conceptual objectives for this chapter.

1. **Discuss (a) covariance, (b) the direction and strength of a correlation coefficient, and (c) one- and two-tailed hypothesis tests.**
   (a) A covariance explains how one variable changes in relation to another. (b) A correlation coefficient measures the direction and strength of covariance. The direction is positive (both variables increase in value together) or negative (one variable increases in value while the other decreases). The strength of the relationship is measured between +1 and –1. The closer the coefficient is to 1, the stronger is the relationship, and vice versa. A coefficient of >.40 indicates a strong linear relationship, but low coefficients can have significant p-values. (b) Researchers use a one-tailed hypothesis test when they predict the direction of the relationship and a two-tailed test when they are not sure of the direction of the association.

2. **Describe the conclusions that can and cannot be made about correlation tests.**
   The correlation coefficient enables the researcher to conclude the direction (positive or negative) and strength (+1 to –1) of a linear association between variables. The researcher uses the p-value to conclude if the relationship is significant and the probability of making a Type I error. However, the researcher cannot conclude that the covariance of one variable is caused by another variable.

3. **Compare the Pearson r and Spearman rank rho correlations.**
   They are similar because they are both tests of association based on a correlation coefficient. They are different because the Pearson r is a parametric test used with

two interval/ratio-level variables, whereas the Spearman rank rho is a nonparametric test of ranking values used with two variables of at least ordinal level. Thus, the Spearman rho is the nonparametric alternative to the parametric Pearson r.

4. **Compare correlation and regression.**
   Correlation and regression are similar because they both measure a linear relationship with a coefficient. Regression is based on correlation but takes it a step further by predicting the dependent variable based on the independent variable(s), rather than just measuring the strength and direction of the relationship.

5. **Write the bivariate regression model and state what the symbols represent.**
   The regression model is: $Y = \beta_0 + \beta_1 X + \epsilon$, where Y = dependent variable, β_0 = constant or intercept, β_1 = the slope of the regression line, X = independent variable, which is the explainer or predictor of Y, and ϵ = the error variable.

6. **Compare the coefficient of determination (R^2) and the error variable.**
   The coefficient of determination measures the amount of variance in the regression dependent variable that is explained by the variance in the independent variables, whereas the error variable is the reciprocal or the unexplained or missing variable(s) from the regression model.

7. **Compare bivariate regression, multivariate regression, and regression with dummy variables.**
   Bivariate regression, multivariate regression, and regression with dummy variables are all similar because they have one interval/ratio dependent variable. However, bivariate regression has only one interval/ratio independent variable, multivariate regression has two or more, and regression with dummy variables has a mix of interval/ratio and nominal variables. Dummy variables are commonly coded 0 and 1. Nominal variables with three groups must be split into two variables, and four groups split into three variables, and so on, so as to have one fewer number of variables than the number of groups in the variable.

8. **Discuss (a) model building, (b) multicollinearity, (c) stepwise regression, and (d) hierarchical regression.**
   (a) Model building is the process of attempting to improve a regression model's predictive powers, primarily by improving the R^2. (b) Multicollinearity exists when the independent variables are correlated with one another. Part of model building is to check for multicollinearity, and if it is problematic (Rs > .7), to eliminate it. (c) Stepwise regression is a model-building method in which the computer adds or removes independent variables from the model to optimize R-square. (d) Hierarchical regression is a model-building method in which the researcher enters variables one at a time or in sets to compare changes in model R-squares and to control for the effects of extraneous variables.

9. **Compare multivariate regression and logistic regression.**
   They are similar because they both develop models with multiple independent variables to predict the value of one dependent variable, and they both provide the level of significance of the model. However, multivariate regression is used with an interval/ratio dependent variable, whereas logistic regression is used with a

nominal dependent variable. Thus, regression is a linear statistic and logistic regression is a nonlinear statistic. Also, logistic regression provides a classification table for determining the percentage accuracy rate of the ability of the independent variables in the model to predict the dependent variable classification.

10. **Define the following key terms.**
    Select one or more methods: (1) fill in the missing key terms from memory, (2) match the key terms with their definitions below, or (3) copy the key terms in order from the list at the beginning of the chapter.

bivariate regression	hierarchical regression	regression
coefficient of determination (R^2)	logistic regression	regression with dummy variables
	multicollinearity	
correlation coefficient	multivariate regression	Spearman rank
covariance	partial correlation	rho correlation
discriminant analysis	Pearson r correlation	stepwise regression

_____ is a measure of the linear relationship between two random variables.

_____ is the measure (+1 to –1) of the strength and direction of the linear relationship between variables.

_____ measures the strength and direction of the linear relationship between two interval/ratio variables.

_____ measures the strength and direction of the ranked linear relationship between two variables that are at least ordinal.

_____ is commonly run with three variables, removing the effect of the third variable from the correlation of the remaining two variables.

_____ predicts the value of one dependent variable on the basis of one or more independent variables.

_____ predicts the value of one interval/ratio dependent variable with one interval/ratio independent variable.

_____ measures the amount of variance in the regression dependent variable that is explained by the variance in the independent variable(s).

_____ predicts the value of one interval/ratio dependent variable with two or more interval/ratio independent variables.

_____ is used when the measurement levels of the dependent variable are interval/ratio and the independent variables are mixed between interval/ratio and nominal.

_____ exists when three or more independent variables are strongly correlated.

_____ is a model-building method in which the computer adds or removes independent variables from the model to optimize R-square.

_____ is a model-building method in which the researcher enters variables one at a time or in sets to compare changes in model R-squares and to control for the effects of extraneous variables.

_____ is used when two or more interval/ratio or mixed independent variables are used to classify observations into categories of a nominal dependent variable with two groups/levels.

_____ is used when two or more interval/ratio or mixed independent variables are used to classify observations into categories of a nominal dependent variable with two or more groups/levels.

WRITTEN ASSIGNMENTS

All three written assignments require selecting the appropriate statistic to test the hypotheses that you develop. However, only the completed study and statistical analysis require running the statistics.

APPENDIX CS, ASSIGNMENTS 3 (RESULTS) AND 4 (DISCUSSION)

Based on your methodology, you may need to complete chapters 9–14 before you can complete the study. If your methodology includes correlations or regression, run them now and write your statistical findings in the Results section of your study.

APPENDIX SA, ASSIGNMENT 5 (CORRELATION AND REGRESSION)

This is a continuation of Assignment 4 in Appendix SA. You will be running a correlation and regression with your data.

DECISION PROBLEMS

PEARSON r CORRELATION

13-1   Continuing our bank loan example, you want to know if there is a relationship between the number of years small-business owners owned their business before applying for a loan and the amount of the loan they applied for.

Instructions

The five steps of hypothesis testing are listed below. For steps 1–5, follow the instructions in Box 13.2 (Example of a Hypothesis for Pearson r).

Solution (Decision)

Step 1. State the hypothesis and action.

Step 2. Set the critical value.

Step 3. Select the methodology of data collection and statistical test.

Step 4. Run the statistics to obtain the p-value.

Step 5. Make the decision.

Correlations

		Years business owned before loan application.	Amount of loan applied for.
Years business owned before loan application.	Pearson Correlation	1	-.006
	Sig. (2-tailed)		.951
	N	94	94
Amount of loan applied for.	Pearson Correlation	-.006	1
	Sig. (2-tailed)	.951	
	N	94	94

13-2 Continuing our bank loan example, you want to know if there is a relationship between the age of business owners and their incomes. In other words, do older owners make more money than younger ones?

Instructions

The five steps of hypothesis testing are listed below. For steps 1–5, follow the instructions in Box 13.2.

Solution (Decision)

Step 1. State the hypothesis and action.
Step 2. Set the critical value.
Step 3. Select the methodology of data collection and statistical test.
Step 4. Run the statistics to obtain the p-value.
Step 5. Make the decision.

Correlations

		Age of the individual.	Income
Age of the individual.	Pearson Correlation	1	.267**
	Sig. (2-tailed)		.009
	N	94	94
Income	Pearson Correlation	.267**	1
	Sig. (2-tailed)	.009	
	N	94	94

**. Correlation is significant at the 0.01 level (2-tailed).

Spearman Rank Rho Correlation

13-3 Continuing our loan example, you want to know if there is a relationship between education (6 scales: elementary to grad school) and income of the small-business owners. In other words, does income go up with education level?

Instructions

The five steps of hypothesis testing are listed below. For steps 1–5, follow the instructions in Box 13.2.

Solution (Decision)

Step 1. State the hypothesis and action.
Step 2. Set the critical value.
Step 3. Select the methodology of data collection and statistical test.
Step 4. Run the statistics to obtain the p-value.
Step 5. Make the decision.

Correlations

			Level of education.	Income
Spearman's rho	Level of education.	Correlation Coefficient	1.000	-.353**
		Sig. (2-tailed)		.000
		N	94	94
	Income	Correlation Coefficient	-.353**	1.000
		Sig. (2-tailed)	.000	
		N	94	94

**. Correlation is significant at the 0.01 level (2-tailed).

13-4   Continuing our bank loan example, you want to know if there is a relationship between education (recall six scales: elementary to grad school) and age of the small business owners. In other words, does income go up with age?

Instructions

The five steps of hypothesis testing are listed below. For steps 1–5, follow the instructions in Box 13.2.

Solution (Decision)

Step 1. State the hypothesis and action.
Step 2. Set the critical value.
Step 3. Select the methodology of data collection and statistical test.
Step 4. Run the statistics to obtain the p-value.
Step 5. Make the decision.

Correlations

			Level of education.	Age of the individual.
Spearman's rho	Level of education.	Correlation Coefficient	1.000	-.164
		Sig. (2-tailed)		.115
		N	94	94
	Age of the individual.	Correlation Coefficient	-.164	1.000
		Sig. (2-tailed)	.115	
		N	94	94

BIVARIATE REGRESSION

13-5 Continuing our bank loan example, you want to know if you can predict a business owner's income based on the amount of the loan applied for.

Instructions

The five steps of hypothesis testing are listed below. Follow the instructions in Box 13.6 (Example of a Bivariate Regression Hypothesis Test, steps 1–4 and 5a–d). Do *not* perform step 5e.

Solution (Decision)

Step 1. State the hypothesis and action.
Step 2. Set the critical value.
Step 3. Select the methodology of data collection and statistical test.
Step 4. Run the statistics to obtain the p-value.
Step 5. Make the decision.

Model Summary

Model	R	R Square	Adjusted R Square	Std. Error of the Estimate
1	.340[a]	.116	.106	17710.174

a. Predictors: (Constant), Amount of loan applied for.

ANOVA[b]

Model		Sum of Squares	df	Mean Square	F	Sig.
1	Regression	3.781E9	1	3.781E9	12.056	.001[a]
	Residual	2.886E10	92	3.137E8		
	Total	3.264E10	93			

a. Predictors: (Constant), Amount of loan applied for.
b. Dependent Variable: Income

Coefficients[a]

Model		Unstandardized Coefficients		Standardized Coefficients	t	Sig.
		B	Std. Error	Beta		
1	(Constant)	33496.473	2561.148		13.079	.000
	Amount of loan applied for.	.218	.063	.340	3.472	.001

a. Dependent Variable: Income

MULTIVARIATE REGRESSION

13-6 Continuing our bank loan example, you want to know if you can predict the amount of the loan applied for, based on the business owner's age, years of prior work experience, and number of years the owner had the business before applying for the loan.

Instructions

The five steps of hypothesis testing are listed below. Follow the instructions in Box 13.10 (Example of a Multivariate Regression Hypothesis Test), but replace step 5(e) with the question: Would your answers change at the .10 or .01 critical value levels?

Solution (Decision)

Step 1. State the hypothesis and action.
Step 2. Set the critical value.
Step 3. Select the methodology of data collection and statistical test.
Step 4. Run the statistics to obtain the p-value.
Step 5. Make the decision.

Model Summary

Model	R	R Square	Adjusted R Square	Std. Error of the Estimate
1	.211[a]	.044	.013	29100.192

a. Predictors: (Constant), Years business owned before loan application., Years of prior work experience., Age of the individual.

ANOVA[b]

Model		Sum of Squares	df	Mean Square	F	Sig.
1	Regression	3.547E9	3	1.182E9	1.396	.249[a]
	Residual	7.621E10	90	8.468E8		
	Total	7.976E10	93			

a. Predictors: (Constant), Years business owned before loan application., Years of prior work experience., Age of the individual.
b. Dependent Variable: Amount of loan applied for.

Coefficients[a]

Model		Unstandardized Coefficients B	Std. Error	Standardized Coefficients Beta	t	Sig.
1	(Constant)	-8253.039	19504.995		-.423	.673
	Age of the individual.	1220.279	740.654	.280	1.648	.103
	Years of prior work experience.	-106.987	1052.910	-.014	-.102	.919
	Years business owned before loan application.	-1180.579	975.456	-.182	-1.210	.229

a. Dependent Variable: Amount of loan applied for.

REGRESSION WITH DUMMY VARIABLES

13-7   Continuing problem 13-6, you decide to add two new dummy variables (*race* and *gender*) to see if the model improves at predicting the amount of the loan applied for based on the business owner's age, years of prior work experience, and number of years the owner had the business before applying for the loan. Coding of the dummy variables are:

race: 0 = African American, 1 = White
gender: 1 = female; 2 = male

Instructions

The five steps of hypothesis testing are listed below. Use problem 13-6, steps 1–4. For step 5, answer these questions: (a) What are the adjusted R-squares with and without the dummy variables? Has the R improved? (b) What are the F and p-values with and without the dummy variables? Has the R improved? (c) Have the p-values of the Xs gotten better or worse with the addition of the two dummy variables? (d) Are the race and gender p-values significant? What do they tell us? Which race and gender has the greater value? (e) Based on the answers to questions a–d, has the model improved or not? Which model is the better predictor of loan amount? (f) Which model should you use to predict amount of loan applied for? (g) What is your conclusion?

Solution (Decision)

Step 1. State the hypothesis and action.
Step 2. Set the critical value.
Step 3. Select the methodology of data collection and statistical test.
Step 4. Run the statistics to obtain the p-value.
Step 5. Make the decision.

Model Summary

Model	R	R Square	Adjusted R Square	Std. Error of the Estimate
1	.225[a]	.051	-.003	29333.253

a. Predictors: (Constant), Gender of the individual., Years business owned before loan application., Years of prior work experience., Race of the individual., Age of the individual.

ANOVA[b]

Model		Sum of Squares	df	Mean Square	F	Sig.
1	Regression	4.042E9	5	8.084E8	.939	.460[a]
	Residual	7.572E10	88	8.604E8		
	Total	7.976E10	93			

a. Predictors: (Constant), Gender of the individual., Years business owned before loan application., Years of prior work experience., Race of the individual., Age of the individual.
b. Dependent Variable: Amount of loan applied for.

Coefficients[a]

Model		Unstandardized Coefficients		Standardized Coefficients	t	Sig.
		B	Std. Error	Beta		
1	(Constant)	3522.774	28087.128		.125	.900
	Age of the individual.	1154.397	757.116	.265	1.525	.131
	Years of prior work experience.	-20.144	1067.607	-.003	-.019	.985
	Years business owned before loan application.	-1097.750	990.868	-.169	-1.108	.271
	Race of the individual.	-3387.062	6134.217	-.058	-.552	.582
	Gender of the individual.	-4918.556	8916.469	-.058	-.552	.583

a. Dependent Variable: Amount of loan applied for.

USING THE COMPUTER

CORRELATION AND REGRESSION: USING DESCRIPTIVE STATISTICS

Instructions

For each of the following problems (13-8 to 13-13) use the data from Chapter 9 about political parties, with a sample size of 10. For each problem, write the steps of the hypothesis testing, similar to the hypothesis examples and problems. For each problem, information about steps 1–4 is as follows:

Step 1. For the *Introduction,* based on the information write the "one hypothesis" (Ho or Ha, one- or two-tailed). Because this is basic research rather than applied research (management decisions), don't state the action.

Step 2. The critical value will be .05 for all problems.

Step 3. For the *Method,* (a) be sure to clearly list Y and X(s) and their measurement levels and (b) state the appropriate test you ran.

Step 4. You actually run the statistics.

Step 5. For all of the problems, label and answer these questions:

(a) What is the R for correlation and R^2 for regression, and what do they tell you? Explain, using the variables.

(b) *Results.* Is the correlation or model significant? How certain are you that there is a relationship (that you aren't making a Type I error)?

(c) *Decision.* Should you fail to reject Ho (accept Ho) or reject Ho (accept Ha)?

(d) *Conclusion.* Put (a)–(c) together to make a clear conclusion about your research.

13-8   Select the two of the five variables that are appropriate to run a Pearson r correlation (assuming true scales are interval-level data). You are not sure of the direction of the relationship.

13-9   Select the one ordinal-level variable and either of the interval/ratio variables to run a Spearman rank rho correlation. You are not sure of the direction of the relationship.

13-10   Select the two interval/ratio-level variables and run a bivariate regression.

13-11 Run the appropriate regression using satisfaction as the Y and age and income (assuming interval level) as the Xs.

13-12 Run the appropriate regression using satisfaction as the Y and age and gender as the Xs. Run the appropriate regression using gender as the Y and age as the X.

YOUR RESEARCH STUDY

13-13 Which tests of association and/or tests of prediction can/will you use for your research study? Explain your answer.

14

Tests of Interaction
and Interrelationship

CONCEPTUAL OBJECTIVES

The conceptual objectives below also appear at appropriate places within the chapter at points when you will have accessed the information necessary to attain them. They appear again at the end of the chapter in the Summary and Glossary section, along with explanations that will enable you to meet the objectives.

After studying this chapter, you should be able to:

1. Compare one-way and two-way analysis of variance (ANOVA). Be sure to explain the main effect and interaction.

2. Compare two-way ANOVA, one-way multivariate analysis of variance (MANOVA), and factorial MANOVA.

3. Discuss the use of tests of interrelationship and the difference between factor and cluster analysis.

4. Explain the use of control variables, and list statistical tests that use them.

5. Define the following key terms (listed in order of their appearance in the chapter).

two-way analysis of variance (ANOVA)   factor analysis
multivariate analysis of variance (MANOVA)   cluster analysis
multivariate factorial ANOVA

SKILL DEVELOPMENT OBJECTIVES

The exercises that apply to particular skill development objectives are indicated directly beneath each numbered objective below. Periodic instructions within the chapter tell you when to stop reading and direct you to the end of the chapter to complete one or more of the skill development exercises.

After studying this chapter, you should be able to:

1. Test a hypothesis using two-way ANOVA.
   Decision problems 14-1 and 14-2, 14-4 and 14-5

2. Test a hypothesis using MANOVA.
   Decision problems 14-3, 14-6 and 14-7

The Research Process

(1) The research question/purpose of the study, literature review, and hypotheses.	(2) Research design methodology for collecting data and statistics.	(3) Data analysis and interpreting results.	(4) Discussing results and making conclusions.
• Introduction	• Method	• Results	• Discussion
Chapters 1–3	Chapters 4–8	Chapters 9–14	Chapters 9–14

In prior chapters we presented the research process shown above. Now we are running statistical tests selected in the Method section to test hypotheses/generate results and aid in decision making.

In this last statistics chapter we discuss advanced statistics, which may not be covered in your course. However, you should read the material to gain a basic understanding of some of the advanced statistics. Understanding p-values does not change, so these tests are not difficult to understand. Also, you will find the information helpful. For example, if you read a journal article that uses any of these statistics, you will understand what is being done and how to analyze the results. (Did any of your literature review articles use any of these techniques?) In addition, a time may come when you may need to use these statistical techniques in your own research. Thus, you can refer to this book for help in running the statistics and analyzing the computer printouts.

We begin this chapter with two-way ANOVA followed by MANOVA, both tests of interaction. We end with factor and cluster analysis, which are tests of interrelationship.

14.1 Two-Way Analysis of Variance (Two-Way ANOVA)

As discussed in Chapter 12, one-way ANOVA is a test of difference. However, when we add Xs, it becomes a test of interaction called two-way (or factorial) ANOVA. *Two-way analysis of variance (two-way ANOVA) tests if there are mean differences and a best combination of two or more nominal independent variables to maximize the value of one interval/ratio dependent variable.* In essence, two-way analysis of variance (two-way ANOVA) runs separate F-tests—one-way ANOVAs between the one Y and each of the Xs. However, with two-way ANOVA the results may be different from those of multiple F-tests, due to multiple comparison procedures. When you run multiple F-tests you increase the chances of finding a significant difference (making a Type I error, saying there is a difference when there really is none). When using two-way ANOVA you can be more confident that you are not making a Type I error.

The major advantage of two-way ANOVA over multiple one-way ANOVAs is the ability to analyze combinations of variables (interaction). It goes a step further than one-way by determining if there is a best combination of X groups/scales to maximize the value of the Y. Sometimes combinations of variables have a different effect than you would expect from each of the variables alone.

Main Effect and Interaction Effect

The *main effect* is the effect of a single X on one or more Ys. With two-way, the results are the same as separate one-way ANOVA tests to determine whether there are significant differences among Y means by the groups/scales of the nominal X. For example, which college class (X1 = 4 scales/groups, first to fourth year) studies more hours per week (Y)? Now let's add an X major (X2 = 3 groups/scales: business, education, psychology) and we have another main effect. However, we now have a two-way ANOVA and a test to determine the interaction.

The *interaction effect* (or Omnibus Test in SPSS) occurs when the effect of an X on some Y depends on the level of another X. An interaction effect occurs when there is a best combination of groups/scales of Xs. Continuing our example, an interaction could be found to conclude that the third-year (X1) business majors (X2) study the most hours (Y). If there is an interaction, you focus on it; if not, focus on main effects.

CONCEPTUAL OBJECTIVE 1
Compare one-way and two-way analysis of variance (ANOVA).
Be sure to explain the main effect and interaction.

Hypothesis testing.
A two-way ANOVA has one H for each X. Ho states no main effect (mean difference); Ha lists the main effect expected. There is also one H test of interaction as shown on the Decision Tree in Chapter 10. Ho states no interaction; Ha lists the expected interaction among the groups/scales of the Xs that will maximize the Y.

Factorial designs.

Factorial designs include two or more Xs (*factor* also refers to the X). Thus, in our example above, *class* and *major* are the two factors (Xs). The design is a 3 × 4 factorial design (based on the groups/scales of the Xs). The terms one-way and two-way also refer to the number of Xs in the design. With unmatched groups, participants are tested under only one scale of the X (male or female); matched group participants are tested repeatedly.

Recall from the Decision Tree that there are three ways to run two-way ANOVA based on the groups. The first is two-way (factorial) ANOVA, used with independent/unmatched groups. The second is repeated measures factorial ANOVA, used with dependent/matched groups. Repeated measures is also known as a *randomized block* design, and it is commonly a true experimental design. The third way is mixed factorial ANOVA, used with both matched and unmatched groups. How the tests are run is often based on how the data are entered into the computer and the software commands. In this chapter we cover only the most commonly used two-way ANOVA. However, if you can read a factorial ANOVA you can read a repeated measures or mixed ANOVA. Refer to the Decision Tree and the material on tests of interaction in Chapter 10 for examples of these three designs.

Two-way ANOVA conclusions.

Two-way conclusions are based on the design of the study. A true experimental design using repeat measures may conclude the cause and effect of a treatment because participants have been randomly assigned to groups. However, with the two-way unmatched groups design, you can conclude understanding and explanations, but not cause and effect. With a mixed design, you have an X that cannot be assigned to a manipulated treatment (participant X), such as gender. Thus, you cannot conclude that a participant X (gender) has a cause-and-effect relationship, but you can infer a causal relationship with the repeated measures X if it is randomly assigned and treatment manipulated.

Two-way ANOVA assumptions.

Two-way ANOVA is a parametric test and therefore assumes interval/ratio Y, independent participant values/score taken randomly from a normal distribution with equal sample size and variance in the populations. Two-way ANOVA is a robust test, and thus the normal distribution with equal variance is not as important as the other assumptions. Also, with a large sample size, 25–30 or more, you can assume a normal distribution with equal variance anyway.

Unlike tests of difference, there are no nonparametric equivalents to tests of interaction. Therefore, using true rating scales is generally considered acceptable with tests of interaction, but keep the scales wide (1–5 acceptable, 1–7 good, 1–9 better).

Sample size (N) needed to effectively run two-way ANOVA.

As with regression, you want to have approximately 10 (or more) participants per X. Thus, with five X you would need a sample of around 50 or more. But remember that the larger the sample size, the greater the chance of finding main effects and interactions (or not making a Type II error by saying there are no differences when there really are).

Now that we have covered the important basics, let's read an example with a two-way computer printout in Box 14.1 below, followed by an example of a two-way ANOVA hypothesis in Box 14.2.

Box 14.1   Reading Two-Way ANOVA Results

Assigning Salespeople to Territories

You are a sales manager. You have four territories and three salaried salespeople. They continually rotate territories; one territory is without sales calls for a period of time. To increase sales, your company has decided to hire another salesperson. You're not sure if you should continue to have your salespeople rotate territories or if you should give each one a territory. If you give them each a territory, you're not sure how to decide who gets which territory. You have decided to determine whether there is a significant difference in the sales ability of your staff, and whether they make significantly greater sales in one territory than in another. If there is a significant difference, you will assign salespeople to the territory in which they are more productive. If not, you will assign the territories based on some other method. Here we have a 4 × 3 factorial design. For the past three periods you calculated the mean sales for each salesperson by territory and two-way ANOVA; see the modified results from SPSS below. We only show the most relevant information.

Omnibus Test[a]

Likelihood Ratio Chi-Square	df	Sig.
26.076	5	.001

Dependent Variable: Sales
Model: (Intercept), territory, salesperson
a. Compares the fitted model against the intercept-only model.

Tests of Model Effects

| | Type III | | |
Source	Wald Chi-Square	df	Sig.
(Intercept)	98.626	1	.000
territory	14.027	2	.001
salesperson	7.321	3	.003

Dependent Variable: Income
Model: (Intercept), territory, salesperson

Estimates

| Salesperson | Mean | Std. Error | 95% Wald Confidence Interval | |
			Lower	Upper
1	144.0			
2	122.6			
3	125.0			

(continued)

Estimates

Territory	Mean	Std. Error	95% Wald Confidence Interval	
			Lower	Upper
A	81.7			
B	91.3			
C	106.0			
D	112.6			

Test of Model Effects. The main effect Wald chi-square and p-values are essentially two separate one-way ANOVAs, calculated with multiple comparisons. We can see that there is a significant difference in the sales by territory (p = .001) and sales by salesperson (p = .003). There are significantly more sales in at least one territory and by salesperson. Ignore the top value of .000 (intercept) because it is not really needed.

2-Way Interaction (Omnibus Test). The two-way interaction tells us if there is a best combination of territory and salesperson to maximize total company sales. There is an interaction (p = .001).

Means. As shown, salesperson 1 has the highest sales (144.0) and territory D (112.6) However, because there is a best combination of territory by salesperson, you need to run descriptive statistics to see the difference, which is shown below.

Sales Means (in Thousands of Dollars)

	Salesperson			
Territory	1	2	3	Totals
A	44	25	12.7	81.7
B	34	28	29.3	91.3
C	32.7	45	28.3	106.0
D	33.3	24.6	54.7	112.6
Totals	144.0	122.6	125.0	391.6

We can see that salesperson 1 has the highest level of sales (144) and that territory D has the most total sales (112.6). Salesperson 1 has the highest level of sales in both territories A and B (44 and 34). Salesperson 2 has the highest level of sales in territory C (45). Salesperson 3 has the highest level of sales in territory D (54.7).

Post Hoc Tests. Note that we just did a comparison of sales Y territory without any statistics. With, or after, two-way ANOVA, you can run test to determine which combination is the best for you, but this is beyond the scope of this book.

Box 14.2   Example of a Two-Way ANOVA Hypothesis

We now present the results of the computer printout in Box 14.1 through hypothesis testing.

Instructions

Clearly list the five steps of hypothesis testing and answer these questions within the appropriate step. For *step 1*, be sure to clearly write the null hypothesis. Remember that you now have multiple hypotheses, one for each X to test differences and one for the interaction. For *step 2*, select .05. For *step 3*, list the dependent and independent variables with their measurement levels and the appropriate statistical test. For *step 4*, see the modified computer printout in Box 14.1; however, write the percentage of confidence that the means are significantly different and for the interaction. For *step 5*, answer the following questions. (a) Which salesperson sells the most? Is the difference significant? (b) Which territory has the highest sales? Is the difference significant? (c) Is there an interaction effect? (d) Should we fail to reject the hypotheses (accept Ho1, Ho2, and Ho3) or reject Ho1–3 (accept Ha1–3)? (e) Conclusion/action—Should you assign specific salespeople to specific territories or use another method? If you assign territories, who should get each territory?

Decision (Solution)

Step 1. State the hypothesis.

   Ho1: All salespeople have equal sales.
   Ha1: All salespeople do not have equal sales.
   Ho2: All territories have equal sales.
   Ha2: All territories do not have equal sales.
   Ho3: There is no interaction effect (no best combination of Xs).
   Ha3: There is an interaction effect.

Step 2. Select the critical value. As researchers, use .05.

Step 3. Select the methodology of data collection and statistical test.

   The Y (sales) is interval/ratio and the two Xs (salesperson and territory) are nominal levels of measurement. Thus, the two-way ANOVA is the appropriate test.

Step 4. Run the statistics to obtain the p-value.

   We are 99% confident that there is a significant difference in salespeople, territory, and interaction (or we are not making a Type I error, saying there are differences and interaction when there are none).

Step 5. Make the decision.

   (a) Sales by salesperson are significantly different (p = .003). Salesperson 1 sells the most (mean = $144,000).

   (b) Sales by territory are significantly different (p = .001). Territory D sells the most (mean = $112,600).

   (c) There is a best combination of salespeople by territory (p = .001). Answer (b) explains it.

   (d) We should reject Ho1, Ho2, and Ho3 (accept Ha 1–3) because there is a significant difference in salespeople and territories; and there is a best combination of salespeople by territory, as shown below.

   (e) Assign people to territories as follows:

   Salesperson 1   Territory A   (sales 44)
   Salesperson 2   Territory C   (sales 45)
   Salesperson 3   Territory D   (sales 54.7)
   Salesperson 4   Territory B   (new person assigned)

   To make this autocratic (not democratic) decision, simply take the highest sales per person per territory. Read down the columns. The new salesperson gets territory B because 1 is highest at both A and B, but the highest of the two is A.

Two-way ANOVA with SPSS 19.

Two-way ANOVA is also called univariate ANOVA.

1. Click *Analyze* on the toolbar.

2. Scroll down to *Generalized Linear Models* and click *Generalized Linear Models* a second time, in the menu to the right.

3. In the Type of Model view, just use the default setting *Scale Response* and *Linear* (or you can skip this step).

4. In the Response view, enter your one Y in the *Dependent Variable* box. Ignore the other boxes.

5. In the Predictor view, enter your two or more nominal Xs in the *Factors* box. Ignore the other boxes.

6. In the Model view move your Xs into the *Model* box.

7. In the EM Means view move the X2 into the *Display Means for* box.

8. You can use the default setting or just skip the other views.

9. Click *OK* to generate the results in the data window.

Multiple comparisons (Tukey).

When we reject the Ho, we need to know which mean(s) is significantly different from the others. By simply looking at the means, we can determine which is larger and smaller, which works well when there are only two groups/scales of X (gender). However, when using two-way ANOVA with three or more groups/scales of X (religion), we cannot conclude which mean(s) are significantly different without performing an analysis by running one or more tests—Tukey. Because race has only two scales/groups, we know which one is larger by simply looking at the means. However, with source of financing there are three groups, so we need a Tukey to be sure of significant differences.

One-way ANOVA (Tukey) with SPSS 19.

As a review from Chapter 12, follow these steps to run one-way ANOVA with three or more groups with Tukey and descriptives. To see the Tukey printout, return to Chapter 12.

1. Click *Analyze* on the toolbar.

2. Scroll down to *Compare Means* and on the menu at the right click *One-Way ANOVA*.

3. Click and drag your scale variable to the right in the *Dependent* list and your nominal independent variable into the *Factors* box.

4. Click *Post Hoc*, check *Tukey*, and click *Continue* to compare the differences between the three means.

5. Click *Options* and check *Descriptive Statistics* and *Continue* to get the means and standard deviations of your Y.

6. Click *OK* to generate the results in the data window.

**STOP READING and turn to the end of the chapter
to complete decision problems 14-1 and 14-2.**

Multiple Comparisons

Recall that when using two-way ANOVA with three or more groups/scales of X (religion), we cannot conclude which mean(s) are significantly different without running one or more tests. To test which means are significantly different, we have two basic options. First, we could run a series of T-tests to compare each set of means. However, the power of individual tests is low, increasing the probability of making a Type II error (saying the means are not different when they really are). A more powerful test is Tukey's multiple comparison method.

Tukey's multiple comparison is run after two-way ANOVA when there is a significant main effect with at least three group means to identify the pairs that are significantly different. As Tukey is an advanced test and Excel does not feature it, we do not present computer printouts, examples, or decision problems. As you can see above, we did not use Tukey with the two-way ANOVA printout, example, or decision problem. Thus, we are not certain which mean pairs of sales by person and territory are significantly different.

14.2 Multivariate Analysis of Variance (MANOVA)

Multivariate analysis means statistical analysis that involves three or more variables and more than one Y. However, multivariate analysis of variance (MANOVA) can have one or more than one X, with or without an interaction effect. There are actually two types of MANOVA, which are based on the number of Xs. When there is only one X, you have what we call one-way MANOVA, or commonly just MANOVA. When there are two or more Xs, you have two-way or factorial MANOVA. Recall that one-way and two-way refer to the number of Xs, and factorial means two or more Xs. In order to have an interaction among Xs, you need at least two Xs (you need a factorial design). Let's discuss both one-way and factorial MANOVA separately in this section after some introductory information.

The *variate* in multivariate means that a set of variables can be represented with one equation. A variate is formed as a linear combination of variables, each contributing to the overall meaning of the variate, based on a function of the measured variables involved in an analysis. So as with multiple regression you have a set of variables and an equation with MANOVA.

Multiple regression with one Y and only covariate control variables (and/or with dummy variables) yields the same inferences as MANOVA, to which it is statistically equivalent. *General (or generalized) linear models* can implement regression models with multiple dependent variables. MANOVA is more appropriate than two-way ANOVA when there is more than one Y and it is inappropriate to do a series of univariate one- or two-way ANOVA tests. There are two major reasons for performing a MANOVA rather than several univariate ANOVAs.

First, there are many measurement instruments/tests that are designed to measure various aspects of one overlying variable/factor (such as SAT scores combining math and verbal), and there are theories of motivation with three levels (ERG theory) and five levels (hierarchy of needs) of motivation. A detailed example appears below.

Second, as a test of interaction factorial MANOVA reports the interaction among the Xs. As two-way (factorial) ANOVA provides new X interaction information that separate one-way ANOVAs do not, factorial MANOVA provides X interaction information that a series of univariate ANOVAs does not provide. Step-down analysis, like stepwise regression, can be run by computing F values successively. Each value is computed after the effects of the previous Y are eliminated. Now that we have some background of the *why* of MANOVA, let's get to the *how*.

One-Way MANOVA (2+ Ys, 1 X, No Interaction Effect)

Multivariate analysis of variance (MANOVA) determines mean differences of two or more interval/ratio dependent variables based on one nominal independent variable. Recall that an interaction takes place between Xs, so you can't have an interaction with only one X. One X means that you can have only one main effect.

In essence, MANOVA runs separate one-way ANOVAs between the two or more Ys and the one X. However, with MANOVA the results may be different from multiple one-way ANOVAs, due to multiple comparison procedures. When you run multiple F-tests you increase the chances of finding a significant difference and making a Type I error (saying there is a difference when there really is none). When using MANOVA you can be more confident that you are not making a Type I error.

MANOVA designs.

There are two MANOVA research designs. As shown on the Decision Tree, there are two methods of running the MANOVA test: (1) independent/unmatched groups, and (2) repeated measures using dependent/matched groups.

Note that you cannot have a mixed design because you only have one X. We illustrate only the unmatched design. However, if you can read the unmatched groups MANOVA, you can read the matched MANOVA as well.

One-way MANOVA and two-way (factorial) MANOVA assumptions.

MANOVA is a parametric test and, therefore, assumes interval/ratio Ys (and nominal Xs), a random sample with a normal distribution, and equal variance in the populations. The new and very critical assumption is that all Ys are measuring parts of the same overall variable/factor; thus, the Ys must be correlated. You should run correlations to test relationships. Therefore, you cannot simply combine any Y to run a MANOVA. A good place to start is to run a correlation with the Ys to see if they are in fact related (measuring the same thing). If not, run multiple univariate ANOVAs.

MANOVA examples.

In the Ski West study, both the personality test and job performance evaluation have multiple parts put together to make one score. But HR never correlated the parts, which is in error. Below is a good example.

John Miner developed the Miner Sentence Completion Scale-Form T as a projective testing instrument, which has been shown to measure motivational factors associated with entrepreneurial success; it is designed to measure entrepreneurial aptitude. The measurement instrument includes five parts: self-achievement, risk avoidance, feedback of results, personal innovation, and planning for the future. The scores of the five parts are combined to provide one aptitude score. Thus, a research study used the total scores and five parts (6 Y) and compared the 6 score results of people who owned their own business to people who were managers working for others (1 X). The results indicated that the business owners did in fact have a higher entrepreneurial aptitude on total scores and all five parts. This research study helps validate the measurement's instrument, as people who own their own business were hypothesized to have a higher entrepreneurial aptitude. Thus, people can take the Miner test to better understand if they have entrepreneurial aptitude before they start their own business.

Unlike with tests of difference, there are no nonparametric equivalents to MANOVA. Therefore, using true Likert scales is generally considered acceptable, but keep the scales wide (at least 1–7 and preferably more).

Sample size (N) needed to effectively run MANOVA and factorial MANOVA.

Similar to all tests using multiple variables, MANOVA requires at least 10 participants per variable and preferably more. Thus, the Miner example with 6 Ys and 1 X requires an N of at least 70 and 140. For factorial ANOVA, you should have at least 10 participants per Y and each additional X. Thus, if we had three Xs in the Minor research design we would need an N of at least 90, and preferably 180.

As you can see, MANOVA is an advanced statistic and factorial MANOVA is even more complex. A MANOVA computer printout appears in Box 14.3 that uses our bank loan example. However, rather than list all the steps of hypotheses testing again, we include the decision at the end of the box.

MANOVA with SPSS 19.

Here are the steps to running MANOVA.

1. Click *Analyze* on the toolbar.

2. Scroll down to *General Linear Model* and click *Multivariate*.

3. Click and drag your two or more scale Ys to the *Dependent Variable* box at the right and your one nominal X into the *Fixed Factor* box. (Ignore the *Covariate(s)* and *WLS* boxes.)

4. If any of your Xs have three or more groups, click *Post Hoc*, move the X into the *Post Hoc Test* box, and check *Tukey* and *Continue* to compare the differences between the Y means.

5. Click *Options* and move your X to the *Display Means for* box, and check *Descriptive Statistics* and *Continue* to get the means and standard deviations of your Y.

6. Click *OK* to generate the results in the data window.

Here is the important printout. As we can see, the race by years business was owned before loan application and the amount of loan applied for are not significantly different between the Whites and African Americans ($p = .593$, $p = .715$).

Box 14.3   Reading MANOVA Results

Continuing with the bank-financing discrimination example, you want to know if there is a difference in income and amount of loan applied for by race.
The SPSS 19 results appear below.

(continued)

Descriptive Statistics

	Race of the individual.	Mean	Std. Deviation	N
Amount of loan applied for.	African-American	29647.06	25451.187	51
	white	27418.60	33543.314	43
	Total	28627.66	29285.482	94
Income	African-American	36649.02	16277.621	51
	white	43383.72	20891.465	43
	Total	39729.79	18733.340	94

Multivariate Tests[b]

Effect		Value	F	Hypothesis df	Error df	Sig.
Intercept	Pillai's Trace	.827	217.560[a]	2.000	91.000	.000
	Wilks' Lambda	.173	217.560[a]	2.000	91.000	.000
	Hotelling's Trace	4.782	217.560[a]	2.000	91.000	.000
	Roy's Largest Root	4.782	217.560[a]	2.000	91.000	.000
race	Pillai's Trace	.044	2.074[a]	2.000	91.000	.132
	Wilks' Lambda	.956	2.074[a]	2.000	91.000	.132
	Hotelling's Trace	.046	2.074[a]	2.000	91.000	.132
	Roy's Largest Root	.046	2.074[a]	2.000	91.000	.132

a. Exact statistic
b. Design: Intercept + race

Tests of Between-Subjects Effects

Source	Dependent Variable	Type III Sum of Squares	df	Mean Square	F	Sig.
Corrected Model	Amount of loan applied for.	1.159E8	1	1.159E8	.134	.715
	Income	1.058E9	1	1.058E9	3.083	.082
Intercept	Amount of loan applied for.	7.597E10	1	7.597E10	87.759	.000
	Income	1.494E11	1	1.494E11	435.346	.000
race	Amount of loan applied for.	1.159E8	1	1.159E8	.134	.715
	Income	1.058E9	1	1.058E9	3.083	.082
Error	Amount of loan applied for.	7.964E10	92	8.657E8		
	Income	3.158E10	92	3.433E8		
Total	Amount of loan applied for.	1.568E11	94			
	Income	1.810E11	94			
Corrected Total	Amount of loan applied for.	7.976E10	93			
	Income	3.264E10	93			

a. R Squared = .001 (Adjusted R Squared = -.009)
b. R Squared = .032 (Adjusted R Squared = .022)

Multivariate Tests. Are income and loan applied for together significantly different by race? No (p = .132).

Tests of Between-Subjects Effects. Is there a significant difference in income (p = .082) or loan (p = .715) separately by race at the .05 level? No (p = .082 and p = .715). Also, the adjusted R-Squares are low (–.009 and .022).

Descriptive Statistics. As we can see, African Americans ask for larger loans than Whites do (M = $29,647.06 vs. $27,418.60) and Whites have a higher level of income (M = $43,383.72 vs. $36,649.02). However, as stated above, the differences are not significant at the .05 level.

Hypothesis Test Discussion

Accept Ho (reject Ha). The conclusion is that the income and amount of loan applied for are not significantly different by race at the .05 level in the sample. However, the difference in income is significant at the .10 level.

STOP READING and turn to the end of the chapter to complete decision problem 14-3.

Factorial MANOVA (2+ Ys, 2+ Xs, Interaction Effect)

Multivariate factorial ANOVA determines mean differences, and whether there are interactions among two or more interval/ratio dependent variables and two or more nominal independent variables. As with two-way ANOVA and MANOVA, you get an interaction multivariate value on the computer printout; it also provides a test of difference in the means of two or more interval/ratio Ys based on two or more nominal Xs. Thus, it is more advanced than two-way ANOVA and MANOVA.

As with two-way ANOVA, the major advantage over running multiple one-way ANOVA is the ability to analyze combinations of variables (interaction). Sometimes combinations of variables have a different effect than you would expect from each of the variables alone.

Factorial MANOVA designs.

The computer prints interactions between Xs and Ys. As shown on the Decision Tree, there are three designs or ways to run factorial MANOVA, based on the groups:

- factorial MANOVA, used with independent/unmatched groups;
- repeated measures factorial MANOVA, used with dependent/matched groups; and
- mixed factorial MANOVA, used with both matched and unmatched groups.

How the MANOVAs are run is based on the method of data entry and the commands used in the computer software/program.

Box 14.4   Reading Factorial MANOVA Results

Continuing with our bank loan discrimination example, from our factorial MANOVA computer printout we get the answers to four things that result in nine hypotheses.

First, is there a difference in income and amount of loan applied for by either race or gender *alone*? This takes four hypotheses (H1–H4) and statistical tests (p-value). In essence, the factorial MANOVA runs four T-tests with one Y (income, then amount of loan applied) and one X (race, then gender).

Second, is there a difference in income and amount of loan applied for by race and gender *together*? This takes two hypotheses (H5–H6) and tests (p-value). In essence, the factorial MANOVA runs two-way ANOVAs with one Y (income, then amount of loan applied for) and two Xs (race and gender).

Third, is race and/or gender alone significantly different than income and amount of loan applied for together? This takes two hypotheses (H7–H8) and tests (p-value). This is the real factorial MANOVA test with two Ys (income and amount of loan applied for) and two Xs (race and gender).

Test of Between-Subjects Effects. This part of the printout answers our first two questions. There is no significant difference in income (H1, p = .162) or amount of loan applied for (H2, p = .268) by race alone. There is no significant difference in income (H3, p = .824) or amount of loan applied for (H4, p = .355) by gender alone. There is also no significant difference in income (H5, p = .781) or amount of loan applied for (H6, p = .257) by race and gender together. Also note that the adjusted R-squares are very low (.002 and –.009), indicating that the factorial MANOVA model is not very good.

Multivariate Tests. This part of the printout answers our second and third questions: Race alone (H7, p = .089) and gender alone (H8, p = .548)

Hypotheses Test Discussion. Accept all nine Ho (reject Ha). As you can see, the only significant finding is for the intercept, which is just a plug-in value that has no meaning. The conclusion is that there is no significant difference in income and the amount of loan applied for by race or gender, and there is no interaction effect.

Multivariate Tests [b]

Effect		Value	F	Hypothesis df	Error df	Sig.
Intercept	Pillai's Trace	.693	100.586[a]	2.000	89.000	.000
	Wilks' Lambda	.307	100.586[a]	2.000	89.000	.000
	Hotelling's Trace	2.260	100.586[a]	2.000	89.000	.000
	Roy's Largest Root	2.260	100.586[a]	2.000	89.000	.000
race	Pillai's Trace	.053	2.492[a]	2.000	89.000	.089
	Wilks' Lambda	.947	2.492[a]	2.000	89.000	.089
	Hotelling's Trace	.056	2.492[a]	2.000	89.000	.089
	Roy's Largest Root	.056	2.492[a]	2.000	89.000	.089
gender	Pillai's Trace	.013	.606[a]	2.000	89.000	.548
	Wilks' Lambda	.987	.606[a]	2.000	89.000	.548
	Hotelling's Trace	.014	.606[a]	2.000	89.000	.548
	Roy's Largest Root	.014	.606[a]	2.000	89.000	.548
race * gender	Pillai's Trace	.020	.916[a]	2.000	89.000	.404
	Wilks' Lambda	.980	.916[a]	2.000	89.000	.404
	Hotelling's Trace	.021	.916[a]	2.000	89.000	.404
	Roy's Largest Root	.021	.916[a]	2.000	89.000	.404

a. Exact statistic
b. Design: Intercept + race + gender + race * gender

Tests of Between-Subjects Effects

Source	Dependent Variable	Type III Sum of Squares	df	Mean Square	F	Sig.
Corrected Model	Income	1.101E9	3	3.669E8	1.047	.376
	Amount of loan applied for.	1.900E9	3	6.332E8	.732	.536
Intercept	Income	6.954E10	1	6.954E10	198.467	.000
	Amount of loan applied for.	4.474E10	1	4.474E10	51.717	.000
race	Income	6.970E8	1	6.970E8	1.989	.162
	Amount of loan applied for.	1.076E9	1	1.076E9	1.244	.268
gender	Income	17437126.459	1	17437126.459	.050	.824
	Amount of loan applied for.	7.467E8	1	7.467E8	.863	.355
race * gender	Income	27125426.679	1	27125426.679	.077	.781
	Amount of loan applied for.	1.125E9	1	1.125E9	1.301	.257
Error	Income	3.154E10	90	3.504E8		
	Amount of loan applied for.	7.786E10	90	8.651E8		
Total	Income	1.810E11	94			
	Amount of loan applied for.	1.568E11	94			
Corrected Total	Income	3.264E10	93			
	Amount of loan applied for.	7.976E10	93			

a. R Squared = .034 (Adjusted R Squared = .002)
b. R Squared = .024 (Adjusted R Squared = -.009)

Factorial MANOVA with SPSS 19.

Here are the steps to run MANOVA. Note that the only difference between MANOVA and factorial MANOVA is that the number of independent variables is two or more, as shown in step 3. Box 14.4 contains an actual printout from SPSS 19.

1. Click *Analyze* on the toolbar.

2. Scroll down to *General Linear Model* and click *Multivariate*.

3. Click and drag your two or more scale Ys to the *Dependent Variable* box at the right and move your two or more nominal Xs into the *Fixed Factor* box. (Ignore the *Covariate(s)* and *WLS* boxes.)

4. If any of your Xs have three or more groups, click *Post Hoc*, move the X into the *Post Hoc Test* box, and check *Tukey* and *Continue* to compare the differences between the Y means.

5. Click *Options* and move your Xs to the *Display Means for* box, and check *Descriptive Statistics* and *Continue* to get the means and standard deviations of your Y.

6. Click *OK* to generate the results in the data window.

14.3 Factor and Cluster Analysis

Research methods with dependent variables are commonly called *dependence methods*, whereas research designs that only include independent variables are commonly called *interdependence methods*. So far we have discussed dependence methods. Now we turn to interdependence methods.

Interdependence Methods

Recall that the two major tests of interrelationship are factor and cluster analysis (see the Decision Tree), and that they only include one variable (or only Xs, no Y). Variables are *interrelated* when they are correlated—they belong together as they have overlapping measurement characteristics. Tests of interrelationship are used to reduce a larger number of Xs into a more manageable number. *Factor analysis reduces a larger number of independent variables into a limited number of interrelated factors by grouping them together. Cluster analysis reduces a large number of participants into a limited number of interrelated groups by classifying them (identifying which group they belong with).* When the groups of variables are put together (factors) and the participants are placed into categories (factors), the factors are not given a name by the computer. When you look at the grouping you have to give it a name, as it essentially becomes a new variable that combines multiple variables or participants. Because factor and cluster analysis are advanced statistics that are not commonly used outside of measurement research, there are no decision problems for the tests of interaction.

Factor Analysis

Factor analysis is commonly used in research to test the validity of a measurement instrument, as discussed in Chapter 8 (Section 8.2, Construct Validity).

Exploratory and confirmatory factor analysis.

There are two major classifications of factor analysis. *Exploratory factor analysis* (EFA) is commonly used when you are not certain how many factors may exist among the set of variables. In essence, you run EFA to find out how many new variables you will have by combining multiple Xs. *Confirmatory factor analysis* (CFA) is commonly used when, based on the literature and the theory you develop, you know how many factors there should be and which variables go with each factor. CFA is used to test construct validity because it confirms that the theory (measurement instrument) does in fact measure what you claim it measures.

In essence, factor analysis develops a matrix of intercorrelations among several Xs, none of which is considered as being dependent on another. The linear combinations of variables are called *factors*. The factors account for the variance in the data as a whole. The best combination makes up the first principal component and is the first factor. The second principal component is defined as the best linear combination of variables for explaining the variance not accounted for by the first factor. This process continues until all the variance is accounted for. There can be any number of factors, but the number is usually small. The correlation coefficients are called *loadings*, and each variable loads on the factor with the highest coefficient. The factor loads appear in the computer printout in Box 14.5.

Box 14.5   Reading Factor Analysis Results

You have decided to empirically test ERG, the need for existence (E), relatedness (R), and growth (G) Motivation Theory developed by C. P. Alderfer in 1972. Ho: ERG Theory is a valid measure of three levels of need satisfaction in organizations. You surveyed 152 participants from all over the U.S. With the need for a minimum of 10 participants per item, your sample is on the small size.

The following material is adapted from an SPSS computer printout that actually had multiple pages. The most important sections to analyze—the Rotated Component Matrix and the Total Variance Explained—appear below. Note that we (not the computer) manually made the numbers **bold** and *italic* to make the factor analysis easier to read and understand.

Total Variance Explained

Component	Initial Eigenvalues			Rotation Sums of Squared Loadings		
	Total	% of Variance	Cumulative %	Total	% of Variance	Cumulative %
1				6.321	42.100	42.100
2				1.519	10.100	52.200
3				1.094	7.300	59.500
4						
5						
6						
7						
8						
9						
10						
11						
12						
13						
14						
15						

Extraction Method: Principal Component Analysis.

(continued)

Rotated Component Matrix[a]

	Component		
	1	2	3
1 Pay satisfaction	055	.191	**.884**
2 Pay increase	093	203	**806**
3 Benefit package	153	**48**	237
4 Working conditions	127	**788**	.006
5 Job security	208	**497**	.236
6 Friendly people	**593**	*464*	.085
7 Socializing	**594**	249	.149
8 Being accepted	**664**	347	286
9 Close friends	**716**	17.0	.059
10 Boss relations	**.734**	.277	.028
11 Advancement	*47.8*	.066	**508**
12 Challenging work	**.544**	.301	285
13 Self-decisions	**621**	*2̶3̶*	187
14 Learning opportunity	**644**	*508*	27.2
15 Job recognition	**.707**	*448*	164

Extraction Method: Principal Component Analysis.
Rotation Method: Varimax with Kaiser Normalization.

Rotated Component Matrix. The matrix values should be the primary analysis in factor analysis. The factor loadings (numbers given) are the correlation of the item with that factor (1, 2, 3) score. Each item correlation between each factor is analyzed. Ideally, the factor loading of each item should be very high on one factor and very low on the others.

The highest correlation, which should be >.40, is considered to be the factor to which the item is grouped (bold values, which are not bold on an actual printout). However, when the difference between the two highest correlations is less than .05, it loads on two factors. Item 11 is an example because the difference in correlations is only .03.

Also, all factor loadings of .40 are considered to be high. (All bold and underlined correlations, done by us and not the computer, are above .40). Thus, even when the difference between the two highest correlations is greater than .05, when both values are greater than .40 the item is considered somewhat problematic because it is highly correlated with multiple factors (multicollinearity). Items 6 and 13–15 are examples. We use italics for the lower of the two values.

The results of factor analysis identified three factors. This is the number we expected—one for E, R, and G. However, E, R, and G items did not group together on separate factors, as needed to be valid. Items 1 and 2 were about pay, and both loaded on factor 3. Items 3–5 loaded on factor 2. To be a valid measure, all five items (1–5) should have loaded on the same factor, without any of the relatedness or growth items.

All five of the relatedness needs items (6–10) loaded on factor 1. Unexpectedly, four of the five growth needs also loaded on factor 1; opportunity for advancement (item 11) primarily loaded on factor 3 as well. Items 6 and 13–15 had factor loads of greater than .40 in factor 2. Item 11 had a double load with the higher value in factor 3, and items 13–15 had factor loads greater than .40 in factor 2, which indicates somewhat problematic correlations (multicollinearity). For ERG to be valid, all five relatedness items should have loaded on one factor that was different than that of Growth. Plus, all five growth items should have also loaded together on a separate factor.

Naming the Matrix Factors. Note that the printout does not use the terms *Factors* (1–3); it just features the numbers 1–3 as column headings in the Component section. It also does not give the factors a name—naming the factors is your job. Overall, based on the factor analysis, factor 1 should be named something like "higher-level needs," as it combines both relatedness and growth needs. Factor 2 should be named something like "other existence needs." Factor 3 should be named "pay existence needs."

Total Value Explained. On the computer printout, the final statistics are given without the numbers that are not needed. In essence, the *Eigenvalue* takes the place of the p-value. An Eigenvalue of >1.0 is considered to be significant. Thus, all three factor Eigenvalues (6.321, 1.519, 1.094) are significant in the printout. In essence, percentage of variance explained is similar to the R-square value in regression. However, unlike regression, in which the Xs explain the variance in Y, the variance is between the factors. Recall that there is no Y with factor analysis.

Decision. Reject the hypothesis (Ha) because the five items for E, R, and G do not load together on three separate factors. Relatedness and growth needs are not clearly separate levels of motivating factors (they appear to measure the same need). Thus, it is more appropriate to think of needs as having two levels, rather than three.

Because ERG is not valid, we cannot take the five measures for E, R, and G and combine them as one standard score and call it an interval/ratio level of measure. Thus, each of the 15 items must be considered as separate variables, and the level of measure of each would be ordinal (or with true scales it would be interval/ratio).

Researchers who develop measurement instruments work to perfect them. For example, some of the questions could be dropped, others could be worded differently, and new ones could be added. Then the instrument is given to a new sample and tested again using factor analysis. This revision process can take several rounds, and the instrument may never be validated. You should understand that it is much easier to use a previously validated questionnaire than to develop and validate your own.

Factor analysis with SPSS 19.

Here are the steps to running factor analysis, using the example above.

1. Click *Analyze* on the toolbar.
2. Scroll down to *Dimension Reduction* and click *Factor*.
3. Click and drag your variables into the *Variables* box. (Ignore the *Selection* box.)
4. Click *Rotation*, and check *Varimax* and *Continue*.
5. You can click *Descriptives* and check *Univariate* and *Correlations* if you want them.
6. Click *OK* to generate the results in the data window.

Cluster Analysis

When using cluster analysis, the participants to be grouped together can be people or objects. Cluster analysis is used as a "classification" device in medicine, biology, engineering, economics, marketing, and other areas. Cluster analysis shares similarities with factor analysis, especially when it is applied to people. Participants are grouped based on similar characteristics they share, resulting in a small number of mutually exclusive and exhaustive groups. It differs from logistic regression and discriminant analysis/function because logistic and discriminant begin with a well-defined nominal Y (two or more groups/scales with distinct sets of characteristics) in search of a set of Xs to separate them.

Cluster analysis starts with an undifferentiated group of people/objects and reorganizes them into homogeneous subgroups. For example, you may want to group employees based on their insurance or retirement needs, or dimensions of job performance. You first select the sample to be clustered. The sample could be buyers, medical patients, inventory, products, animals, employees, and so on. Then you define the Xs on which to measure the people/objects. The Xs could be financial status, political affiliation, market segment characteristics, symptom classes, product competition definitions, productivity attributes, and so on. Now you are ready to run cluster analysis, as in the example below.

Example.

You work for Ford Motor Company and you want to segment the car-buying population into various distinct market segments or types of customers. The next step in cluster analysis is to define the variables on which to measure distinct types of customers. You select age, income, and family size as the variables to measure types of customers to be clustered together. You have a sample of 1,000 people to classify. Box 14.6 contains an SPSS 19 printout of the cluster analysis, and Figure 14.1 contains a graphical representation generated from the SPSS results.

In Box 14.6 and Figure 14.1, the first cluster may be targeted as potential minivan Aerostar buyers, based on larger family sizes (4.125) with moderate incomes ($40,254). The second cluster could be Focus and Mustang—small and sports and performance sedans based on younger people (25.258) with moderate incomes ($35,526) and smaller family size

Box 14.6   Reading Cluster Analysis

Final Cluster Centers

	Cluster 1	2	3	4
Age	33.254	25.158	49.258	35.782
Income	40524.25	35526.01	66000.62	41559.27
Family size	4.125	2.326	2.062	3.633

Number of Cases in each Cluster

Cluster	1	318.000
	2	305.000
	3	142.000
	4	235.000
Valid		1000.000
Missing		.000

Figure 14.1   Cluster Analysis of Car Buyers

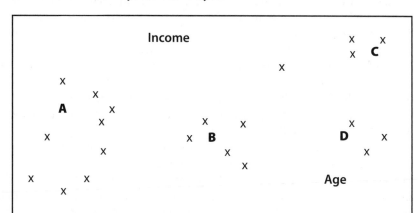

(2.326) who want a smaller car. The third cluster could be Lincoln, luxury buyers with high incomes ($66,000) who are a bit older (49.258) with smaller or older children in their family size (2.062). The fourth cluster would be the Taurus for moderate-income people ($41,559) who want a midsized car.

Cluster analysis with SPSS 19.

Here are the steps to running cluster analysis.

1. Click *Analyze* on the toolbar.

2. Scroll down to *Classify* and click *K-Means Cluster*. You should have at least three variables. Note that you can also select *Two-step* (using both scale and categorical variables) and *Hierarchical* for advanced methods.

3. Click and drag your variables into the *Variables* box. (Ignore the *Selection* box.)

4. You can change the *Number of Clusters* from two to any number of clusters you want.

5. You can click *Options* and select from the menu, depending on your requirements. Cluster information for each case will give you a list of each participant and the cluster to which it belongs in a *Cluster Membership* table (not shown in the SPSS printout).

6. Click *OK* to generate the results in the data window.

CONCEPTUAL OBJECTIVE 3

Discuss the use of tests of interrelationship and the difference between factor and cluster analysis.

14.4 Statistical Tests That Use Control Variables

Recall from Chapter 13 that control variables (also called nuisance variables) are extraneous variables that you are not studying, and you don't want them to affect the results of your study—so you take the effect of the control variable out of the results. With tests of association we discussed partial correlation, and with prediction we discussed the use of partial correlation in regression. In this chapter we discuss control variables used with nonlinear advanced statistics.

Analysis of Covariance (ANCOVA) (a test of interaction), cross-tabulation (chi-square) (a test of difference and association), and its advanced techniques (automatic interaction detection [AID] and chi-square-square automatic interaction detection [CHAID]) are discussed together because they are advanced statistical techniques that use control variables. Control variables are placed in this last text chapter because they are advanced topics, and ANCOVA is an advanced form of ANOVA.

Here we simply describe rather complex statistical procedures in basic terms without giving SPSS 19 steps to run them; and no computer printouts, examples, or decision problems are included. Our main intent is to make you aware of control variables and how they are used in research and statistics. Thus, if you read about control variables and these statistical tests in a research study, you will have some understanding of what you are reading.

ANCOVA, cross-tabluation–X^2, AID, and CHAID are not included in the Decision Tree because they are advanced statistics with a control variable that does not fit within the Decision Tree. However, partial correlation and regression are included in the Decision Tree. The purpose and use of control variables is the same for ANCOVA, partial correlation, cross-tabulation control, and multiple regression. As when using the Decision Tree, the key to knowing which statistic to use with control variables is heavily based on the measurement level of the variables.

Analysis of Covariance (ANCOVA/MANCOVA)

In essence, ANCOVA is an extension of the General Model and Generalized Model ANOVAs; think of ANCOVA as an option when running one-way or two-way ANOVAs and MANOVAs. *Analysis of covariance (ANCOVA)* examines differences between an interval/ratio dependent variable and one or more nominal independent variables while controlling for the effects of one or more covariates. The *covariate* is the term used for the control variable with ANCOVA and MANOVA; the control variable is also called a nuisance variable.

SPSS 19.

Recall that in SPSS 19 both the Generalized Models (two-way ANOVA) and General Models (MANOVA) featured a *Covariate* box in addition to the dependent and independent variable boxes. So when you run ANOVA or MANOVA, add the covariates when entering variables.

MANCOVA. As stated, covariates can also be used with MANCOVA. You are adding one or more covariates to one-way or factorial MANOVA.

ANCOVA examples.

For a university, it may be interesting to see differences in SAT scores between genders after controlling for (taking out the effect of) the IQ level of the student. Also, to compare mean salaries of men and women professors, it would be advisable to control for years of teaching (partialing out), as the difference in salary may be due to seniority pay raises rather than gender.

ANCOVA/MANCOVA assumptions.

In an advanced parametric ANOVA/MANOVA, there must be an interval/ratio Y and a nominal X. The covariate (or control variable) must also be an interval/ratio level of measurement, and it must be strongly correlated with the Y. Thus, you need to run a correlation between the Y and the control variable; the association must be significant, or at least .40. The control variable also must not be correlated with the X, because if the control variable and X are related it becomes impossible to remove the effect of the control variable from the analysis.

Cross-Tabulation (Chi-Square)

Cross-tabulation (X^2) with control variables is essentially a partial correlation. Cross-tabs uses "partial" tables, as discussed below. Again, correlation is commonly used with at least ordinal-level data. Here we are discussing the use of nominal-level X^2 variables.

Use of cross-tabulation control.

Cross-tabulation control is used to measure the association between nominal-level variables while controlling for the effect of another variable. Cross-tabulation (X^2) involves the division of the sample into subgroups according to the categories (nominal variable groups/scales) of the controlled variable. You then reassess the original bivariate relation within each subgroup's scale. By dividing the sample into subgroups, you remove the biasing inequality by computing a measure of association/correlation for groups that are internally homogeneous with respect to the biasing factor.

Partial tables.

The results are shown in *partial tables* because each one reflects only part of the total association. Each pair of parallel cells in the two partial tables adds up to the corresponding cell in the original table. Recall that X^2 uses cross-tabs to indicate frequencies within each cell. The number of rows and columns depends on the number of nominal groups/scales of the variable.

Measuring association (no r or R^2).

To assess the partial association, you compute a measure of relationship for each of the control groups and compare it with the original results. The measurement level of the variable indicates the test—X^2 using the test of correlation, which could include Cramer's V, Mantel-Haenszel, Phi, and/or lambda. None of these correlations provides an r or R^2, as nominal variables do not provide a linear relationship. If the association is close to the original, you can conclude that the control variable does not account for the original relation and that the relationship is direct and real, or nonspurious. If the association vanishes with cross-tabs, the original association is said to be spurious, or due to some other variable. If the partial association is different from the original association or if it is different in each of the partial tables, the X and Y are said to interact.

Cross-tabulation control assumptions.

X^2 is used with nominal-level data. Recall that you can always make interval/ratio and ordinal-level data into nominal-level data by categorizing/grouping the data. For example, income in dollars can be grouped into high or low nominal groups/scales. Thus, in a sense, cross-tabulation can be used with any level of data so long as you have or create nominal groups. We can also run percentages with X^2 to make a comparison based on 100, making it interval/ratio data; we talk about this automatic interaction detection (AID) after we discuss regular cross-tabs.

Generally, only variables that are associated with both the Y and X can potentially bias the results. Thus, as with partial correlation, you select as control variables only those variables that show an association with the Y and X under investigation—unlike ANCOVA, which assumes a relationship with the Y but no correlation with the X.

Partial correlation has an advantage over cross-tabulation.

Recall the rule of 5 (X^2 requires at least five frequencies per cell). To use cross-tab control you need to subdivide the sample into progressively smaller subgroups according to the number of categories/groups of control variable. Subdividing the sample reduces the number of participants that serve as a basis for computing the coefficient, and a small sample size calls into question the validity and reliability of the findings. The problem is a major concern when several variables are controlled simultaneously. Note that this is the same sample size issue between tests of difference and correlation. Again, with correlation you do not create groups, so a sample size of 25–30 is generally a large sample. However, with X^2 tests of difference you break the sample into smaller groups, so with two groups you need an original sample size of 50–60. You need even more participants if you continue to make multiple subgroups of control variables.

Cross-tabulation has an advantage over partial correlation.

Partial correlation provides a single summarizing measure that reflects the degree of correlation between two variables while controlling for a third. Thus, the partial correlation does not reflect variation in the partial associations in different categories/groups of the controlled variable because it averages out the different partials. This average is partial correlation's main disadvantage, as it might obscure otherwise essential information. In studies where you suspect that there are significant differences between the partials of the various subgroups, it is advisable to use the cross-tabulation technique instead, assuming you have a large enough sample.

Automatic Interaction Detection (AID)

An advanced form of cross-tabs is the *automatic interaction detection (AID)*. However, AID is used with all percentages, making the variables interval/ratio level. AID is a sequential partitioning procedure that begins with a Y and a set of X predictors. It searches among up to 300 variables for the best single division according to each predictor X, chooses one, and splits the sample using X^2 tests to create multi-way splits. These subgroups then become separate samples for further analysis. The search procedure is repeated to find the variable that, when split into parts, makes the next largest contribution to the reduction of unexplained variation in each subsample, and so on.

Chi-Square Automatic Interaction Detection (CHAID)

CHAID is an advanced form of AID. *Chi-square automatic interaction detection (CHAID)* is commonly used in segmentation analysis and marketing research to identify subgroups of the Y. For example, a university can use CHAID to determine which of its applicants have a higher probability of enrolling (Y = enroll and not enroll) or whether any segment/

subgroup of its students are at a greater risk of withdrawing (Y = stay enrolled or withdraw) from the university.

CHAID begins with regression by identifying the "best predictor" of the Y and splits the sample into distinct groups/subsamples. After a variable has been defined as the "best predictor" variable, CHAID will attempt to create optimally merged categories of this predictor variable using a form of chi-square analysis. CHAID goes on to perform these operations in an interactive process until all subgroups have been analyzed or contain too few participants.

CONCEPTUAL OBJECTIVE 4
Explain the use of control variables, and list statistical tests that use them.

14.5 Other Advanced Statistics

In this last section we briefly explain linear structural relationships (LISREL), path analysis, conjoint analysis, multidimensional scaling (MDS), and time-series analysis. Again, here we simply describe rather complex statistical procedures in basic terms without showing computer printouts, examples, or decision problems. Our main intent is to make you aware of these advanced statistics and how they are used in research. If you subsequently read about them in a research study, you will have some understanding of what you are reading. None of these advanced tests are on the Decision Tree, partly because they don't fit properly and because they are advanced beyond the scope of this book.

Linear Structural Relationships (LISREL)

Linear structural relationships (LISREL) is used in explaining causality among constructs that cannot be directly measured, such as motivation. LISREL is actually a family of models appropriate for confirmatory factor analysis, path analysis, time-series analysis, recursive and nonrecursive models, and covariance structure models. (Some of these models are discussed in this section.) It is used in the social and behavioral sciences in various ways. LISREL is also used with business issues such as macroeconomic policy formation, racial discrimination in employment, and consumer behavior, among others. LISREL analyzes covariance structures in two parts.

Measurement model.
First, LISREL has a measurement model. Since constructs cannot be directly measured, the measurement model is used to relate the observed/recorded/measured variables to the latent variables/constructs. For example, to understand employee performance, several variables may be used, such as the observations of the manager, measures of work output, and the number of requests for peer assistance from an employee. When combined, these three measures give the researcher a better understanding of performance. Hence, measurement models are important for modeling constructs such as attitude, feelings, and motivation that cannot be directly observed.

Structural equation model (SEM).
Second, LISREL uses regression to develop a structural equation model, which shows the causal relationships among the latent variables (thus commonly called *causal modeling*).

It also describes the causal effects and the variance that are unexplained. However, because it uses regression rather than a true experimental design to test cause-and-effect differences based on a treatment, it is a weaker test. Mathematically, the model is described by a set of linear structural equations, and a causal structure among the variables is assumed.

Path Analysis

Path analysis is actually a second type of causal modeling, with which the causal inter-relationships are examined among a set of variables that have been logically ordered on the basis of time. Logically, a causal variable must precede any variable that it is estimated to affect, establishing the causal ordering of the variables. Path analysis uses linear regression to test the causal relations among the variables specified in the model. Path analysis begins with the researcher developing a diagram with arrows connecting variables and depicting the causal flow, or the direction of cause and effect. It has a substantial advantage over simple models in that both the direct and indirect causal effect can be estimated. The model could have been developed with LISREL. It involves three steps:

1. The researcher draws a path diagram based on a theory or set of hypotheses.
2. The researcher than calculates path coefficients (direct effects) using regression.
3. The researcher determines indirect effects.

Conjoint Analysis

Conjoint analysis determines the importance of attributes and the levels of features that are most desirable. Participants provide preference data by ranking or rating cards. Conjoint analysis is commonly used in marketing research and product development. For example, when buying a home computer you may evaluate a set of attributes that include brand, speed, price, educational values, games, or capacity for work-related tasks. The attributes and their features require you to make trade-offs in the final decision of which computer to buy.

Conjoint analysis commonly includes nominal Ys. Normally, we would use cross-tabulation control tables, as discussed above, to handle such data. However, even multi-way tables become quickly overwhelmed by the complexity. With our computer decision, assume we have 3 prices, 3 brands, 3 speeds, 2 levels of educational value, 2 categories for games, and 2 categories for work assistance. The model would have 216 decisions levels with a $3 \times 3 \times 3 \times 2 \times 2 \times 2$ factorial design. Thus, conjoint analysis solves the complexity problems with various optimal scaling approaches, often with loglinear models, to provide reliable answers that could not be obtained otherwise.

MultiDimensional Scaling (MDS)

MultiDimensional Scaling (MDS) creates a special description of a participant's perception about a product/service or other object of interest. It judges the similarity of objects. For example, how different is a Honda Accord from a Toyota Camry? How different are MBA programs at Harvard, Wharton, Yale, MIT, and Stanford? Which ones are perceived to be the same and which are different? Items that are perceived to be similar will fall close together in multidimensional space, and items that are perceived to be dissimilar will be farther apart. MDS is often used in conjunction with cluster analysis or conjoint analysis. MDS assists the researcher to understand difficult-to-measure constructs such as product quality or desirability, which are perceived and cognitively mapped in different ways by individuals.

MDS was used in a study of 16 companies from the natural resources (fuel) segment. Variables included executive total compensation and return on equity (ROE). Based on these two variables, the 16 companies were graphically mapped as being higher or lower on ROE and executive compensation, or as similar (closer together) or different (farther apart).

Time-Series Analysis

Any variable that is measured over time in sequential order is called a *time series*. We analyze time series in order to detect patterns that will enable us to forecast the future value of the time series. The government uses time series to forecast interest rates, unemployment rates, percentage increases in the cost of living, and demand for housing. Many companies use time series to forecast the demand/sales for their product and their market share.

Components of a time series.

A time series can consists of four components:

1. *Long-term trends (T)*. Long-term means longer than a year, and by trend we mean a relatively smooth pattern or direction exhibited by a series. For example, the U.S. population has experienced relatively steady growth (or a linear line with population by year). However, the trend can be steady growth followed by leveling off and then decline. The easiest way of isolating T is by *regression analysis*, where the X(s) are measures of time.

2. *Cyclical effects (C)*. A cycle is a wavelike pattern describing a long-term trend that is generally apparent over a number of years. You have most likely heard of the business cycle of economic recession and inflation, and monetary and financial cycles. Unlike seasonal variations, Cs are often considered unpredictable as they are difficult to forecast. However, they need to be isolated and the common measure is *percentage of trend*, again using regression.

3. *Seasonal variations (S)*. Ss are like cycles, but they occur over short, repetitive calendar periods and by definition have a duration of less than one year. In many countries sales are much higher during the Christmas holiday season, for example. An S may occur at any short time interval, such as a month, week, or day. To measure the seasonal effect we construct *seasonal indexes*, which attempt to gauge the degree to which the seasons differ. You need at least 4 S for this.

4. *Random variation (R)*. Rs are irregular changes in a time series that are not caused by any other component. They tend to hide the existence of the other more predictable components. R exists in almost all time series. To develop a better forecast it is common to remove the R through *smoothing techniques*.

Forecasting.

When the components of a time series are identified, we can select one of many available methods to forecast the time series. When there is very little or no trend, or cyclical and seasonal variation, exponential smoothing is recommended. When trend and seasonality are present, we can use regression analysis with seasonal indexes or indicator variables to make predictions. We can also use the autoregressive model.

SKI WEST STUDY

As we bring this chapter to a close, you should be able to understand two-way ANOVA, MANOVA, factor and cluster analysis, and other advanced statistics.

Matt McLeish did not use any of the advanced statistics from this chapter because they were not appropriate for his research study.

Chapter Summary and Glossary

The chapter summary is organized in a way that provides you with the answers necessary to help you meet the conceptual objectives for this chapter.

1. **Compare one-way and two-way analysis of variance (ANOVA). Be sure to explain the main effect and interaction.**

   Both one-way and two-way ANOVA compare mean differences of one interval/ratio dependent variable across groups/scales of a nominal independent variable. However, two-way extends the one-way design by using two or more independent variables/factors. Thus, two-way compares the mean differences for each independent variable's main effect, and it also tests for an interaction. The main effect is the difference between means for each independent variable, and the interaction is the best combination of groups/scales of the independent variables to maximize the value of the dependent variable.

2. **Compare two-way ANOVA, one-way multivariate analysis of variance (MANOVA), and factorial MANOVA.**

   Two-way ANOVA and MANOVA are both tests of interaction because they have multiple independent variables. However, their variable count is the opposite. Two-way ANOVA has only one dependent variable and multiple independent variables, whereas one-way MANOVA has multiple dependent variables and only one independent variable. Thus, MANOVA cannot have an interaction. The major similarity between one-way MANOVA and factorial MANOVA is that they are both types of multivariate analysis (they have more than one dependent variable). However, the difference between one-way MANOVA and two-way (factorial) MANOVA is the number of independent variables. Factorial MANOVA extends MANOVA to include multiple independent variables and possible interactions.

3. **Discuss the use of tests of interrelationship and the difference between factor and cluster analysis.**

   Tests of interrelationship are used to reduce a larger number of independent variables into a limited, more manageable number. Factor analysis reduces a larger number of independent variables into a limited number of interrelated factors by grouping them together. Cluster analysis reduces a large number of participants into a limited number of interrelated groups by classifying them (identifying which group they belong with).

4. **Explain the use of control variables, and list statistical tests that use them.**
   Control variables are used to reduce the risk of attributing explanatory power to variables that are not in fact responsible for the variance found in the dependent variable. Control variables are used with partial correlation, multiple regression, analysis of covariance (ANCOVA and MANCOVA), and cross-tabulation control—chi-square and its advanced techniques—automatic interaction detection (AID), and chi-square automatic interaction detection (CHAID).

5. **Define the following key terms.**
   Select one or more methods: (1) fill in the missing key terms from memory, (2) match the key terms from the end of the review with their definitions below, or (3) copy the key terms in order from the list at the beginning of the chapter.

   cluster analysis   multivariate factorial ANOVA
   factor analysis   two-way analysis of variance (ANOVA)
   multivariate analysis of variance (MANOVA)

   _____ tests whether there are mean differences and a best combination of two or more nominal independent variables to maximize the value of one interval/ratio dependent variable.

   _____ determines mean differences of two or more interval/ratio dependent variables based on one nominal independent variable.

   _____ determines mean differences and whether there are interactions among two or more interval/ratio dependent variables and two or more nominal independent variables.

   _____ reduces a large number of independent variables into a limited, more manageable number of interrelated factors by grouping them together.

   _____ reduces a large number of participants into a limited number of interrelated groups by classifying them (identifying which group they belong with).

WRITTEN ASSIGNMENTS

All three written assignments require selecting the appropriate statistic to test the hypotheses that you develop. However, only the completed study and statistical analysis require running the statistics.

APPENDIX CS, ASSIGNMENTS 3 (RESULTS) AND 4 (DISCUSSION)

Based on your methodology, you may need to complete chapters 9–14 before you can complete the study. If your methodology includes correlations or regression, run them now and write your statistical findings in the Results section of your study. It is also time to write the Discussion section.

APPENDIX SA, ASSIGNMENT 6 (TWO-WAY ANOVA AND MANOVA)

This is a continuation of Assignment 5 in Appendix SA. You will be running a two-way ANOVA and MANOVA with your data.

USING THE COMPUTER: TWO-WAY ANOVA AND MANOVA

USING DESCRIPTIVE STATISTICS

Following the five steps of hypotheses testing, complete the following problems in a similar manner to those in chapters 12–13.

TWO-WAY ANOVA DECISION PROBLEMS

14-1   Continuing our bank financing discrimination example, you want to know whether there is a difference in income (Y) between African Americans and Whites and by those who received a loan and those who did not (Xs); you also want to know whether there is a best combination of race and loan to maximize income. Because the two-way ANOVA did not include the means, you used the descriptive statistics.

Mean incomes:
African American $36,449 and White $43,384. "Got a loan" mean $46,385 and "did not get a loan" $37,289.

Step 1. State the 3 hypotheses in both the null and alternative. (See Box 14.2 for an example.)
Step 2. Set the critical value at .05.
Step 3. Select the methodology of data collection and statistical test.
Step 4. You ran the statistics and obtained the p-value below.

Omnibus Test[a]

Likelihood Ratio Chi-Square	df	Sig.
7.754	2	.021

Dependent Variable: Income
Model: (Intercept), race, loan
a. Compares the fitted model against the intercept-only model.

Tests of Model Effects

	Type III		
Source	Wald Chi-Square	df	Sig.
(Intercept)	470.742	1	.000
race	1.650	1	.199
loan	4.774	1	.029

Dependent Variable: Income
Model: (Intercept), race, loan

Step 5. Make the decision.
(a) Which race has the highest income? Is the difference significant?
(b) Which loan status group has the highest incomes? Is the difference significant?
(c) Is there an interaction effect?
(d) Should we fail to reject Ho1–3 (accept Ho) or reject Ho1–3 (accept Ha1–3)?
(e) What conclusion should be made, putting (a)–(d) together?

14-2   You want to know whether there is a difference in income (Y) by gender and by those who received a loan and those who did not (Xs). You also want to know whether there is a best combination to maximize income. You ran the descriptive statistics and got the following mean incomes: males $39,803.70 and females $39,269.23; those who got a loan $46,385 and those who did not get a loan $37,289.

Instructions

For *steps 1–4* of hypothesis testing, follow the instructions in Box 14.2. For *step 5*, answer the following questions: (a) Which gender has the highest income? Is the difference significant? (b) Which loan status group has the highest income? Is the difference significant? (c) Is there an interaction effect? (d) Should we fail to reject H1a,b,c (accept Ho) or reject (accept Ha)? (e) What conclusion should be made?

Solution (Decision) (See Box 14.2 for an example.)

Step 1. State the hypothesis in both the null and alternative.

Step 2. Set the critical value at .05.

Step 3. Select the methodology of data collection and statistical test.

Step 4. Run the statistics and obtain the p-value (see the SPSS printout below).

Omnibus Test[a]

Likelihood Ratio Chi-Square	df	Sig.
6.244	2	.044

Dependent Variable: Income
Model: (Intercept), gender, loan
a. Compares the fitted model against the intercept-only model.

Tests of Model Effects

	Type III		
Source	Wald Chi-Square	df	Sig.
(Intercept)	218.609	1	.000
gender	.125	1	.723
loan	6.446	1	.011

Dependent Variable: Income
Model: (Intercept), gender, loan

Step 5. Make the decision.

(a) Which gender has the highest income? Is the difference significant?
(b) Which loan status group has the highest incomes? Is the difference significant?
(c) Is there an interaction effect?
(d) Should we fail to reject Ho1–3 (accept Ho) or reject Ho1–3 (accept Ha1–3)?
(e) What conclusion should be made, putting (a)–(d) together?

MANOVA DECISION PROBLEM

14-3 Continuing with the bank financing discrimination example, you want to know whether there is a difference in income and amount of loan applied for by gender and whether gender has an interaction effect on income and the amount of loan applied for.

Because the MANOVA does not include the means, you ran the descriptive statistics and got the following mean incomes: for males $39,803.70, and for females, $39,269.23. For amount of loan applied for: males $27,598.77 and females $35,038.46.

Instructions

The five steps of hypothesis testing are listed below. For *steps 1–4*, follow the instructions in Box 14.2. For *step 5*, answer the following questions: (a) Which gender has the largest income, and is the difference significant? (b) Which gender applied for the largest loans, and is the difference significant? (c) Is there an interaction effect? (d) Which hypotheses should you accept and/or reject? (e) What conclusions should you make?

Solution (Decision) (See Box 14.2 for an example.)

Step 1. State the hypothesis in both the null and alternative.

Step 2. Set the critical value at .05.

Step 3. Select the methodology of data collection and statistical test.

Step 4. You ran the statistics and obtained the p-value below.

Multivariate Tests[b]

Effect		Value	F	Hypothesis df	Error df	Sig.
Intercept	Pillai's Trace	.689	100.707[a]	2.000	91.000	.000
	Wilks' Lambda	.311	100.707[a]	2.000	91.000	.000
	Hotelling's Trace	2.213	100.707[a]	2.000	91.000	.000
	Roy's Largest Root	2.213	100.707[a]	2.000	91.000	.000
gender	Pillai's Trace	.010	.440[a]	2.000	91.000	.645
	Wilks' Lambda	.990	.440[a]	2.000	91.000	.645
	Hotelling's Trace	.010	.440[a]	2.000	91.000	.645
	Roy's Largest Root	.010	.440[a]	2.000	91.000	.645

a. Exact statistic
b. Design: Intercept + gender

Tests of Between-Subjects Effects

Source	Dependent Variable	Type III Sum of Squares	df	Mean Square	F	Sig.
Corrected Model	Income	3200014.548[a]	1	3200014.548	.009	.925
	Amount of loan applied for.	6.200E8	1	6.200E8	.721	.398
Intercept	Income	7.004E10	1	7.004E10	197.457	.000
	Amount of loan applied for.	4.395E10	1	4.395E10	51.092	.000
gender	Income	3200014.548	1	3200014.548	.009	.925
	Amount of loan applied for.	6.200E8	1	6.200E8	.721	.398
Error	Income	3.263E10	92	3.547E8		
	Amount of loan applied for.	7.914E10	92	8.602E8		
Total	Income	1.810E11	94			
	Amount of loan applied for.	1.568E11	94			
Corrected Total	Income	3.264E10	93			
	Amount of loan applied for.	7.976E10	93			

a. R Squared = .000 (Adjusted R Squared = -.011)
b. R Squared = .008 (Adjusted R Squared = -.003)

Step 5. Make the decision.

(a) Which gender has the highest income? Is the difference significant?

(b) Which gender asked for the higher loan? Is the difference significant?

(c) Is there an interaction effect?

(d) Should we fail to reject Ho1–3 (accept Ho) or reject Ho1–3 (accept Ha1–3)?

(e) What conclusion should be made, putting (a)–(d) together?

Two-Way ANOVA and MANOVA

For problems 14-4 through 14-7, use the data from Descriptive Statistic Problem 9-1 in chapter 9. Set up each of the problems like problems 14-1 through 14-3 above to test hypotheses.

14-4   Run a two-way ANOVA using satisfaction, party, and gender as variables.

14-5   Run a two-way ANOVA using age, party, and gender as variables.

14-6   Run a MANOVA using satisfaction, age, and party as variables.

14-7   Run a MANOVA using satisfaction, age, party, and gender as variables.

Your Research Study

14-8   Which advanced statistical tests, if any, can/will you use for your research study?

Index